the CULINARIAN

the CULINARIAN

A KITCHEN DESK REFERENCE

BARBARA ANN KIPFER

Illustrations by Kyle Kipfer

WILEY

JOHN WILEY & SONS, INC.

Published by John Wiley & Sons, Inc., Hoboken, New Jersey

Published simultaneously in Canada

For general information on our other products and services or for technical support, please contact our Customer Care Department within the United States at (800) 762-2974, outside the United States at (317) 572-3993 or fax (317) 572-4002.

Wiley also publishes its books in a variety of electronic formats. Some content that appears in print may not be available in electronic books. For more information about Wiley products, visit our web site at www.wiley.com.

Library of Congress Cataloging-in-Publication Data:

Kipfer, Barbara Ann.
    The culinarian : a kitchen desk reference / Barbara Ann Kipfer;
illustrations by Kyle Kipfer.
        p.   cm.
    Includes index.
    ISBN 978-0-470-55424-1 (pbk.), 978-1-118-11059-1 (ebk.), 978-1-118-11060-7 (ebk.), 978-1-118-11061-4 (ebk.)
        1. Food—Dictionaries.   2. Cooking—Dictionaries   3. Cooking—Terminology.
    I. Title.
    TX349.K566   2011
    641.3003—dc22
                                                            2011000435

Printed in the United States of America
10 9 8 7 6 5 4 3 2 1

INTRODUCTION

good cooks and people interested in cooking become obsessed with finding out everything about food. This kitchen desk reference is a compendium of food vocabulary, cooking techniques, ingredient facts, smart tips, and trivia—for novices and experienced cooks alike. It is for those who have cooking intuition and those who watch cooking television shows and Internet videos trying to gain it. The alphabetical arrangement and comprehensive index make it easy to find all the information you need. Offering much more than other cooking reference books, this volume also contains word histories, lists, trivia, and little-known culinary facts.

The book has one main alphabetical section peppered with informational lists and sidebars, as well as factual matter in the front and indexes in the back.

The opening section includes measurements, conversions, food grades and classes, and more.

In the alphabetical section, you will find terms and their origins, the history of food names, food dishes, techniques, equipment, as well as some food lore. (In explanations of word origins, words beginning with an asterisk are not attested in any written source, but they have been reconstructed by etymological analysis; an example is the Indo-European *ped-, the root of words for "foot" in most of its daughter tongues.) A number of entries have descriptions and differentiations of confusable/equivalent terms such as hot dog/frankfurter/wiener.

The many hints and tips following the main entries cover selection, purchase, and storage of foods; preparation and seasoning suggestions; kinds and types of specific foods; and common cooking problems with solutions.

Helpful lists interspersed throughout the frontmatter and alphabetical section will delight trivia lovers, such as U.S.-British food translations, herbs, outfitting a kitchen, and an ultimate grocery list. And food process features reveal the mysteries behind techniques like brewing beer and pressure-cooking.

More than just a special collection of helpful hints, kitchen tips, lists, and descriptions of ingredients, dishes, and other food terms, The Culinarian is also a great browsing book for inspiration and trivia. Whether you're struggling with what to cook for dinner tonight or what to do when you have bought too many eggs, you can count on this book to pinpoint exactly the information you need, or to provide inspiration when you open to any page.

ACKNOWLEDGMENTS

*t*he *Culinarian* came about because I, like millions of others, envisioned myself as a chef. Buying some appliances, tools, and books was the first step. The second step was to use them, whereupon I discovered that I did not have the makings of a chef—I lacked not only the patience, intuition, and common sense, but also the flexibility, daring, and willingness to keep trying while failing. So I settled for acquiring the skills of a good home cook. *The Culinarian* gathers together all the information I personally wanted to know, minus the recipes, of course.

This was my first collaboration with my son, Kyle Kipfer, who created the wonderful illustrations for this book. His drawings are amazing and he has only just started his career.

I thank my husband, Paul Magoulas, for all of his super contributions and work on this. He goes into topics more in depth than I do, so his skill is a great complement to my ability to collect and organize lots of information.

I also thank Bob Amsler and Brad Haugaard, longtime colleagues and friends, who have helped so much with data management on this large project. Thanks, too, to Keir Magoulas, who eats some of the food I cook but is looking forward to college cafeteria fare!

It has been a true pleasure to have Christine McKnight as my Wiley editor. In my twenty-five years of publishing, she has been, by far, the easiest publishing executive to communicate with, which made the writing and compiling process very smooth. Thank you, Christine.

—Barbara Ann Kipfer

HELPFUL INFORMATION

ABBREVIATIONS

Common abbreviations used in recipes:

C: Celsius	kg: kilogram	pt: pint
c: cup	L: liter	qt: quart
cm: centimeter	lb or #: pound	sq: square
doz: dozen	m: meter	tbsp or tbp or T: tablespoon
F: Fahrenheit	mg: milligram	
ft: foot	min: minute	tsp or t: teaspoon
g: gram	mL: milliliter	yd: yard
hr: hour	mm: millimeter	
in: inch	oz: ounce	

FDA LABEL TERMS

ENRICHED: Due to processing, nutrients were lost, so the product was enriched and the nutrients replaced.

FAT-FREE: It contains less than ½ gram of fat per serving.

FORTIFIED: Nutrients have been added that were not in the original ingredients.

HEALTHY: It is low in fat and saturated fat, has limited amounts of cholesterol and sodium, and provides significant amounts of one or more key nutrients: vitamin A, vitamin C, iron, calcium, protein, and fiber.

LIGHT (OR LITE): It is low in fat or calories. (Restaurants may continue to use the term light as in "Lighter Fare" to mean smaller portions, as long as they make it clear how they're using the word.)

LOW-CALORIE: It contains 120 calories or less per 100 grams (about 3½ ounces); also defined as having 40 calories or less per serving and less than 0.4 calories per gram of food.

LOW-CHOLESTEROL: These items must contain less than 20 milligrams of cholesterol per 100 grams and no more than 2 grams of saturated fat.

LOW-FAT: It has less than 3 grams of fat per 100 grams. The phrase *"number %* fat-free" may only be used for low-fat foods.

LOW IN SATURATED FAT: Each serving has 1 gram (or less) of saturated fat, and the number of calories from that source is not more than 15% of the total.

LOW-SODIUM: It has 140 milligrams or less of sodium per 100 grams.

NATURAL: This term generally means that the product has no artificial ingredients or intentional additives. Many "natural" foods have lots of sugar, fat, and preservatives.

NATURAL FLAVORING: It contains flavoring derived from a spice, fruit or fruit juice, edible yeast, herb, bark, bud, root, leaf or similar plant material, or a meat, seafood, poultry, egg, or dairy product whose significant function in food is flavoring rather than nutritional. Those broad parameters include ingredients like hydrolyzed protein and HVP, both of which contain MSG.

NO SUGAR ADDED: There is no table sugar, but there may be other forms of sugar, such as corn syrup, dextrose, fructose, glucose, maltose, or sucrose.

ORGANIC AND NATURAL: This phrase can mean the product is minimally processed, free from artificial ingredients, chemical free, or pesticide free.

REDUCED-CALORIE: It has at least one-third fewer calories than the regular version of the product.

REDUCED-FAT: It has less than 50% of the fat found in the regular version of the product.

REDUCED-SODIUM: It has at least 75% less sodium than the regular version of the product.

SODIUM-FREE: It has less than 5 milligrams per serving.

SUGAR-FREE: It contains no sugar.

VERY LOW SODIUM: It has 35 milligrams or less sodium per serving.

SMOKE POINTS OF OILS

Corn oil: 410°F

Grapeseed oil: 420°F–485°F

Olive oil: 410°F

Peanut oil: 410°F

Rapeseed oil: 437°F

Soybean oil: 410°F

Sunflower oil: 392°F

U.S.-BRITISH EQUIVALENT FOOD NAMES

U.S. = British

bacon = streaky

baked potato = jacket potato

beet = beetroot

bell pepper = green pepper

biscuit = scone

bologna = polony

can opener = key

chop = cutlet

cilantro = coriander

confectioners' or powdered sugar = icing sugar

cookie = biscuit

corn = maize

corned beef = salt beef

cornmeal = Indian meal

corn syrup = golden syrup

cotton candy = candyfloss

cracker = unsweetened biscuit

cupcake = fairy cake

dessert = sweet

doughnut = ring doughnut

eggplant = aubergine

English muffin = crumpet

endive = chicory

fish sticks = fish fingers

French fries = chips

frosting = icing

gingersnap = ginger nut

groceries = stores

ground beef = mince

ham = gammon

hamburger bun = bap

hard cider = cider

ladyfinger = sponge finger

light brown sugar = demerara sugar

light cream = single cream

liverwurst = liver sausage

meatball = faggot

molasses = black treacle

oatmeal (cooked) = porridge

pie = tart

plastic wrap = clingfilm

porterhouse steak = sirloin

potato chips = crisps

roast = joint

romaine = cos

salad dressing = salad cream

sausage = banger

shrimp (small) = prawn

silverware = plate

sirloin = rump steak

soda cracker = water cracker

squash = vegetable marrow

string bean = French bean

taffy = toffee

tenderloin steak = fillet steak

top round = silverside

turnip = Swede

wax paper = greaseproof paper

whipping or heavy cream = double cream

zucchini = courgette

USDA MEAT GRADES

U.S. PRIME: highest in quality and intramuscular fat, limited supply

U.S. CHOICE: high quality, widely available in food service industry and retail markets

U.S. SELECT (FORMERLY GOOD): lowest grade commonly sold in retail markets, acceptable quality but less juicy and tender due to leanness

U.S. STANDARD: lower quality yet economical, lacking marbling

U.S. COMMERCIAL: low quality, lacking tenderness, produced from older animals

U.S. UTILITY

U.S. CUTTER

U.S. CANNER

MEASURES

DONENESS TEMPERATURES FOR MEAT

USDA suggested minimum internal temperatures:

beef, veal, or lamb, ground: 160°F

beef, veal, or lamb, steaks and roasts: 145°F

beef: medium-rare 150°F, medium 160°F, well done 170°F

casseroles with meat or egg: 165°F

chicken breast: 170°F–180°F

chicken or turkey, ground: 165°F

chicken or turkey, leg or thigh: 180°F–185°F

egg dishes: 160°F

fish: 145°F

ham: 140°F

lamb and veal: medium 160°F, well done 170°F

pork: 160°F, medium 160°F, well done 170°F

poultry, general: 165°F

turkey breast, boneless: 170°F

EGG EQUIVALENT MEASURES

1 whole medium egg = ¼ cup

2 egg whites = ¼ cup

2 whole medium eggs = ⅓–½ cup

3 egg whites = ⅜ cup

3 egg yolks = ¼ cup

3 whole medium eggs = ½–⅔ cup

4 egg whites = ½ cup

4 egg yolks = ⅓ cup

4 whole medium eggs = ⅔–1 cup

5 egg whites = ⅔ cup

5 egg yolks = ⅜ cup

6 egg yolks = ½ cup

FISH SINGLE-SERVING SIZES

drawn or dressed fish: 8 ounces

live crabs: 1 pound

lobster meat (cooked): 4–5 ounces

lobster tail: 8 ounces

shelled shrimp: 3–4 ounces

steak or fillet: 4–5 ounces

whole fish: 12–16 ounces

whole lobster: 1–1½ pounds

NUT EQUIVALENT MEASURES

almonds: 1 pound in shell = 1–1¾ cups nutmeats

almonds: 1 pound shelled = 3½ cups nutmeats

peanuts: 1 pound in shell = 2¼ cups nutmeats

peanuts: 1 pound shelled = 3 cups nutmeats

pecans: 1 pound in shell =
2¼ cups nutmeats

pecans: 1 pound shelled =
4 cups nutmeats

walnuts: 1 pound in shell =
1²/₃ cups nutmeats

walnuts: 1 pound shelled =
4 cups nutmeats

SCOOP SIZES

#30 = 2 tablespoons

#24 = 2¾ tablespoons

#20 = 3 tablespoons

#16 = 4 tablespoons

#12 = 5 tablespoons

#10 = 6 tablespoons

#8 = 8 tablespoons

#6 = 10 tablespoons

TEMPERATURES IN THE KITCHEN

0°F: freezer

8°F–40°F: refrigerator

65°F: cool room temperature

70°F–75°F: warm room
temperature

95°F: lukewarm liquid

105°F–115°F: warm liquid

120°F: hot liquid

175°F–225°F: low oven

212°F: boiling water

250°F–275°F: very slow oven

300°F–325°F: slow/warm oven

350°F–375°F: moderate oven

400°F–425°F: hot oven

450°F–475°F: very hot oven

475°F–500°F: extremely hot oven;
broiler

YIELDS AND EQUIVALENTS

apples: 1 cup sliced or
chopped = 1 medium
(6 ounces)

apples: 3 cups
sliced = 1 pound = 3
medium

asparagus: 1 pound =
16–20 stalks

bacon: ½ cup
crumbled = 8 slices,
crisply cooked

bananas: 1 cup
mashed = 2 medium

bananas: 1 cup sliced =
1 medium or 2 small

bananas: 2½ cups
sliced = 3 medium = 1
pound

beans, dried: 5–6 cups
cooked = 1 pound dried

beans, green or wax: 3
cups 1-inch pieces = 1
pound

broccoli: 2 cups flow-
erets, 1-inch pieces, or
chopped = 7 ounces

butter and fats: 2 cups
= 1 pound = 4 sticks

butter or margarine:
½ cup = ¼ pound = 1
stick

cabbage, Chinese
(napa): 1¼ pounds = 1
medium head

cabbage, green or
red: 1½ pounds = 1
medium head

carrots: 1 cup ¼-inch
slices = 2 medium

carrots: 1 cup shredded = 1½ medium

cauliflower: 3 cups flowerets = 1 pound

celery: 1 cup thinly sliced or chopped = 2 medium stalks

cheese, cottage: 2 cups = 1 pound

cheese, cream: 1 cup = 16 tablespoons = 8 ounces

cheese, cream: 6 tablespoons = 3 ounces

cheese, hard: 4 cups grated = 1 pound

cheese, hard, shredded, or crumbled: 1 cup = 4 ounces

coconut, shredded: 5 cups = 1 pound

coffee, ground: 80 tablespoons = 1 pound

corn, sweet: 1 cup kernels = 2 medium ears

cranberries, dried: 1 cup = 4 ounces

cranberries, fresh: 4 cups = 1 pound

cream, whipping (heavy): 1 cup (2 cups whipped) = ½ pint

cream, whipping (heavy): 2 cups (4 cups whipped) = 1 pint

crumbs, finely crushed, chocolate wafer: 1½ cups = 27 cookies

crumbs, finely crushed, graham cracker: 1½ cups = 21 squares

crumbs, finely crushed, saltine cracker: 1 cup = 29 squares

crumbs, finely crushed, vanilla wafer: 1½ cups = 38 cookies

cucumbers: 1 cup chopped = ¾ medium

eggplant: 1½ pounds = 1 medium

eggplant: 2 cups ½-inch pieces = 12 ounces

egg, large, whole: ¼ cup fat-free cholesterol-free egg product

eggs, large, whole: 1 cup = 4 large eggs

eggs, large, yolks: 1 cup = 8 or 9 large eggs

flour, all-purpose: 4 cups sifted = 1 pound

flour, unsifted: 3½ cups = 1 pound

garlic: ½ teaspoon finely chopped = 1 medium clove

lemon or lime: 1½–3 teaspoons grated rind = 1 medium

lemon or lime: 2–3 teaspoons juice = 1 medium

lettuce, iceberg or romaine: 1½ pounds = 1 medium head

lettuce, iceberg or romaine: 6 cups bite-sized pieces = 1 pound

lettuce, iceberg or romaine: 2 cups shredded = 5 ounces

marshmallows: 16 pieces = 4 ounces

meat, cooked: 1 cup chopped or bite-sized pieces = 6 ounces

melon, cantaloupe or honeydew: 3 pounds = 1 medium

melon, cantaloupe or honeydew: 2 cups 1-inch chunks = 1 pound

mushrooms, fresh: 2½ cups chopped = 8 ounces

mushrooms, fresh: 6 cups sliced = 1 pound

nuts (without shells), chopped: 1 cup = 4 ounces

nuts (without shells), whole or halves: 3–4 cups = 1 pound

onions, green, with tops: ¼ cup sliced = 2–3 medium

onions, green, with tops: 2 tablespoons sliced = 1 medium

onions, yellow or white: ½ cup chopped = 1 medium

orange: ⅓–½ cup juice = 1 medium

orange: 1–2 tablespoons grated rind = 1 medium

pasta or macaroni: = 4 cups cooked = 6–8 ounces uncooked/dried

peaches or pears: 2 cups sliced = 1 pound = 3 medium

peas, green: 1 cup shelled = 1 pound in pods

peppers, bell: ½ cup chopped = 1 small

peppers, bell: 1 cup chopped = 1 medium

pineapples, fresh: 4 cups cubed = 1 medium

potatoes, red or white: 1 cup ½-inch pieces = 1 medium

potatoes, red, white, sweet, or yams: 5–6 ounces = 1 medium

potatoes, small red: 1½ pounds = 10–12 small

pumpkin: 1 cup mashed cooked = 1 pound uncooked = 1 cup canned pumpkin

rice, regular long-grain: 3 cups cooked = 1 cup uncooked

shortening: 2⅓ cups = 1 pound

slaw (packaged shredded cabbage): 4 cups = 1 pound

sour cream: 1 cup = 8 ounces

spinach: 4 cups leaves = 6 ounces

spinach: 2 cups shredded = 2½ ounces

squash, summer or zucchini: 2 cups ¼-inch slices, chopped, or shredded = 1 medium

squash, winter: 1½–2½ pounds = 1 medium

strawberries: 4 cups sliced = 1 quart

sugar, brown: 2¼ cups = 1 pound

sugar, confectioners': 3½ cups sifted = 1 pound

sugar, granulated: 2 cups = 1 pound

tomatoes: 1 cup chopped = 1 large

CULINARIAN EQUIPMENT

COOKERS

autoclave (pressure cooker)

baker

barbecue

boiler

brazier

broiler

camp stove

casserole

chafing dish or chafing pan

coffeemaker

convection oven

cookstove

cooktop

corn popper

crockpot

deep fryer

double boiler

Dutch oven

electric cooker

electric frying pan

electric roaster

electric toaster

field range

fireless cooker

fish kettle

fry-cooker

frying pan or frypan

galley stove

gas grill

griddle

grill

haybox (insulated box for keeping things warm)

hibachi

hotplate

infrared broiler

infrared cooker

karahi (round frying pan with two handles)

marmite (large, deep, lidded pot)

microwave

oven

percolator

pipkin (small earthenware cooking pot)

poacher

pressure cooker or pressure canner

pressure saucepan

range

rice cooker

roaster

rotisserie

samovar

saucepan

skillet

slow cooker

smoker

solar box cooker

steamer

stewpot

stockpot

stove

tagine

tian (French gratin dish)

toaster

toaster oven

waffle iron

waterless cooker

wok

COOKING TOOLS (BASIC)

basting/glazing brush

bulb baster

can opener

colander

corkscrew

cutting board

funnel

grater

ladle

measuring spoons and cups

melon baller

mixing bowl

pepper mill

pizza wheel

potato masher

pot holders and oven mitts

salad spinner

scissors

skewers

skimmer

spatula

steamer basket

strainer

thermometer

timer

tongs

vegetable brush

vegetable peeler

whisk

CUPS AND DRINKING VESSELS

balloon glass

beaker

beer glass

beer mug

bottle

bowl

brandy snifter or brandy glass

cannikin

chalice

cocktail or martini glass

coffee cup or mug

copita (Spanish sherry glass)

coupe

cup

demitasse

drinking horn

flagon

flask

flute

glass

globe

goblet

highball glass

jigger

jorum (large drinking bowl)

jug

juice glass

kylix (ancient Greek shallow vessel)

liqueur glass

loving cup

mug

noggin (small cup or mug)

old-fashioned glass

pannikin

pony

rhyton (ancient Greek vessel)

rummer (large glass with short stem)

schooner (large glass for beer or sherry)

seidel (beer glass)

shot glass

sippy cup

snifter

stein

stoup

tankard

taster

tazza (ornamental shallow bowl)

teacup

tumbler

tyg (mug with twelve handles)

water glass

wineglass

yard of ale

CUTLERY, FLATWARE, AND SILVERWARE

after-dinner coffee spoon

Asian-style cleaver

bird's-beak paring knife

bone cleaver

boning knife

bouillon spoon

bread knife

butter knife

butter spreader

carving fork

carving knife

cheese knife

chocolate spoon

chopsticks

citrus spoon

cleaver

cocktail fork

coffee spoon

cook's knife

demitasse spoon

dessert fork

dessert knife

dessert spoon

dinner fork

dinner knife

electric knife

filleting knife

fish fork

fish knife

five o'clock spoon

fondue fork

fork

fruit fork

fruit knife

grapefruit knife

grapefruit spoon

ham knife

ice-cream spoon

iced-beverage spoon

kitchen knife

knife

lobster fork

luncheon fork

luncheon knife

offset knife

oyster fork
oyster knife
paring knife
pastry fork
place spoon
runcible spoon
salad fork
salt spoon

sandwich knife
santoku knife
seafood fork
serrated knife
serving spoon
sheep's-foot paring knife
slicer

soupspoon
spoon
steak knife
sundae spoon
tablespoon
teaspoon
utility knife
vegetable knife

DEEP-FRYING EQUIPMENT

bird's nest basket
deep fryer
frying pan
mesh skimmer
slotted spoon

spatter guard
spider (skimmer)
thermometer
thick, long oven mitts
tongs

wire basket liner
wire rack
wok

DISHES FOR EATING

after-dinner cup and saucer
bowl
breakfast cup and saucer
cereal bowl
coffee cup
cup
demitasse

dessert bowl
dessert plate
dinner plate
dish
eggcup
fruit bowl
luncheon plate
mug

plate
porringer
salad bowl
salad plate
saucer
soup bowl
teacup

DISHES FOR SERVING

boat
bowl
breadbasket
bread tray
buffet plate
butter dish
cake plate

charger
coffeepot
compote
cookie jar
creamer
cruet
decanter

fish plate
gratin dish
gravy boat
jar
jug
lazy Susan
pitcher

platter
punch bowl
ramekin
salad bowl
salt and pepper shakers

salt cellar
salver
service plate
sugar bowl
tea service

teapot
tray
tureen

FORKS

carving fork
cocktail fork
dessert fork
dinner fork
fish fork

fondue fork
fruit fork
lobster fork
luncheon fork
oyster fork

pastry fork
salad fork
seafood fork
toasting fork

GRILL EQUIPMENT

basting brush
drip pan
flame-retardant long
mitts

hinged basket for vegetables, whole fish, and
other items
instant-read
thermometer

skewers
tongs
wire cleaning brush

KITCHEN KNIVES

boning knife
bread knife (average 8 inches)
butchering knife
butter knife
butter spreader
butterfly knife
carving knife
cheese knife
chef's knife or cook's knife (average 8 inches)
citrus knife
clam knife
cleaver
cook's knife

dessert knife
dinner knife
dough knife
filleting knife
fish knife
frozen-food knife
fruit knife
Gorgonzola knife
grapefruit knife
ham knife
luncheon knife
mezzaluna
oyster knife
paring knife (average 3–4 inches)

Parmesan knife
roast beef slicer
salami slicer
salmon slicer
sandwich spatula
scallop knife
serrated knife
shellfish knife
slicing knife
steak knife
table knife
tomato knife
utility knife (average 6–8 inches)

LADLES

bail

dipper or dip

punch bowl ladle

scoop

soup ladle

spatula

POTS AND PANS

baking pan

baking sheet

bean pot

biggin (coffeepot)

boiler

brazier

bread pan

broiler

Bundt pan

cake pan

caldron

coffeepot

coffee urn

cookie sheet

corn popper

crockpot

double boiler

Dutch oven

frying pan or frypan

griddle

jelly roll pan

kettle

loaf pan

muffin pan

muffin tin

omelet pan

paella pan

percolator

pie pan

pie plate

pie tin

pipkin (earthenware pot)

pizza pan

poacher

pressure cooker

quiche pan

roaster or roasting pan

saucepan

sauté pan

skillet

slow cooker

smoker

soufflé dish

springform pan

steamer

stewpan

stew pot

stockpot

tandoor

tart tin

teakettle

teapot

tube pan

wok

SPATULAS

baking spatula

Chinese spatula

crêpe spatula

grilling spatula

narrow spatula

serving spatula

slotted lifting spatula

SPOONS

after-dinner coffee
spoon

bouillon spoon

chocolate spoon

citrus spoon

coffee spoon

demitasse spoon

dessert spoon

five o'clock spoon
(between teaspoon and
tablespoon)

ice-cream spoon

iced beverage spoon

place spoon

salt spoon

soupspoon

sundae spoon

tablespoon

teaspoon

UTENSILS FOR BAKING

baker's peel

baking knife

baking sheet

baking spatula

baking stone

biscuit cutter

breadboard

cookie cutters

cookie sheet

cooling rack

croissant cutter

decorating comb

decorating turntable

dough scraper

doughnut cutter

dredger

egg beater

English muffin rings

flour wand

frosting spatula

icing syringe

jelly roll pan

loaf pan

measuring cups and
spoons

mixing bowls

mixing spoons

muffin tin or muffin pan

pastry bag and nozzles

pastry blender

pastry board

pastry brush

pastry wheel or pastry
cutter

pie pan, pie plate, or
pie tin

pie weights

pizza peel

pizza stone

prep bowls

quiche plate or quiche
pan

removable-bottomed
pan

roasting pan

rolling pin

round cake pans

rubber spatula

scale

scraper

sifter

square cake pan

tart pan

tube pan

whisk

UTENSILS FOR GRINDING AND GRATING

citrus juicer

citrus press

citrus reamer or reamer

coffee mill or coffee
grinder

egg slicer

food mill

food processor

garlic press

grain mill

grater

juice extractor

mandoline

masher

meat grinder

meat hammer or meat
pounder and tenderizer

mincer

mortar and pestle

nutcracker

pasta maker

peeler

pepper mill or pepper grinder

potato masher

potato ricer

pounder

rasp

rolling pin

salt mill

spice grinder

scraper

squeezer

stoner

zester

UTENSILS FOR MEASURING

balance

candy thermometer or jelly thermometer

deep-fat thermometer

digital scale

dough thermometer

dry measuring cups (¼ to 1 cup)

egg timer

hydrometer

kitchen scale

kitchen timer

liquid measuring cups (1 cup, 2 cup, or 1 quart)

measuring spoons (¼ teaspoon, ½ teaspoon, 1 teaspoon, 1 tablespoon)

meat thermometer

oven thermometer

ruler

spring scale

thermometer

UTENSILS FOR STRAINING AND DRAINING

cheesecloth

chinois

colander

draining spoon

egg separator

fat separator

filter

food strainer

funnel

gravy separator

salad spinner

screen

sieve or fine-mesh strainer

sifter

skimmer

skimming ladle

tea ball

MASTER GROCERY LIST

☐ apples

☐ applesauce

☐ asparagus

☐ avocados

☐ baby food

☐ bacon

☐ bagels

☐ baked beans

☐ bakery items

☐ baking powder

☐ baking soda

☐ bananas

- ☐ barbecue sauce
- ☐ basil
- ☐ beans
- ☐ beef
- ☐ beer
- ☐ berries
- ☐ biscuits
- ☐ black pepper
- ☐ blue cheese
- ☐ bouillon
- ☐ bread
- ☐ bread crumbs
- ☐ breakfast food
- ☐ broccoli
- ☐ broth
- ☐ brown sugar
- ☐ butter/margarine
- ☐ cake
- ☐ cake decorating items
- ☐ cake mix
- ☐ candy/gum
- ☐ canned beans
- ☐ canned fruit
- ☐ canned soup
- ☐ canned tomatoes
- ☐ canned vegetables
- ☐ carrots
- ☐ catfish
- ☐ cauliflower
- ☐ celery
- ☐ cereal
- ☐ Cheddar cheese
- ☐ cheese
- ☐ cheese slices
- ☐ cherries

- ☐ chicken
- ☐ chili
- ☐ Chinese food
- ☐ chip or veggie dip
- ☐ chocolate
- ☐ chocolate chips
- ☐ cilantro
- ☐ cinnamon
- ☐ club soda/tonic water
- ☐ cocoa
- ☐ coffee
- ☐ coffee creamer
- ☐ coleslaw
- ☐ confectioners' sugar
- ☐ cookies
- ☐ cooking spray/nonstick cooking spray
- ☐ corn
- ☐ cornmeal
- ☐ cornstarch
- ☐ cottage cheese
- ☐ crab
- ☐ crackers
- ☐ cream (light, heavy, whipping)
- ☐ cream cheese
- ☐ croutons
- ☐ cucumbers
- ☐ cupcakes
- ☐ dairy products
- ☐ Danish pastry
- ☐ deli food
- ☐ dessert
- ☐ dietetic food
- ☐ doughnuts
- ☐ dried beans
- ☐ dried fruit

- [ ] duck
- [ ] egg rolls
- [ ] eggs
- [ ] egg salad
- [ ] English muffins
- [ ] ethnic foods
- [ ] evaporated milk
- [ ] feta cheese
- [ ] fish
- [ ] fish sticks
- [ ] flavoring extracts
- [ ] flour
- [ ] fresh fruit
- [ ] fresh vegetables
- [ ] frosting/cake icing
- [ ] frozen breakfast
- [ ] frozen French fries or other potatoes
- [ ] frozen fruit
- [ ] frozen fruit juice
- [ ] frozen vegetables
- [ ] frozen veggie burgers
- [ ] garlic
- [ ] gelatin mix
- [ ] goat cheese
- [ ] granola bars
- [ ] grapefruit
- [ ] grapes
- [ ] gravy
- [ ] ground beef
- [ ] ground turkey
- [ ] half-and-half
- [ ] ham
- [ ] hamburger rolls
- [ ] hamburgers
- [ ] herbs

- [ ] honey
- [ ] horseradish
- [ ] hot cereal
- [ ] hot chocolate mix
- [ ] hot dog rolls
- [ ] hot dogs
- [ ] hot sauce
- [ ] ice cream
- [ ] ice-cream topping
- [ ] instant mashed potato flakes
- [ ] jam/jelly/preserves
- [ ] juice
- [ ] ketchup
- [ ] kiwis
- [ ] kosher salt
- [ ] lamb
- [ ] lemon/lime juice
- [ ] lemons/limes
- [ ] lettuce/greens
- [ ] lobster
- [ ] lunch meats
- [ ] macaroni
- [ ] macaroni and cheese
- [ ] maple syrup
- [ ] margarine
- [ ] marshmallows
- [ ] mayonnaise
- [ ] meat loaf
- [ ] melons
- [ ] Mexican food
- [ ] milk
- [ ] milk flavoring
- [ ] mineral water
- [ ] mint
- [ ] molasses

- [ ] mozzarella cheese
- [ ] muffin mix
- [ ] muffins
- [ ] mushrooms
- [ ] mussels
- [ ] mustard
- [ ] nectarines
- [ ] nuts/seeds
- [ ] oatmeal
- [ ] olive oil
- [ ] olives
- [ ] onion flakes/powder/salt
- [ ] onions
- [ ] oranges
- [ ] oregano
- [ ] oysters
- [ ] packaged meals
- [ ] pancake/waffle mix
- [ ] paprika
- [ ] Parmesan cheese
- [ ] parsley
- [ ] pasta
- [ ] pasta sauce
- [ ] peaches
- [ ] peanut butter
- [ ] pears
- [ ] peppers
- [ ] pickle relish
- [ ] pickles
- [ ] pie
- [ ] pie crust
- [ ] pie filling
- [ ] pita
- [ ] pizza
- [ ] plums

- [ ] popcorn
- [ ] popsicles
- [ ] pork
- [ ] potato chips/corn chips
- [ ] potatoes
- [ ] potato salad
- [ ] poultry
- [ ] powdered milk
- [ ] pretzels
- [ ] pudding
- [ ] raisins
- [ ] ready-bake breads
- [ ] red pepper flakes
- [ ] relish
- [ ] rice
- [ ] ricotta cheese
- [ ] rolls
- [ ] rye bread
- [ ] salad dressing
- [ ] salad ingredients
- [ ] salmon
- [ ] salsa
- [ ] salt
- [ ] sausage
- [ ] seafood
- [ ] shortening
- [ ] shrimp
- [ ] soda pop
- [ ] sorbet or sherbet
- [ ] soup
- [ ] soup mixes
- [ ] sour cream
- [ ] soy sauce
- [ ] spaghetti
- [ ] spaghetti sauce

- ☐ spices
- ☐ spinach
- ☐ spirits/alcohol
- ☐ sports drinks
- ☐ squash
- ☐ steak
- ☐ steak sauce
- ☐ stuffing
- ☐ sugar
- ☐ sugar substitute
- ☐ Swiss cheese
- ☐ syrup
- ☐ tea
- ☐ tilapia
- ☐ tinned meats
- ☐ tofu
- ☐ tomatoes
- ☐ tomato paste

- ☐ tomato sauce
- ☐ tortillas
- ☐ trail mix
- ☐ tuna
- ☐ turkey
- ☐ TV dinners/frozen entrées
- ☐ vanilla extract
- ☐ veal
- ☐ vegetable oil
- ☐ vinegar
- ☐ wheat bread
- ☐ whipped cream
- ☐ white bread
- ☐ wine (red, white)
- ☐ Worcestershire sauce
- ☐ yeast
- ☐ yogurt
- ☐ zucchini

ABSINTHE is a bitter green liqueur of distilled wine mixed with oil of wormwood (*Artemisia absinthium*), anise, and other herbs. The term comes from the French absinthe, meaning "wormwood plant." It is 68% alcohol (136 proof) and is served diluted with sugared water. The liqueur was invented by Dr. Pierre Ordinaire, a Frenchman living in Switzerland, who sold the recipe to Monsieur Pernod in 1797. Absinthe has a reputation as a mysterious, addictive, and mind-altering drink. It has been seen or featured in fine art, movies, video, music, and literature. The liqueur is often shown as an unnaturally glowing yellow-green liquid that is set on fire before drinking. The United States, along with many other nations, banned absinthe in 1912 because the spirit was thought to spark violent crimes and social disorder. It remained illegal in the United States until 2007. Microdistilleries have started making small batches of high-quality absinthe in the United States.

ACIDIC food contains acid, any of several sour substances that make food sour or bitter in taste. Examples of acidic foods include beans, broth, cheeses (aged), corn, cranberries, eggs, fish, fowl, grains, gravy, meat, plums, prunes, sour cream, and yogurt. Other acidic substances are artificial sweeteners, beer, chocolate, coffee, jams and jellies, liquor, and pastries and cakes made from white flour, sugar, and wine.

> **HINT** Acidic food can be seasoned with salt and pepper or toned down with dairy or fat, or have sweetness added to counter the acidity.

ACORN SQUASH is an acorn-shaped winter squash with a ridged, dark green rind and yellow or orange flesh.

> **HINT** Acorn squash can be kept in the refrigerator for up to one week. Whole acorn squash can be kept in a cool dark place for months.

ACTIVE DRY YEAST is a granular powdered yeast in which yeast cells in dehydrated granules are alive but dormant because of the lack of moisture; it is used to leaven bread.

> **HINT** You can tell that active dry yeast is active by looking at the 10-minute result. The yeast will have expanded and the mixture will look bubbly or foamy. If you do not see bubbles or foam, your yeast has expired. Try another package and proof again. It's very important not to overheat your water, which can kill active dry yeast. Keep the water comfortably warm, but don't overwarm it.

ADAM'S FIG: see PLANTAIN.

ADDITIVE, also called FOOD ADDITIVE, is a substance added directly to food during processing for purposes such as preservation, coloring, or stabilization. To regulate additives and inform consumers, each additive is assigned a unique number. Initially these were the E numbers used in Europe for all approved additives. This numbering scheme has now been adopted and extended by the Codex Alimentarius Commission to internationally identify all additives, regardless of whether they are approved for use.

ADE or **-ADE** is a suffix indicating a sweetened drink produced from a particular fruit, as in lemonade, limeade, and orangeade.

ADOBO SAUCE is a dark red marinade and condiment used in Latin American, Mexican, and southern U.S. dishes, including chipotles, tomatoes, garlic, vinegar, salt, and spices. The term adobo also refers to a Filipino meat dish seasoned with garlic, soy sauce, vinegar, and spices.

ADZUKI, AZUKI, ADZUK, or **ADUKI** (Japanese for "red bean") is a small, round, dark red, edible bean (*Vigna angularis*), first grown in Japan and China. After the soybean, adzuki are the most commonly used beans in Japanese cookery.

AEBLESKIVER are light, nonyeast Danish dumplings filled with apple purée and cooked in a special aebleskiver pan.

AFTER-DINNER DRINK is alcohol for after a meal or any alcoholic beverage served after a meal.

AGAVE is a plant whose sap is used in making tequila. The name is from the Greek *agunos*, "noble/highborn." Tequila is required to be at least 51% agave; the remainder is usually sugarcane or maize.

AGING of meat is done mainly by hanging in cold storage, where the enzyme action improves the flavor and tenderness of the meat. Fresh (unaged) meat is a brighter cherry red, with the fat a creamy white. When meat is aged, the color darkens and the surface dries. Aging of cheese is a very important stage. The aging period (also called ripening, or, in French, *affinage*) lasts from a few days to several years. As a cheese ages, microbes and enzymes transform texture and intensify flavor. This transformation is largely a result of the breakdown of casein proteins and milkfat into a complex mix of amino acids, amines, and fatty acids.

> **HINTS** Only top-quality, whole pieces of meats that are well covered with fat may be aged. Because the surface must be discarded after aging, it would be too wasteful to use small cuts, such as individual chops or steaks, for this process.

> Tenderizing meat before aging improves flavor. If the meat is stored for up to several weeks in an ideal aging environment (34°F–38°F plus ultraviolet light to minimize mold), there is a natural enzymatic change that softens some of the connective tissue. Shrinkage of 10%–20% occurs, which also intensifies flavor. The meat proteins break down into amino acids, which have a stronger flavor, and

the meat loses 1% of its water content (by weight) per day, making the flavor more intense.

AGNOLOTTI is a type of small semicircular pasta stuffed with meat, cheese, or other filling and sealed at the edges. The name is from the Italian *agnello*, "lamb," or *anello*, "ring."

AHI: see YELLOWFIN TUNA.

AIOLI is a type of mayonnaise made with garlic, egg, lemon juice, and olive oil. Aioli is French for "garlic," *ai*, and "oil," *oli*.

ALA: see BULGUR.

À LA or **ALLA** means "in the manner or style of" and indicates that a dish has been prepared or garnished in a certain style.

À LA BROCHE: see BROCHETTE.

À LA CARTE, a French term literally meaning "by the card or menu," refers to a menu from which dishes are ordered as separately priced items, as opposed to a table d'hôte or prix fixe menu.

À LA KING indicates a dish of cubed or diced chicken or turkey in a cream sauce with vegetables such as green peppers and red or pimiento peppers. This dish, originally called chicken à la Keene, was created before 1912 either when Foxhall Keene, the son of a Wall Street broker, requested that the Delmonico's restaurant chef create a chicken dish, or when the chef at the Claridge Hotel in London dreamed it up to honor J. R. Keene, who had won the Grand Prix.

À LA MARENGO: see MARENGO.

À LA MEUNIÈRE: see MEUNIÈRE.

À LA MILANESE: see MILANESE.

À LA MODE, French for "in the current fashion," was first used for beef made in a rich stew, usually with wine and vegetables. À la mode is also a North American term that came into use around 1920 for a topping of ice cream on a pie or other dessert.

À LA NAGE: see NAGE.

À LA NIÇOISE: see NIÇOISE.

À LA POLONAISE: see POLONAISE.

À LA PROVENÇAL: see PROVENÇAL.

À LA RUSSE is prepared "in Russian style," with sour cream and beets.

ALASKA KING CRAB or **ALASKA CRAB**: see KING CRAB.

ALBACORE is a large tuna (*Thunnus alalunga*) with long pectoral fins that is a source of canned tuna. Its name came into English via the Portuguese *albacor* or Spanish *albacora*, but ultimately from the Arabic *albakurah*, meaning "the young cow/heifer." In the United States albacore tuna is the only tuna species that can be marketed as "white meat tuna."

ALBERT SAUCE, also called SAUCE ALBERT, is a rich cream–based horseradish sauce usually served with beef, basically a velouté with horseradish and mustard. The name is attributed variously to Prince Albert of Sax-Coborg-Gotha, the husband of Queen Victoria; Albert (Albrecht) Pfalzgraf (1554); and a French actress, Madame Albert.

ALCOHOL refers to any intoxicating liquor containing the pungent liquid ethanol, with the basic chemical formula of C_2H_5OH. The word is from the Arabic *al-kohl*, "a substance obtained by distillation," and came to be used of any distillate. Its first meaning was "finely ground powder/kohl," and Arabian alchemists inventing the distillation of alcohol by a similar process borrowed the name. When spirits or wine are cooked, the alcohol in them does not completely evaporate. From 5% to 85% of the alcohol may remain, depending on cooking time, temperature, and type of beverage.

ALCOHOLIC DRINKS NAMED AFTER PEOPLE, PLACES, AND SO ON

A person who gives or is supposed to have given his or her name to a people, place, product, or institution is an eponym (from the Greek *epi-*, "upon," and *onuma*, "name"). Jack Daniel bought a still at age thirteen. In 1904 he entered his Old No. 7 Tennessee sipping whiskey at the World's Fair held in St. Louis, Missouri. Of the twenty whiskeys from around the world, his was the only one awarded the World's Fair gold medal and honored as the world's best whiskey. There are many interesting stories like this behind the people and places who have had alcoholic drinks named after them.

BACARDI (Don Facundo Bacardi Masso, rum distiller)

BAILEYS (Name based on Irish brand)

BEEFEATER (Popular name of the Yeoman Warders, the ceremonial guards of the Tower of London)

BENEDICTINE (Benedictine monks)

BLOODY MARY (Appellation of Mary I of England)

BOURBON (Bourbon county in Kentucky)

BRANDY ALEXANDER (Origin unknown)

BRONX COCKTAIL (The NYC borough)

CAPTAIN MORGAN (Seventeenth-century Caribbean privateer)

DOM PÉRIGNON (Benedictine monk)

GIBSON (May be named for Charles Dana Gibson)

GIMLET (Possibly from drill for small holes)

GIN RICKEY (Colonel Joseph K. Rickey [1842–1903], U.S. politician, said to have Invented the drink in a Washington DC bar in the late nineteenth century)

GROG (Nickname of an English admiral)

HARVEY WALLBANGER (A Manhattan Beach, California, surfer)

HENNESSY (Richard Hennessy, founder of a cognac distillery)

JACK DANIEL (Jasper Newton "Jack" Daniel, distillery founder)

JIM BEAM (The Boehm family, who founded a distillery and eventually changed the spelling to Beam)

JOHNNIE WALKER (John Walker, who sold whiskey at his grocery store)

JOSE CUERVO (José María Guadalupe Cuervo, tequila distiller)

MARTINI (May be named for a bartender named Martini)

MARTINI & ROSSI (Alessandro Martini, businessman, and Luigi Rossi, winemaker)

MICKEY FINN (American saloon keeper)

ROB ROY (Robert McGregor, Scottish freebooter)

SCOTCH (Scotland)

SEAGRAM (Joseph Seagram, Canadian distiller)

SMIRNOFF (Pyotr Arsenievich Smirnov, Vodka distiller)

TOM COLLINS (From hoax conversation about the nonexistent Tom Collins)

ALCOHOLIC SPIRITS, CORDIALS, LIQUORS, AND LIQUEURS

A spirit is defined as a liquid that is an essence or extract from some substance, especially one obtained by distillation. A cordial is defined as an aromatized and sweetened spirit used as a beverage. A liquor is a drink produced by fermentation or distillation of a mash of various ingredients, including grains or other plants. A liqueur is a strong alcoholic liquor sweetened and flavored with aromatic substances. The terms are not interchangeable and the differences lie in the way the various flavors are obtained. Liqueurs are spirit-based drinks to which flavors are added, usually by infusion, and are often enhanced by sweetening. Essential oils and extracts are used to flavor many of today's liqueurs. Sometimes spirits are flavored, but unflavored liqueurs do not exist—they are simply known as spirits. Liqueurs are also known as cordials in the United Kingdom and Australia. Some common alcoholic drinks are listed here.

ABISANTE	AMARETTO	ANISETTE
ABSINTHE	AMERICA WHISKEY	APPLE BRANDY
ADVOCAAT OR ADVOKAAT	AMER PICON	APPLEJACK
ALCOOL BLANC	ANGOSTURA BITTERS	APRICOT BRANDY
ALMONDRADO	ANISE	APRY

(continued)

AQUAVIT OR AKVAVIT
ARMAGNAC
ARRACK
ASIAGO
B AND B
BATHTUB GIN
BENEDICTINE
BENEDICTINE CAFÉ
BITTERS
BLENDED WHISKEY
BOURBON
BRANDY
CALVADOS
CANADIAN WHISKEY
CASSIS
CHARTREUSE
CHERI-SUISSE
CHERRY MARNIER
CHERRY ROCHER
CHOCLAIR
CHOCOCO
CHOCOLATE LIQUEUR
COCORIBE
COFFEE LIQUEUR
COFFEE SAMBUCA
COGNAC
COINTREAU
CORDIAL MÉDOC
CORN LIQUOR
CORN WHISKEY
COURVOISIER
CRÈME D'AMANDE
CRÈME DE ABRICOTS
CRÈME DE BANANAS
CRÈME DE CACAO
CRÈME DE CASSIS
CRÈME DE CERISE
CRÈME DE FRAISE OR
CRÈME DE FRAISES
CRÈME DE FRAMBOISE

CRÈME DE MENTHE
CRÈME DE MOKA
CRÈME DE NOYAUX
CRÈME DE ROSE
CRÈME DE VIOLETTE
CURAÇAO
DRAMBUIE
DUTCH GIN
EAU DE VIE
FRAMBOISE
FRANGELICO
GALLIANO
GENEVA
GIN
GLAYVA
GOLDSCHLAGER
GRAIN ALCOHOL
GRAND MARNIER
GRAPPA
GROG
IRISH MIST
IRISH WHISKEY
JAMAICA GIN
JAMAICA RUM
KAHLÚA
KIR
KIRSCH(WASSER)
KUMMEL
MALT LIQUOR
MALT WHISKEY
MANDARINE NAPOLEON
MAO-TAI
MARASCHINO
MARC
MASH
MESCAL
METAXA
MIDORI
MOCHA LIQUEUR
MOONSHINE

NEGRA
OKOLEHAO
ORANGE CAFÉ
OUZO
PARFAIT D'AMOUR
PASHA
PASTIS
PEAR BRANDY
PEPPERMINT SCHNAPPS
PERNOD
PLUM BRANDY
POIRE WILLIAM
PRUNELLA
PULQUE
RAKI
RATAFIA
ROCK AND RYE
ROIANO
RON COCO
RUM
RYE OR RYE WHISKEY
SAMBUCA
SCHNAPPS
SCIARADA
SCOTCH WHISKEY OR
SCOTCH OR SCOTCH WHISKY
SINGLE-MALT SCOTCH
SLIVOVITZ
SLOE GIN
SOUTHERN COMFORT
STREGA
TEQUILA
TIA MARIA
TRIPLE SEC
TUACA
VODKA
WHISKEY
WILD TURKEY
YUKON JACK

AL DENTE describes pasta cooked just long enough to be still firm but not too soft. The term is Italian, literally meaning "to the tooth," and can be applied to other kinds of food besides pasta.

ALE is a general name for beer made with a top-fermenting yeast; in parts of the United States an ale is (by law) a brew of more than 4% alcohol by volume.

Ale is usually stronger and more bitter than beer. Ale is a very old word, descended from Old English and Old Norse. Because of the brewing process, ales tend to take significantly less time to brew than lagers. Typically, ales have a fuller body and sweeter taste than lagers.

ALE/BEER DIFFERENCES

NAMES	DESCRIPTION/COLOR	ALCOHOLIC STRENGTH
ALE (IN UK)	fermented barley flavored with hops/ pale yellow	medium
ALE (IN U.S.)	fermented hops at high temperature/pale yellow	medium
BEER	malt, sugar, hops fermented with yeast/pale yellow to dark brown	low or medium
BITTER	draft beer, strong hops flavor, low effervescence/light brown	low
LAGER	young, effervescent/pale yellow	low or medium
PORTER	black malt/dark brown	medium or strong
STOUT	porter more strongly flavored with malt and hops/blackish brown	strong

ALFREDO is a rich cream-based butter and cheese sauce usually served with pasta such as fettuccine. It is named for Alfredo di Lelio, the Italian chef who invented it in 1914 to satisfy his pregnant wife, who had lost her appetite.

ALLA BOLOGNESE: see BOLOGNESE.

ALLA CARBONARA: see CARBONARA.

ALLIGATOR PEAR: see AVOCADO.

ALL-PURPOSE FLOUR is the finely ground and sifted meal of a blend of high-gluten hard wheat and low-gluten soft wheat, which can be used in most food recipes calling for flour. All-purpose flour comes bleached or unbleached, but they are interchangeable.

ALLSPICE is the ground dried berries of a tropical evergreen tree (*Pimenta dioica*). Allspice is used as a spice and is so named because it is reminiscent of a combination of cinnamon, cloves, and nutmeg. The spice was discovered by Christopher Columbus. Allspice is also called PIMENTO, which should not be confused with the pimiento, and is also called JAMAICA PEPPER because Columbus and other early explorers thought the berries resembled peppercorns. The only spice that is grown exclusively in the Western Hemisphere is allspice.

ALMOND is the edible, oval-shaped, brown-skinned seed of the almond tree (*Prunus dulcis* or *amygdalus*). The word comes from the Latin *amygdala* and the Greek *amygdale*, "almond." Almond should be pronounced without the *l*. True almond paste cannot be made in home kitchens because it contains oil of bitter almonds, and both bitter almonds and apricot pits contain a toxic chemical that must be neutralized by commercial processing. The FDA prohibits the importation or sale of bitter almonds to consumers. Botanically, the almond is related to the cherry, peach, plum, and apricot.

ALUMINUM FOIL: see FOIL.

AMANDINE (French for "almond") indicates that a dish is served or prepared with slivered almonds; an example is sole amandine.

AMARANTH, also called CALLALOO or CHINESE SPINACH, is a high-protein plant grown for its leaves and somewhat peppery seeds, which can be cooked or eaten raw and are used in Asian and Caribbean cuisine. The seeds, which are rich in protein and calcium with a mild peppery flavor, are used as a cereal or can be ground into flour. The word is from the Greek *amarantos*, "not corruptible/not fading," referring to an imaginary flower reputed to never fade, which later became the name for this plant. Amaranth is the only known food to contain 75%–87% of the total human nutritional requirements.

AMARETTO is an almond-flavored Italian liqueur made from apricot pits. The word is Italian and means "little bitter (one)." The original brand, Amaretto di Saronno, dates to 1851.

AMERICAN CHEESE harks back to around 1760 and is a smooth processed cow's milk cheese of white, yellow, or orange color that is in essence a young Cheddar or a blend of cheeses including Cheddar.

AMERICANISMS

These food terms of American origin do not necessarily reflect the origin of the foods:

BAVARIAN CREAM	FRENCH FRIES	RUSSIAN TEA
CANADIAN BACON	FRENCH TOAST	SPANISH RICE
DANISH PASTRY	GERMAN CHOCOLATE CAKE	SWISS CHEESE
ENGLISH MUFFIN	RUSSIAN DRESSING	TURKISH TAFFY

AMERICAN RICE: see B<small>ULGUR</small>.

AMUSE-BOUCHE or **AMUSE-GUEULE** (French for "that which amuses the mouth") is a small bite of food or an appetizer-sized portion; it is often served before a meal, typically without charge at restaurants.

ANADAMA BREAD, AMADAMA BREAD, or **AMMY DAMMY BREAD** is a yeast-raised corn and molasses bread originally made in colonial New England. The word is of unknown origin.

ANCHO CHILE is a dried poblano pepper with a mellow, sweet pepper flavor.

ANCHOVY is a small silvery ocean fish of the herring family whose flesh is used for food; it is often sold pickled or salted and canned in oil. The term is from the Spanish and Portuguese *anchova*; the Greek *aphye*, "small fry"; or from the Basque *anchu*, "dried fish."

> **HINT** Jarred anchovies offer better flavor and texture than canned. Transfer leftover canned anchovies to a covered glass or plastic container and keep for up to one week in the refrigerator. Salted anchovies in a nonreactive container will keep for several weeks in the refrigerator. They must be boned and rinsed before using. Anchovy paste in a tube should be refrigerated after opening.

ANDOUILLE or **ANDOUILLETTE** is a type of pork sausage. Andouille refers to a spicy smoked pork sausage with garlic and Cajun seasonings, and andouillette is a fresh pork sausage made with tripe or chitterlings. The latter is a French diminutive of andouille (the larger version), which is descended from a Latin word meaning "to insert." Though there are many varieties of sausages with the name andouille, Guémené andouille and Vire andouille are the only two authentic varieties. Guémené andouille is protected by a trademark, and Vire andouille's authenticity is guaranteed with a method of production and an area of production.

ANGEL FOOD CAKE or **ANGEL CAKE** is a very airy sponge cake made with egg whites and baked in a tall tube pan. It is so named because it has no fat and is thus a cake even an angel could not resist.

> **HINT** Once an angel food cake is baked, the fragile network of its structure begins to compress. With the pan turned upside down, the air cells stay stretched until the structure solidifies as the cake cools. To slice easily, freeze the cake, then thaw overnight before cutting.

ANGEL HAIR is pasta in very fine, long, thin strands; it is smaller in diameter than vermicelli and capellini.

> **HINT** Since angel hair pasta is so fine, a light or delicate sauce should be used instead of a chunky and dense sauce.

ANGELS ON HORSEBACK are shucked oysters wrapped in bacon and broiled, grilled, or baked and served on buttered toast points or in oyster shells. Angels on horseback is a traditional British hors d'oeuvre and postlude (concluding dish), and it is complemented by devils on horseback, the "hot" version with Tabasco and red peppers. The "angels" are oysters, the saddle is the bacon, and the "horse" is the toast.

ANISE or **ANISESEED** is an aromatic plant with licorice-flavored seeds. The word comes from the Greek *anison*, "anise/dill," and the plant is a native of the ancient Levant and Greece. Anise is one of the world's oldest known spice plants, and it has been used since ancient times for both culinary and medicinal purposes, with some evidence pointing to its use in Egypt around 1500 BC. Today, most of the licorice flavoring in licorice candy comes from anise.

ANJOU is a variety of pear with green skin and firm flesh, named for a former province of France.

> **HINT** Ripen a pear in a paper bag at room temperature, then place it in the refrigerator for up to a few days until you are ready to eat it.

ANTIOXIDANT is a molecule capable of slowing or preventing the oxidation of other molecules. Oxidation reactions can produce free radicals, which start chain reactions that damage cells. Antioxidants are widely used as ingredients in dietary supplements in the hope of maintaining health and preventing diseases such as cancer and coronary heart disease.

ANTIPASTO, literally meaning "before food," is an Italian course of appetizers or a snack consisting of cured meats, cheeses, olives, and sometimes fish. The *pasto* in antipasto is not related to pasta—*pasto* derives from the Latin *pastus*, meaning "food." In traditional European dining, the main purpose of antipasto is to extend the meal. The dining experience is designed to allow people to enjoy food slowly and to encourage conversation.

APERITIF or **APÉRITIF**, also called PREPRANDIAL LIBATION, is a light alcoholic drink taken before a meal. The word aperitif, literally meaning "open the appetite up," comes from the Latin *aperire*, "to open," the idea being that the drink opens the stomach and stimulates the appetite. Consuming an aperitif before a meal did not become a generally accepted custom until the twentieth century.

APHRODISIAC FOODS

An aphrodisiac is a food, drink, or drug that stimulates sexual desire. The word comes from the Greek *aphrodisiakos/aphrodisios*, from Aphrodite, the goddess of love. The following foods are purported to have this effect on some people.

ALMOND	EEL	PEACH
ANISE	FIG	PINEAPPLE
APRICOT	FROG'S LEGS	PINE NUT
ARUGULA	GARLIC	PRUNE
ASPARAGUS	GINGER	RASPBERRY
AVOCADO	GINSENG	SNAIL
BANANA	HONEY	SPICY FOOD
CARROT	LICORICE	SPINACH
CAVIAR	LOBSTER	STRAWBERRY
CELERY	MACARONI	THYME
CHOCOLATE	MUSTARD	TRUFFLE
CLOVES	NUTMEG	VANILLA
CORIANDER OR CILANTRO	OYSTER	
CUTTLEFISH	PARSNIP	

À POINT refers to a food that is cooked just enough so that it is neither overcooked nor undercooked. Applied to steaks, this means medium-rare to medium.

APPETIZER is any small dish of food served at the beginning of a meal to stimulate the appetite. The term derived from the word appetizing around 1862.

> **CONFUSABLE** APPETIZER/HORS D'OEUVRE. An appetizer is a finger food served at the table as a first course, while an hors d'oeuvre is usually a passed finger food.

APPETIZERS AND HORS D'OEUVRES

An appetizer (from the Latin *appetitiare*, "to cause to want food") is any savory foodstuff taken to create an appetite for the main meal. (An aperitif is the drink equivalent of this.) Hors d'oeuvres means "outside the (main) work" because these appetizers are outside the principal task of preparing the meal. Hors d'oeuvres are described by *Larousse Gastronomique* as the first dish to be served at a meal and are, literally,

(continued)

11

"additional to the menu," but they can also be served in between the courses of a meal to whet the appetite or clear the palate. All appetizers and hors d'oeuvres are supposed to be light and delicate, stimulating the appetite for the heavier dishes to follow. There are two main types: hot and cold. The word antipastic means pertaining to appetizers or hors d'oeuvres or the eating of them. The plural of hors d'oeuvre can be hors d'oeuvres or hors d'oeuvre. The following foods are commonly served as hors d'oeuvres.

ANTIPASTO	EGG ROLLS	PICKLES
ARTICHOKE HEARTS	FINGER SANDWICHES	PIMIENTOS
BLINI	FISH BALLS	PIZZA BITES
BRANDIED FRUITS	FRITTERS	POPCORN
BREADS	FRUIT	POTATO CHIPS
CARROT STICKS	FRUIT CUP	PRETZELS
CAVIAR	GHERKINS	PROSCIUTTO
CELERY STICKS	GRAVLAX	RADISHES
CHEESE	GUACAMOLE	RUMAKI
CHEESE BALLS	SLICED HAM	SALAD
CHEESE PUFFS	HOT CANAPÉS	SALMON CANAPÉS OR SMOKED SALMON
CHICKEN WINGS	HUMMUS	SARDINES
CHIPS	KABOBS	SHRIMP COCKTAIL
CHUTNEY	LOBSTER CANAPÉS OR SALAD	SLAW
COCKTAIL HOT DOGS	MEATBALLS	SLICED ROAST BEEF
COCKTAIL SAUSAGES	MELON	SLICED TURKEY
COLD CANAPÉS	MINI QUICHES	SPANAKOPITAS
CORN RELISH	NUTS	STEAK BITES
CRABMEAT	OLIVES	STUFFED MUSHROOMS
CRACKERS	ONION RELISH	STUFFED TOMATOES
CRANBERRY SAUCE	ONIONS	SWEDISH MEATBALLS
CUCUMBER CRUDITÉS	PARTY MIX	TRAIL MIX
DEVILED EGGS	PÂTÉ	TURNOVERS
DEVILED HAM	PEPPER RELISH	
DIPS		

APPLE is a firm round fruit (genus *Malus*) with a central core; red, green, or yellow skin; and white or yellow flesh. It was probably the earliest cultivated fruit. Apple is one of the oldest English words and originally referred to fruit in general. The apple is the most common tree fruit with seven thousand known varieties. An apple has a stem end and a blossom end. About 20%–25% of an apple's volume is air, much more than in most fruits. That's why you can bob for apples. There is space between the cells of an apple's tissue, which is why an apple "cracks" when you bite into it.

APPLE ESSENTIALS

CONFUSABLE APPLE JUICE/APPLE CIDER. Apple juice is a filtered clear liquid, while apple cider is usually an unfiltered caramel-colored cloudy liquid. Apple juice has high sugar content, while apple cider is made from early-harvest apples, making it more tart. In many countries apple cider is an alcoholic drink; in the United States such a drink is called hard cider. Apple cider is popular on the East Coast, but rarely found on the West Coast.

■ When selecting apples, look for fruit with unbroken skin, good color, and no soft brown spots. Seek out newly harvested local apples. Apples continue to ripen at room temperature, so refrigerate them in the cold back part of the refrigerator for one week or more.

■ Use a well-greased muffin tin when baking stuffed apples to help them keep their shape.

■ An apple is ready to eat when the flesh softens slightly and the color deepens.

As an apple ripens, its sweetness intensifies, its acidity drops, and its aroma becomes stronger.

■ Use a peeler to remove the peel from an apple, because a knife takes too much of the flesh with the peel. After removing the stem, start the peeler at the stem end and turn the apple into the blade of the peeler. Angle the peeler at about sixty degrees to spiral the peel off.

■ When preparing baked apples, hollow out the core using a melon baller without going all the way to the bottom.

■ The browned part on an apple, whether on a cut or bruised apple, is safe to eat. Phenolic compounds and enzymes in the apple's cells are just reacting with air.

■ Peeled and sliced apples can be kept in apple juice or lemon juice to prevent them from turning brown.

APPLE VARIETIES

The apple tree, the most widely cultivated fruit tree in the world, originated in Asia Minor and was growing wild in Europe by prehistoric times. Known throughout the ancient world, the apple was cultivated early in many varieties and has been found in ancient recipes. The apple belongs to the family Rosaceae and the genus *Malus* (which includes about twenty-five species); it is one of the pome fruits, in which the ripened ovary and surrounding tissue both become fleshy and edible. Apples fall into three broad classes—cider varieties, cooking varieties, and dessert varieties—which differ by color, size, aroma, smoothness, crispness, and tang. Apples provide vitamins A and C, are high in carbohydrates, and are an excellent source of dietary fiber. These are some popular apple varieties:

(continued)

ADANAC	GOLDEN DELICIOUS	PORTER
AKANE	GOLDEN HARVEST	PRIMA
ALBANY BEAUTY	GOLDEN SUPREME	PRISCILLA
AMERICAN MOTHER	GRANNY SMITH	RAMBO
ANNA	GRAVENSTEIN	RED ASTRACHAN
ARCTIC	GREEN SWEET	RED DELICIOUS
ARKANSAS BLACK	GRIMES GOLDEN	RED ROME
AURORA	HONEY CRISP	REDFREE
BAILEY SWEET	HUBBARDSTON	RHODE ISLAND GREENING
BALDWIN	IDA RED	RIBSTON PIPPIN
BELLE DE BOSKOOP	INGRAM	ROMAN STEM
BELMAC	IRISH PEACH	ROME
BELMONT	JERSEY BLACK	ROME BEAUTY
BEN DAVIS	JERSEYMAC	ROXBURY RUSSET
BLUE PERMAIN	JONAGOLD	RUSSET
BRAEBURN	JONARED	SAINT LAWRENCE
BRAMLEY	JONATHAN	SIR PRIZE
BUCKINGHAM	KIDDS ORANGE RED	SNOWAPPLE
COLLINS	LADY SWEET	SPARTAN
CORTLAND	LIBERTY	SPIGOLD
COX'S ORANGE PIPPIN	LOBO	STARKRIMSON
CRITERION	LODI	STARR
DELICIOUS	LONGFIELD	STAYMAN
DISCOVERY	MACOUN	TWENTY OUNCE
DORSET GOLDEN	MCINTOSH	TYDEMAN'S LATE ORANGE
EARLIBLAZE	MCMAHON	TYDEMAN'S RED
EARLY HARVEST	MISSOURI	VIRGINIA BEAUTY
EIN SHEMER	MONROE	WEALTHY
EMPIRE	MUTSU	WILLIAMS
ENGLISH SWEET	NEWTON PIPPIN	WINESAP
FORTUNE	NORTHERN SPY	WINTER BANANA
FREEDOM	OLDENBURG	WORCESTER PEARMAIN
FREYBURG	ORTLEY	YELLOW NEWTON
FUJI	PERMAIN	YELLOW TRANSPARENT
GALA	PINK LADY	YORK IMPERIAL
GIDEON	PIPPIN	

APPLE PANDOWDY is a deep-dish apple pie or cobbler, usually sweetened with molasses; see PANDOWDY.

APRICOT is a small round fruit of a tree (*Prunus armeniaca*), with a soft, furry, yellowish orange skin and a single pit. The Romans regarded it as a type of early ripening peach and its name comes from the Latin epithet *praecocus*, "early ripening," which became the Byzantine Greek *berikokkia*, then the Arabic *al-birquq/al-barquq*.

The Catalan language adopted this word as *abrecoc/abrecock*, which is the source of the English word. The final *t* came soon after, from the French *abricot*.

> **HINT** Apricots peak in July, but do not travel well. Look for golden color when fully ripe; ripe fruit will indent slightly when pressed. If you must store them, do so in the refrigerator for up to two days. If not fully ripe, leave out at room temperature.

APRICOT VARIETIES AND TYPES

The apricot has very little juice. The smooth stone or pit comes away easily and contains an edible kernel (almond), which is used to flavor apricot jam. The apricot tree grew wild in China several thousand years ago. The ancient Greeks called the apricot the "golden egg of the sun." It was doubtless among the fruits brought into southern California early in the eighteenth century by Spanish missionaries. It continues to be cultivated in warm temperate regions. Apricots are a good source of vitamin A and are high in natural sugar content; dried apricots are an excellent source of iron. Some popular varieties and types of apricots are listed here:

ACME OR CHINESE OR SHENSE

ALEXANDER OR RUSSIAN NO. 2

BERGERON

BLENHEIM OR SHIPLEY'S

BLUSHED APRICOT

BREDA OR ANANAS OR DEHOLLANDE

CHINESE APRICOT

CLINGSTONE

CLUSTER

COMPRESSED APRICOT

CONICAL APRICOT

CRIMSON APRICOT

DESSERT APRICOT

EARLY APRICOT

EARLY GOLDEN OR DUBOIS

FREESTONE

GOLDBAR

GOLDCOT

GOLDSTRIKE

HARGLOW

HARRIS OR HARRIS HARDY

HEMSKIRKE

JUMBOCOT

KITCHEN APRICOT

LARGE APRICOT

LARGE EARLY OR GROS PRECOCE

MARKET APRICOT

MEDIUM APRICOT

MOOR-PARK OR DENANCY OR MOORPARK

NEWCASTLE OR NEWCASTLE EARLY

OBLATE APRICOT

OBLONG APRICOT

ORANGE APRICOT

ORANGE OR EARLY ORANGE

ORANGE DE PROVENCE

PEACH OR ROYAL PEACH

PERFECTION

RED APRICOT

RIVAL

ROUGE DU ROUSSILLON

ROUND APRICOT

ROYAL OR ABRICOT ROYAL

RUSSIAN

SEMICLINGSTONE

SHERIDAN

SMALL APRICOT

ST. AMBROISE

SURPRIZE

TILTON

TOMCOT

VERY LARGE

WENATCHEE-MOORPARK

WHITE APRICOT

YELLOW APRICOT

ARABICA is a species of coffee plant from Ethiopia, the earliest cultivated species of coffee tree and the most widely grown. It produces around 70% of the world's coffee. All fine, specialty, and fancy coffees come from *Coffea arabica*, the species name assigned to the coffee tree by European botanist Linnaeus while categorizing the flora of the Arabian peninsula. Out of all the commercially cultivated species of coffee, Arabica contains the least amount of caffeine. While there are several coffee species, two major commercial beans produce around 90% of the world's coffee: Arabica and robusta. Arabica trees produce around 70% of the world's coffee, and robusta trees produce around 20%.

ARBORIO RICE is short-grain, high-starch, white Italian rice that becomes fat and creamy when cooked and is used for risotto. It is named for Arborio, the town in the Po Valley in Italy where the rice is grown.

> **HINT** A pound of Arborio rice can absorb up to 6 cups of liquid without becoming mushy.

ARCTIC CHAR is a small trout (*Salvelinus alpinus*) that inhabits arctic lakes and streams of the Northern Hemisphere, and its fatty, flaky-textured meat is considered a delicacy.

ARMENIAN CRACKER BREAD: see LAVAS.

AROMA (a word tracing back to Greek) is a pleasant odor or fragrance of a plant, a wine, or cooking.

> **HINT** To rid your hands of pungent ingredient odors, wash your hands with a couple of tablespoons of mouthwash.

AROMATIC refers to any rice with an aroma and flavor like that of roasted nuts or popcorn, such as basmati, jasmine, and Texmati. The word aromatic can also describe fragrant or spicy plants used to flavor food or drink. Aromatics are important items in cooking, even though they add no nutritional value to food.

ARROWROOT or **ARROWHEAD**, also called CHINESE ARROWHEAD, CHINESE POTATO, CI GU, GOO, SEEGOO, TSE GOO, or TSU GOO, is a nutritive, fine-grained starch obtained from the root of the West Indian arrowroot plant. Arrowroot is so called because the fleshy tubers can be used to absorb poison from arrow wounds, and the word is an alteration of Arawak *aru-aru*, "meal of meals." Arrowroot is the clearest and most digestible starch.

ARTICHOKE, also called GLOBE ARTICHOKE, is a thistlelike plant and its edible flower buds. The word has been subject to widespread alteration as a result of folk etymology throughout its history, but is ultimately from the Arabic *al-karsufa/al-kharshof*, "the artichoke." The plant is unique in that the base of the flower head and its bracts are eaten; before the flower opens, it looks like a scaly sphere, which inspired the term globe artichoke. Eating artichokes creates a chemical reaction in the mouth that makes things you eat or drink taste sweeter. The responsible compound is cynarine. An artichoke is actually a flower bud; a flower will develop from the edible bud.

ARTICHOKE ESSENTIALS

CONFUSABLE ARTICHOKE/JERUSALEM ARTICHOKE. Artichoke and Jerusalem artichoke are completely different plants, both used as food.

■ The season for artichokes is early spring, but some are also available in fall and winter. Buy artichokes that are tightly closed and heavy for their size. Try to use jars of marinated artichokes for salads or spreads, but not for cooked preparations.

■ Sprinkle artichokes with a few drops of water and store in a perforated plastic bag in the coldest part of the refrigerator for up to one week. If you are cooking on the day you buy them, cool room temperature is fine.

■ Once opened, marinated artichokes can be kept in the refrigerator for up to two weeks.

■ To eat an artichoke, pull off the leaves one at a time and dip them in butter, lemon juice, vinaigrette, mayonnaise, hollandaise, or another sauce. Remove the flesh from the leaf with your teeth. The choke can be removed with a spoon and you can eat the heart. Fingers are the correct utensil for eating artichoke leaves.

■ Purple tips on an artichoke indicate too much exposure to sunlight or that the artichoke is too mature.

■ The size of an artichoke indicates where the chokes were on the stalk. The larger ones are at the top. Baby artichokes are not immature, but simply smaller ones grown lower down on the plant.

■ To prevent an artichoke from turning brown from cooking, use stainless steel cutting tools and rub the cut surface with a sliced lemon.

■ To sweeten the flavor and improve the color on an artichoke, add a small amount of sugar and salt.

■ Rub an artichoke with your fingers and listen carefully. If it is tender, the leaves will squeak. Brown streaks or scars are fine; these are called "kiss of the frost" and indicate a nice nutty flavor.

■ Smash an artichoke on a countertop to loosen the leaves and spread them apart.

■ Whole trimmed artichokes must remain upright when steamed so that all the leaves cook at an equal rate. You can stack sliced onion rings and set an artichoke upright in them in the pan.

ARTISANAL refers to food, especially bread and cheese, made with care and skill using traditional techniques. This term also applies to expensive small-batch edibles available through mail order.

ARUGULA, also called ITALIAN CRESS, ROCKET, or ROQUETTE, is a Mediterranean annual with pungent leaves harvested when young and tender; Arugula is an Italian dialect word from the Latin *eruca*, "colewort," which became the Italian *ruca*, "rocket." It is pronounced ah-ROO-guh-lah.

> **HINT** To store arugula, trim the stalk ends and rinse the leaves thoroughly under cool water. Wrap the stems of fresh leaves in damp paper towels and put in a loosely sealed plastic bag or kitchen towel in the refrigerator crisper for two days.

ASHCAKE: see JOHNNYCAKE.

ASIAGO is a strong-flavored Italian cow's milk cheese that, depending on different aging, can assume different textures. Asiago comes in small wheels with glossy rinds and is yellow inside with many small eyes. It originally was made from sheep's milk in the northern village of Asiago in the province of Vicenza. There are two forms of Asiago cheese: fresh Asiago (*pressato*), which is matured for twenty to forty days, and mature Asiago (*d'allevo*), which is matured for three to twelve months and sometimes longer.

ASPARAGUS is a plant whose spear-shaped, succulent young shoots are cooked and eaten as a vegetable. It was first called sperage, and also sperach or sparage, in English in the sixteenth and early seventeenth centuries. Around 1600 the influence of herbalists and horticultural writers made the word asparagus familiar in the aphetic form 'sparagus; this was corrupted by folk etymology before 1650 to sparagrass or sparrow-grass, which remained the name during the eighteenth century. Botanists still used the term asparagus, and during the nineteenth century this word returned into literary and polite use. It first appeared as the ancient Greek *asparagos*. Asparagus can cause a disagreeable smell in urine in about 50% of the world's population.

ASPARAGUS ESSENTIALS

- Steam or boil asparagus vertically in an asparagus steamer or horizontally in a large frying pan.

- When selecting asparagus, look for firm stalks and tight, dry tips (purple-tinged is fine). Cut ends should look fresh. Slight spreading at the top of spears is fine. White at the bottom of spears should be cut off before cooking.

- To store asparagus, cut off an inch or so at the base of the stalks and put in a shallow pan of water for up to four days in the refrigerator.

- Bend the cut end of each asparagus spear until it breaks naturally and it will snap right where the tough inedible part starts.

- A can of asparagus should be opened upside down from the bottom to avoid breaking the tips.

- Test the doneness of cooked asparagus by piercing the stalk with the tip of a knife. The stalk should offer little resistance but be tender. Remember that it continues to cook with residual heat once it has left the heat source.

- Salvage limp asparagus pieces by cutting them into one-inch lengths.

- Only the thickest, woodiest asparagus spears need peeling. Peel just two strips on opposite sides of each spear. Tough skin can be peeled up to an inch away from the tips.

- If asparagus is not too large or heavily sauced, it is appropriate to eat the spears with your fingers.

ASPIC, also called GELÉE, is a savory jelly based on fish or meat stock used as a mold for meats or vegetables. The name's origin is likely from the French *asp*, "snake," as the colors of aspic resemble those of a snake.

ASTI SPUMANTI, **ASTI SPUMANTE**, or **ASTI**, also called SPUMANTE, is a sweet sparkling white wine made from fragrant Muscat grapes, often served as an aperitif or dessert wine. Asti Spumanti originated in Asti, Italy, and is Italian for "effervescent/sparkling." Asti Spumanti is meant not to be aged, but to be drunk promptly.

AUBERGINE, also called EGGPLANT or MELONGENE, is an egg-shaped vegetable with a shiny skin that is typically dark purple but occasionally white or yellow. The word is French for "fruit of the eggplant," a diminutive of *auberge* and variant of *alberge*, "a kind of peach," from the Spanish *alberchigo*, "apricot"—but a rival origin of the word is the Catalan *alberginera*, from the Arabic *al-badinjan*, "the eggplant."

> **HINT** To reduce the large amount of oil and/or sauce an aubergine will absorb while cooking, heavily salt then rinse the sliced vegetable. Do not cook aubergine in an aluminum pan because aluminum will cause discoloring. A ripe aubergine should feel heavy at the time you buy it.

AU BLUE or **AU BLEU** is a French term referring to fish prepared immediately after it is killed, as a freshly killed fish is plunged into boiling water and poached until the skin of the fish has a bluish tinge.

AU GRATIN is literally French for "with scrapings/by grating" and originally this term referred to dried or toasted bread that was scraped from the bottom of a pan and mixed with grated cheese. Now the term (also called GRATIN, GRATINÉ, or GRATINÉE) refers to a dish sprinkled with bread crumbs or grated cheese and browned. Gratin as a noun is the term for the brown crust formed on food that has been cooked au gratin, and also for a dish cooked in this manner.

AU LAIT is French for "made/served with milk" and is used in describing coffee drinks.

AUXERROIS: see MALBEC.

AVGOLEMONO is a Greek chicken-stock soup with egg yolks, lemon, and sometimes rice. The name is Greek for "egg-lemon soup."

AVOCADO is a large, usually pear-shaped fruit (*Persea americana*) with green to blackish skin, a single large seed, and soft, light green pulp. The term is derived from Spanish, purportedly from the Aztec/Nahuatl word *ahucatl*, meaning "testicle" (in reference to the shape), and the word guacamole comes from *ahuacatl-molli*, "avocado sauce." The fruit is also called ALLIGATOR PEAR for its shape and rough skin. The avocado is one of the few fruits that contain significant amounts of fat, about 22%. Mexican avocado growers sometimes "store" their crop on the tree for up to one year. Avocados normally ripen only after they have been picked.

> **HINTS** To check an avocado for ripeness, flick the small stem. If it comes off easily and there is green underneath, the avocado is ripe.
>
> ▌ The dark green, dimpled Haas/Hass avocado should have rough skin. The Fuerte variety should have smooth, pale green, unblemished skin. Store ripe avocados at room temperature for up to two days or for a week in the refrigerator. Test ripeness by gentle finger pressure. When it gives, the Fuerte is ready; let the Haas/Hass ripen one more day.

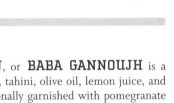

BABA GHANOUSH, **BABA GHANOUJ**, or **BABA GANNOUJH** is a Middle Eastern dish that is a purée of eggplant, tahini, olive oil, lemon juice, and garlic; it is used as a spread or dip and traditionally garnished with pomegranate seeds and mint. The Arabic term translates to "father of coquetry" in reference to its supposed invention by a member of a royal harem, but there is a second theory that it is from the Arabic *baba*, "father," and *gannuug*, perhaps a personal name.

BABY BACK RIBS are the meaty pork ribs that come from the blade and center section of the loin, the lower back rib section; the meat between the ribs is called finger meat. The origin of this term is not from the age but the size of the ribs. A typical rack of baby back ribs consists of ten to thirteen ribs. If the rack has less than ten ribs, it is called a cheater rack.

BABY VEGETABLE describes any immature vegetable, such as corn, that is much smaller than the mature version. Baby corn is also called COCKTAIL CORN. By contrast, baby carrots are simply grown-up carrots chopped into smaller pieces and peeled.

BACK BACON, also called CANADIAN BACON, is relatively fat-free bacon from the loin or rib end of a pig.

BACK OF THE HOUSE is a term for the kitchen and kitchen staff of a restaurant.

BACON is salted, dried, cured, or smoked meat from the back or sides of a pig. The term is derived from the Germanic *bache/backe* "back meat," though at first the word referred to any part of a pig. Flitch (or slab bacon) designates a whole chunk of bacon before it is cut into slices. Burned bacon can be dangerous because burning it will produce carcinogens.

BACON ESSENTIALS

■ Generally, bacon is about 50% fat. As it cooks, the fat becomes liquid and separates from the meat; this process is called rendering. The rendered fat can be put in a tightly covered container and stored in the refrigerator or freezer for sautéing or frying other foods.

■ If you buy bacon from a butcher, you can ask for the rind to be removed and for the bacon to be sliced. A whole slab stays fresher longer. A butcher-cut slab can be stored for two weeks in the refrigerator or two months in the freezer. However, bacon does not freeze well, since its high salt content will prevent satisfactory long-term freezing. In addition, the freezing creates ice crystals, causing the bacon to splatter when fried.

■ Cook bacon in a dry pan, not pre-heated, over medium-low heat. You do not have to separate the slices before cooking them. You can cook a large amount of bacon in a roasting pan at 450°F for around 25 minutes; separate the strips after 10 minutes and turn every 5 to 10 minutes after that. If you

decide to pour off the grease during cooking, do it carefully and not down the kitchen sink.

■ Buying the leanest bacon can be counterproductive, as the fat gives the bacon most of its desirable flavor and crispness. Most of the extra fat melts off during cooking. The fat on bacon should be about one-half to one-third of the total weight. You can freeze rolled-up pieces of bacon in a zip-lock freezer bag. Long-term freezing is not recommended.

■ Use paper towels over bacon when cooking it in the microwave to prevent splattering. Using paper towels under bacon when cooking it in the microwave reduces the nitrosamine level, which is considered to be a carcinogen in animals but does not seem to be an important problem for humans.

■ Microwave bacon cooks without curling. Crisp bacon can be achieved in a microwave if cooked on a bacon plate, that is, one with ridges so that the melting fat drips off.

(continued)

■ Cook bacon and store it wrapped in paper towels and plastic wrap for one week or freeze up to one month. Microwave or warm in a skillet to use. Leftover cooked bacon can be recrisped in a skillet, a microwave, or an oven. It can also be used crumbled in salads, in pasta, or on baked potatoes.

■ Once the vacuum pack is opened, bacon will usually keep for only about a week in the refrigerator, although sometimes it will keep for a couple of weeks. The ends may darken and dry out, and they should be sliced off and discarded before using.

■ Splattering can be minimized when cooking bacon by pouring off the fat as it is rendered. This will also produce crisper meat. Start the frying in a cold pan and cook over moderate heat. If the fat starts to smoke, lower the heat. Or use a bulb baster to remove the bacon fat during cooking to make the bacon extra-crispy. Drain on a rack over a paper towel–covered plate.

■ To prevent bacon from curling, soak the raw slices in cold water for 2 minutes but dry them well with toweling before cooking, or sprinkle with flour or poke a few holes in the slices.

■ Put bacon fat in an empty wax beverage container or an aluminum can, or pour into a foil-lined bowl and when it solidifies, throw it out.

■ To make bacon crumbles, chop the bacon first, then cook it.

■ Save strained bacon fat by freezing it in an ice cube tray. Once frozen, transfer to a zip-lock freezer bag.

■ Oven-cook bacon on foil in a baking pan. Cooking in a skillet yields curly bacon, but cooking it in an oven keeps the strips flat. After cooking and removing the bacon, let the grease cool, then crumple up the foil and discard.

■ Bacon must be turned often when cooking to render the fat.

BAGELS, ring-shaped rolls, take their name from the Austrian-German *beugel/bugel*, "ring," from the Yiddish *beygel*, and from the Middle High German *boug-/bouc-*, meaning "ring bracelet." In ancient Egypt there was a hard cracker with a hole in the middle called *ka'ak* that can be seen as an ancestor of the bagel. From Egypt, ancestry can be traced to classical Rome and then to France, Russia, and Poland. The present-day bagel is purported to have been born in Poland, and its first mention was in 1610 in Krakow when a piece of literature referred to it as something to give to women in labor.

> **HINT** Set a bagel on its side, holding the top steady, and slice downward in a sawing motion.

BAGUETTE, also called FRENCH STICK, is a long, thin loaf of French bread. Baguette means "little rod" and is

derived from the Latin *baculum*, "staff/stick." It is smaller than a flûte. A baguette pan is a long metal pan shaped like two or three half-cylinders joined on the long edge.

BAIN-MARIE or **BAIN MARIE** is a large pan containing hot water in which smaller pans may be set to cook food slowly or to keep food warm; often the bottom of a double boiler is used. It was originally alchemical equipment named for the sister of Moses or for an alchemist, literally "the bath of Mary." A bain-marie may be used for melting chocolate, baking cheesecake, cooking custard, warming sauces like hollandaise, and thickening condensed milk.

BAKE (BAKING) is to cook food by dry heat, especially in an oven; baking is the act or process of cooking food by dry heat in an oven. Specifically, it is to cook by dry heat acting by conduction and not by radiation, hence either in a closed place (oven) or on a heated surface (baking stone, griddle, live coals). The Old English form (c. 1000) of the word traces back to the Proto-Indo-European base **bhog-*, "to warm/roast/bake."

CONFUSABLE **BAKE/ROAST**. We use the word bake for bread and potatoes, and we usually use roast when talking about meat and vegetables cooked in an oven.

■ For many baked recipes, like cakes and cookies, the eggs and butter should be brought to room temperature for a smooth batter.

■ Baking pans should be lightweight because lighter and medium-weight pans transmit heat evenly and more quickly.

■ Do not leave batter sitting for more than 20 minutes before baking.

■ Leave space around foods during oven-baking. Don't put pans directly over each other, but stagger the pans on the different levels.

■ For larger batches of cookies, put the first batch on a liner on the pan. While the first batch bakes, put another batch on a separate liner. Let the hot cookies cool for 5 minutes before removing them from the liner.

■ Adjustments need to be made when baking at high altitudes. If you are baking at an altitude over 3,500 feet, increase the temperature setting by 25°F. Continue adding 1 tablespoon of flour for each 1,500 feet above 3,500 feet. If 1 teaspoon is required at sea level, then use ⅔ teaspoon at 3,500 feet; ½ teaspoon at 5,000 feet; ⅓ teaspoon at 6,500 feet; and ¼ teaspoon above 6,500 feet.

■ Ideally, the ingredients for a batter to be baked should be at 70°F, because at this temperature they can combine and penetrate one another to make a homogenous batter.

■ Don't open the oven too often; you lose up to 70°F each time.

■ If you take out an unneeded oven rack before baking, it can be used as a cooling rack for the baked goods.

BAKEAPPLE BERRY: see CLOUDBERRY.

BAKE BLIND or **BAKE EMPTY** is to bake a pastry shell before it is filled; the shell is often prepared by pricking it to prevent blistering and by putting in weights to keep the crust from rising. Baking blind helps keep the crust from getting soggy when a wet fruit or custard filling is placed in it.

BAKED ALASKA is a dessert of cake topped with ice cream, covered with meringue, and then quickly browned in a very hot oven. Baked Alaska was said to have been created at Delmonico's in New York City to commemorate the purchase of Alaska in 1869; the term dates in print to at least 1905 and was used by Fannie Merritt Farmer in the 1909 edition of her cookbook. When baked Alaska is browned, the meringue acts as an insulator and helps prevent the heat from melting the ice cream.

BAKED BEANS are baked navy (or haricot) beans with onion, brown sugar or molasses, and bacon in a tomato-based sauce, and their "cousin" is pork 'n' beans. In 1895 HJ Heinz first put beans with tomato sauce in a can. BOSTON BAKED BEANS are these beans baked slowly over a long period of time. Before European settlers came to America, Native Americans cooked dried beans in earthenware pots with maple syrup and bear fat.

BAKED ZITI is a dish of ziti and sauce, often topped with cheese, and baked.

BAKER'S CHEESE: see FARMER CHEESE.

BAKER'S PEEL: see PEEL.

BAKER'S RACK is a tall metal or wire shelving unit providing places for trays of baked goods, such as pies and doughnuts, to cool.

BAKERY is a building, part of a building, store, or part of a store where baked goods, such as bread and cakes, are baked and/or sold. The word appeared in English around 1820 for a place for making bread. By 2600 BC the Egyptians, who developed the first ovens and the first intentional use of leavening, were making bread by methods similar in principle to those of today; the Egyptian baking industry eventually developed more than fifty varieties of bread.

BAKEWARE or OVENWARE, is defined as heat-resistant dishes for use inside an oven, such as cake pans, pie pans, loaf pans, and baking sheets. Glass has a natural brittleness. It has low heat flow efficiency. When something hot is poured onto a cold glass bottom, cracking can ensue. Treated glass, such as Pyrex, is less vulnerable, but it has its limitations. Corningware is even less susceptible to cracking.

HINT When using glass bakeware, reduce the oven temperature by 25°F because glass conducts heat better than metal. When a metal pan is put in the oven, the radiated heat warms the pan, which in turn warms the food. If the pan is shiny, it does not heat readily. When a glass dish is put in the oven, the radiated heat passes through the glass directly to the food in the dish, which cooks the food touching the dish more quickly. Accordingly, lowering the temperature when using glass bakeware ensures that the top will brown before the bottom burns.

BAKEWARE AND COOKWARE MATERIALS

ALUMINUM: Aluminum is a great heat conductor that heats evenly and is especially good for baking. Insulated aluminum heats more slowly, which prevents burnt bottoms. Anodized aluminum is treated to make it more dense, hard, and resistant to corrosion.

CAST IRON: Cast iron absorbs and releases heat more slowly than other metals.

CERAMIC AND GLASS: Ceramic and glass conduct and retain radiant heat and are good for browning. Foods bake quickly in ceramic and glass.

COPPER: Copper heats and cools rapidly and evenly. Copper can react with food, so copper lined with stainless steel or alloyed aluminum, or with an aluminum core, is better.

NONSTICK: Nonstick aluminum is a good heat conductor, but it is not as sturdy as other materials. Select double-layer nonstick bakeware and use plastic or wooden utensils with it.

STEEL: Steel, especially heavy-gauge stainless steel, is easy to clean and strong, and is nonreactive. It will not corrode but is a poor absorber of heat. Cladded stainless steel has rapid, uniform heat conduction. Stainless steel with a layered alloyed aluminum or aluminum core, or an aluminum bottom, heats quickly and evenly, is durable, and does not corrode. Tinned steel prevents overbrowning; darkened steel is a good absorber and distributor of heat. Enameled steel is heavy, durable, and nonreactive.

BAKING POWDER is a leavening agent that is a mixture containing sodium bicarbonate (or sometimes ammonium bicarbonate or ammonium carbonate), starch, and acids. Through its effervescence, carbonic acid is diffused through the dough. The word's appearance in English is dated to 1850. Baking powder, a mixture of acid and alkaline substances, releases carbon dioxide when exposed to moisture or heat, causing a baked good to rise.

BAKING POWDER ESSENTIALS

CONFUSABLE BAKING POWDER/BAKING SODA. Baking soda is a principal ingredient in baking powder, with either starch or flour added.

■ Check baking powder's freshness by putting a pinch into some warm water. If it fizzes or bubbles, it is fresh.

(continued)

■ Never dip a moist spoon into the can, as that will deactivate the powder.

■ Make your own baking powder using 1 tablespoon of baking soda, 2 tablespoons of cream of tartar, and 1½ tablespoons of cornstarch.

■ Single-acting baking powder has cream of tartar as the acid, and the batter must be baked immediately after mixing. Double-acting baking powder has cream of tartar and slower-acting sodium aluminum sulfate, so it releases gas in two phases (the batter can sit at room temperature for a few minutes before baking, or it has to be refrigerated or frozen). Double-action baking powder is good for baked items that bake slowly, such as cakes.

■ Store baking powder in a cool, dry place and remove it from the container only with a dry spoon.

■ Cut the seal on baking powder so you have a straight edge for leveling a measuring spoon of powder.

BAKING PAN or **BAKING TIN** is one type of bakeware and the basic varieties are cake pan, loaf pan, pie pan, and sheet pan; see BAKEWARE.

BAKING POTATO: see IDAHO POTATO and RUSSET POTATO.

BAKING SHEET, also called COOKIE SHEET, is a flat rectangular metal tray with at least one rolled-up end, used for baking food in an oven.

> **HINT** Use a baking sheet that allows two inches of space between it and the sides of the oven.

BAKING SODA is a leavening agent of sodium bicarbonate (also called bicarbonate of soda). Baking soda is a principal ingredient in baking powder (with either starch or flour added). Baking soda is activated when mixed with an acid; carbon dioxide bubbles are produced, which causes the dough or batter to rise. Baking soda produces carbon dioxide only in the presence of liquid and acid, or an acidic liquid like buttermilk, yogurt, or vinegar. Baking soda does not deteriorate with age.

BAKING STONE or **BAKING TILE** is a thick, heavy stoneware or ceramic piece(s) placed in an oven and heated with the oven; it is used to replicate the brick floor of a commercial oven.

BAKLAVA is a Middle Eastern pastry made of many layers of paper-thin phyllo dough with a filling of chopped nuts, baked, and then drenched in syrup or honey and sometimes rose water. Baklava is a Turkish word and the dessert originated during the Ottoman Empire. Until the mid-nineteenth century, baklava was considered a treat for special occasions and a food for the wealthy. Since many cultures lay claim to baklava, there are many local versions.

BALLOON WHISK is a handheld implement made of stiff wires that form a loop at one end and are gathered into a covered handle at the other. It works best when whipping egg whites or cream. Balloon whisks are the most common whisks used for preparing and cooking food.

BALLOTTINE or **BALLOTINE** describes a French dish (a type of galantine) in which a piece of meat or poultry has been boned, stuffed, and folded or rolled into an egglike shape, then braised, poached, or roasted. It can be served hot or cold. The term, French for "meat roll," is from *balle*, "bale/package of goods," for the appearance of the dish.

BALSAMIC VINEGAR is made from the juice of white grapes matured in wood for ten to fifty years, giving it a characteristic dark color and rich sweet-sour taste. Bona fide balsamic vinegar (Aceto Balsamico Tradizionale di Modena) is strictly controlled by law and must have aged in wood for at least twelve years. Vinegar aged twenty-five years or more is called *stravecchio*. The word balsamic is from the Greek *balsamon*, "balmlike," denoting its digestive character. Balsamic vinegar is classified into three types: Aceto Balsamico Tradizionale (di Modena or di Reggio Emilia), which is true balsamic vinegar and follows the standards adopted by consortia in Modena and Reggio Emilia; Condimento balsamic vinegar, which is made in the traditional method but is produced outside Modena and Reggio Emilia or produced without consortium approval; and Aceto Balsamico di Modena, which is essentially an imitation of Tradizionale and is the commercial grade—most balsamic vinegars available in America fall into this category. Although balsamic vinegar was enjoyed in Italy for a thousand years, it was relatively unknown outside of the country and was not introduced into the American market until the late 1970s. Balsamic vinaigrette is an oil-based dressing made with balsamic vinegar.

BAMBOO SHOOTS are the young leaves and heart of edible species of bamboo (*Phyllostachys* or *Dendrocalamus*), eaten as a vegetable. The winter harvest is more tender and less fibrous.

> **HINT** Bamboo bought in brine in a container and then opened should be trans-ferred to a glass or plastic container and covered with water; it can then be refrig-erated for up to seven days. Changing the water once a day will keep the bamboo fresh for up to a week longer.

BAMBOO STEAMERS are round or rectangular stackable containers for steaming Asian foods. The steamer is put in a wok or frying pan that has a little water in it; the food is arranged in the steamer and covered, and the water is then heated. Bamboo steamer baskets are designed to fit against the sides of a wok and sit above the water. You can steam different items in one, two, or three separate baskets.

BANANA is a long and slightly curved fruit with soft cream-colored flesh and a skin that turns from green to yellow when ripe. The word is from the Portuguese or Spanish *banana* (the fruit) or *banano* (the tree), although it was probably a tropical African word first and the plant probably first grew in Southeast Asia. But it was the Spanish and Portuguese who took the banana with them from Africa to the Americas. The Cavendish is the familiar yellow variety of banana. They are picked nearly mature but still green. When ripening, they emit ethylene gas, which makes other bananas ripen. The other varieties of bananas include lady's finger, apple, Canary, and Lakatan bananas. Most are small and chubby. Some are yellow but others are rosy red. Bananas are harvested underripe because they ripen less well if left on the tree, and also because they ship better green. When harvested green, bananas contain about 1% sugar and 20% starch, but when they are fully ripened, the starch is converted to sugar and only about 1% starch is left. Up until the 1880s, very few Americans had seen or eaten a banana and it was considered a luxury item.

> **HINTS** If you put bananas in a loosely closed paper bag with tomatoes, avocados, or peaches, the bananas will ripen more quickly. A banana that is yellow with brown spots is fully ripe, sweet, and tender.
>
> ▌ Buy light green or light yellow bananas with few or no brown spots.
>
> ▌ Peel firm ripe bananas, wrap in plastic, and freeze for up to three months for use in recipes. Save overripe bananas peeled or unpeeled in a zip-lock freezer bag in the freezer for use in banana bread.

BANANAS FOSTER is a dessert of lengthwise-sliced bananas sautéed and then flambéed in rum, banana liqueur, and brown sugar and served with vanilla ice cream. The story is that in the 1950s, New Orleans chef Paul Blange made the dessert for Richard Foster, one of his regular customers.

BANANA SPLIT is a dessert of a banana split lengthwise (hence the name) and served with three scoops of ice cream (usually in different flavors) and topped with three different syrups. To that, many add whipped cream, chopped nuts, and/or cherries. It is said that David Evans Strickler, a twenty-three-year-old apprentice pharmacist at Tassel Pharmacy in Latrobe, Pennsylvania, who enjoyed inventing sundaes at the store's soda fountain, invented the banana-based triple ice cream sundae in 1904. The drugstore chain Walgreen's is often credited with promoting the early banana splits in its soda fountains.

BANBURY CAKE or **BANBURY BUN** is a small oval pastry containing currants, candied peel, honey, and spices, usually with three parallel cuts across the top. It was created in Oxfordshire, England, in the early seventeenth century.

BANGER is slang for sausage and bangers and mash, which is sausage and mashed potatoes. The dish is usually served with a rich onion gravy. Bangers became a well-known term in World War II, but the term was actually in use at least as far back as 1919.

BANQUET describes an elaborate meal or feast, often a formal affair. Banquet is literally "little bench" in French and at first it meant "light snack/single course." It has evolved from a snack taken from a small side table to an elaborate ceremonial feast. What we now call dessert was once called a banquet. In ancient Greece, banquets were occasions for philosophical debates, games, and songs, as described by Plato in his dialogue *The Banquet*.

BAOBAB is the edible fruit of a very thick African tree (also called monkey bread tree or thousand-year tree). The edible pulp (known as monkey bread) is used in foods and beverages. The leaves are also edible and the seeds are ground to produce a meal or used for making condiments. The word is probably from an African language; it was first recorded in Latin in 1592 in a treatise on the plants of Egypt by the Italian botanist Prosper Alpinus. Baobab fruit pulp can be used to thicken smoothie drinks.

BARBECUE or **BARBEQUE** has several meanings: a cookout in which food is cooked over an open fire, meat that has been barbecued or grilled in a highly seasoned sauce, and the act of cooking outdoors on a barbecue grill. Technically, to barbecue is to cook outdoors in a closed chamber by indirect heat at a low temperature for a long time. Before cooking, the meat is usually rubbed with a spice mixture (dry rub) or marinated. Barbecue was originally a word for a wooden framework for sleeping or for drying or storing meat or fish, and the word derives from the Arawak or Haitian or Taina *barbacoa*, which became the Spanish *barbacoa*, "wooden frame on posts" or "framework for meat over fire."

> **CONFUSABLE** BARBECUING/GRILLING. Often the words are used interchangeably and usually refer to meat cooked on a grill. Barbecuing is most often done outdoors. The term broiling is also used for grilling, even though broiling refers to a heat source above the food. Barbecuing isn't grilling but is slow-cooking with smoke or liquid.

BARBECUE SAUCE is a sweet-sour and spicy sauce, usually with vinegar, tomato, chiles, sugar, and spices, used to marinate meat or served with meat. Mop is the name of a barbecue tool and a basting solution used to prevent meats from drying out while being cooked over an open flame.

> **HINT** Put barbecue sauce in a squeeze (ketchup) bottle for use with the grill.

BAR COOKIE is a type of cookie made by baking batter in a sheet pan, then cutting into bars or squares.

BARD refers to covering meat with fat before roasting it to prevent it from drying out. The term was first used to describe covering fowl with bacon for cooking. Barding is not recommended for some very tender meats because the strong flavor of the bard will overwhelm the taste of the tender meat.

BARISTA is a preparer/server in a coffee bar. The word is Spanish for "supporter." Barista can be accurately used for both women and men preparers and servers of coffee in a coffee bar.

BARLEY is a hardy cereal plant and it has long heads of whiskered grains; it is used in foods and malt production. It may have been the earliest cereal cultivated by humans, in the Neolithic period. The Old English word for barley was *baerlic*, related to the Latin *farina*, "flour."

BARON is a beef cut of a joint consisting of double sirloins connected at the backbone; the term baron also refers to the hindquarters and both legs of a lamb. Baron was first a cut of beef going back to Henry VII (1457–1509) of England who was so impressed after being presented with a spit-roast double sirloin cut of beef that he named it "Sir Loin, Baron of Beef."

BARQUETTE is French for "small boat" and it denotes a pastry shell shaped like a little boat, then filled with fruit, vegetables, custard, or other fillings.

BAR SUGAR: see SUPERFINE SUGAR.

BARTLETT PEAR is a large, juicy, yellow variety originated in Berkshire, England, in the seventeenth century by a schoolmaster named John Stair. Stair sold some of his pear tree cuttings to a horticulturist named Williams (which is the name it still goes by in the United Kingdom), who further developed the variety and renamed it after himself. The Bartlett pear was not developed by Enoch Bartlett (1779–1860) but promoted and distributed by him. The Bartlett pear is the pear of choice for canning because the pears are well suited for processing. Bartlett pears are handpicked when they are in the mature green stage and ripened off the tree because they become mealy if ripened on the tree. Bartlett pear trees can produce fruit for up to one hundred years, but the average age of production trees ranges from fifty to seventy-five years.

BASIL is an herb with aromatic leaves that is used as a seasoning. The word is from the Greek *basilikon* (*phuton*), "royal (herb)," as early on it was used in some royal ointments or medicines. This herb brings a minty, clovelike aroma to food. More than sixty varieties of basil exist. Although related to mint, basil tastes a little like anise and cloves.

HINTS Basil should be added toward the end of cooking or it will lose flavor.

▌ Basil will keep best if not refrigerated but kept in a cool place, out of the sun, with the stems in water.

▌ Fresh and dried basil cannot be used interchangeably. For example, you cannot make pesto from the dried form.

BASKIN-ROBBINS'S 31 ORIGINAL FLAVORS

In 1945 Irv Robbins opened an ice-cream store in Glendale, California, called Snowbird, which proudly featured 21 exotic flavors. The next year Robbins teamed up with his brother-in-law and competing ice-cream store owner, Burt Baskin, to form Baskin-Robbins. In 1948, after opening six successful Baskin-Robbins ice-cream stores, Baskin and Robbins licensed operations of a store—giving birth to the concept of franchising in the ice-cream industry. In 1953 the big "31" sign made its debut at all Baskin-Robbins stores, announcing to customers that a different ice cream flavor was available for every day of the month.

BANANA NUT FUDGE	COFFEE CANDY	PEPPERMINT FUDGE
BLACK WALNUT	DATE NUT	PEPPERMINT STICK
BURGUNDY CHERRY	EGG NOG	PINEAPPLE SHERBET
BUTTER PECAN	FRENCH VANILLA	PISTACHIO NUT
BUTTERSCOTCH RIBBON	GREEN MINT	RASPBERRY SHERBET
CHOCOLATE	LEMON CRISP	ROCKY ROAD
CHOCOLATE ALMOND	LEMON CUSTARD	STRAWBERRY
CHOCOLATE CHIP	LEMON SHERBET	VANILLA
CHOCOLATE FUDGE	MAPLE WALNUT	VANILLA BURNT ALMOND
CHOCOLATE RIBBON	ORANGE SHERBET	
COFFEE	PEACH	

BASMATI RICE is a high-quality, long-grain Indian rice, literally "fragrant rice" in Hindi. It did not take on its current spelling until the 1960s. Basmati rice is the only rice that has the combination of a nutlike aroma and postcooking elongation. It becomes more than twice its original length postcooking. Basmati rice is the most costly rice in the world.

BASS is the nontechnical name for any of numerous edible marine and freshwater spiny-finned fishes. The original form of the word in Old English was *barse*.

BASTE means to spoon, brush, pour, or cover food with liquid (such as melted butter, fat, or pan drippings) before or during cooking (at intervals) in order to prevent drying, to add flavor, or to glaze the food.

HINTS A metal baster is better than plastic, as the latter can warp or melt.

▌ Stop basting with a marinade at least 5 minutes before the end of cooking to allow time for the heat to kill off any bacteria that the marinade has picked up from the meat.

BATCH is the quantity baked at one time.

BATTER is a thin mixture of flour, eggs, and liquid (usually pourable), especially one used in making cakes and pancakes, and for coating foods before frying.

CONFUSABLE BATTER/DOUGH. In contrast to a batter, which is a thin mixture, a dough is a thick mixture of flour, liquid, and other ingredients.

HINTS Put flour or sugar on nuts or fruits to help distribute them evenly in batter (or dough).

▌ Level the batter in a pan by snap-spinning the pan on a flat surface. For a square pan, put your hands on opposite sides and shake.

▌ An ice-cream scoop works well when filling a muffin tin or papers and also when scooping out cookie dough onto a baking sheet.

BATTER BREAD: see JOHNNYCAKE.

BATTERCAKE: see GRIDDLECAKE and JOHNNYCAKE.

BATTERED means covered with a mixture of egg, milk, and flour and then cooked, usually by frying.

BATTUTO: see SOFRITO.

BAVARIAN CREAM, BAVAROIS, or **BAVAROISE** is a creamy cold dessert made with an egg-custard base, into which are mixed cream, beaten egg whites, a flavoring (such as chocolate or orange), and gelatin, and set in a mold. The dessert has been popular in Britain since the mid-nineteenth century, frequently under the anglicized name Bavarian cream, and the French term is from *fromage bavarois* and *crème bavaroise*. It is not known what its original connection with Bavaria was. Bavarian cream can be served on its own or used as a filling for cold charlottes or molded cakes.

BAY LEAF, also called LAUREL LEAF, is from the bay tree of the laurel family. In ancient Greece the tree was sacred to Apollo, and its leaves were used for crowning victors in the Pythian games. The leaves are valued for their pungent, peppery, woodsy flavor and are a standard component of the bouquet garni and commonly used in slow-cooking dishes. The term bay actually originally denoted the fruit or berry of the laurel, and comes ultimately from the Latin *baca*, "berry."

HINTS Always remove the bay leaves before serving. There are many instances of diners accidentally swallowing a sharp-edged leaf. Even though the flavor of the leaf is good and it is safe to digest, the solid leaf is unwholesome if consumed in more than a small quantity.

▌ Bay leaves should not be crumbled before adding because it will be impossible to remove the pieces.

▌ The flavor of bay leaves may overwhelm a slow-cooked dish if they are left in the pot for the entire cooking period. The ideal cooking time is 30 minutes or less.

BAY SCALLOP is a small scallop (*Aequipecten irradians*) about one-half inch in diameter, inhabiting the Atlantic coast's shallow waters and mudflats, especially eastern Long Island Sound. Many eat the edible adductor muscle of this scallop for its sweet and delicate flavor. Bay scallops are the most expensive scallops because they are the most tender and delicious; compared to sea scallops, they are more succulent, sweeter, less chewy, and less abundant.

BEACH PLUM is a dark purple edible plum native to the New England coast that is used in jams, jellies, and pies. The beach plum plant can grow in poor soil and is used as an erosion-control plant. Humphrey Marshal, the famous plant taxonomist, is credited with giving the beach plum its species name, *Prunus maritima*, in 1785.

BEAN has a couple of meanings: the versatile seed found in pods of leguminous plants, and the seed of various other plants that resemble the common bean (such as coffee). The bean is one of the most ancient of human foods, known to be used by hunter-gatherers more than twelve thousand years ago. The general term bean relates to two genera of plants: *Phaseolus*, which comprises a number of species and varieties, including the haricot bean, French bean, runner bean, and butter bean, all of which originated in Mexico and South America; and *Vicia*, which comprises only one cultivated species, the HORSEBEAN (also called BROAD BEAN or FIELD BEAN), which originated in the Near East before spreading through Europe by the later first millennium BC. The mature seeds of beans used for food, except soybeans, are rather similar in composition, although they differ widely in eating quality. Beans have 22% protein content, as compared to beef's 18%. Beans are used second only to grains in the human diet and have been cultivated for about nine thousand years. The Old English form of the word was of Germanic origin.

BEAN ESSENTIALS

■ Beans cause gas because they contain carbohydrates (oligosaccharides) that humans cannot fully digest. When bacteria in the intestine start to ferment the undigested substance, gas (flatus) results. Since about 80% of the flatulent-causing chemicals are water soluble, you can minimize or eliminate gas production

(continued)

in beans by soaking the beans overnight, discarding the soaking water, and rinsing before cooking.

■ Canned beans have a similar nutritive value compared to dried, uncooked beans. Both are fine sources of protein, vitamin B, and iron. Both have one gram of fat per cup, and both have more fiber than other foods except cereal bran. Canned beans are higher in sodium. Rinsing them will reduce the salt content somewhat. The taste difference is slight.

■ Dried beans should be stored in an airtight container in a cool, dry place or frozen in a zip-lock freezer bag. Most dried beans require presoaking in water. It is best to soak the beans overnight in cold water. If overnight soaking is not possible, then cover the dried beans with cold water, bring to a boil, simmer for 5 minutes, then turn off the heat. Let the beans soak for 2 hours before starting to cook. Remove any "floaters." Always discard the soaking water. You can tell if a bean has been soaked enough by biting one; it should have a crisp, raw texture but no hard core. Red and green lentils and split peas, which are relatively soft, require no soaking or, at most, minimum soaking and 30 to 45 minutes of cooking time.

■ The age of the dried beans makes a difference in cooking them. The older the bean, the harder it is and the longer it needs to be soaked and cooked.

■ When cooking beans, do not mix two batches, even if they are of the same variety. If one batch has been stored longer than the other, it may be considerably more dehydrated and, therefore, require longer cooking time. If different varieties are used, cook them separately because they will have different cooking requirements.

■ When you cook beans in a covered pot, they yield a creamier texture. When you cook beans in an uncovered pot, they stay separate and don't break.

■ To check dried bean damage, put the beans in a bowl of cold water and discard any that float to the surface.

■ Store dried beans in a cool, dry cupboard and they will keep for up to a year. Cooked beans must be refrigerated and can be frozen for up to a year.

■ Fresh beans should have a bright color and be firm. Store in a perforated plastic bag and refrigerate up to five days.

■ Put dried beans in a jar with dried chile peppers to keep insects out.

■ Add salt to soaking water to soften the texture of beans. When cooking beans, wait to add any acidic ingredients like tomatoes, vinegar, or wine. Acids react with the starch in beans and prevent them from swelling. Hold off on adding salt, which inhibits absorption of water by the beans. Add sugar in some form to long-cooking beans to help them retain their shape and not turn to mush.

■ Cook beans a day ahead and cool them in their cooking liquid to get the best flavor and texture.

■ Always begin cooking beans, lentils, and legumes in cold water.

■ Season beans when they are still warm, even if serving them cold.

■ Test doneness by putting a bean on a spoon, then blowing on it. If the skin wrinkles, the bean is cooked thoroughly.

Beans are the seeded pods of various legumes and are among the oldest foods known to humanity. They come in two broad categories—fresh and dried. Some beans can be found in both fresh and dried forms. Peas come in many varieties, all members of the legume family. Some are grown to be eaten fresh, removed from their pods. Others are grown specifically to be used dried. Pod peas are those that are eaten in the pod. Pulses are the edible seeds, usually dried, of several legumes, including beans, peas, and lentils. Legumes furnish food for humans and animals and provide edible oils, fibers, and raw material for plastics. Nutritionally, they are high in protein and contain many of the essential amino acids. These are some common beans, pulses, and peas:

ADZUKI BEAN OR ADUKI BEAN	FRENCH BEAN	PUY LENTIL
APPALOOSA	GARBANZO BEAN	RED BEAN
BAKED BEAN	GARDEN PEA	RED KIDNEY BEAN
BLACK BEAN	GREAT NORTHERN BEAN	ROMAN BEAN OR ITALIAN BEAN
BLACK-EYED BEAN	GREEN BEAN	RUNNER BEAN
BLACK-EYED PEA	HARICOT OR HARICOT VERT	SCARLET RUNNER
BORLOTTI BEAN	HORSEBEAN	SCOTCH BEAN
BROAD BEAN	JACK BEAN	SHELL BEAN
BUSH BEAN	KIDNEY BEAN	SNAP BEAN
BUTTER BEAN	LENTIL	SNOW PEA
CANNELLINI BEAN	LIMA BEAN OR CHRISTMAS/CALICO BEAN	SOYBEAN
CAROLINA BEAN	MANGETOUT	SPLIT PEA
CHICKPEA	MARROWFAT PEA	STRING BEAN
CHINESE LONG BEAN	MEXICAN JUMPING BEAN	STRINGLESS BEAN
CIVIT BEAN	MOTH BEAN	SUGAR BEAN
COWPEA	MUNG BEAN	SUGAR PEA
CRANBERRY BEAN	NAVY BEAN OR PEA BEAN	SUGAR SNAP PEA
DAL	PARTRIDGE PEA	TICK BEAN
ENGLISH PEA	PETIT POIS	WAX BEAN OR WAXPOD BEAN
FAVA BEAN	PINK BEAN	WHITE BEAN
FIELD BEAN	PINTO BEAN	WINDSOR BEAN
FIELD PEA	POD PEA	YELLOW WAX BEAN
FLAGEOLET	POLE BEAN	

BEAN CURD: see TOFU.

BEAN POT is any heavy, covered crockery or metal pot suitable for slow-cooking beans, stews, and other dishes. Bean pots usually have a narrow mouth to minimize evaporation and heat loss and a deep, thick-walled body to facilitate long, slow cooking.

BEAN SPROUTS are the sprouts of certain newly germinated beans, especially those of mung beans, used as a vegetable. They are harvested while crisp and eaten raw or very lightly cooked. Since bean sprouts, and any other sprout, can be a source of bacterial contamination, it is important to thoroughly rinse them before eating to reduce the risk of harmful bacteria.

BEAN THREADS: see CELLOPHANE NOODLES.

BÉARNAISE or **BÉARNAISE SAUCE** is a rich sauce of egg yolks, shallots, tarragon, butter, vinegar (and sometimes white wine and chopped chervil) that is served with meat. It derives from the French *béarnais*, "of Béarn," a region in southwest France.

> **HINT** Béarnaise sauce can be saved if it curdles by gradually beating in a tablespoon of hot water in cold sauce, and a tablespoon of cold water in hot sauce.

BEAT is to stir or mix rapidly in a circular motion with a utensil. One hundred strokes by hand equals about one minute by electric mixer.

BEAUFORT is a hard, rather sharp cheese made from cow's milk, similar to Gruyère. It is produced in the area around Beaufort, high in the French Alps, and it is this high altitude that imparts Beaufort with its unique flavor. Beaufort is commonly used to make cheese fondue because it melts easily. Beaufort has earned itself a protected designation origin, meaning that only cheese produced from Tarentaise cows who are pastured in the summer can be labeled "Beaufort." Beaufort cheese is often produced in huge wheels weighing up to one hundred pounds.

BEAUJOLAIS is a light red wine named for its origination in central France. Wines from the southern part of the region are called Beaujolais. Wines from certain areas in the northern part of the region with the appellation Beaujolais-Villages generally have more color and body and are considered to be superior in quality. Ten villages in the north produce the best Beaujolais, classified as Grands Crus. Traditionally, young Beaujolais is served cool—at cellar temperature. Beaujolais Nouveau is new wine, bottled right after fermentation without aging. It's very light and fruity and should be drunk within a few months.

BEAU MONDE is a seasoning spice of celery, onion, and salt. The name is French for "beautiful world."

BÉCHAMEL is a rich white sauce consisting of a roux made with milk infused with herbs (such as onion and nutmeg). It is named after Marquis Louis de Béchamel, a French financier and a steward of Louis XIV. It is similar to velouté sauce, which is made with stock rather than milk. Béchamel is one of the mother sauces of French cuisine.

HINT When you add milk to béchamel sauce, you should be sure the milk is at room temperature or slightly warmed. Adding cold milk can "break" the sauce, resulting in a lumpy instead of a creamy finish. Milk should be added a few drops at a time and incorporated by whisking constantly. Overcooking can also ruin a béchamel sauce. Keep whisking and keep a careful eye on the thickness. Once the sauce reaches the desired thickness, remove it from the heat.

BEE BALM: see BERGAMOT.

BEECHNUT is the small, triangular nut of the beech tree. The oil extracted from beechnut is considered to be second only to olive oil in quality. Beechnuts have a high oil content; the oil can be extracted for salads and cooking purposes.

BEEF is the meat from bovine animals: cows, steers, bulls more than a year old. The word came from French through the Latin *bos/bov-*, "ox," and also from Greek and Sanskrit. Grass-fed beef is beef from cattle that have been allowed to roam and graze in pastureland. Beef graded as Prime is sold at premium butcher shops. Most of the beef sold to consumers is Choice or Select.

BEEF ESSENTIALS

■ Choose bright red beef with light marbling and nearly white outer fat, but not too much. The more marbling, the more juicy and tender the meat. Press a package of meat through the plastic to make sure it is firm.

■ Leave meat in its wrapper in the coldest part of the refrigerator, usually the back of the bottom shelf. Beef can stay for four days like this or for five days in a refrigerator meat drawer. Ground beef can be kept for two days in the refrigerator. Freeze meat in freezer-weight plastic for up to ten months. When meat is thawing, two hours at room temperature is the maximum, or thirty minutes for ground beef.

■ Just before cooking, trim fat from the outside of beef, leaving a thin layer.

■ Beef that is broiled, grilled, or roasted should "rest" for 5–25 minutes before being carved.

■ Make sure the thermometer does not touch any bone when checking meat for doneness. Remove the meat from the heat source when the temperature reaches the lowest temperature of the desired range, as the meat continues to cook from residual heat when resting.

■ Wash hands, utensils, dishes, and surfaces with hot soapy water if they come into contact with raw beef.

■ Ground beef is more perishable than steak because ground beef is subjected to bacteria that may be on the butcher's hands or grinder, and grinding increases the surface area many times, thus making the meat more accessible to bacteria. Ground beef must contain only beef, but may be from any part of the cow.

BEEF CUTS

Beef, the meat of an adult (over one year) bovine, was not always as popular as it is today. America has had cattle since the mid-sixteenth century, but most immigrants preferred either pork or chicken. Shortages of those two meats during the Civil War, however, suddenly made beef attractive and very much in demand.

Today's beef comes from cows (females that have borne at least one calf), steers (males castrated when very young), heifers (females that have never borne a calf), and bulls under two years old. Common beef cuts are listed here, with the nine primal cuts described in more detail in parentheses.

ARM POT ROAST

BACK RIBS

BLADE RIB ROAST

BLADE ROAST

BONELESS NECK

BONELESS RUMP ROAST

BOTTOM ROUND ROAST

BRISKET (For braises, brisket, corned beef)

CHATEAUBRIAND

CHUCK (Muscular shoulder section; source of chuck steak, chuck roast, stew beef)

CHUCK ARM ROAST

CHUCK SHOULDER POT ROAST

CHUCK STEAK

CLUB STEAK

CROSS RIB ROAST

CROSS RIBS

CROSSCUT SHANK

DELMONICO STEAK

EYE OF ROUND

FILET MIGNON

FLANK (Source of lean flank steak, ground beef)

FLANK STEAK

FLAT BONE TOP SIRLOIN

FLATIRON STEAK

FORESHANK (Cubed or in bone-in slices for braising, stews, stock)

GROUND BEEF

HAMBURGER

HANGER STEAK

HEEL POT ROAST

HINDSHANK

HIP SIRLOIN

LONDON BROIL

MARKET STEAK

MINUTE STEAK

NEW YORK STRIP STEAK

NOISETTE

PLATE (Source of short ribs, stew beef, skirt steak, ground beef, cuts for braising, broiling, grilling)

PORTERHOUSE RIBS

PORTERHOUSE STEAK

RIB (Flavorful, juicy, tender; ribeye steaks, short ribs, rib roasts, ribeye roasts, standing rib roasts)

RIBEYE ROAST

RIBEYE STEAK

RIB ROAST

RIB STEAK

ROUND (Source of round/ rump roast, ground beef)

ROUND BONE TOP SIRLOIN

ROUND STEAK

ROUND TIP ROAST

ROUND TIP STEAK

RUMP ROAST

SHANK

SHELL STEAK

SHORT LOIN (Source of finest steaks: T-bone, porterhouse, club, top loin, tenderloin/filet mignon, fillet, strip)

SHORT PLATE

SHORT RIBS

SIRLOIN (source of sirloin steak, ground beef)

SIRLOIN STEAK

SIRLOIN STRIP STEAK

SKIRT STEAK

STRIP STEAK

T-BONE STEAK

TENDERLOIN

TENDERLOIN ROAST

TOP BLADE STEAK

TOP LOIN STEAK

SPECIAL TYPES OF BEEF

Certified Angus Beef (CAB): a specification-based, branded-beef program started in 1978 to promote Angus cattle as providing consistent high-quality beef with superior taste. The brand is owned by the American Angus Association and its thirty-five thousand rancher members. The terms "Angus Beef" or "Black Angus Beef" are loosely and commonly misused and/or confused with CAB; the brand or name Certified Angus Beef can't be legally used by an establishment that is not licensed to do so.

Certified Hereford beef: beef certified to have come from Hereford cattle.

Grass-fed beef: beef raised primarily on forage rather than in a feedlot.

Kobe beef: cattle of the Wagyu breed raised and fattened in the hills above Kobe, Hyōgo Prefecture, Japan. During the fattening period, the cattle are hand-fed (using high-energy feed, including beer and beer mash) and hand-massaged for tenderness and high fat content.

Halal beef: certified to have been processed in a prescribed manner in accordance with Muslim dietary laws.

Kosher beef: certified to have been processed in a prescribed manner in accordance with Jewish dietary laws.

Organic beef: produced without added hormones, pesticides, or other chemicals, though requirements for labeling a product "organic" vary widely.

BEEFALO is a cross between the domestic cow and the buffalo (genetically three-eighths North American bison and five-eighths domestic bovine); it is raised on grass and does not require supplements and is therefore leaner and sweeter than beef. Beefalo was created to combine the best characteristics of bison and beef cattle. A USDA study showed beefalo meat, like bison meat, to be lower in fat and cholesterol than beef. In 1985, beefalo was approved for public sale by the USDA under the stamp "Beefalo Beef."

BEEFBURGER: see HAMBURGER.

BEEF JERKY, also called JERKED BEEF, is chewy strips of dried beef. The word jerky comes from the Spanish *charqui*, which the Spanish borrowed from the Quechua *c'arqi*. Nothing is actually "jerked" in the preparation of the dried meat, as folk etymology sometimes assumes.

BEEF SHORT RIBS: see SHORT RIBS.

BEEFSTEAK MUSHROOM or BEEFSTEAK FUNGUS, also called OX TONGUE, is an edible bracket fungus (*Fistulina hepatica*) that grows on trees and looks similar to a slab of raw meat. It requires long, slow cooking to be edible.

BEEFSTEAK TOMATO or **BEEF TOMATO** is a large, thick-fleshed tomato; it is the largest variety of tomato. The most common homegrown tomato is the beefsteak variety.

BEEF STROGANOFF: see STROGANOFF.

BEEF WELLINGTON is basically a beef fillet coated in pâté and enclosed in puff pastry. The dish was named for the Duke of Wellington (Arthur Wellesley [1769–1852]), a British soldier and statesman best known for his military victory over Napoleon at the Battle of Waterloo in 1815.

BEER is an alcoholic beverage made by brewing and fermentation from cereals, usually malted barley, and flavored with hops. Beer's etymology is uncertain, but the word came to us through West Germanic, perhaps from the Latin *biber*, "drink," from *bibere*, "to drink." The word beer originally distinguished a drink flavored with hops from (unhopped) ale, but today it is mainly a more general term that encompasses ale, lager, and stout. The enemy of beer is oxygen from the air, which, once the bottle has been opened, is in contact with the beer; the oxidation can generate off flavors. Full-flavored beers are the best to use for cooking.

TYPES OF BEER

Beer is a low-alcohol (usually a maximum of 5% alcohol by weight) beverage brewed from malted barley and other cereals (such as corn or rye) mixed with cultured yeast for fermentation and flavored with hops. Since about nine-tenths of beer's volume is water, the quality of the water is extremely important. Beers from different regions of the United States and other countries take their character from the water used in the brewing. There are many varieties of beer. Before 6000 BC, beer was made from barley in Sumeria and Babylonia. Reliefs in Egyptian tombs dating from 2400 BC show that barley or partly germinated barley was crushed, mixed with water, and dried into cakes. When broken up and mixed with water, the cakes gave an extract that was fermented by microorganisms accumulated on the surfaces of fermenting vessels. Here are some common terms used to identify different types of beer.

ABBEY ALE	COLD-FILTERED BEER	FRUIT BEER
ALE	COPPER ALE	GERMAN LAGER
ALTBIER	CRAFT-BREWED BEER	GOLDEN ALE
AMBER ALE	CREAM ALE	GUEUZE
AMERICAN LAGER	CRYSTAL MALT	HEFE WEIZEN
BARLEY WINE	DARK BEER	HOME BREW
BERLINER WEISSE	DIAT PILS	ICE BEER
BIERE DE GARDE	DOPPELBOCK	INDIA PALE ALE OR IPA
BITTER	DORT	IRISH STOUT
BITTER STOUT	DORTMUNDER	KEG BEER
BITTERSWEET	DOUBLE CREAM SPROUT	KELLERBIER
BLINK BEER	DRAFT BEER	KOLSCH
BOCK BEER	DRAUGHT BEER	KRAUSEN
BOSTON LAGER	DRY BEER	KRIEK
BROWN ALE	DUNKEL BEER	KRISTALL WEIZEN
BRUISED BEER	DUNKEL WEISSBIER	KRUIDENBIER
CALIFORNIA COMMON BEER	EISBOCK	KULMBACHER BEER
CARAMEL MALT	FARO	KUMISS
CASK-CONDITIONED ALE	FESTBIER	KVASS
CHICHA	FIRE-BREWED BEER	LAGER
CHOCTAW BEER	FRAMBOISE	LAMBIC BEER

LIGHT ALE	OBERGARIG	STEAM BEER
LIGHT BEER OR LITE BEER	OLD ALE	STOCK BEER
LOSTER BIER	ORGANIC BEER	STOUT
MAIBOCK	OSCURA	SUMMER ALE
MALT LIQUOR	PALE ALE	TRAPPIST
MARZEN	PILSNER OR PILSENER	TRIPEL BEER
MEAD	POKER BEER	UR-BOCK
MELOMEL	PORTER	VIENNA BEER
MICROBREW BEER	RAUCHBIER	WEISS BEER
MILD BEER	SAISON	WEIZENBIER
MILK STOUT	SCHENK BEER OR SCHENK	WEIZENBOCK
MUNCHENER	SCHWARZBIER	WHEAT BEER
MUNICH BEER	SCOTCH ALE	WHITE BEER
NEAR BEER	SHANDY	WINTER BEER
NEEDLED BEER	SMALL BEER	WITBIER
NONALCOHOLIC BEER	SPECIALTY MALT	ZWICKELBIER
NUT BROWN ALE	SPRUCE BEER	
OATMEAL STOUT	STARKBIER	

STEPS IN BREWING BEER

1. The grains are malted. This process involves steeping and aerating the barley, allowing it to germinate, and drying and curing the malt.

2. The malt is transferred to the mash tun, and water and mixtures of other grains are combined, in preparation for the fermentation process.

3. The unfermented malt, or wort, is filtered.

4. The wort is boiled in brew kettles. Hops are added for flavor at the start of this step, then removed at the end.

5. Yeast is added to the starter tank.

6. The brew ferments in the fermentation tank for about a week.

7. After fermentation, the yeast is removed and the brew is transferred to the aging tank for several weeks of storage.

8. Final filtering is done.

9. The beer is packaged: it is pasteurized and transferred to cans and bottles.

BEET or **BEETROOT** is a plant with a large swollen root that is used as a vegetable and for sugar production. A plant of very early cultivation, the word comes from the Latin *beta*. The beet has the highest sugar content of all vegetables and has varieties that are red, purple, white, gold, and striped.

HINTS Look for firm, rounded vegetables with smooth skins and no bruises. There should be greens and one to two inches of root. Cut the greens off when you get home, but leave the one to two inches of root. Beets are best refrigerated (up to ten days) or stored at cool room temperature for a few days. Cooked and cooled whole beets can be frozen for up to ten months.

❚ Leave the skin on for cooking, as peeling will be easier afterwards and the skin retains nutrients and preserves color. Add lemon juice or vinegar to preserve color during boiling.

❚ To keep beets from staining a salad, toss separately in a vinaigrette and add at the last minute.

BEGGAR'S PURSE is a crêpe made to resemble a miniature purse or sack and containing a savory or sweet filling, such as caviar and crème fraîche, and tied with a chive. It is the American name for the French *aumoniere* (alms purse). Beggar's purses are served at room temperature.

BEIGNET is the French word for "fritter" and it is specifically a square of fried dough sprinkled with powdered sugar and eaten hot. The French colonists of the eighteenth century brought the recipe and custom of making beignets to New Orleans.

BELGIAN ENDIVE, also called French endive or Witloof, is a small, cigar-shaped head of cream-colored, tightly packed, slightly bitter leaves of a variety of the common chicory (*Cichorium intybus*) deprived of light to produce blanched, bitter, curly leaves used in salads.

> **HINT** Buy firm, flat, crisp heads with tight, unblemished, white leaves with red or yellow tips. Refrigerate, wrapped to prevent bruising, for three to five days.

BELGIAN WAFFLE is a thick, sweet waffle with large, deep indentations, often eaten with ice cream or fruit sauce.

BELLINI is a cocktail of one-third peach juice and two-thirds Champagne or Prosecco, though there are now variations. It was concocted at Harry's Bar in Venice in the 1930s, but not named until 1948, when it was named in honor of Venetian artist Giovanni Bellini during a major exhibition of his paintings.

BELL PEPPER, also called Sweet pepper, is a bell-shaped green, red, yellow, or orange fruit (*Capsicum annuum*) used as a vegetable. Red peppers are just more mature and sweeter than green peppers. Other colors are different varieties.

> **HINTS** Buy firm, smooth, and bright-colored bell peppers. Refrigerate immediately in a perforated plastic bag. All kinds keep a week or less.

❚ When preparing stuffed green peppers, place the cut-off tops in between them in the baking pan so they stay upright.

BEL PAESE is a type of rich, mild, creamy cow's milk cheese. It is an Italian proprietary name, literally meaning "fair or beautiful country." Genuine Bel Paese can be determined by the wrapping. It bears an image of the Italian geologist and paleontologist Antonio Stoppani, whose geological treatise *Il Bel Paese* gave its name to the cheese; cheese made in the United States has a map of the Americas, while that made in Italy has a map of Italy.

BELUGA is the Russian name for the white sturgeon (*Acipenser huro*), whose roe makes the most prized caviar. Beluga caviar is considered a delicacy worldwide. The meat of the beluga, on the other hand, is not particularly renowned.

BENTO BOX or **BENTO**, also called OBENTO, is a partitioned or stacking lacquered box made of wood or other material in which a meal consisting of various types of Asian food (bento) is served. Bento also describes a Japanese-style packed lunch consisting of items such as as rice, vegetables, and sashimi. In Japan the bento lunch, which is commonly available at train stations, represents fast food elevated to high culinary art and design. Each of the country's five thousand train stations sells a unique box lunch that reflects the cooking of the region.

BERGAMOT is a dessert pear of a rich and sweet variety. The name is from the French *bergamotte*, from the Italian *bergamotta*, from the Turkish *begarmudu*, "prince's pear." It is also the name of a variety of Seville orange with a roundish or pear-shaped fruit, used as flavoring in Earl Grey tea. The citrus fruit is apparently so called from its resemblance to the pear. The rind of a bergamot (the orange-like citrus fruit) contains an essential oil used in perfumery (the basis for eau-de-cologne) and confectionery; the zest is used in pastries. In addition, bergamot is the name of an herb, a wild or garden mint plant, which is also called BEE BALM or OSWEGO TEA.

BERMUDA ONION is a large, yellow-skinned, mild-flavored onion with a round shape and flattened ends, which originated in the Bermuda Islands.

BERRY denotes any fruit enclosed in a fleshy pulp and having one or more seeds but no stone, including fruits like the banana and tomato, as well as the grape and cranberry. There are simple berries (grape or blueberry) and aggregate berries (blackberry or raspberry). Each blackberry and raspberry has 75–125 plump druplets. In Old English the word was *berie*, of earlier Germanic origin. The word "berry" is also used for any of various kernels or seeds, such as the coffee bean, and also a fish egg or roe of a lobster or similar creature.

HINTS Berries are available all year, but are more affordable, flavorful, and plentiful in spring and summer. Cranberries' season is fall and raspberries have a second harvest in the fall.

▌ When purchasing berries, check the underside of the carton for wetness and mold. Wash berries just before you use them. No berries should be soaked, only rinsed. They should be hulled but left whole. To freeze, rinse and dry completely; they will keep for eight to ten months in the freezer.

▌ Quick-freeze berries on a baking sheet for 10 minutes before folding them into a batter. Using dried fruit instead of fresh also prevents "bleeding" in baked goods.

▌ When using frozen berries in place of fresh in a recipe, slightly increase the thickener (flour, cornstarch, tapioca).

▌ Toss bland-tasting berries in sugar and let stand at room temperature for 30 minutes.

BERRY FRUITS

Berries have a combined mesocarp and endocarp layer. The middle and inner layers of the fruit wall often are not distinct from each other. Any small, fleshy fruit is popularly called a berry, especially if it is edible. Raspberries, blackberries, and strawberries are not true berries but aggregate fruits (or aggregate berries)—fruits that consist of a number of smaller fruits. Berries often have many seeds that each have a tough seed coat (testa). The leathery-rinded berry of citrus fruits is called a hesperidium, and the elongated, tough-skinned, berrylike fruits of the watermelon, cucumber, and gourds are referred to as pepos. Here are some common terms used to identify different berry fruits.

AVIGNON BERRY OR FRENCH BERRY	CLOUDBERRY	JAUNDICE BERRY
AVOCADO	CRANBERRY	JESUIT BERRY
BANANA	CUCUMBER	JUNEBERRY
BANEBERRY	CURRANT	JUNIPER BERRY
BARBADOS CHERRY	DANGLEBERRY	KIWANO
BEARBERRY	DATE	KIWI
BILBERRY	DEWBERRY	LEMON
BLACKBERRY	DINGLEBERRY	LIME
BLACK RASPBERRY	DOGBERRY	LIMEBERRY
BLUEBERRY	ELDERBERRY	LINGONBERRY
BOXBERRY	GOOSEBERRY	LYCHEE
BOYSENBERRY	GOURD	LOGANBERRY
BUFFALO BERRY	GRAPE	MELON
CANDLEBERRY	HEATHBERRY	MULBERRY
CANKERBERRY	HIMALAYA BERRY	ORANGE
CAPER BERRY	HONEYBERRY	ORANGE BERRY
CHECKERBERRY	HUCKLEBERRY	PARTRIDGEBERRY
	INDIAN BERRY	PERSIAN BERRY

PERSIMMON	SALMONBERRY	STRAWBERRY
RAMBUTAN	SERVICEBERRY	TOMATO
RASPBERRY	SHADBERRY	TURKEYBERRY
RED CURRANT	SHOT BERRY	WATERMELON
SALA BERRY	SPICEBERRY	WHORTLEBERRY

BERRY SUGAR: see SUPERFINE SUGAR.

BETEL NUT is the dark red seed of a palm, which is chewed with leaves of the betel pepper and lime as a digestive stimulant in some Asian regions. It was misnamed by Europeans because it is chewed with the betel leaf; in actuality, the nut comes from the Areca palm.

BETTY: see COBBLER.

BEURRE BLANC, literally "white butter" in French, is a creamy sauce made with butter, onions, and vinegar or lemon juice, and usually served with seafood and poultry dishes. There are other "beurre" sauces: beurre manié (a mixture of equal parts flour and butter used for thickening sauces or soups), beurre noir (black butter, a sauce made by heating butter until it is brown, usually mixing it with vinegar or lemon juice, capers, and parsley), and beurre noisette (brown butter, the step before beurre noir).

BEURRE COMPOSÉ: see COMPOUND BUTTER.

BEVERAGE is any liquid suitable for drinking. The word is from the French *be(u)vrage/breuvage*, from *bevre*, "to drink," and goes back to the Latin *bibere*, "to drink."

BHATTI: see TANDOORI.

BIALY is a flatbread roll topped with chopped onions that originated in Bialystok, Poland.

BIBB LETTUCE is a butter lettuce of a variety that has a small head and dark green color, developed by nineteenth-century amateur gardener, John Bibb, in his Kentucky backyard.

> **HINT** Bibb lettuce is regarded for its distinctive, almost buttery, flavor and is considered a delicacy among lettuces. Preparing Bibb lettuce leaves requires a gentle touch. Because they are so delicate, they are easily bruised or damaged. First, carefully remove the core; then immerse the leaves in cold water, drain, and pat dry.

BILBERRY, also called WHINBERRY, or WHORTLEBERRY, is a small, edible, blue-black berry (*Vaccinium myrtillus*) native to northern Europe and of the same genus as the blueberry. It is probably of Scandinavian origin. Bilberries freeze well. They are smaller and tarter than their cousin, the American blueberry, and make delicious jams, jellies, liqueurs, sorbets, syrups, and tarts.

BINDER: see LIAISON.

BING CHERRY is a type of large, dark red, sweet cherry, developed in the 1870s by Oregon horticulturist Seth Lewelling and his Manchurian Chinese foreman, Ah Bing, for whom the cultivar is named. Native Americans first discovered the cherry in about 1530 and used it as a cure for certain ailments, believing it had a special healing power because of its bright red color.

BIOENGINEERED FOOD, also called GENETICALLY ENGINEERED FOOD, is food with foreign genes from other plants or animals inserted into its genetic code. Tomatoes, potatoes, squash, corn, and soybeans have been bioengineered.

BIOFLAVONOID, also called FLAVENOID, is any of a group of water-soluble compounds present in citrus fruits, rose hips, and other plants. In mammals, bioflavonoids maintain the resistance of capillary walls to permeation and change of pressure.

BIRCH BEER is a carbonated soft drink similar to root beer but flavored with oils of birch tree bark and sassafras or oil of wintergreen. Various types of birch beer are available, distinguished by color. The color depends on the species of birch tree from which the sap is extracted (although enhancements via artificial coloring are not uncommon). Popular colors include brown, red, and clear (often called white birch beer).

BIRD: see ROULADE.

BIRD'S BEAK KNIFE, also called TOURNÉE KNIFE, is a tool with a specialized curved blade, usually shorter than that of a paring knife, suited to tasks like carving fruit. From the side, it does resemble the curved beak of a bird. A bird's beak knife can be used to slice soft fruits, such as nectarines, plums, or peaches, and to peel skins or blemishes from a variety of fruits and vegetables. Its alternate name, tournée knife, is a reference to the tournée cut that results in a sculpted piece of fruit or vegetable.

BIRD'S NEST PUDDING: see COBBLER.

BIRD'S NEST SOUP is a Chinese dish made from the dried gelatinous coating of the nest of a bird similar to a swift, which builds its nest in a cave using glutinous spit. The soup includes chicken broth, ham, egg white, and spring onion and was created in 1956 for Margherita di Savoia, a queen of Italy.

BIRYANI or **BIRIANI** is a spicy Indian dish of rice layered with meat, fish, or vegetables and flavored with saffron or turmeric. The word is from the Hindi and earlier Persian *biriyan*, "fried/grilled." Lamb or mutton were the original meats, but chicken or fish may be used. Biryani originated in Persia.

BISCOTTO or **BISCOTTI** is a hard-textured, sweet, almond-flavored Italian cookie that has been baked twice. Biscotti is from the Latin *bis coctus*, "twice cooked" (similar to German's *zwieback*, "twice bake"). Biscotti is actually the plural form. It is typically served with a hot drink, into which it is dipped. Biscotti are perfect for dipping into dessert wine or coffee. Today's biscotti are a popular accompaniment to cappuccino and dessert wine.

BISCUIT is any small, usually round, piece of quick bread that rises with baking powder or soda and is then baked in an oven. This word also means "cookie" in the United Kingdom. Biscuit is from the Latin *biscotum panem*, "twice-cooked bread," which became the Old French *bescuit*, "twice cooked." Biscuits include the following types: baking powder, beaten, Brussels, cream, pilot, raised, rolled, sea, ship, and soda.

> **HINTS** Biscuit dough can be mixed in a food processor with pulsing. The fat should be in chunks the size of small peas. Do not overknead or overwork biscuit dough. Dip a biscuit cutter in flour to make it cut more easily and lift straight up after stamping. You can gather and reroll scraps once.
>
> ▮ For crisp biscuit tops, brush with water before baking; for soft tops, brush with milk.
>
> ▮ To fix the bottom of burnt biscuits, run them over a grater to remove the burnt part.
>
> ▮ Biscuits can be reheated in the oven at a low temperature in a well-dampened sealed paper bag.

BISQUE denotes a rich soup made from shellfish. The term was originally French for "crayfish soup." The shell is used to make the initial purée, and in an authentic bisque the shells are ground to a fine paste and added to thicken the soup.

BISTECCA is Italian for "steak."

BISTRO is French for "small restaurant/wineshop/bar." Originally Parisian slang, the word was first used in English around 1922.

BITTER ORANGE: see SEVILLE ORANGE.

BITTERS is an alcoholic liquid distilled from plant extracts, such as aromatic herbs, barks, and roots. The name comes from the bitter or bittersweet flavor.

BITTERSWEET CHOCOLATE is chocolate liquor with cocoa butter and small amounts of sugar and vanilla, and usually lecithin. The chocolate is dark, but a little sweeter than unsweetened.

BLACK BEAN is a term for any small, black-colored bean that is dried and used in cooking.

BLACKBERRY refers to the fleshy, purple or black, edible aggregate fruit of various brambles of the rose family. To some, the term is synonymous with BLACK CURRANT or BILBERRY. The *Oxford English Dictionary* says that because the blackberry is one of the most common wild fruits in England, it is spoken of proverbially as being typical of what is plentiful and little prized. Boysenberries and loganberries are blackberry hybrids. The blackberry is sweetest when black. Blackberries are fragile and should not be refrigerated more than a day.

BLACKBERRY VARIETIES

The blackberry is the fruit of the bramble (*Rubus fruticosus*) and its varieties. The bush is usually biennial and prickly and has leaves with three to five oval, coarsely toothed, stalked leaflets; white, pink, or red flowers; and black or red-purple fruits, each consisting of numerous drupelets adhering to a juicy core. Blackberries are a good source of iron and vitamin C. There many varieties of blackberries:

AGAWAM	ELDORADO	PURPLE
ALLEN	ERIE	RATHBUN
AMBER	EVERGREEN	RED
APACHE	HERITAGE	REVEILLE
ARAPAHO	HULL	ROUND
BLACK	ICEBERG	SHAWNEE
BLACK BUTTE	ILLINI HARDY	SNYDER
BLACK SATIN	KILLARNEY	STONE
BOYNE	KIOWA	TAYLOR
BRITON	KITTATINNY	THORNLESS
BRUNTON	LATHAM	THORNY
CONICAL	LAWTON	TRIPLE CROWN
CHESTER	LOGAN	TRIUMPH
CHICKASAW	MAMMOTH	WACHUSETT
CHOCTAW	MERCEREAU	WARD
COX	MINNEWASKA	WHITE
CRANDALL	NAVAHO	WILSON
DALLAS	OVAL	YELLOW
EARLY HARVEST	PERRON NOIR	

BLACK BOTTOM PIE is a rich pie with a shell made from crushed chocolate cookies or gingersnaps and filled with rum- or whiskey-flavored chocolate or vanilla filling, and topped with whipped cream.

BLACK COW, also called MUD FIZZ, is a root beer float containing vanilla ice cream. Its popularity has spread from the U.S. Midwest. In some regions the term refers to chocolate milk.

BLACK CURRANT is the small, round, blackish, tart, edible fruit of a shrub of the saxifrage family. There are also red and golden varieties of currant, which can be defined as the raisin or dried fruit prepared from a dwarf seedless variety of grape. The name currant comes from the French *raisins de Corinthe*, as the currants were originally from Corinth, Greece.

BLACKENED FOOD is that which has been coated (fish or meat, for example) with pepper and other spices and then quickly seared in a very hot skillet, thereby producing meat that is black on the outside but tender on the inside. Blackening meats was made popular by chef Paul Prudhomme of New Orleans. Most blackening is done in restaurants, as a very well–ventilated kitchen is needed.

BLACK-EYED PEA, BLACK-EYE(D) BEAN, or **BLACK-EYED SUSAN**, also called BUNG BELLY, CHAWLI, CHINA BEAN, COW BEAN, COWPEA, CREAM PEA, CROWDER PEA, LOBBIA, LOMBIA, POOR MAN'S PEA, or SOUTHERN PEA, is a small beige bean with a black spot. The black-eyed pea is are so named for its black hilum, the scar where the bean attaches to the ovule. Although many of the names for this legume include the word pea, it is not a pea, but a bean. Originally from the Far East, these chewy beans were common fare on slave plantations. They are still popular in the South, where they are traditionally eaten on New Year's Day or combined with rice and sausage to make a dish called hoppin' John.

BLACKFISH refers to any of numerous dark-colored fishes, including the tautog, sea bass, or an edible Siberian or Alaskan freshwater fish of the same order as trout, pike, and salmon.

BLACK FOODS

BLACK BASS	BLACK PEPPER	BLACK VINEGAR
BLACK BEAN	BLACK PUDDING	CAVIAR
BLACKBERRY	BLACK RADISH	LICORICE
BLACK CURRANT	BLACK RASPBERRY	OLIVE (RIPE)
BLACK DUCK	BLACK RICE	SEA URCHIN
BLACK-EYED PEA	BLACK SESAME	TRUFFLE

BLACK FOREST CAKE or **BLACK-FOREST GATEAU** is a rich chocolate layer cake with whipped cream and cherries between each layer. The dessert originated in the Black Forest region of southwestern Germany. *Schwarzwälder Kirschtorte* (its German name, which means "Black Forest cherry torte") was first mentioned in writing in 1934; its English name was first recorded in in 1959.

BLACK FOREST HAM is a smoked boneless German ham with blackened skin and a light smoky flavor. The production of Black Forest ham can take up to three months. Within the European Union, Black Forest ham has an Appellation of Controlled Origin, meaning that only ham from the Black Forest is allowed to be labeled as "Black Forest ham." For European consumers, this appellation ensures that they know what they are buying.

BLACK PUDDING: see BLOOD PUDDING.

BLACK TEA is any variety of tea that is fully fermented before drying. There are five stages in its preparation: withering, when the leaf is dried and softened; rolling, during which the cells of the leaves are broken down to release and mix the constituents; moist fermentation for two to three hours at 81°F; desiccation for twenty minutes at 194°F; and sorting or grading. Black tea is generally stronger in flavor and contains more caffeine than the less oxidized teas, such as green tea, white tea, and oolong tea. While green tea usually loses its flavor within a year, black tea retains its flavor for several years. For this reason, it has long been an article of trade.

BLACK WALNUT is an oily edible nut native to eastern North America with a thick, hard shell that is difficult to crack without disturbing the kernel. While its flavor is prized, the difficulty in preparing the black walnut may account for the wider popularity and availability of the English or Persian walnut. The black walnut is high in unsaturated fat and protein and has no cholesterol.

BLANC, also called COURT-BOUILLON, is a stock made of fat, broth, wine, herbs, and vegetables that is used for braising or poaching fish or meat. Blanc is French for "white," and the term is used in French cooking, as in beurre blanc, "white butter."

BLANC DE BLANC is a white sparkling wine or Champagne made entirely from white grapes.

BLANCH means to boil or scald (food) briefly, as in removing the skins of nuts and fruits, or preparing fruits and vegetables for freezing; scalding almonds to remove their skin is blanching. Blanching onions or garlic can mellow their flavor. Blanching cured meats reduces their saltiness. Some vegetables should be blanched before freezing to disable enzymes that would ruin their color and texture.

HINT Foods may be blanched up to a day ahead, then refrigerated until needed. Blanch vegetables in rapidly boiling water to brighten their taste and enhance their color. To flavor the food, salt the blanching liquid before adding the food.

BLAND DIET is a diet that is free from any irritating or overstimulating foods.

BLAND FOODS

There are times when a bland diet is recommended. These foods are purported to be nonirritating, not overstimulating to the digestive tract, and possibly soothing to the intestines. It is generally suggested that those on a bland diet should also avoid alcohol, strong tea or coffee, pickles, and spices.

APPLESAUCE	FRUIT JUICE	PUDDING
BANANA	GELATIN OR JELL-O	REFINED BREADS
BROTH	LEAN MEAT	REFINED CEREALS
CAKE	MARSHMALLOWS	RICE
COOKED CEREALS	MILK AND DAIRY PRODUCTS	SEEDLESS CANNED FRUIT
COOKIES	PASTA	TOFU
CRACKERS	PEANUT BUTTER (SMOOTH)	WHEAT
DECAF COFFEE	PIE	
EGGS	POTATOES (ESPECIALLY MASHED)	

BLANQUETTE is a French stew or ragout of veal, lamb, chicken, or seafood prepared in a velouté (egg and cream) sauce and usually garnished with croutons or small onions and mushrooms. The word is French for "blanket," from *blanc*, "white."

BLEND or **BLENDING** in cooking is to mix, especially to produce a desired flavor, color, or grade; it is to fuse thoroughly, so that the ingredients merge and are no longer distinct.

CONFUSABLE BLEND/BEAT. Blending differs from beating because its purpose is only to combine the ingredients, not to incorporate air into the mixture.

BLENDER, also called LIQUEFIER or LIQUIDIZER, is an electric appliance with whirling blades that blend, mix, grind, or liquefy foods. With short blades that rotate quickly, a blender can instantly blend, chop, and purée foods.

CONFUSABLE BLENDER/FOOD PROCESSOR. A food processor is an electric kitchen tool that is used to chop, grate, mince, slice, purée, and blend food ingredients, while a blender is an electric kitchen appliance that consists of a tall container with a removable lid and motor-driven blades at the bottom that blend, chop, mix, or liquefy foods depending on the speed setting selected. In general, blenders are better suited to working with liquids, and food processors work better with more solid foods. Therefore, of the two, the food processor is the more versatile. A blender with 290 watts is fine for most tasks except crushing ice, for which you will need a 330–400 watt model.

HINT To make cleaning a blender easier, add warm water and dish soap to the blender and blend for a few seconds before washing.

BLENNY is a small, scaleless, long-bodied fish found in rocky coastal areas and coral reefs. The name is from the Greek *blennos*, "slime," from the mucous coating on its scales.

BLIMPIE: see GRINDER.

BLIND BAKE or **BLIND BAKING** is cooking a pie crust or pastry shell before adding the filling; also called BAKING EMPTY.

BLIND TASTING is a method of wine tasting in which an impartial judgment is ensured by serving the tasters without their having seen the label or bottle shape. Blind tasting may also involve serving the wine from a black wineglass to mask the color of the wine. Tasting a wine blind is one of the best ways to formulate an unbiased opinion about the wine. Any knowledge that you have about a wine can cloud your judgment or influence your assessment. Tasting a wine blind forces the taster to concentrate on every tiny aspect of the wine.

BLINI or **BLINTZE** or **BLINTZ** are small pancakes made with yeast and buckwheat flour, filled with sour cream and caviar or smoked salmon (or other fillings), and folded. Blini (pronounced BLEE-ne) is Russian for "pancake"; they originated in Russia and are popular in Eastern Europe. The singular form is blin, and the Yiddish form is blintz or blintze. The blintze may have fruit for the filling and then be sautéed or baked.

BLOOD ORANGE is a type of orange (citrus fruit) with red-streaked or dark red flesh, which is colored by the presence of anthocyanins—the same pigment as in red grapes—in the juice vesicles. Blood oranges are generally seedless and the skin color ranges from bright orange to orange with red areas.

BLOOD PUDDING or **BLOOD SAUSAGE**, also called BLACK PUDDING, is a sausage made from pig's blood, suet, a thickening agent, and herbs. Although it is already cooked, it is usually sliced and fried. One of the oldest-known cooked meats, black pudding is said to have been invented by Aphtonite, a cook of ancient Greece.

BLOODY MARY, a drink of vodka and spicy tomato juice, is named for Mary Tudor, the English queen (Queen Mary I) remembered for her bloody persecution of

Protestants; it was called the Red Snapper before it came to New York from Paris. A Bloody Mary without liquor in it is called a Virgin Mary or Contrary Mary.

BLT is a bacon, lettuce, and tomato sandwich. The abbreviation was first recorded in 1941. The BLT is said to be the second-most-popular sandwich in the United States, after the ham sandwich.

BLUEBERRY is the purplish blue fruit of high and low bushes belonging to the genus *Vaccinium*. The word was written as blue-berry when it came into English around 1772. The blueberry is the most widely distributed fruit in the world, and its wild growth is the reason that cultivation started only recently. The fruit is also mistakenly called HUCKLEBERRY. Wild blueberries, about one-third the size of cultivated blueberries, have a more intense flavor and hold up better in baking. Maine produces more wild blueberries than any other state in the United States. Blueberries' color is derived from the high amount of the plant pigment anthocyanin (from the Greek for "blue plant"). The blueberry is a native fruit of America. Some botanists consider it to be a pome like an apple and pear, and not a berry.

> **HINTS** Blueberries should be dark blue and have a powdery white bloom. They can be kept in the refrigerator for up to one week.
>
> ▌ Blueberries should be frozen by putting them in a single layer on a baking sheet in the freezer. When frozen, put them in a zip-lock freezer bag or container.
>
> ▌ Fresh blueberries in blueberry muffins baked in muffin tins turn greenish brown because the baking soda in the recipe causes an alkaline balance in the batter that creates the discoloration. This can be avoided by using 1 teaspoon of baking powder for every 1¼ teaspoon of baking soda in the recipe.

BLUE CHEESE or **BLEU CHEESE**, also called FROMAGE BLEU, is any Roquefort-type cheese marked with veins of blue mold. The first versions came from the Roquefort area in southeastern France. Maytag blue cheese is an artisanal cheese that has been produced in Iowa since 1941.

> **HINT** Blue cheese should be brought to room temperature before serving.

BLUE CRAB is a bluish edible crab of the Atlantic and Gulf coasts of North America. The blue crab is a swimming crab, which differs from the common crab in that its fifth pair of legs has developed to form paddles and its body is lighter. Blue crabs have blue claws and dark blue-green, oval shells. You can tell the difference between male and female blue crabs by looking at the design located on the apron (belly). The male blue crab's design is in the shape of the Washington Monument, while the female blue crab's apron resembles the U.S. Capitol.

BLUEFIN TUNA is the largest tuna known, weighing up to 1,500 pounds. It is found mostly in temperate seas; it is known to feed in polar regions but breed in the tropics. Bluefin tuna are one of the most endangered fish in the world; the decline has largely been driven by Japanese demand for sushi and sashimi.

BLUEFISH is a predatory blue-colored marine game fish.

BLUE FOODS

BLUEBERRY	BLUE POTATO	POPPY SEED
BLUE CHEESE	BLUE TROUT	SCOTCH BLUE HARE
BLUEFISH	BORAGE	
BLUEPOINT OYSTER	MUSSELS	

BLUE-PLATE SPECIAL or **BLUE PLATE SPECIAL** is a specially priced main course of the day, as of meat and vegetables, listed as an item on a menu, especially in an inexpensive restaurant. The first use of the term was in 1892 on a menu of the Fred Harvey restaurants, which were built at stations to serve the traveling public on the Atchison, Topeka, and Santa Fe Railroad. The blue-plate set meal was designed to rapidly serve passengers whose trains stopped only for a few minutes. The plates used were inexpensive replicas of the sturdy blue plates of Josiah Wedgwood.

BLUSH WINE is pink table wine from red grapes whose skins were removed after fermentation began. Blush wine should be served chilled, but not icy. In the United States the phrase blush wine has almost replaced that of rosé, which is considered somewhat passé.

BOCK is a very strong lager traditionally brewed in the fall and aged through the winter for consumption in the spring. The word is from the German *bock/bockbier,* shortened from *Einbecker bier,* as it was first made in Einbeck, a town in Hanover, Germany.

BODY in reference to food and drink describes a full, rich, complex flavor and texture that lingers in the mouth.

BOIL means to cook foods or liquids at 212°F (called the BOILING POINT). For liquids, this means a change from a liquid to a gaseous state, which produces bubbles of gas that rise to the surface of the liquid, agitating it as they rise. When bubbles are small and cling to the edge of the pot, a simmer has been reached. When bubbling cannot be halted by stirring, a rapid, full, or rolling boil has been reached. A moderate boil is in between these stages and at this point stirring temporarily stops the boiling. A large pot of water can take up to fifteen minutes to boil.

BOILED DINNER, also called NEW ENGLAND BOILED DINNER, is a meal of meat and vegetables, such as corned beef or smoked ham, cabbage, and potatoes and other root vegetables, prepared by boiling—it is a specialty of New England. New England boiled dinner is traditionally accompanied by horseradish and mustard. New England boiled dinner was originally made with salted beef; today it more commonly contains corned beef, ham, or salt pork.

BOILED DRESSING is any cooked salad dressing thickened with egg yolks; it often contains mustard and is used on dishes like potato salad. Boiled dressing is not actually boiled, but gently cooked in the top of a double boiler.

BOK CHOY or **BOK CHOI**, also called CHINESE CABBAGE, PAK CHOI, or PAK CHOY, is a Chinese cabbage with long white stalks and narrow green leaves. Bok choy is Chinese for "white vegetable."

> **HINT** Refrigerate bok choy in a zip-lock bag for up to four days. Trim the stalks' rough ends.

BOLETES: see PORCINI.

BOLLITO MISTO, Italian for "boiled mixed," is a dish of vegetables and various meats (traditionally a piece of beef, a shoulder of veal, a chicken, an ox tongue, half a calf's head, and a pork sausage) simmered together in a broth and usually served with an anchovy-garlic sauce.

BOLOGNA, also called POLONY (British), is smoked sausage made with a variety of finely ground seasoned meats, usually including beef and pork, or a similar sausage made with chicken or turkey. True Italian bologna sausage is called mortadella.

BOLOGNESE, also called ALLA BOLOGNESE, is, literally, "in the style of Bologna" (Italy), though in Italy the dish is known as RAGU. It is spaghetti (or another type of pasta) served with a thick tomato-meat sauce. Curiously, given the popularity of the pairing elsewhere, meat sauce in Bologna is never served over spaghetti, but with tagliatelle or lasagna.

BOMBAY DUCK is a fish (the bummalo), not a fowl; the dish is South Asian and the fish is dried, salted, grilled, and served as a pungent relish or curry. "Bombay" is an alteration of *bombila*, which comes from the Marathi term for the fish, presumably influenced by Bombay, India. Some speculate that "duck" comes from the way the fish skims the surface of the water. Bombay duck's great claim to notoriety is its extraordinarily pungent smell, which manages to seep out of the most airtight container and is nothing at all like the aroma of duck. Despite the rather unpleasant odor of the fish, it is often considered to be a delicacy by connoisseurs of Indian cuisine.

BOMBE is a frozen or set dome- or ball-shaped dessert. It is French for "bomb," referring to the shape of the original copper mold used. Plain ice cream is used to line the mold and then a second, more strongly flavored ice cream mixture is used as a filling. The bombe is usually decorated with crystallized fruit, then frozen.

BOMBER: see GRINDER.

BON APPÉTIT, "Good/hearty appetite!" in French, is a salutation to a person about to eat.

BONBON, also called SUGARPLUM, is a candy with chocolate or fondant (sugar paste) coating and a fondant center that sometimes contains fruits and nuts. Even though bonbon (from the French *bon*, "good") is a registered name belonging to the Hershey Company, the use of bonbon in Europe and especially France is so common that it isn't necessary to include a trademark sign unless you are referring specifically to the Hershey product.

BONED or **BONELESS**, also called DEBONED, means having had the bones removed.

BONING KNIFE is a small (six- to eight-inch) kitchen knife having a narrow curve-edged blade for boning meat, poultry, or fish. A stiff boning knife is good for boning beef and pork, but a very flexible boning knife is preferred for poultry and fish. Using a boning knife ensures that the maximum amount of meat is taken off the bone cleanly, reducing waste in the kitchen.

BONITO (plural is bonito or bonitos) is the flesh of a game fish related to tuna, with dark stripes on its back, though the word often refers to other similar fish. The word origin is unknown, though bonito is Spanish for "pretty good/pretty."

BONNYCLABBER: see CLABBER.

BORAGE is the leaves of a hairy blue-flowered European herb used to flavor sauces and punches; the young leaves are eaten in salads or cooked like spinach. Borage is from the Latin *borago*, "rough hair/short wool," referring to the roughness of the foliage, which tastes like cucumber and produces oil for pharmaceuticals. The flowers of borage are often used to garnish gin drinks. The flower has a sweet honey-like taste and is one of the few truly blue-colored edible things.

BORDEAUX WINE is any of several red or white wines produced around Bordeaux, France, or wines resembling them.

BORDELAISE is a brown-colored red wine sauce flavored with shallots and garnished with bone marrow and parsley. Bordelaise is the feminine form of Bordeaux. Traditionally, bordelaise sauce is served with grilled beef or steak, though it can also be served with other meats that pair well with demi-glace-based sauces made with red wine.

BORSCHT, BORSCH, BORSHT, or **BORSHCH** is a Russian or Polish soup made with beets and usually served with sour cream. It is based on a meat stock and often contains other vegetables like cabbage. The name indicates that beets were not originally its main ingredient; it is from the Russian *borshch* (related to the English bristle), literally "cow parsnip," a plant of the carrot family, which was the soup's original base. Borscht can be served hot or cold.

BOSC PEAR, also called KAISER PEAR, is a winter pear with a long, tapering neck; dense flesh; and a golden-brown and often russeted skin. A cultivar of the European pear, it is named after Louis Bosc d'Antic (1759–1828), a naturalist. The Bosc pear holds its shape well when baked or poached. Color on a Bosc pear doesn't change as it ripens.

BOSTON BAKED BEANS are a variety of baked beans cooked slowly and sweetened with maple syrup or molasses and flavored with salt pork or bacon. The Pilgrims baked these beans on Saturday because of the religious mandate that dictated Sunday as a day of rest.

BOSTON BROWN BREAD is a dark steamed bread made of cornmeal, rye flour, graham flour, or wheat or whole wheat flour and sweetened with molasses; it often contains raisins. Boston brown bread's color comes from the addition of dark-colored sweetener or coffee and the use of a mixture of flours. The bread is cooked by steam in a can or cylindrical pan.

BOSTON CREAM PIE is actually a cake: it is a round sandwich cake filled with cream or custard and covered with chocolate icing. It is cut into wedges like a pie. The Parker House Hotel claims to have served Boston cream pie since 1856, when French chef Sanzian created it. This cake was probably called a pie because in the mid-nineteenth century, pie pans were more common than cake pans.

BOUCHE or **BOUCHET**: see CABERNET.

BOUILLABAISSE (pronounced BOOL-yuh-BAYZ) is a highly seasoned Provençal soup or stew made of several kinds of fish and shellfish with tomatoes and onions or leeks and seasoned with saffron, garlic, and herbs. The fish is served separately from the broth, which is seasoned with rouille (spicy sauce) and poured over garlic-rubbed toast. Bouillabaisse is from the French *bouiabaisso*, "to boil and settle/lower," which is how this fish soup/stew is cooked. In fact, bouillabaisse is more a method of rapid cooking than an actual recipe; there are as many authentic bouillabaisses as there are ways of combining fish.

BOUILLON is a clear seasoned beef, chicken, or vegetable broth; the word is literally French for "liquid in which something has boiled." A bouillon cube is a cube of bouillon extract with seasonings; there is also powdered bouillon.

> **CONFUSABLE** BOUILLON/CONSOMMÉ. A bouillon and a consommé are different in that the latter's ingredients are browned before simmering. In French cookery the term bouillon applies principally to the liquid part of a pot-au-feu.
>
> **HINTS** Bouillon cubes or granules can keep for years in a cool, dry place.
>
> ▌Dropping a quartered potato into boiling bouillon can reduce saltiness. Simmer for several minutes, then strain.

BOUNCEBERRY: see CRANBERRY.

BOUQUET, also called NOSE, is used to describe the aroma or smell of wine. In referring to a bouquet, aromas are frequently described in terms of fruits, honey, nuts, spices, or wood, depending on the age and style of each wine.

BOUQUET GARNI, also called FAGGOT, is a bunch of herbs used to flavor a soup or stew; it consists of sprigs of parsley and thyme and a bay leaf, tied together if fresh or wrapped in cheesecloth if dried, and combined with celery, fennel, garlic, leek, marjoram, and/or orange peel, among other additions. Instead of being tied together, the bunch can also be enclosed in a porous container and cooked with a dish but removed before serving. The term is French for "garnished bunch/bouquet."

> **HINT** Tying or bagging the herbs in a bouquet garni allows for their easy removal before the dish is served. A paper coffee filter may also be used to wrap the herbs. Put the herbs in the filter, stem end up; tie at the top with string. An easier way to enclose the herbs is to put them in a tea infuser.

BOURBON is a kind of American whiskey distilled from a mash made up of not less than 51% corn, plus malt and rye. It is America's only native spirit and was first distilled in Kentucky just after the Revolutionary War at a mill in Bourbon County. The term straight bourbon means it has been aged for at least two years. Bourbon can legally be made only in the United States.

BOURGUIGNONNE or **BOURGUIGNON** means cooked in a red wine sauce with small mushrooms, onions, and bacon, a style that originated in Burgundy (Bourgogne), France.

BOURSIN is a trademarked French triple cream cow's milk cheese, often flavored with garlic, pepper, and other herbs. It is similar to cream cheese in texture and taste and was created in 1957 by Francois Boursin, a cheesemaker in Normandy. Boursin cheese is wrapped in foil because Boursin's unique packaging was designed to keep Boursin fresh, make it easy to unwrap and rewrap, and make an attractive presentation on a cheese board.

BOUTIQUE WINE is produced by a small company specializing in its own products.

BOWL is a round vessel or dish that is open at the top, is more wide than deep, and is used for holding or serving food or liquids. In Old English the word was *bolla*, descended from Teutonic, Germanic, and Proto-Indo-European forms.

BOX GRATER is a usually stainless-steel kitchen tool that is a slightly tapered, four-sided pyramid with an open bottom and a handle on top. It has coarse, fine, and superfine grating surfaces (perforations and slits) and a slicing surface for use on spices, vegetables, cheese, and other items.

HINTS Spray nonstick cooking spray on the box grater before you start grating the cheese.

To clean a box grater, first brush off as many of the loose bits as you can, both on the inside and outside of the grater. Soak the grater in hot soapy water, then take a nylon scrub pad or toothbrush and scrub away, or grate a raw potato or apple after you're done grating cheese.

EARNING A BOY SCOUT COOKING BADGE

THE BADGE REQUIREMENTS ARE AS FOLLOWS:

PLAN nine menus for three days of camping, including a three-course dinner; a one-pot dinner; and breakfast, lunch, and dinner for a backpacking trip.

MAKE a shopping list for the above.

LIST utensils for cooking and serving.

FIGURE and record the weight of food used for the backpack menus.

BUILD a fireplace, including supports for utensils.

PREPARE and cook meals.

CLEAN up thoroughly.

BOYSENBERRY is a large raspberry-flavored fruit that is a cross between the loganberry and various blackberries and raspberries. The boysenberry is named after Rudolph Boysen (1895–1950), an American horticulturist who developed the berry in the early 1920s; he later turned it over to Walter Knott of Knott's Berry Farm for commercial development. All boysenberries in the world can be traced to Knott's Berry Farm.

BRACIOLA: see ROULADE.

BRAEBURN is a tart-sweet, crisp-fleshed, red dessert apple named for the Braeburn Orchard in New Zealand, where it was first commercially grown. Braeburn apples originated in the early 1950s as a chance seedling, with Lady Hamilton and Granny Smith apples as possible parents.

BRAINS refers to beef, pork, and lamb brains sold for food; they are usually plump and firm, with a bright, pinkish white color. They are usually poached, fried, baked, or broiled, and should be prepared and eaten on the day of purchase.

> **HINT** Brains must be well washed, then blanched in acidulated water. Brains need to be handled with care to be eaten safely, because they may contain prions, the proteins that cause spongiform diseases like Creutzfeldt-Jakob disease (the human form of mad cow disease).

BRAISE (BRAISING) originally meant to fry food lightly and then simmer it in a closed container; the word is French for "live coals," in which this container was placed. Braise now refers to any method in which a food is cooked slowly with fat and little moisture in a closed pot. Braising is a slow-cooking method for tough cuts of meat or poultry and some stringy vegetables. Braised foods often taste better the next day, after the flavors have had a chance to meld.

> **HINT** Meat to be braised is generally browned in fat for color and flavor before braising. Because of reverse osmosis, salting and seasoning meat and poultry up to 24 hours before braising actually helps keep them moist and flavorful. The tougher (less tender) meats, such as those cut from the leg, shoulder, rump, or neck, which are suited for long, slow cooking, are the best cuts of meats for braised dishes. In this slow process, the muscles in these meats release natural gelatin, which both tenderizes the meat and enriches the stock. Make sure the meat can be cut into regular, larger pieces. A roast with lots of fat and poultry with the skin on are not recommended for braised dishes.

BRAMBLE refers to a prickly bush of the rose family, especially blackberry or raspberry, and the fruit of a bramble. The word is also used to refer to jellies—when the fruit is used in pies, crumbles, or tarts, it is known as a "blackberry," but when made into jelly, it becomes "bramble." Bramble jelly may also include crab apples; bramble pie is a deep-dish pie made from blackberries.

BRAMBLE FRUITS

BLACKBERRY	LOGANBERRY	TAYBERRY
BOYSENBERRY	RASPBERRY	WINEBERRY
CLOUDBERRY		

BRAN is broken husks of the seeds of cereal grains (barley, oats, wheat) that are separated from the flour by sifting; the term also refers to food prepared from bran. The word is very old but of unknown origin.

BRANDY is a spirit distilled from the fermented juice of the grape or other fruit. The *Oxford English Dictionary* says the name comes from the distillation process: the wine is heated, or "burnt," to separate out the alcohol, so the Dutch called it *brandewijn*, literally "burnt wine." The English borrowed the word in the early seventeenth century as brandewine or brandwine, which became brandy wine and then, around 1657, brandy. True brandy is from grapes, but fruit brandies may be created from any other type of fruit, though some, like apricot brandy, are really considered to be liqueurs. It is appropriate to cup a brandy snifter in your hands to warm the liquor and inhale the fragrance.

BRASSERIE, French for "brewery," usually denotes a small, inexpensive French-style restaurant serving beer and wine as well as food.

> **CONFUSABLE** BRASSERIE/BISTRO. Both a brasserie and a bistro serve inexpensive food, but a bistro has less formal and quicker service than a brasserie. The distinction of all brasseries is that they serve a limited menu at any time of day and often until fairly late at night. Typically, a brasserie is open every day of the week and serves the same menu all day.

BRATWURST is a German pork sausage, though sometimes veal is added. The word is from the German *brat*, "fried meat," and *wurst*, "sausage." Bratwurst is a very popular form of fast food in German-speaking countries, where it is often cooked and sold at small stands.

BRAUNSCHWEIGER is a spicy smoked liver sausage (liverwurst) created in Braunschweig, Germany; the term literally means "Brunswick sausage." Braunschweiger is soft enough to be spreadable and is usually served at room temperature.

BRAZIER denotes a simple cooking device consisting of a container of live coals covered by a grill upon which the food is cooked. A HIBACHI (Japanese for "fire bowl/pot") is a portable brazier. The word brazier comes from the French *brasier*, from *braise* ("hot coals").

BRAZIL NUT, also called CREAMNUT or PARANUT, is a three-sided South American nut with an edible white oily meat and a hard brown shell. The tree yields three to four pounds of pods with thick shells that must be broken open with a machete; inside are twelve to twenty Brazil nuts. It is technically a seed, not a nut.

> **HINT** Brazil nut shells are extraordinarily hard and must be tempered so they're easier to crack. To do so, you can freeze the nuts for 6 hours or bake them at 400°F for 15 minutes (cool for 15 minutes), or put the nuts in a pan and cover with water. Bring to a boil, then boil for 3 minutes. Drain off the hot water, then cover with ice water and let stand for 3 minutes before draining and cracking.

BREAD is a food made from a dough of flour or meal and usually raised with yeast or baking powder and then baked. The simplest breads are made from grains (barley, corn, millet, oats, rye, wheat) mixed with milk or water. These ingredients are mixed into a dough, shaped, and cooked, usually by baking. Salt, eggs, sugar, and other ingredients may be added to give the bread flavor, change its texture, or increase its nutritional value. A special ingredient called a leavening agent is often added to make the bread rise by enlarging air pockets in the dough, giving it a lighter texture and more volume. The simplest unleavened breads, including matzo and tortillas, are made from only flour and water. During baking, heat converts the water in the bread dough to steam, which creates tiny bubbles that cause the bread to rise. Leavened breads also use the physical action of steam to create rise, but they receive an additional lift from leavening agents, such as baking powder, baking soda, or yeast. Leavening agents produce carbon dioxide, a harmless gas that enlarges air bubbles inside the dough. Bread was an Old English word meaning "piece/fragment," but its meaning of "baked dough" is comparatively recent. The standard word in the Old English period for bread was *hlaf*, which evolved into "loaf." It was not until around 1200 that the word bread was used in its current sense, leaving loaf to mean just an "individual mass of bread."

BREAD ESSENTIALS

■ Presliced, store-baked bread should still be good two days after its sell-by date. If you refrigerate bread, put it in a zip-lock freezer bag and then bring to room temperature before serving.

■ Slightly stale bread produces a firmer-textured toast.

■ For baking bread, it helps to have warm hands, a warm kitchen, and a hot oven.

■ To test if kneading is complete, insert a finger in the dough and if the indent springs back, the dough is well kneaded.

■ To test a loaf for doneness, tip it out of the pan into a mitted hand and tap it on the bottom. If it does not sound hollow, return it to the oven and check in 5–7 minutes.

■ About ½ cup of bread crumbs is produced from one slice of bread.

■ When you make bread, be sure to include the relax step before shaping the loaf. Form the bread into a tight round and wrap with plastic wrap or a damp cloth for 10–15 minutes. Then shape the dough, or roll or press it out.

■ Cool freshly baked bread before storage. Store yeast bread at room temperature or freeze it. Very moist or fruit bread can be stored in the refrigerator after cooling.

■ Freshen a stale loaf of bread by putting it in a paper bag, sealing the bag, and lightly moistening the bag with water. Put on a baking sheet in a 350°F oven for 5 minutes. You can also revive stale bread by wetting the outside and putting in a 400°F oven for 15 minutes, or put bread in a steamer insert or on a splatter screen and steam it.

■ Turn a crusty bread loaf on its side for easier slicing.

- Place a pan of boiling water in the oven while bread is baking to ensure a crisp crust.

- To keep commercial loaves of bread fresh, twist the end of the bread bag and fold the excess back on the bag itself, over the remaining bread. You can do this as soon as a few slices are removed.

- For dough that is to rise in a loaf pan (second rise), slip the pan into a zip-lock bag. Put the loaf pan inside another loaf pan so the inflated bag rises about the dough, giving it room to expand. This affords draft-free rising for the dough.

- A bread loaf can be slashed with kitchen shears or a razor blade.

HOW DOES BREAD RISE?

Yeasts are one-celled fungal organisms. One ounce of yeast contains two hundred billion cells.

1. Yeast is mixed with flour, water, salt, and other ingredients. Yeast first produces glucose (a form of sugar) and then breaks down or ferments the glucose into alcohol and carbon dioxide. The proteins in wheat flour form gluten, an elastic substance.

2. The dough is kneaded and the proteins in the flour arrange them-selves so that they trap the carbon dioxide produced by the yeast as it ferments the sugars in the flour.

3. The trapped carbon dioxide creates a large number of pores or bubbles in the bread that make it rise.

4. As the dough rises, the yeast cells become separated from the nutrients and the process starts to slow down.

5. Kneading the dough again will restart the process, causing the dough to rise again.

6. Heat in the oven causes the gases like carbon dioxide to expand, making the bread rise even more. The alcohol that is created by yeast during this process is released as the bread is baked. The heat also drives off the carbon dioxide, leaving a light, soft loaf.

BREAD VARIETIES

Bread is a basic food made from a flour-and-water dough, normally with yeast added, and baked in an oven. No other food is as redolent of myth, rite, and tradition as bread. Central to meals until almost the end of the second millennium (more so than meat), it is indeed the "staff of life." Bread making dates back to at least 9000 BC; the first breads were cooked on heated baking stones, many of which survive. The invention of leavened bread (around 5000 BC) is attributed to the

(continued)

Egyptians, who made bread from millet and barley. They may have discovered fermentation by chance when a piece of dough become sour. It was in the Middle Ages that the bakery trade developed and from that time on, there have been many types of bread. A bread's crumb and the thickness and quality of its crust are affected by oven temperatures and times. Humidity also plays a part. Manipulating these factors and the careful choice of ingredients is part of the baker's art. These are some common varieties of bread:

ALTAR BREAD	ENGLISH MUFFIN	POPPY SEED PLAIT
ANADAMA	ENRICHED BREAD	PORTUGUESE BREAD
BAGEL	FINGER ROLL	POTATO BREAD
BAGUETTE	FLATBREAD	PRETZEL
BANANA BREAD	FOCACCIA	PULLED BREAD
BANNOCK	FRENCH BREAD	PUMPERNICKEL
BATTER BREAD	GARLIC BREAD	RAISIN BREAD
BIALY	GRAHAM BREAD	ROLL OR SMALL BREAD
BLACK BREAD	GRISSINI	RUSK
BLEEDING BREAD	HOLIDAY BREAD	RUSSIAN RYE
BOSTON BROWN BREAD	HUSH PUPPY	RYE BREAD
BOULE	IRISH SODA BREAD	SALT-RISING BREAD
BREADSTICKS	ITALIAN BREAD	SCONE
BRIOCHE	JEWISH RYE	SEMOLINA
BROWN BREAD	KAISER ROLL	SEVEN-GRAIN BREAD
BUN	LANDBROED	SODA BREAD
CARAWAY SEED BREAD	LAVASH	SOURDOUGH BREAD
CHALLAH	MATZO, MATZOH, OR MATZAH	STOLLEN
CHAPATI		SWEET BREAD
CINNAMON BREAD	MELBA TOAST	TEA BREAD OR TEABREAD
CORN BREAD	MONKEY BREAD	TORTILLA
CORN PONE	MUFFIN	UNLEAVENED BREAD
COTTAGE LOAF	NONWHEAT BREAD	VASILOPITA
COUNTRY-STYLE BREAD	NONYEAST BREAD	VIENNA BREAD
CRACKLING BREAD	NUT BREAD	WAFER BREAD
CRESCENT ROLL	OATCAKE	WHITE BREAD
CROISSANT	OATMEAL BREAD	WHOLE-GRAIN BREAD
CROUTON	OIL-RICH BREAD	WHOLE MEAL BREAD OR WHOLEMEAL BREAD
CRUMPET	ONION ROLL	
DARK BREAD	PARKER HOUSE ROLL	WHOLE WHEAT BREAD
DINNER ROLL	PITA	ZWIEBACK
EGG BREAD	PLAIN WHITE ROLL	
	POPOVER	

BREAD-AND-BUTTER PICKLE or **BREAD AND BUTTER PICKLE** is an unpeeled thin slice of cucumber pickled with vinegar, salt, celery seed, cloves, mustard, turmeric, and sugar. Bread-and-butter pickles are sweet and may be so called because they are "basic" pickles (pickled cucumbers). Bread-and-butter pickles likely got their name during the Great Depression when they were cheap and shelf-stable, and could become a meal when sandwiched between bread and butter.

BREADFRUIT is the large round green fruit of a tropical tree of the fig family that grows on South Pacific islands; it is so named because the soft white pulp resembles freshly baked bread. The fruit was discovered in 1688 on the Pacific island of Guam by William Dampier. It is used as a vegetable and sometimes as a substitute for flour. Breadfruit is one of the highest-yielding food plants, with a single tree producing up to two hundred or more fruits per season.

BREADING is a coating of crumbs applied before cooking to add a crisp texture to fried foods. Bread crumbs are most commonly used, but crumbs from crackers, breakfast cereals, Melba toast, matzos, pretzels, and corn chips are also used. When a food is breaded, the food is dried completely; dusted with a light coating of flour; dipped in eggs mixed with a little milk, water, or oil; and dredged in the breading.

> **HINT** To help breaded food brown evenly, pat the food dry before breading. Roll in flour or cornstarch, then a wet mixture, then the crumbs. Put the seasoning in the wet mixture. Let the food sit on a rack for 15 minutes before cooking.

BREAD KNIFE is a knife designed or suitable for slicing bread; it usually has a long, serrated blade that is straight, not curved. The serrations on the blade make it ideal for cutting bread and other foods with a hard surface and soft interior, enabling it to pierce a hard crust or skin without bruising or crushing the delicate insides.

BREAD MACHINE is a small appliance for baking bread. It has a boxlike shape and contains a computer-run combination mixer and oven. In most models all of the bread ingredients are put into the container, which automatically mixes and kneads, makes the dough rise twice, shapes it, and bakes it. Most bread machines have different cycles for different kinds of dough/bread.

> **HINTS** It's important to follow manufacturer's directions, which can vary, for adding and layering ingredients. Failing to do so could prevent the yeast from mixing with the liquid, which would result in a failed loaf of bread. Ingredients should be at room temperature (70°F–80°F).
>
> If a cooled bread is hard to remove from the container, gently rap the pan on the side of the counter, or use a rubber mallet to tap lightly on the sides of the pan.

BREAD PUDDING is a dessert made of bread cubes or slices soaked in a mixture of milk, eggs, sugar, and spices; fruit and nuts are often added. Bread pudding is served hot or cold. Food historians generally attribute the origin of basic bread pudding to frugal cooks who did not want to waste stale bread.

BREADSTICKS or **BREAD STICKS**, also called GRISSINI, are slender, sticklike pieces of crisp, dry bread.

BREAKFAST is the first meal of the day, usually in the morning. It literally means "break the fast" of the night, as it is the first meal after sleeping. The word first appeared in English around 1463.

BREAKFAST FOODS

BACON	FARINA	ROLL
BAGEL	FRUIT	SAUSAGE
BREAKFAST BURRITO	GRITS	SCRAPPLE
CEREAL	JUICE	STRUDEL
COFFEE	MILK	TEA
CROISSANT	OATMEAL	TOAST
DOUGHNUT	PANCAKE	WAFFLE
EGG	PASTRY	YOGURT

BREAST refers to meat carved from the chest of poultry, the front of the thorax or chest, or the forepart of the body between the neck and the belly.

BREATHE, as used for wine, means to allow the wine to reach full flavor by leaving it to stand and absorb air after having been uncorked. Typically, red wines are the ones that benefit most from breathing before serving. However, there are select whites that will also improve with a little air exposure. In general, most wines will improve with as little as fifteen to twenty minutes of air time. When wine is allowed to mix and mingle with air, the wine warms up, its aromas open up, its flavor profile softens and mellows out a bit, and its overall flavor characteristics usually improve.

BREW is any drink made by steeping and boiling and fermenting rather than distilling, and the verb means to prepare a drink in this manner. It is a very old word, the original sense being "make a drink by boiling." The word brewery did not enter English until 1658, when it replaced the earlier brewhouse. Today, brew mainly refers to the preparation of beer by using yeast as a catalyst in the alcoholic fermentation of liquors containing malt and hops.

BREWIS is a dish with a few variations: bread soaked in broth, drippings of roast meat, milk, or water and butter; broth thickened with bread; or bread soaked in milk, broth, or gravy. It is from an Old French word meaning "soup made with broth of meat."

BREWPUB or **BREW PUB** is a restaurant that sells beverages brewed on the premises. A small brewery is attached to this pub or restaurant.

BRICK CHEESE is a semisoft, sweet American cheese made from the whole milk of cows and produced in brick form. This surface-ripened cheese is mild when young, but very pungent when aged. Brick is an American original. It was "invented" in 1877 by John Jossi, a Swiss-born American cheese maker and called BOX CHEESE. Brick cheese is said to have gotten its name from the bricklike shape of the weights that were originally used to press the cheese.

BRIDGE MIX is so called because it is typically served during card games. It is generally a mixture of various ingredients such as candies (caramels, chocolates, jujubes), fruits, malt, nougat, and nuts (almonds, cashews, macadamia, peanuts, pecans).

BRIE is a soft, surface-ripened, cow's milk cheese with a whitish rind and a pale yellow interior, named for a district in France. When Brie is at room temperature, it is runny. It is an ancient cheese, dating back to at least the thirteenth century, and it is traditionally named after the particular place where it was made, such as Brie de Meaux. True Brie must be made from unpasteurized milk and is therefore unavailable in the United States, where the USDA prohibits raw milk cheese under sixty days old. Brie is served toward the end of a meal.

> **HINT** Because Brie is drained on an inclined surface, the finished cheese is sometimes of uneven thickness. The thinnest part is the most matured.

BRIGADE: See FRONT OF THE HOUSE.

BRINE is a variable strong solution of salt and water that is used for curing, preserving, canning, pickling, and developing flavor in food. To brine is to steep food in brine. The term fresh brine means nitrite may be added; live brine contains microorganisms that convert nitrate to nitrite (as in pickling salts). Salt from salt springs was formerly known as BRINE SALT. Lean meats like chicken, pork, and turkey are best for brining, as they benefit most from the process, which prevents the meat from drying out. Salmon and duck are also good candidates for brining.

BRIOCHE (pronounced BREE-ohsh) is a soft, light-textured French roll or bun enriched with eggs and butter. The word is from the Old French *brier*, "knead." A BRIOCHE PAN has fluted sides with a narrower base and a broader lip; brioche pans with six cups on a tray are also available.

> **HINT** Since brioche is made with butter, it is best to handle the dough while it is cool, to prevent melting. Many cooks chill the dough intermittently while they work on it, and the dough is set to rise under refrigeration. While the rising will take longer, it also yields a better brioche.

BRISKET is a cut of meat, especially beef, that is the breast of the animal, which extends from the forelegs back beneath the ribs. It is a fairly firm cut, usually inexpensive, and benefits from long, slow cooking. Sold on the bone, or boned and rolled, it is often cooked in one piece. The word brisket seems to be from the Old Norse *brjosk*, "cartilage/gristle." Brisket is usually divided into two sections. The flat cut has minimal fat and is usually more expensive than the more flavorful point cut, which has more fat. In the United States the whole brisket has the meat-cutting classification NAMP (North American Meat Processors Association) 120. The brisket is made up of two separate muscles (pectoralis major and pectoralis minor), which are sometimes separated for retail cutting: the lean first cut or flat cut is NAMP 120A, while the fattier second cut, point, deckel, fat end, or triangular cut is NAMP 120B.

BRITTLE is a candy made of caramelized sugar, sometimes with nuts like peanuts, cooled in thin sheets. Named for its texture, brittle was created around 1892. Brittle-type recipes were quite possibly the first candies. These simple combinations composed of honey and sesame seeds were favorites of ancient Middle Eastern cooks.

BROAD BEAN, also called FAVA BEAN, FIELD BEAN, or HORSEBEAN, is the large, flat, edible seed of an Old World plant (*Vicia faba*). This vegetable was known to the Greeks as *pháselos*, the Romans as *faba*, and the Anglo-Saxons as bean.

BROAD-LEAVED ENDIVE: see ESCAROLE.

BROCCOLI is a plant in the cabbage family with tight heads of green, purple, or white flower buds that are cooked and eaten as a vegetable. Broccoli comes from the Latin *brachium*, "strong arm/branch," in reference to its shape; broccoli is the Italian plural of *broccolo*, "cabbage sprout/head," and literally means "little shoots."

> **HINTS** The broccoli heads should be dark green or purplish and tightly clustered; the stalks should be fresh looking, not tough or woody.
>
> ▌ Refrigerate broccoli for up to five days in a perforated bag. Broccoli can be blanched and frozen for a year.
>
> ▌ Soak a head of broccoli upside down in a bowl of cold water for 20 minutes to remove dirt. Cut or peel off any stalk parts that are tough. Cut into spears. Broccoli can be precooked by blanching or parboiling.

BROCCOLINI is a hybrid of broccoli and Chinese kale (gai lan) with small florets and a peppery or nutty-sweet taste. Broccolini, known in Europe as asparation and in the United States as BABY BROCCOLI, is a trademark of the Mann Produce Company, which developed the hybrid.

> **HINT** Store broccolini in a plastic bag in the refrigerator for up to five days.

BROCCOLI RABE, BROCCOLI RAAB, BROCCOLETTI DI RAPE, or **BROCCOLETTO**, also known as RAPINI, is a leafy green vegetable with broccoli-like buds and thin bitter-flavored greens, related to the cabbage and turnip.

> **HINT** Avoid yellowing florets on broccoli rabe. The season is fall and winter.

BROCHETTE, also known as À LA BROCHE, KEBAB, or SHISH KEBAB, is a skewered dish of meat, chicken liver, or seafood, usually sautéed or grilled. Food cooked en brochette is cooked on a skewer. The word brochette is derived from the French *broche*, "pointed tool," and literally means "little skewer."

BROIL (BROILING) means to cook by direct exposure to radiant heat (as over a fire or under a grill). To pan-broil means to cook food in a pan on top of the stove, dry and with only enough oil to prevent the food from sticking. The word is of uncertain origin and history.

BROILING ESSENTIALS

- Generally, foods are placed four to eight inches from the broiler element. Thicker meat cuts need to be farther away to cook properly (or they will char).

- Keep the oven door ajar to prevent the oven from overheating. Most grill recipes can be done in a broiler. Spray the upper pan with nonstick cooking spray and line the bottom pan with heavy-duty foil.

- Turn meat with tongs or a spatula, not a fork, which will puncture.

- Pan-broiling is done over high heat, without liquid, without a cover, and with little or no fat. Use a heavy pan and preheat it to very hot before adding the food.

- To soak up grease and prevent flare-ups, scatter pieces of bread in the pan under the broiler rack.

- When broiling, move thicker foods that take time to cook *away* from the heat source. Lowering the rack allows them to cook through without burning.

BROILER has two meanings: an oven, or part of a stove or oven, that is used for broiling (using a BROILER PAN, a pan on which to broil food); and a small, young chicken that is intended for broiling.

BROOK TROUT: see CHAR.

BROTH is a liquid made by cooking vegetables, meat, seafood, or poultry in water for a long time, and used as a base for soups and sauces; it is also the word for this liquid as a clear soup. Broth etymologically means "that which has been brewed," coming from the Indo-European *broþ*, "heat/boil."

> **CONFUSABLE** BROTH/STOCK. Broth is made from whole or large pieces of poultry, meat, or fish. Stock is made from bony parts—such as necks and backs, feet, and giblets—which are rich in minerals and collagen. Stock is cooked longer than broth and you will rarely see salt in a stock recipe.

> **HINT** Look for low-sodium versions of bouillon cubes, bouillon powder, or canned broths, as store-bought products tend to be saltier than homemade

broth or stock. Refrigerate any unused broth in glass or plastic for up to one week. Broth can be frozen for up to three months.

BROWN (BROWING) means to fry, sauté, or scorch slightly in cooking, especially in a pan.

> **HINT** Before browning, wipe meat dry with a paper towel and do not crowd the food in the pan. Keep the heat high.

BROWN BETTY or **BETTY** is a baked pudding of chopped or sliced apples (or other fruit), bread crumbs, sugar, butter, spices, and sometimes raisins. The name first appeared in print in 1864 in the *Yale Literary Magazine*.

BROWNIE is a rich, chewy chocolate cake, sometimes containing chopped nuts, that is baked in a square or rectangular pan. The first mention of brownies was in the Sears Roebuck catalog in 1897.

> **HINTS** When cutting brownies containing nuts or chocolate chips, you should use a serrated knife.
>
> Line a brownie pan with overlapping perpendicular pieces of foil if you want to lift the whole thing out easily.
>
> You can make individual brownies by pouring the batter into greased muffin tins.

BROWN MUSHROOM: see CREMINI.

BROWN RICE, also called UNPOLISHED RICE, is whole grain rice from which the germ and outer layers containing the bran have not been removed. Brown rice requires more water and longer cooking than white rice. Only the outermost layer, the hull, is removed to produce what we call brown rice. This process is the least damaging to the nutritional value of the rice and avoids the unnecessary loss of nutrients that occurs with further processing. Because the outer coating of brown rice contains added minerals and protein, brown rice is considered to hold greater food value than its white-grain counterpart. The presence of the bran means that brown rice is subject to rancidity, which limits its shelf life to only about six months.

BROWN SAUCE is a sauce of brown roux, dark meat stock, herbs, and Worcestershire sauce that is reduced and strained. In the United Kingdom, the term also refers to a commercially bottled relish containing vinegar and spices. The classic brown sauce is one of the five French mother sauces from which an infinite host of variations are spun.

BROWN STOCK (also called ESTOUFFADE or FOND BRUN) is any dark stock made of beef, poultry, or veal bones and root vegetables. Sauces made from brown stock are called brown sauces, for example, espagnole, bordelaise, Bercy, or piquante. Brown stock is used to make brown sauces, gravies, braised dishes, and brown stews; to deglaze fried meats; and to make glazes by reduction.

BROWN SUGAR is unrefined or partially refined sugar that retains some molasses or white refined sugar to which varying amounts of molasses have been added to make either light brown or dark brown sugar.

> **HINTS** Soften brown sugar by putting a piece or slice of apple in the container or bag of sugar for one day. Another method is to put brown sugar in a heatable container and sprinkle with water, then put it in a 200°F oven for a few minutes.

> ▌ To soften brown sugar in a microwave, put it in a glass bowl or plate, cover with wax paper, and put a piece of bread on top. Cover loosely with plastic wrap and microwave for 30 seconds.

BRÛLÉE or **BRÛLÉ** is French for "burned" and usually refers to caramelization of the top of food.

BRUNCH is a meal usually eaten in the morning, combining a late breakfast and an early lunch. The term was a British student slang portmanteau of the words breakfast and lunch, first found in print in 1896. Brunch is commonly eaten on Sundays between 10:00 a.m. and 3:00 p.m. The practice of having brunch did not really take hold in the United States until the 1930s.

BRUNOISE is the term for food that is finely diced into approximately ⅛-inch (very tiny) cubes, especially for garnishes and soups. The term is also used for any food garnished with vegetables cut this way. The vegetable must first be julienned, then precisely diced into tiny uniform lengths.

> **HINT** Brunoise is generally used as soon as it is ready, but it can be kept briefly under a damp cloth.

BRUNSWICK STEW is a southern U.S. stew of vegetables and usually chicken and/or wild game meat like squirrel or rabbit. It is named for Brunswick County, North Carolina, its purported place of origin, but some people contend that the dish came from Virginia or Georgia. The key distinguishing factor between soup and Brunswick stew is the consistency. Brunswick stew must be thick; otherwise, it would be vegetable soup with meat added. Most variations have more meat and vegetables than liquid. Unlike soup, the stew is usually allowed to simmer and cook for long periods of time. This may be attributed to the older tradition of putting wild meats into the stew, which, depending on the meat, might require longer cooking times to become tender.

BRUSCHETTA (pronounced broo-SKEH-tah) is an Italian appetizer of toasted bread slices rubbed with olive oil and garlic; topped with diced tomatoes, basil, salt, and pepper; and served warm or with melted cheese on top. The word is Italian, from *bruscare*, "to roast over coals." Bruschetta, a Tuscan dish, was designed to show off the new season's olive oil at the time of the olive harvest.

BRUSH is to apply a liquid, such as melted butter or beaten egg yolk, to the surface of a food with a brush.

> **HINT** Clean kitchen brushes in a glass of liquid dish soap and very hot water. Then put the brushes in a cup and cover the bristles with coarse salt. This will dry out the brushes and keep them fresh.

BRUSSELS SPROUT is a thick-stalked plant lined with small, green, swollen buds (resembling tiny cabbages) that are eaten as a vegetable. Brussels sprouts are a relatively new vegetable, only about four hundred to five hundred years old; they are said to have originated near Brussels, Belgium. The French call Brussels sprouts *choux de Bruxelles*, "Brussels cabbages," and in Italian they are *cavolina di Brusselle*, "the little cabbage of Brussels."

> **HINTS** Brussels sprouts are at their sweetest after the first frost. Buy green ones with tight leaves/heads, and choose small heads, if possible. Store in the refrigerator for up to four days. Rinse and dry the heads, and trim the stem ends. Cut a shallow X into the stem end before cooking.
>
> It is not necessary to cut an X in all Brussels sprouts. While the X will allow steam to penetrate the stem better, it is not necessary with small sprouts. Avoid overcooking and cook within three days of purchase to prevent bitterness. Add celery rib or caraway seeds to the cooking water to eliminate odor.

BRUT is French for "unsweetened" and it refers to wine that is extremely dry, especially sparkling wine and Champagne. The term extra brut denotes a wine that is extremely (sometimes totally) dry.

BUBBLE AND SQUEAK is a British dish consisting of leftover cooked potatoes and cabbage chopped up and fried together; the dish gets its name from the sounds made in the cooking process.

BUCKLE, also called COBBLER, CRUMBLE, etc., is a streusel-topped coffee cake with berries added to the batter. Some cooks prefer to split the batter, layering half in the bottom of the pan and mixing the other half with the fruit before pouring it in.

BUCKWHEAT is the dark flour produced from any of several plants of the buckwheat family (genus *Fagopyrum*). The word buckwheat comes from a Middle Dutch word meaning "beech wheat," as its grains are shaped like beech mast, the nuts of the beech tree. Buckwheat is unsuitable for making bread. Despite the common name and the grainlike use of the crop, buckwheat is not a cereal or grass. It is actually a fruit seed that is related to rhubarb and sorrel.

BUFFALO WINGS or **BUFFALO CHICKEN WINGS** are small deep-fried chicken wings cooked in spicy hot cayenne pepper sauce and served with celery sticks and blue cheese dressing. They are so named because they were first served in the Anchor Bar in Buffalo, New York, in 1964.

> **CONFUSABLE** BUFFALO WINGS/CHICKEN WINGS. Buffalo wings are spicy; chicken wings are not.

BUFFET has several meanings: an elongated table (also called a SIDEBOARD), a meal set out on a buffet, and a meal consisting of several dishes from which guests serve themselves. Buffet was first the sideboard or cupboard, then the food served on it. For a buffet, set foods right next to the accompanying condiments or sauces. The utensils should be placed at the end of the buffet.

BÚLGAROS: see KEFIR.

BULGUR, **BULGHUR**, **BULGAR**, or **BURGHUL**, also called ALA or AMERICAN RICE, is wheat that has been parboiled, dried or parched, and cracked into small pieces. Bulgur is the oldest processed food known, originating in Persia; the term comes from a Persian word meaning "bruised grain." Often confused with cracked wheat, bulgur differs in that it has been precooked. Unlike cracked wheat, bulgur is ready to eat with minimal cooking; it can be soaked in water or broth, then mixed with other ingredients without further cooking. Bulgur is often used in vegetarian cooking—in soups and gruels with pulses and flavorings, in stuffed vegetables (in place of rice), or as a salad garnished with raw vegetables in vinaigrette. Bulgur can also be used in pilafs and baked goods. Its high nutritional value makes it a good substitute for rice or couscous.

BULKIE ROLL: see KAISER ROLL.

BUN is any small roll of bread, either plain or sweet.

> **HINT** Toast hot dog or hamburger buns on top of a toaster's slots.

BUNCHING ONION: see GREEN ONION and SCALLION.

BUNDT CAKE is a ring-shaped pound cake baked in a type of tube pan with fluted sides. Once a proprietary name, the word Bundt is from the German *Bund*, "ring-shaped cake."

BUNG BELLY: see BLACK-EYED PEA.

BURBOT, also called CUSK or EELPOUT, is a freshwater fish (*Lota lota*) of the cod family that looks like an eel with a flat head and barbels. Burbot tastes like lobster and has the same texture. It is sometimes called POOR MAN'S LOBSTER, although this term usually refers to monkfish.

BURGER: see HAMBURGER.

BURGOO, also called BURGOUT, is a southern U.S. term for a thick spicy stew of whatever meat and vegetables are available; it is also the outdoor event at which this stew is served. The term also refers to an old seafaring dish: a thick oatmeal gruel or porridge.

BURGUNDY WINE is red wine or unblended white wine from the Burgundy region of France, or a blended red wine from another region made in the style of red wine from Burgundy. (The term is also used loosely for any dry red table wine.) Burgundy sauce is made with red wine and thickened with an espagnole sauce or kneaded butter.

BURMA BEAN: see LIMA BEAN.

BURRITO is a Mexican dish of a flour tortilla rolled or folded around a filling, such as meat, refried beans, and cheese. The burrito, literally meaning "little donkey/small burro," was named for its curved shape when filled, which resembles a donkey's back. Burritos are a north-of-the-border Tex-Mex invention.

BUTCHER KNIFE is a broad-bladed, heavy-duty knife for butchering and cutting meat.

BUTCHER'S STEAK or **BUTCHER'S TENDERLOIN**: see HANGER STEAK.

BUTT is the lean upper cut of a pork shoulder or the large end cut of a beef loin.

BUTTER is a dairy product that is an edible emulsion of fat globules made by churning the fat from milk or cream until it solidifies. Butter was known by 2000 BC; at first it was churned in skin pouches thrown back and forth or swung over the back of trotting horses. Later, hand churns were devised. Butter making on the farm consists of allowing the milk to cool in pans, letting the cream rise to the top, skimming the cream off, and letting it ripen by natural fermentation; the cream is then churned. Exclusively made on farms until about 1850, butter is now made mainly in factories. Chemistry and bacteriology contribute to making butter of uniform quality. Commercial butter usually contains 80%–85% milk fat, 12%–16% water, and about 2% salt. The Old English form of the word was *butere,* from the Latin *butyrum*, from the Greek word *boútyron*. The ancient Greek historian Herodotus described how butter was made, but credit for recording its name goes to the physician Hippocrates, who called it *boútyron*. That word was formed from *bous*, "cow," and *tyros*, "cheese," and was probably a translation of the term for butter in some non-Indo-European language, such as Scythian.

BUTTER ESSENTIALS

■ Use a cold pan to heat butter; heat the pan and butter simultaneously. Butter melts and then foams. The best time to add the food to be cooked is when the foam starts to subside but the butter is not yet brown.

■ Butter can be frozen for up to six months in the original packaging.

■ To soften butter in the microwave, put it in a glass dish and cover with wax paper. Microwave (on defrost) for 15–30 seconds and check, repeating if necessary.

■ To soften cold butter, run a small stainless-steel bowl under hot water; when the bowl is hot, put it upside down over the butter. To soften a wrapped stick of butter, hold it in your hands and massage gently for about 4 minutes.

■ Shave butter onto food with a vegetable peeler.

■ To check if butter is soft enough for creaming, bend the stick; if it bends with little resistance, it is ready. The butter should also give slightly when pressed.

■ Cut butter into tablespoon-sized pieces and it will soften in about 15 minutes.

■ If serving bread and corn on the cob for dinner, butter the bread and then roll the ear of hot corn in it to coat the corn with butter.

■ To prevent milk from boiling over when you are heating it, rub butter along the top edge of the pan.

■ You can refrigerate compound butter for a few days or freeze it for 1-2 months in two to three layers of plastic wrap.

■ Unsalted butter is best for baking because too much salt could increase the gluten beyond the desired amount.

■ One-half stick of butter is ¼ cup, 4 tablespoons, or 2 ounces. One stick of butter is ½ cup, 8 tablespoons, or 4 ounces. One and a half sticks of butter is ¾ cup, 12 tablespoons, or 6 ounces. Two sticks of butter is 1 cup, 16 tablespoons, or 8 ounces.

BUTTER TYPES

BROWN BUTTER: Butter cooked over low heat until it turns light brown.

BUTTER/MARGARINE BLEND: Blend of usually 60% margarine and 40% butter.

CLARIFIED BUTTER: The clear liquid obtained by slowly melting butter so that the pure butterfat separates from the milk solids and water; any foam on the surface is also skimmed.

CULTURED CREAM BUTTER: Butter made from fermented cream (lactic acid added).

DRAWN BUTTER: Melted butter to which an acid, such as lemon juice or vinegar, or a flour thickener is added.

EUROPEAN-STYLE BUTTER: Cultured butter with higher than 80% butterfat.

RAW CREAM BUTTER: Rare butter made from unpasteurized cream.

SALTED BUTTER: Butter made from fresh cream with added salt, with no less than 80% butterfat.

(continued)

SPECIALTY BUTTER: Butter made by melting butter, adding other ingredients, then recooling.

SWEET CREAM BUTTER: Most common butter; made from pasteurized fresh cream with at least 80% butterfat and no more than 16% water.

UNSALTED OR SWEET BUTTER: Made from fresh cream but with no salt, with no less than 80% butterfat.

WHIPPED BUTTER: Butter with air or nitrogen gas whipped into it to increase the volume, lighten the texture, and make it easier to spread.

BUTTER BEAN: see LIMA BEAN.

BUTTER BREAD: see SPOON BREAD.

BUTTERCREAM is a mixture of softened butter, powdered sugar, egg yolk, and vanilla that is used as cake frosting or filling.

BUTTER CURLER is a kitchen tool with a ridged, curved edge used to create textured balls or scalloped shapes of butter. A BUTTER MOLD is a wood or plastic tray with designs used to mold butter into decorative shapes. Once butter garnishes have been sculpted with a butter curler, they should be kept in ice water or under refrigeration so that the shape does not collapse.

BUTTERFAT is the fatty substance of milk or cream from which butter is made. It refers to the natural fat contained in milk and dairy products. Butterfat is mainly the glycerides of oleic, stearic, palmitic, and butyric acids. Milk and cream are often sold according to the amount of butterfat they contain.

BUTTERFLY or **BUTTERFLIED** means to split a piece of food, such as meat or fish, along its length, separating it into halves that remain joined, like the wings of a butterfly, so the piece opens up and is thinner. This may be done to prepare the meat for stuffing or rolling. Any kind of thick meat cut can be butterflied, including chicken breasts or thighs, lamb chops, steaks—and even seafood. The meat must be thick enough to slice nearly in half, with two fairly thick sides coming from it. The butterfly method is generally used on boneless cuts of meat, so the meat can lie flat in the pan or broiler. Another advantage of the butterfly method is that it allows the cook to brown all sides of the meat, then fold a stuffing into the crease, seal the meat with a toothpick or kitchen string, and cook the meat with the stuffing mixture inside.

BUTTER KNIFE or **BUTTER SPREADER** is a small knife with a dull blade for cutting or spreading butter. The point of the butter knife, which is often shared, is to avoid using your own knife to slice pieces off the shared butter. You use the butter knife to cut the butter you need, then you use your own knife to spread the butter where you wish. The butter knife should not be used for cutting bread; bread should be broken with the fingers.

BUTTERMILK originally referred to residue from making butter from sour raw milk or cream. Buttermilk now refers to pasteurized skim milk curdled or thickened by adding culture (bacteria or other microorganisms). Buttermilk is slightly acidic, with a distinctive flavor due to the presence of diacetyl and other substances. The word was first recorded in the early sixteenth century. In baking recipes, buttermilk acts as a leavener when its acid reacts with alkaline baking soda to create gas bubbles. There is no butter in buttermilk.

> **HINTS** To substitute for buttermilk when you have none, add 1 tablespoon of cider vinegar, distilled white vinegar, or lemon juice to 1 cup of milk and let the mixture sit at room temperature for 10 minutes. The milk will curdle and can then be used in place of buttermilk.

> For baking, ½%, 1%, and 1½% buttermilk are interchangeable.

BUTTERNUT, also called WHITE WALNUT, is the edible nut of the white walnut tree (*Juglans cinerea*); the nut's rich, oily meat is used in candies and baked goods. Because of the high oil content, butternuts become rancid quickly. The word butternut was recorded in 1753 for the nut and was transferred to the tree itself in 1783. The nut's color is a brownish gray; hence the word was used in 1861 to describe the color of the Southern uniforms in the American Civil War.

BUTTERNUT SQUASH is a type of pear-shaped winter squash (*Cucurbita moschata*) with a smooth, tan rind and edible yellow or orange flesh. Butternut squash bears some resemblance to a nut of the butternut tree, hence the name.

> **HINTS** Butternut squash will store well for several months in a cool, dark, dry place, as long as they are blemish free and have an inch of their stalk still attached (this reduces the likelihood of rotting).

> Butternut squash can be easily peeled with a standard vegetable peeler. To remove the seeds, cut the squash in half lengthwise and spoon them out.

BUTTERSCOTCH is a toffee-like candy made with butter and brown sugar, or with a sauce or syrup flavored with butter or brown sugar. It is boiled at a higher temperature than caramels. Butterscotch has no liquor in it; perhaps "scotch" appears in this term because the toffee was first made by the Scotch, or the root may be "cut butter squares" from scotch's meaning of "to score/cut." The major difference between butterscotch and toffee is that the sugar is boiled to the soft-crack stage for butterscotch and the hard-crack stage for toffee. The butterscotch mixture is boiled until the temperature reaches 270°F–290°F (soft-crack stage). If the same mixture is heated another 15°F–20°F, it will result in a product with a higher sugar concentration, and thus become toffee.

BUTTON MUSHROOM, also called TABLE MUSHROOM or WHITE MUSHROOM, is a variety of cultivated mushroom (*Agaricus bisporus*) with white flesh and a round, half-ball-shaped head that is cultivated for food. The term is also used for any young unopened mushroom. The common grocery store form is completely white, but in recent years the mushroom industry has developed brown strains of the species, which it markets as "cremini" and "portobello" mushrooms (the distinction is simply that the portobellos have been allowed to mature past the button stage).

CABBAGE refers to various cultivars of the genus *Brassica oleracea* grown for their roundish heads of closely layered green, white, or red leaves that are eaten raw or cooked as a vegetable. Cabbage means "head" (from the Latin *caput*), and it is probably the most ancient of vegetables. The phrase "head of cabbage" is actually redundant.

HINTS Buy firm, heavy heads with close-furled leaves. The average head weighs two pounds. Make sure the stem has not cracked around the base. A cabbage wedge can be kept from breaking apart by skewering it first with one or two toothpicks.

❚ You can refrigerate green or red cabbage for up to two weeks, but savoy and Chinese cabbage stay fresh in the refrigerator only for five to six days. Unused cabbage (after some has been cut from the head) should be wrapped in plastic wrap, refrigerated, and used within two days.

❚ To minimize gassiness from eating cabbage, parboil the cabbage for 4–5 minutes, discard the water, rinse, and finish cooking in fresh water.

❚ To help crisp cabbage for slaw, immerse it in ice water for an hour or so, then drain, blot dry, and slice.

CABBAGE FAMILY

ARUGULA	COLLARD GREENS	RUTABAGA
BOK CHOY	KALE	SWISS CHARD
BROCCOLI	KOHLRABI	TURNIP
BRUSSELS SPROUTS	MUSTARD GREENS	TURNIP GREENS
CAULIFLOWER	RADISH	WATERCRESS

CABBAGE TURNIP: see KOHLRABI.

CABERNET, also called BOUCHE, BOUCHET, PETIT-CABERNET, SAUVIGNON ROUGE, and VIDURE, is a premium red grape, originally of the Bordeaux region, used to make wine. *Cabernet Sauvignon* is the major ingredient in the blend of grapes used to produce claret in the Médoc. The name Cabernet originated in the Médoc dialect, but it is not clear where it came from. Cabernet Franc is one of the parent grape varieties that gave rise to the Cabernet Sauvignon cultivar. The acids and tannins in Cabernet are the basis for its longevity and structure and contribute to its complexity (multiple layers and nuances of bouquet and flavor).

CABINET: see MILKSHAKE.

CACAO is a tropical American tree (*Theobroma cacao*) bearing large seedpods containing the seeds (beans) from which cocoa and chocolate are made. For many years the cacao tree was confused with the coco tree because of a printing error in Samuel Johnson's dictionary, which listed the two trees together in the cocoa entry. The word cacao comes from the Mexican *caca-uatl*, "caca-tree." The cacao tree thrives only in latitudes no more than 20° north or south of the equator. High-quality chocolate manufacturers will actually choose their cacao beans as carefully as a winery chooses its grape varieties.

CACCIATORE is an adjective indicating that a dish is cooked with mushrooms, onions, tomatoes, and herbs. It means "hunter" in Italian and possibly alludes to the ingredients a hunter might have handy or to a hunter's game dishes that might be topped with this sauce.

CACIOCAVALLO (pronounced kah-choh-kuh-VAH-loh) is a type of firm Italian cow's or sheep's milk cheese with a smoky flavor, like provolone. The word is Italian for "cheese on horseback," from the custom of draping two cheeses over a pole to dry. The cheese has a mild, slightly salty flavor and a firm, smooth texture when young. As the cheese ages, the flavor becomes more pungent and the texture more granular.

CACTUS FIG: see PRICKLY PEAR.

CAESAR SALAD consists of cos or romaine lettuce leaves and garlic croutons dressed with a mixture of olive oil, lemon juice, raw or coddled (gently boiled) eggs, Worcestershire sauce, Parmesan cheese, and seasonings. Sometimes the dressing is prepared in a flamboyant ceremony at the table. The salad was invented in 1924 by Caesar Cardini, who ran a restaurant in Tijuana in northern Mexico. It is said that on Fouth of July weekend, Cardini was running low on food and he put together this salad. In 1948 Caesar Cardini established a patent on the dressing, which is still packaged and sold as Cardini's Original Caesar dressing mix. The original salad was prepared at tableside. When the salad dressing was ready, the romaine leaves were coated with the dressing and placed stem side out, in a circle, and served on a flat dinner plate so that the salad could be eaten with the fingers.

CAFÉ, also called BISTRO, LUNCHROOM, or TEAHOUSE, is a coffeehouse or restaurant, often small and unfussy, sometimes with an outdoor section. It is also a French word for "coffee." The first café (in the modern sense) was the Café Procope, opened in 1686 by an Italian in Paris.

CAFÉ MOCHA is a drink of typically one-third espresso and two-thirds steamed milk with chocolate added, either cocoa powder or chocolate syrup; see MOCHA.

CAFETERIA is a restaurant where you serve yourself and pay a cashier. Cafeteria is literally Latin American Spanish for "coffee shop/coffeehouse."

CAFFÈ is the Italian word for "coffee."

CAFFÈ LATTE: see LATTE.

CAJUN indicates food cooked with a blend of seasonings and ingredients that generally includes chiles, celery, garlic, mustard, onion, and pepper. This style of cooking originates from the French-speaking Acadian or Cajun immigrants deported by the British from Acadia in Canada to the Acadiana region of Louisiana. An authentic Cajun meal is usually a three-pot affair: a main dish; steamed rice, skillet corn bread, or some other grain dish; and a vegetable.

CAKE mainly denotes a baked good made from or based on a sweet mixture of flour, fat, sugar, and eggs, but there is also the meaning of a small, flat mass of ground or chopped food. Cake is a Viking contribution, from the Old Norse *kaka*, and is related to "cook." Cake first meant a small, flat bread roll baked on both sides by being turned—as in a pancake or potato cake. There are foam cakes and butter cakes. Foam cakes are high in eggs, sugar, and liquid, and contain very little fat. Angel food and sponge cake are of the foam variety. Layer cakes and pound cakes are butter cakes. Chiffon cakes and génoise are combination cakes.

CAKE ESSENTIALS

- When lining the pan for chocolate cake, use cocoa powder instead of flour.

- A cake is done when its top springs back when you press the center, or when a toothpick inserted into the center comes out clean. You can also insert an uncooked strand of spaghetti in the center of a cake to test it for doneness. Cool on a wire rack. Place the rack on top of the cake and invert. Let the cake cool completely before frosting. A plastic-wrapped unfrosted cake can be stored at room temperature for two days or in the refrigerator for three days. It can be frozen for six months, but a foam cake can be frozen for only two months. A frosted cake can be frozen, then wrapped and kept frozen for one month. Thaw a frosted cake in the refrigerator or on the counter, removing the wrap when partially defrosted.

■ When preparing a cake, start with room-temperature ingredients. When creaming butter with sugar, thoroughly cream the butter, then add the sugar and continue creaming until the mixture is light and fluffy. Add eggs one at a time.

■ Whisk together the dry ingredients for cake batter before mixing with the wet ingredients. This ensures even distribution of salt and leavening.

■ Before baking a foam cake, gently run a kitchen knife through the batter to pop any large air bubbles.

■ For light, airy cakes, bake in the bottom third of the oven.

■ Toss fruit, nuts, and chocolate chips in flour before adding to cake batter so they will not sink to the bottom.

■ Put a hot cake pan on a wet kitchen towel for 5 minutes so the steam will loosen the cake.

■ To frost a soft or crumbly cake, freeze the cake for 15 minutes first. Then frost with a thin layer of frosting and put the cake back in the freezer for 15 minutes. Finish with a thicker layer of frosting.

■ Put toothpicks with miniature marshmallows on top of a cake and lay plastic wrap over that to protect the cake during transport.

■ Use tongs to grab and turn cake pans during baking. Cakes need to be rotated to ensure even browning.

■ You can blow-dry a frosted cake with a hair dryer to give it a smooth, lustrous appearance.

■ Store a cut cake with half an apple to keep it moist.

■ An inverted salad spinner can be used to protect a cake.

■ Cakes filled or frosted with whipped cream should be assembled no more than 2 hours before serving to keep them from getting soggy. If your cake filling or frosting contains whipped cream, cream cheese, yogurt, or eggs, store it in the refrigerator; cover loosely if you don't have a cake cover.

■ A 9-inch cheesecake or 13 x 9-inch cake will serve twelve.

CAKE VARIETIES

AMERICAN LAYER CAKE	CASSATA	COFFEE CAKE
ANGEL FOOD CAKE	CHARLOTTE	CUPCAKE
BAKLAVA	CHARLOTTE RUSSE	CUSTARD
BATTENBERG CAKE	CHEESECAKE	DEVIL'S FOOD CAKE
BAVARIAN CREAM	CHIFFON CAKE	DOUGHNUT
BROWNIE	CHOCOLATE CAKE	FRUITCAKE

(continued)

FUNNEL CAKE	MARBLE CAKE	SPONGE CAKE
GATEAU	PANETTONE	STRAWBERRY SHORTCAKE
GÉNOISE	PETIT FOUR	STREUSEL
GINGERBREAD	PINEAPPLE UPSIDE-DOWN CAKE	TEA CAKE
HONEY CAKE		TIRAMISU
HOT CROSS BUN	POUND CAKE	TORTE
JELLY ROLL	RUM BABA	TRIFLE
KUCHEN	SALLY LUNN	UPSIDE-DOWN CAKE
LADYFINGER	SAVARIN	VACHERIN
LAYER CAKE	SHORTCAKE	WEDDING CAKE
LOAF CAKE	SIMNEL CAKE	WHITE CAKE
MADEIRA CAKE	SOUFFLÉ	YELLOW CAKE
MADELEINE	SPICE CAKE	ZUPPA INGLESE

CAKE FLOUR is finely ground, soft wheat bleached with chlorine gas, which whitens the flour and makes it slightly acidic. This acidity makes cakes set faster and gives them a finer texture. The delicate, fine texture of cake flour is achieved by heavy milling. The fine grain absorbs fat readily, ensuring that butter and other fats in cakes are well distributed throughout the batter.

> **HINTS** Cake flour should not be used to make breads and other leavened products, as it is not strong enough.
>
> In a pinch, a substitute for cake flour can be made with ¾ cup of sifted bleached all-purpose flour and 2 tablespoons of cornstarch.

CAKE KNIFE is a very long knife that makes it easier to cut a cake at such occasions as a wedding, and also facilitates cake decorating. Sometimes cake knives are included in a serving set consisting of a knife to cut a cake and a server to place it on the plate.

> **HINT** A cake knife will cut more easily if you soak the blade first in very hot water for a couple of minutes; dry thoroughly before using.

CAKE PAN is a type of bakeware available in various shapes (round, square, rectangular) and sizes, often made of heavy-gauge nonstick materials so it will facilitate even browning but will not warp.

> **HINT** You should grease a cake pan by brushing melted, unsalted butter over the bottom of the pan with a pastry brush. Then lightly dust the pan with flour to prevent sticking. You should not grease the sides of the pan when baking a cake. Most cakes rise more evenly when they can cling to the ungreased sides while baking.

CAKE TESTER is a kitchen utensil, usually a simple stainless-steel wire, inserted into the center of a cake. If the tester comes out clean, the cake is ready. It takes the place of a toothpick.

CALAMARI are squid prepared as food, especially deep-fried. Calamari, from the Latin *calamarium*, "ink pot," is Italian for the inky substance a squid secretes.

CALAMATA: see KALAMATA.

CALF FRIES: see PRAIRIE OYSTER.

CALIFORNIA ROLL is a popular form of sushi made of avocado, crabmeat, carrot, cucumber, and smelt or flying fish roe wrapped in vinegared rice and nori (dried seaweed). The story is that a California chef created the dish in the 1970s; most people in Japan have never heard of the California roll.

CALLALOO: see AMARANTH.

CALZONE is a turnover made of pizza dough and filled with a savory combination of tomatoes, cheese, herbs, and sometimes meat. It is folded over itself and then baked or fried. The word is from the Italian for "trouser/pant leg," ultimately from the Latin *calza*, "sock/stocking." It is a Neapolitan specialty.

CAMBRIC TEA is a beverage for children containing hot water, milk, sugar, and a small amount of tea. Cambric tea derives its name from its resemblance to cambric cloth, a very thin white fabric often used to make lightweight garments.

CAMEMBERT is a rich, soft, surface-ripened, creamy cheese with a thin grayish white rind and a yellow interior. The cheese in its modern form can be dated to 1792, when Marie Harel launched her version, which she passed on to her daughter, who sold it in the village of Camembert, France. Before fungi were properly understood, the color of Camembert rind was a matter of chance, most commonly blue-grey with brown spots. Since the early twentieth century, the rind has more commonly been pure white, but it was not until the mid-1970s that pure white became standard. Camembert's crust should look like a thin white down and may be covered with very small red dots. Under the crust the cheese should be supple, with a beautiful light yellow color. A Camembert cheese that has reached the correct ripeness will yield like bread dough to the light touch of a thumb.

CANADIAN BACON is boneless cured meat with little fat that comes from the loin or rib end of a pig. In Canada it is called BACK BACON.

> **HINT** Sliced Canadian bacon keeps for three to four days, unsliced for one week, and frozen for up to two months.

CANAPÉ is any small piece of bread, cracker, or pastry with a savory topping such as cheese, vegetable, caviar or relish, meat or fish. The figurative word entered English around 1890 and is based on French for "sofa/couch." Cold canapés are served at buffets or lunches or with cocktails or apéritifs; hot canapés are served as entrées or used as foundations for various dishes.

CANDIED: see GLACÉ.

CANDIED FRUIT is fruit cooked in sugar syrup and encrusted with sugar crystals. The fruit is put into increasingly concentrated syrup solutions so that the syrup gradually replaces the water in the fruit. The impregnation must be progressive so that the fruit flesh does not break or shrivel up. Whole fruit, smaller pieces of fruit, or pieces of peel are placed in heated sugar syrup, thereby absorbing the moisture from within the fruit and eventually preserving it. Depending on the size and type of fruit, this process of preservation can take from several days to several months. The continual process of drenching the fruit in syrup causes the fruit to become saturated with sugar, thereby preventing the growth of spoilage microorganisms. The high sugar content of candied fruit allows it to stay fresh essentially indefinitely under the right conditions.

CANDY is any rich sweet or piece of confectionary made with sugar. The word is a shortening of "sugar candy," which is a translation of the French *sucre candi*, borrowed from the Arabic *sukkar qandi*, from the Sanskrit *khanda*, "sugar in pieces." The stages of candy making are thread, soft ball, firm ball, hard ball, soft crack, hard crack, light caramel, and dark caramel.

> **HINTS** The best candy thermometer has a mercury bulb and column mounted on a protective metal casing and has a clip for attaching to the pan.
>
> ▌ The goal of candy making is usually to prevent crystals from forming, so use a wooden spoon to mix the sugar and water, and when the syrup boils, let it do so undisturbed.
>
> ▌ Cook sugar syrup on cool, dry days if possible. Cook in a heavy pan smaller than the burner. Use a clean brush dipped in hot water to brush sugar crystals down the pan sides back into the syrup.

CANDIES, CONFECTIONS, AND SWEETS

Confections are food products based on sugar. Confection is a French term for something mixed or composed that can be applied to sweets and candies. Numerous raw materials are used in making confections: sugar, glucose syrup, honey, milk, animal and vegetable fats, fruit, cocoa, gum arabic, pectin, starches, gelatin, and natural or artificial products and colorings. Some confections are particular to occasions, such as holidays. Here is a sampling of well-known candies, confections, and sweets:

BARK	FONDANT	MARZIPAN OR MARCHPANE
BOILED SWEET	FRANGIPANE	MINT
BONBON	FRUIT ROLLUP	NONPAREIL
BRITTLE	FUDGE	NOUGAT
BUBBLE GUM	GANACHE	PASTILLE
BUTTERSCOTCH	GLACÉ	PEANUT BRITTLE
CANDIED FRUIT	GOBSTOPPER	PEANUT BUTTER CUP
CANDY BAR	GUM	PENUCHE
CANDY CANE	GUMDROP	PEPPERMINT
CANDY CORN	HALVAH	PRALINE
CANDY FLOSS	HARD CANDY	RED HOT
CARAMEL	HOREHOUND	ROCK CANDY
CHEWING GUM	JAWBREAKER	SALTWATER TAFFY
CHOCOLATE	JELLY BEAN	SUGARPLUM
CHOCOLATE BAR	JIMMIES	TAFFY
CHOCOLATE DROP	JUJUBE	TOFFEE
COMFIT	KISS	TRUFFLE
COTTON CANDY	LEMON DROP	TURKISH DELIGHT
CRYSTALLIZED FRUIT	LICORICE	TURTLE
DIVINITY	LOLLIPOP	TUTTI-FRUTTI
DRAGÉE	MARSHMALLOW	

CANDY APPLE, also called CARAMEL APPLE or TAFFY APPLE, is an apple on a stick coated with a mixture of caramel, taffy/toffee, or other melted candy.

> **HINT** Choose smaller apples when making candy apples—they'll be easier to make and easier to eat, and will give you a better candy to apple ratio. Store-bought apples are usually coated with wax, which makes it more difficult to coat them. If you have no choice but to use wax-coated apples, quickly dip them in boiling water and then wipe away the wax coating. Chill the apples in the refrigerator until you're ready to start making candy apples.

CANDY FLOSS or **CANDYFLOSS**: see COTTON CANDY.

CANE SYRUP is a very sweet, thick syrup made from sugarcane. Corn syrup is not as sweet or flavorful, but can generally be substituted for cane syrup. You can also substitute a sugar syrup made of 1¼ cups of sugar and ⅓ cup of water, boiled until syrupy.

CANISTER is any container, usually airtight, for storing dry foods, such as flour or sugar. The word is ultimately from the Greek *kanastron*, "wicker basket," from *kanna*, "cane/reed."

CANNELLINI, also called WHITE KIDNEY BEAN, is a medium-sized, white oval bean with a thin skin and mild flavor. The word is Italian for "small tubes."

CANNELLONI is plural for rolls of pasta stuffed with a meat or vegetable filling and served in a cheese or tomato sauce. Cannelloni is Italian for "large tubes."

CANNING is the act or process of preserving foods in cans or jars, often with a hermetic seal to keep out air. Often such foodstuffs are heated to a specific temperature for a specified time to destroy disease-causing microorganisms and prevent spoilage. Canning was invented in 1809 by Nicholas Appert.

CANNOLI are Italian tube pastries that are deep-fried and filled with a soft cheese like sweetened ricotta and sometimes other ingredients, such as chocolate, nuts, fruit, or liqueur. Cannoli's origin is the Italian *canna*, "reed." Cannoli are sometimes called cannolis, but this is not the correct plural. Cannolo is the correct terminology for a single pastry and cannoli is the name given to two or more pastries.

> **HINT** When making cannoli, always fill them right before serving to keep the shells crisp. Cannoli are best served fresh; the fried pastry dough does not remain crisp, especially when filled, for more than a day. Refrigeration, essential because of the cheese filling, can sometimes help retain the crispness of the outer shell.

CANOLA OIL is an edible vegetable oil made from canola (oilseed rape) grown in Canada and northern North America; the name canola was derived from "Canadian oil, low acid." Canola is high in monounsaturated fatty acids. Canola was derived from rapeseed in the early 1970s but has a different chemical composition from rapeseed. Canola oil is lower in saturated fat (about 6%) than other oils; in comparison, the saturated fat content of peanut oil is 18% and that of palm oil is 79%. Canola oil contains more cholesterol-balancing monounsaturated fat than any oil except olive oil. It also has the distinction of containing omega-3 fatty acids, the polyunsaturated fat reputed not only to lower both cholesterol and triglycerides, but to contribute to brain growth and development as well.

CANTAL is a firm cow's milk cheese, similar to Cheddar, made in the Auvergne region of France. One of the oldest cheeses in France, Cantal dates back to the Gauls of Roman times. There are two types of Cantal cheese: Cantal Fermier, a farmhouse cheese made from raw milk, and Cantal Laitier, the commercial mass-produced version made from pasteurized milk. Cantal cheese has a fat content of 45%.

CANTALOUPE is a variety of muskmelon vine that bears fruit with a tan, netted rind and orange flesh. Cantaloupe was first cultivated outside Rome at a villa called Cantalupo, hence the name. However, the cantaloupes you buy in stores are actually muskmelons—why grocers prefer to call them by the wrong name is unclear, as real cantaloupes are rarely grown or sold in the United States.

> **HINT** The cantaloupe peaks in midsummer to early fall. Choose a melon heavy for its size and free from blemishes, shriveling, or soft, moldy areas. Ripe melons have a strong, sweet smell and give slightly when pressed at both ends. The netting should be pronounced, have undertones of green, and be evenly distributed.

CAPE COD TURKEY is a facetious name for dried salt cod.

CAPER is a bush (*Capparis spinosa*) with spiny trailing stems that is cultivated for its green flower buds, which are pickled or salted and used as a flavoring. The word is derived directly from the Latin name of the plant, *capparis*.

> **HINTS** Before using dried capers, rinse them in water to remove excess saltiness and then dry them.
>
> ❙ Brined capers are often used directly from the jar. Pour out the liquid and replace it with undiluted plain white vinegar, which will double or triple the storage life of the capers. After opening, store the jar in the refrigerator. When capers are past their prime, they begin to acquire a brownish tint. Even with the best of care, after the jar has been opened, capers can become mushy after a few months, so replace them on a regular basis.

CAPON is a fattened, castrated male chicken or the flesh of that chicken. Capons often weigh six to eight pounds and are more flavorful, juicy, and denser-textured than regular chickens. The history of capons dates to 162 BC, when Roman law forbade the eating of fattened hens as a way to save grain, so breeders castrated the cocks, which caused them to grow to twice their normal size. It was within the law to eat these castrated chickens. The word may have descended from the Greek *koptein*, "to cut." Capon is still a popular Christmas roast in Italy. The abundance and great delicacy of the flesh of a capon is due to the accumulation of fat, which is stored in successive layers in the muscles. Capons have fattier, more tender flesh because they are not as active as roosters are. They have no sex drive, so they just eat and rest in the shade until they are about ten to twenty weeks old. The process of turning a rooster into a capon is known as caponization.

CAPONATA is a Sicilian dish similar to ratatouille; it is a relish composed of chopped eggplant, olives, onions, celery, and herbs in olive oil, usually served as an antipasto. The word is Italian, from the Sicilian *capunata*, "sailor's dish of biscuit steeped in oil and vinegar with chopped vegetables," from the Catalan *caponada*, "dry bread soaked in oil and vinegar." Caponata should be served only the day after it is made, so the flavors will have had time to blend and settle.

CAPPELLETTI, literally Italian for "little hats," are small, triangular hat-shaped cases of dough with cheese and/or meat fillings. Cappelletti has three double consonants and can take a singular or plural verb.

CAPPUCCINO is espresso coffee mixed with steamed milk and often topped with cinnamon or chocolate and whipped cream. Its "formula" is one-third espresso, one-third steamed milk, and one-third foamed/frothed milk; others say it is one-third espresso and two-thirds microfoam (foamed milk made with a steam wand). Cappuccino commemorates the dull gray-brown clothing of the Italian Capuchin monks.

> **CONFUSABLE** CAPPUCCINO/LATTE. A cappuccino differs from a latte, which is mostly milk and little foam. Caffè latte is half espresso and half steamed milk. Cappuccino is one-third espresso, one-third steamed milk, and one-third foamed/frothed milk.

> **HINT** To foam the milk for cappuccino, heat the milk on a stove and beat with a handheld mixer. Because of the foam on a cup of cappuccino, it cools more slowly than a cup of regular coffee.

CAPSAICIN is a colorless, pungent crystalline compound derived from capsicums; it is the source of the hotness of hot peppers of the genus *Capsicum*, such as cayenne, chile, and jalapeño. The Scoville scale is the measure of the level of capsaicin in a pepper. Most of the capsaicin (up to 80%) is found in the seeds and membranes of a chile. Since neither cooking nor freezing diminishes capsaicin's intensity, removing a chile's seeds and veins is the only way to reduce its heat.

> **HINT** Capsaicin, the "hot" component of chile peppers, is not water soluble—it is soluble in fat and alcohol. So don't drink water to cool your mouth after eating very hot chiles. Drink milk or beer, or eat some ice cream or guacamole, if your mouth is on fire.

CAPSICUM, also called PEPPER, is any member of the nightshade family and the genus *Capsicum*, tropical American herbs and shrubs, that is cultivated for its many-seeded, usually fleshy-walled berries (fruit). These are eaten raw or cooked as a vegetable and are often dried. Capsicum is also the term for an oleoresin derived from the fruit of some capsicums. The name comes from the Greek *kapto*, "to bite." Green capsicum is the least mature type and has a fresh, raw flavor. Red capsicum is basically a matured or ripened green capsicum and is distinctively sweeter. Yellow and orange capsicums are similar in taste to red capsicum, although not quite as sweet.

CARAFE is a glass bottle with a flared lip and sometimes a stopper that is used to hold and serve beverages, such as wine, water, and coffee. A full carafe contains one liter; a demi-carafe or half carafe contains a half liter. The word is French, from the Italian *caraffa*, probably from the Arabic *ghurruf*, "drinking cup," or the Persian *qarabah*, "large flagon." A carafe is closely related to a decanter, which is designed specifically for alcoholic beverages. The wine carafe is also used to eliminate the sediment from the wine. Pouring the wine slowly from the original bottle into a carafe allows you to watch carefully as the sediment approaches the neck of the bottle—at that point you are finished pouring.

CARAMBOLA is the acidic, orange, fleshy fruit of a small shrub of the wood sorrel family; the fruits have five prominent ridges and in transverse section appear as a five-pointed star and thus are also called STAR FRUIT or STARFRUIT. Portuguese writers of the sixteenth century said carambola was the native name of the fruit in Malabar.

> **HINTS** Carambolas naturally fall to the ground when fully ripe. For marketing and shipping they should be handpicked while pale green with just a touch of yellow.

> **❙** Carambolas do not require peeling. The fruit is entirely edible, including the slightly waxy skin. Ripe carambolas are eaten plain, sliced and served in salads, or used as a garnish on avocado or seafood dishes. They are also cooked in puddings, tarts, stews, and curries.

CARAMEL is burnt sugar used to color or flavor food and drink, but it is also a chewy candy made from burnt sugar, milk or cream, and butter. Caramel was first recorded in 1725, arriving via French from the Spanish *caramelo*, "honey cane," but its earlier history is uncertain. A likely source is the Late Latin *calamellus*, a diminutive form of the Latin *calamus*, "reed/cane." Caramel should be pronounced KAR-uh-muhl, KAR-uh-mel, or KAHR-muhl.

> **HINT** Caramel requires careful attention. Heated above 300ºF, sugar syrup changes color, gradually losing its sweetness and giving off an increasingly strong burnt odor. Eventually it becomes inedible. The end product is determined by temperature, depending on what the caramel is to be used for. When heated, sugar is very sticky and hot and easily burns, so take tremendous care when making caramel on your own. Caramel burns can be very serious. Keep ice water readily available to use on caramel burns, should they occur.

CARAMEL APPLE: see CANDY APPLE.

CARAMELIZE is to convert to caramel by cooking over moderate heat until the natural sugars break down and leave a sweet flavor. Caramel is formed by heating carbohydrates in the presence of acid or alkali. Caramelize has a second meaning in relation to meats and vegetables: it refers to the heating of these until the natural sugars in them break down and turn light brown (as in caramelizing onions).

THE PROCESS OF CARAMELIZATION

Caramelizing means heat-induced browning of sugar or a food that contains sugars but no proteins.

1. When sugar is heated to about 365°F, it dehydrates and melts into a colorless liquid.

2. Further heating turns it yellow, then light brown, then darker brown.

3. If the sugar or starch heated is in the presence of proteins or amino acids, then Maillard reactions take place. Part of the sugar molecule reacts with the nitrogen of the protein molecule.

4. A series of complex reactions lead to brown polymers and highly flavored (though as-yet unidentified) chemicals.

5. Heating makes some of the starch break down into free sugars, which then truly caramelize.

CARAWAY is a Eurasian plant with small, white flowers yielding caraway seeds. The ultimate source of the word is perhaps the Greek *karon*, "cumin," as caraway and cumin seeds are very similar, but the word can only be traced definitely to the Latin *carui*. Caraway is a native to northern Africa, the Mediterranean, and much of Europe. It falls into both categories of herb and spice because the leaves and root are also edible. Caraway has been found in food dating back to 3000 BC, making it one of the oldest cultivated spices.

CARBOHYDRATE is any compound—such as sugars, starch, and cellulose/fiber—that contains carbon, hydrogen, and oxygen; occurs in foods and living tissues; and can be broken down to release energy in the body. Carbohydrates are the primary metabolic fuels: they form the major part of the diet, providing 50%–70% of the energy intake, mainly from starch and sucrose. There are two classes of carbohydrates: simple and complex. Simple carbohydrates are the sugars, which include glucose and fructose from fruits and vegetables, sucrose from beet or cane sugar, and lactose from milk. Simple carbohydrates are absorbed by the body very quickly. Complex carbohydrates include starches and fiber and are most commonly found in whole grains and legumes. Complex carbohydrates, which are generally large chains of glucose molecules, take longer to digest and provide more nutrients than simple carbohydrates.

CARBOHYDRATES

The body's main fuel, carbohydrate, comes in the form of sugars and complex carbohydrates, which include starch and cellulose. Carbohydrates are probably the most abundant and widespread organic substances in nature, and they are essential constituents of all living things. Carbohydrates are formed by green plants from carbon dioxide and water during the process of photosynthesis. In addition to being an energy source, carbohydrates are part of the structure of nucleic acids, which contain genetic information.

The word carbohydrate literally means "watered carbon," from its general formula $C_x(H_2O)_x$.

ALDOSE	FRUCTOSE OR FRUIT SUGAR	POTATO SUGAR
ALTROSE	FUCOSE	POWDERED SUGAR
AMINO SUGAR	FURANOSE	RAFFINOSE
ANHYDROUS SUGAR	GALACTOSE	RAW SUGAR
ARBINOSE	GLUCAGON	REFINED SUGAR
BAMBOO SUGAR	GLUCOSE	RHAMNOSE
BARLEY SUGAR	GLYCOGEN	RIBOSE
BEET SUGAR	GRANULATED SUGAR	SACCHARIDE
BRITISH GUM	GRAPE SUGAR	SACCHAROSE
BROWN SUGAR	GULOSE	SIMPLE SUGAR
CANE SUGAR	HEXOSE SUGAR	SORBOSE
CASTOR SUGAR OR CASTER SUGAR	IDOSE	SPUN SUGAR
CELLOBIOSE	INULIN	STARCH
CELLULOSE	LACTOSE	SUCROSE
CLINICAL DEXTRAIN	LEVULOSE	SUPERFINE SUGAR
COMPOUND SUGAR	LYXOSE	TABASHEER
CONFECTIONERS' SUGAR	MALTOSE	TABLE SUGAR
CORN SUGAR	MALT SUGAR	TAGATOSE
DATE SUGAR	MANNOSE	TALOSE
DEMERARA SUGAR	MAPLE SUGAR	TREE MOLASSES
DEOXYRIBOSE	MELIBIOSE	TREE SUGAR
DEXTRAN	MILK SUGAR	TRELIALOSE
DEXTRIN	MOLASSES	TRISACCHARIDE
DEXTRO-GLUCOSE	MONOSACCHARIDE	TURBINADO SUGAR
DEXTROSE	NIPA SUGAR	VANILLA SUGAR
DISACCHARIDE	PALM SUGAR	WHITE SUGAR
ERYTHROSE	PENTOSAN	WOOD SUGAR
	PENTOSE SUGAR	XYLOSE

CARBONARA, also called ALLA CARBONARA, is a white Italian pasta sauce of cream, egg, Parmesan cheese, small pieces of bacon or ham, onions, pepper, and sometimes vegetables, such as peas. The word is Italian for "(all) on the charcoal grill."

> **HINT** When carbonara is served, it is important that the pasta be very hot so that when the sauce is poured over it, the eggs will briefly continue to cook. In all versions of the recipe, the eggs are added to the sauce raw and are cooked (coagulated) by the heat of the pasta itself.

CARBONATED BEVERAGE is any effervescent drink that releases carbon dioxide under conditions of normal atmospheric pressure. Carbonation may occur naturally in spring water that has absorbed carbon dioxide at high pressures

underground, and it can also be a by-product of fermentation, such as beer and some wines. Soft drinks are artificially carbonated. In 1767 Englishman Joseph Priestley invented carbonated water when he first discovered a method of infusing water with carbon dioxide by suspending a bowl of water above a beer vat at a local brewery in Leeds. Priestley found that water thus treated had a pleasant taste, and he offered it to friends as a refreshing drink.

CARBONATED WATER or **CARBONATED MINERAL WATER**: see SELTZER.

CARDAMOM, CARDAMUM, or **CARDAMON** is a rhizomatous herb of the ginger family that has aromatic pods and seeds used as seasoning or spice. Arabic coffee is flavored with ground cardamom seeds. Cardamom is from the Greek *kardamomon*, a blend of *kardamon*, "peppergrass," and *amomon*, referring to a variety of Indian spice. Each cardamom pod is a green, three-sided, oval capsule containing fifteen to twenty dark, reddish brown to brownish black, hard, angular seeds. Green cardamom is one of the most expensive spices by weight, but little is needed to impart the flavor. Cardamom is often named as the third most expensive spice in the world (after saffron and vanilla), and the high price reflects the high reputation of this most pleasantly scented spice.

> **HINT** Cardamom is best stored in pod form because once the seeds are exposed or ground, they quickly lose their flavor. Ground cardamom is not as full flavored because the seeds begin to lose their essential oils as soon as they're ground.

CARDOON is a leafy vegetable of the thistle family (which also includes the globe artichoke) that looks like celery; both the fleshy root and the ribs and stems of the inner (blanched) leaves are eaten. Extracts from the dried flowers are used in cheese making. The word comes from the French *carde*, "edible part of an artichoke," from the Latin *cardus/carduus*, "thistle/artichoke."

> **HINT** When purchasing cardoons, look for stalks that are firm, wide, plump, and creamy white or silvery gray-green in color. Cardoons are sold with the leafy part and top of the root. They can be blanched first in cold salted water and refrigerated for up to two weeks, or simply refrigerated in a zip-lock bag for up to five days.

CARIBBEAN LOBSTERETTE: see PRAWN.

CARNITAS, Mexican Spanish for "little meats," is a dish of browned, shredded, tenderized pork, served with salsa and sometimes used as a filling for burritos, tacos, or tamales. Carnitas is made from an inexpensive cut of pork that is simmered in a small amount of water until tender, then finished by cooking the pieces in pork fat until nicely browned all over.

CAROB is a Mediterranean evergreen tree with edible pods, whose powder is used as a chocolate substitute because it is sweet and tastes similar to chocolate. The carob bean has a nutritious, refreshing pulp, as rich in sugar as molasses.

CARP is any of various freshwater fish of the family Cyprinidae; carp are often farmed and their lean flesh is baked or braised.

> **HINT** When buying carp, choose a plump one that is carrying eggs, or milt.

CARPACCIO is an appetizer consisting of very thin slices of raw beef or fish served with a vinaigrette or a mustard sauce. The dish was named for artist Vittore Carpaccio (c. 1460–1525), whose art was bright red like thinly sliced raw meat.

CARRAGEEN or **CARRAGHEEN**, also called IRISH MOSS, is dark purple edible seaweed of the Atlantic coasts of Europe and North America. It is named for Carrageen, Ireland. A complex-carbohydrate food additive, carrageenan, is obtained from carrageen.

CARROT is the deep orange, edible, tapering root and herb of the cultivated carrot plant (*Daucus carota*) of the parsley family; it is commonly used as a vegetable. The common garden carrot (*Daucus carota sativa*) is a root crop, probably derived from some variety of the wild carrot. The word is from the Greek *karoton*.

> **HINTS** Limp carrots or celery can be revived by a 30-minute soak in ice water.
>
> ▌Buy smooth, firm, bright-colored carrots without cracks, whitening, or sprouting. Store carrots in their original plastic bag or in a partially open plastic bag in the refrigerator for up to two weeks. Do not store near bananas or apples. Scrub under cold running water. Nutrients are lost with the peel, so don't peel organic carrots. Peel nonorganic carrots and trim at least an inch from the stem end.
>
> ▌As soon as possible after you buy carrots, remove the carrot tops, because they draw out the internal juices.
>
> ▌Smaller carrots are best for eating raw; the larger ones are good for cooking and slicing.
>
> ▌Cut a thin slice off the lengthwise side of a carrot to give it a flat base for easier slicing.

CARRYOVER COOKING is any further cooking that continues after a food has been removed from heat, especially for larger, denser foods, such as a roast or turkey. After a food is removed from the heat source, the internal temperature can continue to increase. This means that to avoid overcooking large roasts or turkeys, one must often pull the bird out of the oven just before it attains the desired internal temperature. During carryover cooking, the temperature of meat increases 5°F–15°F.

CARTE is the list of dishes available at a restaurant.

CARVE (CARVING) is to cut a piece of meat, such as turkey, ham, or beef roast, into pieces or slices. The word in Old English was *ceorfan*, "cut/carve," ultimately of West Germanic origin. A carving fork and carving knife are large utensils used in carving cooked meat.

CARVER: see SLICER.

CASABA, CASSABA, or **CASABA MELON** is a winter melon (*Cucumis meloinodorus*) with usually yellow rind and sweet white or yellow flesh. The name comes from Kasaba (now Turgutlu), Turkey, from which it was first exported.

> **HINT** Choose a casaba heavy for its size and free from blemishes, shriveling, or soft, moldy areas. Ripe melons have a strong, sweet smell and give slightly when pressed at both ends. The skin should be smooth; if it is green, then the melon is not ripe. When fully ripe, there may be tiny cracks at the stem end.

CASHEW is a tropical American evergreen tree bearing kidney-shaped nuts that are edible only when roasted. The cashew's nuts are at the end of an edible pear-shaped receptacle called a cashew apple or cashew pear. The shell of the nut consists of three layers; the middle layer contains an extremely acrid and irritating brown oil, which is rendered harmless by roasting the nuts before eating—this is why cashews are never sold in their shells. The cashew originated in Central and South America, and the name comes from *caju* or *acaju* in the language of the Tupi people of the Amazon basin. Not only do cashews have a lower fat content than most other nuts, but approximately 75% of their fat is unsaturated fatty acids, and about 75% of this unsaturated fatty acid content is oleic acid, the same heart-healthy monounsaturated fat found in olive oil. Technically, the cashew nuts are actually the kidney-shaped seeds that adhere to the bottom of the cashew apple.

> **HINT** It is necessary to refrigerate an open package of cashews because they contain almost 50% fat and they can easily become rancid.

CASSAVA, also called MANIOC, MANIOCA, or YUCCA, is any of several plants of the genus *Manihot* having a tuberous root yielding a nutritious starch. The word is from Taino, a Caribbean language. Cassava is a very hardy plant whose root contains cyanide, and before the root can be eaten it must be grated and left in the open to allow the cyanide to evaporate. The leaves can be eaten as a vegetable, and the tuber is the source of tapioca. There are many varieties of cassava, but only two main categories: sweet and bitter. Both contain a poisonous compound, which is why cassava should never be eaten raw. The toxins found in sweet cassava are concentrated in the skin, so peeling is mandatory. The bitter form is specially processed to make cassareep and TAPIOCA.

CASSEROLE is any food cooked and served in a deep dish (also called a casserole). The word casserole is a diminutive of *casse*, "spoonlike container," which probably comes from the Greek *kuathos*, "serving cup." The word was first used for the pan (by 1725) and later denoted the pan's contents (by 1960).

> **HINTS** You can cook a casserole, cool to room temperature, and freeze. Most casseroles can be reheated directly from the freezer in a 350°F oven for about an hour. To brown the top, uncover for the final 10–15 minutes of baking.

> A casserole recipe can be halved, but when halving, reduce the amount of liquid by a third instead of a half. A casserole recipe can also be doubled, but when doubling, multiply the liquid by 1½, not 2, to avoid a soupy dish.

> Use heavy-duty rubber bands to secure a casserole lid during transport.

CASSOULET is French for "small stewpan" and describes a French stew or ragout of white beans and various meats, sausage, and other vegetables cooked in a casserole. The dish is either slowly simmered or baked in a slow oven. The word, just like casserole, was first used for the pan itself. During the cooking of cassoulet, a film develops and this film must be broken seven times to create the perfect cassoulet according to culinary folklore.

CAST IRON is an alloy of iron containing so much carbon that it cannot be wrought but must be melted and shaped by casting. Cast iron generally has 1.8%–4.5% carbon, 0.5%–3% silicon, and small amounts of sulfur, manganese, and phosphorus. The word was first recorded in English in 1664. Cooking with cast-iron pans significantly increases the iron content of food, as the surface releases fine particles. Some foods cooked in cast iron contain up to double their original iron content.

> **HINT** You must keep cast-iron pans well seasoned. It is all right to wash a pan briefly with a little soapy water after it has been seasoned, as long as the pan is then thoroughly dried.

CASTOR SUGAR or **CASTER SUGAR** is a British term for white sugar with finer grains than those of granulated sugar; the sugar is usually sprinkled with a castor, a shaker with a perforated lid used for sprinkling or "casting" the sugar onto food. The American equivalent is *superfine sugar*. Castor sugar dissolves faster than granulated and is especially useful for making meringues and for sweetening fruits and ices.

CATFISH is any of numerous mostly freshwater (often farmed) fishes of Eurasia and North America with barbels like whiskers around the mouth; the flesh of this scaleless fish is eaten as food. So named for its catlike whiskers, catfish should be skinned before cooking. The easiest method is to nail the head of the dead fish to a board, hold onto its tail, and pull the skin off with pliers.

CATSUP or **CATCHUP**: see KETCHUP.

CAULDRON or **CALDRON**, also called KETTLE, is a very large metal pot used for boiling food. The word derives from the Latin *caldarius*, "hot water."

CAULIFLOWER is a plant with a large, compact, edible head of crowded undeveloped white flower buds that is eaten as a vegetable. Cauliflower, collard greens, kale, and kohlrabi are all derived from the Latin *caulis*, "cabbage," and cauliflower literally means "flowering cabbage"; the original English form in the sixteenth century of cauliflower was *colieflorie* or *cale-flory*. The plant seems to have been originally developed by the Arabs.

> HINTS Buy firm, tight heads of cauliflower without brown spots or bruises. Don't buy any with loose or spreading florets. Store loose in a perforated plastic bag in the refrigerator for up to one week.

> Lightly cooking cauliflower will break down the high fiber content, and this will free the nutrients that are stored in the raw product and make them more available. Overcooking diminishes the nutritive value.

> To preserve cauliflower's white color, add vinegar, lemon juice, or milk to the cooking water.

CAVIAR or **CAVIARE** is the pickled roe of sturgeon or other large fish, which is eaten as a delicacy. Caviar started out as a four-syllable word, following the Italian *caviale/caviaro*; the modern pronunciation was influenced by French. The three main types are sevruga, asetra (ocietre), and beluga, the prime variety. The ovaries of the fish are beaten to loosen the eggs, which are then freed from fat and membranes by being passed through a sieve. The liquid is pressed off, and the eggs are mildly salted and sealed in small tins or kegs. The eggs—black, green, brown, and the rare yellow or gray—may be tiny grains or the size of peas. Caviar is known for its subtle, buttery flavor and high price; it should always be served cold.

> HINTS Store caviar in the coldest part of the refrigerator—the back bottom shelf or the meat drawer.

> Choose caviar labeled "*malossol*" (lightly salted). The salt acts both as a preservative and a curing agent on the caviar. Raw caviar is almost without texture. After the salt "curing," however, the eggs become firmer.

> Because silver and steel bowls may alter the flavor of caviar, it's classically served in containers made of mother-of-pearl, wood, horn, or gold. Caviar should be spooned with a bone, horn, crystal, or mother-of-pearl utensil. Metal spoons impart a metallic taste.

▌ Caviar's flavor and texture are greatly diminished by cooking, so add it to a hot dish just before serving, stirring gently to keep the eggs from breaking and turning mushy.

CAYENNE or CAYENNE PEPPER, also called CHILE or RED PEPPER, is a

pepper plant (*Capsicum frutescens* or *annuum*) bearing usually red pods and seeds. The word also refers to the pods and seeds themselves and to a very hot, spicy pepper made by grinding these. Cayenne is distinctly hot, and it is the seeds that make the difference; without them you have the relatively mild paprika. In use in English since the eighteenth century, the word comes from the Tupi *kyynha/quiynha*, although it was later associated through folk etymology with the city of Cayenne in French Guiana.

HINT Give your hot cocoa a traditional Mexican flair by adding a tiny bit of cayenne.

CELERIAC, CELERY KNOB, CELERY ROOT, or CELERI-RAVE, also

known as TURNIP-ROOTED CELERY, is the thickened, edible, aromatic root of a variety of celery plant; it tastes like celery, with an earthy pungency.

HINT To prevent darkening, soak celeriac for 15 minutes in acidulated water.

CELERY is a widely cultivated plant (*Apium graveolens*) of the pars-

ley family, with aromatic leafstalks that are eaten raw or cooked. The word is from the French *celery*, from the Greek *selinon*, "parsley."

HINTS Store celery for up to two weeks in a perforated plastic bag, the original plastic bag, or a partially open plastic bag in the vegetable crisper of the refrigerator.

▌ Slice a rib of celery crosswise, then slice each half lengthwise before dicing. To chop quickly, keep the stalk intact and slice, then put pieces in a colander to be rinsed clean (and remove the leaves).

▌ You can revive limp celery by cutting a little off the ends and submerging it in a tall glass of ice water for 30 minutes.

CELERY SEED is a spice made from the seed of the celery plant. Celery seed

tastes similar to table celery, with its warm, slightly bitter, aromatic flavor. Celery salt is a mixture of fine white salt and ground celery seeds.

HINT Use caution when adding celery seeds to soups or long-cooked items like braising liquids—it is best to add them at the end of cooking, as the slow-cooking process can pull out bitter flavors and infuse them into the food.

CELLOPHANE NOODLES, also called BEAN THREADS, CHINESE VERMICELLI, CRYSTAL NOODLES, or GLASS NOODLES, are thin, translucent Asian noodles made from mung bean starch. The name for the noodles is a reference to their resemblance to cellophane, a crinkly transparent plastic. Cellophane noodles are sold dried, then must be soaked briefly in hot water before being used in most dishes. Presoaking isn't necessary when they're added to soups. Cellophane noodles can also be deep-fried.

CEP or **CÈPES**: see PORCINI.

CEREAL has two meanings: a breakfast food prepared from grain, and any grass whose starchy grains are used as food, such as buckwheat, corn, oats, rice, rye, or wheat. The ancient Roman goddess of agriculture was Ceres, giving us the word cereal. Commercial cereals like Rice Krispies often have tiny air bubbles. When milk is added, it is unevenly absorbed, which causes the kernels to unevenly swell and produce a snap, crackle, and pop.

CEREAL POPPING

1. Cereal grains contain starch and they are processed to many times their normal size to make air pockets surrounded by the starch. The structure of the cereal grains is similar to that of a very fine glass crystal.

2. Adding the cold milk changes the temperature in the cereal grains, causing "heat stress." The snap, crackle, and pop is caused by the uneven absorption of milk by the air pockets in the cereal grains.

CEVICHE or SEVICHE is a Latin American dish of raw fish or seafood marinated in lemon or lime juice with oil and served as an appetizer or salad with chopped onions, peppers, tomatoes, chiles, and seasonings. In American Spanish the word is seviche, probably from the Spanish *cebo*, "fish pieces used for bait," from the Latin *cibus*, "food." Ceviche is marinated in a citrus-based mixture, with lemons and limes most commonly used. The action of the acid in the lime juice "cooks" the fish, thereby firming the flesh and turning it opaque. But the acid does not kill bacteria and parasites as well as heat does, so it's important to start with the freshest, cleanest fish possible.

CHAAT or CHAT is an Indian dish of spiced boiled fruits and vegetables, typically served at roadside stalls or carts in Southeast Asia. The word was first used in English around 1954.

CHABLIS is a dry white wine named for the small town of Chablis in Burgundy, France. Chablis is made only of Chardonnay grapes. The French word chablis literally means "deadwood," such as wood fallen from a tree through age or brought down by wind. The name Chablis has acquired common usage in the United States and Australia as a generic term to describe any dry white wine of unspecified origin. Though the United States, Australia, and South Africa all make a wine labeled "Chablis," only France creates a true Chablis, made entirely from Chardonnay grapes.

CHAFING DISH is any type of metal pan over a heat source or with an outer pan of hot water; it is used to cook or to keep things warm at the table. The term derives from the now obsolete sense of chafe, which was "become warm/warm up." The heat source for a chafing dish can be provided by a candle, electricity, or solid fuel like Sterno or butane.

CHAI, also called Masala chai or Spiced tea, is tea boiled with milk, sugar, cardamom, and other spices. Chai (pronounced CHIE) and tea are really the same word, borrowed from two different Chinese dialects. Chai latte is a hot drink similar to chai, made with spiced tea and steamed milk; it originated in North America. Chai is the word for tea in many other parts of the world.

CHALLAH is a white bread containing eggs and leavened with yeast, usually formed into braided or twisted loaves and glazed with eggs before baking. Challah is traditionally eaten by Jews on Friday evening at the Sabbath meal and on holidays. On Rosh Hashanah, the Jewish new year, raisins are added to the dough and the challah is braided into a special crown shape, representing God's crown. The term also applies to the portion of dough set aside and given to the priest. The word is from the Hebrew *hallah*, "form of bread," probably from the Hebrew *hll*, "hollow/pierce," perhaps a reference to its original shape.

CHALUPA is corn tortilla dough fried in a boat shape and filled with shredded meat, vegetables, or cheese and a spicy or hot sauce. Chalupa is a Mexican Spanish word meaning "boat/launch," from the French *chaloupe*, "sloop," ultimately related to the Dutch *sloep*, "sloop."

CHAMOMILE or **CAMOMILE** refers to plants with strong-smelling foliage belonging to two genera, whose dried flower heads are used in making tea. The word derives from the Greek *chamaimelon*, "earth apple," from *chamai*, "on the ground."

CHAMPAGNE is the name of a province in eastern France and the varieties of still or sparkling wine made from the grapes there. As defined by French law, only sparkling wine from Champagne can be called Champagne. The word entered English by 1664, promoted by Benedictine cellar master Dom Pierre Pérignon at the Abbey d'Hautvilliers. Champagne glasses that are tall and narrow are called flutes or tulips, and the old-fashioned wider shape is called a coupe or saucer. Statistics say that you are more likely to be killed by a Champagne cork than a poisonous spider. A raisin dropped in a glass of Champagne will bounce up and down, bottom to top, in the glass. It takes six twists to remove the wire cage from a cork in a bottle of sparkling wine. The cork should be pulled from the bottle with a sigh, not a bang. The average bottle of Champagne contains forty-nine million bubbles.

> **CONFUSABLE** CHAMPAGNE/SPARKLING WINE. Only sparkling wine that comes from the Champagne region (northeast) of France can be called Champagne—by law. But in the United States, where the Treaty of Versailles was never ratified, it is perfectly legal to call sparkling wine "Champagne."

> **HINT** To chill Champagne quickly, put it in a bucket of ice and cold water for 30 minutes.

CHAMPIGNON is an edible species of mushroom (*Agaricus campestris*), including the meadow mushroom, with a light brown cap. The word is French for "mushroom," diminutive of the Old French *champagne*, "open country." The term aux champignons refers to dishes garnished with mushrooms or served with a mushroom sauce. Champignons are classified according to the places they grow naturally: dace champignons grow in muck soil and can be found close to housing or farms, in kitchen gardens, and in parks; forest champignons grow in mixed and coniferous forests; field champignons grow on forest glades and in pastures. Cultivated champignons are the most popular cultivated champignon species.

CHANTERELLE, also called GIROLLE, is an edible woodland mushroom (*Cantharellus cibarius*) that is yellow in color with a smooth funnel-shaped cap and a pleasant aroma. The word comes via French from the Modern Latin *cantharellus*, "little cup," and from the Greek *kantharos*, "drinking vessel."

> **HINT** When you select chanterelles, the aroma should be fruity—like fresh apricots. Fresh chanterelles should be clean and (almost) dry to the touch. They keep well if allowed to remain in a wax paper or brown paper bag in the refrigerator until they are cleaned. It is important to clean young chanterelles by brushing. Alternatively, you can wash them quickly and drain on paper towels. Cleaned chanterelles may also be stored in the refrigerator for a few days. They should be loosely arranged in a bowl lined with cloth or paper towels and covered lightly with towels.

CHANTILLY or **CHANTILLY CREAM** is a sweetened vanilla-flavored whipped cream. It was named after the chateau of Chantilly, near Paris, and the word is sometimes used attributively for a confection containing the cream.

CHAPATI, CHAPATTI, CHAPPATI, or **CHUPATTI** is a flat, pancakelike Indian bread made of unleavened whole meal and cooked on a griddle. The word is Hindu for "roll out." The plural is chapatis.

CHAR is a troutlike small-scaled northern freshwater or marine fish of the salmon family, including Arctic char, BROOK TROUT, and LAKE TROUT. The word's origin is unknown.

CHARBROIL means to broil on a grill over charcoal.

CHARCUTERIE is a shop that specializes in meats, especially those cured or otherwise processed, such as as sausages and pâtés. The word can also be applied to cold cooked meats collectively. The word is from the French *char cuite*, "cooked flesh."

CHARD or **CHARD BEET**, also called SILVER BEET and SWISS CHARD, is a type of beet (*Beta vulgaris* or *cicla*) whose large leaves and thick stalks are used as food. Chard is from the French *chardon*, "thistle."

> **HINTS** Chard is available year-round but is best during the summer. Chard is extremely perishable. Store in a plastic bag in the refrigerator for up to three days.
>
> ▌Do not cook chard in an aluminum pot since the oxalates contained in the chard will react with the metal and cause the pot to discolor.

CHARDONNAY is a variety of white wine grape used for making Champagne, Chablis, and other wines. The word also denotes a full-bodied, dry white wine from this grape; oaked and unoaked Chardonnays are produced. Chardonnay is believed to have originated in the Burgundy wine region of eastern France, but is now grown wherever wine is produced.

CHARGER, also known as CHOP PLATE, SERVICE PLATE, or UNDERPLATE, is a large, flat serving dish, often made of wood. A charger is considered "decorative" because it never directly touches any food; instead it functions as an aesthetic resting place onto which food-bearing dishes and bowls are placed. A charger is usually larger than a dinner plate but smaller than a food-serving platter.

CHARLOTTE has two meanings: a dessert with several variations served hot or cold and commonly made by lining or layering a mold with strips of bread, LADYFINGERS, or biscuits and filling or layering it with fruit, whipped cream, custard, or gelatin; and the mold used in making this dessert. Charlotte may be based on a corruption of the Old English word *charlyt* meaning a "dish of custard," or may be based merely on the feminine name. The charlotte russe is a dessert invented by the French chef Marie-Antoine Carême (1784–1833), who named it in honor of his Russian employer, Czar Alexander I (*russe* being the French word for "Russian").

CHARRED means scorched and this term refers to meat cooked at high temperatures to the point of burning and charring.

CHASSEUR is a seasoned sauce made from mushrooms, shallots or onions, white wine, and butter. A dish designated chasseur or à la chasseur is served with this sauce. In French, chasseur literally means "hunter," and the recipe probably originated as a way of serving game. The equivalent term in Italian cookery is cacciatore. It is thought that chasseur was invented by Duke Philippe de Mornay (1549–1623), governor of

Saumur, and Lord of the Plessis Marly in the early seventeenth century, who may also have created béchamel sauce, lyonnaise sauce, Mornay sauce, and porto sauce.

CHATEAUBRIAND is a large (double-cut center section) beef tenderloin steak, usually grilled or broiled and served with a sauce (such as béarnaise). The dish was named after French diplomat and writer Vicomte François René de Chateaubriand (1768–1848).

CHAUD-FROID is French for "hot-cold" and it pertains to a dish, often meat, that is cooked with heat then chilled and glazed with aspic or jelly before serving.

CHAWLI: see BLACK-EYED PEA.

CHAYOTE or **CHAYOTE SQUASH**, also called CHRISTOPHENE, MIRLITON, or VEGETABLE PEAR, is a climbing plant of tropical America that bears a pear-shaped, furrowed, green or white gourd that is cooked and eaten as a vegetable. The word is Spanish, from the Nahuatl *chayotli*, and the plant was cultivated by the Aztecs and Maya. The chayote (pronounced chi-OH-tay) is not eaten raw; its large seed is edible as is the thick skin, but many prefer to remove the skin.

CHEDDAR is a hard, smooth, pale yellow or orange-red cheese with a flavor that ranges from mild to very sharp, depending on its maturity. Cheddar cheese originated in the town of Cheddar Gorge, England. In its natural form it is cream colored, but it is often dyed orange. Cheddar is usually classified by age. The classifications are mild (usually 2–4 months old), medium (4–8 months old), sharp (9–12 months old), and extra-sharp (1–4 years old). Cheddaring is a unique multistep process that gives Cheddar its unique flavor. The curds are allowed to set for a few minutes. "Loaves" of curds are cut about six inches wide along each side of the vat. After ten minutes, the loaves are turned and stacking begins. Every ten minutes, when the loaves must be turned, they are stacked. The first time, two loaves are stacked together. The next time the loaves are turned, two stacks of two are put together. When the stacks get large enough (generally four high), stacking stops, but the loaves are still turned every ten minutes. This process is complete when the acidity of the whey is between 0.5 and 0.7, so the acidity is checked constantly.

> **CONFUSABLE** ORANGE/WHITE CHEDDAR CHEESE. Orange Cheddar cheese and white Cheddar cheese are the same cheeses. The only difference is that annatto has been added to the orange version, usually for aesthetic reasons only, as annatto is a natural product that is practically tasteless.

> **HINT** Four ounces of cheddar cheese will yield 1 cup of grated cheese.

CHEESE is basically a solid food prepared from the pressed curd of milk from any milk-producing animal. It is most commonly made from the milk of cows, goats, or sheep, with a small fraction from water buffalo. The differences between cheeses come from the way the curds are drained, cut, flavored, pressed, cured, and refrigerated. Archaeologists found cheese as far back as 6000 BC, made from cow's and goat's milk and stored in tall jars. When the Pilgrims came to America in 1620, they stocked the *Mayflower* with cheese. Cheese derives from the Latin *caseus*, "to ferment or become sour," which became *queso* in Spanish.

There are two main types of cheese—fresh and ripened/aged. A third type is processed cheese, such as American cheese. The proper order for eating cheese selections on a cheese plate is from most delicate to most assertive in taste.

CHEESE ESSENTIALS

CONFUSABLE FARMER/POT/COTTAGE CHEESE. Farmer, pot, and cottage cheese are all made from pasteurized cow's milk and are all low in fat and nutritious. Sometimes the same cheese is called by any of the three names. However, there are some differences. Farmer cheese is cottage cheese from which most of the liquid has been pressed out, and it is grainy, firm enough to cut, and curdless. Pot cheese is cottage cheese that has been drained of whey for a longer period. Cottage cheese is moist and milky and has curds. When a cheese is made with milk from animals on the farm where the cheese is made, it is called farmstead cheese.

■ Do not substitute light or whipped cream cheese when a recipe calls for full-fat block cream cheese.

■ Avoid buying cheeses with cracks or color changes near the rind. Soft cheese keeps for seven to ten days, while harder cheeses can keep for two to four weeks. Parmesan may keep for up to ten months. Wrap cheese in wax paper and then double-wrap in plastic wrap or foil.

■ To serve cheese at room temperature, remove from the refrigerator 45–60 minutes before serving.

■ Dry natural cheese rinds are generally not eaten.

■ Firm cheeses are cheeses ripened utilizing a bacterial culture throughout the whole cheese, and slow cured with very low moisture and higher salt content.

■ To remove mold from cheese, rub it with salt.

■ Coat the grater with oil to prevent cheese from sticking and make cleanup easier.

■ A zester can be used to grate a little hard cheese.

■ Cold water is best for cleaning up clinging cheese on dishes, utensils, and appliances.

■ When making grilled cheese, instead of buttering the bread, melt 1 tablespoon of butter or oil in a medium-heat skillet. Once the skillet is hot, put the bread and cheese sandwich in the skillet, cover with a plate, and weigh down the plate with a can of soup or another heavy object; then turn and repeat.

■ Cheese paper, with a shiny side to protect and a matte side to breathe (and sometimes tiny holes), is a wrapping that allows cheese to breathe but not dry out.

CHEESE VARIETIES

Cheese making goes back to the earliest livestock farmers, who discovered that letting the milk curdle, then beating it with branches, pressing it on stones, drying it in the sun, and sprinkling it with salt was an excellent way of converting surplus milk into a form that could be stored. A distinction is made between soft fresh cheeses (cream, curd cheeses), fermented cheeses, and processed cheeses. The hundreds of varieties of cheese can be distinguished first by the type of milk used: cow, goat, or ewe (or sometimes mixed), or even mare or buffalo. Also, the milk can be whole, skimmed, or enriched. The four stages of basic cheese making are acidification, coagulation or curdling, cutting and draining of the curds, and ripening. These are some popular cheese varieties:

AMERICAN

ANGELOT

APPETITOST

ASIAGO

BAKER'S CHEESE

BANON

BAVARIAN BLUE CHEESE

BEAUFORT

BEL PAESE

BLEU DE BRESSE

BLUE CHEESE OR BLEU CHEESE

BLUE CHESHIRE

BLUE VINNY OR DORSET

BONDON

BOULE

BOURSAULT

BOURSIN

BRICK

BRIE

BRILLAT-SAVARIN

BRYNZA

BUCHERON

CACIOVALLO

CAERPHILLY

CAMEMBERT

CANTAL

CHAROLAIS

CHEDDAR

CHESHIRE

CHÈVRE

CHEVRET

CLABBER

COLBY

COOK CHEESE

COTTAGE CHEESE

CREAM CHEESE

CRÈME FRAÎCHE

CROTTIN

CUP CHEESE

DANISH BLUE

DERBY

DEVON

DOLCELATTE

DUNLOP

DUTCH

EDAM

EDELPILZKASE

EMMENTAL OR EMMENTHALER

EPOISSES

EXPLORATEUR

FARMER CHEESE

FETA

FONTINA

FROMAGE (FRENCH FOR "CHEESE")

FROMAGE BLANC

FULL-CREAM CHEESE

GAMMELOST

GERVAIS

GJETOST

GLOUCESTER

GOAT CHEESE

GORGONZOLA

GOUDA

GREEN CHEESE

GRUYÈRE

HAND CHEESE

HAVARTI

HOOP CHEESE

JACK CHEESE

JARLSBERG

KEBBUCK OR KEBBOCK

KUMMINOST

LANCASHIRE

LEICESTER

LEIDEN

LIEDERKRANZ

LIMBURGER

LIPTAUER

LIVAROT

LOAF CHEESE

LONGHORN CHEESE

MANCHEGO

MAROILLES

MASCARPONE

MAYTAG BLUE

MIMOLETTE

MONTEREY JACK OR MONTEREY CHEESE

MONTRACHET

MOZZARELLA

MUENSTER

NEUFCHÂTEL

NEW ENGLAND SAGE

OSSAU-IRATY

PANEER

PANNERONE

PECORINO	RACLETTE	ST. MARCELLIN
PECORINO ROMANO	RAT CHEESE	ST. NECTAIRE
PETIT-SUISSE	REBLOCHON	STILTON
PIMENTO CHEESE	RED WINDSOR	STORE CHEESE
PINEAPPLE CHEESE	RICOTTA	STRING CHEESE
PONT L'ÉVÊQUE	RICOTTA SALATA	SWISS
PORT SALUT	ROMANO	TELEME
POT CHEESE	ROQUEFORT	TILLAMOOK
PRESSED CHEESE	SAGE CHEESE	TILSIT
PROCESS OR PROCESSED CHEESE	SAMSOE	TOMME AU RAISIN
	SAPSAGO	TRAPPIST CHEESE
PROVOLONE	SCAMORZA	VACHERIN
QUARGEL	SHROPSHIRE	WASHED-CURD CHEESE
QUESO BLANCO	SMOKED CHEESE	WHITE WENSLEYDALE
QUESO FRESCO	SOUR MILK CHEESE	YORK

CHEESE TYPES

BLUE OR BLUE-VEINED (Gorgonzola, Roquefort, Stilton)

DOUBLE- AND TRIPLE-CREAM (Boursault, Boursin, Petit-Suisse)

DUTCH-STYLE (Edam, Colby, Gouda, Jack)

ENGLISH-STYLE (Cheddar, Cheshire, Gloucester, Leicester)

FRESH FIRM (Paneer, Queso Fresco)

FRESH SOFT (Cottage Cheese, Cream Cheese)

GOAT'S MILK (Banon, Bucheron, Feta)

HARD OR FIRM (Asiago, Fontina, Gruyère, Emmental, Parmesan, Pecorino, Romano)

PICKLED (Feta, Teleme)

SEMIHARD OR SEMIFIRM (Cheddar, Manchego, Ossau-Iraty)

SEMISOFT (Havarti, Monterey Jack)

SHEEP'S MILK (Feta)

SOFT (Camembert, Goat Cheese)

SOFT-RIPENED (Brie, Camembert)

STRETCHED-CURD (Mozzarella, Provolone)

WASHED-RIND (Limburger, Muenster)

Whey (Gjetost, Ricotta)

CHEESECAKE is a dessert consisting of a layer of sweetened soft cheese (cream cheese, Neufchâtel, cottage cheese, and ricotta) mixed with cream, sugar, eggs, and flavorings and set in a cracker-crumb or pastry base. The word entered English around 1440.

HINTS Cheesecake can be made in a greased cake pan with the bottom lined with wax or parchment paper.

If baking cheesecake in a springform pan, wrap the cheesecake in foil and put in a water bath. This helps promote creaminess, or unmold by wrapping the pan in a hot damp towel for a few minutes.

Take cheesecake out of the oven when the center still quivers. Cut cheesecake with a long, thin knife that has been dipped in hot water.

CHEESECLOTH is a coarse, loosely woven, unsized cotton gauze, originally used to wrap cheeses to drain cheese curds and/or line cheese molds.

CHEESE KNIFE is a tool designed for slicing. It has a thicker handle that is intended to be held like a standard knife. The blade of the cheese knife, however, is almost in the reverse shape of a typical knife, as it starts out thinner at the top of the handle and gradually widens as it reaches the tip of the blade. In addition, the blade of a cheese knife is typically somewhat square in shape, rather than curved or tapered, and has various-sized holes in the blade that allow the cheese to be cut more easily and help prevent it from sticking. The type of material used for the blade of the cheese knife is also important, with stainless steel usually being the best to make it easier for the cheese to slide off the blade without getting stuck. There is an etiquette for using a communal cheese knife: If cheese is served on a board for more than one person, leave the cheese knife on the board for use by other guests. If the host puts out a separate knife for each cheese, use this.

CHEESE PLANE is a type of cheese slicer invented and patented in 1925 by Thor Bjørklund, a carpenter from the city of Lillehammer in Norway. The design was based on the carpenter's plane. There are many other styles of cheese slicer. Most cheese slicers have a thin handle with two tines at the top that are spread apart and a firm wire that is stretched between the two tines; the wire is used to slice the cheese (this type of slicer is also called a cheese wire).

CHEESESTEAK or **CHEESE STEAK**, also called PHILADELPHIA CHEESESTEAK or PHILLY CHEESESTEAK, is an American sandwich of sautéed beef and onions with melted cheese on an Italian or French hard roll. It originated in Philadelphia in the 1930s and is credited to Pat and Harry Olivieri.

CHEESE STRAW is a long, thin baked strip of cheese-flavored pastry or cracker, sometimes with a twisted shape.

CHEF is a cook, especially a professional one, or the head cook. The word is short for the French *chef de cuisine*, "head of the kitchen." It first appeared in English in 1842. Much of the chef's uniform has developed out of necessity: hat, necktie, double-breasted jacket, apron, houndstooth (checkered) trousers, and steel- (or plastic-) toe-capped shoes or clogs. A chef's hat (toque) is tall to allow for the circulation of air above the head and also provides an outlet for heat. Neckties were originally worn to allow for the mopping of sweat from the face, but as this is now against health and safety regulations (due to hygiene), today they are largely decorative. Capped shoes protect the feet from falling pans and knives. The double-breasted feature allows the coat to be reversed if it becomes stained. It also gives an extra measure of protection from heat and burns due to the extra insulation.

CHEF GARDE MANGER: see GARDE MANGER.

CHEF'S KNIFE or **CHEF KNIFE**, also called Cook's knife, French chef's knife, or French knife, is a large knife with a blade at least 8 inches long and 1½–2 inches wide, although individual models range in length from 6–12 inches. It is a basic tool for cutting, carving, and chopping (dicing, julienning, mincing) most foods. There are two types of blade shape: French and German. The far more common German design features a pronounced curve (or belly) toward the tip of the blade that allows the user to rock the knife up and down, chopping the food with the belly and heel of the blade. The French design is more triangular, with much less curve at the tip and a longer straight section of blade; it is designed to be pulled toward the user, slicing the food instead. The chef's knife evolved from the butcher knife and was originally designed to slice and disjoint large cuts of beef.

CHEF'S SALAD is composed of tossed greens and cold julienned meats and cheeses, sliced vegetables, and hard-cooked eggs, topped with dressing. It is often offered as a main course. Some trace this salad's roots to salmagundi, a popular meat and salad dish originating in seventeenth-century England and popular in colonial America. Others say chef's salad is a product of the United States, possibly created by chef Louis Diat of the Ritz-Carlton in New York City during the 1940s.

CHEF'S STEEL: see Steel.

CHENIN BLANC, also called Pinot blanc, is a white grape grown in the lower Loire Valley of France and also in California and South Africa, named for Mont-Chenin in Touraine, France. This hard, acidic grape is slow to mature, but is then made into fine sweet wines that age well for at least ten years in the bottle. This is one of the nine classic grape varieties used for winemaking.

CHERIMOYA is a tropical American tree bearing large fruits with scaly, leathery skin; smooth black seeds; and soft pulp. The fruit is closely related to custard apples and has a flavor similar to pineapple. Its name is from an American Spanish adaptation of *chirimuya*, "cold seeds," from the Quechua language.

> **HINT** Cherimoya is ripe when the skin turns a brownish green and the fruit gives slightly when pressed. When purchased, it should have even-colored green skin. It is in season from November to April. Ripen at cool room temperature and store in plastic wrap or plastic bag in the refrigerator for up to three days.

CHERRIES JUBILEE is a dessert of vanilla ice cream topped with black cherries that have been flambéed with brandy or kirsch. The cherries are usually prepared in a chafing dish at the table and flamed with great flourish. When the initial large flame has died down, a small blue flame will continue to burn for several seconds. Shake or stir the cherries gently to expose more alcohol to the flame, being careful that they do not burn.

CHERRY is a small, soft, round stone fruit that is typically bright or dark red, from a tree native to the Near East, western Asia, and eastern Europe. Cherry comes ultimately from the Greek *kerasós*, "cherry tree," which became the Latin *cerasus* before being borrowed into the Germanic languages as *kirsche*, then into Anglo-Saxon as *ciris* and Old Northern French as *cherise*. English speakers misinterpreted *cherise* as a plural, so the new singular cherry was coined. Cherries are most closely related to plums. Sour cherries need to be cooked. Sweet cherries should be large, plump, smooth, and dark colored, and have firm stems (preferably, the stems should be attached). The darker the cherry, the sweeter it is.

HINTS The freshest cherries have bright green stems. Keep them uncovered in the refrigerator. Let them get to room temperature, though, before serving.

▌A drop of almond extract in cherry pie, cobbler, sauce, and other dishes enhances the cherry flavor. It takes about 250 fresh, tart cherries to make a cherry pie.

▌Pit cherries with a pastry bag tip, with needle-nose pliers, or with a drinking straw. You can remove cherry stains with a cut lemon.

CHERRY TYPES AND VARIETIES

The cherry is a pulpy drupe of a species of the genus *Prunus*. The wild sweet cherry tree was known to the Egyptians, Greeks, and Romans; the bitter cherry was apparently brought to Rome by Lucullus after the campaigns against Mithridates, around 75 BC. There are many varieties and types of cherries:

AMARELLE	CENTENNIAL	ELTON
AMERICAN	CERISE	ENGLISH
ANGOULEME	CHAPMAN	EUGENIE
ARCHDUKE	CHOISY	EUROPEAN BIRD
AUSTRALIAN	CHOKECHERRY	FLORIDA
BALDWIN	CLEVELAND	GEAN
BARBADOS	COE	GROUND
BESSARABIAN	CORNELIAN	HEART
BIGAROON	DOWNER	HEDELFINGEN GIANT
BIGARREAU OR HARD CHERRY	DUKE	HORTENSE
BING	DYEHOUSE	HOSKINS
BITTER	EAGLE	IDA
BLACK	EARLY BASLE OR CERET	JAPANESE
BLACKHEART OR BLACK HEART	EARLY BURLAT	KEARTON
CARNATION	EARLY PURPLE	KERMES
CAYENNE OR SURINAM	EARLY RIVERS	KERMESITE
	ELKHORN	KING

KNIGHT	MAY-DUKE	HEART
LARGE MONTMORENCY	MAZZARD	QUEENSLAND CHERRY
LATE DUKE	MERRY	RED
LATE KENTISH	MONTMORENCY	REVERCHON
LITHAUER	MORELLO OR ENGLISH	SAND
LUTOVKA	MORELLO	WHITEHEART
MANCHU OR NANKING	NAPOLEON	WILD
MARASCA	NATIVE	WILLIAM
MARASCHINO	PIN OR PIGEON OR PIGEON'S	WINTER

CHERRYSTONE CLAM is a small (half-grown) quahog larger than a littleneck, eaten raw or cooked as in clams casino. The most popular cooking method for cherrystone clams is steaming and baking, especially for clams casino. There are about three cherrystone clams to a pound.

CHERRY TOMATO is a small, round/orb-shaped, red or orange fruit of a plant (*Lycopersicon esculentum cerasiforme*).

> **CONFUSABLE** CHERRY TOMATO/GRAPE TOMATO. A cherry tomato is orb shaped, about 1 inch in diameter, and available in red, orange, yellow, and green varieties. A grape tomato is grape-shaped or oval, ½–¾ inch long, and almost always red. Grape tomatoes are easier to spear and pop in your mouth, and don't squirt like cherry tomatoes.

CHERVIL is an aromatic Old World herb of the parsley family cultivated for its delicate fernlike leaves and used as a garnish and flavoring. It is one of the main ingredients in fines herbes, and it has a flavor similar to parsley with a hint of tarragon. English borrowed the word in Anglo-Saxon times from the Latin *chaerephyllum*, from the Greek *khaírephullon*, from *khaírein*, "rejoice," and *phúllon*, "leaf."

> **HINT** Chervil loses its flavor with prolonged heating, so it should be added at the end of cooking. Chervil keeps well when frozen.

CHESHIRE is a mild yellow cow's milk cheese with a crumbly texture, similar to Cheddar, and originating in Cheshire, England. Cheshire's particular taste is due to the deposits of salt in the pastures where the cows graze. There are three varieties: red (the best known), white, and blue (fairly rare).

CHESS PIE is a pastry shell filled with a mix of eggs, sugar, butter, some flour or cornmeal, and various flavorings; sometimes fruit or nuts are added. It is a southern U.S. specialty, but the origin of the name is uncertain. What sets chess pie apart from many other custard pies is the substitution of cornmeal for flour. Chess pie is often served with coffee to offset its sweetness.

CHESTNUT is the smooth-shelled, sweet, edible nut of any of a genus (*Castanea*) of trees of the beech family. Chestnut comes from a Greek word meaning "nut of Castanaea/Castana" (Pontus or Thessaly), and in English it was first chesten nut, which was soon reduced to chestenut, chestnut, and chesnut until 1820, when Samuel Johnson adopted chestnut. Chestnuts contain very little fat compared to other nuts.

> **HINT** Chestnuts turn rancid in a short time because they have a high moisture content, and they are susceptible to mold and bacteria and therefore perishable. They should be refrigerated if bought in advance, but it is better to freeze them.

CHÈVRE is French for any cheese made with goat's milk. (The word is French for "goat.") "*Pur chèvre*" on the label ensures that the cheese is made entirely from goat's milk; "*mi-chèvre*" means that it's composed of at least 50% goat's milk, with the remainder typically cow's milk. The plural is chèvres.

> **HINT** Store chèvre, tightly wrapped, in the refrigerator for up to two weeks.

CHIANCARELLE: see ORECCHIETTE.

CHIANTI is a dry red wine produced in a region of Italy or a similar wine made elsewhere from the Sangiovese grape. Chianti is named for the Chianti Mountains in Tuscany. In 1932 the Chianti area was completely redrawn and divided into seven subareas: Classico, Colli Aretini, Colli Fiorentini, Colline Pisane, Colli Senesi, Montalbano, and Rùfina. The squat bottle enclosed in a straw basket that Chianti has been historically bottled in is called a fiasco.

CHICKEN is a domestic fowl (*Gallus domesticus*) bred for flesh or eggs. Chicken meat should have even coloring and be firm and resilient. Chickens have both light and dark meat, while ducks and geese have all dark meat. The coloration comes from oxygen-storing myoglobin. The muscles that require a large amount of oxygen have more myoglobin to retain the oxygen brought by the blood until needed by the muscle cells. Since chickens do a lot of standing and walking and practically no flying, the breast muscles aren't exercised and thus don't need much oxygen and accordingly have little myoglobin. The legs do more exercise. This distinction is also true for turkeys. Ducks and geese fly, using their breast muscles; therefore, the breast meat is dark. Dark meat has 2%–10% more calories than light meat, depending on the bird. Chickens in a foreign country taste different than chickens from the United States because many foreign countries don't allow fowl to be raised as they are in the United States, where great coops hold ten thousand or more birds housed in a box with food and light available day and night so that they can eat at any hour. A fryer/broiler is a chicken six to eight weeks old, weighing 3–4½ pounds. Fryers are more caloric than roasters. A roaster is two to six months old and can weigh up to 8 pounds.

CHICKEN ESSENTIALS

■ Thaw chicken in the refrigerator or in a microwave on low and be careful not to overheat. Plan to cook within two days or freeze it (for up to six months after washing, drying, and wrapping).

■ When chicken is done, there is no pink color at the bone, the juices run clear when a thigh is pricked, and the breast meat is opaque. An instant-read meat thermometer inserted in the thick part of the thigh, not touching the bone, is best for determining doneness. Chicken is safely done when it reaches 165°F.

■ A roasting chicken should be turned with a large kitchen fork inserted in the main cavity so that no holes are made in the meat, which would cause loss of juice.

■ Basting prolongs cooking time when roasting a chicken, but it increases the attractiveness of the skin.

■ Boneless chicken cutlets are pounded before sautéing or grilling so they will cook faster and more evenly. If uniformly pounded, no one part will be over- or undercooked.

■ To make boning easier, partially freeze the chicken first.

■ Fresh chickens are better to buy than frozen ones because the frozen ones lose a fair portion of their internal juices during thawing. The catch is that federal regulations say that the chicken is not frozen until it reaches 0°F. Sometimes the price of a frozen chicken will be low enough to compensate for the juice loss.

■ If you want crisp skin on a chicken, do not salt the exterior until near completion of the cooking, since the salt draws out the juices, keeping the skin moist, which hinders browning and crisping. You can also rub chicken with mayonnaise or butter before roasting to get crisp, golden skin.

■ To pound a piece of chicken to an even thickness, remove the breast tender, place between two sheets of wax paper, and pound.

■ It is easier to skin a chicken before cutting it up. The skin can be pulled off in one piece, with the exception of the wings, which are very difficult to skin before they are cooked.

■ It is important to handle chicken carefully because it can carry pathogenic bacteria like salmonella. Work on the chicken in a confined area that is easy to clean, or spread a plastic or paper bag on the work surface and use poultry shears to cut the chicken. Then discard the bag. When done, wash your hands and all surfaces that the raw chicken has touched with hot soapy water. Store uncooked chicken in the coldest part of the refrigerator.

■ The best way to refrigerate a chicken is to wrap it in wax paper instead of plastic wrap.

(continued)

■ The older and larger the chicken, the lower the cooking temperature and the longer the roasting period should be.

■ The term "organic chicken" is not tightly defined, but usually refers to a chicken fed only pesticide-free and chemical-free grains and raised on land that has not been treated with pesticides, herbicides, or chemical fertilizers for at least three years. Organic chickens are almost always free-range and of high quality.

■ When roasting a stuffed chicken, you can protect the stuffing from burning by covering the cavity with a small piece of foil during the end of the roasting time.

■ When you cook a chicken with the bone in, the meat will be juicer and tastier.

■ For boneless chicken, buy 1 extra ounce for every 4-ounce cooked serving, for example, a 5-ounce boneless breast to make a 4-ounce serving. For bone-in chicken, add 3 ounces, so buy a 7-ounce chicken leg to make a 4-ounce serving.

■ Put frozen chicken in the refrigerator to thaw, either on a plate or in a bucket of cool water.

■ Use tongs to dip chicken cutlets into each of the ingredients for breading. Use fingers to press the bread crumbs or cornmeal into the food surface.

■ When making chicken salad, wait until the meat is fully cooled before adding any type of salad dressing or mayonnaise.

■ Many people think that raw chicken should be washed, but if there are any germs, they will be killed when the chicken is cooked thoroughly.

■ Letting breaded cutlets dry on a rack for 5 minutes makes the breading stay attached to the cutlets during cooking.

■ Partially freeze chicken cutlets before cutting for stir-fries or potpies.

■ White meat cooks faster than dark.

CHICKEN BREEDS

Chickens are one of the most widely domesticated fowl, raised worldwide for meat and eggs. Chickens are descended from the wild red jungle fowl of India and belong to the species *Gallus gallus*. They have been domesticated for at least four thousand years. Not till about 1800, however, did chicken meat and eggs start to become mass-production commodities. Some well-known chicken breeds are listed here.

AMERICAN GAME FOWL	BOOTED	CREVECOEUR
ANCOBAR	BRAHMA	DELAWARE
ANCONA	BRESSE	DOMINICK
ANDALUSIAN	BUCKEYE	DOMINIQUE
ARAUCANA	BUTTERCUP	DORKING
AUSTRALORP	CAMPINE	FAVEROLLE
BANTAM	COCHIN OR COCHIN CHINA	FRIZZLES
BARRED PLYMOUTH ROCK	CORNISH	HAMBURG

HOLLAND	NEW HAMPSHIRE OR NEW HAMPSHIRE RED	SPANISH
HOUDAN		SULTAN
IXWORTH	ORLOFF	SUMATRA
JERSEY GIANT	ORPINGTON	SUSSEX
LANGSHAN	PHOENIX	TURKEN
LEGHORN	PLYMOUTH ROCK	WELSUMER
LESSER PRAIRIE CHICKEN	RHODE ISLAND RED	WHITE LEGHORN
MALAY	RHODE ISLAND WHITE	WHITEBELLY
MILLE FLEUR	ROCK	WYANDOTTE
MINORCA	ROCK CORNISH	YOKOHAMA
MODERN GAME	RUMPLESS	
MODERN LANGSHAN	SILKIE	

CHICKEN TYPES

BROILER: Small young chicken weighing up to 2.5 pounds; good for broiling.

BROILER-FRYER: Small young chicken weighing 2¾–4 pounds; good for braising, broiling, frying, grilling, roasting.

BROILER HEN: Older chicken weighing 4–6 pounds; good for braising, stewing, stock.

CAPON: Castrated male chicken weighing 5–8 pounds; good for roasting.

FREE-RANGE: Permitted to graze or forage rather than being confined to a feedlot.

ORGANIC: Grown or raised without synthetic fertilizers or pesticides or hormones.

POUSSIN (also called **SPRING CHICKEN**): Youngest chicken eaten, weighing 1 pound; good for broiling, grilling, roasting, sautéing.

ROASTER: Meaty chicken weighing 3½–5 pounds; good for braising, roasting, stewing.

CHICKEN À LA KING is a dish of diced poultry in a cream (béchamel) sauce with vegetables such as peas, mushrooms, and peppers or pimientos. Chicken à la king was said to be named after E. Clark King, proprietor of a hotel in New York.

CHICKEN-FRIED STEAK or **COUNTRY-FRIED STEAK** is a thin tenderized steak dipped in batter, fried like chicken, and served with country gravy; the dish is so named because it is prepared like fried chicken.

CHICKEN KIEV is a boned and flattened chicken breast that is rolled around a chilled piece of herbed butter, then breaded and fried. Chicken Kiev was originally called chicken cutlet Kiev, from the Russian, *Tsiplenokovo Po-Kievski*, "cutlets in the Kiev manner."

CHICKEN TETRAZZINI is diced chicken in a sherry cream sauce with mushrooms and almonds, baked in a casserole with noodles and cheese. There is also a turkey Tetrazzini version. The dish was created for Luisa Tetrazzini (1871–1940), an Italian opera singer, in the 1920s.

CHICKPEA or **CHICK-PEA**, also called GARBANZO, is a plant of the pea family that bears round yellowish edible seeds. The word chickpea is not related to chicks but is from the Latin *cicer*, the Roman name for the plant—which became *chichepease* until the eighteenth century. The chickpea, along with wheat and barley, is one of the oldest foods known to humankind and one of the first crops to be cultivated, dating back to 4000 BC.

CHICORY, or ENDIVE and sometimes called RADICCHIO, is an herb with crisp, spiky green leaves that have a somewhat bitter taste; it is used in salads. The root of the chicory plant is roasted and ground to substitute for or flavor coffee. The word came to English from the French *cichorée*, from the Latin *cichoreum*, from the Greek *kikhorion*, "endive," and possibly from the Egyptian *keksher*. Radicchio is a type of chicory, and it has white-veined, reddish purple leaves.

> **CONFUSABLE** CHICORY/ENDIVE. What the British call endive, Americans call chicory and vice versa. Americans say chicory is synonymous with radicchio and endive is synonymous with escarole.

> **HINT** Store chicory in a perforated bag in the refrigerator for up to four days.

CHIFFON denotes a food with a light, fluffy texture, usually created by adding whipped egg whites or gelatin. Chiffon cake is a light-textured cake made from a batter of flour, sugar, oil, and egg yolks folded into beaten egg whites, usually baked in a tube pan. Chiffon pie has a light-textured jelled filling into which beaten egg whites have been folded. Chiffon cake owes its unique texture to the use of vegetable oil instead of butter, and the effect of the oil on the foam structure of the beaten egg whites used in this cake. The chiffon cake was invented in 1927 by Harry Baker, a California insurance salesman turned caterer. Mr. Baker kept the recipe secret for twenty years, until he sold it to General Mills.

CHIFFONADE is a term for vegetables that have been shredded or finely chopped or cut into ribbons and used as a garnish. Chiffonade, literally meaning "made of rags," is from the French *chiffonnade*, from *chiffonner*, "to crumple." *Chilaquiles* is a Mexican dish of fried softened tortilla chips covered with salsa or mole and cheese and broiled. The word is from the Nahuatl language. Because it was invented to use up leftovers, chilaquiles is sometimes called "poor man's dish." Usually, chilaquiles are eaten at breakfast or brunch.

CHILES RELLENOS (literally "stuffed chile peppers") is a Mexican dish of mild green chiles (with skins removed) filled with cheese, dipped in batter, and fried. It is pronounced CHIL-ee ruh-YEY-nohz.

HINT When making chiles rellenos, use cold eggs for the batter. Use a very light coating of flour. Test the oil with a drop of batter before putting a whole chile in. If the drop of batter sizzles and floats to the top, the oil is the right temperature. If the batter sinks, the oil is not hot enough. Fillings can be made ahead of time and refrigerated, then brought to room temperature before stuffing the chiles.

CHILE, CHILI, CHILLI, or **CHILI PEPPER** is the name of a fiery vegetable, the pungent pod of any of several species of *Capsicum*. The (dried) red pod of the pepper is used in sauces and relishes and made into a hot cayenne. The U.S. spelling is chile (plural chiles) or chili (plural chilis), while the British spelling is chilli (plural chillies). The word comes from Spanish, from the Nahuatl *chilli*, "sharp/ pointed." Christopher Columbus was the first European to write about chiles. He wrote an entry in his journal dated January 15, 1493, describing his eating experience and the importance of chiles to the local people. The smaller and more pointed the chile, the hotter it tends to be. The heat of a chile in a dish increases over time. The bite in the pepper comes from capsaicin, which causes the heat of chile peppers to vary from mild to firebombs. Capsaicin is located in the placenta, the part just under the stem where the seeds attach, and down the white- or yellow-veined ribs or membranes. The seeds are not a source of heat, although they may carry capsaicin because they rub up against the hot parts. There is a difference between green and red chile peppers. The color indicates the ripeness of the pepper when it is picked. All varieties are green when young. They lose chlorophyll as they ripen, and previously hidden red, yellow, or orange colors become visible as the green disappears. The heat takes longer to come on when chiles are green. Peppers and chiles are synonymous in most places, but in Mexico all peppers are called chiles. In America only sweet peppers are called peppers and only fiery ones are called chiles.

CHILE ESSENTIALS

■ Dried chiles should have flexible pods with good color. They can be hung up but are better off in an airtight container in a dark place.

■ Fresh chiles can be kept at room temperature for two days, and in a perforated bag in the refrigerator for one week. You can also wrap them in paper and then in a zip-lock freezer bag and store in the freezer for up to six months.

■ Wear rubber gloves when working with chiles, or hold a chile with chopsticks or tweezers while slicing and cleaning out the seeds and veins, or hold it by its stem. Coat your non-knife-wielding hand with vegetable oil and use only that hand to touch or move the chiles. Wash your hands, all surfaces, and the knife with hot soapy water. Do not touch your face!

■ To reduce the chile's heat, scrape out the veins inside the chile's flesh. You can also soak chiles in heavily salted water for several hours.

(continued)

■ Soothe hands that accidentally touched chiles by making a paste of baking soda and water, rubbing the paste over your hands, then rinsing your hands with cold water.

■ Add dairy or sugar to a dish that is too chile-pepper hot.

■ Chiles should be stored in zip-lock bags in the vegetable crisper of the refrigerator. If you plan to keep them for more than a couple of days, pierce the bag in several places.

■ The capsaicin that causes the heat in chiles is not water soluble, so water does not relieve the pain. Milk with its butterfat, ice cream, or starches such as rice or potatoes are best at relieving the burn pain. Beer and wine will not cool the mouth either. In fact, they will have just the opposite effect, for alcohol increases the absorption of capsaicin. Rice and tortillas absorb chile oils from the mouth, while sour cream, yogurt, and milk neutralize chile oils and cool the burn.

CHILE PEPPERS

Chile peppers are native to South America, where Portuguese and Spanish explorers found them. The explorers introduced chiles to Asia, and chiles were then transported to the Middle East, Africa, and Europe. There is now a vast array of different chiles, ranging from mild to very fiery.

AJI	ESPANOLA	NUMEX BIG JIM
ANAHEIM	FRESNO	PASILLA
ANCHO	GUAJILLO	PEPERONCINI OR PEPPERONCINI
ARBOL OR CHILE DE ARBOL	GUINDILLA	PEQUIN OR PIQUIN
BAHAMIAN	HABANERO	PIMIENTO OR PIMENTO
BANANA OR SWEET BANANA	HAIMEN	POBLANO
BIRD'S EYE OR BIRD	HIDALGO	PULLA
BONNET OR SCOTCH BONNET	HONTAKA	PUYA
CAPSAICIN	HOT WAX	RED SAVINA HABANERO
CAROLINA CAYENNE	HUNGARIAN CHERRY PEPPER	ROCOTILLO
CASCABEL	JALAPEÑO	SANDIA
CAYENNE	JALORO	SANTA FE GRANDE
CHERRY	JAMAICAN HOT	SANTAKA
CHILTECPIN OR CHILTEPIN	KUMATAKA	SERRANO
CHIPOTLE	MALAGUETA	SHIPKAS
CHORICERO	MANZANO	SUPER CHILE
CORONADO	MIRASOL	TABASCO
DE ARBOL	MULATO	TABICHE
EL PASO	NEGRO	THAI
	NEW MEXICO	TOGARASHI
	NORA	YATSAFUSA

CHILE POBLANO: see POBLANO.

CHILI CON CARNE or **CHILI** is a Mexican dish of chiles or chili powder, ground or diced beef, chopped onion and pepper, kidney beans, and tomatoes, although meatless versions are also made. It was first called carne con chili, literally meaning "meat chunks with chile" or "chile pepper with meat."

> HINT Cook chili longer to thicken it and deepen the flavors. You can also add 2 tablespoons of cornstarch or cornmeal for 8 cups of chili and the chili will thicken in 5 minutes.

CHILI POWDER, CHILE POWDER, or **CHILLI POWDER** is a hot-tasting seasoning consisting of ground red chiles (often cayenne) blended with other seasonings, such as cumin and oregano.

> HINT You can increase the hotness of commercial chili powder by adding cayenne pepper to it.

CHILI SAUCE is a piquant sauce made from tomatoes, cayenne (peppers), spices, onions, garlic, and salt, simmered in vinegar and sugar.

CHILL is to make cool, cooler, or cold.

> HINT Try to cool foods down before putting them in the refrigerator, but don't let them sit out for more than two hours. Some items can be set into a pot or sink of ice water to lower the temperature before refrigerating. Food can be divided into smaller portions for chilling.

CHIMICHANGA is a crisp deep-fried or grilled tortilla containing a spicy meat filling, usually served as an appetizer with sour cream, green chili sauce, and melted cheese. Chimichanga means "trinket" in Mexican Spanish. El Charro, which opened its first Mexican restaurant in downtown Tucson in 1922, claims it invented the chimichanga. A story printed on its menus says that the original owner, Monica Flin, accidentally dropped a burrito into a deep fryer. She was about to swear in Spanish, but stopped herself because nieces and nephews were nearby. The word she used instead came out as "chimichanga," which roughly translates to "thingamajig" in Spanish. Flin liked the way the fried burrito tasted, and decided to name it after her blundered word.

> HINT To prevent the filling from spilling out when frying a chimichanga, the flour tortilla must be rolled around the filling with the ends tucked in.

CHIMICHURRI is an Argentinean sauce of chopped parsley, oregano, red chiles, garlic, lemon zest, vinegar, and olive oil that is used as a marinade or served with grilled meat. The word is from American Spanish but the origin is unknown. One story about the chimichurri's origin is that in the mid-nineteenth century an

Englishman and bon vivant, Jimmy Curry, arrived in Argentina. He fell in love with the aroma and taste of the roasted meats of the traditional *criollo* Argentine barbecue and set about to create a spicy accompaniment. He gathered chile peppers, sweet red peppers, tomatoes, onions, and garlic and combined them with rosemary, oregano, thyme, and salt to make a sauce to scent and flavor the meat.

CHINA BEAN: see BLACK-EYED PEA.

CHINESE ARROWHEAD: see ARROWROOT.

CHINESE BLACK MUSHROOM: see SHIITAKE.

CHINESE CABBAGE: see BOK CHOY.

CHINESE FIVE-SPICE POWDER, also called FIVE-SPICE or FIVE-SPICE POWDER, is a blend of five powdered spices, typically cinnamon, cloves, fennel seed, Szechuan peppercorns, and star anise, used in Chinese cuisine. The formula for five-spice powder is based on the Chinese philosophy of balancing the yin and yang in food. Five-spice powder should be used in moderation because the flavor can be quite pungent and intense, and it is easy to ruin a dish by using too much of it.

CHINESE GOOSEBERRY: see KIWI.

CHINESE PARSLEY: see CILANTRO.

CHINESE POTATO: see ARROWROOT.

CHINESE RADISH: see DAIKON.

CHINESE SPINACH: see AMARANTH.

CHINESE VERMICELLI: see CELLOPHANE NOODLES.

CHINESE WATER CHESTNUT: see WATER CHESTNUT.

CHINOIS (pronounced sheen-WAH) is a conical fine-mesh sieve with a handle that is used for straining sauces and soups. The chinois with a metallic mesh is used for straining broths, sauces, fine creams, syrups, and jellies, which need to be very smooth. The perforated tinplate chinois is used to strain thick sauces, which are pressed through with a pestle to remove the lumps.

CHIP is most often thought of as a thin, crisp slice of a starchy food, such as potato or corn, fried in deep fat, but in the United Kingdom chip is synonymous with French fry. Another meaning is a small cone-shaped bit of food often used for baking, such as a chocolate chip. The word in English first applied to a thin, irregular slice of fruit, found in writing by 1769.

CHIPOLATA or **CHIPPOLATA** is a very small and thin Italian pork sausage flavored with chives, cloves, coriander, thyme, and sometimes red pepper. The word is Italian for "little fingers."

CHIPOTLE (pronounced chi-POAT-lay) is a ripe red chile pepper that has been dried and smoked for use as an appetizer or seasoning. The word is Mexican Spanish, from the Nahuatl *xipotli*, "smoked chile."

> **HINT** Dried chipotle chiles can easily be reconstituted by soaking them in warm liquid for just a few minutes.

CHIPPED BEEF is thin slices of smoked, dried beef, often served with cream sauce over toast. It was recorded before 1850 as an American creation and takes its name from the early usage of the word chip as "to strip or pare away." During World War II, creamed chipped beef was such a mainstay in U.S. military mess halls that it took on the humorous name "shit on a shingle."

CHITTERLING or **CHITLIN** is the small intestines of pigs cooked as food, sometimes filled with mincemeat or forcemeat as a kind of sausage. The word, which appeared by the late thirteenth century, may be a diminutive of the Old English *cieter*, "intestines." Chitterlings must be thoroughly cleaned in order to remove all fecal matter and bacteria. This labor-intensive process, which requires turning the intestines inside out, can take hours.

CHIVE is a bulbous perennial plant (the smallest species of *Allium schoenoprasum*) related to the leek and onion, with long, slender, hollow leaves that are used as a seasoning. The word chive is derived from the Latin *cepa*, "onion."

> **HINTS** Look for fresh chives with a uniform green color and no signs of wilting or browning. Wrap chives in a paper towel and store in a plastic bag in the refrigerator up to a week. For frozen chives, keep them in their original container, then put in a zip-lock freezer bag and freeze; frozen chives will keep for up to six months. For dried chives, store in a cool, dark place and use within three months.

> ▌ Fresh chives should be added toward the end of the cooking time to retain their delicate flavor. If chives are added to a dish too soon, their flavor becomes harsh and slightly sour.

> ▌ Keep a pot of chives on a well-lit windowsill and have fresh chives on hand whenever you want. Snip off whole chives close to the base, rather than lopping off the tops of the entire bunch.

CHOCOLATE is a food made from husked, roasted, fermented, ground cacao beans (seeds); cocoa nibs are the pieces of husked, roasted beans. Chocolate is often refined with added sweetener or flavoring. The word also describes confections or beverages made with this food. Spanish explorers first found chocolate in Central America as *xocoatl*, an Aztec cold drink of cocoa, honey, vanilla, and other spices. The Aztecs also used the word *chocolatl* for an edible substance made from the seeds of the cacao tree. The Spanish explorers seem to have gotten these mixed up and first used the word chocolate for the drink, the first sense of the word in English (1604). By the middle of the seventeenth century, however, the solid confection made from roasted ground cacao seeds was becoming familiar and became the main meaning of the word. Columbus brought the cacao bean to Europe, but it was the mid-nineteenth century before chocolate was made for eating instead of as a beverage. The percentage of chocolate necessary for a fine semisweet or bittersweet chocolate is a minimum of 35% according to USDA standards, but premium chocolates contain over 60%.

CHOCOLATE ESSENTIALS

CONFUSABLE BITTERSWEET CHOCOLATE/ SEMISWEET CHOCOLATE. The difference between bittersweet chocolate and semisweet chocolate is that bitter-sweet (baking) chocolate has no sugar added and semisweet chocolate has sugar added. However, they are both dark chocolates.

CONFUSABLE SWEET CHOCOLATE/ SEMISWEET CHOCOLATE. The difference between sweet chocolate and semisweet chocolate is that sweet chocolate must contain at least 15% chocolate liquor, while semisweet or bittersweet chocolate must have at least 35%. But one manu-facturer's bittersweet chocolate may turn out to be sweeter than another's semi-sweet chocolate. Sweet chocolates vary greatly in aroma, flavor, consistency, and texture; this is because they vary in the quality and blend of the beans, the roast, and the amount of cocoa butter added.

■ Make sure chocolate is not stored near foods with strong odors or flavors, as it will pick them up.

■ Seized chocolate is that which has turned hard and grainy because it has been affected by moisture. You can salvage seized chocolate by taking it off the heat and working in a tablespoon of water at a time. It will become good enough to use in fillings and icing, but not for candy making. Melting chocolate in a microwave prevents seizing.

■ Chopped-up chocolate can be melted in less than a minute in a microwave in a wide, shallow bowl. Heat both dark and milk chocolate on low to medium power. White and milk chocolate should be chopped more finely than dark so they melt without getting gritty.

■ Wrap chocolate well in foil and plastic wrap and store at cool room tempera-ture. Chocolate can be refrigerated or frozen, but wrap in a double layer of plastic wrap. When thawing, let the chocolate come to room temperature before unwrapping. Dark chocolate can keep for up to one year; milk and white chocolate keep for up to eight months at cool room temperature.

HOW DO THEY GET THE CREAM CENTER IN CHOCOLATE?

Creamy-centered chocolates contain fondant, which is made by mixing sugar with a quarter of its own weight in water.

1. The fondant is heated slowly until the sugar dissolves.

2. The remaining syrup is boiled until it reaches 240°F. The hot, sticky, clear solution is poured out and cooled on a slab to 100°F, becoming a mass of tiny sugar crystals.

3. The fondant is reheated to 110°F, making it pliable enough to knead in natural or artificial colors and flavorings.

4. The enzyme invertase is also added. It assists chemical changes later in the process.

5. The kneaded fondant is again re-heated until it is just liquid and poured into corn flour molds.

6. A shallow, flat bed of corn flour passes under a machine that stamps indentations for the shapes, which

are then filled with the liquid fondant.

7. As the fondant cools and hardens, the fondant centers pull away from the corn flour slightly and are then turned out onto another conveyor.

8. The fondants go through a bath of melted chocolate, which covers the base, while a curtain of melted chocolate covers the rest of the shape.

9. When the chocolate has hardened, the sweets are heated to 86°F—not hot enough to melt the chocolate, but hot enough to activate the invertase.

10. Invertase breaks down the sugar in the fondant into glucose and fructose.

11. The glucose and fructose combine with the water in the fondant to liquefy the centers and make them creamy.

CHOCOLATE TYPES

BAKING COCOA: Dried chocolate liquor with the cocoa butter removed, ground into unsweetened cocoa.

BITTERSWEET CHOCOLATE: Chocolate liquor with cocoa butter and small amounts of sugar and vanilla; lecithin is usually added and it is dark and sweeter than unsweetened.

CHOCOLATE CHIP: Small piece of chocolate used especially in making cookies and desserts.

COCOA POWDER: Powdery remains of chocolate liquor after cocoa butter is removed.

COUVERTURE CHOCOLATE: Chocolate with a higher percentage of cocoa butter than ordinary chocolate, which makes for glossier coatings and a richer flavor; available in bittersweet, semisweet, milk, and white varieties.

DARK CHOCOLATE: Slightly bitter chocolate with a deep brown color, without any added milk.

DUTCH COCOA: Cocoa treated with an alkali, making it milder yet richer tasting.

GERMAN CHOCOLATE: Dark chocolate, but sweeter than semisweet.

(continued)

MILK CHOCOLATE: Chocolate made from chocolate liquor with sugar, cocoa butter, whole or skim powdered milk solids, vanilla, and (usually) lecithin.

SEMISWEET CHOCOLATE: Slightly sweeter than bittersweet chocolate.

SWEET CHOCOLATE: Any chocolate that contains added sugar.

UNSWEETENED CHOCOLATE (also called BAKING CHOCOLATE, BITTER CHOCOLATE, PAIN CHOCOLATE): pure chocolate liquor.

WHITE CHOCOLATE: Not legally chocolate because it contains no cocoa powder.

HOW CHOCOLATE IS MADE

1. Dried, fermented whole cacao beans are roasted, and the shells are discarded. The resulting pieces of husked, roasted beans are called cocoa nibs.

2. The roasted nibs are then ground into chocolate liquor.

3. The chocolate liquor is refined and pressed, producing cocoa butter and cocoa cake.

4. The cake is pulverized into sweet chocolate with the addition of chocolate liquor and sugar, or into milk chocolate with the addition of milk solids.

5. After all the ingredients have been added, the chocolate is conched, which means that it is heated in tubs while huge rollers plow back and forth to smooth and refine it. In some European plants, this process goes on for seventy-two hours to develop a special creaminess. This conched chocolate also has a more nutlike flavor.

6. Finally, the chocolate is tempered: it is heated and cooled to develop a bright finish, durability, and good melting quality. Chocolate that has not been tempered properly will melt into a sticky mess or tighten.

CHOICE is a grade of government-classified meat between Prime and Good. For beef, Choice grade is high quality, but has less marbling than Prime. Choice roasts and steaks from the loin and rib are very tender, juicy, and flavorful and are suited to dry-heat cooking. For veal, Choice (and Prime) grades are juicier and more flavorful than the lower grades. For lamb, Choice grade has slightly less marbling than Prime, but is still of very high quality. Within the Choice grade, there are three different levels of quality, which are usually called Small marbling, Modest marbling, and Moderate marbling. Moderately marbled USDA Choice is the top cut, just one step short of Prime.

CHOP is a slice of lamb or pork cut from the rib, loin, or shoulder, along with a piece of bone. (When cut from the neck, it is a cutlet.) Beef cuts from these areas are very large in comparison and are not referred to today as chops. The word chop was first recorded in reference to an individual portion of meat in the seventeenth century, and the chop can be seen as a forerunner of the hamburger; in the United Kingdom there were chophouses for serving muttonchops and beefsteaks. Chop (or chop up) is also to cut up into pieces, often small. To chop roughly means to cut into pieces up to 1 inch; "regular" chopped refers to pieces that are ½–¼ inch.

HINTS You can determine whether a chop (noun) is rare, medium, or well done by touching it instead of cutting into it. Rare: when touched it is soft with very little resistance. Medium: when touched there is slight resistance that springs back into place. Well done: when touched it is firm.

❚ When chopping (verb) with a food processor or knife, spray the knife or food processor blades with nonstick cooking spray to keep sticky foods from adhering to the blade.

CHOP PLATE: see CHARGER.

CHOPSTICKS are a pair of small, thin, tapered sticks of wood, bamboo, ivory, or plastic that are held in one hand and used as eating utensils for Asian food. The word is from the Chinese *k'wai tse*, "nimble/fast ones." The synonym in Japan is HASHI. Japanese chopsticks have pointed ends; Chinese chopsticks have blunt ends. The broad ends of chopsticks are used for picking up food from a communal serving plate.

CHOP SUEY is a Chinese-style dish of small pieces of meat or chicken stewed and fried with bean sprouts, bamboo shoots, and onions, and served with rice. The term chop suey is an alteration of the Cantonese *tsaap sui*, "various or mixed bits." Chop suey does not exist in China, but originated in the United States; Chinese cooks served it to laborers who worked on the Pacific Railroad in the late nineteenth century.

CHORIZO (pronounced CHORE-ee-so) is a highly seasoned Spanish or Mexican pork sausage with garlic, paprika, and other spices like hot peppers. Mexican chorizo is made with fresh pork; the Spanish version uses smoked pork. Sausages tied with red string are hotter than those with ordinary string.

CHOUX PASTRY is a soft, glossy, egg-rich pastry that puffs up into a hollow case when baked and is used for making cream puffs, éclairs, and profiteroles. The French word choux literally means "cabbage/rosette," as the pastry has layers similar to a cabbage's leaves. This special pastry is made by an entirely different method from other pastries. The dough is very sticky and pastelike. It is based on a paste of flour and water that is enriched with butter, then lightened with egg and by thorough beating.

HINT Uncooked choux pastry freezes well. Shape and freeze the mixture, then pack the pieces in zip-lock freezer bags when firm. Cook from frozen, allowing slightly longer time. Unfilled cooked pastry also freezes well, but it tends to soften, so should be placed in a hot oven for 1–2 minutes to crisp up before any filling is added.

CHOW is an informal (pidgin English or slang) term for food or a meal. It was originally a verb meaning "to eat," and derives from the Cantonese *chaau*, "fry/cook."

CHOW-CHOW is a Chinese preserve of fruit, orange peel, and ginger; it is also a relish of chopped pickled vegetables in mustard sauce. The word origin may be a reduplication of the Chinese/Cantonese *tsaip*, "food/mixture." Chow-chow, the mixed vegetable and pickle relish, is thought to have been brought to America by the Chinese railroad laborers.

CHOWDER is a soup or stew of seafood (fish, clams) usually made with milk or tomatoes, salt pork, onions, and other vegetables like potatoes; it is also a soup resembling chowder (such as corn chowder). The word derives from the French *chaudière*, "stew pot," a descendant of the Latin *caldarium* (which produced the English cauldron). Chowder was originally a hodgepodge prepared in the fishing villages of Brittany, and then the custom was carried to Newfoundland, from which it spread to Nova Scotia, New Brunswick, and New England.

CHOW MEIN is fried noodles served with a thick sauce to which other ingredients (meat, seafood, vegetables) are added after being stir-fried separately. The word is an alteration of the Chinese *ch'ao mein*, "fried flour." Chow mein was introduced in the American West in the early twentieth century.

CHRISTMAS PUDDING: see PLUM PUDDING.

CHRISTOPHENE: see CHAYOTE.

CHUCK describes a cut of beef extending from the neck to the shoulder blade to the first few ribs. The term appears to be a specialization of an earlier chuck that meant simply "lump." Chuck as in chuck wagon (food or provisions wagon) also derives from that usage. This traditional cut for casseroles and stews is gelatinous and best braised slowly in dishes. For maximum tenderness, chuck cuts must be cooked slowly, as in stewing or braising.

CHUMBO FIG: see PRICKLY PEAR.

CHURCH KEY is a type of small metal can opener with a triangular pointed end that pierces the tops of cans. In the mid-1930s, when beer cans were first invented, they had instructions on them on how to use a church key to open the can so people would not get mad or frustrated when using the new device and can.

CHURN means to stir cream vigorously in order to make butter; it also refers to a vessel in which cream is agitated to separate butterfat from buttermilk. It derives from the Old English word *cyrnel*, "kernel," from the grainy appearance of churned cream. The traditional churn barrel is made of teak, while modern churns are made of stainless steel.

CHURRO is a thick fritter of dough made in a coiled shape, similar to a cruller. The word is an Americanism from Spanish, perhaps from the dialectal name for the inhabitants of the mountainous parts of Valencia (literally, the word refers to a kind of coarse-wooled sheep), the approximate area where the pastry originated.

CHUTNEY is a spicy condiment or relish made of ripe fruits or vegetables with vinegar or lemon juice, soured herbs, spices or chiles, and sugar. Chutney, a term from Indian cookery, is from the Hindi *chatni*, "a hot, spicy condiment." American chutneys tend to be less spicy and sweeter than their Indian counterparts. Chutneys can range in texture from chunky to smooth, and in degrees of spiciness from mild to hot. Sweeter chutneys make interesting bread spreads, can be served on crackers, and are delicious served with cheese. Chutney can be served as an accompaniment to a variety of cheeses, from Cheddar to chèvre.

> **HINT** Chutney can be stored for well over a month. In fact, the flavor improves with age. You can actually make it and allow it to mature for a month before using it.

CIABATTA is a flat white Italian yeast bread made with olive oil. Ciabatta is Italian for "slipper," from the shape of the loaf. The bread has a moist, open texture and is often used as the base for bruschetta. A toasted sandwich made from small loaves of ciabatta is known as a panino; the plural is panini.

> **HINT** Ciabatta bread tastes best when it is fresh. Wrapping the bread in plastic tends to make it slightly soggy, which can be an undesirable or unacceptable trade-off. To refresh ciabatta bread that is slightly stale or soggy, sprinkle it with water and toast it in the oven immediately before serving.

CIDER is a beverage made from fermented juice pressed from apples. Apple juice if unfermented is cider or sweet cider; if fermented, it is hard cider, which is 4%–8% alcohol. In the United Kingdom, the term cider refers to hard cider. Pears and sweet cherries are also made into cider. The term entered English early on, from French and the earlier Latin *sicera*, a Vulgate rendition of the Hebrew *shekhar*, "strong drink." Several hundred varieties of apple are used for the manufacture of cider; some are sweet, but most are rather bitter or even sour. The cider maker's skill lies in blending different varieties to obtain an agreeable and well-balanced cider. Cider can be classified from dry to sweet. Fermentation, which occurs naturally without the addition of yeasts or sugar, takes about a month.

CIDER VINEGAR is vinegar produced from fermented apple cider.

> **HINT** Cider vinegar should be stored in a cool, dark place such as a cabinet until ready for use.

CI GU: see ARROWROOT.

CILANTRO, also called CHINESE PARSLEY, is the leaves of coriander, an Old World herb resembling parsley, which are used as an herb for garnish or seasoning. The seeds of this plant are called CORIANDER; ground coriander seed is also called CUMIN. Originally grown in Greece, cilantro has been used as an herb since at least 5000 BC. It is mentioned in Sanskrit texts and the Bible; Latin used the word *coliandrum*, "coriander." Coriander is one of the herbs thought to have aphrodisiac qualities; the Chinese used it in love potions, and in *The Thousand and One Nights* a man who had been childless for forty years is cured with a coriander concoction. There are people who despise cilantro, describing the aroma and flavor as "soapy," and some scientists believe that there is a specific gene that causes such a reaction.

> **HINT** Cilantro loses flavor during long exposure to heat. Since the stems are tender, they can be used along with the leaves.

CINNAMON is a spice from the dried aromatic bark of a tropical Asian evergreen tree (genus *Cinnamomum*); it is used as rolled strips or ground. Cinnamon is split from the shoots, cured, and dried, then shrinks and curls into a cylinder or "quill." The source of the word cinnamon is the Semitic or Hebrew *qinnamon*, which was borrowed into Greek as *kunnamon*, a word for the inner bark of the tree. Cinnamon is thought to be the oldest of spices. By the Middle Ages it was essential to the culinary arts. Controlling the island of Ceylon, the Dutch were exporting 270 tons per year. When the British took over the island and increased the planting and cultivation of the trees, their export rose to 1,000 tons per year by around 1850. Cinnamon is sometimes called a health food due to studies suggesting that it may help regulate blood sugar and that its fragrance may enhance brain activity. It is responsible for much world exploration and was thought to inspire love.

> **HINT** Cinnamon sticks come from the upper branches of the tree and are lower in flavor than ground cinnamon. The ground cinnamon comes from the lower, older bark and is more intense in flavor.

CIOPPINO is a spicy stew of fish and various shellfish, tomatoes, onions, green pepper, red or white wine, and garlic. It was developed in the late nineteenth century by Italian fishermen who settled in the North Beach section of San Francisco, though the origin of the word is unknown and speculated to be Italian American for "chip in."

CIPOLLINI or **CIPOLLINA**, also called WILD ONION, are the bulbs of grape hyacinth, which resemble small onions/chives and are used in Italian cuisine.

> **HINT** For peak flavor, fresh cipollini should be slowly simmered or braised. They can be served as an appetizer or vegetable.

CITRON is a large, thick-skinned, pale yellow fruit resembling the lemon/lime, from a thorny Indian evergreen shrub or tree (*Citrus medica*). The fruit is often candied and used in confections and fruitcakes. The citron tree is of Asian origin and was brought to Rome about the beginning of the Christian era. Citrons give little juice, which can be used like lemon juice. Citron pulp is very sour and not suitable for eating raw. The most important part of the citron is the extremely thick, lemon-perfumed peel, which is a fairly important article in international trade. The fruits are halved, depulped, and immersed in seawater or ordinary saltwater to ferment for about forty days, with the brine being changed every two weeks; they are then rinsed and put in denser brine in wooden barrels for storage and export. The candied peel is widely employed in the food industry, especially as an ingredient in fruitcake, plum pudding, buns, sweet rolls, and candy.

> **HINT** Citron should be stored in the freezer for maximum freshness.

CITRUS FRUIT denotes any of numerous fruits of the genus *Citrus* having aromatic thick rind and juicy pulp. The Latin *citrus* signified the citron, an Asian tree with lemonlike fruit. Citrus fruits include bergamot, citron, clementine, grapefruit, lemon, lime, mandarin, orange, pomelo, tangelo, tangerine, and ugli fruit.

> **HINT** Citrus fruit that is heavy for its size will be juicier than its lightweight counterparts. Room-temperature citrus fruit yields more juice than refrigerated fruit. Using the palm of your hand, roll citrus fruit around on the countertop a few times before squeezing to maximize juice yield. Microwaving the fruit for 15 to 20 seconds before squeezing will also help extract more juice.

CITRUS FRUITS

Citrus fruits, rich in vitamin C, have an acid flavor to varying degrees. There are many varieties.

AFRICAN CHERRY ORANGE	FORBIDDEN FRUIT	ORANGELO
BERGAMOT OR BERGAMOT ORANGE	GRAPEFRUIT	ORTANIQUE
	ICHANG LEMON	OTAHEITE ORANGE
BITTER ORANGE OR SEVILLE ORANGE	KING ORANGE	POMELO, PUMMELO, OR SHADDOCK
	KUMQUAT	
CALAMONDIN	LEMON	RANGPUR OR LEMANDERIN
CITRANGE	LIME	SATSUMA
CITRANGEDIN	MANDARIN LIME	SWEET LIME
CITRANGEQUAT	MANDARIN ORANGE	TANGELO
CITRON	NAARTJE	TANGERINE
CLEMENTINE	ORANGE	UGLI FRUIT

CITRUS ZESTER: see ZESTER.

CIVET is a thick, rich game stew, usually made with hare, that is cooked and thickened in wine and the animal's blood. A key ingredient is small green onions, in French, *cives*, which give the dish its name.

CIVET BEAN: see LIMA BEAN.

CLABBER, also called THICK MILK, is thick curdled sour milk; it is short for BONNYCLABBER, the Irish word. Clabber is milk that has naturally clotted on souring. Clabber cheese is curd or cottage cheese. With the rise of pasteurization, the making of clabber virtually stopped, except on farms that had easy access to unprocessed cow's milk. A somewhat similar food can be made from pasteurized milk by adding a couple of tablespoons of commercial buttermilk or sour milk to a glass of milk.

CLABBER CHEESE: see COTTAGE CHEESE.

CLAM refers to a large marine mollusk with a hard or soft bivalve shell, and the edible flesh of this mollusk. The word's origin is the Old English *clamm*, "bond/fetter," from an earlier Proto-Germanic form, but the word clam-shell was used in English until the sixteenth century. In North America the term refers especially to two species, the hard or round clam (*Venus mercenaria*), and the soft or long clam (*Mya arenaria*), both found in great abundance on sandy or muddy shores. Atlantic hard-shell clams are quahogs, which vary from littlenecks to large chowder clams. Pacific hard-shell clams are unrelated. The Atlantic has soft-shell steamer clams and the Pacific has soft-shell razor clams. The appetizer clams casino—clams baked in the shell with bacon and green pepper and in some regions stuffed with bread crumbs—was created in 1894 by Julius Keller at Louis Sherry's Narragansett Casino in Narragansett, Rhode Island.

CLAM ESSENTIALS

- If you harvest clams yourself, they need to be purged of sand and grit. If using commercially sold clams, you do not need to purge them, for they are usually purged before reaching the market. To purge clams, soak them in a generous amount of lightly salted water with a couple of tablespoons of flour or cornmeal stirred in. After a few hours, the clams will have purged themselves of sand.

- Hard-shell quahogs should have firm, fine-textured gray shells with no yellowing. Other hard-shell clams should have firm, even-colored shells. An open shell means the clam is dead. Shucked hard-shell clams should be plump and moist and have clear liquor (liquid) and a fresh, briny aroma.

- Soft-shell clams should be oval with a protruding neck/siphon and be evenly colored. Tap the neck, which should pull back into the shell, to test for freshness.

- Quick-frozen clams are second-best after fresh.

- Put fresh clams on a tray or in a shallow bowl covered with a damp cloth in the refrigerator. (They can also be put in a mesh bag in a large bowl.) Serve within two days. This is true for ready-shucked clams too, but they should be kept in a sealed container in the back of the refrigerator. Once canned clams are opened, keep for no more than two days in the refrigerator.

- Scrub clamshells under running water with a soft-bristled brush. Briefly steaming clams to open them is easier than shucking. If there is sand in the liquor, you can strain it with a coffee filter or a fine-mesh sieve.

- If the shell of a clam does not open while cooking, it indicates that the clam was not alive in the first place and should be discarded.

BUTTER (also called WASHINGTON): Sweet edible clam of the Pacific coast.

CHERRYSTONE: Small quahog larger than a littleneck, of the Atlantic coast; eaten raw or cooked as in clams casino.

GEODUCK: Large edible clam of the Pacific coast, usually weighing two to three pounds but can be over ten pounds.

LITTLENECK: Small young quahog of the Atlantic coast, usually eaten raw.

MAHOGANY (also called OCEAN QUAHOG): Hard-shell clam of the Atlantic coast.

MANILA (also called JAPANESE): Small sweet clam of the Pacific coast with an elongated, flattened shell.

PISMO: Thick hard-shell clam of the Pacific coast.

QUAHOG: Edible clam with a large, thick, hard shell, often three or more inches in diameter, of the Atlantic coast.

RAZOR: Long, narrow, razor-shaped soft-shell clam of the Pacific coast.

STEAMER (also called FRYER, LONG-NECK, MANINOSE): large oval-shaped soft-shell clam of the Atlantic coast, with sweet, mild meat.

SURF (also called BAR, SEA, SKIMMER): Large hard-shell clam of the Atlantic coast.

CLAMBAKE or **CLAM BAKE** is a cookout at the seashore where clams, fish, and other foods are cooked, usually on heated stones and covered with seaweed. The fire is built in a deep pit with flat rocks on top of burning wood, with those layers repeated a couple of times. About six inches of wet seaweed goes on top of that and then the food is added, covered with wet canvas, and cooked.

CLAM CHOWDER is a chowder containing clams and either potatoes or tomatoes. There are two basic types: white (milk or cream based) and red (tomato based). Manhattan clam chowder is a chowder made from clams, tomatoes, and other vegetables and seasoned with thyme, while New England clam chowder is a thick chowder made from clams, potatoes, onions, sometimes salt pork, and milk or cream. Rhode Island clam chowder uses clear broth. Clam chowder was brought to New England by French-Canadian fishermen.

> **HINTS** Cream is best to use to get a creamy clam chowder. So much milk would be needed that the clam flavor would be lost.

> When making clam chowder, use fresh or frozen clams, not canned clams. Add minced clams only during the last minutes of cooking. Simmer, don't boil, the chowder or the clams will toughen.

CLARET first pertained to wine that was light red in color (from the French *clair*, "clear/light/bright") to distinguish it from white wine and red wine. Now the word describes dry red wine in general or the red wines of Bordeaux, France.

CLARIFY (CLARIFICATION) means to make clear by removing impurities or solids, as by heating. Clarified butter is unsalted butter that has been heated to remove the milk solids. Other fats and liquids are also clarified by heating or filtering.

HINT Butter can be clarified in the oven by heating 1 pound (4 sticks) in a deep dish at 300ºF for 1 hour. The microwave can also be used by first melting the butter in a small measuring cup and then letting it stand for 5 minutes to separate.

CLARIFYING BUTTER

1. Butter is heated over low heat.

2. As the butter melts, most of the water evaporates and the milk solids separate and sink to the bottom.

3. The foam that rises to the top is skimmed off.

4. The clear or clarified liquid below is poured off.

CLEAVER is a heavy knife with a large squarish or broad blade, especially one used by butchers for cutting meat into joints or pieces. The name of the tool is not old and was first recorded by 1580. A cleaver's flat sides can be used for pounding, as in tenderizing meat. The butt end can be used as a pestle to pulverize seeds or other food items; the flat side is also great for crushing garlic.

CLEMENTINE is a variety of small, deep orange-red orange created as an accidental hybrid of the tangerine and a Seville orange. It was first cultivated around 1900 near Oran, Algeria, by a French priest, Père Clément. The clementine is first mentioned in an English text in 1926. Clementines are easy to peel and have only occasional seeds. They have been called zipper oranges and kid-glove oranges because they are so easy to peel. Simply apply gentle pressure with a fingertip to the top or bottom of the fruit's skin.

HINT Store clementines in the refrigerator if you are planning to keep them beyond a few days. Clementines will last at room temperature for two to three days.

CLINGSTONE is a term for any peach or nectarine variety in which the flesh adheres to the stone, as opposed to freestone. The flavor of clingstone fruits tends to be more complex than that of freestone fruits. Clingstone are the best varieties for canning and cooking since the flesh tends to be a bit firmer.

CLOTTED CREAM is cream made thicker and richer by heating milk until scalded, then cooling it and skimming off the cream; until the nineteenth century, clotted cream was known as clouted cream or DEVONSHIRE CREAM. It has at least 55% butterfat, giving it a pale yellow color, often topped with a deeper yellow crust. Clotted cream is traditionally served with tea and scones in England.

HINT Fresh clotted cream can be refrigerated, tightly covered, for up to four days. Clotted cream is not sweet. It tastes like thick whipping cream or unsalted butter and has the consistency of soft cream cheese.

CLOUDBERRY, also called SMALL CAPS BAKEAPPLE BERRY, MOUNTAIN BERRY, and YELLOW BERRY, is a type of creeping perennial raspberry (of the rose family) that grows in northern temperate regions and has yellow or light orange berries. Cloudberry may derive from the obsolete sense of cloud, "hill," combined with berry as the berry grows on hills in the north. The berries of cloudberries are too tart to eat plain but make excellent preserves, jams, and jellies.

CLOVE has two definitions: it is one of the small bulbs that make up the compound bulbs of garlic and shallots; it is also the pungent aromatic spice of the dried flower bud of a tropical evergreen (*Eugenia aromatica*). The word comes from the Old French *clou de girofle*, "nail of gillyflower (clove tree)"; the nail refers to the clove's shape and gillyflower was the original name of the spice. Cloves are among the strongest of spices.

CLOVERLEAF ROLL is a bread roll with three sections, named for the three-lobed leaf of a clover plant.

> **HINT** To make a cloverleaf roll, divide the dough into several equal portions and roll each portion into ropes of equal diameter—about ¾ to 1 inch. Cut the ropes into equal-sized pieces and roll each piece into a ball. (This technique ensures that the balls of dough will be of equal size.) For experienced home cooks, it is often just as easy to make the dough balls simply by pulling off similar-sized pieces of dough from the whole. Place three balls into each cup of a lightly greased muffin tin. The balls will join and form a cloverleaf pattern during the proofing and baking time.

CLUB SANDWICH is any sandwich consisting of two layers of fillings between three slices of bread. There is usually a sliced meat like chicken or turkey, bacon, tomato, lettuce, and a dressing like mayonnaise. The sandwich is often cut into quarters and held together by cocktail sticks. There are several possible origins of the name: club sandwiches may be named for the country clubs where they were first popular, or the double-decker club cars of early American railways. Perhaps the sandwich got its name because the word club suggests a "combination to make a total." The oldest recipe for the club sandwich was published in the *Good Housekeeping Everyday Cook Book* by Isabel Gordon Curtis in 1903.

CLUB SODA, also called SODA WATER, is a flavorless soft drink that gets its effervescence from an infusion of carbon dioxide. The term started out as a trademark in 1877 for "Cantrell & Cochranes Super Carbonated Club Soda (specially prepared) Works by Dublin & Belfast."

> **CONFUSABLE** CLUB SODA/SELTZER. The distinction between club soda and seltzer is that club soda also contains a bit of sodium bicarbonate. The small amount of sodium bicarbonate that is in club soda can help neutralize an acidic stomach because of its alkalinity.

CLUB STEAK, also called DELMONICO STEAK, SHELL STEAK, KANSAS CITY STRIP STEAK, NEW YORK STEAK, NEW YORK STRIP, STRIP LOIN STEAK, or STRIP STEAK is a small steak from the front of the short loin of beef.

> **HINT** You can tell the quality by looking at the steak's "eye"—the meat should be fine in texture with delicate marbling; avoid cuts that seem coarse or contain fat chunks.

COARSE SALT, COARSE-GRAINED SALT, or COARSELY GROUND SALT, also called GROS SEL, is a large-grained, somewhat refined sea salt crystal that is used in cooking.

> **HINTS** Most recipes calling for salt intend finely ground salt (table salt), but many professional chefs prefer cooking with coarse salt because they can easily measure it with their fingers. It is less moisture sensitive, so it resists caking and is easily stored.
>
> ▮ The jagged edges and large crystals make coarse salt a good choice for sprinkling on pretzels or corn on the cob because the edges tend to cling and the salt does not readily melt.
>
> ▮ It is acceptable to substitute 1 tablespoon of coarse salt for 2 teaspoons of table salt.

COAT means to cover a food completely in a layer of liquid, paste, or ground foodstuff, especially before baking or frying.

> **HINT** Use crushed stuffing mix as a coating for chicken.

COBBLER, also called BETTY, BIRD'S NEST PUDDING, BUCKLE, CRISP, CROUSTADE, CROW'S NEST PUDDING, CRUMBLE, GRUNT, PANDOWDY, SLUMP, or SONKER, is a fruit pie with a crust of biscuits or scones; some versions are enclosed in the crust, while others have a biscuit or crumb topping. This American dessert may have gotten its name from its top crust's resemblance to cobblestones. But the first culinary use of the word was for an iced drink consisting of a spirit, liqueur, or fortified wine mixed with fruit, ice, and sugar. This first usage may be short for cobbler's punch.

COBB SALAD is a salad with chopped poultry, tomatoes, avocado, bacon, hardcooked eggs, and sometimes onions and mushrooms, dressed in vinaigrette and topped with Roquefort, Cheddar, or blue cheese. The most popular story about the salad is that around 1937 a Los Angeles restaurant owner, Robert Cobb of the Brown Derby, threw together a salad of leftovers and named it after himself. The Cobb salad and the Caesar salad were the first modern "main course" salads in the United States. Up until the 1920s and 1930s, most salads were side dishes composed of greens with a simple dressing of vinegar, oil, and salt.

COCK-A-LEEKIE is a Scottish soup made of chicken and leeks. The words in the name are diminutives, and the earlier spelling was cocky-leeky.

COCKTAIL is a broad term for any mixed alcoholic drink, one consisting of a spirit or spirits mixed with other ingredients. The word cocktail first appeared at the beginning of the nineteenth century in the United States. It was not until the 1920s that the cocktail became complicated and adventurous. The word's origin remains obscure: cocktail was also used in the nineteenth century to mean a "horse with a docked tail that stood up in the air," usually nonthoroughbreds that raced, and this may have led to the sense of "lack of purity/adulteration" and the use of the word cocktail for an "adulterated" spirit —but the connection between the horse and the drink has not been firmly established. Cocktails that are based on spirits without much dilution are usually served in a small stemmed glass. Longer drinks, such as juleps, Pimm's, and recipes incorporating soda or sparkling wine, may be served in tall glasses, large goblets, or tumblers.

ALCOHOLIC MIXED DRINKS AND COCKTAILS

Mixed drinks and cocktails seem to be preferred by middle-class and upper-class drinkers and by women. There are many more in existence than appear on this representative list, but it is interesting to read the creative names for these drinks. Some books, like bartenders' guides, offer some interesting stories behind the names given to mixed drinks and cocktails.

ADAM AND EVE	BELMONT COCKTAIL	BRANDY CASSIS
ALABAMA SLAMMER	BERMUDA ROSE	BRANDY FIZZ
ALASKA COCKTAIL	BETSY ROSS	BRANDY HIGHBALL
ALEXANDER	BETWEEN-THE-SHEETS	BRANDY SMASH
ALLEGHENY	BIJOU COCKTAIL	BRANDY SWIZZLE
AMERICAN BEAUTY COCKTAIL	BLACK MARIA	BRANTINI
AMERICANA	BLACK RUSSIAN	BRIGHTON PUNCH
ANGEL'S KISS	BLACK VELVET	BRONX COCKTAIL
APRICOT COOLER	BLOODY CAESAR	BUCK'S FIZZ
B&B	BLOODY MARY	BULL AND BEAR
B-52	BLUE CANARY	BULL'S EYE
BACARDI COCKTAIL	BLUE HAWAIIAN	BULLSHOT
BAHAMA MAMA	BLUE LAGOON	BULL'S MILK
BANANA DAIQUIRI	BLUE MARGARITA	BUTTERED RUM
BANSHEE	BLUE WHALE	CAPE CODDER
BARBIE'S SPECIAL COCKTAIL	BOCCE BALL	CAUDLE
BASIN STREET	BOMBAY COCKTAIL	CEMENT MIXER
BAY BREEZE	BOSOM CARESSER	CHAMPAGNE COCKTAIL
BEACHCOMBER	BOSTON COCKTAIL	CHAMPAGNE COOLER
BEER BUSTER	BOSTON COOLER	CHAPEL HILL
BEE STINGER	BOURBON AND WATER	CHERRY BLOSSOM
BELLINI	BOURBON ON THE ROCKS	CHERRY FIZZ
	BRANDY ALEXANDER	CHICAGO COCKTAIL

(continued)

CHI-CHI
CLAMATO COCKTAIL
CLUB COCKTAIL
COBBLER
COFFEE GRASSHOPPER
COFFEE OLD-FASHIONED
COOLER
COOPERSTOWN COCKTAIL
COSMOPOLITAN
CUBA LIBRE
DAIQUIRI
DAISY DUELLER
DAMN-THE-WEATHER COCKTAIL
DEPTH CHARGE
DESERT SUNRISE
DINGO
DIRTY BANANA
DIXIE JULEP
DREAM COCKTAIL
DRY MARTINI
EGGNOG
ENGLISH HIGHBALL
FANCY GIN
FIFTH AVENUE
FIREFLY
FIZZ
FLIP
FLYING SCOTCHMAN
FOXY LADY
FRAPPE
FRENCH CONNECTION
FRENCH MARTINI
FROZEN DAIQUIRI
FROZEN MARGARITA
FUZZY NAVEL
GENTLEMAN'S COCKTAIL
GEORGIA MINT JULEP
GEORGIA PEACH
GIBSON
GIMLET
GIN AND BITTERS
GIN AND SIN
GIN AND TONIC
GIN COOLER
GIN FIZZ
GIN HIGHBALL
GIN RICKEY

GIN SLING
GIN SOUR
GIN SWIZZLE
GLUHWEIN
GODFATHER
GODMOTHER
GOLDEN CADILLAC
GRASSHOPPER
GREEN DRAGON
GREYHOUND
GROG
HARVARD COCKTAIL
HARVARD COOLER
HARVEY WALLBANGER
HIGHBALL
HOLE-IN-ONE
HOLLYWOOD
HONOLULU COCKTAIL
HOT BUTTERED RUM
HOT TODDY
HURRICANE
INCOME TAX COCKTAIL
INDIAN SUMMER
IRISH COFFEE
IRISH WHISKEY
JACK-IN-THE-BOX
JACK ROSE
JERSEY LIGHTNING
JOCOSE JULEP
JOURNALIST COCKTAIL
KAMIKAZE
KENTUCKY BLIZZARD
KENTUCKY COCKTAIL
KING ALPHONSE
KIR
KIR ROYALE
KISS ON THE LIPS
LADY FINGER
LIBERTY COCKTAIL
LONDON COCKTAIL
LONG ISLAND ICED TEA
LOUISVILLE COOLER
LOUISVILLE LADY
LOVER'S KISS
MADRAS
MAI-TAI
MANHATTAN

MARGARITA
MARTINI
MARY PICKFORD COCKTAIL
MELON BALL
MELON COOLER
MERRY WIDOW
METROPOLITAN COCKTAIL
MEXICAN COFFEE
MIDNIGHT COCKTAIL
MIMOSA
MIND ERASER
MINT JULEP
MISSISSIPPI MUD
MORNING COCKTAIL
MOSCOW MULE
MUDSLIDE
NARRAGANSETT
NEW YORK COCKTAIL
NIGHT CAP
NIGHTMARE
NINETEENTH HOLE
NUTCRACKER
NUTTY PROFESSOR
OLD-FASHIONED
ORANGE BLOSSOM
ORGEAT
PARK AVENUE
PASSION MIMOSA
PEACH SANGAREE
PEPPERMINT PATTIE
PETER PAN COCKTAIL
PIMM'S CUP
PIÑA COLADA
PINK LADY
PINK PUSSY CAT
PINK SQUIRREL
PLANTER'S PUNCH
POLO COCKTAIL
POSSET
POUSSE CAFÉ
PRAIRIE OYSTER
PRINCETON COCKTAIL
PUNCH
RAMOS GIN FIZZ
RED DEATH
RICKEY
ROB ROY

RUM AND COKE	SLAM DUNK	TROPICAL SPECIAL
RUM COOLER	SLOE GIN FIZZ	UNION JACK COCKTAIL
RUM EGGNOG	SMASH	VELVET HAMMER
RUM OLD-FASHIONED	SNAKE BITE	VIRGIN MARY
RUM RUNNER	SNOWBALL	VODKA AND TONIC
RUM SOUR	SOCIETY COCKTAIL	VODKA COOLER
RUSTY NAIL	SOMBRERO	VODKA GIMLET
SALTY DOG	SOOTHER COCKTAIL	VODKA MARTINI
SANGRIA	SOUTHERN LADY	VODKA ON THE ROCKS
SAN JUAN COOLER	SOUTHERN PEACH	WASSAIL
SCARLETT O'HARA	SPRITZER	WHISKEY HIGHBALL
SCOTCH AND SODA	STINGER	WHISKEY SOUR
SCOTCH HIGHBALL	STRAWBERRY DAIQUIRI	WHITE LADY
SCOTCH ON THE ROCKS	STRAWBERRY MARGARITA	WHITE RUSSIAN
SCOTCH SOUR	SYLLABUB	WHITE SATIN
SCREWDRIVER	TEQUILA SUNRISE	WHITE SPIDER
SEABREEZE	THANKSGIVING SPECIAL	WIDOW'S KISS
SEVEN AND SEVEN	THOROUGHBRED COOLER	WILD THING
SEX ON THE BEACH	TOASTED ALMOND	WINE COOLER
SHANDY	TODDY	WU-WU
SHRUB	TOM AND JERRY	YALE COCKTAIL
SIDECAR COCKTAIL	TOM COLLINS	ZOMBIE
SINGAPORE SLING	TO THE MOON	

COCKTAIL CORN, Baby corn, or Candle corn are very small corn ears harvested when the ears are very small and immature, less than 3 inches long. Varieties of specialized corn plants are used to produce baby corn, an important crop in Southeast Asia.

COCKTAIL FRANKS IN PASTRY: see Pigs in blankets.

COCKTAIL SAUCE is any of various sauces served with a seafood cocktail, typically consisting of ketchup, Worcestershire sauce, Tabasco, lemon juice, horseradish, and seasonings.

> **HINT** Chilling cocktail sauce improves its flavor.

COCOA or **COCOA POWDER** is made from cacao seeds after they have been fermented, roasted, shelled, ground, and defatted, but the word also describes a beverage made by mixing this powder with sugar in hot water or milk (this beverage was originally called chocolate). Cocoa was originally known as cacao, an adaptation of *cacahuatl*, the term for "cocoa bean" in the Nahuatl language, and the later change in the spelling was influenced by the word coconut. Used in Latin and South America long before European explorers arrived, cocoa made its way to Europe in the early sixteenth century. Early spellings were cacoa and cocao, which were pronounced with three syllables, but by the end of the eighteenth century cocoa became the established spelling.

COCONUT or **COCOANUT** is a large, hard-shelled, oval nut with a fibrous husk containing thick white meat with fluid/milk when fresh. Coconut is the nut or seed of the coco-palm (coconut palm); the word comes from the Portuguese *côco*, literally meaning "bogeyman/bugbear," from the resemblance of a coconut to a grotesque head or mischievous monkey face. The outer fibrous husk yields coir; the dried nut is called copra. The coconut is the world's largest nut. Coconut palms migrated not only by means of ancient traders and explorers, but also by means of the ability of coconuts to float and easily travel along ocean currents for long stretches, ending up on land on tropical beaches.

HINTS Choose heavy coconuts and shake them near your ear to listen for liquid. The more liquid, the fresher the coconut is. The liquid is coconut water; coconut milk or cream is often made with it.

Coconut meat does not keep well and becomes rancid quickly when exposed to air, since it is high in oil content. Revive coconut flakes by covering with milk and refrigerating for a few hours. Drain and pat dry to use.

Coconut cream is not part of the water that comes out of a coconut. It is made from the white meat of the coconut, which is grated and moistened with water. The liquid from the coconut is drained off from the grated white meat, which is then left to stand until the cream rises to the surface and can be scooped off. This is put into cheesecloth and wrung out. This thick, rich cream can be used for sweet dishes or as a thickener for sauces. The water that comes out of the pierced eyes of the coconut is a sweet liquid that is good for drinking but only infrequently used for cooking.

COCONUT MILK is the clear to whitish fluid found in a fresh coconut or the white liquid obtained from compressing fresh coconut meat. Coconut cream is the rich, dense milk found at the top of a can of coconut milk.

HINT Store opened coconut milk in an airtight container for up to three days in the refrigerator. Coconut cream is at the top of an unshaken can.

COD is a major food fish of Arctic and cold-temperate waters, known for its lean white flesh. The word is from an Old English word meaning "bag fish." The cod's delicate flesh requires careful cooking because of the whitish liquid that seeps from it. Prolonged cooking harms both the flavor and the presentation. Cod is rarely grilled (broiled) because of the flaky texture of its flesh.

CODDLE means to cook slowly in nearly boiling water, or to cook just below the boiling point. Coddling is a cooking method most often used with eggs, though other foods can be coddled as well. Coddling is usually done by placing the food in a covered individual-sized container, setting the container in a large pan of simmering water, and placing the pan either on the stovetop or in the oven at very low heat.

COEUR À LA CRÈME is a heart-shaped dessert of cream cheese with whipped cream or sour cream, made in a wicker or cheesecloth-lined mold to allow the whey or liquid to drain, and garnished with berries. Coeur à la crème is traditionally associated with Valentine's Day.

> **HINT** To make coeur à la crème, you can rig up makeshift molds by cutting the sides of four twelve-ounce paper cups to three inches high. With a toothpick, poke twelve holes in the bottom of each. Line with cheesecloth; fill as directed in the recipe. Be sure to place the molds on another dish to catch the liquids.

COFFEE is a moderately stimulating drink made by infusion or decoction from the roasted and ground seeds of a shrub (genus *Coffea*). Coffee was discovered around 850 AD, according to legend, when a goatherd noticed that a goat became frisky after chewing the berries of the plant. By the fifteenth century the Arabs had learned to roast the beans and make a hot beverage. The word coffee may derive from the Arabic qahwah, a word originally used for wine or a drink made by infusion; when coffee first arrived in Europe, it was known as "Arabian wine." However, there are others who say the source is the name *Kaffa*, familiar in the Ethiopian highlands where the plant originates. The European languages appear to have gotten the name around 1600 from the Turkish kahveh: Dutch koffie, Italian caffè, French and Spanish café, German kaffee, and Danish and Swedish kaffe. A regular cup of coffee has a little more caffeine than an espresso shot. Black tea has less caffeine and green tea has the least. There are two main kinds of coffee beans: Arabica, which accounts for about three-quarters of production, is the main type that comes to the United States. It is grown in high altitudes in tropical and subtropical areas that have plenty of rainfall. Robusta makes up about one-quarter of production and is a stronger-flavored bean. It is grown at lower altitudes, also in tropical and subtropical areas. This varietal is easier to grow and is a heavier producer than the Arabica. Coffees grown at higher altitudes mature more slowly and develop better-flavored oils. The tiny opening on an aluminized heat-sealed bag of coffee beans is a one-way degassing valve. This valve is designed to release carbon dioxide created by the beans so the bag does not inflate, while keeping out oxygen, which will make the coffee beans stale. The first patent in the United States was granted in 1833.

■ Store everyday coffee beans in a cool cupboard in an airtight container for up to two weeks or in the refrigerator for up to one month. The beans can be frozen for up to three months. Preground coffee can be kept for up to two weeks in airtight container in a cool, dry place.

■ Coffee should not be ground in advance because the grinding increases the surface area that is exposed to air, causing the coffee to oxidize more quickly. Also, grinding releases some of the carbon dioxide that is part of the body and bouquet. Packing ground coffee in sealed cans slows coffee's deterioration until the can is opened. Refrigeration slows the oxidative process; freezing slows it even more.

■ Coffee should not be left on the warming plate of a coffeemaker for more than 10–15 minutes. It is best to pour brewed coffee into a preheated, insulated carafe because the flavors start to deteriorate within 10–15 minutes if left on the warmer. Coffee will keep in a thermos almost an hour if the container has been preheated with hot water and drained.

■ The best water for brewing coffee is cold, naturally soft, and free of any water softener residue or odor such as chlorine. Filtered water is best. Instead of buying bottled water, use a filtration pitcher.

■ The different coffee grinds vary from one store to the next, and some stores use numbers, such as 1, 2, or 2½, instead of names. But there are general guidelines for the different coffee grinds. Fine: use for drip or espresso. Medium: use for metal filters. Coarse: used for boiling types or percolators. Extra-fine: used in vacuum types or for Turkish coffee. The finer the grind, the stronger the coffee.

■ Use a dark roast for iced coffee. Brew it for a few hours before serving.

■ If coffee is overcooked, add ½ teaspoon of salt.

■ When you put hot coffee in a cold mug, the mug absorbs the heat, making the coffee cool off faster. Preheat the mug with hot tap water and let it sit while the coffee brews, preparing it for the hot coffee.

■ The flavor compounds in coffee are released at 195°F–200°F. Once water has boiled, coffee enthusiasts let it rest for 10–15 seconds to bring it down to this temperature before using it to make coffee.

■ To test beans for freshness, put ½ cup into a zip-lock bag, press the air out, seal it, and leave it overnight. If the beans are still fresh, the bag will puff from the carbon dioxide they release. If the beans are not producing gas, they are no longer fresh.

■ Coffee beans stored in the refrigerator will pick up off-flavors from the other foods. If you plan on using the beans within twelve days, storing them away from heat and light in the original bag is fine.

■ The proper temperature to brew coffee is 195°F–205°F. The most desirable flavor compounds of coffee are released when the water is heated to this level.

- A standard guideline for brewing coffee is 2 tablespoons of ground beans for every 6 ounces of water. Depending on your taste, you can adjust the amount of ground beans to make the coffee weaker or stronger.

- It is important to clean your coffee pot on a regular basis because a little of the oil in coffee beans is left behind each time you brew a pot of coffee. After a while, the coffee will taste rancid if the oil is not removed.

CAFFEINE'S EFFECTS

Adenosine is the chemical in your brain that makes you sleepy. Adenosine binds to adenosine receptors on nerve cells in the brain. This slows nerve cell activity and causes drowsiness.

1. Caffeine enters your system through a beverage, chocolate, or over-the-counter remedy.

2. The nerve cells in the brain recognize caffeine as adenosine. Caffeine then binds to the adenosine receptors. The nerve cells can no longer detect adenosine because caffeine is taking up all the receptors that adenosine binds to.

3. Caffeine works in the opposite way that adenosine does, by increasing the neuron firing in the brain. The nerve cells also speed up because the adenosine is blocked.

4. The pituitary gland senses this is an emergency situation and releases hormones that tell the adrenal glands to make adrenaline (epinephrine).

5. The pupils dilate, breathing tubes open up, the heart beats faster, blood vessels constrict on the surface, blood pressure rises, blood flow to the stomach slows, and muscles tighten.

6. The liver releases sugar into the bloodstream for extra energy.

COFFEE DRINKS

CAFÉ AU LAIT (COFFEE WITH MILK): Equal parts steamed milk and strong brewed coffee (not espresso), or one-third dark roast coffee and two-thirds scalded milk.

CAFÉ FILTER: Coffee made by pouring hot water through ground coffee beans in a filter, often served black in demitasse cups.

CAFÉ MOCHA: Espresso with chocolate syrup or cocoa powder or steamed chocolate with espresso poured into it, topped with a sprinkle of cocoa.

CAFÉ NOISETTE (FRENCH FOR "HAZELNUT"): Espresso with a little bit of hot milk—the equivalent of the Italian macchiato.

CAFFÈ LATTE OR CAFÉ LATTE (COFFEE-MILK OR LATTE): Espresso poured into steamed milk.

CAFFÈ MACCHIATO OR CAFÉ MACCHIATO: espresso coffee topped (marked) with teaspoons of foamed milk, often with added flavoring like caramel.

(continued)

CAPPUCCINO: Espresso coffee mixed with frothed hot milk or cream, often flavored with cinnamon.

ESPRESSO (PRONOUNCED ES-PRES-OH): strong black coffee made under steam pressure.

FRENCH PRESS: Coffee brewed using a device that separates spent grounds from brewed coffee by pressing them to the bottom of the brewing receptacle with a mesh plunger.

GREEK COFFEE: Very strong coffee served with fine grounds in it.

IRISH COFFEE: Coffee with Irish whiskey and cream.

TURKISH COFFEE: Coffee made from pulverized coffee beans, usually sweetened.

COFFEE OR COFFEE BEAN VARIETIES

There are many complex factors involved in the production of coffee, from the wide variety of conditions—the mountains and valleys, the jungles and plantations and different soils—to the different species and varieties of plants. These, combined with national styles of harvesting, processing, marketing, and transportation, have resulted in a tangle of nomenclature. The more than forty coffee-exporting countries all use different systems of classification for more than a hundred types of coffee. A sampling of coffee varieties is listed here:

AFRICAN	DECAFFEINATED	JAVA
ALTURA	ECUADOR	KAUAI
AMERICAN	EL SALVADOR	KENYAN
ANGOLA	ESPRESSO	KONA
ARABICA	ESTATE	LIBERICA OR LIBERIAN
BLENDED OR BLEND	ETHIOPIA	MALAWI
BLUE JAVA	EXOTIC	MEXICO
BLUE MOUNTAIN	FLAVORED	MOCHA
BRAZILIAN	FRENCH ROAST	MYSORE
BURUNDI	GREEK	OAHU
CAMEROON	GRAND CRUS	OAXACA
CARIBBEAN	GROUND	ORGANIC
CELEBES	GUATEMALA	PANAMA
CHAGGA	HAITI	PUERTO RICO
CHICORY	HAWAIIAN	REUNION
COLOMBIAN	HONDURAS	ROBUSTA
CONTINENTAL ROAST	INDIA	SANTOS
COSTA RICAN	INDONESIAN	SOUTH AMERICAN
CUBA	ITALIAN ROAST	SUMATRA
DARK ROAST	JAMAICAN	TURKISH

COFFEE CAKE or **COFFEECAKE** is a sweet rich bread that may contain spices, nuts, raisins, and fruit and is often iced or glazed. Coffee cake is so called because it was first served with coffee. According to Stuart Berg Flexner in the book *Listening to America*, it wasn't until 1879 that the term coffee cake became a common term.

COFFEE CREAM: see LIGHT CREAM.

COFFEE WHITENER: see NONDAIRY CREAMER.

COGNAC (pronounced KOHN-yak or KON-yak) is brandy distilled from white wine and produced in the vicinity of Cognac, a town in western France. French law limits the use of the name to brandy made from the wine of a specified grape variety, distilled twice in special pot stills, and aged for a prescribed period in Limousin oak. Every step in the production of cognac must take place within seven areas of the Charente and Charente-Maritime departments. Cognac traces its origins to the seventeenth century, when wines of the Charente region were distilled to withstand shipment to distant European ports. Minimum age is indicated by certain words or symbols, as follows: Three Star or VS, two years; VSOP (very superior old pale, an English phrase), four years; Napoleon, five years. When cognac is drunk by itself, as an after-dinner liqueur, it should be served in a small balloon glass, which can be held in the hand, the only means of slightly warming the spirit and releasing the bouquet. The heating of the glass is anathema to anyone who appreciates fine brandy of any kind. Some people, however, prefer to drink cognac quite cool.

COHO SALMON, also called SILVER SALMON or MEDIUM RED SALMON, is a small salmon with light-colored flesh, found in the Pacific and Great Lakes. Its name is an alteration of *cohose*, from Halkomelem, the Salishan language of southwestern British Columbia. Coho salmon adults migrate from a marine environment into the freshwater streams and rivers of their birth in order to mate (anadromy). They spawn only once and then die (semelparity). The flesh of the Coho salmon is light pink and has a very delicate flavor. Coho is a very difficult salmon to keep fresh because of its feeding habits; its flesh tends to soften very quickly unless dressed immediately after being caught.

COINTREAU (pronounced KWAHN-troh) is a colorless, sweet, orange-flavored liqueur named after the Cointreau family, liqueur producers of Angers, France. In addition to being imbibed as an aperitif, Cointreau is sometimes used as a digestif.

COLA refers to an African tree whose seeds/nuts contain a high amount of caffeine and yield an extract; it is also a sweet carbonated beverage flavored with this extract. Cola is from West African *Temne k'ola*, "cola nut." Cola nuts are used to make Coca-Cola and Pepsi-Cola. Rich in caffeine, the cola nut is chewed for its stimulating effects. The caffeine content is similar to that of coffee, but its tonic effect is less harsh and more prolonged.

COLANDER is a perforated bowl or bowl-shaped kitchen strainer used to drain liquid from food after cooking or washing. The word is based on the Latin *colare*, "to strain/sieve."

> **CONFUSABLE** COLANDER/STRAINER. A colander and a strainer both strain, but the colander has larger holes and also has legs so that it can stand up by itself. A strainer must be held by hand or set over a pan. A colander is best for cleaning and draining larger pieces of food.

COLBY is a mild cheese similar to Cheddar but softer and creamier. Colby jack cheese is a combination of Colby and jack cheese. Colby cheese was invented in 1885 by Joseph Steinwand in his father's cheese factory near Colby, Wisconsin. He named it for the township in which his father, Ambrose Steinwand Sr., had built northern Clark County's first cheese factory three years earlier. It is considered to be one of the first truly American cheeses, as it was developed by an American in the United States and it is not intended to be an imitation of a European cheese. Colby cheeses made in an elongated shape or thick half-moon shape are known as Longhorn. Because it is such a mild cheese, Colby is seldom used in cooking. It is used as a table cheese, for grating and grilling, and in snacks and salads.

> **HINT** Colby should not be aged. It is best used shortly after purchase; otherwise, it soon dries out.

COLD CUTS, also known as LUNCHEON MEATS or LUNCH MEAT, are assorted slices of unheated cooked meats, such as bologna, ham, liverwurst, salami, and turkey. Cold cuts are American in origin. Cold cuts may also be known as cooked meats, cold meats, deli meats, sandwich meats, and sliced meats.

COLD SMOKING or **COLD-SMOKING** is adding a smoked flavoring to foods but not during the cooking process, and also curing meat (bacon, fish, ham, sausage) in the smoke of smoldering wood or corncobs at temperatures from 60°F to 100°F. Cold smoking is very difficult, and even impossible in the summer months, because the outside air temperature is normally as hot as or hotter than the temperature needed for true cold smoking. The best time to use cold smoking is during the winter months when the days are typically cooler. Unlike hot smoking, cold smoking can take days or weeks to complete, and it tends to yield drier, saltier foods. The prolonged smoking process yields a complex flavor development, but it also requires careful work to do correctly, as the perfect conditions for cold smoking are also ideal for the promotion of bacterial growth.

COLESLAW, also called SLAW, is a salad of finely shredded raw cabbage and sometimes shredded carrots, dressed with mayonnaise or vinaigrette. The word is from the Dutch *koolsla*, "cabbage salad," but it was called cold slaw in England until the 1860s.

> **HINT** When making coleslaw, mix the vegetables and dressing and refrigerate for at least 1 hour before serving.

COLLARD, COLLARDS, or **COLLARD GREENS** is a variety of kale (*Brassica oleracea acephala*) with a rosette of green leaves; it is eaten as a vegetable called collard greens. Collards take their name from the Anglo-Saxon *coleworts*, "cabbage plants." In the United Kingdom they are known as GREENS or SPRING GREENS. Collard is a variety of cabbage, but it does not have a head; it grows instead in a loose rosette at the top of a tall stem. Collards are among the easiest of all vegetables to grow.

> **HINTS** When purchasing collard greens, look for crisp green leaves with no evidence of yellowing or browning, wilting, or insect damage. Leaves that are smaller in size will be more tender and have a milder flavor.
>
> ▌ Store unwashed collard greens in a damp paper towel in a plastic bag. They should be placed in the vegetable crisper of the refrigerator, where they will keep for three to five days, but the sooner they are eaten, the less bitter they will be.

COLLOP is any small slice of meat, or a fried or grilled slice or piece of meat, such as fried bacon. The word is likely from the Scandinavian *kolhuppadher*, "roasted on coals." There is also an obsolete meaning of egg fried on bacon or fried ham and eggs. Ash Wednesday was preceded not just by Shrove Tuesday, but also by Collop Monday, which was two days before Ash Wednesday and the last day to cook meat before Lent. On Collop Monday slices of meat were used up, usually along with eggs for breakfast, before Lent began.

COMBINATION COOKING is simply using two or more methods for cooking a foodstuff. With combination cooking methods (as in a stew or braise), tough pieces of meat or vegetables are first seared (browned with very high heat) and then simmered in liquid. Searing gives a good flavor and brown color to the outside, then slow-cooking in liquid gives more flavor and softens the inside.

COMBINATION OVENS are either microwave with convection or halogen with microwave, to combine the speed of microwave with either the even cooking of convection baking or the oven-quality browning and crisping of light waves. Convection uses a fan to circulate hot air through the oven, enabling the food to cook faster and more evenly. Halogen light waves can cook food four times faster than a conventional oven.

COMMON CUMIN: see CUMIN.

COMPOSED SALAD is a salad in which the components are elaborately put together or arranged, rather than tossed; the goal is a more formal, elegant-looking salad. A successful composed salad should have a balance of colors, flavors, and textures. In addition to general appearance and taste, color is an important aspect of a composed salad. The colors generally complement each other, and they may be arranged in layers or concentric rings in some salads. Cooks should not forget the impact of the dressing on the color of the salad.

COMPOTE is fruit cooked in sugar or syrup as a hot or cold dessert; the word is from the French for "mixture." Compote is also the word for a long-stemmed dish used for holding fruit, nuts, or candy.

> **HINT** Compote does not keep as long as jam. Slow cooking is important because it helps the fruit retain its shape.

COMPOUND BUTTER, also called BEURRE COMPOSÉ, FINISHING BUTTER, or FLAVORING BUTTER, is a chilled mixture of whole butter and flavoring ingredients, such as herbs, that is used to flavor and color dishes.

> **HINTS** To make compound butter, allow butter to soften at room temperature and then stir in the ingredients. Put the finished butter back into the refrigerator to cool (some cooks make it into a log or block for easy slicing). As a general rule, the compound butter should be used within a few days, or frozen for up to a month.
>
> When using cooked ingredients such as roasted garlic in compound butter, allow them to cool completely. Mixing warm ingredients into the butter could cause it to separate, rendering the compound butter useless.

CONCENTRATE denotes a substance made by removing or reducing the diluting agent; it also refers to a liquid that has been made denser, as by the removal of some of its water. A familiar example is orange juice concentrate.

CONCORD GRAPE is a variety of bluish black sweet grape (*Vitis labrusca*) from the eastern United States, named for Concord, Massachusetts. It is used in grape juice, wine, jelly, and jam. In 1849 in Concord, Ephraim Wales Bull achieved his goal of developing the "perfect" sweet and palatable grape: the Concord. In 1853 Bull felt ready to put the first bunches of his Concord grapes before the public—and won first prize at the Boston Horticultural Society exhibition. In 1869 Dr. Thomas Bramwell Welch, a physician and dentist by profession, successfully pasteurized Concord grape juice to produce an "unfermented sacramental wine" for fellow parishioners at his church in Vineland, New Jersey, where he was communion steward. His achievement marks the beginning of the processed fruit juice industry.

CONDENSED MILK, also called sweetened condensed milk, is whole cow's milk thickened by evaporation and then sweetened. According to the writings of Marco Polo, the Tartars were able to condense milk. Gail Borden (1801–1874), American dairyman and inventor, came up with the idea during a transatlantic trip on board a ship in 1852, when the cows in the hold became too seasick to be milked during the long trip. He was granted a patent for sweetened condensed milk in 1856. Condensed milk was very popular during World War II because of how well it kept.

> **CONFUSABLE** CONDENSED MILK/EVAPORATED MILK/SWEETENED CONDENSED MILK. Evaporated milk undergoes a more complex process than condensed milk and it is not sweetened. Sweetened condensed milk is whole milk from which about 60% of the water has been removed. This condensed milk is then mixed with sugar, which makes up about 40% of its volume. Sugar helps to fight bacteria, making condensed milk particularly shelf-stable.

> **HINT** Store unopened condensed milk at room temperature for up to six months. Once opened, transfer the unused milk to an airtight container, refrigerate, and use within five days.

CONDIMENT is a broad term for a preparation, such as an herb, relish, sauce, or spice, used to enhance the flavor of a dish. Condiment is from the Latin *condimentum*, from *condire*, "to pickle/preserve."

CONDIMENTS

Condiments are food substances used to heighten the natural flavor of foods, stimulate the appetite, aid digestion, or preserve certain foods. The use of condiments is as ancient as cookery itself. Condiments were first used as a means of preserving and were mainly of vegetable origin. In the United States large quantities of bottled sauces and condiments are used to accompany salads, meats, and vegetables. Some popular condiments are listed here.

AIOLI	BÉARNAISE SAUCE	CAPER
ANCHOVY	BLACK PEPPER	CHEESE
ANGOSTURA BITTERS	BREAD-AND-BUTTER PICKLE	CHEESE DIP
ASPIC		CHILI SAUCE
BARBECUE SAUCE	BUTTER	CHOCOLATE

(continued)

CHUTNEY	LEMON	SALSA
CLAM DIP	LEMON CURD	SALT
CORNICHON	LEMON PEEL	SASHIMI
CRANBERRY SAUCE	LIME	SAUCE
CREAM CHEESE	MAPLE SYRUP	SEASONING
DILL PICKLE	MARINADE	SHALLOT
DIP	MARMALADE	SOUR CREAM
DRESSING	MAYONNAISE	SOY SAUCE
DUCK SAUCE	MINT SAUCE	SPICE
GHERKIN	MUSTARD	STEAK SAUCE
GUACAMOLE	ONION	STUFFING
HERB	PEPPER	SUGAR
HOISIN SAUCE	PEPPER SAUCE	SWEET PICKLE
HONEY	PICANTE SAUCE	TABASCO
HORSERADISH	PICKLE	TACO SAUCE
HOT PEPPER	PIMIENTO	TAHINI
JALAPEÑO PEPPER	PRESERVES	TARTAR SAUCE
JAM	RADISH	VINEGAR
JELLY	RELISH	WORCESTERSHIRE SAUCE
KETCHUP OR CATSUP	RÉMOULADE	ZEST
LEEK	SALAD DRESSING	

CONFECTION is a broad term for a sweet dish or a food rich in sugar. The term chocolate confectionery refers to chocolates, sugar confectionery to the various sugar-based products, and flour confectionery to such products as cakes and pastries. Confectionery items include candy bars, chocolate, cotton candy, lollipops, and other sweet snack foods.

CONFECTIONERS' SUGAR or CONFECTIONER'S SUGAR, also called
ICING SUGAR or POWDERED SUGAR, is finely ground and sifted sugar with added cornstarch. Confectioners' sugar must generally be sifted before using. It is the fastest-dissolving sugar. Confectioners' sugar labels have an X designation, which refers to the fineness of the sugar particles. The range goes from 4X (large particles) to 10X (the finest; ground ten times); the latter is the type commonly found in supermarkets. The different types can be used interchangeably.

> **HINTS** Store confectioners' sugar in an airtight container at room temperature indefinitely; it will absorb moisture from the surrounding area if left unprotected.

> Never sprinkle confectioners' sugar over a moist cake, pudding, or other dessert until just before serving. The moisture will liquefy the sugar and turn it an unappealing pale gray color.

CONFIT (pronounced kon-FEE) has two culinary definitions: a meat, such as duck, goose, or pork, that has been salted and then cooked slowly and preserved in its own solidified fat; and a jamlike condiment made by cooking seasoned fruit or vegetables in sugar and alcohol or vinegar. The meat version is derived from an ancient method of preserving meat in which the confit was packed into crocks and sealed with more fat. The word is from French the *confire*, "preserve." Confit is one of the oldest forms of preserving food. The long life of confit, the fact that it can be eaten hot or cold, and its delicate flavor make it a very practical way of preparing food.

> **HINT** Once preserved, confit is good for six months if kept stored in an air-tight container in the refrigerator. Because the preparation method also creates a salty taste, it is wise to serve confit with something sweet or sour in taste.

CONFITURE, also called CONSERVE, JAM, or PRESERVE, is fruit preserved or candied in sugar.

CONGEE is a Chinese rice soup or gruel, usually served at breakfast; it can be sweet or savory. The word's origin is the Tamil *kañci*.

> **HINTS** Congee can be made in a rice cooker. Some rice cookers even have a congee setting, allowing users to cook their breakfast congee overnight.

> When you make congee, it is better to use too much water than too little. Also, the longer congee cooks, the more powerful it becomes.

CONSERVE is jam or marmalade made of fruits stewed in sugar.

> **HINTS** When making conserve at home, make sure to cook it until it becomes thick. If you are adding nuts, add them during the last 5 minutes of cooking.

> Fruit for conserve should always be as freshly picked as possible and slightly underripe, because it is at this stage that the fruit contains the highest amount of pectin, which occurs naturally in fruit. When pectin is cooked with sugar and the naturally occurring acid in the fruit, it thickens and sets the conserve. High-pectin fruits include apples, citrus fruits, blackberries, quinces, red currants, plums, and cranberries. If you are making conserve with fruits low in pectin, then fruits with a higher level need to be added. Alternatively, a few squeezes of lemon juice will help low-pectin fruits to set.

CONSOMMÉ is a clear soup made with concentrated stock. The word is from French and literally means "something consummated"—in this case, by boiling down meat or vegetables so that the flavors become completely concentrated. Consommé is made in two steps—first the broth, then the clarification. Clarification is the process that removes all the traces of small and bigger particles floating in the soup, resulting in a perfectly clear consommé.

> **HINTS** Consommé can be served hot or cold as a soup course. Cold consommés are normally placed in the refrigerator for 1–2 hours before serving.

▌ A double consommé has been reduced until it is half the volume and twice the flavor of regular or single consommé. This takes a little longer to prepare, but many gourmets find the experience well worth it.

CONTINENTAL BREAKFAST describes a light breakfast made up of coffee or tea and a roll, pastry, or other baked good. The term came into use because this is the type of breakfast eaten on the European continent, especially in France.

CONTINENTAL CHOCOLATE: see DARK CHOCOLATE.

CONTREFILET: see NEW YORK STEAK.

CONVECTION OVEN is a kitchen appliance that heats/cooks food by the circulation of hot air with a fan, so that food cooks faster and more uniformly than in a conventional oven.

> **HINT** To convert conventional oven recipes for a convection oven, put the convection oven 25°F lower and expect the food to be done in 25% less time.

CONVERTED RICE is white rice prepared from brown rice by soaking, steam pressure, drying, and milling. The steam pressure forces water-soluble nutrients into the starchy endosperm. The method began as a trademark in the United States. Converted rice is a good compromise between nutritious brown rice and tender, fast-cooking white rice. When cooked, the grains are more nutritious, firmer, and less clingy than white rice grains. Converted rice takes a little longer to cook than regular rice, but the grains will be very fluffy and separate after they have been cooked.

COOK (COOKING) as a verb generally means to transform a foodstuff and make it suitable for consumption by heating; as a noun, a cook is someone who cooks food. The Old English version, *coc*, came from the Latin *cocus*, "cook," from *coquere*, "to cook/prepare food/ripen/digest/turn over in the mind," from a Proto-Indo-European base *pekw-*, "to cook." The noun was first; the verb was first recorded around 1380.

> **HINTS** When cooking from a recipe, prepare the ingredients according to the ingredient list before going on to the method. That means chopping, slicing, or measuring ingredients. Taste dishes as you cook and adjust the seasonings. Clean up as you go. Keep a garbage bowl for peelings and trimmings and empty it when you are all done.

▌ You should write in your cookbooks—noting the recipes you have used and the ingredients and procedures you have changed.

▌ To avoid splattering your cookbooks with food when using them to cook, tape together two clear page protector sheets (these can be purchased at any office supply store) and place this over your cookbook. The protective cover can be easily cleaned and reused. If you get liquid on cookbook pages, blot it dry with paper towels and slip a piece of wax paper between the pages before closing the book.

COOKING METHODS

Many foods must be cooked before they can be eaten. When food is heated, chemical changes take place that improve its taste and make it easier to digest. Early people ate raw food until they discovered cooking, probably by accident. These are some commonly used cooking methods:

BAKE	FRICASSEE	SAUTÉ
BARBECUE	FRY	SCALLOP
BASTE	GRIDDLE	SCRAMBLE
BLANCH	GRILL	SEAR
BOIL	HEAT	SHIRR
BRAISE	MARINATE	SIMMER
BREW	MICROWAVE	SLOW-COOK
BROAST	OVEN-ROAST	SMOKE
BROIL	PAN-BROIL	SPIT-ROAST
BROWN	PAN-FRY	STEAM
CARAMELIZE	PARBOIL	STEW
CASSEROLE	PICKLE	STIR-FRY
CHARBROIL	POACH	SWEAT
CODDLE	POT-ROAST	TANDOORI
CURE	PRECOOK	TENDERIZE
CURRY	PRESSURE-COOK	THICKEN
DEEP-FRY	REDUCE	TOAST
DEVIL	REHEAT	
FIRE	ROAST	

TYPES OF COOKS AND FOOD SERVERS

BAKER	DISHWASHER	SCULLERY MAID
BARKEEPER	HEADWAITER	SERVER
BARMAID	HOST	SHORT-ORDER COOK
BARMAN	HOSTESS	SODA JERK
BARTENDER	INNKEEPER	SOMMELIER
BUSBOY	KITCHEN MAID	SOUS-CHEF
CARHOP	MAÎTRE D'HÔTEL OR MAÎTRE D'	STEWARD
CATERER		WAITER
CHEF	PASTRY CHEF	WAITPERSON
CHEF DE CUISINE	PASTRY COOK	WAITRESS
CHIEF COOK	PREP COOK	WAITRON
CONFECTIONER	PUBLICAN	WINE STEWARD
COOK	RESTAURATEUR	

COOKIE denotes a small, sweet cake, usually flat and either crisp or chewy, with many variations. In the United Kingdom and Australia, this item is called a biscuit, but only for a flat version; anything raised has now become cookie or cake in those countries. The word was introduced into the United States in the late eighteenth century by Dutch immigrants and derives from the Dutch *koekje*, a diminutive form of *koek*, "cake." A stiff, sweet dough is usually rolled and sliced or dropped by spoonfuls onto a baking sheet. The earliest cookie-style foods are thought to date back to the seventh century AD in Persia (now Iran), one of the first countries to cultivate sugar. Toll House cookies, created around 1930 by Ruth Wakefield, were the first chocolate chip cookies. The Trefoil was the first official Girl Scout cookie, introduced in 1932.

COOKIE ESSENTIALS

- Set the timer for the least amount of time if a range is given in a cookie recipe.

- If baking more than one sheet of cookies at a time, switch the baking sheets (rotate) halfway through the baking time.

- Line the pan with foil to ease removal of bar cookies.

- Cookie dough can be refrigerated for up to 24 hours before cooking (but not bar cookie dough). Many cookie doughs can be frozen, especially those that are rolled for slicing.

- Baked cookies can be frozen for up to three months when wrapped snugly. Most will defrost within two hours.

- Bake cookies on cool, dry days or chill the dough before rolling out.

- Remove cookies from the baking sheet 2–3 minutes after removing from the oven, to avoid sticking.

- Soft cookies should be kept in an airtight container with half an apple or a slice of bread, changing the half apple or slice of bread regularly.

- You can avoid overbaking cookies by taking the pan out of the oven a few minutes before they are done, since the hot pan will continue to bake them.

- You can store crisp cookies by placing them in a container with a loose cover.

- Shape cookie dough between your palms like meatballs, then use the bottom of a drinking glass that is buttered and sugared to flatten the balls.

- Between cookie batches, you should let baking sheets cool completely. Succeeding batches can be prepared on parchment paper, which can then be moved to a cooled baking sheet.

- To remove stuck cookies, put the baking sheet on a hot, moist towel or over a large pan of simmering water. Spraying nonstick cooking spray on the spatula helps, too.

- Frost bar cookies with chocolate by placing chocolate bars on top of the hot cookies; when the chocolate is softened, spread it on the cookies.

- To avoid dark spots on the bottom of cookies, loosen them from the baking sheet using a metal spatula about halfway through the baking, allowing heat to be distributed evenly at the top and bottom.

- Flour the edges of cookie cutters to prevent the dough from sticking.

The cookie started out as a staple food of soldiers, sailors, and explorers. The industrial manufacture of cookies began in Britain with the Carr establishment in 1815. Today, there are a multitude of popular cookies.

ANIMAL CRACKER	GINGERSNAP	PEANUT BUTTER COOKIE
BAR COOKIE	GRAHAM CRACKER	PETIT BEURRE
BISCOTTI	HARDTACK	PRETZEL
BISCUIT	HERMIT	RATAFIA
BRANDY SNAP	JUMBLE	SHORTBREAD OR SHORTCAKE
BROWNIE	LADYFINGER	SPRITZ
BUTTER	MACAROON	SUGAR COOKIE
CHOCOLATE CHIP COOKIE	MADELEINE	TOLL HOUSE
FIG BAR	OATCAKE	TUILE
FLORENTINE	OATMEAL COOKIE	WAFER
FORTUNE COOKIE	OATMEAL-RAISIN COOKIE	
GARIBALDI	PALM LEAF	
GINGERBREAD MAN	PANETTONE	

COOKIE SHEET, also called BAKING SHEET, is a flat, usually rectangular, metallic sheet with at least one rolled-up end, used for baking food such as cookies in an oven. The darker the cookie sheet, the faster the cookies will brown because a dark cookie sheet absorbs heat more readily and transfers the heat directly to the cookies. Aluminum cookie sheets are good conductors of heat but are not good for ensuring that the cookies will brown. Insulated cookie sheets will ensure evenly baked cookies no matter how they are spaced on the sheet

> **HINT** If you're baking successive batches of cookies and using the same cookie sheet, always let it cool to room temperature before putting more dough on it. Quick-cool the sheet by running cold water over it. Otherwise, the cookie dough can begin to melt and spread, which will affect the cookies' final shape and texture. Using a hot cookie sheet can also cause the cookie bottoms to brown before the inside is done.

COOKING BANANA: see PLANTAIN.

COOKING OIL is any of various vegetable oils used in cooking. The oil, a purified fat that is liquid at room temperature, is usually extracted from the kernel or nut of the plant. Common types include canola oil, corn oil, grapeseed oil, olive oil, palm oil, peanut oil, safflower oil, sesame oil, soybean oil, and sunflower oil. The oils with the least saturated fat are canola (6%), grapeseed (7%), and safflower (9%). Oil and fats with high levels of saturated fat include olive oil (14%), shortening (26%), and butter (54%).

Sesame and olive oils have the oldest origins, having been used by both the ancient Egyptians and the ancient Greeks. Oils provide the fatty medium for many cooking methods; are an ingredient in dressings, sauces, and condiments; and are used to pre-serve, moisten, and flavor foods. Fats are also used as a cooking medium for frying and roasting, for basting during grilling, for moistening ingredients and mixtures, and as dressings and sauces. Fats make starches and dry ingredients taste better and also improve or enhance the flavor of many foods, either raw (bread spread with butter) or cooked (potatoes fried in oil). There are many types of oils and fats used in cooking:

ALMOND OIL	GRAPESEED OIL	RICE BRAN OIL
AVOCADO OIL	HAZELNUT OIL	SAFFLOWER OIL
BACON FAT	LARD	SCHMALTZ
BUTTER	MARGARINE OR OLEOMARGARINE	SESAME OIL
CANOLA OIL		SHORTENING
CHICKEN FAT	OLIVE OIL	SOLID VEGETABLE SHORTENING
COCOA BUTTER	PALM OIL	
COCONUT OIL	PARTIALLY HYDROGENATED VEGETABLE OIL	SOYBEAN OIL OR SOYA OIL
CORN OIL	PEANUT OIL	SUET
COTTONSEED OIL	POPPY SEED OIL	SUNFLOWER SEED OIL
DRIPPINGS	PUMPKIN OIL	VEGETABLE OIL
EXTRA-VIRGIN OLIVE OIL	RAPESEED OIL	VIRGIN OLIVE OIL
GHEE	RENDERED CHICKEN FAT	WALNUT OIL
GOOSE GREASE		WHEAT GERM OIL

COOKING WINE is any inexpensive grape or rice wine used for cooking rather than drinking; some wines are especially made for this purpose, often with salt added. The salt in cooking wine inhibits the growth of acetic acid–producing micro-organisms. Most professional chefs prefer to use inexpensive but drinkable wine for cooking. The function of wine in cooking is to intensify, enhance, and accent the flavor and aroma of food—not to mask the flavor of what you are cooking but rather to fortify it. As with any seasoning used in cooking, care should be taken in the amount of wine used; too little is inconsequential and too much will be overpower-ing. During cooking, most of the alcohol in wine evaporates, leaving only the flavor behind. The exposure to the alcohol is greatly diminished.

HINTS Never cook with a wine you would not drink, and be sure the wine's flavor complements the food with which it is paired. The flavor of the wine in a dish should be subtle and never overpower the central essence.

If you want a nice, rich wine flavor without a lot of liquid, boil 1 cup of wine until it's reduced by half or two-thirds. Wine should be reduced slowly over low heat. This method takes more time and effort, but will achieve a superior sauce because the flavor compounds present in the wine are better preserved.

For best results, wine should not be added to a dish just before serving. If added late in the preparation, it could impart a harsh quality. Wine should simmer with the food or in the sauce while it is being cooked; as the wine cooks, it reduces and becomes an extract that enhances the flavor of the dish. A wine needs time to impart its flavor, so wait 10 minutes or more to taste a dish before adding more wine.

COOK'S KNIFE: see CHEF'S KNIFE.

COOK'S SPOON: see SLOTTED SPOON.

COOKWARE is a general term for any pot, pan, or dish in which food can be cooked.

> **HINT** Coat cookware with cooking spray to prevent stains, especially from acidic ingredients.

COOLER is an iced drink usually consisting of white wine, fruit juice, and soda water, though it can also refer to other chilled drinks like iced coffee. The word also denotes a compartment or container in which something is cooled or kept cool, especially any portable insulated container.

COOLING RACK is a flat grid of closely spaced wires with formed feet, used for cooling baked goods. A cooling rack can be used as a drainer when set over a sink. Blanched vegetables can also be cooled quickly on such a rack.

COPPER is a ductile, malleable, reddish brown, corrosion-resistant metallic element, the only metal that occurs abundantly in large masses as well as within various minerals. Of all metals used for cooking, copper offers the most even and the quickest cooking.

> **HINT** To remove tarnish from copper cookware, use a paper towel to coat the tarnished area with a layer of ketchup. Wipe off and rinse after 5 minutes.

COQ AU VIN (pronounced coke-aw-VAN) is a dish of chicken, onions, and mushrooms braised in red wine and seasonings. The term is French for "cock in wine." Coq au vin is considered a French comfort food. The traditional recipe for coq au vin did not include chicken, but rather a coq, which is a rooster. Many recipes originally called for old barnyard fowl, roosters, capon (a castrated rooster), and old laying hens. Coq au vin was originally considered peasant food, and the farmers would make do with what they had on hand.

COQUILLE is French for "scallop/shell" and a dish made en coquille is a seafood or chicken dish served in a scallop shell, or served in a shell-shaped dish. The word coquille is also used for a shell-shaped serving dish or casserole.

CORDIAL is any of various strong, highly flavored, sweet liqueurs or liquors usually drunk after a meal. Fruits, flowers, herbs, seeds, roots, plants, or juices with sweetener are used to create cordials. Most cordials are colorful and concentrated in consistency. Cordials are supposed to have a tonic effect, as the etymology of the word suggests (from the Latin *cor*, "heart").

CORDON BLEU (pronounced kor-dohn-BLUH), literally meaning "blue ribbon," is used to describe a master chef or a cook or cooking of the highest class. The blue ribbon once signified the highest order of chivalry during the reign of the Bourbon kings. The Cordon Bleu cooking school in Paris was established in 1895 and the Grand Diplome of the school is the highest credential a chef can have. The term also refers to a dish, chicken or veal cordon bleu, in which a thin scallop of veal or chicken is topped with a thin slice each of prosciutto or other ham and Gruyère or other Swiss cheese, then another meat scallop. The stacked meats and cheese are then breaded and sautéed until golden.

CORE is the center of an object, as in a fruit like an apple or pear that contains the pips or central membrane, and in cooking to core is to remove the core of a foodstuff. This is done with a knife or a special tool called a corer.

CORIANDER is an Old World herb resembling parsley whose leaves and seeds are used for garnish or seasoning; the word is derived from Greek. The seeds of this plant are called coriander; the leaves are called CILANTRO. The flavors of the seeds and the leaves bear no resemblance to each other. The tiny seeds have an aromatic flavor somewhat like a combination of lemon, sage, and, caraway. Whole coriander seeds are used in pickling and for special drinks, such as mulled wine. Ground coriander seeds are also called CUMIN. Coriander is the oldest known herb, dating back to about 5000 BC.

CORKSCREW is a device for pulling corks out of bottles, usually made of a spiral-shaped piece of steel with a point at one end and a handle on the other. The spiral must be 2¼–3½ inches long so that the cork, which is quite long in a good bottle, is pierced all the way through. The type of corkscrew most often used in restaurants is also called a WAITER'S FRIEND. It is very useful because it folds up and fits in a pocket without any sharp or pointed ends showing; an arm extends to brace against the lip of the bottle for leverage when removing the cork. Some corkscrews have two steps on the lever, and often also a bottle opener. A small hinged knife blade is housed in the handle end for removing the foil that wraps the neck of many wine bottles.

> **HINT** If you have a cork in a wine bottle that is crumbly and in danger of breaking, it is recommended that you use a type of corkscrew that operates with two blades of unequal length, which are inserted between the

neck and the cork so you do not have to pierce the cork while you pull the cork up.

CORN, also called MAIZE, is an important North American cereal plant, a tall-growing plant (*Zea mays*) bearing long ears (cobs) of kernels. In the United Kingdom the term corn normally refers to wheat, in North America to maize, and in Scandinavia to barley. The word corn came through Germanic languages from the Indo-European *grnóm*, "worn-down particle." The grain that Americans call corn was originally known to the British as maize or Indian corn. The word corn is also used in different parts of the United Kingdom for whatever is the most important grain of the region; only in the United States did it come to refer exclusively to maize.

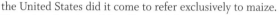

The original notion of "small particle" survives in the term corned, as in corned beef, where corned refers to the grains of salt used for preserving the meat. The word maize was the Taino name used in the West Indies. Generally, white corn is more tender and more subtly flavored; yellow, fuller flavored and more robust. White corn usually comes on the market in the first part of the season.

CORN ESSENTIALS

- Choose ears of corn with green husks with no browning or drying. The silk should be pale yellow and moist. If possible, don't buy prehusked ears of corn, for they lose quality quickly. Fresh sweet corn should be kept in its husks in the refrigerator or a cooler for no more than a few days.

- You can remove corn silk with a vegetable brush under cold running water. Alternatively rub the ear with a slightly moistened paper towel, or rub it with your hand under running water.

- Corn can be cooked without removing the husk. This results in steaming instead of boiling, which yields sweeter corn. The corn also retains the heat until serving but is somewhat messy at the table. Cook in the microwave with the husks on; when finished, dehusk the corn and remove the corn silk with a paper towel.

- To microwave corn without the husks, remove the silk, wash the cobs but don't dry them, and loosely wrap in wax paper. The amount of time will vary with the power of the oven and the number of ears being cooked together.

- Stand an ear or half ear of corn on end and then use a sharp knife to cut the kernels off onto a plate.

- To grill corn, remove all but the innermost layer of husk, snip off the tassel, and grill. When the husk picks up the dark silhouette of kernels, it is ready.

- Cut corn on the cob into chunks, run a corkscrew through each, then put on a skewer to grill the corn.

CORN VARIETIES

Corn (or maize) is a cereal with white, yellow, red, blue, pink, black, or rust-colored grains attached to a cob and protected by layers of fibrous leaves with tasseled tops. It originated in North America and was discovered by Christopher Columbus. The inedible parts of the corn plant are used in industry. Stalks are made into paper and wallboard; husks are used as filling material; cobs are used for fuel, for making charcoal, and in the preparation of industrial solvents. These are many words used to describe the varieties of corn:

BABY	GRAIN MAIZE	SQUAW
BLUE	GREEN	SUGAR
DENT	HULLED	SWEET
EDIBLE	INDIAN	WHITE
FIELD	MAIZE	YANKEE
FLINT	POPCORN	YELLOW
FLOUR	SOFT	

CORN BREAD or **CORNBREAD** is any bread made wholly or partly of cornmeal; cornmeal is corn (maize) ground to the consistency of fine granules. Corn bread is especially associated with the cuisine of the southern U.S. states. Because corn lacks elastic gluten, it cannot be raised with yeast; consequently, most corn breads are leavened with baking powder or baked unleavened, even when made partly of wheat flour. The term was first recorded in English in 1775.

> **HINTS** For crispy side and bottom crusts on corn bread, put 1 to 2 tablespoons of vegetable oil or bacon drippings in an 8- or 9-inch square pan, tilting the pan so the oil coats the sides and bottom. Place the pan in a preheated 400°F oven for 10 minutes. Remove the pan from the oven and immediately fill with corn bread batter (it will sizzle); bake as usual. Also, a dark pan will make crustier corn bread than a light pan. For the crustiest corn bread, use a skillet.

> For slightly sweet corn bread, add 2 tablespoons of brown sugar and ¼ teaspoon of ground nutmeg to the dry ingredients.

> Corn bread does not keep well. It is best used on the day it is baked. Store leftovers wrapped in plastic wrap and then foil and place in the refrigerator. Corn bread can be frozen for six weeks.

CORN DODGER: see HUSH PUPPY.

CORN DOG or **CORNY DOG**, also called DAGWOOD DOG, PLUTO PUP, or POGO, is a hot dog (frankfurter) covered in cornmeal batter that is deep-fried or baked and served on a stick; it is an American invention dating to around 1939. The corn dog has its own holiday. National Corndog Day is a celebration of basketball, the corn dog, Tater Tots, and beer that occurs every March on the first Saturday of the NCAA Men's Division I Basketball Championship.

CORNED BEEF is beef brisket that has been cooked, preserved in salt or brine, and often canned. It contains no corn, but gets its name from corn's sense of "particle/granule," from the particles of salt that permeate the beef as it soaks in brine. The dish is of British origin, dating to around 1881.

CORNET (from Latin meaning "cone") is a cone-shaped pastry shell that is often filled with whipped cream. Cornet is also the word in the United Kingdom for an ice-cream cone, and for a slice of ham or salmon rolled up, filled with a cold preparation, and served as an hors d'oeuvre. A cornet is also the name for a small piping bag made from parchment paper, usually used to make fine decorations.

> **HINT** To close a cornet once it has been filled, fold it away from the seam; this will keep the seam from opening. Use a pair of scissors or a sharp knife to cut an opening at the tip of the cornet to the desired size.

CORNICHON, also called GHERKIN, is a tiny, tart pickled cucumber. Cornichons are a traditional accompaniment to pâtés, as well as smoked meats and fish.

> **HINT** If you are making cornichons yourself, try to use very small cornichons that were processed the same day they were harvested, whether you have grown them yourself or are lucky enough to have found them in a produce market or farmers' market. Their thin skins make them quite perishable.

CORNMEAL is maize ground to the consistency of fine granules, or any meal ground from dried corn. (However, in other countries, such as Scotland, it is meal made from some other grain, such as oats.) The corn used can be yellow, white, or blue and fine, medium, or coarse in texture. Corn can be ground by millstones or steel rollers and with or without the germ and husk. There is no difference in taste or usage between white and yellow cornmeal, though yellow has more vitamin A. Stone-ground cornmeal contains the germ, has more nutrients, and has a nutty flavor.

> **HINT** Stone-ground cornmeal must be stored in the refrigerator (it can be stored for up to four months). Degerminated cornmeal can be kept in an airtight container at cool room temperature for up to a year.

CORN OIL is an almost tasteless oil extracted from the germ of the corn kernel. Corn oil is excellent for cooking because it can withstand high temperatures without smoking and is high in polyunsaturated fat. For health reasons, corn oil has replaced a significant amount of saturated fat and is also a top choice for transfat reduction in numerous food products. Corn oil contains very little cholesterol. Its fatty acid content is 13% saturated, 62% polyunsaturated, and 25% monounsaturated.

CORN PONE or **CORN CAKE** is a plain, simple oval loaf of corn bread, often without eggs or milk; pone is from a Native American word for "bread." The bread may be fried or baked on a griddle like a pancake.

CORN SALAD, also called FELDSALAT, FIELD LETTUCE, FIELD SALAD, LAMB'S LETTUCE, LAMB'S TONGUE, or MÂCHE, is a name given to several annual herbs (genus *Valerianella*) whose edible young leaves are used in salads or as a potherb. It is considered a gourmet green and is expensive and hard to find.

> **HINTS** Corn salad must be carefully washed and dried, leaf by leaf, before it is eaten. The best way to dry it is to pat it dry by hand gently. You can also dry it gently in a salad spinner.
>
> ▌ To store corn salad, wrap it in plastic wrap and place it in the vegetable crisper of the refrigerator; it should remain fresh for two to three days.

CORNSTARCH is a fine, dense, white, powdery thickener made from corn and used in foods like pudding, as well as in making corn syrup and sugars. Cornstarch has nearly twice the thickening power of flour.

> **HINTS** You can keep cornstarch in its original package in a cool, dry cupboard for up to a year after the sell-by date, but if you live in a humid climate, you should also enclose it in a plastic bag.
>
> ▌ Cornstarch should be whisked with water (1 part cornstarch, 3 parts liquid) to make a slurry before adding it to a gently cooking dish.
>
> ▌ Cornstarch will actually thin a dish when there is too much heat, vigorous stirring, or a too-long cooking time.

CORN SYRUP is a thick syrup made from cornstarch and containing dextrins, dextrose, and maltose. It is produced when starch granules from corn are processed with acids or enzymes and varies in color from clear white to amber. Light corn syrup is clarified to remove any color and cloudiness; dark corn syrup is more strongly flavored and has coloring and caramel flavoring added. Corn syrup does not crystallize when heated, which is very desirable for candy making.

> **HINTS** Unopened, corn syrup can stay in a cool, dark cupboard for up to six months after the sell-by date. Opened, it can keep for up to six months.
>
> ▌ Light corn syrup can be used in place of dark corn syrup, honey, or granulated sugar (but not for baking). Dark can be used in place of light, but it will add too much flavor to some dishes calling for light. Dark can be substituted for molasses, though it is not as sweet.

CORTLAND is a large, dark red, cultivated variety of apple, originally grown in Cortland County in New York.

HINT Good-quality Cortland apples will be firm with smooth, clean skin and have good color for the variety, which is mostly red with some yellow blush and occasional green streaks. Test the firmness of the apple by holding it in the palm of your hand. (Do not push with your thumb.) The apple should feel solid and heavy, not soft and light. Avoid apples with soft or dark spots. Also, if the apple skin wrinkles when you rub your thumb across it, the apple has probably been in cold storage too long or has not been kept cool. To store, keep apples as cold as possible in the refrigerator. Apples do not freeze until the temperature drops to 28.5°F. Cortland apples are wonderful for kebabs, fruit plates, and garnishes because they don't turn brown quickly when cut.

COS or **COS LETTUCE**, also called ROMAINE, is lettuce with long, narrow leaves in a loosely packed, elongated head. Cos lettuce is named for the Aegean island of Cos/Kos, where it originated, and is the more common term in the United Kingdom.

HINTS Avoid heads of cos lettuce with any signs of rust; avoid oversized butt ends; avoid older plants with large, strong, milky ribs. Choose heads that are cut close to leaf stems and are free from decay and browning.

‖ Store cos lettuce at a temperature around 33°F–35°F. Do not allow the temperature to go below 32°F, as this will damage the leaves. Store the unwashed, whole heads in plastic bags to retain natural moisture and keep the leaves crisper. Uncut, whole heads of lettuce retain nutrients best; cos lettuce will keep for seven to ten days this way. Surface water from washing encourages bacterial growth, so do not wash the lettuce before storing. Keep cos lettuce away from apples, as ethylene gas they give off will turn the lettuce brown.

CÔT: see MALBEC.

COTTAGE CHEESE, also called CLABBER CHEESE, CURD CHEESE, DUTCH CHEESE, POT CHEESE, SMEARCASE, or SOUR-MILK CHEESE, or is a soft, white curd cheese made from soured skim milk; it comes in small, medium, and large curd, and is usually mixed with milk or cream. Cottage cheese was supposedly named for its origins in U.S. farm-cottage kitchens and the term originally referred to any spreadable cheese.

HINT Cottage cheese should be stored with the container upside down in the refrigerator.

COTTAGE FRIES, COTTAGE-FRIED POTATOES, or COUNTRY FRIES

is a regional U.S. name for home fries, which are usually thinly sliced potatoes fried in butter or oil.

HINT When making cottage fries with onions, cook the onions separately. As potatoes need to cook quite a bit longer than onions, this prevents them from becoming burnt specks by the time the potatoes are ready.

COTTAGE PIE: see SHEPHERD'S PIE.

COTTON CANDY, also called CANDY FLOSS, CANDYFLOSS, SPUN SUGAR, or SUGAR COTTON WOOL, is a light, very sweet candy made of spun sugar threads, often tinted with food coloring and twirled onto a stick. Its origin is uncertain. New Orleans claims that Josef Delarose Lascauz, a dentist, was the inventor of cotton candy and the cotton candy machine, and that it was first introduced at the 1830 World's Fair. But Thomas Patton received a patent for the cotton candy machine in 1900 and that cotton candy first appeared in 1900 at the Ringling Bros. Circus. The machine used to make cotton candy has a small sugar reservoir bowl into which sugar is poured and food coloring is added. The sugar reservoir bowl is spun at high speed while heaters near the rim melt the sugar, which is squeezed out through tiny holes by centrifugal force. The molten sugar then solidifies in the air and is caught in a large metal bowl surrounding the central sugar reservoir bowl. The operator of the machine twirls a stick, cone, or their hands around the rim of the large catching bowl, gathering the sugar strands into portions. Modern cotton candy machines work in much the same way as older ones.

COULIS (pronounced koo-LEE) is a thin sauce of strained, puréed, raw or cooked vegetables or fruit, used especially as a garnish. Its original meaning was a broth, jelly, or gravy made from the juices of roasted or grilled meat. Coulis is French for "strained sauce, gravy, or broth," from *couleri*, "to flow."

> **HINT** As a general rule, coulis should be used within a few days if it is not going to be frozen.

COUNTRY GRAVY, also called CREAM GRAVY or MILK GRAVY, is a white sauce made from pan drippings, flour, and milk and popularly served with country-fried steak.

> **HINT** Country gravy can be thick to thin, depending on the amount of milk added. If you like a thinner gravy, you can substitute water for milk. When making country gravy, you should continuously stir it because it will burn quickly.

COURGETTE is the British term for ZUCCHINI. It is French for "little gourd."

> **HINT** Courgettes are best eaten fresh or they can be stored for a few days in the refrigerator.

COURT-BOUILLON: see BLANC.

COUSCOUS is from North Africa and is a pasta made of crushed and steamed semolina. Couscous is often served with spicy meat or vegetables. Its name came to English by 1600 from the Arabic *kaskasa*, "to pulverize."

Couscous can be cooked in a special double-tiered pot, a couscousière. Meat, vegetables, and spices cook in the lower tier and the couscous steams in the upper tier.

Couscous can be stored in a cool, dry cupboard for at least three months and keeps indefinitely in the refrigerator.

COUTEAU D'OFFICE: see PARING KNIFE.

COW BEAN or COWPEA: see BLACK-EYED PEA.

COWBERRY: see LINGONBERRY.

CRAB denotes any of various decapods with four pairs of legs, grasping pincers, a flattened shell, and a short, broad abdomen (tail) folded under its thorax. Crabmeat (or crab meat) is the flesh of a crab used as food. Crab cake (or crabcake) is a round patty made from shredded crabmeat and other ingredients, then baked or fried. There are four thousand species of crab, of which four are generally seen in our markets: Dungeness, king, soft-shell, and stone. People on the Atlantic and Gulf coasts prefer the blue crab; Florida, the stone crab; Pacific, Dungeness; and Alaska, king crab and snow crab. Female blue crabs are she-crabs when young and snooks when mature. Male blue crabs are jimmies.

HINTS Like lobsters, crabs must be kept alive until cooking. Live hard-shell crabs should look moist and soft, and should move their claws vigorously when poked. If the claws drop, don't buy it. Properly packed, crabs can be kept in the refrigerator for up to two days. Put the crabs in a shallow bowl, inside a larger one filled with ice. Cover with a damp kitchen towel or with the seaweed that came with them, and replace the ice as needed.

Lump crabmeat is the most desirable as it is the white meat from the center and legs. The advantage of the male crab is the large quantity of white meat in its claws. The advantage of the female crab is its pink coral (roe or eggs).

Fresh-cooked crabmeat keeps in the refrigerator for up to two days. Pasteurized crabmeat in sealed bags keeps for three to four weeks.

Look at the small flap (apron) on the underside of a crab. If it is thin and pointed, the crab is male; a rounded apron indicates a female. Males tend to have more meat.

CRAB MEAT GRADES

CLAW	LUMP OR BACKFIN LUMP
JUMBO LUMP OR LUMP	WHITE

CRAB TYPES

ALASKAN KING/NORWEGIAN	KING	SOFT-SHELL (BLUE CRABS THAT HAVE SHED THEIR HARD SHELL)
BLUE	ROCK	
DUNGENESS	SNOW	STONE

CRAB APPLE or **CRABAPPLE** is the small sour/tart cultivated or wild apple of some trees of the *Malus* genus; it is used to make jelly and preserves.

> HINTS Good-quality crab apples will be very firm, but will not have many of the other hallmarks of other apples. They are often scabbed or misshapen and can vary in color from almost black to red, and even to rich yellow. Test the firmness of the apple by holding it in the palm of your hand. (Do not push with your thumb.) The apple should feel solid and heavy, not soft and light. Avoid crab apples with soft or dark spots. If the skin wrinkles when you rub your thumb across it, the crab apple has probably been in cold storage too long or has not been kept cool.

> To store crab apples, keep them as cold as possible in the refrigerator. Crab apples do not freeze until the temperature drops to 28.5°F.

CRACKED WHEAT is grains of whole wheat that have been crushed or broken roughly into tiny pieces before being used in a food product.

> HINTS Cracked wheat should be stored in a cool, dry place so that it does not go rancid. If not used within one year, cracked wheat should be discarded.

> As with all grains, cracked wheat should be washed before use, to remove residual dirt and other compounds that may have adhered to the wheat during growing, processing, and shipping. The easiest way to do this is to measure the wheat out into a fine-holed colander and run water over it, gently stirring it with a spatula or by hand to make sure that each grain is washed. Soaking the washed cracked wheat will also make it cook more quickly.

CRACKER denotes a thin, crisp wafer made of flour and water with or without leavening and shortening. This is chiefly a U.S. term, dating to 1739. Crackers need holes to be crisp.

CRACKER BREAD: see LAVASH.

CRACKLINGS are the crisp residue left after rendering fat from meat or frying or roasting the skin of a chicken, goose, or pig.

CRANBERRY is the very tart red berry from a low-growing evergreen plant of the heath family. Cranberry was first known as crane berry, and it was so named because the plant grows on a stalk (stamen) that looks like a crane's neck. The fruit is used to make jelly, juice, relish, and sauce. Since a cranberry bounces when it is ripe, it is also called BOUNCEBERRY. Cranberries, blueberries, and Concord grapes are North America's only true native fruits. The cranberry has been cultivated since 1810 in large, sandy bogs in northern North America. The first written recipe that recommended serving cranberries with turkey was in the first American cookbook, *American Cookery*, written by Amelia Simmons and published in 1796.

> **HINT** Cranberries should be plump, firm, and dry. Keep in the refrigerator for up to one month or freeze for ten months.

CRAPPIE

CRAPPIE denotes a small sunfish of central U.S. rivers, including the black crappie and white crappie, which both have protruding spines. Crappies have lean flesh that is particularly suited to broiling or sautéing. Most cooks choose to skin and fillet crappies before cooking.

CRAYFISH, CRAWFISH, or CRAWDAD

CRAYFISH, **CRAWFISH**, or **CRAWDAD**, also called MUDBUG, are tiny, lobsterlike freshwater crustaceans eaten as food, especially in Cajun and Creole cooking. The term is also another name for the SPINY LOBSTER, a type of lobster lacking large pincers and having a spiny shell.

> **HINT** Store live crayfish in the refrigerator, covered with a damp towel for one to two days. Frozen crayfish can be kept for up to three months. Cooked crayfish will keep in the refrigerator for up to three days.

CREAM

CREAM is a high-fat liquid product separated from milk: it is the liquid that rises to the top when fresh milk is left to stand. Creams vary according to the amount of butterfat they have (see Cream by Fat Content on page 164). Lightest of all is half-and-half, which is half milk and half cream and has a 10.5%–18% butterfat content. Light cream, like half-and-half, can't be whipped. Light whipping cream, heavy cream, double cream, and heavy whipping cream are all heavy enough to whip. Use heavy cream for making sauces. Extra-thick double cream and clotted cream (or Devonshire cream) can be spread like butter. Cream, the oily or butyraceous part of milk, is converted into butter by churning. The word cream did not appear in English until 1332.

> **CONFUSABLE** HEAVY CREAM/WHIPPING CREAM. Heavy cream and whipping cream are similar, but heavy cream must have a minimum of 36% butterfat, while whipping cream (which may be labeled "light whipping cream") must have 30%–36% butterfat.

> **HINTS** Cream should be kept in the coldest part of the refrigerator. Once opened, use within four to seven days.

> ▌ Cream that is almost ready to dispose of forms flecks in hot coffee.

> ▌ Whip heavy or light whipping cream in a metal bowl that has been chilled for 15 minutes with ice cubes and cold water and thoroughly dried, or has been

placed in the refrigerator with the beaters or whisk for about 1 hour. Whip until it rises in the bowl and thickens and forms soft peaks. A peak should gently fall to one side.

CREAM BY FAT CONTENT

EXTRA-THICK DOUBLE CREAM AND CLOTTED CREAM (OR DEVONSHIRE CREAM): Around 60% butterfat; can be spread like butter.	**LIGHT WHIPPING CREAM:** 30%–36% butterfat.
HEAVY WHIPPING CREAM: At least 48% butterfat.	**LIGHT CREAM:** 18%–30% butterfat; can't be whipped.
DOUBLE CREAM: 48%-60% butterfat.	**HALF-AND-HALF:** Half milk, half cream; 10.5%–18% butterfat; can't be whipped.
HEAVY CREAM: At least 36% butterfat.	

CREAM CHEESE is a soft, smooth white cheese made of cream and nonskim milk, similar to unripe Neufchâtel cheese but with a higher fat content. The first American cream cheese was developed in 1872 by William Lawrence, a Chester, New York, dairyman. Because Philadelphia bore a remarkable reputation for high-quality food products at that time, the first cream cheese received its name as a marketing tool. A cheese distributor soon commissioned the enterprising dairyman to produce the cream cheese in volume under the trade name Philadelphia Brand. By law, cream cheese must contain at least 33% milk fat and not more than 55% moisture, as specified by the USDA. Reduced-fat cream cheese has a milk fat content of 16.5%–20%; light or low-fat cream cheese can have no more than 16.5% milk fat; nonfat cream cheese has zero fat grams. Manufacturers make whipped cream cheese soft and fluffy by whipping air into it.

> **HINT** Cream cheese can absorb odors. It should be refrigerated, even unopened, and tightly wrapped. Consume within two weeks, or no later than the sell-buy date.

CREAMED POTATO: see MASHED POTATO.

CREAMERY is a place where dairy products are produced or sold, especially butter and cheese. The first establishment using this name was in Vermont around 1872.

CREAM GRAVY: see COUNTRY GRAVY.

CREAMNUT: see BRAZIL NUT.

CREAM OF TARTAR, also called POTASSIUM HYDROGEN TARTRATE, is another name for potassium bitartrate, which is a natural component of grapes. It is obtained as a by-product of wine fermentation. Crystalline acid deposits form on the inside walls of wine barrels, these deposits are purified, and tartaric acid is made into a fine powder. It is added to baking soda to create baking powder and it is also used as a leavener by itself. Cream of tartar in baking powder adds acidity, which reacts with the alkali of the powder to set loose the bubbles of gas that cause the dough to rise.

> **HINT** Cream of tartar acts as a stabilizer when beaten with egg whites and helps make a higher, lighter cake. It adds hydrogen ions to create a more stable molecular structure and works as a coagulant.

CREAM PEA: see BLACK-EYED PEA.

CREAM PUFF is any type of puff choux pastry filled with whipped cream or a light cream or custard filling; it is often sprinkled with powdered sugar. It seems to be an American invention dating from around 1889.

> **HINTS** To reduce the likelihood of cream puffs deflating, some bakers poke holes into the finished cream puffs right after they have come out of the oven. Then the cream puffs are placed back into the still-warm, but turned-off, oven. The heat in the oven makes most of the wet dough inside the cream puffs dry out and helps keep their shape. Always cut one of the cream puffs in half at the end of baking to make sure they have dried out, because if the inside dough is still very wet, the choux pastry will deflate upon cooling. But don't worry if the cream puffs have just a small amount of moist dough in them, as this can simply be removed before filling them.

> ▌ When cream puffs are done, immediately slash into each of them with a serrated knife. This lets out the steam and prevents the inside from getting soggy. You can then return the cream puffs to the oven for a few minutes. To ensure there will be no sogginess whatsoever, some people cut open the cream puffs and let them dry out a bit in the oven, but if you like some softness inside, omit this step.

> ▌ Do not add the filling to cream puffs until just prior to serving; if you do, they will become soggy. Keep in a cool place until serving time, but not in the refrigerator.

> ▌ Unfilled cream puffs may be stored in an airtight container at room temperature for several days, but first cut them open and remove the strands of dough to prevent sogginess. To freeze unfilled cream puffs, wrap them tightly in plastic wrap or put them in zip-lock freezer bags. Do not cut cream puffs open or remove the strands of dough before freezing. Thaw at room temperature.

CREAM SODA is a soft drink made with vanilla-flavored carbonated water. It is often colored with caramel or other flavoring and can be clear, light brown, pink, red, or blue. The first patent for cream soda in the United States was granted to Francis John Higgins in Chicago; he later sold his company to Hires Root Beer. Cream soda doesn't actually have cream in it, but it earned that name because it used to be commonly served with a dollop of ice cream floating at the top.

CREAM SOUP is any soup with a milk or other dairy product as the base, as opposed to clear soups, which have broth as their base. Traditionally, cream soups are based on a roux of fat and flour with stock and milk added. This is used to cook the main ingredients for the soup until tender.

CRÈME ANGLAISE is a rich vanilla-flavored custard sauce often containing a liquor such as rum, orange liqueur, or kirsch; it is served hot or cold with cake, fruit, or another dessert. The term is French for "English cream."

> **HINTS** Crème anglaise is stirred with a spoon until it is thick enough to coat the back of a spoon, and then must be removed from the heat. If the sauce reaches too high a temperature, it will curdle. Check to see if it is the right consistency by holding a wooden spoon sideways that is covered with the custard and running your finger along the back of the spoon. If the streak remains without the cream running down through the streak, it is ready. If the sauce is overheated and curdling occurs, pour instantly into a blender and process until smooth before straining. If necessary, add a little heavy cream to the mixture before blending.

> ▮ Cover crème anglaise with plastic wrap and it will keep in the refrigerator for about five days. Do not freeze it.

CRÈME BRÛLÉE is a custard dessert made with cream and eggs; the custard is topped by a layer of sugar and put under a broiler or flame to caramelize the sugar and form a brown crust on top. Crème brûlée is usually served in an individual RAMEKIN. Ramekins are built to withstand high temperatures, such as those that occur when crème brûlée is exposed to the flare of a cooking torch. Crème brûlée can also be prepared in any type of heatproof dish, such as a custard cup or baking dish.

> **CONFUSABLE** CRÈME BRÛLÉE/CRÈME CARAMEL. The difference between crème brûlée (literally "burnt cream") and crème caramel lies in the method of achieving the caramel topping. Crème caramel is a custard baked in a caramel-lined dish and coated with caramelized sugar, which forms a sauce; the custard is then cooked in a mold.

> **HINTS** Once you heat the sugar, you have to serve the crème brûlée as quickly as possible, because the hard layer of caramelized sugar will turn soft again when it absorbs moisture from the crème underneath. It should be served within 30–60 minutes, depending on whether or not it is refrigerated. The most appealing part of this dessert is the contrast between the crisp, hard layer of sugar and the soft, creamy custard.

> ▮ The best test for doneness of crème brûlée is the so-called "wobble" test: as the ramekins cook, carefully reach in the oven and gently shake one with tongs or an oven mitt. It is perfect when the edges are set but the rest of the custard jiggles like gelatin/Jell-O. Cooking the custards past this point will lead to a harder, pastier consistency.

CRÈME CARAMEL is a custard baked in a caramel-lined dish and coated with caramelized sugar, which forms a sauce, then cooked in a mold.

> **CONFUSABLE** FLAN/CRÈME CARAMEL. Flan and crème caramel, both a mixture of sugar, flavorings, and a milk product, differ in that flan is Spanish in origin and is made with sweetened condensed milk, while crème caramel is French in origin and is made with whole milk or cream.

CRÈME DE MENTHE (French for "cream of mint") is a sweet peppermint-flavored liqueur, which can be colorless, green, or white. The term was first recorded in English in 1903; it is pronounced krem-duh-MENTH. Traditionally, it is made by steeping dried peppermint leaves in grain alcohol for several weeks. Peppermint leaves from different parts of the world, each with its unique flavor, are blended. This is followed by filtration and the addition of sugar. If green, the color comes naturally from the leaves.

> **HINT** Because crème de menthe is a concentrated liqueur syrup, a small amount will go a long way in flavoring just about any sweet, hot or cold.

CRÈME FRAÎCHE (literally "fresh cream") is cream that is slightly soured and thickened by lactic acid from buttermilk, sour cream, or yogurt. It is used as a topping or as an ingredient in sauces. It is pronounced krem-FRESH and was recorded in English by 1936.

CREMINI or **CRIMINI**, also called BROWN MUSHROOM, ITALIAN BROWN MUSHROOM, or ITALIAN MUSHROOM, is a cultivated, meaty, tan or brown mushroom (*Agaricus bisporus*). Cremini mushrooms are the immature version of portobello mushrooms, harvested before the cap has opened. Once the cremini mushroom grows to a diameter of four to six inches, it is called a portobello mushroom. Unlike some mushrooms, the stems are completely edible. Cremino is the singular and cremini is the plural.

> **HINT** The best way to store loose cremini mushrooms is to keep them in the refrigerator either placed in a loosely closed paper bag, wrapped in a damp cloth, or laid out in a glass dish that is covered with a moist cloth. These methods will help them to preserve their moisture without becoming soggy and will keep them fresh for several days. Cremini mushrooms that are purchased prepackaged can be stored in the refrigerator for up to one week in their original container. Do not seal cremini mushrooms in plastic, as plastic doesn't "breathe."

CRENSHAW MELON or **CRANSHAW MELON** is a variety of winter melon that is a cross between a Persian and a casaba melon; it is large and oval shaped, with a greenish yellow rind and sweet, usually salmon pink flesh. The origin of the name is unknown.

> **HINT** To select a good Crenshaw melon, look for one that feels heavy for its size, and yields slightly at the end where the flower once was. Good-quality Crenshaw

melons will be fairly large and firm, with a small amount of softness at the stem end. The coloring will be rich yellow with green tinges on the skin. The skin will have a slightly waxy feel when the melon is ripe.

CREOLE CUISINE is a style of cooking originating in Louisiana, especially New Orleans, and is based upon French stews and soups and influenced by Spanish, African, Native American, and other South American groups. The word originally described people of mixed French and Spanish blood who migrated from Europe or were born in southeast Louisiana. It now refers especially to food cooked in a spicy, garlicky sauce containing tomatoes, onions, and peppers.

> **CONFUSABLE** CREOLE/CAJUN. Creole cuisine uses a wider variety of spices than Cajun cuisine and is considered more sophisticated and complex. It is vaguely similar to Cajun cuisine in ingredients. Cajun tends to be spicier than Creole. Both Creole cuisine and Cajun cuisine use the "holy trinity" of ingredients: chopped onions, green peppers, and celery.

CRÊPE is a thin, delicate pancake, usually served rolled or folded with a sweet or savory filling. The word was first seen in English around 1877; it is French for "pancake," derived from the Latin *crispa*, "curled," and is pronounced KRAYP. A crêpe pan is a shallow, usually ten-inch, nonstick pan. A dessert crêpe should be eaten with a spoon (for cutting and eating) and fork (for stabilizing).

> **HINTS** Crêpe batter must be made ahead, as it needs to chill for at least an hour (or up to 24 hours) to allow the flour to expand and absorb the liquid, which makes the crêpes tender. Make the batter in a blender or food processor for the smoothest batter. Beat the eggs into the batter one at a time and add the milk gradually while stirring. Crêpes can be made ahead, refrigerated, and then wrapped in foil and reheated in a 325°F oven.

> ▌ To cook a crêpe, put ½ teaspoon of butter in the pan and add enough batter (3–4 tablespoons) to film the bottom. It is not necessary to grease a nonstick pan.

> ▌ If you cannot flip a crêpe by shaking the pan, slip a small knife or spatula under it and turn it.

> ▌ Put squares of wax paper in between finished crêpes. Crêpes can be stacked on a plate and covered with plastic wrap.

CRÊPE SUZETTE, also called SUZETTE PANCAKE, is a crêpe rolled in an orange sauce and served with flaming brandy or liqueur (flambé). There are a number of stories, none substantiated, about the naming of the dessert; the name was first recorded in 1922.

> **HINT** The most common way to make crêpe Suzette is to pour liqueur (usually Grand Marnier) over a freshly cooked crêpe with sugar and light it. This will make the alcohol in the liqueur evaporate, resulting in a fairly thick, caramelized

sauce. In a restaurant, crêpe Suzette is often prepared in a chafing dish in full view of the guests. As soon as the flames subside, serve the crêpe.

CRESS is a general term for the pungent, peppery-flavored leaves of any of various plants of the crucifer/cabbage family, such as watercress, which are used in salads and as garnishes. The word cress comes from the Proto-Germanic *krasjon* and was used in Old English.

> **HINTS** Cress can be eaten raw or cooked. When eating cress raw, pick it over carefully; remove the thicker stems and yellowing leaves, wash the rest of it, and drain carefully. Cress should not be left to soak in water.

> ▌ Choose cress with dark green leaves and no sign of yellowing.

> ▌ Refrigerate cress in a plastic bag (or stems down in a glass of water covered with a plastic bag) for up to five days.

CRIMP, in cooking, means to make ridges/pleats by pinching or pressing together the edges of pastry to form a seal or for decoration. A pastry crimper (or pastry crimper and cutter) is a tool used to seal the edges of pie crusts, ravioli, tarts, and similar layered food items, or to cut fluted edges into the pie crust. The crimper can be a hollow wheel with indentations for crimping or a thin-bladed wheel with scalloped edges for cutting fluted edges on pie crusts. Crimp can also mean to cut gashes at one- or two-inch intervals along both sides of a freshly caught fish. The fish is then soaked in ice water for up to an hour. Crimping a fish creates a firmer-textured flesh and skin that quickly becomes crisp when cooked, by making it easier for heat to penetrate the flesh.

> **HINT** You can crimp pastry edges with your fingers, a fork, or another utensil.

CRISP is a dessert consisting of fruit baked with a crumbly topping (streusel), such as flour, sugar, and butter or other fat, until the top is crunchy. CRUMBLE is the British name for this dessert, and it is also called BUCKLE and COBBLER in some areas.

CRISPER indicates the compartment for storing fruits and vegetables in a refrigerator, which works to make or keep them crisp by lowering the humidity in the compartment. A crisper will not only lengthen the life of your food, but also help preserve its firmness or crispness, as well as the taste and nutritional value of your vegetables. Crispers that include temperature and moisture controls are perfect for storing different varieties of foods, including fruits, which typically require a less humid environment than vegetables. As a general rule, vegetables require high-moisture storage and fruits low-moisture storage. The crispers in a refrigerator will perform better if they are at least two-thirds full.

CROCKPOT or **CROCK POT** started as a trademarked term (Crock-Pot) for a type of electric SLOW COOKER and now it is used more generically. The pot has a tight-fitting lid and is used for cooking meats and other dishes at a low temperature, usually between 200°F and 325°F, for a long time. Crockpots range from one to six quarts in size.

HINTS When cooking in a crockpot, use recipes that call for less tender meat cuts, which benefit from long, slow cooking. Cut vegetables into uniform, bite-sized pieces so they will cook evenly. If using larger pieces of meat, place the meat on top of the vegetables in the pot. Thaw meat completely before adding it to the crockpot. Do not cook very large pieces of meat in a crockpot; cut roasts in half that are larger than 2½ pounds.

A crockpot should be at least half full and no more than two-thirds full for best results.

Resist peeking in the crockpot because every time you open the lid, you lose heat. The crockpot is already at low heat, so opening it reduces the temperature dramatically.

CROISSANT (French for "crescent") is a piece of baked dough or pastry shaped into a crescent; it is usually moist, flaky, and very rich in fat. A Viennese baker created croissants by copying the shape of the Islamic crescent symbol on the Turkish flag to commemorate the raising of the siege of Vienna by the Turks. The French word croissant was used as a translation of the German *Hörnchen*, the name given by the Viennese to this pastry. The proper pronunciation of croissant is krwah-SSAHN.

HINT When baking croissants, it is important to keep the dough and butter cold in order to get good results. Cooking in cold weather always helps the process.

CROOKNECK SQUASH or **CROOKNECK** is a yellow summer squash with a long curved neck and somewhat warty skin. These are commonly seen at farm stands close to Halloween.

HINTS Crookneck squash average from eight to ten inches long, but are best when a youthful six inches. Avoid a crookneck squash that is too large, as it may be woody and tasteless. Choose crookneck squash that are firm with no sign of shriveling; the skin should be easily pierced with a fingernail. Avoid crookneck squash that are soft, wrinkled, blemished, or dull in appearance.

The skin does not have to be peeled on crookneck squash. Most of the nutrients are in the skin. The seeds in the crookneck squash are also edible.

Store unwashed crookneck squash in the vegetable crisper of the refrigerator for no more than three to four days. Do not wash them until you're ready to prepare them, since moisture promotes decay. The flesh may be diced or grated and then frozen for long-term storage, but freezing breaks down the texture. Unless you intend to use frozen squash for baking, it should be blanched for 2 minutes prior to freezing.

CROQUEMBOUCHE or CROQUE-EN-BOUCHE (French for "crunches in the mouth") is a French dessert made up of small cream puffs or profiteroles glazed with caramelized sugar and stacked in a conical tower or pyramid. The profiteroles can be decorated with threads of caramel, sugared almonds, chocolate, flowers, and/or ribbons, and are often covered in macarons, a small pastry with ganache between two layers. It is considered the traditional French wedding cake, known as a *piece monte*; it is also seen at French baptisms and christenings. French chef Marie-Antoine Carême (1784–1833) is credited with popularizing croquembouche.

> **HINT** When making a croquembouche, always work with a bowl of cold water and a cold, wet cloth to wipe sugar drips. In the event that you do touch the hot sugar, immediately dip your hands in the cold water. Do not rub them.

CROQUE MONSIEUR is a toasted or fried ham and cheese sandwich that is dipped in beaten egg before being prepared, like French toast. When topped with a fried egg, it is called croque madame. Croque monsieur is said to have first been served in a Paris café toward the end of the nineteenth century.

CROQUETTE is a small cake, ball, or cylinder of minced food (fish, meat, vegetable) that is usually coated in bread crumbs and deep-fried. The minced items may be mixed with a rich sauce or panada (thickish paste) before shaping and breading. Croquettes get their name from their crisp exterior; the word derives from the French *croquer*, "to crunch."

CROSIER: see FIDDLEHEAD.

CROSS-CUT or CROSSCUT describes a steak that is cut from two parts of the animal. Porterhouse steak is a cross-cut containing part of the tenderloin and part of the top loin, which are separated from each other with a T-shaped bone. T-bone steak is a cross-cut containing part of the tenderloin and part of the top loin, but less tenderloin than a porterhouse.

CROSTINI (plural of the Italian *crostino*, "little crust") are small or thin pieces of toasted or fried bread. Crostini are often served with a topping as an hors d'oeuvre.

CROUSTADE is a small casing of bread or pastry hollowed to hold a savory filling. It is French, from the Italian *crostata*, "tart," from *crosta*, "crust."

CROUTE or **CROÛTE** or **EN CROÛTE** literally means "in a crust," so in reference to a dish, it means fish or meat served in a pastry case or surrounded by sliced bread. The French croûte comes from the Latin *crusta*. En croûte describes a food (usually partially cooked) that is wrapped in pastry and baked. Whether fully cooked beef, partially cooked fruit or vegetables, or uncooked salmon, the filling is wrapped in pastry and then baked to complete the dish.

CROUTON is a small, often cubed, piece of toasted or fried bread that is served as an accompaniment to soup or salad; crouton is a diminutive form of the French *croute* "crust or hunk," so it literally means "little crust."

> **HINT** To prepare bread for croutons, toss or brush the bread with melted butter or olive oil and season with salt and pepper. Put the bread in a single layer on a baking sheet and bake at 350°F for 15 minutes, or cook the bread in a skillet with olive oil, salt, and pepper.

CROWDER PEA: see BLACK-EYED PEA.

CROWN ROAST is a roast of lamb, pork, or veal with the ribs arranged like a crown; the bones are in a circle pointing upward. A crown roast often involves two or more rib sections of meat. The dish is of American origin, and the term was first recorded in 1934, though in a 1912 cookbook a "roast crown" was mentioned.

> **HINT** Purchase ¾ pound of crown roast per person, which is approximately one rib bone per person. The average roast will serve eight to ten people.

CROW'S NEST PUDDING: see COBBLER.

CRUDITÉS are bite-sized pieces or strips of raw vegetables eaten as an appetizer or snack, often served with a dip. The term is the plural of the French crudité, "rawness," and is ultimately from the Latin *cruditas*, "undigested food."

CRUET is a small, usually glass, container (often with a stopper) for holding a condiment, such as vinegar, oil, vinaigrette, or another liquid dressing. The word is an Anglo-French diminutive form of *crue/cruie*, "earthen pot," and dates to 1382.

> **HINT** To clean a cruet, empty the contents and invert over a paper towel so any remaining vinegar or oil drips out. Use a skinny bottle brush or a baby bottle brush along with some dishwashing detergent or soap, or soak the cruet in a solution of dishwashing detergent or soap and hot water. Then thoroughly rinse out the cruet with hot water. Alternatively, you can place 2 tablespoons of uncooked rice in the cruet along with either ½ cup of white vinegar, or hot water

and dishwashing detergent. Cover the opening and shake well, then empty and discard the rice and vinegar or soap mix. Rinse the cruet under warm running water until it is completely free of vinegar scent, and wash the exterior with a sponge and hot soapy water.

CRULLER, also spelled Kruller, is a rich, light doughnut twisted or curled into various oblong shapes and deep-fried; it is often glazed or sugar-coated. A French cruller is the same type of doughnut, but it is often ring-shaped with a ridged surface and sometimes topped with white icing. The word is from the Dutch *cruller*, from *crullen*, "to curl."

CRUMB in culinary terminology is the soft inner part of a bread roll, slice, or loaf. The verb to crumb means to cover with bread or cracker crumbs. A crumber is an appliance used to remove bread crumbs from a table, as at a restaurant. By looking at the way the cell structure of the crumb in a baked good is formed, and the shape and size and color of the cells, a baker can analyze the hydration, flour types, and yeast amounts, as well as how the dough was mixed and shaped.

CRUMBLE: see Buckle, Cobbler, and Crisp.

CRUMPET is a spongy, yeast-raised British griddlecake with small holes, and is a cross between a pancake and an English muffin; it is eaten toasted with butter. The batter is poured into special rings and baked on a stovetop. In certain parts of United Kingdom, this item can be called muffin or Pikelet, though the latter can be thinner and bigger than a regular crumpet. Crumpets are toasted whole (unlike English muffins, which are split). Although the crumpet and the English muffin share some characteristics, the two foods and their recipes are in fact very different, with crumpets being made from batter and English muffins being made from a dough.

CRUST has a few definitions: the hard, crisp outer part of bread; the pastry shell of a pie or tart; or the sediment that develops as wines mature. Crust is from the French *crouste*, from the Latin *crusta*, "rind/shell/incrustation." Highly saturated fats, such as animal fats or shortening, produce the crispiest crusts.

> **HINTS** The colder the better for making pie crust. All ingredients (even the flour) should be ice-cold before mixing. It is especially important for the fat you are using (butter, lard, and/or vegetable shortening) to be very cold. Professionals say pie dough should never get warmer than 60°F. If you are making the dough in a food processor, you can even freeze the fat before using it. Cold ingredients and limited handling are the key to preparing a wonderful pie crust.

> If you roll out pie crust dough on wax paper or parchment paper, it makes cleanup easier. To keep wax paper from slipping, sprinkle a few drops of water on the countertop before arranging the paper.

❚ Always make deep slits in the top crust of fruit pie. If you do not do this, the filling will be soft and soggy. To prevent the crust from getting too dark, you can cover it with a strip of foil or a pie shield. You also have the option of reducing the oven temperature if you notice the crust getting too dark.

❚ Prepare your pie crust ahead of time—it keeps for about three days in the refrigerator and three months in the freezer.

CRYSTALLIZE means to coat with sugar, often as a preservative step.

CRYSTAL NOODLES: see Cellophane noodles.

CUBAN SANDWICH: see Grinder.

CUBE means to cut or dice food into half-inch pieces (on all sides), larger than diced or mirepoix.

CUBEB, also known as Java pepper, Tailed cubeb, or Tailed pepper, is the small, dried, unripe, brownish, spicy berry of a climbing plant (*Piper cubeba*) with heart-shaped leaves, native to Southeast Asia. Cubeb is ground into a gray pepper with a pungent camphor-like flavor.

CUBED STEAK or **CUBE STEAK** is a thin cut of bottom or top round tenderized with an instrument that scores it with squares to make it more tender. Cube steak would be too tough to eat without being tenderized. After cube steak is tenderized, either by hand and mallet or mechanically, it ends up looking like it is made up of cubes, but it is still just one piece of meat. A common way to cook cube steak is to fry it, cooking it for a few minutes on each side. Cube steak should not be well done because it will look and taste like leather.

CUCUMBER is a long cylindrical green fruit of the gourd family with a thin green rind and seeded white flesh; it is eaten as a vegetable. Cucumber is gathered before fully mature and used in salads or preserved as pickles. The word is from the Latin *cucumis*. There are slicing varieties and pickling varieties, with slicing varieties further divided into outdoor and hothouse/English varieties.

HINTS Look for slender, dark green slicing cucumbers without yellowing. Try to buy unwaxed cucumbers, as removing the skin removes the vitamin A. Hothouse cucumbers should be twelve to sixteen inches long and have smooth skin.

❚ Store cucumbers in a perforated bag in the refrigerator for up to five days, but not in the coldest area. Sliced cucumber keeps for about two days.

❚ Pickling cucumbers should be scrubbed with a vegetable brush under cold running water.

❚ The easiest way to seed a cucumber is to cut the cucumber in half lengthwise and scrape out the center seeds with a small spoon or the handle of a vegetable peeler.

❚ You can tell if a cucumber has been waxed by lightly scraping the skin with your fingernail or knife. If a string comes off, it is wax. If a cucumber has been waxed, peel it or scrub it.

CUISINE is a manner or style of cooking. The word is French for "kitchen" and first meant "kitchen/culinary establishment" (c. 1483).

CUISINE AND RESTAURANT TYPES

CUISINE TYPES

AMERICAN FOOD
ASIAN FOOD
BARBECUE
BRITISH FOOD
CAJUN FOOD
CALIFORNIA FOOD
CARIBBEAN FOOD
CHINESE FOOD
CONTINENTAL CUISINE
CONVENIENCE FOOD
CREOLE FOOD
CUPHOLDER CUISINE
DIETETIC FOOD
FONDUE
FRENCH FOOD
FUSION CUISINE
GERMAN FOOD
GOURMET CUISINE
GREEK FOOD
HAUTE CUISINE
HEALTH FOOD
HUNAN FOOD
HUNGARIAN FOOD
INDIAN FOOD
ITALIAN FOOD
JAMAICAN FOOD
JAPANESE FOOD
JUNK FOOD
KOREAN FOOD
KOSHER FOOD
MACROBIOTIC
MANDARIN FOOD

MIDWESTERN FOOD
NEW ENGLAND FOOD
NOUVELLE CUISINE
PIZZA
SOUL FOOD
SOUTH AMERICAN FOOD
SOUTHERN FOOD
SOUTHWESTERN FOOD
SPANISH FOOD
SWEDISH FOOD
SZECHUAN FOOD
TAPAS
TEX-MEX FOOD
THAI FOOD
TURKISH FOOD
VEGAN FOOD
VEGETARIAN FOOD
VIETNAMESE FOOD

RESTAURANT TYPES

À LA CARTE
ALFRESCO
ALTERNATE RESTAURANT
BEANERY
BISTRO
BLUE-PLATE SPECIAL
BOX LUNCH
BRASSERIE
BREAKFAST RESTAURANT
BREWPUB
BRUNCH-ONLY RESTAURANT
BUFFET RESTAURANT
CAFETERIA

(continued)

CANTEEN	ICE-CREAM PARLOR
CARRYOUT RESTAURANT	LUNCH RESTAURANT, LUNCH COUNTER, OR LUNCHEONETTE
CARVERY	
CHARCUTERIE	MESS
CHOPHOUSE	MOBILE CANTEEN OR CANTEEN ON WHEELS
CHUCK WAGON	PIZZERIA OR PIZZA RESTAURANT
COCKTAIL LOUNGE	PRIX FIXE RESTAURANT
COFFEE BAR, COFFEE SHOP, OR COFFEEHOUSE	RESTAURANT CHAIN
	SALAD-BAR RESTAURANT
COMMISSARY	SELF-SERVICE RESTAURANT
DELICATESSEN OR DELI	SIT-DOWN RESTAURANT
DINER	SMORGASBORD
DINNER-ONLY RESTAURANT	SNACK BAR
DRIVE-IN	STEAK HOUSE
DRIVE-THROUGH RESTAURANT	TAKE-OUT RESTAURANT
EARLY-BIRD SPECIAL RESTAURANT	TAPAS RESTAURANT
FAST CASUAL RESTAURANT	TAVERNA
FAST-FOOD RESTAURANT	TEAROOM OR TEAHOUSE
FONDUE RESTAURANT	THEME RESTAURANT
GREASY SPOON	TO-GO RESTAURANT
GRILLROOM	TRATTORIA
HAMBURGER JOINT	TRUCK STOP
HASH HOUSE	WHITE-TABLECLOTH RESTAURANT

CULINARIAN is an adjective meaning pertaining to a kitchen, or a noun meaning cook or chef. The word is pronounced KUHL-uh-nair-ee-uhn, but it has pronunciation variants of kyoo-luh-NAIR-ee-uhn and COO-luh-nair-ee-uhn.

CULINARY means related or relating to or used in a kitchen or cooking. The word came into English around 1638 and derives from the Latin *culinarius,* from the earlier *culina,* "kitchen." Culinary should be pronounced KULL-i-ner-ee, KYOO-li-ner-ee, or COOL-i-ner-ee. The second pronunciation is older, but the first pronunciation appears to be more common now in both American and British English.

CULTURED, in terms of food, means naturally fermented; the term is used especially in relation to cheese, yogurt, and milk. Cultured foods like kefir, cultured vegetables, and naturally fermented probiotic liquids, such as lactic acid, contain beneficial bacteria for the colon along with essential enzymes, vitamins, and minerals. Cultured foods and naturally fermented probiotic liquids contribute to efficient digestion in three ways: by breaking down foods to make digestion and assimilation easier, by providing enzymes to aid digestion, and by supplying and nourishing the correct intestinal bacteria. Every traditional cuisine has developed some sort of naturally fermented or cultured food, for example, Japanese miso, Bulgarian yogurt, Polish sauerkraut, Indian lassi, and Korean kimchi. Cultured can also refer to a foodstuff created using an artificial method, such as laboratory-grown meat or cultured meat.

CUMBERLAND SAUCE is a cold British sweet-and-sour sauce made of red currant jelly, port, lemon and orange zest or juice, and seasoning; it is served on game, goose, ham, pâté, and sausages.

> **HINT** Homemade Cumberland sauce can be stored for up to one month in the refrigerator.

CUMIN, also called COMMON CUMIN, GARDEN CUMIN, or ROMAN CUMIN, is a small annual herb (*Cuminum cyminum*) of the carrot family cultivated for its aromatic seedlike fruits, which are used as a spice. The Greek name for cumin became the English name for caraway, as caraway actually resembles cumin seeds. Cumin was known to the Egyptians five millennia ago; the seeds have been found in the Old Kingdom pyramids. Cumin is an ingredient of most curry powders and many savory spice mixtures.

CUMQUAT: see KUMQUAT.

CUP is a small container, usually with a handle, used to hold liquids for drinking. Until the Age of Exploration in the seventeenth century, Europeans took beverages cold. The new international trade brought hot beverages to the table, especially coffee, tea, and chocolate. Whereas cold beverages were served in tall cylindrical vessels such as goblets, beakers, and tankards, hot drinks brought a need for bowl-shaped vessels called cups, from the Sanskrit *kupa*, meaning "water well," and the Latin *cupa*, meaning "cask/tub."

CUPCAKE first denoted a cake baked from ingredients measured by the cupful; now it refers to a cake baked in small, usually paper, cups or cup-shaped molds. Cupcakes are often iced. The term dates to 1828.

CURAÇAO is an orange-flavored liqueur that originated around 1810 on the Caribbean island of Curaçao. It is made from the peel of bitter oranges and flavored with cinnamon and mace. Curaçao is usually amber in color, but a few brands are colorless, yellow, orange, or even blue.

CURD is the coagulated, semisolid residue of milk and whey, formed by the action of acids. These thin, watery remains occur naturally or can be created artificially by adding rennet. Curds are the result of caseins (milk proteins) clumping together after they are exposed to starter bacteria, which raise the acid level of the milk. When rennet is introduced, the curds further solidify and become cheese. The word curd dates to before 1362 and may come from the Old English *crudan*, "to press/drive," from the Proto-Indo-European base **greut-*, "to press/coagulate." Curd is also a creamy mixture made from juice (usually lemon, lime, or orange), sugar, butter, and egg yolks. The ingredients are cooked together until the mixture becomes quite thick.

CURD CHEESE: see COTTAGE CHEESE.

CURDLE is to coagulate, especially to separate into curds and whey, as in milk; this is done by permitting or encouraging bacterial action. The verb was originally curd in the fourteenth century, but evolved to curdle around 1590.

> **HINT** To avoid curdling, as for eggs, heat gently and slowly to the point of thickening. Eggs to be added to hot liquids should be tempered by adding a little hot liquid to them first. Fat also prevents curdling, so use full-fat versions of liquid in recipes.

CURE is to dry, salt, smoke, or chemically process in order to preserve; the term mainly pertains to meat and fish. Curing refers to various food preservation and flavoring processes involving the addition of a combination of salt, sugar, nitrates, or nitrites. Historically, people have cured meat in order to prevent the waste of valuable food and to ensure against poor harvests or hunting seasons. Curing is also synonymous with AGING or RIPE in cheese making.

CURLY ENDIVE is a widely cultivated herb with leaves valued as salad greens. There are three types: one with crisp, frilly leaves, also called ENDIVE or FRISÉE; one with lightly bitter broad flat leaves, also called ESCAROLE; and the less common Belgian endive or FRENCH ENDIVE, with cream-colored, broad bitter leaves. Endive is grown by painstakingly forcing chicory roots to sprout in a darkened humid room, and is very fragile.

CURRANT is any of several tart black or red berries of the genus *Ribes* used primarily for jellies and jams. Currant is also the word for a small seedless raisin, produced chiefly in California and the Mediterranean region. Currant developed from the Middle English *raisins of Corauntz*, "raisins of Corinth," as they were first exported from southern Greece. By 1578 the word was applied to an unrelated European berry based on its resemblance to the raisin.

> **HINT** Currants, in season in July and August, should be small and firm. They can be refrigerated for two days.

CURRANT VARIETIES

BLACK	GOLDEN	SKUNK
BUFFALO	INDIAN	SPICE
CHERRY	MISSOURI	WHITE
CLOVE	MOUNTAIN	WILD
FETID	NATIVE	WINTER
FLOWERING	RED	
GARDEN	RED AND WHITE	

CURRY refers to a pungent dish or stew of vegetables or meats flavored with curry powder made of various spices and usually eaten with rice. To curry means to prepare with such a sauce. Curry is from the Tamil *kari*, "sauce/relish"—as it first meant spicy sauce for wheat cakes or rice; the term had entered English by 1600. Though curry is mainly thought of as spicy, there are also many mild curries. Curry does not exist in traditional Indian cooking as a particular dish seasoned with a set mixture of spices. However, the name has been adopted by some Indian restaurants, often to describe a range of dishes prepared by simmering different ingredients in a standard sauce.

CURRIES

Curry was adapted by British settlers in India from the traditional spice mixtures of Indian cuisine. The word also applies to any dish using such seasoning. The basic ingredients of commercial curry powder are cayenne (red) pepper, coriander, cumin, and turmeric. Other ingredients may be allspice, anise, bay leaf, black pepper, cinnamon, cloves, fennel, fenugreek, ginger, mace, mustard seed, nutmeg, poppy seed, roasted and finely ground chiles, or white pepper. Curries are also part of South Asian cookery. These are some common curry dishes:

BALTI	JALFREZI	PHAL
BHUNA	KARAHI	RHOGAN JOSH
BIRYANI	KASHMIR	THAL
CEYLON	KORMA	TIKKA MASALA
DHANSAK	MADRAS	VINDALOO
DOPIAZA	MASALA	
GOBI MASALA	PASANDA	

CURRY POWDER is a mixture of bruised spices and turmeric. There are many variations in curry powder blends, but generally it contains six or more of the following: cardamon, chili powder/cayenne pepper, cloves, coriander, cumin, dill, fenugreek, ginger, mace, pepper, and turmeric.

> **HINTS** Since commercial curry powder quickly loses its pungency, it should be stored in an airtight container for no longer than two months.

> Authentic Indian curry powder is freshly ground each day and can vary dramatically, depending on the region and the cook. Such curry powder is a pulverized blend of up to twenty spices, herbs, and seeds.

> Curry powder is one of those spices that gets hotter the longer it stands, so use discretion when adding it to foods that may stand before being eaten.

CUSK: see BURBOT.

CUSTARD, also called EGG CUSTARD, is a dessert or sweet sauce made with milk and eggs and thickened, either by baking, boiling, or freezing. Custard was originally an open pie with meat or fruit in thickened and spiced sweetened milk or broth. The term was originally crustarde/custarde (from the French *crouste*, "crust"); today custard refers to a thickened, sweetened sauce. Custard's mixture of dairy items is cooked until the proteins thicken to form a soft, smooth dish. Custard sauces include sugar and are pourable. Pastry cream (crème patisserie) is another type of custard.

> **HINTS** Custard needs to cook slowly, but not simmer or boil, and the liquid should be hot.

> ▌ If a recipe says to cook until the mixture coats a spoon, run a finger along the custard on the spoon and if the place stays clear and custard doesn't run back onto it, the mixture is ready to be removed from the heat. Use a wooden spoon or silicone rubber spatula to stir custard sauce as it cooks. Stir gently. When custard sauce settles, looks glossy, and is noticeably thicker, it is ready. Stir for a few minutes after removing it from the heat. Let it cool on the countertop, then in the refrigerator. Once chilled, put parchment or wax paper directly on the custard surface and keep for up to two days.

> ▌ Custard baked in a water bath cooks evenly. When done, the center should still wiggle or a knife in the center should come out moist. After removing custard from the oven, let it cool in the water bath. When the water bath is lukewarm, remove the custard baking container. But if the oven test shows it is over-cooked, remove it from the oven and water bath and put it halfway into a pan or sink of cold water and ice cubes.

CUSTARD APPLE is a native South American heart-shaped fruit (*Annona reticulata*) with a dark brown rind, and a yellowish pulp resembling custard in appearance and flavor. The term was used in English by 1657. The skin is thin but tough, and may be yellow or brownish when ripe, with a pink, reddish, or brownish red blush; the skin may be faintly, moderately, or distinctly reticulated.

> **HINT** The flesh of a custard apple may be scooped from the skin and eaten as is or served with light cream and a sprinkling of sugar. Often it is pressed through a sieve and added to milkshakes, custards, or ice cream. It can also be used in sorbets and fruit salads.

CUSTARD CUP is a heat-resistant porcelain or glass cup in which an individual custard is baked; see RAMEKIN.

CUSTARD MARROW: see PATTYPAN SQUASH.

CUT in cooking most often refers to any of the segments of the carcass of a meat animal, a sense that entered English around 1600. Cut as a verb means to divide into pieces with a knife or other sharp implement. Cut (or cut in) has a second meaning of a method of mixing: to mix a solid, cold fat (such as butter or shortening) with dry ingredients (such as a flour mixture) until the combination is in the form of small particles. Cutting terms include: Minced: ⅛ inch or smaller. Chopped fine: ⅛–¼ inch. Chopped medium: ¼–½ inch. Chopped coarse: ½–¾ inch. Cut into chunks: ¾ inch or larger. Sliced: cut into flat, thin pieces. Diced: cut into uniform cubes. Cut on the bias: cut at an angle. Almost all cutting skills require a rocking motion, the way a paper cutter works.

CUTLERY, also called FLATWARE, is a term for the eating utensils knives, forks, and spoons. It also has the sense of tools with blades, including knives. The word is from the Old French *coutelier*, "cutler's art," from *coutel*, "knife." A cutler is one who makes, repairs, or sells knives and similar cutting utensils. The knife is the earliest-known implement, a tool used as an eating utensil before it evolved as a weapon. The term flatware refers to domestic cutlery, especially in the United States.

CUTLET is a thin, tender cut of meat (usually from chicken, lamb, pork, or veal) taken from the leg or rib section. Cutlets are often flattened and served breaded. The word, in English since 1706, is from the French *côtelette*, "little rib," a double diminutive of *coste/côte*, "rib," and the diminutive suffix *-ette*. A cutlet bat is a kitchen tool used for flattening or pounding meat into cutlets. The word cutlet has a second food meaning of a small, flat croquette of chopped meat or fish.

CUTTING BOARD is a piece of flat wood, or a piece of rigid plastic, acrylic, or other material, that is used to protect a countertop or table while cutting food. The term first appeared in English in 1825. Wooden cutting surfaces are the softest cutting surface and therefore the most desirable. Though softwood does less harm to the knife than hardwood, softwood doesn't last as long and is more absorbent of juices, so hardwood is more commonly used and is considered better.

CUTTING BOARD ESSENTIALS

■ Every couple of months, rinse the cutting board in 4 cups of water with 1 teaspoon of bleach, then rinse with hot water. Use mineral oil to season a wooden board, first letting it soak for 5–10 minutes and rubbing it in with fine steel wool. Wipe dry with a soft cloth. Repeat once a month. To remove odors, clean the board with lemon juice, salt, or both together.

■ Use separate cutting boards for animal products and for produce, and use a nonwooden board for poultry to avoid bacterial contamination.

■ After each use, a plastic cutting board should be cleaned with soap and water, rinsed, then dried with paper towels. Periodically put it in the dishwasher, vertically, and let it go through the complete cycle. A microwave can be used to disinfect a microwave-safe plastic cutting board. Wash the board well with hot water, rub with the cut side of a lemon, then heat in the microwave for 1 minute. Plastic cutting boards are safe to use when working with chickens if they are cleaned afterward with a bleach solution or put through the dishwasher drying cycle.

(continued)

- A wooden cutting board should be cleaned with soapy water, rinsed quickly, then wiped dry with paper towels. Don't soak it or run it through the dishwasher. If used for cutting meat, occasionally scour it with a paste of baking soda and water.

- If the surface of a plastic cutting board loses its smoothness or becomes chipped or badly cut, discard it, because the breaks in the surface become good nesting places for bacteria that can poison food.

- Polyethylene boards work quite well, except for the molded ones, which often deliberately do not have a smooth surface, cannot be cleaned as easily, and can become unsanitary.

- The cutting surface of a cutting board affects a knife's sharpness. The harder the surface, the more quickly a knife dulls. Hard surfaces include metal, marble, granite, tile, china, and most countertops.

- Remove onion odor from a cutting board with a paste of baking soda and water.

- A damp paper towel under a cutting board can keep it stable.

CUTTLEFISH is a ten-armed, oval-bodied, nonswimming, squidlike cephalopod with a calcareous internal shell (cuttlebone). The word comes from the Old English *cudele*, from the Germanic *codd*, "bag," referring to its ink sac, which ejects ink when there is danger. Like the squid, the cuttlefish can be cooked in its ink. However, the flesh is quite tough and exceedingly chewy and has to be beaten vigorously in order to tenderize it before cooking.

CYMLING: see PATTYPAN SQUASH.

DAB is any of several flounders (genus *Limanda*), a small flatfish with edible, sweet, lean, firm flesh.

DAGWOOD DOG: see CORN DOG.

DAGWOOD SANDWICH or **DAGWOOD** is a very thick, multilayered sandwich made with a variety of meats, cheeses, lettuce, and condiments. It is named after Dagwood Bumstead, a character who made such sandwiches in the comic strip *Blondie* by Murat Bernard "Chic" Young (1901–1973).

DAHL or **DAL** is a thick, creamy stew made from lentils or other legumes, onions, and spices, and originating in South Asia. The word is from the Hindi *dal/dahl*, "split pulse," from the Sanskrit *dal*, "to split." Dal is also a word used for any of various kinds of pulse used as food in India.

DAIKON, also called CHINESE RADISH, JAPANESE RADISH, MOOLI, or ORIENTAL RADISH, is a long, white, carrot-shaped radish that is crunchy with a mild peppery flavor similar to watercress. It is from Asia and is eaten raw, pickled, or cooked. The word comes from the Japanese *dai*, "large," and *kon*, "root." Today, more land in Japan is devoted to the cultivation of daikon than any other vegetable. Perhaps this is because daikon is one of the best vegetables for storage. Unbruised daikon will keep for at least four months in a cool root cellar. When cut, fresh daikon will be crisp and juicy, like an apple.

> **HINT** Choose a firm, unwrinkled, moist daikon, without cracks or bruises. It should also feel heavy for its size. Refrigerate in a plastic bag for up to a week.

DAIQUIRI is an iced cocktail made from rum, lemon or lime juice, and sugar or simple syrup; it is named for Daiquiri, Cuba, where it had originated by 1920. F. Scott Fitzgerald was the first to write about it.

DAIRY PRODUCT is a general term for milk and foodstuffs produced from milk, including butter, cheese, ice cream, and yogurt. Eggs are sometimes categorized as a dairy product as they are a food other than meat that is produced by animals. Milk has been used by humans since the beginning of recorded time, and cow milk is by far the principal type used throughout the world. Sheep and goats are also raised for their milk. Dairying in North America began with the earliest European invasions. Spaniards brought cattle to Veracruz (Mexico) in 1525; English cattle reached Jamestown in 1611.

DAIRY PRODUCTS

BONNYCLABBER	FROZEN YOGURT	MILK
BUTTER	GOAT'S MILK	OLEO
CHEESE	HALF-AND-HALF	SOUR CREAM
CLABBER	HEAVY CREAM	SWEET BUTTER
CREAM	ICE CREAM	WHEY
CRÈME FRAÎCHE	KEFIR	WHIPPING CREAM
CURDS	LEBEN	YOGURT
EGGS	LIGHT CREAM	

DAMSON is a plum tree that yields a small, sour, dark purple fruit that is made into jam or jelly. Damson plums were named for Damascus, Syria, where they originated. The skin of the damson can be heavily acidic, rendering the fruit unpalatable to some for eating plain.

> **HINT** Damsons will stay fresh for a week or two in the refrigerator. For longer storage, they can be made into an excellent jam (stronger flavored than jam from regular plums) and bottled.

DANISH LOBSTER: see Prawn.

DANISH PASTRY or **DANISH** is a type of rich yeast cake often decorated with icing or sugar and containing fruit or nuts. The term Danish pastry dates to 1934 and the shortened form Danish is from 1963. Danish are popular and were perfected in Denmark, but are said to have originated in Austria. The Danes call this pastry *Wienerbrod*, "Viennese bread."

> **HINTS** Danish pastry may be kept at room temperature for up to two days; cover with foil or plastic wrap to prevent drying out. Danish pastry will keep for an additional week in the refrigerator, covered with foil or plastic wrap or in a plastic bag. To freeze Danish pastry, wrap tightly in foil or freezer-weight plastic wrap, or place in a zip-lock freezer bag. They will stay good in the freezer for up to three months.

> When making Danish pastry dough at home, refrigerate the dough any time that it becomes soft during the rolling and shaping. You will be more than compensated for the extra time by how much easier the dough will be to handle. Keep the dough refrigerated for 2–24 hours after preparing it. If you want to keep it longer, or use only part of the dough, freeze it. Allow it to rest in the refrigerator for several hours, then remove it from the refrigerator, deflate it by pressing it gently with the palms of your hands, and cut off the amount you wish to freeze. Double-wrap that portion in freezer-weight plastic wrap and freeze it for up to several weeks. Defrost the frozen dough in the refrigerator overnight before using it.

DARJEELING is a high-quality black tea grown at about seven thousand feet in the mountainous regions of northern India and named for a city there. Darjeeling is considered one of India's finest teas and cannot be grown or manufactured anywhere else in the world, just as Champagne can be produced only in a particular region of France. The Darjeeling tea story started way back in 1835 through the initiative of the British governor general, Lord Bentinck. Dr. Campbell, the first superintendent of Darjeeling, planted the first seeds in his garden.

> **HINTS** When buying Darjeeling tea, make sure that "Darjeeling," "Pure Darjeeling," or "100% Darjeeling" appears on the label.

> To brew a perfect cup of Darjeeling tea, bring a pot of water to a furious boil and pour it over 1 level teaspoon of tea in each cup. Let the tea steep for 3–4 minutes. If adding milk or sugar, extend the brewing time to about 5 minutes. The quantity of tea and the brewing time can be altered according to personal preferences.

DARK CHOCOLATE, also called Continental chocolate, Luxury chocolate, or Plain chocolate, is chocolate that has no added milk and is darker in color and less sweet than milk chocolate. The cocoa content of commercial dark chocolate bars can range from 30% (sweet dark) to 70%, 75%, or even above 80% for extremely dark bars. Common terms used to distinguish the cocoa content of dark chocolate bars include bittersweet, semisweet, and sweet dark chocolate. The U.S. government has no definition for dark chocolate; it defines only "sweet chocolate," which requires a 15% concentration of chocolate liquor. European rules specify a minimum of 35% cocoa solids for dark chocolate.

> **HINTS** The key to storing chocolate is to keep it in a cool, dry place. Wrap it tightly in a couple of layers of plastic wrap and stash it in a dark cupboard away from strong-smelling foods. Chocolate, like butter, will absorb strong aromas. Stored improperly, chocolate will develop a white film called bloom. Bloom happens because the chocolate has gotten too warm, causing the cocoa butter to separate out, or because some condensation has taken place, melting sugar in the chocolate's surface. If bloom happens, the chocolate will not have that luxurious melt-in-your-mouth feel, but will be fine for baking.

> ▌ If you are using chocolate bars with more than 60%–70% cacao in a recipe not specifically designed for them, follow this general rule: use 25%–35% less chocolate than called for in the recipe and add up to 1½ teaspoons more granulated sugar for each ounce of chocolate in the original recipe.

DARK MEAT denotes the thighs and legs of a cooked chicken or turkey, which has a darker color than the meat of the breast; it also refers to meat that is dark in appearance after cooking. The term seems to have been coined in the nineteenth century. Dark meat is made dark by two proteins involved in the process of converting the fat into energy for the muscles. Dark meat has a stronger and more gamelike flavor than white meat. This is due to the activity of those muscles and the various chemicals, proteins, and fats that activity builds in the muscle tissue. The more compact and sheltered dark meat takes longer than white meat to cook.

DASH is a small amount or quantity of something added to something else, especially to improve the flavor of food. This term was used by 1611. Generally, a dash can be considered ⅟₁₆ to ⅛ teaspoon, but most consider it to be ⅛ teaspoon.

DASHI, Japanese for "broth," is clear broth or stock, usually with a fish or vegetable base.

> **HINT** Dashi is best used on the day it is made. If you have some leftover dashi, you can keep it in a covered container in the refrigerator for up to two weeks. You can also freeze it for longer storage.

DATE is the edible oblong or oval fruit of the date palm (*Phoenix dactylifera*). Dates are sweet and rich with a chewy, sticky texture and a long, hard seed. Fresh dates are plump and dark brown with a glossy sheen. The word is from the Greek *daktulos*, "finger," from its shape. Dates are classified as being soft, semidry, or dry. Dry dates are also known as bread dates. The most common semidry dates are Deglet Noor and Zahidi; Thoory is the most common dry date; Medjool, Khadrawy, and Halawy are popular soft dates. The date palm may very well be the oldest food-producing plant in the world.

HINTS When cutting sticky dates, oil the knife blade or shears and cut or snip into pieces, or dust the knife blade with flour before chopping. Don't finely mince the dates or they will form a paste. You can also separate dates by microwaving for 30 seconds.

▌ Tightly wrap soft and semidry dates in plastic and refrigerate for up to 3 weeks. Dry dates can be refrigerated for ten to twelve months. Pits must be removed for eating or cooking.

▌ The peak season for dates is October through January. Choose dates that are plump and shiny, not covered with crystallized sugar—though the Medjool has a dusting of natural sugar.

DAUBE is a stew of meat (usually beef, but also lamb or mutton) braised in red wine with vegetables, herbs, and spices. Daube is also the pot or casserole in which such a stew is cooked. Daube can be served hot or cold. For best flavor, it is cooked in several stages, and cooled for a day after each stage to allow the flavors to meld together.

DAU BEAN: see LIMA BEAN.

DAUPHINE POTATOES or **DAUPHINOISE** is a dish of potatoes baked in cream, milk, butter, garlic, and often Gruyère cheese. The potatoes can also be puréed, combined with choux pastry, and formed into balls to create croquettes, which are then rolled in bread crumbs and deep-fried. It is named for the Dauphiné area of France, near the Italian border, where the dish originated.

DEBONED: see BONED.

DECAFFEINATED or **DECAF** indicates that most or all of the caffeine has been removed from coffee or tea. Coffees are decaffeinated in their green state and there are three main processes used: the traditional or European process, the water-only or Swiss Water Process, and the carbon dioxide or sparkling water process. All are consistently successful in removing all but a trace (2%–3%) of the resident caffeine. The first commercially successful decaffeination process was invented by Ludwig Roselius and Karl Wimmer in 1903. It involved steaming coffee beans with a brine (saltwater) solution and then using benzene as a solvent to remove the caffeine.

DEEP-DISH refers to a fruit pie or pizza pie that has been prepared in a deep-sided dish and has a thicker than normal crust, allowing for more filling. The deep-dish pizza was invented in Chicago by Ike Sewell at his restaurant Pizzeria Uno.

DEEP-FRY (DEEP-FRYING) means to fry food in an amount of fat or oil sufficient to cover the food completely. Foods that are deep-fried include doughnuts, chicken wings, and French fries. An average fat temperature for deep-frying is 375°F, and a special deep-fat thermometer should be used. There is an electric appliance for deep-frying called a deep fryer, which usually consists of a deep pan or pot with a basket, often of mesh, inside.

DEEP-FRYING ESSENTIALS

■ Really fresh oil will not cook food as well as oil that has broken down a little. Use more oil than you might think necessary.

■ Salt food to be deep-fried before applying the batter and then again after-frying.

■ It is best to only deep-fry small tender pieces of food due to the intense heat and quickness of deep-frying. Larger pieces or too much food lowers the temperature of the oil.

■ Keep the liquid batter ice-cold to improve its ability to stick to the food.

■ If the oil is old and deteriorated, the food will be greasy, the color of the food will be dark, a rancid taste will develop, and a toxicity may develop. Heat, sunlight, iron and copper pans, and exposure to air (oxygen) are all conditions that cause the fat/oil to deteriorate.

■ If the oil temperature is too hot when deep frying, the oil will smoke and the food will burn. If the oil temperature is too low when deep frying, the food will be greasy and it will take too long to cook. The best way to tell if the cooking temperature is correct is with a thermometer; the bulb should be completely immersed but should not touch the sides or bottom of the pan.

■ If you reuse oil and it is not strained before using it again, the debris from previous cooking will scorch and produce a bad flavor. When reused oil begins to smoke at 360°F or lower, it should be discarded.

■ Items can be prepared in advance for deep-frying, but it is best if they are refrigerated until cooking time.

DEEP-FRYING PAN: see SAUTÉ PAN.

DEGLAZE is to remove the bits of sautéed or roasted meat (called the FOND) and the juices from a pan by adding stock, water, or wine and scraping. The resulting liquid is usually used in or as a sauce or gravy. The resulting sauce is called a reduction sauce or pan sauce.

DEGREASE is to remove excess fat from the surface of a sauce, soup, or stew. One way to degrease food is to use a spoon to skim the fat, or a bulb baster to suck the fat, from the surface of a hot liquid. Another way is to chill the mixture until the fat becomes solid and can be easily lifted off the surface.

DELICATESSEN or **DELI** is a store selling ready-to-eat foods, such as meats, cheeses, and salads; it is also the name for the delicacies sold. Delicatessen is from the German *delikat Essen*, "fine foods/good things to eat," from the French *delicat*, "delicacy." The word did not appear in English until 1877, with the shortened deli first recorded in 1954. America's first delicatessen opened around 1868 on Grand Street on the Lower East Side of Manhattan (a heavily populated German area) in New York City.

DELMONICO STEAK, also called CLUB STEAK, KANSAS CITY STRIP STEAK, NEW YORK STEAK, NEW YORK STRIP, STRIP LOIN STEAK, SHELL STEAK, or STRIP STEAK, is a small steak cut from the front of the short loin of beef. It was named in the mid 1800s after Delmonico's restaurant in New York City, which served a tender strip of boneless top loin. There are at least eight different cuts that are claimed to be the original for the Delmonico steak.

DEMERARA SUGAR or **DEMERARA** is a light brown to yellowish brown raw cane sugar grown in the Demerara region of Guyana, whose large sparkling crystals feel slightly moist. There is also fine demerara sugar. In the United States, this sugar is sold as TURBINADO SUGAR.

> **HINTS** Although demerara makes an excellent textural addition to recipes, it should not be substituted for certain sugars. Recipes that call for confectioners' or castor sugar should not be made with demerara, since the sugar will have a negative impact on the end texture. In addition, demerara sugar will discolor meringues and other pale, fine foods, and it tends not to make terribly good caramels.

> Store demerara sugar so it is dry; if it gets moist, it will become hard. If the sugar becomes hard, pour it into a medium bowl and cover with a damp towel. Leave overnight and the sugar will reabsorb the moisture, and the next morning it will be soft, moist, and ready to use.

DEMI-GLACE, literally meaning "half glaze," is a mixture of equal portions of brown stock and beef-based sauce that is reduced until it is a rich, glossy brown sauce. It is referred to as espagnole sauce when it is made with extra beef stock that has been partly reduced and seasoned with dry wine or sherry.

> **HINT** Demi-glace keeps very well, about six months refrigerated or almost indefinitely frozen.

DEMITASSE, French for "half cup," is a small coffee cup or its contents. The term had entered English by 1842.

DESSERT is a broad term for a usually sweet course served at the end of a meal. In this category fall cakes, cookies, frozen treats, pies, and puddings. The word, first recorded in 1600, is from the French *dessert*, "(course following) clearing the table" from *desservir*, "remove what has been served." It was not until about 1850 that the word dessert took on its present meaning.

DESSERTS

Dessert is the last course of a meal. In the United States dessert is likely to consist of pastry, cake, ice cream, pudding, or fresh or cooked fruit. In countless surveys, apple pie has been chosen as the favorite dessert in the United States. Here is a tasty sampling of desserts.

AMBRETTE
AMBROSIA
ANGEL FOOD CAKE
ANGEL PIE
APPLE COBBLER
APPLE CRISP
APPLE PANDOWDY
APPLE PIE
BAKED ALASKA
BAKLAVA
BANANA SPLIT
BANANAS FOSTER
BAVARIAN CREAM
BLANCMANGE
BLINTZE
BOMBE
BOSTON CREAM PIE
BRANDY SNAP
BREAD PUDDING
BROWNIE
CAKE
CANDY
CANNOLI
CHARLOTTE
CHARLOTTE RUSSE
CHEESECAKE
CHERRIES JUBILEE
CHESS PIE OR CHESS CAKE
CHOCOLATE CHIP COOKIE
CHOCOLATE MOUSSE
CLAFOUTI
COBBLER
COFFEE CAKE
COMPOTE
COOKIE
COTTAGE PUDDING
COUPE
CREAM PUFF

CRÈME BRÛLÉE
CRÈME CARAMEL
CRÊPE SUZETTE
CRISP
CRULLER
CUPCAKE
CUSTARD
DANISH PASTRY
DEEP-DISH PIE
DESSERT CHEESE
DEVIL'S FOOD CAKE
DOUGHNUT
ÉCLAIR
EGG CREAM
ESKIMO PIE
FIG BAR
FLAN
FLOATING ISLAND
FLUMMERY
FRANGIPANE
FRAPPE
FROZEN CUSTARD
FROZEN DESSERT
FROZEN YOGURT
FRUITCAKE
FRUIT CUP
FRUIT DESSERT
FRUIT PIE
FRUMENTY
GALATOBOUREKO
GATEAU
GELATIN
GELATO
GINGERBREAD
GINGERSNAP
GRANITA
HALVAH
ICEBOX CAKE
ICE CREAM

ICE-CREAM BAR
ICE-CREAM CAKE
ICE-CREAM FLOAT
ICE-CREAM SANDWICH
ICE-CREAM SODA
ICE-CREAM SUNDAE
INDIAN PUDDING
ITALIAN ICE
JELL-O
JELLY ROLL
JUNKET
KEY LIME PIE
KUCHEN
LADYFINGER
LAYER CAKE
LEMON MERINGUE PIE
MACAROON
MARBLE CAKE
MARSHMALLOW
MELA STREGATA
MERINGUE
MILKSHAKE
MOUSSE
MUD PIE
NAPOLEON
NESSELRODE
PANDOWDY
PARFAIT
PASTRY
PATISSERIE
PAVLOVA
PEACH MELBA
PECAN PIE
PIE
POUND CAKE
PROFITEROLES
PRUNE WHIP
PUDDING
PUMPKIN PIE

(continued)

RHUBARB CRUMBLE	SOUFFLE	TART
RICE PUDDING	SPICE CAKE	TIRAMISU
SACHER TORTE	SPONGE CAKE	TOLL HOUSE COOKIE
SCONE	STRAWBERRY SHORTCAKE	TORTE
SHERBET	STREUSEL	TRIFLE
SHOOFLY PIE OR SHOOFLY CAKE	STRUDEL	TURNOVER
	SUGAR COOKIE	UPSIDE-DOWN CAKE
SHORTBREAD	SUGAR WAFER	VACHERIN
SHORTCAKE	SUNDAE	WAFER
S'MORES	SWEET POTATO PIE	WEDDING CAKE
SNOW CONE	SWEET ROLL	ZABAGLIONE
SNOW PUDDING	SYLLABUB	ZUPPA INGLESE
SORBET	TAPIOCA	

DESSERT WINE is a sweet wine served with or after dessert. Dessert wines contain high levels of both sugar and alcohol. Dessert wines, which are 17%–21% alcohol, are classified by alcoholic strength, not sweetness.

> **HINTS** White dessert wines are generally served somewhat chilled, but can be easily served too cold. Red dessert wines are served at room temperature or slightly chilled.

> ▌ Dessert wines go by the rule that a little goes a long way. An average pour is two ounces and is usually served in a smaller, stemmed wineglass or cordial glass.

DEVEIN is to remove the main central vein (which is the digestive tract) from a shrimp or prawn. It is a dark, thready gut vein from the back of the tail meat. In theory, it is okay to eat the "vein" because any bacteria will be killed during cooking.

> **HINT** Deveining can be done with the tip of a sharp knife or a special tool called a deveiner. The vein is relatively easy to remove. It is easier to devein shrimp prior to cooking them. If you plan on cooking your shrimp with the shell still on, you can still devein them. In this case you will need a shrimp deveiner, a knifelike kitchen tool made specifically for deveining shrimp with their shells on. Start by holding the shrimp back side up, and place the deveiner under the tip of the shell. Gently slide the deveiner up the back of the shrimp, toward the tail. The deveiner has a serrated edge that the vein will adhere to, as the deveiner cuts the shell with its sharp, upper edge.

DEVIL (DEVILED) means to prepare food, often chopped or minced, with hot or savory seasoning; examples are deviled ham and deviled eggs. Deviled eggs are halved hard-cooked eggs with the yolk mashed with mayonnaise and seasonings and returned as a filling in the white. The term deviled, used in relation to food, dates back to at least 1786, when it was defined in the *Oxford English Dictionary* as "various highly-seasoned broiled or fried dishes, also for hot ingredients."

DEVIL'S FOOD CAKE is a rich, but light-textured, dark chocolate cake, named for its color contrast with angel's food cake. The cake has a reddish brown color; the first recipe for it appeared in 1905.

> **HINT** Devil's food cake is best the day it is made, although it's fine the next day. Store at room temperature under a cake dome or loosely wrapped with plastic wrap for up to two days. Be sure to keep the cake out of the sun in the meantime.

DEVILS ON HORSEBACK is oysters wrapped in bacon, sometimes with a pitted prune or date stuffed with mango chutney, and served with hot pepper sauce on toast points. First recorded in 1909, it is also the term for a prune or plum wrapped in a bacon rasher and served on fried bread.

DEVONSHIRE CREAM: see CLOTTED CREAM.

DIANE describes a thin-sliced tenderloin steak (like filet mignon) pan-cooked with cream, brandy, and seasonings, especially Worcestershire sauce. It dates to 1957 and *Larousse Gastronomique* says it is named for the goddess Diana, the huntress, and originally was a way of serving venison.

> **HINT** When making steak Diane, you may want to slightly undercook the filet mignon steaks prior to adding the cream and brandy so that the reduction process of making the sauce doesn't overcook them.

DICE is to cut into cube-sized pieces (like playing dice), especially meat and vegetables. The verb was first recorded around 1390. The dimension of the dice varies, with recipes calling for ingredients to be cut into anywhere from ⅛- to ½-inch dice.

DIGESTIF is a type of alcoholic drink taken to aid digestion, such as brandy, cognac, or another liqueur drunk after a meal. A digestif can be served plain or with ice. Digestifs tend to be stronger than aperitifs.

> **HINT** For your digestif bar, choose sweet liqueurs over astringent liqueurs as a rule. While sweet liqueurs and cordials would cloy the taste buds before dinner, a sweet finish provides a satisfying ending to a meal. Select amber spirits over clear spirits. Amber spirits such as dark rum and brandy have a robust taste that the diner can tolerate on a full stomach. Match the digestif with the cuisine. For example, grappa and sambuca are popular finishes to an Italian meal. French diners enjoy a cocktail prepared with cognac and amaretto in a three to one ratio. Enhance digestion by adding aromatic bitters to your digestif preparations.

DIJON MUSTARD or **DIJON** is a mild-to-medium hot, pale yellow French mustard made with brown and black varieties of seeds, white wine or unripe grape juice (verjuice), and seasonings. Dating to 1869, it was originally made in Dijon (pronounced DEE-zhon).

> **HINTS** The flavor difference between Dijon mustard and yellow mustard is so great that they cannot be substituted for each other.

> ▌ Refrigerate prepared mustards after opening and use by the expiration date. If water pools at the top of the container, simply shake or stir well. It is still fine to use.

> ▌ Since heat causes the pungent flavor of mustard to dissipate, mustard is generally added near the end of a dish's cooking time and gently heated.

DILL, DILL SEED, DILL WEED, or **DILLY** is an aromatic Old World herb (*Anethum graveolens*) of the parsley family with threadlike leaves and seeds used as seasoning, especially for pickling. Its first mention in English was before AD 700.

> **HINTS** Fresh and dried dill are not equivalent. They are quite different and cannot be used interchangeably. Fresh dill is assertive and works well with fish (such as salmon) and in salads and sauces. Fresh dill leaves are beautiful as a garnish. Dried dill is used in pickling because of its strong flavor, and in smoking fish.

> ▌ Refrigerate dill in a covered jar with the stem ends sitting in a one-inch layer of water, or wrap the stem ends in a moist paper towel and seal in a plastic bag, then refrigerate.

DILL PICKLE is a cucumber or gherkin that is pickled and flavored with dill weed, a U.S. invention dating to around 1906. Deep-fried dill pickles first appeared in Arkansas in 1963 and can now be found throughout the country on restaurant and pub menus, as well as at food vendor booths at state and county fairs. The dill pickle is by far the most popular variety of pickle.

> **HINT** If you are making your own dill pickles, soak the cucumbers in ice for 2–8 hours before putting them in the brine to make sure the pickles are crisp. Refresh the ice as necessary. They have to sit in the jar for 8 weeks after pickling before you can eat them.

DIM SUM, also known as YAM CHA or YUM CHA, is a variety of dishes, including several kinds of steamed or fried dumplings or rolls with savory fillings, served in small portions as a meal. The term dim sum comes from the Cantonese *dim sam*, "touch the heart" or "dot heart/small center." The dishes are usually served in tiers of bamboo steamers or small- to medium-sized plates or are served like desserts on trolley carts. In China dim sum is usually served from midmorning right through the afternoon and is a standard fare in Chinese teahouses, but some eateries begin serving it in the early morning. The drinking of tea is as important to dim sum as the food. In a dim sum restaurant, diners point to what they want from trays of small dishes.

DINER is a type of restaurant that originally resembled a railway dining car, where customers eat at the counter or in booths. Diner is also the term for a person eating a meal, especially in a restaurant. The term was used in the United States in 1890 for the railway dining car, then by 1935 for a restaurant; for a person who dines, the term was recorded in 1815. According to the American Diner Museum, Walter Scott of Providence, Rhode Island, began serving meats from a horse-drawn lunch wagon to late-shift workers in 1872, giving birth to this concept.

DINNER is the main meal of the day served in the evening or at midday, a term first recorded in 1297. The word is also used for a banquet or formal meal in honor of a person or event, or for the food prepared for either of these meals. In Middle English dinner meant "breakfast," the first big meal of the day, derived from the Old French *disner/diner*, from the Latin *disinre*, "to break one's fast." Over time, the chief meal of the day has become the last meal of the day.

> **CONFUSABLE** DINNER/SUPPER. Dinner is the main meal of the day, while supper is the last meal of the day. Supper is lighter than dinner. Supper is in the early evening if dinner is at midday. Supper is just before bedtime if dinner is later than midday.

DINNER FORK is the largest fork in a table setting, measuring about seven inches in length. It is used to eat the main course. The continental-size fork is about a half inch longer than the American-size dinner fork. Long tines are used for a dinner fork so that thick morsels of food can be easily speared. When setting a formal table, the dinner fork is placed on the left side along with all other forks being used. The forks are placed in order of what is being eaten, beginning farthest away from the dinner plate. So if you were serving salad, the main course, and dessert, beginning from outside, you would have the salad fork, then the dinner fork, then the dessert fork next to the dinner plate. The first dinner forks were made with two flat prongs.

DINNER PLATE is the plate used to serve the main course to an individual and varies from 9½ to 11 inches in diameter. When you set a formal table, the first items to be placed on the tablecloth should be the dinner plates. These should be in the middle of each place setting, and everything else should be placed around the dinner plate.

DIP is a thick sauce or dressing in which pieces of food are dipped before eating; to dip is to put something briefly into a liquid or soft mixture and take it out again. The verb is fairly old, but the use of the noun in this sense did not become popular until around 1960. It is proper etiquette, when sharing dip with other people, not to double-dip the food. In a 2008 study performed by the *Journal of Food Safety*, in which scientists tested double-dipping in salsas, cheese dips, and chocolate sauces, it was determined that double-dipping just once added fifty to one hundred germs to the food. So to be polite, keep things clean and refrain from double-dipping. Also, if the dip requires a skewer, do not use the same skewer twice. Just as double-dipping adds germs to the dip, so too does your skewer. This is why hosts often provide a large quantity of disposable skewers. After enjoying your freshly dipped food, throw out the skewer and take a new one. This is the polite way to dip your morsel.

DIRTY RICE is white rice cooked with onions, peppers, celery (these three are referred to as the "holy trinity"), herbs, Cajun spice, and chicken giblets (livers and gizzards). The name was first recorded in 1949 and is derived from the appearance of the finished dish. In these more health-conscious days, livers and gizzards are not used often. Instead, small amounts of ground pork or beef are used, but the inclusions and spices remain the same. Some cooks also throw in a little bacon grease for extra flavoring.

DISH is a container for serving food, usually a bowl. The first eating "dishes" were probably stones with a concave top, but by 10,000 BC ancient peoples knew how to make pottery and our dinnerware evolved from there. The word dish is from the Latin *discus*, "circular shape," and is an all-encompassing term for the items we put our food on and in. There are two other culinary meanings of dish: a serving or plateful of food, especially one that forms only part of a larger meal; and a special recipe or style, or a food prepared to a recipe or in a recognized style.

DISTILL (DISTILLATION) is to remove impurities from, increase the concentration of, and separate through boiling. Distillation purifies a liquid by heating it so that it vaporizes, then cools and condenses the vapor to produce a nearly pure or refined substance. The word is from the Latin *destillare*, "to drip or trickle down." The apparatus that performs distillation is called a still. There are two types of still: a pot still and a continuous still. The pot still works in relatively small batches, while the continuous still is used in mass production. The condensation from distillation has a higher alcohol concentration than the original mixture. It is a method of increasing the alcohol content over and above that possible by normal fermentation.

DOGGY BAG is a U.S. term dating from around 1964 for a bag or container provided by a restaurant for taking home leftover food.

> **HINT** Food placed in a doggy bag may become unsafe if it stays in the temperature danger zone (41°F–140°F) for too long. It can have increased levels of food-poisoning bacteria. Food from a restaurant that is put into a doggy bag should be put into the refrigerator or eaten within two hours (preferably sooner) of the food leaving the hot plate, the oven, or the chiller at the restaurant. To reduce the risk of food poisoning, it is important that the doggy bag be refrigerated to below 41°F

as soon as possible after leaving the restaurant. It can be kept in the refrigerator for up to two days. It is safe to reheat the food one time. Do not reheat a second time for safety reasons; just toss it out.

DOUBLE BOILER is two saucepans, one fitting or nesting inside the other, designed so that the water-filled lower pan facilitates the slow, even cooking or heating of food in the upper pan, eliminating the possibility of scorching or overcooking. The BAIN-MARIE is the bottom pan. Double boilers are used to warm or cook heat-sensitive foods, such as custards, delicate sauces, and chocolate. If a recipe calls for a double boiler, you can set a bowl over a pot or pan of water or just use a smaller saucepan inside a larger one.

DOUBLE CREAM is thick cream with a high fat content or fresh soft cow's milk cheese enriched with cream and containing 48%–60% butterfat. Double cream is a little thicker than U.S. whipping cream. Double cream works really well when it is added to hot foods because the fat content acts as a binder, making it less likely to separate or curdle. This is why it is often used in making hot sauces and desserts, such as crème caramel.

> **HINTS** Other heavy or whipping creams can be used in recipes that call for double cream, although the end result may not be as rich. Double cream whips up very easily, but it is difficult to work with because it separates if you beat it too much and it can become very stiff.
>
> ▌ You can freeze double cream for up to two months, but when you thaw it, you can use it only for cooking and not as a topping.

DOUBLE-CRUST indicates a pie or tart with a lower and upper crust. The two crusts on a pie form a seal around the ingredients. This can help prevent juice from coming out of the pie, though a little bit might escape from the vents in the top crust. Sealing the two crusts together is important, since otherwise any liquid in the pie ingredients may leak underneath the bottom crust, dripping into the oven or onto the baking sheet upon which the pie sits.

DOUBLE GLOUCESTER (pronounced GLOSS-ter) is a smooth, firm, mild, orange-yellow cheese, originally made from Gloucester cattle milk and so named because two milkings are used to make the cheese. The main difference between Single Gloucester and Double Gloucester cheese is that Single Gloucester is made with skimmed evening milk and whole morning milk, while Double Gloucester is made with whole milk. Single Gloucester is more crumbly, lighter in texture, and lower in fat, and Double Gloucester has a firmer, denser texture. Double Gloucester rounds are larger.

DOUGH is flour or meal combined with water and/or milk and sometimes other ingredients into a thick mixture for baking. It may contain yeast or baking powder as a leavening agent and is usually kneaded, shaped, and baked to make bread or pastry. The word is from the Old English *dag*, "dough," from the Proto-Germanic **daigaz*, "something kneaded," from the Proto-Indo-European **dheigh-*, "to mold/to form/to knead." Lean dough is formed with only flour, yeast, and water. Rich dough has flour, yeast, and water—plus shortening or tenderizing ingredients, such as sugars, syrups, butter, oil, whole eggs, egg yolks, milk, or cream.

DOUGH ESSENTIALS

■ A good place to put dough for rising is in a slightly warm oven. Turn on the oven to the lowest setting for a few minutes, then turn it off. Place the covered bowl on the oven rack and close the door.

■ You can tell that dough has risen sufficiently when it no longer springs back when poked lightly in the center with two fingers, that is, when it holds the indentations.

■ To monitor dough's rise, use a skewer, marking the dough's first position and also marking where it needs to rise to once doubled.

■ To maintain a loaf's shape while cooking, poke holes in the top with a metal skewer before baking.

■ Cover a bowl of dough that is to rise with plastic wrap rather than a damp kitchen towel.

■ Put a fat rubber band (or a few bands) on the ends of a rolling pin so you can roll dough uniformly but not too thin.

■ When bread dough has enough flour, your hands will pull away cleanly when kneading.

■ If you overmix dough, the gluten polymers will begin to break down, making the dough sticky and then too dense.

DOUGHNUT or **DONUT**, also called DUNKER or SINKER, is a deep-fried or baked, usually round, piece of sweetened dough, sometimes filled or topped with icing or glaze. The doughnut was first called oly-cook/oli-cook, from the Dutch *olykoek*, "oilcake." The word was first recorded in 1809 in Washington Irving's *Knickerbocker's History of New York*. The original doughnuts were small, nut-sized balls of fried dough; the toroidal shape became common in the twentieth century. There are two types of doughnuts: raised, which are leavened with yeast; and cake, which are leavened with baking powder. The first Dunkin' Donuts shop was opened by Bill Rosenberg in 1950 in Quincy, Massachusetts.

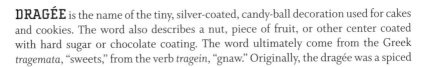

DRAGÉE is the name of the tiny, silver-coated, candy-ball decoration used for cakes and cookies. The word also describes a nut, piece of fruit, or other center coated with hard sugar or chocolate coating. The word ultimately come from the Greek *tragemata*, "sweets," from the verb *tragein*, "gnaw." Originally, the dragée was a spiced lump of sugar eaten to sweeten the breath and as a digestive after meals. Dragées are traditionally given at christenings, first communions, anniversaries, birthdays, holidays, and weddings. Throwing or handing out these candies at such occasions dates back centuries and is meant to ensure prosperity, fertility, happiness, and good luck. Dragées were hand-made by craftsmen until 1850, then, with the invention of the mechanical turbine, the process became more automated.

DRAINING SPOON: see SLOTTED SPOON.

DRAMBUIE is a sweet Scottish liqueur of malt whisky flavored with heather honey and herbs. The name comes from the Scottish Gaelic *dram buidheach*, "satisfying drink." The actual ingredients and the exact method of Drambuie's creation are kept secret from the general public. The secret selection of herbs, spices, and Scottish heather honey is then infused by hand into the Scotch whisky base. In 1909 Drambuie was first bottled in mainland Scotland, with the first batch created in secret and labeled for sale to the public. To this day, that recipe has remained a closely guarded secret. Drambuie was first commercially distributed in 1910.

DRAWN BUTTER is butter that is melted, clarified, and seasoned with herbs or lemon juice. This butter is often served as a sauce on cooked vegetables. The term comes from an obsolete sense of draw, which once meant "to bring to a proper consistency." Drawn butter is also called clarified butter, although there does appear to be some confusion or disagreement about whether butter must be clarified to be considered drawn, or merely melted with the surface foam skimmed away, or even simply melted. However, most culinary experts consider drawn butter to be the same as clarified butter.

> **HINTS** Because the milk solids, which make butter burn when used for frying, have been removed, drawn butter or clarified butter has a higher smoke point than regular butter and therefore may be used to cook at higher temperatures.
>
> Drawn butter can be covered and stored for one month in the refrigerator. It can also be frozen. If you freeze it, do so in small batches. Serve warm.

DREDGE means to lightly coat food with a dry substance, such as bread crumbs, cornmeal, flour, or sugar, before frying or browning. Most foods that are breaded are first dredged in flour and dipped in egg, then dredged again in the breading. This term actually derives from the same source as dragée.

> **HINT** Don't dredge too far ahead of the cooking time or the coating will become gummy. Put dredged food on a wire rack to prevent this.

DREDGER is a container with a perforated top used for sprinkling confectioners' sugar, flour, or sugar onto food. The sense dates to 1666. Using a dredger means the cook does not have to handle the meat as much, which translates to a lower risk of contracting foodborne diseases and results in a higher level of food safety.

DRESS is to clean, eviscerate, and otherwise prepare fish, fowl, game, or meat for the purpose of cooking and eating. Dress also means to put mayonnaise, vinaigrette, or another sauce on a salad or vegetable dish.

DRESSING, also called SALAD DRESSING, is a sauce for salads, usually one consisting of oil and vinegar or a mayonnaise base with herbs or spices. In addition, dressing, also called STUFFING, is a mixture of bread and seasoned ingredients used to stuff meats and vegetables or as an accompaniment to meat. The term salad dressing dates to writing by Charles Dickens in 1836.

DRIED FRUIT is any fruit preserved by drying, especially fruit with 75%–85% of the moisture removed. Fruits commonly found in dried form include apples, apricots, bananas, cherries, currants, dates, figs, grapes/raisins, peaches, pears, prunes, and strawberries. Drying fruit greatly concentrates both sweetness and flavor, and the taste is much changed, as from grape to raisin or from plum to prune. Fruit can be dried in the sun or by machine. Machine-drying usually takes no more than twenty-four hours. Sun-drying can take three to four times as long, causing additional loss of nutrients through heat and time. Dried fruit contains four to five times the calories by weight of fresh fruit.

> **HINTS** Most dried fruit can be stored in an airtight container at room tempera-ture for up to three months, or refrigerated or frozen for up to one year. Do not store new dried fruit with older dried fruit. The container keeps out any dust and germs, and prevents infestation by fruit flies. It also keeps the fruit moist and soft, helping it keep its color, flavor, and nutritional value. Temperature is critical for storage; ideally dried fruit should be kept at the cool temperature of 50°F. When storing dried fruit in the refrigerator, keep containers away from pungent foods, such as garlic or onions.

> If you need to chop dried fruit, freeze it for an hour or so and it will be easier to chop. You can use a knife, food processor, or kitchen shears to chop dried fruit. It is a good idea to also spray the knife, food processor, or kitchen shears with nonstick cooking spray to minimize sticking.

> Soften hardened dried fruit by covering it with boiling water and letting it stand for 15 minutes. Drain and blot the fruit dry before using. If dried fruit, such as raisins or dates, clumps together, put it in a strainer and spray hot, running water over it. You can also pop it in the microwave and heat on high for 10–20 seconds.

DRIED MILK or **DRY MILK**, also called MILK POWDER or POWDERED MILK, is dehydrated milk from which about 95% of the moisture has been evaporated and the milk has been reduced to powder.

> **HINTS** Dried nonfat milk and buttermilk can be kept in an airtight container in a cool, dry place for up to six months. Refrigerating opened packages will

help retain their freshness. Dried whole milk must be refrigerated because of its fat content.

▎ Dried milk dissolves readily in water but once reconstituted should be treated as fresh milk. Reconstituted dried milk can be refrigerated for up to three days.

▎ Dried milk tends to dissolve more readily in cool water. Stir the milk vigorously to dissolve the powder. Then let the milk sit for a little while and stir again; the protein in the dried milk blends most easily if it gets a chance to stand after mixing. Chill the milk whenever possible. If you have fresh milk available, then it may be mixed half-and-half with reconstituted milk to improve the flavor.

DRIPPINGS, also called PAN JUICES, are the juices and fats that drip from roasting or frying meat. Drippings are used for basting, for making gravy, or as a cooking fat. A metal pan called a dripping pan is used to catch juices or melted fat when roasting poultry or other meat, or when grilling or broiling food.

> **HINT** If you plan to make gravy or sauce from drippings, it's a good idea to accumulate as much of the drippings as you can when you're roasting meat. Place the meat on a rack above the pan or set it in the pan, so that the cooking meat doesn't reabsorb the drippings or block them from dropping. A rack will help your meat yield the most juice, resulting in lots of flavor for your gravy or sauce.

DRIZZLE means to pour in a fine stream or drops, as in slowly pouring butter or icing on top of a food. This word may come from the Old English *dreosan*, "to fall."

> **HINT** To drizzle, put the liquid in a small ladle or cup and gently swirl over the food surface. Another method is to dip a fork in the liquid and drizzle from the tines. For something like olive oil, put your thumb over the bottle opening, leaving a small gap, and then shake the bottle over the food.

DRUMSTICK is the meaty lower half of the leg of a chicken, duck, turkey, or other poultry. It is named for its shape and the term had appeared by 1764.

DRUPE is a fruit with a thin outer skin, soft pulpy middle, and hard stony central part that encloses a seed.

DRUPES

ALMOND	COCONUT	NECTARINE
APRICOT	DATE	OLIVE
BETEL PALM	ELDERBERRY	PEACH
BLACKBERRY	MANGO	PLUM
CHERRY	MULBERRY	RASPBERRY

DRY has two culinary meanings: pertaining to food served without butter, jam, gravy, or garnish; and pertaining to wine that is not sweet as a result of the decomposition of sugar during fermentation.

DRY-CURE is to dehydrate a food (such as meat or olives) by covering or infusing it with salt, sugar, and sometimes saltpeter or another nitrate/phosphate combination, rather than curing it with a liquid. Dry-curing meat produces a more intense flavor than liquid-curing and deepens the color of the meat.

DRY RUB is a mixture of spices, herbs, salt, sugar, and various other seasonings that is used to flavor meat to be barbecued or grilled, instead of using a sauce. The moisture from the meat mixes with the rub to make a kind of thick sauce on the surface of the meat. Dry rub may have originated with cowboys in the American West.

> HINT A dry rub will flavor meat just as a wet marinade does, but the advantage is that because a dry rub does not drain off, all the flavor stays with the meat and the rub cooks into a crisp crust. The best types of meat for dry rub are cuts that are fat enough to hold their moisture when cooked a long time. Dry rub can be added long before grilling or just before.

DU JOUR, French for "of the day," is from the French *plat du jour*, "dish of the day," and by the early twentieth century appeared on restaurant menus for dishes offered or served as a special of the day.

DUBLIN BAY PRAWN: see PRAWN.

DUCHESS POTATOES or **DUCHESSE POTATOES**, also called POMMES DUCHESSE, are mashed potatoes, butter, egg yolks, and seasonings piped onto a baking pan or made into small cakes, topped with grated cheese, and baked or fried. The first recipe was published in 1930. The term à la duchesse refers to dishes garnished with duchess potatoes.

> HINT The mixture for duchess potatoes can be made up to 24 hours in advance and stored in a refrigerator, covered. For that matter, you can also make the shapes in advance and store in the same way.

DUCK is a relatively small waterfowl with edible flesh. There are many types of duck; wild ducks differ from domesticated ducks in that wild ducks are often gamey in flavor and are very low in fat.

> HINTS Buy duck with smooth skin and no discoloration. Store in the coldest part of the refrigerator and cook within two days. Frozen duck, tightly wrapped, keeps for up to six months. Let frozen duck defrost in the refrigerator for a day

or (in its packaging) in cool water for 2–3 hours, changing the water every 30 minutes. Do not refreeze.

▌ Basting is not enough to ensure moistness in a wild duck during roasting. The birds are often so lean that they need to be barded with a layer of fat; this means covering the breast with salt pork or bacon during cooking.

▌ Before roasting a duck, prick the skin so the juices and fats can escape to the surface where they will caramelize in the heat and coat the skin with flavor and crispness. Duck can be microwaved. Do about three-quarters of the cooking in the microwave and then finish in a very hot oven. A properly prepared duck breast will be pink in color.

DUCK SAUCE, also called PLUM SAUCE, is a thick sweet-and-sour condiment of apricots, plums, seasonings, and sugar served with deep-fried items in Asian cuisine, such as noodles, egg rolls, and chicken. It was first served with the pancakes that accompany Peking duck.

> **HINT** If you make your own duck sauce, let it cool, then chill it. Duck sauce tastes best if refrigerated, covered, overnight to allow the seasonings to mellow, and it will keep in the refrigerator for several days. Use homemade duck sauce within a few days, as it doesn't keep as well as store-bought sauce.

DULCE DE LECHE is a Latin American concoction of caramel and sweet cream, used as a spread or flavoring for foods like ice cream. Dulce de leche, from the Latin *dulcis*, "sweet," is literally Spanish for "milk candy/sweet milk." It is prepared by slowly heating sweetened milk to create a product that is similar in taste to caramel. In 1997 Häagen-Dazs introduced a dulce de leche–flavored ice cream; in the same year Starbucks began offering dulce de leche–flavored coffee products.

DUM means cooked by steaming and is a term in South Asian cuisine. The *handi*, a spherical-shaped clay pot with a thick bottom and a wide-mouthed opening, is used for dum cooking. There is no handle, so the pot is lifted by grabbing the rim. A clay saucer is used as a lid and placed on the top. The lid is sealed with a hard paste made of flour and water. The *handi* is left on the charcoal for several hours, until the food is to be served. The heat creates the steam, then the steam condenses and rolls down the curved walls.

DUMPLING refers to a small ball or package of seasoned dough that is boiled, fried, baked, or steamed and, sometimes, filled. Dumplings may be served in soup or as an accompaniment. A second meaning of dumpling is a baked dessert of sweet dough wrapped around fruit, such as an apple. The word, which dates to around 1600, may be a diminutive of *dump*, which has obsolete meanings of "lump" as a noun and "the consistency of dough" as an adjective.

> **HINTS** To prevent dumplings from becoming heavy with soggy bottoms, cook them in liquid that bubbles gently but continuously.

❙ If you freeze dumplings, store them in a zip-lock freezer bag and place a sheet of wax paper between each layer to prevent the dumplings from sticking to each other. When you are ready to use the dumplings, thaw them at room temperature.

DUNGENESS CRAB is a large edible crab (*Cancer magister*) of the Pacific coast of North America, named for Dungeness, Washington. Dungeness crabs can range from one to four pounds in weight. Dungeness crabs are one of the largest edible crabs along the Pacific Coast of America. These larger crabs are valued for their high meat to shell ratio.

HINT When buying Dungeness crabs, you can test their freshness by feeling the outer parts of the legs. If the legs bend easily, the crab isn't fresh. Do not use crabs that have been dead for more than a couple of hours without being cooked. Dungenesses are not sold as soft-shells.

DUNKER: see DOUGHNUT.

DURIAN is the fruit of a Southeast Asian tree; it has a hard, prickly rind containing a creamy pulp with an offensive smell but a good taste. The word is a derivative of the Malay *duri*, "thorn." Durian fruit are large and can grow to ten to eleven pounds.

HINT A durian fruit is ready to eat when its husk begins to crack. The various preferences regarding ripeness among consumers make it hard to issue general statements about choosing a "good" durian. A durian that falls off the tree continues to ripen for two to four days, but after five to six days, most people would consider it overripe and unpalatable. The usual advice for a consumer choosing a whole fruit in the market is to examine the quality of the stem or stalk, which loses moisture as it ages: a big, solid stem is a sign of freshness. Reportedly, unscrupulous merchants wrap, paint, or remove the stalks altogether. Another frequent piece of advice is to shake the fruit and listen for the sound of the seeds moving within, indicating the durian is overripe and the pulp has dried out a bit. The unpleasant and distinctive smell of a durian becomes nauseating when the fruit is overripe.

DURUM WHEAT or **DURUM**, also called MACARONI WHEAT, is a hardy emmer wheat (*Triticum turgidum* or *Triticum durum*) used mainly for making pasta. Durum wheat gets its name, which was first recorded in 1908, from the Latin *durus*, "hard." Durum wheat is not suitable for baking because in most baking you need to use a soft wheat to prevent toughness. American-grown durum wheat is considered among the best in the world. Durum wheat is used almost exclusively for making pasta and is most often ground into a granular flour with a light yellow color known as semolina, which has the ideal properties for making the best pasta. (Italian pasta makers never refer to semolina as flour—they refer to it as grain.) Durum is high in protein and gluten, which are necessary for making good pasta.

DUST is to coat lightly with a dusting of a powdery substance, such as flour or confectioners' sugar.

DUTCH CHEESE: see Cottage cheese.

DUTCH OVEN is a large pot of earthenware or cast iron with a tight-fitting lid or cover, for making casseroles, roasts, and stews. Originally, this oven was a metal box with an open front, which cooks heated in a fire by heaping coals around it. Dutch ovens are said to be of Pennsylvania Dutch heritage, dating back to the eighteenth century, but the casting process for these ovens originated in Holland. Dutch ovens are well suited for long, slow cooking and moist-cooking methods such as braising and stewing, but other types of dishes, such as breads, can also be cooked in a Dutch oven.

> **HINT** If you have a small amount of light rust in a cast-iron Dutch oven, gently rub it with a dry steel wool pad. The rust should easily come off. The other method is to soak the rusted area in cola; the soaking time depends on how rusty the Dutch oven is. To keep your Dutch oven rust-free and ready to use, season it with a thin film of oil.

DUXELLES is a stuffing or garnish made from chopped, sautéed mushrooms, onions, shallots, and parsley. It is named after the Marquis d'Uxelles, a seventeenth-century French nobleman. Duxelles can be made with any cultivated or wild mushroom, depending on the recipe. Duxelles made with wild porcini mushrooms will be much stronger flavored than that made with white or brown mushrooms. Fresh mushrooms are usually used, but reconstituted dried varieties can be used as well. If you want a stronger flavor, use a mixture of both dried and fresh, heavy on the fresh mushrooms.

EARL GREY TEA is a blend of Indian and Sri Lankan black teas flavored by oil of bergamot, a small acidic orange. It was probably named for the second Earl Grey (1764–1845), said to have been given the recipe by a Chinese mandarin.

> **HINTS** Earl Grey tea is used as a flavoring for many types of cakes and confections, such as chocolates, as well as savory sauces. For sauces, the flavor is normally created by adding tea bags to the basic stock, boiling for a few minutes, and then discarding the bags. For sweet recipes, loose tea is often added to melted butter and strained after the flavor is infused.
>
> ▌Since bergamot is a strong flavoring, it can cover up for tea of a lesser quality. For that reason, people who are concerned about the grade of their tea should

read the label carefully. When shopping for Earl Grey, make sure to double-check the grade of the tea before making your choice. Loose-leaf tea tends to be of better quality, and some bagged teas can be quite unpleasant. Earl Grey is not a kind of tea; it is just black tea with the flavor of bergamot infused through it. Almost any black tea can be used to make it.

EARTHNUT: see PEANUT.

EARTHY is a descriptive term for food or drink with a texture, odor, or color suggestive of the earth. It denotes a heartiness reminiscent of freshly plowed soil or forest litter. Wine, coffee, and cheese may be described with this term.

EASTER FOODS

BORSCHT	LAMBROPSOMO, PANETTONE, SIMNEL, TSOUREKI)	EGGS
EASTER BREADS (SHAPED)		HAM
	EASTER CANDY	LAMB WITH MINT SAUCE
EASTER CAKES (HOT CROSS BUN, KULICH,	EASTER COOKIES	NEW POTATOES

EATING

Your body is extremely efficient at capturing and storing excess calories. Whenever your body has extra calories, it converts them to fat and stores them. A body with a more active metabolism will use up this store more rapidly.

HERE IS WHAT HAPPENS TO CARBOHYDRATES:

1. When you eat a carbohydrate, glucose flows into the bloodstream and is available to every cell in your body.

2. However, when you eat fiber, it simply passes straight through your system, untouched by the digestive system.

3. Cells perform a set of chemical reactions on glucose to create adenosine triphosphate (ATP), which has a phosphate bond that provides energy for the cells.

4. When you eat a carbohydrate containing fructose or galactose, your liver converts these sugars to glucose.

5. Glucose, fructose, and galactose can be absorbed into the bloodstream through the intestinal lining.

6. Lactose, sucrose, and maltose are converted by enzymes in the digestive tract before entering the bloodstream.

7. When you eat a complex carbohydrate or starch, your digestive system breaks it down into its component glucose molecules so that the glucose can enter your bloodstream.

8. Eating any carbohydrate causes your body to secrete insulin, which decreases blood sugar levels. If there is an insulin imbalance, your body will release extra adrenaline.

HERE IS WHAT HAPPENS TO FATS:

1. Fats that you eat enter the digestive system and meet with an enzyme called lipase.

2. Lipase breaks the fat into its two parts: glycerol and fatty acids.

3. These components are reassembled into triglycerides for transport in the bloodstream.

4. Muscle cells and fat/adipose cells absorb the triglycerides, either storing them or burning them as fuel.

HERE IS WHAT HAPPENS TO PROTEINS:

1. The digestive system breaks down all proteins into their individual amino acids or short amino acid chains so they can enter the bloodstream.

2. Cells then use the amino acids as building blocks.

ÉCLAIR is a type of long cream puff filled with whipped cream or custard and topped with chocolate frosting. Éclair is French for "lightning bolt"— perhaps for the speed with which one is eaten. The éclair probably originated in France during the nineteenth century.

EDAM is a mild yellow cow's milk cheese made into slightly elongated spheres encased in a red wax covering. It is named for Edam in the Netherlands, where it was originally made. Outside the Netherlands you will sometimes see Edam cheese with a black paraffin coating; these cheeses have been matured for at least seventeen weeks.

EDAMAME or **EDA MAME** (pronounced eh-dah-MAH-meh) is the Japanese term for fresh, immature green soybeans. These are boiled and often served in the pod as an appetizer. Edamame may be served hot or cold. Some call edamame the super or wonder vegetable because it is the only vegetable that contains all nine essential amino acids. This makes edamame a complete protein source, similar to meat or eggs. Edamame also contains isoflavonoids, which are found in all soy products and are being studied for their health benefits.

> **HINTS** To eat edamame, push the beans out of the pod and into your mouth. Discard the outer shell.

> ▌ In Japan, edamame is sold as whole plants. Pods are also sold removed from the stalks and packed in plastic net bags. Fresh beans are harvested by cutting the entire plant at about two inches and bunching stalks together in groups of four to six plants. The top leaves and small damaged pods are removed, while whole plants with leaves, pods, stems, and roots are packed in bundles or cartons. This form is considered the most desirable and brings the highest prices, since Japanese consumers believe this method best preserves pod quality. To maintain freshness, speedy harvesting and packaging are crucial. Beans are also shelled and marketed fresh or—more often in the United States—frozen.

EDIBLE means suitable for eating by human beings.

EDIBLE CRUSTACEANS AND GASTROPODS

Usually crustaceans are viewed as a luxury food rather than a staple source of protein. But this was not always so. In the first half of the twentieth century, rock lobsters, then more commonly referred to as crayfish, were not reserved for the rich. The crayfish, also known as the crawfish, owes its name to a misunderstanding. The actual source of the word may be the Old High German word *krebiz*, "edible crustacean." These are some common edible crustaceans and gastropods:

CRAB	LOBSTER	SEA URCHIN
CRAYFISH	PERIWINKLE	SHRIMP
LANGOSTINO, LANGOUSTE, LANGOUSTINE	PRAWN	SPINY LOBSTER
	ROCK LOBSTER	TURBAN SNAIL
LIMPET	SCAMPI	WHELK

EDIBLE FLOWERS

Most herb flowers have a taste that is similar to the leaf, but spicier. The concept of using fresh edible flowers in cooking is not new. Flower cookery has been traced back to Roman times and was especially popular in the Victorian era. Today, many restaurant chefs and innovative home cooks garnish their entrées with flower blossoms for a touch of elegance. *Inedible* flowers include daffodil, hydrangea, lily of the valley, narcissus, oleander, poinsettia, rhododendron, sweet pea, and wisteria. The following flowers are edible:

ALLIUM	CHRYSANTHEMUM	HYACINTH
ANGELICA	CITRUS BLOSSOM	HYSSOP
ANISE HYSSOP	CLOVER	IMPATIENS
APPLE BLOSSOM	COURGETTE	JASMINE
ARUGULA	DAISY	LAVENDER
BANANA BLOSSOM	DANDELION	LEMON VERBENA
BASIL	DAYLILY	LILAC
BEE BALM	DIANTHUS	LINDEN
BEGONIA	DILL	LOTUS
BERGAMOT	ELDERFLOWER	MARIGOLD
BORAGE	EVENING PRIMROSE	MARJORAM
CALENDULA	FENNEL	MINT
CARNATION	FUCHSIA	MUSTARD
CHAMOMILE	GARDENIA	NASTURTIUM
CHERVIL	GERANIUM	OKRA
CHICORY	HIBISCUS	ORCHID
CHIVE	HOLLYHOCK	OREGANO

PANSY	ROCKET	SUNFLOWER
PEACH BLOSSOM	ROSE	THYME
PEAR BLOSSOM	ROSEMARY	TIGER LILY
PEONY	SAFFLOWER	TULIP PETAL
PETUNIA	SAFFRON	VIOLA OR JOHNNY-JUMP-UP
PRIMROSE	SAGE	VIOLET
QUEEN ANNE'S LACE	SAVORY	YUCCA PETAL
RADISH FLOWER	SNAPDRAGON	
REDBUD	SQUASH BLOSSOM	

EDIBLE MOLLUSKS

Shellfish is the popular name for certain edible mollusks. All mollusks are more or less edible. The principal edible mollusks are oysters; clams, including the hard-shell clam or quahog and the soft-shell clam of the Atlantic; and several Pacific species—the scallop, mussels, and the abalone.

ABALONE	GOLDEN NECK CLAM	NEW ZEALAND ROCK OYSTER
ATLANTIC OYSTER	GREAT SCALLOP	OCTOPUS
ATLANTIC SEA SCALLOP	GREENLIP MUSSEL	OLYMPIA OYSTER
BASKET COCKLE	HARD-SHELL CLAM, QUAHOG, OR QUAHAUG	OYSTER
BAY SCALLOP	HOG ISLAND OYSTER	PINK SCALLOP
BLOOD CLAM	JAPANESE SEA SCALLOP	PIPI CLAM
BLUE MUSSEL	KUMAMOTO OYSTER	RAZOR CLAM
BORING CLAM	LITTLENECK CLAM	SCALLOP
CALIFORNIA MUSSEL	MANILA CLAM	SOFT-SHELL CLAM
CLAM	MEDITERRANEAN MUSSEL	SQUID
COCKLE	MUSSEL	SURF CLAM
EUROPEAN FLAT OYSTER	NEW ZEALAND COCKLE	
FRESHWATER CLAM		
GEODUCK CLAM		

EELPOUT: see BURBOT.

EGG in cooking refers to the thin-shelled reproductive body laid by female birds that is used as food. An egg consists of a hard, porous calcium carbonate shell enclosing a thin membrane, a small air pocket at one end, and a transparent egg white (albumen) surrounding a yellow yolk anchored by two threads called chalazae. The word was borrowed from the Old Norse *egg* and is akin to the Old English *aeg/egg*, Old High German *ei*, Crimean Gothic *ada*, Latin *ovum*, Welsh *wy*, Greek *omacrion*, and Old Persian *xamacrya*. Five eggs yield the following volumes: 5 large eggs = 1 cup, 5 large yolks = ⅓ cup, 5 large whites = ⅔ cup.

CONFUSABLE WHITE EGG/BROWN EGG. A white egg comes from hens with white feathers, while brown eggs come from hens with reddish brown feathers. Contrary to popular belief, brown eggs are not a healthier alternative to white eggs.

■ Cold eggs are easier to separate. So separate the eggs first and if the eggs need to be room temperature for the recipe (as for batters), let them come to room temperature after separating. To separate egg yolks from the whites, crack the egg and let the whites run through your fingers into a bowl, keeping the yolk in your hand. This method will not break the yolks like passing them back and forth between the shell halves may.

■ Buy large AA eggs if possible. All eggs sold commercially have been washed and coated with a natural mineral oil to prevent the introduction of bacteria. Eggs should be stored in their carton or in an egg rack with the large end up and pointed end down. This way they will stay fresh longer, for upright storage helps to retard spoilage, as it minimizes the distance between the yolk and the natural egg space. The gaseous space is potentially the more prolific environment for pathogenic bacteria. AA grade eggs cost more than A, which cost more than B; the higher the grade, the plumper the yolk, and the thicker the white, which is desirable for frying or poaching because the cooked eggs will be more compact and visually pleasing. AA eggs will have a thick white that doesn't spread much and the yolk will stand up. A eggs will have a white that is a little less thick and a round yolk that will stand high. B eggs will have a thick white with wide spread and probably an enlarged-looking yolk that is somewhat flattened. C eggs will have an even wider spread and a thin, somewhat watery white. C eggs may be used for baking and general cooking with other ingredients but not for frying or poaching. The grade of an egg is determined by candling, in which a light is held in back of the unbroken egg to illuminate the interior for visual inspection.

■ Use older eggs for baking, and fresher eggs for cooking; use older egg whites for meringue, and fresh eggs for emulsified sauces. Use fresh eggs for poaching. Use older eggs for boiling. You can tell how fresh an egg is by putting it in several inches of water. If it lies on its side, it is fresh. If it tilts, it is about three to four days old. If it stands upright, it is about ten days old or more. A fresh egg sinks to the bottom of a bowl of water and an old egg floats due to moisture loss through evaporation.

■ Eggs should be put into cold or lukewarm water before hard-cooking them because otherwise the air space in the shell expands too fast and the eggs may crack.

■ Hard-cooked eggs should be kept no longer than three days for health considerations, although they will taste good past this point. To protect hard-cooked eggs during transport, put a rubberized shelf/drawer liner in a dish. Hard-cooked eggs is the more appropriate term than hard-boiled eggs because eggs should not be hard-boiled, but rather cooked with simmering water (always just below the boiling point) until the eggs are solid. To remove hard-cooked eggs from their shell, peel soon after the cooking. If necessary, do it under running cold water to make the egg cool enough to handle. Start peeling at the large end. If you add salt to the water when hard-cooking an egg, the egg will be easier to peel. An old egg will be easier to peel when hard-cooked than a fresh egg. Another way to remove the shell from a hard-cooked eggs is to tap it all over on a counter, then roll it on the counter until it is cracked everywhere. Start peeling from the end with the air pocket. Alternatively, drain the water from the pot used to simmer hard-cooked eggs, then shake the pot back and forth to crack the eggs. You can also add ice water to cover the eggs to cool; water seeps under the shells, making it easy to remove them.

■ Only at 70°F can eggs and liquids combine and penetrate one another to give a smooth, homogeneous batter.

■ To rescue an egg that cracks while being boiled, add a tablespoon of salt or teaspoon of vinegar to the water. This helps coagulate the white and stop the seeping.

■ Press hard-cooked eggs through a sieve to get an even crumble.

■ Put nonstick cooking spray on the spatula to ease the flipping and removing of cooked eggs.

■ Crack an egg on a flat surface (like a countertop) rather than the edge of a mixing bowl for cleaner cracking.

■ Boiled eggs should be called poached because the water should never be at a real boil, which just bounces the eggs and cracks the shells. When poaching eggs, use a saucepan big enough for water to circulate freely.

■ To beat egg whites with a mixer, use the whisk attachment and a spotless metal or glass bowl, and make sure the whites contain no yolk whatsoever. When adding eggs while whipping by machine, do so one at a time to keep the batter creamy and airy.

■ When making scrambled eggs, heat the eggs with some of the butter on low heat. When the eggs start to thicken, beat in more cold butter. For scrambled eggs, after you add beaten eggs to the pan, let them sit untouched for a full minute to puff. Then gently push one edge to the center and allow uncooked egg to flow into the bare spot.

■ When making fried eggs, use medium heat rather than high.

■ Open the carton at the store and check each egg, making sure none are stuck to the carton. There is a Julian date on USDA-graded eggs, so 001 means the eggs were packed on January 1. Don't confuse it with the three-digit packing date, which is preceded by a *P*. You can decipher this and add five weeks to determine how long the eggs can be kept.

EGG DISHES

Eggs are among the most versatile ingredients used in cooking—a component of pasta, cookies, cakes, pastries, and sauces. Eggs can be cooked in a great variety of ways. They can be served plain or with an array of garnishing ingredients, sauces, or other accompaniments.

The nutritive value of eggs ensured they would become part of the human diet all over the world from the earliest times; they are also associated with the rites and traditions of holidays, such as Lent and Easter. Some popular egg dishes are listed here:

(continued)

209

BAKED	EN COCOTTE	QUICHE
BENEDICT	FLORENTINE	SCOTCH
BOILED	FRIED	SCRAMBLED
CODDLED	FRITATTA	SHIRRED
CREAMED	HARD-COOKED	SOFT-COOKED
CURRIED	HUEVOS RANCHEROS	SOUFFLÉ
DEVILED	NEPTUNE	STUFFED
DROPPED	OMELET	
EGGS IN A MOLD	POACHED	

EGG WHITE WHIPPING STAGES

FOAMY: The whites are lightly whipped to a frothy but still fluid consistency, consisting of large bubbles on the surface that readily pop. The foam does not hold any peaks when the whisk is lifted from it.

SOFT PEAKS: The foam is moist, shiny, and bright white. When the whisk or beaters are lifted, the foam forms a dull peak, then piles softly or gently curls over. Soft peaks flow when the bowl is tilted.

STIFF PEAKS: The foam maintains its glossy sheen and holds an upright peak when the whisk or beaters are lifted; it has reached its maximum volume.

OVERBEATEN: The foam begins to look dry and granular. Add an extra fresh white and beat until you have a glossy foam that holds the desired peaks.

EGG BREAD: see SPOON BREAD.

EGG CREAM is a carbonated drink made with milk, flavoring syrup (often chocolate), and seltzer (soda) water. An egg cream contains neither egg nor cream, but is probably so named for its frothy top that resembles beaten egg white. An egg cream will lose its head and turn flat if not drunk within minutes. This New York City soda fountain drink was invented by 1841.

EGGCUP, **EGG CUP**, **EGG-CUP**, or **EGG SERVER**, is simply an egg-shaped container to hold an egg, such as a soft-boiled one. The eggcup is a collectible item. Collecting eggcups is called pocillovy. Eggcups can be made of china, pottery, wood, plastic, glass, various metals, or Bakelite. The main function of an eggcup is to hold the egg in place while the top of the shell is tapped and opened. Once the top portion of the shell is removed, it is possible to salt and pepper the hard- or soft-cooked egg and scoop out the contents with a spoon. The bottom section of the shell can be discarded with ease once the contents are consumed.

EGG CUSTARD: see CUSTARD.

EGG FOO YONG or **EGG FU YUNG**, also called FOO YOUNG or FU YONG, is a pancakelike omelet with onions, celery or bean sprouts, and chopped meat or fish. The term has been used in English since 1917. Foo yong means "in a sauce made with eggs and other ingredients," from the Chin *fúrong*, "egg white," literally the name of a kind of lotus. Egg foo yong is one of the few Chinese dishes for which a sauce is prepared separately and served over the dish.

EGGNOG or **EGG-FLIP**, also called FLIP, is a thick drink made of sweetened milk or cream beaten with eggs and flavored with nutmeg and sometimes liquor like rum, bourbon, or brandy. Eggnog is from Old English *nog*, "strong ale," as the drink was originally made with hot beer, cider, wine, or spirits. A traditional Christmas drink, eggnog has been around since before 1825. It can be served either hot or cold.

> **HINT** For commercial eggnog, refrigerate for up to a week after the sell-by date. For homemade eggnog, cover tightly and refrigerate for up to two days.

EGG NOODLE is any narrow strip of pasta dough made with eggs.

EGGPLANT, also called AUBERGINE or MELONGENE, is an egg-shaped vegetable with a typically dark purple, shiny skin, though some are yellow or white; eggplant was so named because the delicate white varieties resemble eggs. Eggplant grows on a plant (*Solanum esculentum*) in the nightshade family. Eggplant is actually a fruit and not a vegetable; it is technically a berry. Eggplants have not always been popular. They were once known as "mad apples," because it was thought that they caused insanity or death. They have been used in China since 600 BC. Thomas Jefferson first brought the eggplant to America from France in the eighteenth century. Male eggplants are rounder, and smoother at the blossom end. They have fewer seeds, which are bitter. Female eggplants are more oval, and the blossom end is usually deeply indented. They tend to have more bitter seeds.

EGGPLANT ESSENTIALS

- Eggplants are at their best from July through September. Select smooth, firm, glossy-skinned eggplants with green caps and stems. Smaller eggplants are sweeter than large ones. The fewer the seeds in an eggplant, the sweeter the eggplant; the more seeds, the older the eggplant.

- Store eggplant in a perforated plastic bag in the vegetable crisper of the refrigerator for four to five days.

- Eggplant should be cooked immediately after peeling or cutting because the exposed flesh discolors rapidly because of oxidation. To prevent this, start cooking as soon as you have cut it. If there is an unavoidable delay, promptly coat the surfaces with lemon juice or submerge the pieces in acidulated water.

- Salt the flesh of a large cut-up eggplant to draw out any bitterness. For frying, it is always good to salt eggplant or otherwise remove excess moisture. Only eggplants with tough, thick skin need to be peeled.

(continued)

■ Eggplants should be cooked in only the minimum of fat or oil, or without any oil. Because they have inner air pockets, eggplants can absorb several times their weight in oil, even when breaded.

Cooking with too much oil or fat breaks down the eggplant's texture.

■ You can slice eggplant more easily with a serrated knife.

EGG ROLL is a Chinese egg-dough wrapper filled with diced meat or shrimp, shredded cabbage, and other vegetables, and deep-fried or steamed. Egg rolls are so named for their casings of thin egg dough.

CONFUSABLE EGG ROLL/SPRING ROLL/SUMMER ROLL. A spring roll has a thin, often transparent, flour wrapper, while egg rolls have thicker wrappings. Spring rolls tend to be vegetarian, while egg rolls sometimes contain meat. Spring rolls, so named because they're traditionally served on the first day of the Chinese New Year (in early spring), are smaller, more delicate versions of the egg roll. The summer roll contains pork, herbs, lettuce, chives, and rice vermicelli and is wrapped in moistened rice paper; it is served cold with dipping sauce called nuoc cham.

HINTS Egg roll wrappers are available in many markets. Prepare the vegetables for the egg rolls ahead of time; this gives them time to drain properly. Use fresh meat. Make sure the filling is not too soggy.

❙ You can freeze egg rolls, either before or after deep-frying. To keep the egg rolls moist, wrap them in foil and store in a zip-lock freezer bag in the freezer for up to four months. (If the egg rolls have already been deep-fried, wait until they have cooled before freezing.) Thaw uncooked egg rolls in the bag in the refrigerator before deep-frying. Reheat cooked egg rolls briefly in the oven or deep-fry them again.

EGG SALAD is a sandwich spread or dish made primarily of chopped hard-cooked eggs mixed with mayonnaise, often including other ingredients, such as celery, pickles, mustard, and seasonings.

HINTS Celery, onions, and cucumbers all add the necessary crunch that will make your egg salad taste fresh and will really add another layer of flavor to it. Just chop whichever vegetables you are adding, and mix them with the eggs before you add the mayonnaise. Make sure to cut the vegetables into pieces smaller than the eggs—since the eggs are in small pieces, you do not want to have large vegetable pieces dominating your salad. Also, control the amount of mayonnaise that you use. A general rule is about a tablespoon of mayonnaise for every four eggs. But this is entirely up to your taste. Finally, if you are making an egg salad sandwich, make sure to use fresh bread to complete the dish.

❙ Egg salad can be stored in the refrigerator for two to three days in a covered container.

EGGS BENEDICT (or eggs Benedict or eggs benedict) is a dish of toasted English muffin halves topped with grilled ham and a poached egg (or an oyster) and hollandaise sauce. Eggs Benedict was probably named for a customer who requested the combination at either Delmonico's restaurant or the Waldorf-Astoria Hotel, both in New York City.

EGG SLICER is a utensil used to slice peeled, hard-cooked eggs quickly and evenly. It usually consists of a slotted dish for holding the egg and a hinged plate of wires or blades that can be closed to slice it. Since slicing a hard-cooked egg can be a messy process, cooks who handle a large number of hard-cooked eggs often appreciate an egg slicer. The uniform slices look neater, which is important for professional presentations at restaurants and catered events. In addition, using an egg slicer means that the egg does not need to be handled beyond the peeling stage, which is more sanitary. As the white flesh of eggs tends to accumulate dirt, the hands-off approach also keeps the egg cleaner.

> **HINT** An egg slicer can also be used to slice soft fruits (strawberries) and vegetables (mushrooms), as well as soft cheese (mozzarella).

EGG WASH is a mixture of beaten raw egg, usually the yolk, with water or milk and a little salt, used for glazing pastry or bread to give it a shine when baked. In addition to being used as a sort of glaze, an egg wash also seals flavors in.

> **HINTS** When you prepare an egg wash, it is important to make sure that the egg is completely beaten, since otherwise chunks of egg may disturb the surface of the finished product. A robust whisk is a great tool for this. As ingredients are added, the egg wash should be whisked or whipped to fully incorporate them.

> Follow these general guidelines for different surface results: Whole egg and salt—provides a shiny surface. Whole egg and milk—provides a medium-shiny surface or faint shine. Whole egg and water—provides a golden-amber surface or a matte, golden-brown surface. Egg yolk and water—provides a shiny, golden-amber surface. Egg yolk and cream—provides a shiny, darker brown surface. Egg white—provides a crispy, lighter-colored surface. Egg yolk with salt—provides a shiny, golden-brown surface. Egg white with salt—provides a matte, golden-brown surface.

ELBERTA PEACH is a variety of large freestone peach with sweet flesh and red-blushed yellow skin. Elberta peaches are good both for eating plain and for cooking. Elberta peaches are also a high-quality canning peach.

> **HINT** Aromatic, slightly soft or semifirm, red and yellow Elberta peaches with velvety skin are best. Avoid Elberta peaches that have a green hue or that feel very hard, as they will not ripen. Bruises can accelerate and reveal spoilage. Use

ripe Elberta peaches as soon as possible, or store them for three to four days at room temperature or in the refrigerator. Wash Elberta peaches only immediately before serving to preserve the integrity of the fruit.

ELEPHANT EARS are a variety of fried bread made from a yeast dough and have sweet varieties with icing, powdered sugar, and so on, or savory versions served with marinara, soy sauce, or other toppings. They are popular for breakfast but also as a snack at fairs, amusement parks, and other venues.

ELEVENSES is a British term for a coffee or tea break taken around 11:00 A.M. Elevenses is generally less savory than brunch, and might consist of some cake or biscuits with a cup of tea. The name refers to the time of day that it is taken.

EMMENTAL, EMMENTHAL, EMMENTALER, or **EMMENTHALER** is a type of mild Swiss cow's cheese with large walnut-sized interior holes; it originated in Emmental, Switzerland. Emmental is Switzerland's oldest and most important cheese. The only true Emmental is produced in Switzerland, but the name isn't protected, so you'll also find Emmentals from other countries. Authentic Emmentals will always have the words "Emmental" and "Switzerland" stamped on the rind. Emmental cheese is the original Swiss cheese, although Swiss cheese is not necessarily Emmental. It is considered to be one of the most difficult cheeses to produce because of its complicated hole-forming fermentation process.

HINT Emmental needs to be refrigerated. Wrap it in wax or parchment paper and then plastic wrap, and store it in the refrigerator for up to sixty days.

EMPANADA is a type of a deep-fried or baked turnover with a spicy or sweet filling in Latin American or Spanish cuisine. The word, which entered English around 1939, is from the Spanish *empanar*, "bake/roll in pastry." Empanadas can also be filled with fruit and served as dessert. Empanadas range in size from the huge empanada gallega, large enough to feed an entire family, to empanaditas, tiny, ravioli-sized pastries.

HINTS If you want to keep empanada dough longer than twenty-four hours, you can freeze it.

If empanada dough gets too soft to handle, refrigerate it for about 15 minutes. Store the unused portion in the refrigerator if the kitchen is particularly warm.

Be careful to avoid overstuffing empanada rounds. If an empanada has too much filling, cut two slits into the top of it or poke a fork into the top. The steam will be more likely to exit through the vents instead of making the empanada explode.

EMPIRE is a type of juicy, dark red apple that is a cross between McIntosh and Red Delicious apples. It is named for New York, the Empire State, and was first produced in 1945 by Lester C. Anderson, a Cornell University fruit nutritionist.

HINTS Buy Empire apples that are brightly colored, firm, and free of bruises or damaged skin. If the flesh gives under pressure, the Empire apple will be soft. The skin on the Empire apple should be taut and show no signs of shriveling. Select individual Empire apples over prebagged apples so that you can see what you are selecting and have an opportunity to smell the apples to make sure they have a fresh smell and are not musty.

For best results, place Empire apples in a perforated plastic bag, sprinkle with water, and store in the coldest area of the refrigerator for two to three weeks. Empire apples give off a gas called ethylene that speeds up ripening, so they should be kept away from other fruits and vegetables to prevent them from ripening prematurely. Empire apples can be stored at room temperature for a short period of time, but should be checked regularly because they will ripen more rapidly than if stored in the refrigerator.

EMULSIFY is to convert something into an emulsion, which is a suspension of one liquid in another, such as oil in water or fat in milk. In cooking, an emulsion of two immiscible liquids will stay mixed only as long as they are stirred together, unless an emulsifying agent is added. For example, both mayonnaise and hollandaise sauce are oil-in-water emulsions that are stabilized with egg yolk's lecithin.

HINT Emulsifying is done by slowly adding (sometimes drop by drop) one ingredient to another while at the same time mixing rapidly. This disperses and suspends minute droplets of one liquid throughout the other.

ENCHILADA is a tortilla filled with meat or cheese, rolled and fried, then topped with a chili-flavored sauce. Enchilada comes from American Spanish and means "season with chili."

HINTS Enchiladas can be refrigerated and reheated, but the signature texture will be absent or altered, as the tortillas continue to absorb the sauce during storage.

Lightly fry the tortillas before filling them, about 5 seconds per side, and set on paper towels to prevent them from becoming soggy. You can also or spray the tortillas on both sides with nonstick cooking spray, place them in a plastic tortilla warmer, and heat in the microwave on high for 45 seconds, until very hot.

ENDIVE is a widely cultivated herb with leaves valued as salad greens. There are three types: one with crisp, frilly leaves, also called CURLY ENDIVE or FRISÉE; one with lightly bitter, broad, flat leaves, also called ESCAROLE; and the less common BELGIAN ENDIVE or FRENCH ENDIVE, with bitter, cream-colored, broad leaves. Endive is grown by a painstaking method in which chicory roots are forced to sprout in a dark, humid room, and it is fragile.

CONFUSABLES ENDIVE/CHICORY/CURLY ENDIVE/ESCAROLE. Endive is often confused with chicory, as they are both in the genus *Cichorium*. Curly endive (often mistakenly called chicory) has a loose head of lacy, green-rimmed outer leaves that curl at the tips and off-white center leaves that form a compact heart. Escarole has broad, slightly curved, pale green leaves with a milder, less bitter flavor.

▌ ENDIVE OR BELGIAN ENDIVE/CHICORY OR SUCCORY. Endive or Belgian endive in the United States is called chicory or succory in the United Kingdom. Another variety of this plant is called escarole in the United States and endive in the United Kingdom.

ENERGIZING FOODS

These foods are good for stimulating alertness. The best energizing foods are those that are rich in complex carbohydrates, protein, antioxidants, fiber, vitamins, minerals, and other health-promoting substances. Put these foods together along with small amounts of healthy fats for a balanced diet that is sure to provide you energy all day long.

APPLE	LOWFAT YOGURT	SKIM MILK
BEANS	MANGO	SOY
BLUEBERRY	NUTS	SPINACH
BROCCOLI	OATMEAL	STRAWBERRY
CANTALOUPE	PEACH	SWEET POTATO
CHICKEN	PEANUTS	TOFU
CITRUS FRUIT	PEAR	TOMATO
FISH	PEPPER	WHOLE GRAIN
GRAPES	POULTRY	
LEAN BEEF	SALMON	

ENGLISH BREAKFAST TEA is a traditional blend of Ceylon, Kenyan, and Indian teas that is served at breakfast. English breakfast tea is more robust, full-flavored, and full-bodied than a single black tea.

ENGLISH MUFFIN is a flat, round, spongy muffin made from yeast dough baked on a griddle and usually eaten split, toasted, and buttered. The muffin is almost always dusted with cornmeal, and the holes are referred to as nooks and crannies. The English muffin dates to the tenth century in Wales, though it is just referred to as muffin in the United Kingdom. To get the proper texture when split in half, an English muffin should not be cut with a knife, but rather with a fork or the fingers.

HINT Instead of using a fork to split an English muffin, you can use an English muffin splitter to split it perfectly and create nooks and crannies to capture butter, honey, or your favorite topping without ever ruining one.

ENOKI, ENOKI MUSHROOM, ENOKIDAKE, or **ENOKITAKE** is an edible white mushroom with a small yellowish cap and a long, thin stem, native to northern Japan. It is sold in a cluster of slender stems and tiny caps and is often used as an uncooked garnish. There are actually two different kinds of enoki mushrooms, although both are botanically classified as *Flammulina velutipes*. One is a wild type, which looks and tastes radically different from the other type, a cultivated mushroom. The cultivated mushroom is raised under specific conditions in order to modify its look and flavor. While both versions are perfectly palatable, many consumers prefer the cultivated mushrooms, since they have a more intense flavor.

> **HINTS** Choose fresh enoki mushrooms that are firm and white. Refrigerate, wrapped in a paper towel within a plastic bag, for up to five days. Before using, cut the mushrooms away from the mass at the base of the stems.
>
> ▌ Enoki are particularly good raw in salads. They may also be used to garnish soups or other hot dishes. If used as part of a cooked dish, they should be added at the last minute, as heat tends to make them tough.

ENOLOGY: see OENOLOGY.

ENRICHED means that a nutrient lost during an early stage of processing has been restored to a food. It can also mean that vitamins and minerals were added to food to enhance its nutritive value. Enriched is a term usually applied to flour that, after the milling has stripped it of the wheat germ and other nutritious elements, has had niacin, riboflavin, and thiamin added back into it. U.S. law requires that flours not containing wheat germ must have these nutrients replenished.

ENTRAILS are internal organs collectively, especially the intestines.

ENTRECÔTE (literally "between the ribs" in French) is a boned steak cut from the middle part of the sirloin of beef, from the long strip of tender muscle underlying the ribs. Entrecôte is a very tender and expensive cut of beef. In the United States, this cut is also called a RIB STEAK.

ENTRÉE in America refers to any dish served as the main course of a meal. However, in the United Kingdom it is a light dish served before the main course. In other parts of Europe it refers to the dish served between the fish and meat courses during formal dinners. In Australia the entrée is the first course or appetizer.

ENTREMETS is another name for side dish, especially a dainty dish of sweetmeats or a relish; it also refers to a dish served between the main courses. The word is from French and literally means "between courses of viands (dishes)." In modern French cuisine, entremets is a small dish served between courses or simply a dessert. Originally, it was an elaborate form of entertainment dish common among the nobility and upper middle class in western Europe during the later part of the Middle Ages and the early modern period. According to *Larousse Gastronomique*, the word entremets indicates the "sweet course," which is always served after the "cheese course" in France. Entremets is also the name for mousse cakes that are staples in French patisseries.

EPICURE is any person devoted to refined sensuous enjoyment of food and drink, or a person who has developed a refined taste for food. The term is named for Epicurus, a Greek philosopher (341–270 BC), who said that the highest good is pleasure.

ESCALOPE or **ESCALLOP**, also called SCALLOP, refers to a thin (beaten) slice of white meat (especially veal), usually coated and fried or broiled and served in a sauce; the term comes from a French word meaning "shell," probably because the meat curls into a shell shape in cooking. The typical size of an escalope used in the food industry ranges from four to eight ounces. The cooking time is very short because it is so thin. A tender escalope requires only a few seconds of sautéing on both sides. To escalope is to bake food cut into pieces in a sauce or other liquid, often with crumbs on top. To escalope is also to bake fish, potatoes, or other foods in scallop shells.

ESCARGOT is the snail as an appetizer or entrée. Snails were among the first animals to be eaten by man, on the evidence of the heaps of shells found in pre-historic sites. Escargot is a French word, pronounced ehs-kahr-GOH. While people who are not from France think that the word refers to a specific dish, in fact it is a generic term for edible snails.

> **HINTS** Snails collected from the wild need to be starved for about ten days to ensure they are rid of any poisonous leaves they may have eaten. Fresh American-cultivated snails do not require the purification period that European snails do, but should be used the same day they are purchased. Be sure that all snails are alive before cooking. A single dead snail will ruin the entire batch. Live escargots are slightly orange in color; when deceased they are brighter.

> Snails can be purchased fresh or canned. You should use six to eight snails per serving. Refrigerate fresh snails for no more than one day. Canned snails can be stored unopened at room temperature for up to a year; refrigerate after opening for up to three days. Fresh or canned escargot can be safely frozen, if certain precautions are taken (although, as with shell-fish, prolonged freezer storage can lead to a loss of flavor over time). Before freezing canned escargot, check with the manufacturer to see how long they can be safely frozen.

ESCAROLE or BROAD-LEAVED ENDIVE has broad, pale flat leaves with frilled edges and is less bitter than other varieties; it is used in salads or cooked. The word literally means "something edible" and is based on the Latin *edere,* "eat."

> HINT If escarole leaves look thick or tough, do not buy that head. Store in the refrigerator in a perforated plastic bag for up to four days.

ESPAGNOLE is the French word for "Spanish" and it refers to a simple brown sauce, considered one of the mother sauces that are the basis of sauce making in classic French cooking. Espagnole is a very dark brown roux, to which veal stock or water is added, along with browned bones, pieces of beef, vegetables, and various seasonings. Espagnole has a strong taste and is rarely used directly on food. As a mother sauce, however, it serves as the starting point for many derivative sauces.

> HINT Cooking espagnole takes several hours, and the sauce needs to be skimmed, stirred, and strained when a particular stage in the cooking is reached. Carefully monitor the sauce as it simmers for the final 30 minutes. If the heat is too high or the roux is too stiff, the sauce will overthicken and burn. Don't be afraid to pull the sauce off the heat early if it appears to be thickened enough. The finished sauce should have the consistency of loose gravy and should coat the back of a spoon.

ESPRESSO (pronounced es-PRES-oh) is strong black coffee made by forcing steam through finely ground coffee beans. The word literally means "pressed out" or "expressed," and it was first recorded in English in 1945.

> CONFUSABLE ESPRESSO/CAFFÈ LATTE/CAPPUCCINO/CAFÉ AU LAIT. Espresso, a strong, thick brewed coffee, is the base of caffè latte, cappuccino, and sometimes café au lait. Café au lait has steamed/scalded milk, cappuccino has foamed/frothed milk, and caffè latte has steamed/heated milk.

ESSENCE is a concentrated plant extract, such as vanilla, containing the plant's unique flavor and scent. Essence is used in small amounts either to enhance the flavor of certain culinary preparations or to flavor certain foods that have little or no flavor of their own. Essences sold commercially sometimes contain artificial flavorings and colorings. Like extracts, essences will keep indefinitely if stored in a cool, dark place. Natural essences are obtained by extracting the essential oil of a fruit or a spice, by reducing an infusion or a cooking liquid, or by infusing or marinating items in either wine or vinegar.

> CONFUSABLE ESSENCE/EXTRACT. The distinction between extract and essence isn't always clear-cut, so read the labels carefully. All essences are extracts,

but extracts are not all essences. Essence is defined as a substance possessing the qualities of something in concentrated form, and extract is a solution (as in alcohol) of essential constituents of a complex material. Strictly speaking, this means that an extract should be natural and an essence may be a chemical imitation; however, as commercial products they may actually be the same.

EVAPORATED MILK is unsweetened milk thickened by evaporating its water content to approximately half the original weight. It is then sterilized and canned. This process can be done with full-fat, skimmed, or partly skimmed milk. To reconstitute evaporated milk, combine it with an equal amount of water. Evaporated milk is less expensive than fresh milk and is therefore popular for many cooked dishes.

> **CONFUSABLE** EVAPORATED MILK/CONDENSED MILK. Evaporated milk is concentrated and unsweetened; condensed milk is reduced, thick milk with sugar added.

> **HINTS** As it comes from the can, evaporated milk is used to enrich custards, sauces, and soups, or to add a creamy texture to many dishes.

> ▌ Swollen cans or containers of evaporated mik should be avoided at all costs. Also avoid purchasing cans that are dented. Canned milk can be stored at room temperature until opened for up to six months. Once opened, transfer to an airtight container and use within five days. The stored milk keeps better if you flip the cans every month; this helps to prevent the fat from settling.

> ▌ When slightly frozen, evaporated milk can be whipped and used as an inexpensive substitute for whipped cream.

EXTRACT is a concentrated form of food or flavoring, whether solid, viscid, or liquid. It is basically a concentrate containing the active principles of, for example, an aromatic plant. An extract labeled "pure" must contain only essential oils distilled from natural plants.

EXTRA-VIRGIN or **EXTRA VIRGIN** is the designation for olive oil with the least acid and the best flavor, aroma, and color; it is made from the first pressing of highest-quality olives. It contains a maximum of 1% oleic acid. Virgin olive oil, by contrast, has an acidity of less than 2%.

> **HINT** Extra-virgin olive oil is better for a marinade than regular olive oil because it has more emulsifiers, which penetrate meat and fish better. It is also better than canola oil as a marinade.

EYE OF ROUND, EYE, or **EYE ROUND**, is a cut from the round primal of a beef hindquarter (back hip), sold as a roast or steak. Eye of round is a very tough and inexpensive piece of meat, so it requires moist, long, and slow-cooking methods.

FAGGOT: see Bouquet Garni.

FAJITA is a dish consisting of strips of marinated and grilled meat, poultry, or vegetables served in a soft tortilla, usually with spicy condiments and accompaniments. Fajita is Spanish for "little strip or belt," as the dish includes small strips of meat. The word is pronounced fuh-HEE-tuh and first appeared in print in 1971. Though originally only skirt steak was used, popular meats today also include chicken, pork, shrimp, and all cuts of beef. The term fajita has completely lost its original meaning and has come to describe just about anything that is cooked and served rolled up in a soft flour tortilla. The only true fajitas, however, are made from skirt steak.

FALAFEL or **FELAFEL** is a spicy mixture of seasoned ground vegetables like chickpeas or fava beans formed into balls or patties and then deep-fried. A sandwich is often made of falafel stuffed into the pocket of a pita and served with tahini sauce. The plural is falafel or felafel. Falafel comes from the Arabic *falafil*, "pepper," and entered English around 1951. Falafel is a popular form of street food or fast food in the Middle East. In Egypt, McDonald's serves its own version of a falafel sandwich.

FARFALLE is pasta shaped like bow ties or butterflies; it is the Italian plural for "butterfly."

> **HINTS** Farfalle are best suited to cream and tomato dishes. Some cooks also use farfalle in baked dishes such as casseroles, since the pasta bakes and holds its shape well. Some producers call their farfalle bow tie pasta. A smaller version of farfalle pasta is called farfalline.
>
> ❙ When making farfalle at home, after cutting the pasta dough with jagged-edge shears so that the rectangles also have a jagged edge, pinch each rectangle in the middle to form the classic bow tie shape.

FARINA is fine meal or flour made from cereal grain, especially wheat, but also from nuts or vegetables such as potatoes; it is often used as a cooked cereal or in puddings. Farina is bland tasting and, when cooked in boiling water, makes a hot breakfast cereal. The word comes from *far*, the Latin word for "spelt/grain." Farina cereal is one of the best single sources of dietary iron available, especially for vegetarian diets, with most brands offering as much as 50% of the recommended daily value in a single 120-calorie serving. Farina is also a trademarked brand name for cereal produced by the Malt-O-Meal Company.

> **HINT** Keep unopened farina in a cool, dry place and use within four to six months. After opening, store in a tightly covered container. Do not store above the refrigerator or stove, and do not store next to soap products or products with strong odors, such as onions. Store cooked farina in a tightly covered plastic container in the refrigerator. Use within three days.

FARMER CHEESE, FARM CHEESE, or **FARMER'S CHEESE,** also called BAKER'S CHEESE, HOOP CHEESE, or PRESSED CHEESE, is unripened cheese made by pressing milk curds. Farmer cheese is drier, firmer, and usually less creamy than cottage cheese; the curds are often smaller and the taste is more sour.

> **HINT** Farmer cheese is an all-purpose cheese that can be eaten as is or used in cooking. Farmer cheese can be kept in the refrigerator for about two weeks. You can freeze your fresh farmer cheese as well. Either freeze it in its original packaging, or wrap it tightly in plastic wrap and put it in a zip-lock freezer bag. Frozen farmer cheese should be eaten within about two months, and should be thawed in the refrigerator first.

FAST FOOD is an Americanism that entered the language around 1951 for food that is prepared and dispensed quickly in quantity by a standardized method at inexpensive restaurants or snack bars as a quick meal or to be taken away. Carl's Jr. and McDonald's were the first fast-food restaurants.

FAT refers to any of various mixtures of solid or semisolid triglycerides found in adipose animal tissue or in plant seeds and then used in cooking. Fats are used in baking, frying, and sautéing, and as flavorings or spreads. Fat also means animal tissue (meat) consisting chiefly of cells containing greasy or oily matter. True fats, neutral fats, or triglycerides are lipids formed by the combination of glycerol and three fatty acids. In more general use, the term fats refers to the neutral fats, which are triacylglycerols, mixed esters of fatty acids with glycerol. The word fat is from the Old English *fætt*, "well fed/plump" or "fatty/oily," and is of West Germanic origin. With 9 calories per gram, fat yields 2¼ times as much energy by weight as protein or carbohydrate. All fats do not have the same amount of fat. Shortening and lard are 100% fat; butter and margarine are about 80% fat. The temperature to which a fat can be heated before it begins to break down and smoke is its smoke point.

FAT ESSENTIALS

> **CONFUSABLE** FATS/OILS. Oils are fats that are liquid at room temperature. The difference between a fat and an oil is that at 68°F the fat is solid and the oil is liquid.

> **CONFUSABLE** FAT-FREE/LOW-FAT. The difference between fat-free and low-fat is about 3 grams of fat per 100 grams. That is the limit for low-fat foods. Fat-free foods have less than ½ gram of fat per serving. Reduced-fat means the food has 25% less fat than a comparable product. Light/lite means the food has 50% less fat than a comparable product. Low-calorie usually means a food has 40 calories or less per serving.

- Keep fats (butter, lard, margarine, shortening) away from heat, light, and water when storing them. Unopened packages of fats can be frozen for up to six months.

- Fat makes baked goods tender by coating the proteins in flour and preventing them from joining together to form tough strands of gluten. Fat also contributes to moistness.

- These cooking fats are arranged from lowest to highest, in terms of percentage of saturated fats: canola, safflower, corn, olive, soybean, peanut, margarine, palm, butter, and coconut.

- If oil is rancid, it will have a sharp, bitter odor.

- You can use the displacement method to measure solid fat. If you need ½ cup of solid fat, fill the measuring cup with ½ cup of water and add shortening or butter until the water level rises to 1 cup.

- Cover an oil spill with flour, let it sit for a few minutes, then clean it up with a paper towel.

- Dispose of excess cooking fat in an empty milk or cream container.

- When fat is creamed with sugar, the dough is aerated and lightens.

TYPES OF FAT

ANIMAL	MARGARINE	SOLID
BUTTER	MILK	SUET
BUTTERFAT	MONOUNSATURATED	TRANS
EDIBLE	POLYUNSATURATED	TRIGLYCERIDE
HYDROGENATED	SCHMALTZ	UNSATURATED
LARD	SHORTENING	

FAT SEPARATOR: see GRAVY SEPARATOR.

FAVA BEAN, also called BROAD bean, or FIELD bean is one of the oldest plants under cultivation; the beans were eaten in ancient Greece and Rome. Fava beans are easily distinguished from kidney beans because they lie across the pod, so the contact point is on the end. Dried beans are more nutritious than fresh ones because they are allowed to grow to full size before being harvested. Fava beans contain a chemical substance to which some people, particularly in the Mediterranean, are allergic.

> HINTS Fava beans can be purchased dried, frozen, canned, and, infrequently, fresh. If you find fresh fava beans, choose those with pods that aren't bulging with beans, which indicates age.

> Refrigerate fresh, in-season beans and prepare within one week. Once cooked, all fava beans should be used or frozen within two days.

FELDSALAT: see CORN SALAD.

FENNEL is a perennial in the carrot family; a commonly cultivated form (*Foeniculum vulgare dulce*) produces aromatic leaves used as an herb and seeds used as a spice. Fennel is from the Latin *faeniculum*, "little hay."

CONFUSABLE FENNEL/SWEET ANISE. Although the two names are commonly used interchangeably in markets, sweet anise is an incorrect synonym for fennel, which is sweeter and more delicate than sweet anise. Fennel gives a slight, subtle licorice flavor to foods.

HINT Fennel bulbs should be smooth and tightly layered, with no bruises. Avoid dried, cracked, or wilted bulbs and leaves. Keep in a perforated plastic bag in the refrigerator up to five days. The bulb, stalk, leaves, and seeds are all edible.

FENUGREEK is a cloverlike plant of the legume family cultivated for its seeds, which are used in curry powder. Fenugreek literally means "Greek hay," as the Romans used this dried plant for fodder. Fenugreek seeds are very hard, resembling tiny stones, and can only be ground using a heavy mortar and pestle or in a special grinder. The seeds, which have a slightly bittersweet taste, are roasted and ground, then used as a flavoring. Their flavor is distinct and easily recognized as one of the ingredients of curry pastes and powders. Fenugreek is also used in maple syrup.

HINT Fenugreek seeds should be stored in a cool, dark place for no more than six months. Store ground fenugreek in the refrigerator; ground fenugreek loses its fragrance rather quickly, so check the quality before you use it. Whole fenugreek seeds will keep quite well for up to two years at room temperature.

FERMENTATION is a process in which an agent (ferment), such as bacteria or yeast enzymes, causes the complex molecules in an organic substance to break down into simpler substances, especially the anaerobic breakdown of sugar into alcohol. Fermentation is the process by which milk transforms into cheese and other milk products such as sour cream and yogurt. The microorganisms are either naturally present in the food or are added because of the requirements of a particular process. The type of fermentation varies depending on the type of food, the nature of the fermenting agent, and the length of time the process takes; however, all types of fermentation result in the formation of acids or alcohols. The main foods that are fermented include dough, milk products (curds, yogurt, buttermilk, and cheese), meat (raw sausage), vinegar, and alcoholic drinks, such as beer, wine, and cider. Fermented vegetables include sauerkraut (cabbage), cucumbers, and beets.

FETA is a white, semifirm, crumbly, salty cheese made from sheep's or goat's milk and cured in brine. Originally from Greece, feta translates to "slice," for one of the stages in its making. The word came into English around 1956. Feta is one of the world's oldest cheeses; it has been made in Greece and other Balkan countries for centuries. Homer himself wrote about it, describing how the gods made their cheese.

HINTS Consumers who dislike feta's salty taste may soak the cheese in fresh water to leach out some of the salt, or tone down the salt in dishes that feta is used in, allowing the cheese to supply the salt.

The finest feta cheese should be purchased direct from its brine bath. If it is prepackaged, it should have some of the brine in the packaging to keep it moist. Feta cheese is best when eaten fresh, so always check the date. If you will not be consuming it immediately, store feta cheese in a brine or milk bath in the refrigerator. The milk bath will reduce the saltiness and help keep the cheese moist and mild in flavor. Properly stored in brine or milk and refrigerated, feta cheese will last for up to three months. Feta cheese is not a candidate for freezing. Barrel-aged feta sold straight from the barrel may be wrapped in lightweight paper, then wrapped in a plastic bag or plastic wrap and stored in the refrigerator. Keep the feta in the paper, even when the paper gets soggy from the cheese moisture.

Allow a good 30 minutes for feta cheese to come to room temperature, to fully enjoy its rich, tangy flavor and creamy texture.

FETTUCCINE is pasta made in ribbons or strips; the word is the Italian plural and diminutive of *fetta*, "slice/ribbon." It is sometimes called TAGLIATELLE, though tagliatelle can be wider than fettuccine.

HINT Cream sauce is better for fettuccine than for spaghetti because the width of the pasta carries the sauce better.

FEUILLETÉ is a French baked pastry made using flaky or puff pastry dough. The word is from the French *feuille*, "leaf."

FIDDLEHEAD or FIDDLEHEAD FERN, also called CROSIER, is a type of fern with woolly, cinnamon-colored, spore-bearing fronds. The early uncurled tip of the young fern is often cooked and eaten as a vegetable. The fiddlehead fern resembles the spiral end of a violin/fiddle. The shoots are in their coiled form for only about two weeks before they unfurl into graceful greenery. Fiddleheads are not generally cultivated (not many farms specialize in growing them) and are available only seasonally; they grow naturally in the wild. An early-spring delicacy, fiddleheads are available in the market for only a few weeks in springtime, and are fairly expensive.

HINTS Choose small, firm, brightly colored fiddleheads with no sign of softness or yellowing. Refrigerate, tightly wrapped, for no more than two days.

Do not eat fiddleheads raw. You should boil fiddleheads for at least 15 minutes or steam them for 10–12 minutes, though some fiddlehead fans think 5 minutes is enough. It is also recommended that you wash the ferns in several changes of cold water.

Because of the short season for fiddleheads, some people like to preserve them for later use. To freeze fiddleheads, clean them as you would for the table. Blanch a small amount at a time for 2 minutes in 4–6 cups of water. Cool and drain in cold water or in an ice-water bath (half water and half ice). Pack into moisture- and vapor-proof containers and freeze. Thaw and boil for 10 minutes before serving.

FIELD BEAN (or BROAD BEAN, HORSE BEAN) is an Old World plant grown for its large, flat, edible seeds. These beans are commonly used in many dishes and cuisines.

FIELD LETTUCE or **FIELD SALAD**: see CORN SALAD.

FIG is the fleshy, sweet, pear-shaped, yellowish or purple fruit of the Mediterranean tree *Ficus carica*; it is eaten fresh, preserved, or dried. Figs are the only fruit to fully ripen and become semidry on the tree. Figs were probably one of the first fruits to be dried and stored by man. There was a fig tree in the Garden of Eden, and it is the most-mentioned fruit in the Bible. The soft pear-shaped fruit is actually a flower swollen and turned in on itself, and the tiny seeds constitute the actual fruit. There are more than 150 varieties of fig. Fresh figs are available twice a year. They do not ripen off the tree. The fig is the sweetest fruit, with 55% sugar.

HINTS Choose figs that are soft but not bruised, mushy, or wrinkled; they should be plump with good color and have no gray or tan spots. The best ones have a webbing of delicate fissures. Avoid figs with a sour aroma. Figs can be refrigerated for one to two days in a single layer on paper towels.

Dried figs will keep in an airtight container or bag in a cool, dry place for one to two months, or in the refrigerator for up to six months.

FIG TYPES AND VARIETIES

The fig probably originated in Asia Minor, but is now widespread in the Mediterranean region. The varieties of figs grown in various parts of the world run into the hundreds. Their nomenclature is confused since the same fig is often grown in neighboring provinces under entirely different names. Here are some of the names for fig varieties and types:

ADRIATIC	COMMON	HARDY CHICAGO
ALMA	CONADRIA	HUNT
AMBER	DARK	ISCHIA
BEALL	DAUPHINE VIOLETTE	KADOTA
BELLONE	DEANNA	KING
BLACK ISCHIA	DESSERT	LATTARULA
BOURJASOTTE	DRIED	LIGHT
BOURJASSOTTE GRISE	EARLY VIOLET	MARSEILLES
BROWN TURKEY	ENDRICH	MISSION
BRUNSWICK	EXCEL	MONACO BIANCO
BUISSONE	FLANDERS	MONSTRUEUSE
CAPRIFIG	FRESH	NEGRONNE
CELESTE OR CELESTINE	GENOA	OSBORN PROLIFIC
COL DE DAME	GREEN	PANACHEE

PURPLE	SAINT JEAN	SMYRNA
RED	SAN PEDRO	TENA
REINE BLANCHE	SAN PIETRO	WHITE

FIGGY PUDDING is a European-style pudding resembling a white Christmas pudding containing figs or raisins. The pudding may be baked, steamed in the oven, boiled, or fried.

FILBERT or HAZELNUT is the term for the edible fruit or nut of the cultivated hazel tree (*Corylus avellana* or *maxima*). Filberts were named for Saint Philibert, the Frankish saint whose feast day (August 22) falls in the height of nut-harvesting season. Filberts can be eaten fresh or dried. Shelled filberts can be eaten whole, chopped, or ground. They can be added to cookies, cakes, and other desserts, or used in salads or to make a savory butter to flavor entrées and side dishes. As with many nuts, roasting filberts brings out their flavor. One pound of shelled filberts is equal to 3½ cups.

> **HINTS** An easy rule of thumb is that the more filberts are processed, the shorter the shelf life they will have. It is best to process (roast, chop, slice, grind) just before use. However, if your goal is to have filberts handy for addition to a huge variety of dishes, then simply roast the kernels, dice them, and freeze them in an airtight container away from foods with strong odors. They will keep for over a year in the freezer and you can remove the amount you need, bring them to room temperature, and use immediately. Filberts are sold shelled and unshelled. Shelled filberts can become rancid quickly and should be used within a week, refrigerated for up to four months, or frozen for up to one year. Unshelled filberts can be stored in a cool, dark place for up to one month.

> To remove the paper skin, spread shelled filberts in a single layer on a baking tray and roast at 275°F, stirring occasionally, for about 15 minutes, until the skins begin to break. Roll in a clean kitchen towel, let rest for 10 minutes, and then gently rub back and forth to remove the skins. Some bits of the skin may remain.

FILET MIGNON is a small, round, tender cut of beef from the thick end of the tenderloin. The term, which in French literally means "dainty fillet," has been in fairly common use in American English since around 1906. The plural forms are filet mignons or filets mignons. The filet is the most tender cut of beef, and the most expensive. The average steer or heifer provides no more than four to six pounds of filet.

> **HINTS** When selecting filet mignon, choose the lighter color over dark red. This indicates more marbling, which makes it more tender. This cut is so tender that it should never be cooked beyond a medium-rare stage. The longer you cook it, the less tender and more dry it becomes.

▌ Bring filet mignon to room temperature before cooking. High heat is the usual method for cooking the filet. Grilling, pan-frying, broiling, or roasting is preferred. Traditionally, filet mignon is seared on each side, using intense heat for a short time, and then transferred to a lower heat to cook the meat all the way through. Filet mignon is often served rarer than other meats. Those who prefer a more well-done steak can request a "butterflied" filet, meaning that the meat is cut down the middle and opened up to expose more of the meat to heat during the cooking process. Allow the meat to rest for 5 minutes before serving.

▌ Wrap filet mignons in bacon, if desired, for extra flavor and juiciness. Filet mignon is often wrapped in bacon (this wrapping is called barding) because this particular cut of meat has no layer of fat around it. The bacon not only adds extra flavor to the filet mignon, but also gives it the fat necessary to keep the meat from drying out. This is a concern because the strips are so small in filet mignon and they have less fat than most cuts of beef.

▌ Since filet mignon is drier than other cuts, you will not want to cut the meat to check to see if it is done. Instead, you should touch it. The touch method of checking is not as hard as it may sound: If the meat feels hard or firm, it is too done. When the filet mignon feels soft when you touch it and your finger leaves an imprint, it is rare. If it is still soft but leaves no imprint and is slightly resilient, then it is medium-rare (best for this particular type of meat).

FILLET (pronounced FIL-it or fi-LAY) or **FILET** (pronounced fi-LAY) is a lean, boneless piece of meat/fish cut from the tenderloin or from a longitudinal boned side of a fish. The word is from the Latin *filum*, "thread," as in a band of nerve or muscle fiber. Fillet can also be used to describe a piece of veal or other meat that has been boned, rolled, and tied for roasting.

FILLING is a general term for a food mixture used to fill pastries, sandwiches, and other foods.

FILO: see PHYLLO.

FINES HERBES (French) is a mixture of equal parts finely chopped chervil, chives, parsley, tarragon, and thyme. The mixture is used to flavor sauces, cream cheese, meat, sautéed vegetables, and omelets.

> **HINTS** Fines herbes quickly lose their flavor, so they should be added to a cooked mixture shortly before serving. Fines herbes are minced very fine, so that they will be almost invisible in the final dish. They are almost smelled rather than tasted, suffusing a dish with flavor rather than appearing in chunks. The fine cut of the herbs also ensures even distribution, so that diners do not encounter a sudden change in seasoning.

Dried fines herbes generally keep for six months to one year before they lose flavor. They should be stored in a dark, cool, dry place. To determine whether or not dried herbs are still usable, shake the bottle gently before opening it. A cloud of flavor should waft out, indicating that the herbs have retained their potency. If the fines herbes have a very light or nonexistent smell, they should be discarded in favor of fresh ones.

FINGERLING is the term for any young or small fish, especially salmon or trout less than one year old; it is so named because a small fish is about the length of a finger. Fingerling is also a type of small, usually white, finger-shaped potato.

FINISH in cooking is the taste of a wine on the back of the tongue as it is swallowed. To finish a dish is also a term, meaning to arrange, garnish, and present the dish.

FINISHING BUTTER: see COMPOUND BUTTER.

FINNAN HADDIE or **FINNAN HADDOCK** is smoked haddock, usually halved and baked (but sometimes broiled) with lots of butter over green oak, turf, or peat, so that the flesh takes on a pale yellow color. It is named for Findon, Scotland, a fishing village or Findhorn, a river. It entered English around 1774.

> **HINT** Finnan haddie can be refrigerated, tightly wrapped, for up to two weeks. It can also be quick-frozen and kept satisfactorily in cold storage; a shelf life of at least seven months for finnan haddie in first-class condition is possible at –22°F.

FINO (Spanish for "fine") is a type of dry sherry. Fino is the driest and palest of the traditional varieties of sherry.

FIOR DI LATTE: see SCAMORZA.

FIREPOT: see HOT POT.

FISH is any of various mostly cold-blooded aquatic vertebrates usually having scales and breathing through gills—and the flesh of this vertebrate eaten as food. As a general rule, the deeper in the water the fish lives, the leaner the fish. For example, tuna is a top dweller and fatter; sole and cod are bottom dwellers. Fish digest food by a chemical process that continues even after they are caught and die, so it is important that they be gutted immediately. Otherwise, the digestive juices will continue to act, cutting through the intestinal wall and starting decomposition of the flesh. Fish flesh is more delicate than meat. The muscles of mammals and birds are composed of very long fibers in bundles. The connective tissue is about 15% by weight in land animals. Fish muscles consist of rather short fibers separated by large sheets of very thin connective tissue, which is very fragile and easily converted to gelatin. Connective tissue is about 3% by weight in fish. This is why fish meat is so tender and tends to fall apart when cooked. Fish is low in fat. Its omega-3 fatty acids have an anticlotting effect and help limit blood triglycerides, a type of fat linked to heart disease. They also help prevent the buildup of artery-plugging plaques that block blood vessels leading to the heart. River fish usually taste better than lake fish because exercise builds flavor into a fish, and since a river fish has to swim just to stay stationary, it expends more energy than a lake fish. Also, a bottom fish that doesn't have to fight against as much of a current will not exercise as much as, for example, a trout in a cold, swiftly moving mountain brook. The safest (least contaminated) fish to eat are halibut, skip jack, sole, and tuna, or commercially raised trout and turbot.

FISH ESSENTIALS

■ Fish should be chosen with your eyes and nose. They should look moist and bright and have a fresh, clean smell. Whole fish should look almost alive. Fish should be displayed on crushed ice or in a case with the temperature displayed at 33°F or lower. If a whole fish is placed in cold water and it floats, it has been recently caught. If you hold a whole fish by the head and tail, the fresher the fish, the less the sag in the middle for its size. The gills of the fish give a clue to its freshness. In a properly stored fish, the oxygen in the air will help keep the gills bright red for a few hours. Then overoxygenation gradually changes the hemoglobin from bright red to pink to brownish red and finally to grayish brown. Also, because gills are more perishable than other parts of the fish, they will develop off-odors faster, which is an early warning system.

■ Ideally, cook fish the day you buy it. If you must keep it a day, refrigerate the package in a baking pan and cover the package with ice. The fish package should be plastic so that the flesh does not get freezer burn.

■ Frozen fish will keep for one to two months in the freezer. To defrost, put the fish on a plate for 24 hours in the refrigerator, then in a pan or tray of ice until ready to cook.

■ Lean fish should be cooked with some kind of liquid or fat. Oily fish should be cooked with a dry-heat method. Any piece of fish should cook for 10 minutes per inch of thickness at its widest point. Start checking doneness after 8 minutes. Use the tip of a small, sharp knife or a fork to separate the flakes or cut into the thickest area. The fish should be opaque but moist and easy to flake (unless you are aiming for medium or medium-rare).

■ Get rid of fish odor by rubbing your hands or cooking utensils with lemon juice. If a pot has a pronounced fish odor, boil ½ cup of vinegar in it for 10 minutes, or place a small amount of vinegar in the pot before washing.

■ In fish, the bones impart a rich flavor to the surrounding flesh, so bone fish after cooking for a tastier dish.

■ Juices can be retained in fish when cooking by using tongs or a spatula instead of a fork to turn the fish, so that the juices won't ooze out of the fork holes. Quickly brown the fish over high heat, then finish cooking at moderate heat, turning only once.

■ Rubbing lemon juice on fish before cooking enhances flavor and helps maintain a good color.

■ Scaling a fish should be done before cooking for a better-tasting fish. You can make the scaling of fish easier by rubbing vinegar on the scales and wetting the fish with water. The direction the knife or scaler moves when scaling a fish is not important. Some say it is best to scale from the tail toward the head. Others say just the opposite. Scaling should be done under running water to keep the loosened scales from flying all over.

■ The center cut of fish is superior to the tail end. The center usually has a higher fat content and is more tender. Even though the tail end does more exercise and thus develops a more intense flavor, the gain in quantity of flavor doesn't begin to match the loss in flavor quality.

■ To evenly bread fish, first dip in flour, shaking off the excess, then dip in liquid, and finally in crumbs.

■ You can keep fish from sticking to the pan without extra fat or oil by sprinkling the bottom of the pan with a little salt.

■ Whiten fish when poaching by adding an acid (lemon juice) to the liquid.

■ Fatty fish include bluefish, herring, mackerel, pompano, and salmon. Lean fish include cod, flounder/sole, haddock, halibut, pike, pollack, and snapper.

■ There are ways to fight the fishy aroma of cooked fish. Start with very fresh fish and wash it well to remove oxidized fats and bacteria-generated amines. Enclose the fish in a covered pan, foil or parchment, a pastry crust, or poaching liquid to reduce the exposure of the fish's surface to the air. After cooking, do not immediately unwrap the fish; let it cool down to reduce the vapors that will escape. Do not bake, broil, or fry the fish, which propels the fishy aroma into the air.

■ Buy 1 pound per serving if purchasing whole fish, ½ pound if purchasing dressed fish, and ⅓ pound if purchasing fish fillets or steaks.

FISH AND SEAFOOD AROMAS

COOKED FISH:

BOILED CRAB, CRAYFISH, LOBSTER, SHRIMP: Nutty, popcorn-like aroma.

FRESHWATER WHITE FISH: Strong aroma from fatty-acid fragments and earthy aroma from ponds, tanks.

SALMON AND SEA-RUN TROUT: Fruity, flowery aroma from carotenoid pigments they accumulate.

SALTWATER WHITE FISH: Mildest aroma.

TUNA, MACKEREL, AND THEIR FAMILY MEMBERS: Meaty, beeflike aroma.

FRESH FISH, ALL TYPES (FROM MOST DESIRABLE AROMA TO LEAST DESIRABLE):

FRESH AND PLANTLIKE, like crushed plant leaves or cut grass; some smell like cucumbers or melons

SMELL OF THE SEACOAST, bromophenol

MUDDINESS, an unpleasant smell from geosmin and borneol

FISHINESS, due to TMA (Trimethylamine)

FISH CUTS

BUTTERFLY FILLETS: Double fillet held together by skin.

DRAWN: Entrails removed, may or may not be scaled.

DRESSED: Entrails, head, tail, fins removed; ready to cook.

FILLETS: Sides cut lengthwise, usually boneless, may or may not be skinned.

PAN-DRESSED: Small sizes of dressed fish with heads and tails removed.

STEAKS: Cross-section/crosscut slices of large dressed fish.

STICKS: Uniform pieces of fillets.

WHOLE OR ROUND: Exactly as cut.

FISH AND SEAFOOD DISHES AND EDIBLE FISH

Fresh fish is generally purchased either whole or gutted, or as steaks or fillets. Freshness is extremely important because fish is subject to quick decay by bacterial action and often can cause food poisoning if not absolutely fresh. Most methods of preserving fish date back to ancient times: freezing (practiced by the Romans), drying (for herring and cod), smoking (for salmon, haddock, and other fish), and salting in casks or barrels. We now have canning and freezing as preservation methods as well. For culinary purposes, fish can be divided into white fish, white flatfish, perch family, or oily fish. These are some names of popular fish dishes and common edible fish.

ABALONE	CHOWDER	FLOUNDER
ANCHOVY	CLAM	GEFILTE FISH
ANGELFISH	COD, CODFISH	GOUJONS
ARBROATH SMOKIE	CODFISH STEW	GRAVLAX
ATLANTIC OCEAN PERCH OR REDFISH	CONCH	GROUPER
BACALAO	COQUILLES ST. JACQUES	GRUNION
BAKED FISH	CORAL	HADDOCK
BASS	COULIBIAC	HALIBUT
BLACKFISH	CRAB	HERRING
BLOATER	CRAB CAKES	JOHN DORY
BLUEFISH	CRAB IMPERIAL	KEDGEREE
BOMBAY DUCK	CRAYFISH	KIPPER
BONITO	DEEP-FRIED FISH	LAKE TROUT
BOUILLABAISSE	EEL	LANGOUSTINE
BRISLING	ESCARGOT	LOBSTER
BROILED FISH OR GRILLED FISH	FILLET OF SOLE	LOBSTER THERMIDOR
BUTTERFISH	FINNAN HADDIE	LOTTE
CALAMARI	FISH AND CHIPS	LOX
CATFISH	FISH CAKE	MACKEREL
CAVIAR	FISH FRITTER	MAHI MAHI OR DOLPHINFISH
	FISH MOUSSE	MATELOTE
	FISH STICKS	MILT

MONKFISH	SALMON	SOLE
MUSSEL	SAND DAB	SOLE BONNE FEMME
MUSSELS MARINIÈRE	SARDINE	SOLE MEUNIÈRE
OCTOPUS	SCALLOP	SPRAT
ORANGE ROUGHY	SCALLOPS BONNE FEMME	SQUID
OVEN-FRIED FISH	SCAMPI	STEAMED FISH
OYSTER	SCROD	STRIPED BASS
OYSTERS ROCKEFELLER	SCUNGILLI	STURGEON
PAN-FRIED FISH	SEA BASS	SURIMI
PERCH	SEA URCHIN	SWORDFISH
PIKE	SHAD	TERRAPIN
POACHED FISH	SHARK OR MAKO	TILAPIA
POMPANO	SHELLFISH	TILE
PRAWN	SHRIMP	TOMALLEY
RAINBOW TROUT	SHRIMP COCKTAIL	TROUT
RED SNAPPER	SKATE	TUNA
RISSOLES	SMELT	TUNA SALAD
ROCKFISH	SMOKED SALMON	TUNA TETRAZZINI
ROE	SNAIL	TURBOT
ROLLMOPS	SNAPPER	WHITEFISH
SABLE	SOFTSHELL CRAB	YELLOWTAIL

FISH AND CHIPS is fried fish fillet and French-fried potatoes. The term was first recorded in 1876. Joseph Malin opened the first shop to combine fish and chips as a dish in London in 1860.

FISH BALLS: see GEFILTE FISH.

FISH KNIFE is a broad-bladed, blunt table knife used for eating or serving fish. The terms was first recorded in 1403.

FISH POACHER is a long (fourteen to twenty-four inches) cooking pan with handles to hold a whole fish for poaching, a cooking method that imparts moisture to the food without masking the flavor. A fish poacher is fitted with a steel rack on which the fish sits above the poaching liquid.

> **HINTS** Poaching is a technique that cooks food delicately and evenly in a barely simmering liquid—a healthier option than frying or broiling in butter and oil. Poached fish retains its natural flavors and is tender and moist, with skin that slips off easily for an attractive presentation at the dinner table. It's a good preparation method for fish with delicate flavors, such as bass, cod, haddock, halibut, orange roughy, pomfret, pompano, salmon, snapper, sole, tilapia, trout, and turbot.

> When poaching on the stove, straddle the poacher across two burners if it is too large for one. Do not allow the poaching liquid to heat above a simmer. Remember, cooking times will vary with the size and thickness of the fish.

FISH SAUCE is a spicy liquid flavoring or condiment made from the fermented liquid of salt-cured fish, especially anchovies or oysters, and used in Southeast Asian cookery. It is called NAM PLA in Thailand, NUOC MAM in Vietnam, PATIS in the Philippines, TUK TREY in Cambodia, NGAN-PYA-YE in Myanmar, KETJAP IKAN in Indonesia, and SHOTTSURU in Japan. The term fish sauce dates to 1728 in English. Fish sauce is cooked with fish and also as a part of curries and sauces. A similar fish sauce was part of ancient Roman cooking, where in Latin it was called *garum* or *liquamen*. The original Worcestershire sauce is a related product because it is fermented and contains anchovies. Light-colored fish sauce is best as a condiment and for dipping. Dark-colored fish sauce is used for cooking.

FISH STICK or **FISH FINGER** is generally any elongated or rectangular breaded and deep-fried whitefish fillet; fish stick is the U.S. term and fish finger is the British term. Fish sticks may be made of mixed compressed ground fish pieces; they date to the 1950s.

FIVE-SPICE or **FIVE-SPICE POWDER**: see CHINESE FIVE-SPICE POWDER.

FLAGEOLET is a type of French green kidney bean with light-colored seeds. Flageolet beans were developed in 1872 by Gabriel Chevrier in Brittany, and in France are often termed *chevriers* in his honor; the origin of the word is the Latin *phaselus*, "kidney bean." Flageolet beans are very popular in French cooking, and are a traditional accompaniment to leg of lamb. Store in a cool, dry area.

FLAKY means made up of flakes or breaking easily into flakes, a term often referring to the texture of pastry and breads.

FLAMBÉ is literally "singed," as food that is flambéed is passed through a flame. The usual method is to cover the food with spirits (like brandy) and set alight briefly, often in a special flambé pan.

> **HINT** In a flambé, burning off the alcohol tempers its harshness and accentuates the flavor. Brandy or other 80-proof liqueur is best; a higher proof is dangerous and a lower proof won't flame correctly.

FLAN is a custard dessert topped with caramel syrup; it is important in Spanish cooking. Flan comes from a Latin word meaning "flat cake" and was first written as flawn. Flan is also a type of open tart filled with fruit, a cream, or a savory mixture. For this, the shell is baked in a bottomless band of metal (flan ring) on a baking sheet, then removed from the ring and filled.

> **CONFUSABLE** FLAN/CRÈME CARAMEL. Flan and crème caramel, both a mixture of sugar, flavorings, and a milk product, differ in that flan is Spanish in origin and is made with sweetened condensed milk, while crème caramel is French in origin and is made with whole milk or cream.

FLANK is a cut from the fleshy part of an animal's side between the ribs and the hip/leg.

> **HINTS** Flank is usually tenderized by marinating, then broiled or grilled whole. It is significantly tougher than the other beef cuts; therefore, many recipes use moist cooking methods such as braising. It is best prepared when cut across the grain.

> Flank steak should be stored in its original packaging in the coldest part of the refrigerator, where it will keep for three to four days. It also can be frozen in this packaging for up to two weeks.

FLAPJACK or **FLANNELCAKE** or **FLANNEL CAKE**, also called BATTERCAKE, GRIDDLECAKE, HOTCAKE, JOHNNYCAKE, or PANCAKE is a flat cake of thin, sweet batter fried on both sides on a griddle. The term flapjack dates to around 1600 and is from flap, which once meant "flip." In the United Kingdom flapjack is a sweet, dense cake made from oats, golden syrup, and melted butter, served in rectangles.

FLASH-FROZEN, also called QUICK-FROZEN, means preserved by freezing sufficiently rapidly to retain flavor and nutritional value. Freezing cooked or uncooked food rapidly permits it to be stored almost indefinitely at freezing temperatures. American inventor Clarence Birdseye developed the quick-freezing process of food preservation in the early twentieth century. During flash-freezing, items are frozen so fast that only small ice crystals are able to form. The cell walls are not damaged, and the frozen food, when thawed, keeps its maximum flavor, texture, and color.

FLATBREAD or **FLAT BREAD** is a general term for any bread made from unleavened dough, often in round, flat loaves or forms. Examples are chapatis, naan, pita, and tortillas. Flatbreads are the oldest breads of all. Quickly cooked, extremely delicious, highly portable, and incredibly versatile, flatbreads originated in places where fuel was scarce. Many cultures have a version of flatbread. Some of the oldest extant examples of food found in tombs and archaeological sites have been flatbreads.

FLATULENCE-CAUSING FOODS

APPLE	DAIRY PRODUCTS	PEA
APRICOT	DRIED FRUIT	PEACH
AVOCADO	FRIED FOOD	PEAR
BEANS	HIGH-FIBER CEREAL	PRUNE
BRUSSELS SPROUT	LEGUME	RADISH
CABBAGE	LIMA BEAN	RAISIN
CORN	MELON	TURNIP
CUCUMBER	ONION	

FLATWARE: see CUTLERY.

FLAT WHISK is a type of whisk with wires arranged in a flat configuration, like a spatula, rather than in a balloon shape. It is best for blending flour into fat and for mixing sauces in low pans. It is not spun in the hands like the round whisk, but used to scrape ingredients from one side of the pan to the other. This makes it especially useful when you are making a sauce like gravy and need to bring together drippings from meat you have just cooked. The scraping action of the whisk helps incorporate these flavorful bits together in order to make delicious gravy. The flat whisk with its scraping action can also keep sauce from collecting or burning on the bottom of the pan.

> **HINT** When selecting a flat whisk, make sure it has a sealed surface where the wires enter the handle, to prevent food from accumulating in hard-to-clean areas.

FLAVOR has two meanings. It is an identifiable or distinctive quality of food or drink perceived with the combined senses of taste and smell. It is also any substance adding flavor to food, or a substance used to give food or drink an identifiable or distinctive taste.

FLAVORS IDENTIFIABLE BY HUMANS

ASTRINGENT: Containing tannin, which contracts mouth tissues.

BITTER: Having a sharp, often unpleasant taste, such as of quinine or peach stones.

COOLING: Containing menthol, which has a refreshing effect.

PUNGENT: Spicy-hot, producing a sharp sensation.

SALTY: Having or tasting of salt.

SOUR: Having the sharp, acidic taste of lemon juice, vinegar, or green fruit.

SWEET: Having a taste of sugar.

UMAMI: Brothlike or meaty, a taste that is characteristic of monosodium glutamate, meat, and high-protein foods like soy products and some Asian foods.

FLAVONOID, also called BIOFLAVONOID, is any of a large group of pigments, such as anthocyanin. Flavonoids supply antioxidants, which neutralize free radicals that can damage bodily tissue, and also have anti-inflammatory and antiviral properties. Flavonoid-rich foods include almonds, apples, apricots, beets, black beans, black tea, blackberries, blueberries, broccoli, Brussels sprouts, carrots, cayenne, chocolate, coriander, cranberries, cucumbers, dark cherries, extra-virgin olive oil, fennel, fresh oregano, fresh parsley, garlic (raw), green tea, herbs, kale, kiwi, leeks, oranges, pears, peppermint, pink grapefruits, pinto beans, plums, prunes, raspberries, red cabbage, red grapes, red peppers (raw), red wine, spices, spinach, squash, strawberries, tangerines, tomatoes (ripe), watercress, and watermelon.

FLAVORING is a term for any substance that gives flavor to a food or drink, such as an essence, extract, herb, or spice.

FLAVORING BUTTER: see COMPOUND BUTTER.

FLIP: see EGGNOG.

FLIPPER: see OFFSET SPATULA and TURNER.

FLOAT is a beverage consisting of a soft drink with ice cream floating in it.

FLOATING ISLAND, also known as SNOW EGGS (*oeufs à la neige* in French), is a cold dessert consisting of custard with pieces of meringue, whipped cream, or whipped egg whites and sometimes jelly or crème anglaise floating on or around the custard's surface. The first mention of this dessert was by Benjamin Franklin in 1771.

> **HINT** Floating island is served at room temperature or cold, usually in a bowl. Once the dessert has been assembled, it should be served immediately. You can make both the crème anglaise and the meringue puffs in advance and keep them chilled, but the assembled dessert won't keep.

FLORENTINE means containing spinach, and the term is applied to dishes of eggs or fish or other white meat served on a bed of spinach or cooked with spinach. A Mornay sauce often accompanies such dishes. Florentine is also the name of a type of cookie made with orange peel or candied fruit and almonds, and coated with chocolate.

FLORET or **FLOWERET** is one of the tightly clustered flowering stems that make up a head of broccoli or cauliflower.

FLORIDA LOBSTERETTE: see PRAWN.

FLOUNDER, also called FLUKE, is any of various edible marine flatfish of two families (Bothidae and Pleuronectidae), including halibut, plaice, and turbot. You can distinguish flounder from other fish because both eyes are on the same side of the head.

FLOUR has two main meanings: a powder obtained by grinding grain (mainly wheat), which is used to make bread, cakes, and pastry; and a powder (usually fine and soft) obtained by grinding the seeds or roots of starchy vegetables. Etymologically, flour originally meant "flower" and later took on the differentiated sense of "finest or best part of the meal" of wheat or another grain. Flour is one of the oldest foods, ground at least fourteen thousand years ago. Stone-ground flour retains more flavor and nutrients than that milled with steel rollers. The bran and germ that contain oils that spoil quickly are removed from white flour, but vitamins and minerals are then added. Soft wheat from milder climates has less protein and more starch. Hard wheat from colder climates has more protein and is ground for bread making and pasta making. Gluten-free grains include buckwheat, corn, and rice. The higher the percentage of protein in a flour, the more gluten will be developed, and the stronger the gluten structure will be. Durum flours are high in protein and cake flours are low; all-purpose flours are in between.

FLOUR ESSENTIALS

■ Flour is best when fresh, so buy only what you need for four to six months. Store in an airtight container in a cool, dark, dry place. Whole wheat flour must be kept in the refrigerator or freezer. Store flour in its bag in the freezer during summer or in humid climates to eliminate bug infestation.

■ Sifting the flour (even presifted flour) gives a lighter, smoother texture to baked goods.

■ Do not substitute whole wheat flour in a recipe calling for all-purpose flour, but you can try using one-quarter to three-quarters whole wheat flour mixed with all-purpose flour. The same goes for substituting with oat or rye flour; no more than one-third of the wheat flour can be replaced with one of these.

■ The starch in flour acts as a thickener in gravies and sauces. Flour can be substituted for cornstarch in sauce. But when you substitute cornstarch for flour in a sauce, the cornstarch produces a more transparent, glistening sauce than flour. To substitute flour for cornstarch as a thickener, use 2 tablespoons of flour for each 1 table-spoon of cornstarch.

■ To substitute cake flour for all-purpose flour, use 1 cup plus 2 tablespoons of cake flour for each 1 cup of all-purpose flour.

■ To substitute all-purpose flour for self-rising flour, use 1 scant cup of all-purpose flour plus 1½ teaspoons of baking powder and 1 teaspoon of salt for each 1 cup of self-rising flour.

FLOUR PROTEIN CONTENTS

HIGH-GLUTEN FLOUR: 14%–15%

WHOLE WHEAT FLOUR: 14%

BREAD FLOUR: 12%–13%

ALL-PURPOSE FLOUR: 9%–12%

SELF-RISING FLOUR: 9%–11%

PASTRY FLOUR: 8%–9%

FLOUR VARIETIES

Flour is finely ground cereal grains or other starchy portions of plants, which is used in various food products and as a basic ingredient of baked goods. Flour is made mainly from wheat but also from other starchy plant materials, including barley, buckwheat, chickpeas, lima beans, oats, peanuts, potatoes, rice, rye, and soybeans. Some common varieties of flour are listed here:

ALL-PURPOSE FLOUR	FARINA	RED-DOG
ALMOND FLOUR	FORTIFIED FLOUR	REFINED FLOUR
BARLEY FLOUR	GRAHAM FLOUR	RICE FLOUR
BLEACHED FLOUR	HARD WHEAT FLOUR	RYE FLOUR
BOLTED FLOUR	HIGH-GLUTEN FLOUR	SELF-RISING OR SELF-RAISING FLOUR
BREAD FLOUR	LIMA BEAN FLOUR	SEMOLINA FLOUR
BREAK	MASA HARINA OR MASA	SOFT WHEAT FLOUR
BUCKWHEAT FLOUR	NONWHEAT	SOY OR SOYBEAN FLOUR
BULGUR	NUT FLOUR	UNBLEACHED FLOUR
CAKE FLOUR	OAT FLOUR	WHEAT FLOUR
CAROB FLOUR	ORGANIC FLOUR	WHEAT GERM OR WHEAT BRAN
CHESTNUT FLOUR	PASTRY FLOUR	WHITE FLOUR
CHICKPEA FLOUR	PEA FLOUR	WHOLE-GRAIN OR WHOLE-MEAL FLOUR
CORN FLOUR	PEANUT FLOUR	
DURUM	PHOSPHATED FLOUR	WHOLE WHEAT FLOUR
ENRICHED FLOUR	POTATO FLOUR	

FLUKE: see FLOUNDER.

FLUMMERY is a soft, sweet, bland food, usually a custard or pudding made from boiled and strained oatmeal, flour, or rice. Sometimes flummery is set with gelatin, mixed with stewed fruit, or flavored with Madeira and lemon.

FLUTE (FLUTING) means to make furrows or rounded grooves in something, such as a pie crust's edge. Fluting or flute is any groove or furrow, as on a pie crust's edge.

> **CONFUSABLE** CRIMP/FLUTE. Crimping differs from fluting in that you use a tool to press down and seal the dough. Fluting involves using the fingers to create a decorative shape or edge.

FOAM is a mass of small bubbles formed in or on a liquid; in cooking this can be created by agitation (beating an egg white, or whipping cream), fermentation (a glass of beer), or heating (steamed milk on cappuccino).

FOCACCIA (pronounced foh-KAH-chee-ah) is a flat, crisp Italian bread made with olive oil and herbs. Focaccia is Italian for "bread baked in the hearth." Focaccia doughs are similar in style and texture to pizza doughs. The plain flatbread evolved into a flatbread topped with olive oil, spices, herbs, vegetables, meats, and cheese, paving the way for the ever-popular pizza.

> **HINT** Cooks commonly poke small holes on the surface of uncooked focaccia dough (this technique is called dotting) to help retain moisture and produce a savory bread. Olive oil is then spread on top and allowed to sink in as the dough rises and is eventually baked.

FOIE GRAS (pronounced FWAH-grah) is a pâté made from the liver of fattened geese (or ducks). These fowl are force-fed a corn diet in a confined living space, making them obese and producing enlarged, fatty livers. Foie gras is French for "fat liver" and the dish has been around since ancient times. The liver is soaked overnight in water, milk, or port; drained; marinated in Armagnac, port, or Madeira mixed with seasonings; then cooked.

> HINTS Store well-wrapped foie gras in the refrigerator for up to two days or freeze for up to two months.

> Trim all traces of green bile and white fat from foie gras; separate the lobes and pull out all the veins.

FOIE GRAS GRADES

GRADE A: Weighs 14 ounces or more, has no imperfections, is smooth and buttery.	GRADE C: Weighs 7–10 ounces, is meaty but small.
GRADE B: Weighs 11–13 ounces, has slight imperfections, is softer than grade A.	

FOIL, also called ALUMINUM FOIL or TIN FOIL, is a piece of thin and flexible sheet metal. It withstands high heat and extreme cold, making it perfect for everything from grilling to freezer storage. Foil minimizes cleanup and ensures that food stays moist. Some popular uses of foil are lining pans before making foods like roasts, covering casseroles, or making foil packets to enclosed foods.

> HINTS Line the oven or firebox of a grill with heavy-duty foil to deflect heat and ease cleanup. The shiny side should face up.

> If you don't want the food you are cooking to stick to the foil covering it, spray the foil with nonstick cooking spray.

FOLD or **FOLD IN** is to blend an ingredient gently with other ingredients, using gentle cutting or lifting strokes with a utensil, so as to include it in the mixture without stirring or beating. The technique mainly applies to gently mixing a light, airy mixture (such as beaten egg whites) into a heavier, denser mixture (such as whipped cream or custard), without deflating the mixture, which could ruin the recipe. The lighter mixture is placed on top of the heavier one in a large bowl. Folding requires a specific mixing motion that gently turns the mixtures over on top of each other, combining them in the process. Starting at the back of the bowl, using the edge of a rubber spatula, cut down through the middle of both mixtures, across the bottom of the bowl, and up the near side. Rotate the bowl a quarter turn and repeat, taking care not to overmix.

FOND is the French word for stock, the base for a stew, sauce, and other dishes. In classic French cooking, there is *fond blanc*, "white stock," made from veal and poultry meat and bones and vegetables; *fond brun*, "brown stock," made with browned beef, veal and poultry meat and bones and vegetables; and *fond de vegetal*, "vegetable stock," made with butter-sautéed vegetables.

FONDANT is a type of candy or icing made of a thick, creamy sugar paste; it is also the name of the paste itself. The word is from the French *fonder*, "to melt."

> **HINTS** Fondant can be refrigerated, tightly wrapped, for up to three months.
>
> ❚ Heating fondant makes it soft enough to be used as an icing to coat large and small cakes. A fondant on a cake acts as an airtight seal that keeps the cake inside fresh and moist. When it comes time to eat the cake, you can peel the fondant off like you would an orange peel, if you do not like the taste of fondant.

FONDUE or **FONDUE POT** generally refers to a hot sauce of melted cheese or chocolate in which bread or fruits are dipped, but it also refers to dipping raw pieces of meat or fish into boiling oil/fat to cook them before dipping in sauces. Fondue is from the French *fonder*, "to melt." The cheese sauce is often seasoned with liquor and herbs. The fondue sits above a heat source, and skewers or long fondue forks are used to dip foods into the pot. Fondue is also a term for a baked soufflé-like cheese dish with bread or cracker crumbs. The etiquette of fondue requires that each person have his or her own color-coded fondue fork and that the fork never touch the lips.

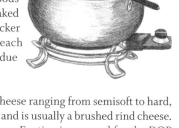

FONTINA is a pale yellow Italian cow's milk cheese ranging from semisoft to hard, and from mild to medium-sharp. It has tiny eyes and is usually a brushed rind cheese. It has a milk fat content of around 45%. The name Fontina is reserved for the DOP cheese made with unpasteurized milk from the Aosta Valley in Italy, even though the cheese is made throughout northern Italy and in several other countries, including France, Denmark, Sweden, and the United States. Outside of Aosta Valley, it is made mainly from pasteurized milk.

> **HINTS** Young Fontina is served at the end of a meal or on canapés; it is also used in cooking. The cheese also melts very well, and it is sometimes included in fondue and similar dishes. When matured, it is grated and used like Parmesan cheese.
>
> ❚ When selecting Fontina cheese in the store, look for an evenly textured specimen without discoloration. Older Italian cheese may have a strong aroma, but young cheese should have a relatively neutral aroma, especially in wrappings. An Italian Fontina stamped with the mark of the consortium will have a high quality, although it may cost more than imitations of the cheese made in other parts of Italy and the rest of the world.
>
> ❚ Before you store Fontina cheese at home, examine the cheese block and make sure that it is free of blemishes and signs of mold. Except with blue cheeses, visible mold means that the cheese is spoiled and must be discarded. Choose an

appropriate container for the cheese. Rindless, semisoft cheeses like Fontina should be stored in a plastic food container that maintains a humid environment for the cheese. A plastic container can also isolate these softer cheeses from other foods, decreasing the risk that it will absorb their flavors. The ideal temperature for storing Fontina is 35°F–40°F, which is close to the average temperature of a home refrigerator. Fontina has a relatively short shelf life; once removed from the wrapper it will last for about ten days in the refrigerator. Make sure to keep unused Fontina wrapped in plastic wrap or wax paper and sealed in a ziplock plastic bag. Fontina also tends to freeze better than other cheeses. Freezing, rather than refrigerating, can extend the life of the cheese for a number of weeks. Frozen Fontina should be defrosted in the refrigerator overnight.

FOOD refers to substances, or a particular substance, providing nourishment for people or animals, especially in solid as opposed to liquid form.

FOODS AND BEVERAGES NAMED FOR PLACES

AMERICAN CHEESE	CURRANT	PARMESAN CHEESE
BAKED ALASKA	EDAM CHEESE	PILSNER BEER
BIALY	FIG NEWTON	PORT WINE
BISQUE	FRANKFURTER	ROMAINE LETTUCE OR COS LETTUCE
BOLOGNA OR BALONEY	GORGONZOLA CHEESE	ROMANO CHEESE
BOMBAY DUCK	GOUDA CHEESE	ROQUEFORT CHEESE
BORDEAUX WINE	GRUYÈRE CHEESE	SCOTCH WHISKEY
BOURBON WHISKEY	HAMBURGER	SELTZER WATER
BRIE CHEESE	HOLLANDAISE SAUCE	STILTON CHEESE
BRUSSELS SPROUTS	JALAPEÑO	SWISS CHEESE
BURGUNDY WINE	JAVA	TABASCO SAUCE
CAMEMBERT CHEESE	LIMA BEAN	TANGERINE
CANTALOUPE	LIMBURGER CHEESE	THOUSAND ISLAND DRESSING
CAYENNE PEPPER	MADEIRA WINE	TOLL HOUSE COOKIE
CHAMPAGNE	MAYONNAISE	TURKEY
CHEDDAR CHEESE	MOCHA	WORCESTERSHIRE SAUCE
CHIANTI WINE	MONTEREY JACK CHEESE	
COGNAC BRANDY	MUENSTER CHEESE OR MUNSTER CHEESE	
COLBY CHEESE		

FOOD CLICHÉS

APPLE OF ONE'S EYE	CREAM OF THE CROP	EGG ONE ON
BRING HOME THE BACON	CURRY FAVOR	EGG ON ONE'S FACE
BUTTER ONE UP	CUT THE MUSTARD	FULL OF BEANS
COOK ONE'S GOOSE	EASY AS PIE	FULL OF BOLOGNA
COOL AS A CUCUMBER	EAT CROW	FULL OF VINEGAR

GOING BANANAS	IN A PICKLE	PIE IN THE SKY
HAPPY AS A CLAM	IN THE SOUP	RED AS A BEET
HIGH ON THE HOG	NUTTY AS A FRUITCAKE	SLOW AS MOLASSES
HOT ENOUGH TO FRY AN EGG	PACKED LIKE SARDINES	TWO PEAS IN A POD
IN A JAM	PIECE OF CAKE	WARM AS TOAST

FOODS AND BEVERAGES NAMED FOR PEOPLE (EPONYMS)

BEEF STROGANOFF	DOM PÉRIGNON	MELBA TOAST
BEEF WELLINGTON	EARL GREY TEA	MIREPOIX
BOYSENBERRY	EGGS BENEDICT	NAPOLEON
CAESAR SALAD	FETTUCCINE ALFREDO	OYSTERS ROCKEFELLER
CARPACCIO	FILBERT NUT	PEACH MELBA
CHATEAUBRIAND	GRAHAM CRACKER	PRALINE
CHICKEN TETRAZZINI	LOBSTER NEWBURG	SALISBURY STEAK
COBB SALAD	LOGANBERRY	SANDWICH
CRÊPES SUZETTE	MACADAMIA NUT	

FOOD ADDITIVE is any natural or artificial substance added to food during processing for the purposes of coloring, preservation, or stabilization. Additives make food look or taste better, or last longer. Under European and American law, each food item must show clearly each food additive on the label or packet under its own E number. Ninety-eight percent (by weight) of all food additives used in the United States are in the form of baking soda, citric acid, corn syrup, mustard, pepper, salt, and vegetable colorings.

FOOD MILL is a hand-operated kitchen tool used to grind/mash and purée soft foods through perforated disks controlled by a crank. This tool fills the gap between a sieve and an electric blender or food processor. Its function is similar to that of a RICER or SPÄETZLE MAKER and it is also used to remove seeds or pulp from some fruits and vegetables. There are several parts to a food mill. The first is a large bowl propped up on sturdy feet. A perforated disk is designed to fit into the bottom of the bowl, and a large, flat blade attached to a crank handle clips onto the top of the disk. Typically, a food mill comes with a selection of disks in an assortment of sizes. This allows chefs to create foods of varying consistencies or to make several passes with a particularly stubborn food.

> **HINT** Look for a food mill that can be easily disassembled and cleaned, and try to find one that is capable of standing up to hard use. If the legs can be easily bent or twisted, the food mill will not hold up through extended projects. The disks and blade of a food mill should also be very strong, as they may undergo large amounts of pressure. Look for solid construction and strong materials, and avoid cheap alternatives as they will be ultimately frustrating.

The best models feature deep hoppers and paddles that fit snugly against the disks. They have interchangeable disks with various hole sizes, so you can control how finely strained your food is. If the disk becomes clogged during milling, turn the crank backward and the paddle will become a scraper that clears the clog.

FOOD PROCESSOR is an electric kitchen appliance with interchangeable revolving blades used to chop, grate, mince, slice, purée, and blend food ingredients. The first American food processor was introduced in 1973 by Cuisinart.

FOOD PROCESSOR ESSENTIALS

CONFUSABLE FOOD PROCESSOR/ BLENDER. A blender is an electric kitchen appliance that consists of a tall container with a removable lid and motor-driven blades at the bottom that blend, chop, mix, or liquefy foods depending on the speed setting selected. In general, blenders are better suited to working with liquids (they are also called liquefiers or liquidizers), and food processors work better with solid foods. Of the two, the food processor is considered more versatile.

■ Use a flexible rubber or plastic mat under heavy appliances like food processors and mixers, and just pull on the mat to move the appliance.

■ A food processor should not be used for mashing potatoes, for beating egg whites, or for whipping cream. Very dense dough will overheat this machine if the motor is not powerful enough.

■ When using a food processor, start with the dryer, milder ingredients and work up to processing the moister, stronger-flavored ingredients to avoid

washing the bowl between steps. Instead, wipe the work bowl with a dry paper towel between ingredients.

■ Lightly coat the blades/disks and bowl of a food processor with vegetable oil when processing sticky foods.

■ If the work bowl of a food processor leaks, there is too much liquid, and smaller batches should be processed.

■ Hold the work bowl of a food processor with your thumb inserted in the bottom hole and press it to one side to prevent the blade from falling out when you are removing foods from the bowl.

■ Keep the lid of the food processor clean by covering the bowl with plastic wrap before running the machine.

■ Only firm/semihard cheese like Swiss and Cheddar can be sliced in a food processor, and only when it is semi-frozen/chilled first.

■ After removing most of the food from a food processor, put the blade back in and pulse to clean the blade and get the rest of the food out.

FOOD SAFETY refers to the conditions and practices that preserve the quality of food to prevent contamination and foodborne illnesses. Food can be contaminated in many different ways. Some food products may already contain bacteria or parasites. The germs can be spread during the packaging process if the food products are not handled properly. Failure to cook or store the food properly can cause further contamination. Properly handling and preparing food greatly reduces the risks of foodborne illnesses. Higher-risk foods include red meats, poultry, eggs, cheese, dairy products, raw sprouts, and raw fish or shellfish.

FOOD SAFETY ESSENTIALS

■ Wash hands with warm water and soap before handling ingredients. Wash tools, surfaces, and dishware with warm water and soap after using.

■ Do not leave perishable food out of the refrigerator for more than two hours, or no more than one hour in warm weather.

■ The rule of thumb for carefully handled leftovers is to keep them in the refrigerator for a maximum of four days.

■ Use fresh kitchen towels as much as possible.

■ Run sponges, scrubbing pads, and brushes through the dishwasher every week or so to sterilize them, or boil or microwave them for two minutes.

■ According to the FDA and other food safety experts, bagged prewashed lettuce and other greens, organic or conventional, need not be washed before eating. If you do choose to wash a product marked "prewashed" or "ready to eat," be sure to use safe handling practices to avoid any cross-contamination. Wash your hands for twenty seconds with warm water and soap before and after handling the product, and wash the produce under running water just before preparing or eating.

■ If there is a power outage, keep the refrigerator and freezer doors closed. Refrigerated foods are safe for four to six hours. Move foods to an ice-filled cooler after that for up to two days. Foods in a fully stocked freezer are safe for up to two days. If the freezer is only half full, frozen food will keep for just twenty-four hours.

■ Avocados, Brussels sprouts, cabbage, cauliflower, corn, green peas, and sweet potatoes are least likely to contain pesticide residue, while American apples, cherries, nectarines, pears, raspberries, and strawberries and Mexican carrots are most likely to have pesticide residue.

■ Make sure a frying pan or deep fryer's handle is turned away from the front of the stove.

■ For a fire in a stovetop pan, turn off the heat and cover the pan with a tight lid to smother the flames. Use no water. Extinguish a fire by smothering with a pot lid, smothering with baking soda, or using a class A, B, or C fire extinguisher. Keep one of these handy when deep-frying.

■ Canned goods with dents or bulging lids may indicate a serious food-poisoning threat.

■ The expiration date is the last date that the food should be consumed. A sell-by or pull-by date is the last date the food should be on the store shelf.

■ If kitchen items have not been used for sixty days, sell or donate them unless they are party or seasonal items, such as an ice-cream maker or waffle iron. If these specialty items are not used after another six months, out they go.

FOOL is a British dessert of crushed or puréed stewed fruit mixed with sugar and whipped cream. Foole was first mentioned as a dessert synonymous with trifle in 1598, though the gooseberry fool may date to the fifteenth century. The word comes from the French word *foulé*, meaning "pressed/crushed," and refers to the combination of crushed fruits and thick cream.

> **HINT** When making fool, take care not to overwhip the cream, because over-whipped cream is difficult to blend with the fruit.

FOO YOUNG: see EGG FOO YONG.

FORCEMEAT is finely chopped, highly seasoned meat, fish, or vegetables used for stuffing or as a garnish. The term, first recorded around 1688, was first written as forced meat and comes from the French word *farce*, "stuffing." There are three major categories of forcemeat: those made with vegetables; those made with meat, game, or poultry; and those made with fish. In addition, there is a fourth, more minor, category of forcemeat, based on egg yolk.

FORK is a pronged eating and serving instrument derived from the agricultural tool. The word fork comes from the Latin *furca*, "pitchfork." The two-prong twig was probably the first "fork." In Egyptian antiquity, large bronze forks were used at religious ceremonies to lift sacrificial offerings. One of the earliest dinner forks was used in Constantinople in AD 400. By the seventh century, small forks were used in Middle Eastern courts. The fork was once censured for being an "affront to God's intention for fingers" and was slow to gain reacceptance because it was considered a feminine utensil. The modern table setting is attributed to Charles I of England who in 1633 declared, "It is decent to use a fork." The first dinner forks had two flat prongs and it took a while for three- and four-prong forks to gain popularity. Today, a set of flatware may contain five forks: dinner fork, fish fork (for leverage in separating fish from the body), luncheon fork, salad or dessert fork, and seafood fork (for shrimp cocktail and other seafood). There are specialized forks for specific foods like berries, birds, cake, cold meat, cucumbers, ice cream, lettuce, pickles, sardines, shellfish, strawberries, soufflé, terrapin, and tomatoes, and to pass sliced bread. Sometimes a tine is wider and has a notch to provide extra leverage when cutting food that normally does not require a knife. A fork with its prongs pointing down, crossed over a knife on a plate, tells the food server that the diner is not finished. This is known as the "rest" position.

FORMAGGIO is the Italian word for "cheese."

FORTIFIED (FORTIFY), also called ENRICHED, in terms of cooking, refers to a food supplied with added ingredients, such as vitamins and minerals, to increase its nutritional content. Common fortified foods are milk (fortified with vitamin D), salt (iodine), yogurt (calcium, vitamin D), ready-to-eat cereals (vitamins, minerals), orange juice (calcium), bread (vitamins B_1 and B_2, niacin, iron), and infant formula (iron). In reference to wines, fortified means having a higher than normal alcohol content due to the addition of brandy or spirits. Fortified wines include port, sherry, Marsala, vermouth, and Madeira. Fortified wines were born of the need to preserve European wines on long trade voyages during the sixteenth and seventeenth centuries. Measures of brandy were added before or during the fermentation process to stabilize the wine. On long sea voyages, fortified wines were able to withstand the wildly fluctuating temperatures and constant motion they were subjected to in the ship's hold.

> **HINT** Fortified wines last much longer after opening than traditional wines do, allowing people to use and serve them in small amounts. Ultimately, however, the wine will go off, becoming unpleasant to drink. Storing fortified wines under refrigeration after opening can help to slow this process, as will using a good replacement cork.

FORTUNE COOKIE describes a thin dough cooked and folded when warm around a slip of paper bearing a prediction or maxim. These cookies are sold or given in Chinese restaurants, though the fortune cookie did not originate in China. Noodle manufacturer David Jung is credited with the invention by some, but a San Francisco court ruled that Makota Hagiwara, manager of Golden Gate Park's Japanese Tea Garden, created the cookies as thank-you notes in the early twentieth century. The concept became so popular that Chinese restaurants in San Francisco's Chinatown appropriated the idea. The *Oxford English Dictionary* dates the written word to 1962.

FOUR FRUITS

The following summer fruits are traditionally served together or combined into preserves or syrups.

QUATRE-FRUITS	QUATRE-FRUITS JAUNES
CHERRIES	CITRONS
RASPBERRIES	LEMONS
RED CURRANTS	ORANGES
STRAWBERRIES	SEVILLE ORANGES

FOUR SPICES is a mixture of white pepper, ginger, nutmeg, and cloves or cinnamon used in French cooking, especially in charcuterie and in dishes that need long simmering, such as stews. The tern is a translation of the French *quatre-épices*.

FOWL is a general term for any of various domestic gallinaceous birds used as food (eggs and flesh): chickens, ducks, geese, pheasants, and turkey. The term is also used for their flesh. POULTRY is the general term for farmyard birds, as opposed to wild game birds, kept for eggs and/or meat.

FOXBERRY: see LINGONBERRY.

FRAMBOISE is French for "raspberry," which originated in Europe. Dating to the twelfth century, the word may be a corruption of the Dutch *braambezie* or the Latin *fraga ambrosia*, "ambrosial strawberry." The term is also applied to a white brandy distilled from raspberries. Framboise is usually served in a small glass that resembles a Champagne glass, only shorter.

FRANGIPANE was first an almond cream flavored with jasmine perfume used as a cake or pastry filling. Now the word refers to a pastry with this filling invented by Count Cesare Frangipani in Rome in 1532.

FRANKFURTER or **FRANK** is a smooth-textured smoked sausage of minced beef, pork, or turkey, often served on a bread roll. First recorded in 1877 in American English, the word comes from the German *Frankfurter wurst* because a sausage somewhat like a U.S. hot dog was originally made in Frankfurt am Main, Germany. The true frankfurter was a cold-smoked sausage made of pork and salted bacon fat.

> **CONFUSABLE** FRANKFURTER/HOT DOG/WIENER. Hot dog describes a frankfurter served in a bun or roll, and wiener is short for wienerwurst or Vienna sausage and is now a synonym for frankfurter.

FRAPPÉ is the term in parts of New England for a thick ice-cream milkshake. It has other meanings: a partly frozen fruit-flavored ice drink, or an alcoholic drink served over or mixed with crushed or shaved ice. As an adjective, it means iced or chilled in reference to a drink. The word comes from from the French *frapper*, "to ice."

FREE-RANGE is a term used to indicate that poultry and cattle have been kept or raised in an area where they may move around freely, and is used to mark egg and meat products of such animals. Dating to 1912, the term suggests these animals have access to open air and grass during the daytime.

> **CONFUSABLE** FREE-RANGE/GRASS-FED. Free-range is a misleading term that really indicates only access to the outdoors. Grass-fed describes poultry or cattle that subsist largely on grasses rather than on grain. Grass-fed generally means

more tender meat. Pastured is a subset of grass-fed, indicating poultry or cattle that graze on living grasses and insects.

FREESTONE is fruit, especially the peach and plum, whose flesh/pulp does not cling to the pit; the word is also used to refer to the pit itself. The opposite is the CLINGSTONE. Freestone varieties of fruits are preferred for uses that require careful removal of the stone, especially if removal will be done by hand. When uniform and attractive slices of fruit are needed, freestones are better to use.

FREEZE (FREEZING) is to expose to a temperature of less than 32°F. The word goes back to an Indo-European base of the Latin *pruina*, "hoarfrost," and the Sanskrit *prusva*, "frozen drop." Freezing is a common method of food preservation that slows both food decay and the growth of microorganisms. In addition to decreasing reaction rates, freezing makes water less available for bacterial growth. The method has been used for centuries in cold regions. Freezers were first developed as appliances in the mid-nineteenth century and shortly thereafter food was frozen for transport via ship and train. In the twentieth century, flash-freezing was found to be especially effective with certain kinds of food.

FREEZING ESSENTIALS

■ To keep delicate fruits and vegetables separate when frozen, freeze them on a baking sheet before putting them in zip-lock freezer bags or containers.

■ Cool all foods before putting in the freezer. Remove as much excess air as possible from containers. Divide large batches into smaller quantities. Mark the date and contents on packages with tape or permanent marker. Don't pack food tightly until it is completely frozen. Once the food is frozen, a full freezer is the most efficient.

■ Use only heavy-duty freezer foil or freezer paper. First wrap in plastic wrap or wax paper. Heavy-duty plastic bags and wrap are also good.

■ Allow for circulation of chilled air around the containers in the freezer. Don't tightly stack them in the freezer or refrigerator until cooled or frozen.

■ Plastic wrap should be used in freezing by placing the plastic wrap directly on the food surface to protect it against the dry freezer air. If using plastic, use two layers, or one layer of plastic and an outer layer of foil.

■ Raw meat and poultry are easier to slice if you freeze them for 30 minutes first.

■ After freezing leftovers in plastic containers, loosen them with a little hot water and transfer the food to a zip-lock freezer bag.

■ Thaw frozen foods in the refrigerator. To quickly thaw, put food in a zip-lock bag and into a large bowl of cool water. Defrosting frozen meat in the refrigerator takes around 48 hours.

FOOD THAT DOES NOT FREEZE WELL

In other words, do not freeze these.

CHEESE (ESPECIALLY COTTAGE AND RICOTTA)	FRIED FOODS	SOUP AND STEW THICKENED WITH CORNSTARCH OR FLOUR
COOKED CHUNK POTATOES (EXCEPT FRENCH FRIES)	EMULSIFIED SAUCES	SOUP AND STEW WITH POTATOES (WHICH DARKEN AND BECOME MUSHY)
COOKED EGG WHITES	FROSTING WITH EGG WHITE OR BUTTER	
COOKED RICE	GELATIN	SOUR CREAM
CREAM SAUCES AND GRAVIES WITH FLOUR OR CORNSTARCH	MAYONNAISE	STUFFED PORK CHOPS AND STUFFED CHICKEN BREASTS
	MERINGUE	
CUSTARD AND CREAM PIES OR DESSERTS WITH CREAM FILLINGS	PASTA	WHOLE EGGS IN THE SHELL, RAW OR COOKED
	RADISHES AND TOMATOES (HIGH WATER CONTENT)	
CUSTARDS AND FILLINGS	SALAD GREENS, CABBAGE, CELERY, AND CUCUMBER (HIGH WATER CONTENT)	
DELICATE BATTERED AND		

FROZEN TREAT TYPES

The method of freezing food has been used for centuries in cold regions, and a patent was issued in Britain as early as 1842 for freezing food by immersion in an ice and salt brine. Iced desserts were introduced into Europe from the East, and Marco Polo brought back descriptions of fruit ices from his travels in China. Italian cooks developed recipes and techniques for making both water and milk ices, too. It was not, however, until the introduction of mechanical refrigeration that the process of freezing became widely applicable commercially. Today, we create an infinite variety of frozen foods, with sweets and treats being a favorite category.

BOMBE	ICE	MOUSSE
FLAVORED ICE	ICEBOX CAKE	PARFAIT
FRAPPE	ICE CREAM	POPSICLE
FROZEN CUSTARD	ICE-CREAM BAR	SHERBET
FROZEN PUDDING	ICE-CREAM CAKE	SORBET
FROZEN YOGURT	ICE-CREAM CONE	SPLIT
GELATO	ICE-CREAM SANDWICH	SUNDAE
GLACE	ICE LOLLY	WATER ICE
GRANITA	ICE MILK	

FREEZE-DRIED (FREEZE-DRYING), also called LYOPHILIZATION, is preserved by rapidly freezing and then drying in a high vacuum to remove the ice. The process of FREEZE-DRYING was invented around 1944 and it is done mainly for preservation, as for coffee and astronaut food. The foodstuff is placed in a vacuum chamber where the water frozen in the food evaporates through sublimation. The basic process of freeze-drying foods was known to the Peruvian Incas of the Andes. During World War II, the freeze-drying process was developed commercially when it was used to preserve blood plasma and penicillin. Hundreds of different types of freeze-dried foods have been commercially produced since the 1960s. The food for freeze-drying is treated in three stages: the product is deep-frozen; it is subjected to a vacuum, which sublimates the ice trapped in it; and the water vapor is removed, leaving the product dry and stable. A solid food that has been processed in this way becomes extremely light because it contains only 1%–2% of its original water content, but it retains its volume. Of all the techniques for drying food, freeze-drying has the least impact on flavor and texture. Freeze-dried foods have proven invaluable for military and astronaut use, as well as for hikers.

> **HINT** Moisture contributes to decay and freeze-dried foods have almost no moisture, which means they may be stored at room temperature for many years.

FREEZER BURN is discoloration and light-colored spots on frozen foods due to surface-moisture evaporation when inadequately packaged or wrapped. Freezer burn is not dangerous. Since the burn occurs from oxygen, the food is safe to eat, but it will probably be dry and not taste very good.

FRENCH BEAN is any young, green string bean; in British English, it is specifically the pod of a green bean or wax bean eaten as a vegetable. The descriptor French or Frenched indicates the beans have been cut lengthwise into very thin strips. French beans are also a variety of thick, fleshy, stringless green or yellow beans. The yellow beans are usually juicier than the green ones. The smaller the beans when picked, the better the taste: the pods start to dry out as soon as they are picked and become limp and bendy within a few hours. This means that unless you grow French beans for yourself, you never get a chance to taste them at their best.

> **HINT** When choosing French beans, keep in mind that they are past their best when the skin is coarse textured and the beans inside begin to show through like small marbles. French beans will keep in the refrigerator for three days or so.

FRENCH BREAD or **FRENCH ROLL** is a type of white bread made from yeast-raised dough containing soft wheat flour and relatively little water and baked in long, usually thin, loaves or baguettes; the bread has a crisp golden-brown crust, an open texture, and a light crumb. The term dates to 1686. A French roll is an individual serving size made of this dough. The golden-brown, intensely crisp crust of French bread is created by brushing or spraying the loaf's exterior with water during the baking process.

FRENCH CHEF'S KNIFE: see CHEF'S KNIFE.

FRENCH DRESSING in the United States is a creamy, mayonnaise-based, often sweet salad dressing, usually orange in color and tomato-flavored. However, in the United Kingdom, where French dressing is an alternative name for VINAIGRETTE, it is a salad dressing prepared chiefly from oil, vinegar, and seasonings. In the United States, the FDA sets Standards of Identity for French dressing, and the modified mayonnaise called salad dressing that is used as the basis for most creamy dressings. French dressing must contain at least 35% vegetable oil by weight, along with vinegar and tomato and/or paprika products.

FRENCHED or **FRENCH** is used in two different senses, depending on the context. In both cases, the food is cut with a specific cooking technique in mind. First, frenched means a food like green beans or potatoes have been cut lengthwise into very thin strips or slivers. It can also mean to cut the meat away from the end of a rib or chop, so that part of the bone is exposed. Frenching is often used on roasts and chops for aesthetic reasons. The frenching ensures that the food cooks evenly while also looking attractive when it is presented. For frenching of the first type, many cooks prefer to use a mandoline or julienne slicer. Using kitchen tools like these ensures that the cuts are even and perfect. This can be very important when presenting food at a formal event, and it also ensures that the food cooks properly. In the second instance, frenching is done with a sharp knife, although the type of knife varies depending on the cut. It does require skill, however, as the meat needs to be trimmed neatly and efficiently from the bone.

FRENCH ENDIVE: see BELGIAN ENDIVE.

FRENCH FRY (FRENCH FRIES) or **FRENCH FRIED POTATO** is a strip of potato fried in deep fat. The "French" in French fry comes from a method called frenching, which is slicing vegetables into long, thin strips. French fries may have originated in Belgium, not France. Thomas Jefferson is credited with introducing French fries in America in the late eighteenth century. They are called CHIPS in the United Kingdom.

moisture content makes them less apt to splatter the oil or to absorb grease. Dry the potatoes well to prevent splattering of the oil by the water.

❚ When making French fries, soak cut potatoes in cold water, or cut into ¼-inch fries with skin on and soak at room temperature. This step ensures maximum crispness when they are cooked.

FRENCH KNIFE: see CHEF'S KNIFE.

FRENCH STICK: see BAGUETTE.

FRENCH TOAST is a dish made of sliced bread dipped in egg and milk mixture, lightly fried or grilled, and served with maple syrup and/or confectioners' sugar and sometimes preserves. The dish dates to 1882. The French call it PAIN PERDU, "lost bread," because the dish is a way of using slightly stale French bread. In England, French toast is simply sliced bread fried in bacon fat or butter on one side, a dish also called "poor knights of Windsor."

> HINTS When making French toast, put a piece of bread between the batter dipping bowl and the frying pan to catch drips after you dip the bread.
>
> ❚ For unsoggy French toast, bake bread in a 300ºF oven for 16 minutes, flipping halfway through.

FRICASSEE is a dish of chicken or other meat sliced and fried or stewed in a gravy made with its drippings. The word, which dates to 1568, is from the French *fricasser*, "cut up and cook in sauce." The verb fricassee refers to preparing meat by this method. The end result of fricassee is a thick, chunky stew, often flavored with wine.

FRIED DOUGH is a variety of fried bread made from a yeast dough and has sweet varieties with icing, powdered sugar, and so on or savory versions served with marinara, soy sauce, or other toppings. Fried dough is popular for breakfast but also as a snack at amusement parks, fairs, and other venues.

FRIED RICE is a dish of boiled rice fried with onions/scallions, scrambled egg, soy sauce, oyster sauce, and seasonings, and sometimes minced meat (chicken, pork), shrimp, or vegetables (bean sprouts, carrots, corn, peas). There are dozens of varieties of fried rice.

> HINT The secret to good fried rice is starting with cold cooked rice. If you can, cook the rice by boiling the day before and refrigerate. This will turn the grains firm and get rid of the excess moisture. They will also be much easier to separate. If you cook with freshly made rice, all you will get is "fried mush" instead of fried rice. If you can't wait a day, at least let the rice cool for a few hours in an airy spot.

FRIGGITELLO: see PEPPERONCINI.

FRIJOLES, **FRIJOLE**, or **FRIJOL** (the singular is frijol, pronounced FREE-hohl) are any beans (genus *Phaseolus*), especially the black, kidney, or pinto bean, used for food in Mexican or southwestern U.S. cuisine. The word is derived from the Greek *phaselos*, "legume."

FRISÉE or **FRISÉE LETTUCE** is a kind of curly-leaved endive (*Cichorium endivia*) used in salad. It is a French term recently introduced into English and is short for *chicorée frisée*, "curly chicory."

> **HINTS** Choose frisée with crisp leaves and no sign of wilting. Look for nice green leaves with no yellowing. Refrigerate in a plastic ventilated bag for up to five days. Wash just before using. Tightly closed packaging does not allow the lettuce to breathe and will make it rot. Be sure that air can circulate around the leaves. Frisée lettuce is fragile and will not tolerate freezing. Do not dress it until just before serving, since vinegar will make it wilt.

> Never cut the frisée lettuce with a knife: tear it by hand. Separate the leaves from each other. Wash them and then spin them well, or dry them immediately with a kitchen towel, since the leaves tend to soften quickly. Remember that the inner leaves are the most tender and are better to use than the tougher outer leaves.

FRITES: see POMMES FRITES.

FRITTATA is a thick Italian omelet with diced vegetables and meat that is cooked until the bottom is set, then inverted into another pan to cook the top. Frittata is from the Italian *fritto*, "fried."

> **CONFUSABLE** FRITTATA/OMELET. There is a difference between an omelet and a frittata. In an omelet, the filling is spooned on top of partially set eggs, cooked a few seconds more, folded, and then turned onto the plate and served warm. An omelet can also be made without a filling. In a frittata, the filling is prepared in the pan and the egg mixture is poured over it and then cooked until the eggs are set. A frittata can be finished on the stovetop or in the oven; it can be served hot, warm, or at room temperature.

FRITTER is small quantity or patty of fried batter containing vegetables, meat, or fruit; the word is from the French *friture*, "to fry."

> **HINT** When you cook fritters, plenty of oil must always be used because the fritters drop to the bottom of the pan when they are placed in the oil and then rise to the surface as the heat cooks the batter. Fritters should be turned halfway through cooking.

FRITTO MISTO is a dish of various small foods, especially meat, seafood, or vegetables, coated with batter and deep-fried. Sometimes sweet foods, like cake, are included. The word is pronounced FREE-toh MEE-stoh and is Italian for "mixed fry."

> **HINT** The food for fritto misto should be in small pieces so that it cooks quickly. Cook it in small batches, so that you don't drop the temperature of the oil. The oil is at the right temperature when a small piece of bread rises to the surface right away. If the oil temperature drops, your food could come out heavy and greasy.

FROGS' LEGS are considered a delicacy in Chinese and French cuisine; the back and legs of *Rana esculenta* are the edible portion. Frogs' legs are often said to taste like chicken.

> **HINTS** All frogs' legs are sold skinless. Look for frogs' legs that are plump and slightly pink. Store, loosely wrapped, in the refrigerator for up to two days. Fresh frogs' legs can be found from spring through summer in many gourmet markets. Frozen frogs' legs can usually be purchased year-round, thought the flavor does not compare to fresh. Store frozen frogs' legs for up to three months. Thaw frozen frogs' legs in the refrigerator overnight before cooking.

> ▌ Because their flavor is so subtle, frogs' legs should be cooked simply and briefly. Overcooking frogs' legs will cause them to toughen.

FROMAGE is French for cheese. A fromager is a cheese maker, though the word is sometimes used to describe a cheese wholesaler or retailer.

FROMAGE BLEU: see BLUE CHEESE.

FRONT OF THE HOUSE includes the areas of a restaurant open to the public or public view, such as the lobby, bar, and dining room. BACK OF THE HOUSE is the crew and the area where they work. The BRIGADE is the name for the executive chef, sous-chef, line cook, maître d', headwaiter, captain, and front waiter.

FROSTED: see GLACÉ.

FROSTING is a flavored sugar topping used to coat, fill, and decorate cakes and cookies. To frost means to ice a cake or cookies. In some parts of the United States, the word ICING is used for this.

> **CONFUSABLE** FROSTING/ICING. Frosting is thick and gooey with a cream or butter base.

Icing may be thinner, often with just a sugar base. Frosting goes on cakes; icing goes on pastry or as a glaze on cakes.

▌ Quickly frost cupcakes by dipping into frosting. Never frost a cake before it has cooled completely.

FRUIT is the edible (raw or cooked) plant structure of a mature ovary or ovaries of a flowering plant; it also refers to the sweet and fleshy product of a tree or other plant that contains seeds and can be eaten as food. Many plants that are botanically fruits are not sweet, so we think of them as vegetables or non-fruits: acorn, almond, beans, buckwheat, chestnut, coconut, corn, cucumber, eggplant, green pepper, okra, peas, pumpkin, rice, sugar pea, string bean, and tomato. The word fruit is from the Latin *fructus*, "fruit/produce/profit," from the Indo-European *frui*, "to use/ enjoy." Pectin is a substance contained in some fruit, used for making jam and jelly thicker. High-pectin fruits include the apple, cranberry, currant, lemon, orange, plum, and quince. Low-pectin fruits include the banana, cherry, grape, mango, peach, pineapple, and strawberry.

FRUIT ESSENTIALS

■ Discoloring happens most commonly in low-acid fruits, such as apples and bananas, and vegetables like artichokes and eggplant. Lemon juice, vinegar, or acidulated water (1 tablespoon of acid to 1 quart of water) slows the discoloring and the acidulated water does not impart an acidic bite to the food. Other fruits and vegetables that discolor are avocado, cauliflower, celery, cherry, fig, Jerusalem artichoke, mushroom, nectarine, parsnip, peach, pear, potato, rutabaga, and yam.

■ When a fruit is bruised, the cell walls break down and discoloration starts, but this process can be slowed down by refrigeration.

■ Rinse fruit in cold running water and scrub as needed before cooking or eating. Soaking fruit in water for more than a few minutes can leach out water-soluble vitamins.

■ A good way to peel a thick-skinned fruit is to cut a small amount of peel from the top and bottom of it, then on a cutting board cut off the peel in strips from top to bottom.

■ A good way to peel thin-skinned fruit more easily is to place the fruit in a bowl with boiling water, let stand for 1 minute, drain, and cool in ice water. You can also spear the fruit with a fork and hold over a gas flame until the skin cracks, or quarter the fruit and peel with a sharp paring knife or potato peeler.

■ Wax can be removed from the surface of fruits by washing them with a mild dishwashing soap and then thoroughly rinsing them. This will remove most of the wax.

■ Buy these fruits fully ripe: berries, cherries, citrus, grapes, and watermelon. All except berries can be refrigerated without losing flavor.

■ Apricots, figs, melons, nectarines, peaches, and plums develop more complex flavors after picking. Store them at room temperature until they are as ripe as you want them.

- You can refrigerate apples, ripe mangoes, and ripe pears as soon as you buy them.

- Winter is the season for citrus; fall is for apples and pears; late spring is for strawberries and pineapples. Summer is great for blueberries, melons, peaches, and plums.

- Predry fruit with paper towels or kitchen towels and then use a blow dryer on "cool" setting to completely dry fruit.

- A microwave can be used to get more juice from citrus fruits. Microwave citrus fruit for 20 seconds before squeezing the fruit for juice.

FRUIT VARIETIES

Simple fruits have a single ovary; compound fruits have more than one. When ripe, some fruits remain succulent and others become woody and hard, or dry and papery. False fruits (such as apples and pears) develop from other flower parts in addition to the ovary. There are also berries, drupes and drupelets (such as raspberries and plums), and dry fruits (such as dandelion and larkspur). Some familiar and not-so-familiar fruit varieties are listed here:

APPLE	CITRON	JUNEBERRY
APPLE BANANA	CLEMENTINE	KIWI
APRICOT	COCONUT	KUMQUAT
APRICOT PLUM	CRAB APPLE	LEMON
ATEMOYA	CRANBERRY	LIME
AVOCADO	CURRANT	LONGAN
BANANA	CUSTARD APPLE	LONGANBERRY
BAYBERRY	DAMSON	LOQUAT
BEACH PLUM	DATE	MANDARIN ORANGE
BERRY	DATE PLUM	MANGO
BILBERRY	DURIAN	MAYAPPLE
BLACKBERRY	ELDERBERRY	MAYPOP
BLACK CURRANT	FIG	MEDLAR
BLOOD ORANGE	GOOSEBERRY	MELON
BLUEBERRY	GRANADILLA	MULBERRY
BOYSENBERRY	GRAPE	MUSKMELON
BREADFRUIT	GRAPEFRUIT	NANNYBERRY
BULLACE PLUM	GREENGAGE	NAVEL ORANGE
CALMYRNA	GROUND CHERRY	NECTARINE
CAMU CAMU	GUAVA	OLIVE
CANISTEL	HAW	ORANGE
CANTALOUPE	HONEYDEW MELON	PAPAYA
CARAMBOLA	HUCKLEBERRY	PARTRIDGEBERRY
CHERIMOYA	JACKFRUIT	PASSION FRUIT
CHERRY	JUJUBE	PAWPAW

(continued)

PEACH	PRICKLY PEAR	SOURSOP
PEAR	PRUNE	STRAWBERRY
PEPINO	QUINCE	TAMARILLO
PERSIAN MELON	QUINOA	TAMARIND
PERSIMMON	RAISIN	TANGELO
PINEAPPLE	RAMBUTAN	TANGERINE
PITAYA	RASPBERRY	TOMATO
PLANTAIN	SAPODILLA	UGLI FRUIT
PLUM	SAPOTE	VALENCIA ORANGE
POMEGRANATE	SATSUMA	WATERMELON
POMELO	SEA GRAPE	WILD CHERRY

FRUIT OR VEGETABLE OR FRUIT VEGETABLE?

Some cookbooks make a distinction between fruit, vegetables, and fruit vegetables. Fruit vegetables are foods that are botanically fruits but are most often prepared and served like vegetables. The following fruits are considered fruit vegetables:

AUBERGINE	GHERKIN	SEEDLESS CUCUMBER
AUTUMN SQUASH	GREEN BEAN	SQUASH
AVOCADO	GREEN SWEET PEPPER	SWEET PEPPER
BITTER MELON	HOT PEPPER	TOMATILLO
CANTALOUPE	MARROW	TOMATO
CHAYOTE	MUSKMELON	WATERMELON
CHILE	OKRA	WAX GOURD
COURGETTE	OLIVE	YELLOW SWEET PEPPER
CUCUMBER	PUMPKIN	ZUCCHINI
EGGPLANT	RED SWEET PEPPER	

FRUITS THAT DO NOT RIPEN AFTER PICKING

A number of years ago, scientists discovered how the ripening process works and now use it to control the ripening of fruit by carefully controlling the storage atmosphere. So now we can enjoy fruit almost year-round, rather than just around harvesttime. And because the ripening process can be controlled and halted, we can also enjoy fruit from around the world shipped by boats and trains to our neighborhood supermarket. The fruits in the following list are picked ripe and the ripening process stops when they are picked.

BLACKBERRY	GRAPE	LIME
BLUEBERRY	GRAPEFRUIT	LYCHEE
CHERRY	LEMON	OLIVE

ORANGE	RASPBERRY	TANGERINE
PINEAPPLE	STRAWBERRY	WATERMELON
PLUM	TANGELO	

FRUITS THAT CONTINUE TO RIPEN AFTER PICKING

When fruits ripen, they undergo a series of changes that alter the way they look, feel, taste, and smell. These changes are good because they make fruits more enjoyable to eat—they become softer and taste better. Unfortunately, the ripening process is difficult to stop and if fruits ripen too much, they spoil. Fruit ripens by producing enzymes that break down the sugar polymers and also neutralize the acids. Fruits know it is time to ripen because they produce an odorless, colorless gas, ethylene, that triggers the production of enzymes. The fruits listed here continue to ripen after they are picked.

APPLE	KIWI	PEAR
APRICOT	MANGO	PERSIMMON
AVOCADO	MUSKMELON	SAPOTE
BANANA	PAPAYA	SOURSOP
CHERIMOYA	PASSIONFRUIT	
FIG	PEACH	

FRUITS WITH LOW SUGAR CONTENT

The energy fruit contains is in the form of sugars (glucose). Your body turns this glucose into energy by using oxygen. Fruit juice takes only about fifteen minutes to digest and raw fruit takes about thirty minutes. The following fruits have low sugar content, as compared to other fruits.

APRICOT	GRAPEFRUIT	PEACH
AVOCADO	HONEYDEW MELON	PLUM
BLACKBERRY	LEMON	PRICKLY PEAR
CANTALOUPE	LIME	STRAWBERRY
CASABA MELON	OLIVE	TANGERINE
CRANBERRY	PAPAYA	TOMATO
GOOSEBERRY	PASSIONFRUIT	WATERMELON

FRUIT BUTTER is a sweet spread made of fruit, such as apples, cooked to a paste, then sweetened. Fruit butter is similar to conventional jams, jellies, and preserves, but is much lower in sugar. The term fruit "butter" derives from its spreadability and the thick consistency of the finished product. There is no butter in the product.

HINT Because fruit butter is low in sugar compared to other jams/preserves, it can generally only be stored for three weeks. Once the jar has been opened, it must be eaten within a few days. Fruit butter can be frozen for up to one year. It can also be stored for one year if processed in a water bath.

FRUITCAKE is a rich, dense cake containing dried or candied fruit, nuts, citron/citrus peel, and spices. The British began their love affair with fruitcake when dried fruits from the Mediterranean first arrived. It is a cake associated with weddings and holidays like Christmas. Dark fruitcakes are generally made with molasses or brown sugar and dark liquor, such as bourbon. Dark-colored fruits and nuts, such as prunes, dates, raisins, pecans, and walnuts may also contribute to the blend. Light fruitcakes are generally made with granulated sugar or light corn syrup and light-colored ingredients such as almonds, dried apricots, golden raisins, apples, pineapples, cardamom, ginger, nutmeg, and macadamias.

HINTS Fruitcakes are baked slowly, and after cooling are usually covered in cheesecloth moistened with liquor or brandy and tightly wrapped in foil or a heavyweight plastic bag. To prevent overbrowning, line the bottom and sides of the pan with foil. If you leave extra foil overlapping the sides, it will be easier to remove the cake. When baking, set the fruitcake pan in a 13 × 9-inch baking pan half-filled with water to prevent burning around the edges.

Fruitcakes taste better with age, a process called ripening. Be sure to ripen fruitcakes a few weeks before freezing. To store for a long period of time, wrap the cake in brandy- or wine-soaked towels, and then wrap in either plastic wrap or foil, or bury the liquor-soaked cake in powdered sugar and place in a tightly covered tin in a cool place. Check liquor-soaked cakes periodically and rewrap in liquor-soaked cloth. Liquor-based fruitcakes may be stored several months in a cool place prior to serving.

Fruitcakes without liquor and non-liquor-soaked cakes may be kept in a cool place or in the refrigerator for short-term storage, or in a freezer for long-term storage.

Fruitcake will slice more easily if it's cold. Use a thin, nonserrated knife.

FRUIT COCKTAIL or **FRUIT CUP** is a mixture of sliced or diced fruits, often packaged with a syrup or juice. FRUIT SALAD is a salad composed of fruits, but it is also used as a synonym for fruit cocktail. The term fruit salad was first recorded in 1861, fruit cocktail in 1922, and fruit cup in 1931. Traditionally, a syrup was used to coat the fruit, but fruit cocktails are often served unsweetened, moistened with fruit juice. The use of the word cocktail in the name does not mean that it contains alcohol, but refers to the secondary definition of cocktail as an appetizer made by combining pieces of food, such as fruit or seafood. In the United States the USDA stipulates that canned fruit cocktail must contain pears, grapes, cherries, peaches, and pineapples; otherwise it cannot be called fruit cocktail. It should contain fruits in the following percentages: 30%–50% diced peaches, any yellow variety; 25%–45% diced pears, any variety; 6%–16% diced pineapple, any variety; 6%–20% whole grapes, any seedless variety; 2%–6% cherry halves, any light sweet or artificial red variety. A less expensive alternative is fruit mix, which contains only peaches, pears, and grapes (no pineapple or cherries). Fruit cocktail comes in grade A and grade B quality.

> **HINT** Store a fruit cocktail in a sealed container in the coldest part of the refrigerator.

FRUIT LEATHER, FRUIT ROLL-UP, or FRUIT ROLLUP is a snack food

made of flavored puréed fruit that is dried and rolled. It gets the name leather from the fact that when puréed fruit is dried, it is shiny and has the texture of leather.

> **HINTS** Fruit leather is a nutritious treat for young and old alike. The leathery sheets of dried fruit purée are easy to make at home using either fresh or canned fruits. The advantages of making your own fruit leathers are that it saves money and allows you to use less sugar and to mix fruit flavors.
>
> ▌ Homemade fruit leather will keep at room temperature for one month, or in the freezer for up to one year. When making homemade fruit leather, use plastic wrap, not wax paper or foil.

FRUIT(S) DE MER is a French term for seafood or any edible crustacean. The

English translation is "fruit(s) of the sea."

> **HINT** Because fruits de mer is served cold, it is common practice for the dish to be served on a tray with a bed of ice underneath. Such trays can be very elaborate and decorative, containing multiple tiers. This is both for visual effect and because the shellfish are often served in the shell, or on the half shell, which causes them to take up a large area while containing only a bite or two of meat.

FRUIT SALAD is a salad composed of fruits, but it is also used as a synonym for

Fruit cocktail.

FRUIT SOUP is any soup with a cream and puréed fruit, most often served cold.

Many recipes for cold soups are served when fruit is in season during hot weather. Some, like Norwegian *fruktsuppe*, may be served warm and rely on dried fruit, such as prunes and raisins, and so can be made in any season.

FRY is to cook a food in fat over high heat; the word is from the Latin *frigere*,

"to roast/fry." There is also a euphemistic noun referring to an animal's testicles, such as a lamb's, prepared for eating—typically by frying. Chefs often toss foods in a frying pan to cook the food quickly over high heat without burning.

FRY

FRYING/SAUTÉING. Frying/pan-frying generally uses more fat, more time, and less heat than sautéing. Coatings often are used in frying to provide a crisp crust.

■ Use refined fats and oils with high smoke points for frying. Frying is done at 350°F–375°F and not over 400°F. Use a deep-frying thermometer.

■ When deep-frying or frying, gently lower food into the oil. Hold the cooked food above the pan to let oil drip off before transferring it to a plate.

■ Have foods at room temperature for deep-frying. Remove excess moisture from the food. Use a slotted spoon. Fry only a small amount of food at a time.

Skim/strain out remains of food from the oil.

■ Drain fried food on a rack over a baking sheet or on layers of paper towels.

■ Keep fried foods warm for up to 30 minutes in a 225°F oven.

■ Do not reuse oil more than three times; if needed, you can clarify the oil by frying a thick slice of potato before you start cooking.

■ Use only very tender cuts of meat for shallow frying. Salt the meat and let it sit for 5 minutes before frying. The salt will draw juices to the surface, where they can caramelize.

FRYING PAN or **FRYPAN**, also called SKILLET, is a shallow, long-handled pan used for frying foods. The word frying pan was first recorded in 1382 and is from the Middle English *fryinge panne*. The term SPIDER originally denoted a type of frying pan that had long legs to hold it up over the coals.

HINT Consider using a ridged-bottom frying pan, as the ridges keep fatty foods away from their juices during cooking.

FUDGE is a soft, creamy candy usually made of sugar, milk/cream, butter, and flavoring such as chocolate, peanut butter, or penuche. The word first appeared in the United States at the end of the nineteenth century as a term for a kind of chocolate bonbon.

FUMET is highly flavored and reduced stock made from fish, chicken, or game, and sometimes vegetables; the word often refers to a concentrated stock made from fish or mushrooms. Fumet is used to add flavor to less intensely flavored stocks or sauces. The word is pronounced FYOO-mit and literally means "aroma"; it is from the Latin *fumus*, "fume of meat/smoke."

HINT Fish fumet can refrigerated for up to one week, or frozen for up to three months.

FUNGO PORCINI: see PORCINI.

FUNNEL is a kitchen utensil that is a tube or pipe wide at the top and narrow at the bottom, used for guiding liquid or powder into a small opening.

> **HINT** You can improvise a funnel by cutting a corner off of a plastic bag, or you can make a funnel out of a double thickness of foil.

FUNNEL CAKE is a deep-fried Pennsylvania Dutch pastry made by spiraling batter through a funnel into hot fat or oil. It is served hot with powdered sugar, syrup, or honey. Fruit toppings or jam can also be added to top off funnel cakes. Funnel cakes are popular around the United States at ballparks, carnivals, fairs, festivals, and seaside amusement resorts. ELEPHANT EARS and FRIED DOUGH are similar to funnel cakes, but are made with yeast dough. Funnel cakes are made with unleavened batter.

FUSILLI, Italian for "little spindles," is short, spiral-shaped pasta. The term had appeared in English by 1948.

FUSION CUISINE is a term for dishes combining ingredients or methods of two or more regional or ethnic culinary traditions. Tex-Mex is the most well known of fusion cuisines. The term fusion cuisine or fusion food originated in the United States in the 1970s, but the practice of combining the cuisines of multiple cultures has existed for centuries.

FU YONG: see EGG FOO YONG.

GALANGAL is a Chinese plant of the ginger family grown for its edible underground stem, which is sold in three forms: fresh, dried and ground, or dried and sliced. Galangal is used as a spice in Asian cooking and has a ginger-pepper flavor. The word derives from the Chinese *ko liang kiang*, "good ginger from Gaozhou."

> **HINTS** Galangal powder should be stored in an airtight container and used within a short space of time. Store fresh galangal in the refrigerator for up to one week. Fresh galangal freezes well in a zip-lock freezer bag; cut it into smaller (two to three inches) chunks first. One slice of the root is equivalent to ½ teaspoon of powder. Dried galangal also comes in the form of slices that must be reconstituted in warm water; this form is closer to fresh galangal in flavor than the powder is.
>
> When purchasing fresh galangal, choose plump, light red roots with smooth, taut skin. Avoid shriveled or moldy galangal.
>
> Galangal reduces the fish smell in foods.

GALANTINE is a French dish of boneless, seasoned, poached fish, meat, or poultry that is stuffed with forcemeat, rolled, and served cold with aspic glaze made from its own gelatin. It is often garnished with items that are part of the stuffing, such as olives, pistachios, and truffles. The term is from the French *galatine/galentine*, "aspic/fish sauce." Galantines are usually pressed into a cylindrical shape.

GALETTE is a French term for a round, flat cake, or pancake made of pastry or yeast dough and usually filled or topped with jam, whipped cream, cheese, meat, or other foods. The word may also be used for a type of grated potato pancake or savory or sweet tart.

GAME is wild birds or animals hunted for sport or for use as food, and also refers to the flesh used as food. Game includes deer, duck, grouse, hare, partridge, pheasant, quail, rabbit, pigeon—and the availability of many of these is governed by the seasons in which shooting is allowed. Game is traditionally hung for several days to soften the meat and develop the flavor.

GAME HEN is any very young domestic fowl, especially one weighing less than two pounds and used for roasting.

> **HINT** Packaged game hens should not have liquid in the package; frozen game hens should not have pink-tinged ice. If stored in the refrigerator, use within two days.

GAMMELOST, **GAMALOST**, or **GAMMALOST** is a pungent Norwegian cheese; the word translates to "old cheese." Gammelost is usually served as a dessert cheese and goes well with alcoholic beverages such as gin or aquavit. It is also noted for its low fat content, which is usually around 5%.

GANACHE is a whipped icing or filling for cakes or sweets, made from chocolate and heavy cream. The word is French, literally meaning "jowl," from the Italian *ganascia*, from the Greek *gnathos*, "jaw." Ganache is used to decorate desserts, to fill cakes or sweets, and to make truffles or petits fours. Ganache can also be allowed to cool and then it can be whipped to increased volume and spread over a cake.

> **HINT** Ganache can be frozen for up to nine months. Thaw it by heating it over a water bath or double boiler. A classic ganache can generally stay at room temperature for two days, as long as it's kept in a cool place. Store ganache in an airtight container and refrigerate for up to two weeks. Also, refrigerate the ganache if you need to thicken it.

GARAM MASALA is Urdu for "hot spice" and is a mix of spices used in Indian cooking—usually cardamom, cinnamon, cloves, coriander, cumin, and pepper. For garam masala, the whole spices are roasted together before being ground. Because it is roasted, unlike raw spices that are generally cooked in the first stages of the preparation of dishes, garam masala is one of the spice mixtures that may be added to dishes in the final stages of cooking or sprinkled over dishes as a final seasoning before serving.

> **HINT** Garam masala is best made fresh just before you begin cooking. It should be stored in a cool, dry place for no more than six months.

GARBANZO, also called CHICKPEA, is an edible legume and among the fattiest of the beans. One cup contains a little over 4 grams of fat and 270 calories. The beans are high in fiber, folic acid, protein, and iron. The word *garbanzo* came to English as "calavance" in the seventeenth century, from Old Spanish.

GARDE MANGER or **GARDE-MANGER**, also called CHEF GARDE MANGER or PANTRY CHEF, is French for "keeper of the food" and the term is used for the professional kitchen's chef or cook in charge of cold foods. The garde manger's responsibilities typically include salads, hors d'oeuvres, dressings, cold soups, aspics, and charcuterie. The term can also be used for a cool room used for storing foods and for preparing certain cold dishes. Garde manger is considered by many to be the most demanding station/job in any kitchen. Garde mangers need to be able to apply proper seasoning to food that is going to be served cold, and in other cases season food that is going to be served hot.

GARDEN CUMIN: see CUMIN.

GARIBALDI: see GRINDER.

GARLIC is an herb (*Allium sativum*) of the lily family whose bulbs have ten to twenty strong-smelling sections called cloves; garlic is used in cooking and also made into garlic powder and garlic salt, as well as extract, flakes, and juice. The word garlic comes from the Old English *gar*, "spear," and *leac*, "leek." Garlic's essential oils permeate the lung tissue, allowing it to remain in the body long after consumption, affecting breath and skin odor. Garlic flavor comes from a compound called allicin, which is not formed until after the garlic cells are ruptured.

GARLIC ESSENTIALS

- Choose plump garlic heads with smooth cloves. Avoid those with green sprouts. Keep whole heads in an open container in a cool, dark, well-ventilated area for up to two months, leaving the papery skin on. A separated unpeeled clove will last for one week. Garlic should not be stored in the refrigerator because refrigeration promotes rot.

- Crush a clove of garlic with the side of a chef's knife to loosen skin for removal, or blanch in boiling water for about 10 seconds and peel. Mince garlic in a garlic press.

- Substitute ¼ teaspoon of garlic powder or ½ teaspoon of garlic salt for one garlic clove. If possible, use fresh garlic instead of garlic powder or garlic salt,

(continued)

because of the diminished garlic quality or a bitterness in the powder or salt.

■ Larger pieces of garlic give a long-cooking dish a mellow garlic flavor. Minced garlic gives a more volatile flavor. Minced is good for uncooked or quickly cooked food. Crushed garlic is even more aromatic.

■ Sauté garlic lightly until golden, as any scorching makes it bitter. Crushed garlic can be cooked in oil to flavor the oil, then discarded before adding other ingredients.

■ Insert slivers of garlic into meat to add flavor.

■ Garlic can be handled so that it is sweet and creamy by slicing about ½ inch from the head so that the tips are exposed. Poach in milk and then give a quick rinse before roasting.

■ If garlic is squashed (as with the flat of a knife or by a hammer), the juice is released, producing a very pronounced garlic flavor. However, the oils in the juice turn rancid rather quickly, especially if heated, so the garlic flavor can turn bitter during extended cooking. The longer the cooking time, the larger the pieces of garlic should be (such as sliced broadly).

■ Minced garlic can be kept from spoiling and made easily available by forming it into a log shape, wrapping tightly in plastic, and freezing. Then slice as needed.

■ The advantage of large garlic cloves is that they require less peeling time than small ones on an ounce-per-ounce basis. The minced yield of an average-sized clove of garlic is about ½ teaspoon.

■ The garlic flavor can be kept from being excessive by putting garlic flakes into a tea ball and immersing it in the cooking soup or stew. Taste periodically while cooking until the desired flavor level is reached. Fresh garlic can be mellowed by first simmering peeled cloves in a little water for 1–2 minutes.

■ The strongest-flavored garlic is the small white-skinned variety. Next are the violet-skinned heads. The oversized elephant variety is the mildest.

■ To minimize the garlic odor on the cutting board, if the recipe calls for both garlic and parsley, chop the garlic first. Then chop the parsley. The chlorophyll in the parsley will neutralize much of the garlic scent. If that doesn't do the job, rub the board with lemon juice.

■ When chopping a garlic clove, the garlic will stick less to the chopping knife blade if you sprinkle salt on the garlic, but be sure to reduce the quantity of salt used in the recipe accordingly. This also means that the sprinkled salt will absorb the garlic flavor that normally would be lost on the chopping board. When herbs and garlic are chopped together, the garlic clings to the herbs rather than to the knife.

■ When strong garlic flavor is desired in tomato sauce, cook the garlic in oil until it just turns golden. If the garlic gets too brown, it is bitter.

■ To get rid of onion or garlic on your breath, chew raw parsley or cilantro, or drink lemonade or wine. Eat some lemon or lime sherbet to combat garlic breath.

■ Dry-toast garlic for a less harsh flavor. Place unpeeled cloves in a dry skillet over medium-high heat. Toast, shaking the pan, until the skins are golden brown, about 5 minutes. Let the cloves cool on a cutting board, then peel off the skins and cut as needed.

■ Remove any green sprouts from a garlic clove before cooking.

GARLIC PRESS is a small, usually metal, kitchen tool that minces a garlic clove by squeezing it through a grid of small holes. It is an alternative to mincing garlic with a knife, though it is generally believed that pressed garlic has a different flavor than knife-minced garlic—since more cell walls are broken during pressing, more of the garlic's strong flavor compounds are released. A garlic press can also be used to mash other small items.

> **HINTS** There is no need to peel garlic that will be put through a press. Simply insert the whole clove, skin and all, and squeeze. Remove and discard the skin before pressing the next clove.

> ▌ Clean a garlic press right after using it, before any residual garlic dries and clogs the holes. Most garlic presses are difficult to clean. Without thorough scrubbing, residual oil from the garlic can cling to the utensil. The oil, which quickly turns rancid, can easily pass its foul flavor to the next garlic clove you press. A stainless-steel garlic press that can be put through the dishwasher is relatively easy to keep clean. A garlic press can also contain teeth that push garlic fragments back out through the holes, making cleaning much easier. Pressing with the peel on makes cleaning the press easier, too.

GARNACHA: see GRENACHE.

GARNISH is a food item, such as mint or parsley, added to or put on a dish for color, decoration, or flavor. To garnish is to decorate food or a plate with ornamental foods or herbs. Garnish food at the last minute. It will look fresher than if you garnish a dish, then let it sit in the refrigerator several hours.

GASTRONOMY generally refers to the art and practice of choosing, preparing, eating, and appreciating good-quality food. The term can also mean a particular style of cooking or dining, such as a style characteristic of a particular country or region, for example, Midwestern gastronomy. The word is from the Greek *gastrologia*, "study of the stomach." MOLECULAR GASTRONOMY is the application or study of scientific principles and practices in cooking and food preparation.

GÂTEAU is French for "cake" and it is a light sponge cake consisting of several layers held together with a rich cream or custard filling. The plural forms are gâteaux and gâteaus.

GAUFRE is French for "waffle," especially a thin batter cake on which a honeycomb pattern is stamped by the iron plates between which it is baked.

GAUFRETTE is a thin, crisp, fan-shaped, almond-flavored French wafer, often served alongside a dessert. Another form of gaufrette is a waffle; Belgian waffles are called gaufrettes. Waffled French-fried potatoes are called pommes gaufrettes.

HINT Before cooling and crisping, gaufrettes are sometimes curled to form an ice-cream cone.

GAZPACHO is a cold, spicy, tomato-based Spanish soup made with chopped onions, cucumber, peppers, and other raw vegetables. The origin of the word gazpacho is uncertain, but etymologists believe it might be derived from the Mozarab word *caspa*, meaning "residue/fragments," an allusion to the small pieces of bread and vegetables in gazpacho.

HINT After making gazpacho, refrigerate for at least 1 hour to allow the flavors to blend.

GEFILTE FISH, also called FISH BALLS, is finely chopped fish mixed with bread crumbs, eggs, and seasonings that is formed into balls or oval-shaped cakes, cooked in fish stock, then usually served chilled. The word is Yiddish, from the German *gefüllte*, "stuffed," as it was originally a dish of finely chopped or minced fish stuffed in a fish's body cavity before boiling or poaching; the word was first recorded in English in 1892. Gefilte fish is a classic Jewish cold fish dish, suitable for the Sabbath, when according to the strict rules of the religion, cooking is not allowed.

HINT Store gefilte fish in an airtight container in the refrigerator for up to seven days. You can also successfully freeze gefilte fish. The key is to thaw it thoroughly, squeezing out the excess liquid if necessary.

GELATIN is the tasteless, odorless, brittle mixture of proteins extracted by boiling skin, bones, and horns, although sometimes it is made from vegetables. The word also refers to a jelly made with gelatin. Gelatin dissolves in hot water and then forms jelly when the substance cools. The word gelatin is from the Italian *gelata*, "jelly."

HINTS Raw fig, ginger, guava, kiwi, papaya, and pineapple contain enzymes that keep gelatin from setting. Canned or cooked versions of these will work with gelatin, though.

To make gelatin set quickly, dissolve one envelope of powdered gelatin in ¼ cup of boiling water and 1¾ cups of ice water and stir until the mixture starts to thicken. Then remove any remaining ice and refrigerate until totally set.

GELATO is a type of rich Italian-style ice cream made of whole milk, gelatin, sugar, and fruit or flavoring and containing little or no air. Because it is made with milk, its fat content is 3%–10%, as opposed to North American ice cream made with heavy cream, which has a fat content of 16%–30%. Gelati is the plural of gelato and the word is from the Latin *gelare*, "to freeze." Gelato is said to have been created by Bernardo Buontalenti for the court of Francesco de' Medici in 1565. An Italian ice-cream parlor is called a gelateria.

HINT Gelato is served slightly warmer than ice cream. While both gelato and ice cream are served well below the freezing temperature of 32°F, gelato is served 10°F–15°F warmer than ice cream. Because gelato is less solidly frozen, its taste is further enhanced as it melts in the mouth.

GELÉE: see ASPIC.

GEMELLI, literally meaning "twins" in Italian, is a type of pasta made of two strands of pasta twisted together into short pieces. Gemelli are great with any sauce, or in pasta salads or casseroles.

GENERAL TSO'S is a sweet and spicy deep-fried chicken dish popularly served in American Chinese restaurants. General Tso's chicken is usually dark-meat pieces of chicken that are battered, deep-fried, and seasoned with ginger, garlic, soy sauce, rice vinegar, Shaoxing wine or sherry, sugar, sesame oil, scallions, and hot chile peppers; it is often served with steamed broccoli and white rice. The dish is believed to have been introduced in New York City in the early 1970s as an example of Hunan- and Szechuan-style cooking; it was possibly the invention of Taiwanese immigrants and may have been named after General Zou Zong-Tang (1812–1885), a general of the Qing (Manchu) dynasty of China. It is pronounced DJO with the tongue hard against the teeth.

GENETICALLY ENGINEERED FOOD: see BIOENGINEERED FOOD.

GÉNOISE or **GENOISE** (pronounced zheyn-WAHZ) is a type of delicate, buttery sponge cake typically layered, filled, and frosted or made into petits fours. It is named for Genoa, Italy.

HINTS The key to a light génoise is air—when it comes time to whip the eggs, the more air you incorporate, the lighter the génoise will be. Be sure to beat the eggs on high speed until they are pale white have doubled in volume, and hold a thick ribbon.

Wrap a génoise in plastic wrap and refrigerate for several days, or double-wrap and freeze for up to one month.

GERMAN CHOCOLATE CAKE is an American creation made first with Baker's German Sweet Chocolate. Sam German was an employee of Baker's who developed the sweet chocolate in 1852. The layers of the cake are frosted and filled with a caramel made with egg yolks and evaporated milk, with coconut and pecans stirred in. Sometimes frosting is spread on the sides of the cake and piped around the circumference of the layers to hold in the filling. Maraschino cherries are an added touch.

GERMAN POTATO SALAD is a hot or warm potato salad including bacon, onion, celery, and green pepper mixed with seasonings, sugar, and bacon fat. German potato salad is actually from southern Poland. German potato salad contains no eggs or mayonnaise and will keep well for picnics and other outdoor meals.

GETMESOST or **GETOST**: see GJETOST.

GEWÜRZTRAMINER (pronounced guh-VURTS-tra-MEE-ner) is a medium-dry white wine that is crisp and spicy, with a perfumed bouquet. Its name derives from the German *Gewürz*, "spice," and *Traminer*, the name of a village in northern Italy.

> **HINT** Gewürztraminer is best when drunk fairly young because even the vintage versions will not usually age well over five years. It should be served at around 50°F. Gewürztraminer is often considered a dessert wine.

GHEE or **GHI** is the name of clarified butter used in Indian cooking. It is the liquid butter remaining when butter from cow's or buffalo's milk is melted, boiled, and strained. The word was first recorded in English in 1665 and derives from a Sanskrit word meaning "sprinkled." The best ghee is made of butter from buffalo's milk, which is twice as rich in fat as cow's milk.

> **HINTS** Because of the steps used to make ghee, it has a longer life and much higher smoke point than regular clarified butter, making it practical for a variety of sautéing and frying uses. A good-quality ghee adds a great aroma, flavor, and taste to food. Ghee is considered a saturated fat, since it is derived from animals. Nevertheless, some studies suggest that it is healthier overall than traditional Western fats, such as lard and margarine.

> ❚ Tightly wrapped ghee can be refrigerated for up to six months and frozen for up to a year. Ghee can be stored without refrigeration for four to six months. As long as ghee is stored in airtight containers, it does not spoil easily. Ghee uses a natural process to maintain stability without refrigeration, unlike the hydrogenated and partially hydrogenated vegetable oils used in Western cooking.

GHERKIN is a small, immature cucumber used for pickling, but it is also a plant (*Cucumis anguria*) of the gourd family that has a small, prickly, cucumberlike fruit. Almost all gherkins are used to make little pickles called cornichons. The word is from the Dutch *gurkkijn*, a diminutive of *gurk*, "cucumber."

GIBLETS are the edible internal organs of fowl/poultry, including the gizzard, heart, and liver, and sometimes kidneys. Giblets is an adaptation of the French *gibelet*, "game stew," as those parts of a bird usually went into such a stew.

> **HINTS** When you purchase a whole turkey or chicken, or other type of poultry carcass, the giblets will often be sealed in a plastic bag that is placed inside the carcass's cavity. According to the USDA, when cooking whole poultry, you

should remove the giblet pack from the cavity as soon as you can loosen it. Cook the giblets separately for food safety reasons.

❚ Select fresh giblets just before checking out at the register at the store. They should feel cold to the touch. Place them in a disposable plastic bag (if available) at the store to contain any leakage that could contaminate cooked foods or produce. At home, immediately place giblets (or poultry containing giblets) in a refrigerator that maintains 40°F or below and use within one to two days, or freeze at 0°F or below. If kept frozen continuously, giblets will be safe indefinitely. For best quality, use giblets within three to four months of freezing.

❚ There are three safe ways to thaw giblets and poultry containing them: in the refrigerator, in cold water, or in the microwave. Never thaw giblets on the kitchen counter.

GIMLET is a cocktail made of gin or vodka and lime juice. The word comes from a Dutch word meaning "auger/drill," and the name of the cocktail may have something to do with its penetrating effect.

GINGER is an Asiatic herb (*Zingiber officinale*) grown in the tropics for its aromatic underground stem rhizome. The hot-tasting rhizome is eaten fresh, pickled, or candied, or made into powdered form and used as a spice, especially in Asian cooking. Fresh and dried (powdered) ginger cannot be used interchangeably.

HINTS Fresh ginger should be hard and heavy and should have an unbroken peel that is light colored, shiny, smooth, and thin. Mature ginger is available year-round and requires peeling. Young ginger is available in springtime and early summer, and is juicier and has a creamy pink color and a thin, pale skin that doesn't require peeling. Store ginger in a cool, dry place for up to three days, or for three weeks in the refrigerator, wrapped in a paper towel or in a small paper bag inside a plastic bag. Ginger can be frozen.

❚ You can peel ginger easily with the bowl of a teaspoon. A ginger grater is a tool for grating ginger. Crushed or grated ginger will have a more intense flavor than sliced or chopped.

❚ Fish is often cooked with ginger because it not only flavors the fish, but helps to counteract fishy odors.

GINGER ALE is a sweetened carbonated soft drink flavored mainly with ginger extract. It was first mentioned in print in 1886 and it became very popular in the United States during Prohibition. Ginger ale turned out to be a perfect mix to mask the taste of strong alcoholic home brew. Ginger ale is often used as a home remedy to relieve motion sickness and upset stomachs.

GINGERBREAD is a cake flavored with ginger and molasses, and is also a soft molasses and ginger cookie cut in various shapes and sometimes elaborately decorated. In origin, gingerbread (the cake) has nothing to do with "bread" but derives from *gingebras*, "ginger paste," and gingerbread was originally a word for preserved ginger or a stiff pudding containing it. By the fifteenth century, the cake had been created, based on the term's association with "bread." According to some researchers, the first gingerbread houses may have appeared as a result of the popular Grimm's fairy tales. Other food historians postulate that the brothers Grimm were writing about something that already existed.

HINTS When making gingerbread cookies, you can use a toothpick to make a hole in the top of the cookies so that you can hang them on a Christmas tree. You can also make paint out of egg yolks and food coloring to make them more colorful. Let gingerbread cookies cool completely before you decorate them, unless you are using egg yolk and food coloring, which is done before baking. When making gingerbread cookies, keep cookie cutters from sticking to the dough by misting them very lightly with cooking spray or dusting them in flour.

Gingerbread cookies can be prepared up to two weeks ahead and stored in single layers between sheets of wax paper in airtight containers. Display your gingerbread house in a cool, dry place. You may wish to cover it at night with plastic wrap to seal out moisture, dust, and bugs.

GINKGO is a large shade tree (*Ginkgo biloba*) native to China that bears seeds with edible kernels, called ginkgo nuts. The word dates to 1727 and comes from the Japanese *ginkyo*, from the Chinese *yin-hing*, "silver apricot."

GINSENG is the aromatic forked root of a Chinese plant; it is believed to have medicinal powers and is used in tonics. The term is from a Chinese word in which the first part means "man," probably because of the supposed resemblance of the forked root to a person.

HINT Keep fresh ginseng in a cool refrigerator at 32.9°F. Make sure that you use it within two weeks after purchase. Keep ginseng extracts or powders in a sealed container in a cool, dry place.

GIROLLE: see CHANTERELLE.

GJETOST is Norwegian for "goat's cheese" and is just that, a Scandinavian boiled-whey goat's and cow's milk cheese with a caramel-like flavor.

HINT Gjetost cheese should be well wrapped and kept in the warmest section of the refrigerator.

GLACÉ, also called CANDIED, FROSTED, or ICED, means coated with a sugar solution to create a glazed finish; it also means frosted, as a cake. Glacé (with the accent), is pronounced glah-SAY and is French for "iced/frozen." Glace (without the accent) is pronounced GLAHS and is French for "ice cream." Glacé can also refer to frozen desserts or drinks.

GLASS is a container without a handle made from glass, for drinking from. In 50 BC, the glass blowpipe was invented and this enabled glass to be blown to a given shape rather than being formed around a central core. In its natural state, glass is greenish or brownish amber. Its color derives from the impurities inherent in the material, such as aluminum and iron. By AD 2, Roman artisans had figured out how to make glass clear. Glass drinking vessels were originally made with rounded or pointed bases. It was not until the late Middle Ages that vessels with horizontal or domed bases were made. Today, the bowls of drinking glasses come in three main shapes: bucket shaped, tulip shaped, and flared.

DRINKING GLASSES

ALSACE GLASS	GOBLET	SHERRY GLASS
BAKER	HEAVY GOBLET	SHOT GLASS
BEER GLASS	HIGHBALL GLASS	SHOT SNIFTER
BEER MUG	JIGGER GLASS	SNIFTER
BORDEAUX GLASS	JUICE GLASS	SOUR GLASS
BRANDY SNIFTER	LIQUEUR GLASS	SPARKLING-WINE GLASS
BURGUNDY GLASS	MUG	STEIN
CHAMPAGNE COUPE	MUG STEIN	STEMWARE
CHAMPAGNE FLUTE	OLD-FASHIONED GLASS	TANKARD
CHAMPAGNE SAUCER	PARIS GOBLET	TOBY
CHAMPAGNE TULIP	PILSNER GLASS	TULIP GOBLET
COCKTAIL GLASS	PONY	TUMBLER
CORDIAL GLASS	PORT GLASS	WATER GOBLET
DEEP-SAUCER CHAMPAGNE GLASS	PUNCH CUP	WHISKEY SOUR GLASS
	RED-WINE GLASS	WHITE-WINE GLASS
FLAGON	RUMMER	WINEGLASS
FOOTED PILSNER	SEIDEL	YARD OF ALE

GLASS NOODLES: see CELLOPHANE NOODLES.

GLAZE is any of various thin, shiny coatings (savory or sweet) applied to foods; to glaze is to coat with something sweet. Glaze can also refer to coating food with milk or egg or sugar before baking in order to produce a shiny, brown finish. Glaze can then be described as a shiny, brown finish on food or the substance used for achieving this effect.

GLOBE ARTICHOKE: see ARTICHOKE.

GLOGG or **GLÖGG** is a Swedish word (from *glödga*, "to burn/mull") for a hot punch of brandy, red wine, and sherry, flavored with fruit pieces, blanched almonds, sugar, and spices. It was originally served in Scandinavia at Christmastime. Glogg is either served as a predinner drink in the winter, or served at a separate event, usually at about 4:00 or 5:00 P.M. Gingerbread (also called PEPPARKAKOR) is often an accompaniment. The extract keeps very well, so you can make more and keep it in a bottle; it will keep for at least a year.

> **HINT** When heating glogg, the temperature should not be allowed to rise above 173.12°F, in order to avoid evaporation of the alcohol.

GLUTEN is the tough, viscid, nitrogenous substance remaining when the flour of wheat or other grain is washed to remove the starch; it is the mixture of proteins found in grains. Gluten is not soluble in water and gives dough its elastic texture. Its presence in flour helps make the production of leavened, or raised, baked goods possible because the chainlike molecules form an elastic network that traps carbon dioxide gas and expands with it. Gluten is the "glue" that holds dough together and imparts texture. Proteins are the building blocks of gluten. When the flour is moistened, mixed, and kneaded, gluten forms an elastic and stretchable product. Light, airy breads and chewy pasta owe their texture to the presence of gluten. The absence of gluten, or low gluten content, makes flaky pie crusts. Higher sugar content slows gluten formation. Celiac disease is an inherited autoimmune digestive disorder in which people cannot tolerate gluten.

GLUTINOUS RICE, also called PEARL RICE, STICKY RICE, SWEET RICE, or WAXY RICE, is a variety of sticky, milky-colored, short-grain Asian rice containing amylose and amylopectin. Glutinous rice does not contain dietary gluten, but is so called because it is gluelike or sticky. It is called sticky, but should not be confused with other varieties of Asian rice that become sticky to one degree or another when cooked. The history of glutinous rice goes back to at least AD 900, and possibly earlier in Laos.

> **HINTS** When you cook glutinous rice, it helps to use slightly less water than one might normally use, as the rice can start to fall apart if it gets too moist. Many cooks prefer to steam glutinous rice, wrapping it in cheesecloth and keeping it above the water level. Unlike many other varieties of rice, glutinous rice also benefits from being stirred once or twice as it cooks.
>
> Store glutinous rice in a cool, dry area in a sealed glass or plastic container, away from the open air and moisture. Cooked glutinous rice can be refrigerated for up to seven days, or stored in the freezer for six months.

GNOCCHI (pronounced NYAWK-ee) are dumplings made of flour and potato and served with sauce. Gnocchi get their name from the Italian *nocchio*, "knot in wood." The smaller forms are called gnocchetti. The original flour and water mixture for gnocchi is still used today in many regional recipes in Italy, where they have a number of different names and shapes. There are also other types of gnocchi made with flour, semolina, ricotta cheese, spinach, or bread crumbs.

HINTS It is important to choose the right type of potato for gnocchi. The potato needs to be floury, with minimum water content. The best are old russet potatoes, which are low in water and high in starch. Round (white or red) or Yukon potatoes would be too waxy, which would make the gnocchi either too heavy or too gummy, or would cause them to break apart in the boiling water. The addition of egg to the dough, not always necessary, serves the purpose of holding the preparation together better. The choice of the right potato potentially makes the use of the eggs optional.

▮ Uncooked gnocchi will not keep for long after they are prepared, and they must be cooked soon. They can be kept covered on a floured cloth for few hours. Soon after, they may start releasing their moisture content and become gummy and sticky. Placing them in the refrigerator will not help since the humidity may cause additional damage. However, uncooked gnocchi can be easily frozen. The most common mistake in freezing gnocchi is to place them all together in a bag and place them in the freezer. When you are ready to eat them, you will discover they have become one big frozen dumpling. Instead, place the gnocchi on a baking sheet, spreading them out so they don't touch each other. Place the baking sheet in the freezer for 10 to 15 minutes. Remove all the gnocchi, which are now just starting to freeze, from the baking sheet and place them in a zip-lock freezer bag. Place the bag in the freezer right away. At this point the gnocchi will not melt together. When you want to eat them, just boil some salted water in a pot and drop them in the pot while still frozen. When ready, they will float. Let them float for about 2 minutes before removing them.

GOAT CHEESE or GOAT'S MILK CHEESE, also called CHÈVRE, is a general term for any cheese made with goat's milk, either alone or mixed with cow's milk. The term first appeared in writing in 1893.

HINT Slice a log of goat cheese neatly with dental floss. Place a goat cheese log in a covered butter dish for easy storage and use.

GOLDEN DELICIOUS is a bright yellow, sweet eating apple. It is not genetically related to the Red Delicious apple. It is sweeter than the Granny Smith. The original tree was found in West Virginia and was locally known as Mullin's Yellow Seedling and Annit apple. The Golden Delicious was designated the official state fruit of West Virginia.

HINTS Good-quality Golden Delicious apples are firm with smooth, clean skin and range in color from light green to pale or creamy yellow. Less mature apples are light green and have a somewhat tart flavor. More mature goldens have a clear yellow color and are sweeter. Some goldens have a wash of pink color or blush across the "shoulders," the result of warm, sunny days and cool nights. Avoid goldens with "russeting," a bronze-colored, rough, and scablike condition principally on the stem end of the apple.

❚ Test the firmness of the apple by holding it in the palm of your hand. (Do not push with your thumb.) It should feel solid and heavy, not soft and light. Avoid apples with soft or dark spots. Also, if the apple skin wrinkles when you rub your thumb across it, the apple has probably been in cold storage too long or has not been kept cool.

❚ Golden Delicious apples are prone to bruising and shriveling, so they need careful handling and storage, but have an extended shelf life if handled correctly. Store Golden Delicious apples in a plastic bag in the refrigerator away from strong-odored foods, such as cabbage or onions, to prevent flavor transfer.

GOLDEN GREEK PEPPER: see PEPPERONCINI.

GOLDEN OAK MUSHROOM: see SHIITAKE.

GOLDEN RAISIN, also called SULTANA, is a small, light-colored, seedless raisin made from white grapes, that is more tart than ordinary raisins.

GOLDEN SYRUP, also called TREACLE, is a pale, mild, amber mixture of molasses, corn syrup, and invert sugar that looks and tastes like honey.

HINTS If you cannot obtain golden syrup, you can substitute honey or corn syrup in recipes requiring it. This will produce a somewhat different taste, however, and the finished product will lack the characteristic flavor of the golden syrup.

❚ Unlike the crystallized form of table sugar, golden syrup is primarily composed of sucrose, fructose, and glucose. This means that you can store it without worrying that sudden cold temperatures in the house will cause hardness or crystallization of the syrup.

GOO: see ARROWROOT.

GOOBER: see PEANUT.

GOOSE is any domesticated waterfowl, generally larger than ducks, and its flesh used for food. The plural is geese.

HINT The USDA grades the quality of geese A, B, and C; the highest grade is A and geese of this grade are generally found in markets. Grade B geese are less meaty. The grade stamp can usually be found within a shield on the package wrapping. Most geese marketed in the United States are frozen; the packaging should be tight and unbroken. The goose should be thawed in the refrigerator and can take up to four days to defrost, depending on the size of the bird. Fresh geese can be found in some specialty markets and are available from early summer through December. Goslings (especially small) are the most tender. Check a goose's bill for pliability, which indicates that it is young. Choose a goose that is plump, with a good fatty layer and skin that is clean and unblemished. Store, loosely covered, in the coldest section of the refrigerator for two to three days; remove any giblets in the body cavity and store separately.

GOOSEBERRY is a small, sour, yellowish green or red berry of various prickly shrubs of the saxifrage family; it looks like a large currant. It is used in making preserves and pies.

> HINT Choose large, firm berries and store for up to three days in the refrigerator.

GORGONZOLA is a type of rich, moist, sharp-flavored, blue-veined Italian cow's and/or goat's milk cheese that was first made in Gorgonzola, a village near Milan. It has been made since the early Middle Ages, but became marbled with greenish blue mold only in the eleventh century. As with most blue-veined cheeses, Gorgonzola was originally aged in caves and the blue veins of mold developed from spores naturally present in the caves. After the whey is removed, it is aged at low temperatures. During the aging process, metal rods are inserted and removed, creating air channels that allow the mold spores to germinate and cause the characteristic veining. Gorgonzola is aged for two to three months and sometimes up to six months. When aged over six months, the flavor and aroma can be quite strong, sometimes downright stinky. Younger cheeses are sold as Gorgonzola dolce, while longer-aged cheeses are sold as Gorgonzola naturale or Gorgonzola piccante. Gorgonzola dolce (also known as Dolcelatte) is a newer variety. It is creamier and much milder because it is not aged as long as the picante, only three to five months; the rind is gray. Gorgonzola picante (mountain Gorgonzola) is the original; this firm, crumbly cheese is sharper than Gorgonzola dolce because it is aged for about a year.

> HINTS When looking for Gorgonzola, determine how old you want it to be, and look for paler cheese if you want a sweet Gorgonzola, and darker versions if you want a cheese with more bite. Gorgonzola should never be brown in appearance, as this is an indication that the cheese has gone bad. The cheese is usually wrapped in foil to keep it moist. It's best to buy Gorgonzola in small quantities. Because the cheese is a "live" product, it is continuously maturing. To ensure you're buying authentic Italian Gorgonzola, look for foil-wrapped wedges marked with a lowercase "g."

> Once you get your Gorgonzola home, remove any crust, wrap the cheese in foil, and refrigerate in an airtight container. If you leave Gorgonzola in the refrigerator too long, it may become too strong to eat plain. It should stay good for three to four weeks in the refrigerator.

GORP: see TRAIL MIX.

GOUDA is a flat, round, mild, whole or skimmed milk cheese with a yellow rind, originally made in Gouda in the Netherlands. Gouda is a good melting cheese. Some Goudas are now made with goat's milk but most are cow's milk. It is pronounced GOW-duh or GOO-duh. The cheese is from milk that is cultured and heated until the curd is separate from the whey. Some of the whey is then drained and water is added. This is called "washing the curd," and creates a sweeter cheese, as the washing removes some of the lactic acid. About 10% of the mixture is curd, which is pressed into circular molds for several hours. These molds are the essential reason behind Gouda's traditional, characteristic shape. The cheese is then soaked in a brine solution, which gives the cheese and its rind a distinctive taste. The cheese is dried for a couple of days before being coated to prevent it from drying out. Next, the cheese is aged, which adds a caramel sweetness, and it is classified depending on the number of weeks or years it is aged.

> **HINT** A semisoft cheese, Gouda may be wrapped tightly in foil or placed in a zip-lock plastic bag and refrigerated for several weeks after opening. Unopened Gouda in wax will remain stable in the refrigerator for up to one year.

GOUGÈRE is a savory French choux pastry like a cheese puff. Grated cheese (typically Gruyère) may be mixed into the batter, cubes of cheese may be pushed into the top, or both. Gougères may be small and filled with ingredients such as mushrooms, beef, or ham.

GOULASH or **HUNGARIAN GOULASH** is a meat stew made of beef (or veal), assorted vegetables, paprika, and other seasonings. Goulash is from the Hungarian *gulyashus*, "herdsman's meat."

GOURMAND describes a person who loves good food but also describes a gluttonous eater.

> **CONFUSABLE** GOURMAND/GOURMET. A gourmand rates quantity higher than quality, while the gourmet adopts the opposite approach; a gourmand is one whose chief pleasure is eating and a gourmet is a connoisseur of food and wines.

GOURMET, also called EPICURE, is a person who likes and is a connoisseur of fine food and drink. *Groumet*, a servant who tasted wine for his wealthy employers, became the English gourmet, which originally meant wine taster or wine merchant's assistant. Gourmet as an adjective describes something suitable for a gourmet, such as a gourmet meal. The word did not appear in written English until around 1820.

GRAHAM CRACKER is a slightly sweet, usually rectangular cracker made with GRAHAM FLOUR, a whole wheat flour that has been produced by grinding the entire wheat berry, including the bran. Graham flour and the graham cracker are named for Sylvester Graham (1794–1851), a dietary reformer who developed the whole-grain cracker out of concern for health and nutrition.

GRAIN denotes the dry seed or fruit produced by cereal grasses and plants, such as wheat, barley, corn (maize), oats, rice, and rye. Grain also describes the plants themselves.

> **HINTS** Store whole grains in an airtight container in the refrigerator for up to six months. Polished grains in an airtight container at cool room temperature keep for up to 1 year.

> A simple test for the nutritive quality of a batch of grains is to pour a quantity into a pot of water. If the majority of the grains sink to the bottom, they still contain most of their nutrients.

EDIBLE GRAINS AND CEREALS

AMARANTH	GROATS	PUFFED RICE
BARLEY	GRUEL	PUFFED WHEAT
BLUE CORNMEAL	HOMINY	QUINOA
BRAN	INDIAN CORN	RAISIN BRAN
BROWN RICE	KAMUT	RICE
BUCKWHEAT	KASHA	RICE GRASS
BULGUR OR CRACKED WHEAT	MAIZE	ROLLED OATS
	MASA	RYE
CORN	MILLET	SEMOLINA
CORNFLAKES	MUESLI	SHREDDED WHEAT
CORNMEAL	MUSH	SORGHUM
COUSCOUS	OAT BRAN	SPELT
EINKORN	OATMEAL	TEFF
FARINA	OATS	TRITICALE
FARRO	POLENTA	WHEAT
FLOUR	POPCORN	WHEAT GERM
GRANOLA	PORRIDGE	WILD RICE
GRITS		

GRAIN TERMS

BERRY: The dry individual whole grain or seed, especially of rye and wheat.

BRAN: The edible broken seed coats of cereal grain, separated from the flour or meal by sifting or bolting.

ENDOSPERM: The soft inner tissue of a grain, where most nutrients are.

FLAKE: Flat edible piece of grain formed by slicing or high-pressure rollers.

GERM: The oil-rich embryo within a whole cereal grain, separated from the endosperm during milling and eaten separately.

HULL: The outer covering or husk of some grains, especially barley, oats, and rice.

PEARLED: Describes polished grain, from which a tough hull or bran has been removed.

ROLLED: Describes grain that has been pressed or spread with a roller.

WHOLE: Describes grain in which bran, germ, and endosperm of grain are intact.

GRANADILLA: see PASSION FRUIT.

GRANITA is a type of Italian ice, a frozen liquid with sugar that is stirred frequently during freezing so it has a granular consistency. This coarse fruit ice is similar to sorbet, without the meringue, and is often flavored with liqueurs. Its origin is *grana*, "grain," from its texture.

> **CONFUSABLE** GRANITA/SORBET. The difference between a granita and a sorbet is mainly one of texture. Granita is a fruit purée, made with simple syrup and perhaps a little lemon juice and a pinch of salt, that is frozen. It has less sugar, which means larger ice crystals and a grainy texture. A sorbet is like a granita with the addition of beaten egg white and is usually finished in an ice-cream machine, which gives it a silky, creamy texture.

GRANNY SMITH is a type of green-skinned apple with hard, tart flesh. Granny Smith was Australian gardener Maria Ann Smith, who purportedly developed it.

> **HINT** A good-quality Granny Smith apple is firm with smooth, clean skin. Granny Smith apples are a deep green with an occasional pink blush on the cheeks. Test the firmness of the apple by holding it in the palm of your hand. (Do not push with your thumb.) It should feel solid and heavy, not soft and light. Granny Smith apples are great in salads because the cut apples keep their color longer than other varieties.

GRANOLA is a breakfast cereal made of rolled oats, wheat germ, cornmeal, sesame seeds, brown sugar or honey, raisins and other dried fruits, and nuts, invented by Dr. James Caleb Jackson, who ran a health facility in Dansville, New York. It was originally a proprietary name, registered in 1886. Granola is important to outdoorspeople as it is lightweight, high in calories, and easy to store like trail mix or muesli.

> **CONFUSABLE** GRANOLA/MUESLI. Granola is usually coated with some type of sugary substance or honey and toasted. Muesli is generally untoasted and often unsweetened.

GRANULATED SUGAR is white sugar in the form of a coarse powder with large particles, so called because the last step in processing white table sugar is sending it through a granulator where it is dried and formed into the grains. Before the sugar refining process was perfected, granulated sugar was almost impossible to produce, because the crystals of sugar would clump together due to its high moisture content. Sugar was made in loaves or blocks that had to be broken up for use. Cooks shaved off the amount of sugar they needed, storing the block in a cool, dry place. Once refineries figured out how to dry sugar so that it would not clump, sugar blocks were largely abandoned.

> **HINT** Sugar should be stored in a cool, dry place away from heat and moisture to ensure that the grains stay separated.

GRAPE is a general word for any of numerous woody vines of the genus *Vitis* bearing bunches of edible, juicy, purple- or green-skinned fruit. The grape is named for the hook that the French used to harvest them (Old French *grape, grapple*). They are eaten fresh and made into juice and wine. Bloom is the natural white powdery substance on grapes. Grapes do not get sweeter once harvested.

HINTS Choose bunches of grapes with firm, plump fruits. Green grapes with a little amber/yellow are ripest and sweetest. Red grapes should have no green on the skin. When a bunch of grapes is shaken and a few grapes drop off, it means that the bunch is not fresh. The stem of fresh grapes should be green and very pliable.

To clean and store grapes, rinse well, drain on paper towels, and remove bruised or rotten grapes. Put the grapes in a perforated plastic bag in the refrigerator for up to one week. Remove from the refrigerator 30 minutes before serving. Whole grapes can be frozen on a baking sheet, then transferred to an airtight container in the freezer for six months.

GRAPE TYPES AND VARIETIES

Grape is the fruit of a vine that grows in bunches on a stalk. The skin, which may be green, yellow, red, or purple, encloses a sweet pulp with one to four seeds. Both white and black grape varieties are used to make wine, and there are other varieties cultivated as dessert grapes for fruit or cooking. It is known that in the Stone Age, wild vines were already established in the Caucasus, where grapes originated, as well as in the Mediterranean. Early on, people discovered how to make a fermented drink from grapes.

ALICANTE GOUSCHET	CHENIN BLANC	LADYFINGER
ALMERIA	CHICKEN GRAPE OR FROST GRAPE	MALVASIA
ARROYO GRAPE	CINSAUT GRAPE	MERLOT
BARBERA GRAPE	CONCORD GRAPE	MOUNTAIN GRAPE
BIRD GRAPE	DELAWARE GRAPE	MUSCADET
BLUE GRAPE	DOWNY GRAPE	MUSCADINE GRAPE
BULLACE GRAPE	EVERBEARING GRAPE	MUSCAT GRAPE
BUSH GRAPE	FOX GRAPE	PIGEON GRAPE
CABERNET SAUVIGNON GRAPE	GEWÜRZTRAMINER	PINOT BLANC
CANYON GRAPE	ISABELLA GRAPE	PINOT GRAPE
CATAWBA GRAPE	ITALIA GRAPE	PINOT GRIGIO OR PINOT GRIS
CHARDONNAY GRAPE	LABRUSCA GRAPE	PINOT NOIR

(continued)

PLUM GRAPE	SAUVIGNON	THOMPSON SEEDLESS GRAPE
POST-OAK GRAPE	SAUVIGNON GRAPE	TOKAY GRAPE
RAISIN GRAPE	SEEDLESS GRAPE	VINIFERA GRAPE
RED GRAPE	SEMILLON	WILD GRAPE
RIBIER GRAPE	SHIRAZ GRAPE	WINE GRAPE
RIESLING GRAPE	SPANISH GRAPE	WINTER GRAPE
RIVER GRAPE	SUMMER GRAPE	ZINFANDEL
SAND GRAPE	SYRAH	

GRAPEFRUIT is a large yellow citrus fruit (*Citrus paradisi*) with somewhat acidic, juicy pulp. It was likely a cross between the orange and the POMELO (also called SHADDOCK), and it may be that its growth in clusters gave it its name. The term, from the French *grappe*, "cluster," was first used in Jamaica in 1814, though another source says 1750. The grapefruit was introduced in Florida in 1823, but was slow to achieve popularity as its bitter flavor is an acquired taste and it was difficult to peel compared to fruits like the orange. Grapefruit juice can cause serious problems when consumed with some prescription medications because it is metabolized by the same enzyme in the liver that breaks down many drugs. Many prescription medications include a warning about drinking grapefruit juice when taking the medicine.

> **HINTS** Choose firm, heavy grapefruits without soft spots. They can be stored at room temperature for one week or in the refrigerator for up to three weeks. Bring to room temperature before serving.
>
> ▌ To remove the white pith, drop the whole grapefruit in a pot of boiling water, remove from heat and let sit for 3 minutes. Remove and cool the fruit. Then peel the fruit and the white pith will easily come off.
>
> ▌ To get the maximum amount of juice from a grapefruit, pierce the skin in several places with the tines of a fork, then microwave for 20 seconds.

GRAPE LEAVES are from grape vines and are available in jars, packed in brine. Grape leaves are used in the cuisines of a number of cultures, including Arab, Greek, Romanian, and Turkish. The leaves are most often stuffed with a mixture of rice, meat, and spices, and then cooked by boiling or steaming.

GRAPESEED OIL is a very light, relatively bland oil extracted from the seeds of the grape; it has a relatively high smoke point (420°F). Although known to Europeans for centuries, grapeseed oil was not produced or used on a large scale until the twentieth century, largely because grape seeds contain a lower percentage of oil as compared to other oil-producing seeds, nuts, or beans.

GRAPE TOMATO is a grape-shaped or oval, ½–¾ inch long, tomato and almost always red. Grape tomatoes are easier to spear and pop in your mouth, and don't squirt like cherry tomatoes.

GRAPPA is an Italian brandy made from the fermented residue (lees) of grapes that have been pressed in winemaking. Grappa is Italian for "grape stalk."

GRATE (GRATING) is to rub hard- or semihard-textured food, such as cheese, against a grater. A grater is a kitchen utensil with small, rough, sharp-edged holes or perforations used to reduce the food into fine particles or shreds. The word grate derives ultimately from the Proto-Germanic *krattojan*, "to scratch/scrape." Grated cheese is a type of cheese that has gone through the process of being grated. Typically, aged hard cheeses are used for this purpose. A hand grater can be used to manually grate the cheese, or cheese can be bought already grated. A MICROPLANE is a registered trademark for a type of grater whose holes are not punched out of a metal sheet but are formed using a photochemical process.

> **HINT** To clean a grater more easily, lightly spray the grater with nonstick cooking spray before using, rub a raw potato over it before washing, or use a pastry brush, toothbrush, or vegetable brush to remove citrus zest or other grated material. For easier cleanup of your work area, grate onto a piece of wax paper. It helps to use a clean, thin, green scrubbing pad to hold food that you are trying to grate.

GRATIN, **GRATINÉ**, **GRATINE**, or **GRATINÉE**, also called AU GRATIN, refers to a cooked dish with a bread crumb or melted grated-cheese crust. A gratin dish is a shallow ovenproof dish used for cooking a gratin; it is often oval in shape with some type of handles.

GRAVLAX is a Scandinavian dish of thin slices of dried salmon marinated in sugar, salt, pepper, dill, and other herbs; it is often served as an appetizer. Gravlax is Swedish for "trench/buried salmon," as the salmon was originally marinated and fermented in a hole in the ground.

GRAVY is a term for the fats and juices that drip from cooking meats, but also for a sauce made from these juices together with flour, stock, seasonings, and other ingredients. Familiar types include brown gravy, white gravy, milk gravy, pan gravy, meat gravy, and au jus. Gravy is served with meat, potatoes, and vegetables.

> **HINTS** Flour can be used in making gravy. To prevent the flour from diluting the flavor, use as little flour as possible and dissolve it in a little water to make a paste before adding.
>
> ▌ When making gravy, pour the liquid from a roasting pan into a glass measuring cup, then use a baster to suck out the pan juice, avoiding the fat. Squeeze the pan juice into a saucepan to make the gravy.

❚ If gravy doesn't brown properly, you can add a small amount of coffee to the gravy to get a richer brown color. You can also cook some flour separately over low heat until the desired darkness is achieved. To thicken gravy without producing lumps, add 1–2 tablespoons of instant mashed potato flakes.

❚ Whisking in a tablespoon of butter or heavy cream just before serving will give gravy a rich, satiny texture.

GRAVY BOAT or **GRAVY SERVER**, also called SAUCE BOAT, is a small elongated dish, often boat shaped, or a pitcher for serving gravy or sauce. A model with a tall, narrow foot may be called a dressing server. A fat-and-lean gravy boat has spouts that pour off either the fat (top) or the lean sauce (bottom); its function is similar to that of a GRAVY SEPARATOR.

GRAVY SEPARATOR or **GRAVY SKIMMER**, also known as FAT SEPARATOR, is a heat-resistant kitchen utensil with a strainer attached on top, into which gravy is poured directly from a pan. The strainer filters out undesired fat, gristle, and debris for disposal, leaving smooth gravy in the container.

GREEK COFFEE, also called TURKISH COFFEE, is very strong and is served with fine grounds in it. It is made by boiling finely ground coffee, sugar, and water three times and cooling between boilings.

GREEK SALAD is a term for a concoction of lettuce, tomatoes, cucumbers, olives, onions, feta cheese, and oregano and other herbs that is served with a vinaigrette. In Greek it is called *horiatiki salata*, "country-Attic salad," for an area near Athens.

GREEN BEAN, also called SNAP BEAN and STRING BEAN, is a general term for a bean plant cultivated for its slender, green, edible pods, and for the immature bean eaten complete with its pod as a vegetable.

HINTS If possible, purchase green beans at a store or farmers' market that sells them loose, so that you can sort through them to choose the beans of best quality. Purchase beans that have a smooth feel and a vibrant green color, and that are free from brown spots or bruises. They should have a firm texture and should "snap" when broken. Store unwashed fresh bean pods in a plastic bag in the vegetable crisper of the refrigerator. Whole beans stored this way should keep for about seven days.

❚ Just prior to using green beans, wash them under running water. Remove both ends of the beans by either snapping them off or cutting them with a knife. Add a pinch of sugar to the cooking water to keep the beans green.

GREENGAGE is a variety of sweet, green or greenish yellow, oval plum, named for Sir William Gage (1657–1727), an English botanist. It is a dessert plum.

GREEN GODDESS DRESSING is a mayonnaise-based dressing with sour cream, chervil, tarragon vinegar, lemon juice, anchovies, parsley, chives, scallions, garlic, pepper, and tarragon. The salad dressing was created for actor George Arliss in the 1920s when he performed in a play called *The Green Goddess*. Before ranch dressing was invented, Green Goddess was one of the most popular salad dressings in the western United States.

GREEN ONION, also called BUNCHING ONION or SCALLION, is an immature onion pulled up before the bulb has developed. Green onions have a white base that has not fully developed into a bulb, and green leaves that are long and straight; both parts are edible and are often used in salad. The term green onions originally referred to a specific type of green bunching onion from Ascalon in ancient Palestine (the word scallion derives from Ascalon).

> **HINT** Choose green onions with crisp, bright green tops and a firm white base. Remove any rubber bands or damaged leaves, put in a plastic bag, and store in the vegetable crisper of the refrigerator for up to two weeks. Store away from odor-sensitive foods such as corn and mushrooms, which will absorb the odor of the onions.

GREEN PEPPER STEAK: see PEPPER STEAK.

GREENS is a general term for any of various leafy plants or their leaves and stems that are eaten as vegetables, especially cabbage, lettuce, and spinach in salad. Greens is also a British term for COLLARD.

> **HINTS** When purchasing greens, select leaves free of blemishes, yellow spots, and insect holes and avoid wilted or dried leaves. For heads, choose those that are heavy and densely packed. Remove any brown or wilting leaves when you get home from the market—the rest will stay fresh longer. Some salad greens can be stored in a plastic bag in the vegetable crisper of the refrigerator. Romaine will keep for up to ten days. Rinse greens thoroughly before using. If you choose to wash a product marked "prewashed" or "ready to eat," be sure to use safe handling practices to avoid any cross-contamination. Wash your hands for twenty seconds with warm water and soap before and after handling the product, and wash the produce under running water just before preparing or eating.

> Wrap unwashed greens in a damp kitchen towel or paper towel, covered loosely with a plastic bag, and keep in the refrigerator for three to five days. Wash well in cool water, though lukewarm water is better than cold for removing sand from greens.

❚ For salad, make sure the greens are as dry as possible so they are ready for the dressing. Put in the refrigerator to crisp. Tear leaves, instead of cutting them, to prevent discoloration (romaine can be cut). Use one handful of greens per person or two heads for a main-course salad for four.

❚ Soaking in ice water revives wilted greens because the membranes allow water back in, restoring texture.

TYPES OF GREENS

DARK	LIGHT/SALAD	
BEET GREENS	ARUGULA	MÂCHE
BROCCOLI RABE	BABY SPINACH	MESCLUN
COLLARD GREENS	BELGIAN ENDIVE	MIZUNA
DANDELION GREENS	BIBB LETTUCE	OAKLEAF LETTUCE
ESCAROLE	BOSTON LETTUCE	RADICCHIO
KALE	BUTTER LETTUCE	RED CABBAGE
MUSTARD GREENS	CURLY ENDIVE	RED ENDIVE
SORREL	ESCAROLE	RED-LEAF LETTUCE
SPINACH	FRISÉE	ROMAINE
SWISS CHARD	GREEN-LEAF LETTUCE	SALAD SAVOR
TURNIP GREENS	ICEBERG LETTUCE	SPINACH
		WATERCRESS

GREEN TEA is tea leaves that have been steamed and dried without fermenting; because the leaves are not fermented, they are a pale green color.

> **CONFUSABLE** GREEN TEA/BLACK TEA. Green tea is tea made from unfermented leaves, and black tea is tea made from fermented leaves.

> **HINT** Green tea needs cooler water than black tea, around 175°F, as boiling water will produce bitter green tea. Green tea also doesn't need to steep terribly long—2 minutes is usually fine.

GREMOLADA or **GREMOLATA** is a mixture of finely chopped fresh parsley, garlic, and lemon zest used as a garnish on osso bucco, grilled fish, or grilled chicken.

GRENACHE, also called GARNACHA, is a sweet red wine grape variety from Spain and France. Grenache is one of the most widely planted red wine grape varieties in the world. Grenache is known as Garnacha in Spain, where it is the most planted grape in the country.

GRENADINE is a red syrup made from pomegranate juice and sugar and used mainly for flavoring cocktails. The word comes from the French *grenade*, "pomegranate." Grenadine syrup is commonly used to mix cherry colas, pink lemonade, Shirley Temple cocktails, and around five hundred alcoholic drinks, and to soak and flavor cherries, making all of these bright red. Today, grenadine is usually made from a mixture of artificial color, sometimes berry or cherry juice for flavoring, and corn syrup or sugar. Grenadine is extremely sweet and high in calories, and should be used in small amounts.

GRIDDLE is a type of heavy cooking pan or metal plate with a flat surface on which food is cooked, especially on a stove. The word is ultimately from the Latin *craticula*, "small gridiron," and the word gridiron was actually the predecessor of griddle, with gridiron meaning a cooking utensil formed of parallel bars of iron or other metal in a frame, usually supported on short legs, and used for broiling flesh or fish over a fire.

> **HINT** Straddle a roasting pan over two stove burners to sub as a griddle.

GRIDDLECAKE, also called BATTERCAKE, FLANNEL CAKE, FLAPJACK, HOTCAKE, JOHNNYCAKE, or PANCAKE, is a flat, thin batter cake cooked on a griddle, but the word can also mean a scone made by dropping a spoonful of batter on a griddle. Griddlecake is an American term dating from around 1775.

GRILL is a type of cooker that radiates heat downward for cooking food, a gridiron used for cooking food on an open fire, a dish of grilled food (such as meat), and a type of restaurant serving grilled food (also called a Grillroom). The verb form means to cook on a grill; grilling is cooking by direct exposure to radiant heat (such as over a fire or under a grill). Grill is not an old word; the verb meaning to cook on a gridiron dates to 1668 and the noun for food cooked this way was first seen in print in 1766.

GRILLING ESSENTIALS

CONFUSABLE GRILL/BROIL/ BARBECUE. Grilling generally means cooking meat on a metal grate directly over the heat source. Broiling means cooking meat in a pan below the heat source. Because of the high temperature of the heat source (3,000°F for gas and around 2,000°F for coals and electrical elements), thin and tender cuts (chops, fish, steaks, poultry parts) can be grilled with success. Barbecuing is different from grilling because it is a low-temperature, slow-heating method in a closed chamber. For barbecue, the meat must be fresh and never frozen.

Good barbecue meat needs to have a layer of fat on it. Lots of marbling helps the meat stay tender, since the fat keeps the juices from escaping and melts into the meat as you cook. Barbecue meat also needs to have an even thickness.

■ If the grill rack is not clean when you start the grill, let the residue burn off and then put the food on. Preheat and oil the rack, too. Starch from a potato can be used to coat the rack so delicate foods don't stick and tear. Scrape the grill clean with a wire brush or crumpled tin foil.

(continued)

■ To measure the propane level in a gas grill's tank, pour boiling water down the side of the tank. Where there is propane, condensation and coolness will form on the tank.

■ Place raw food on a foil-covered platter, then once the food is on the grill, throw away the foil and use the platter for the cooked food.

■ Oil a grill grate with a wad of paper towels dipped in vegetable oil using tongs.

■ The grill should be very hot when cooking fish fillets. The high temperature keeps the fish from sticking to the grill by melting any fat or heating the oil to form a coating, and thus keeps the fish from falling apart.

■ Marinating meat in herbs, beer, or wine can reduce the carcinogens that form during grilling by as much as 88%.

■ Direct-heat grilling is for thinner cuts of meat, fish, and vegetables that take less than 25 minutes to cook. Indirect-heat grilling is for whole poultry, roasts, and large cuts. For indirect-heat grilling, the coals are placed on the opposite side from the food or the grill is set on low. A drip pan is used in the area of low heat to catch juice and reflect heat.

■ Opened grill vents will allow more air and make a hotter fire.

■ Put sugar-based glazes or sauces on toward the end of grilling to prevent burning.

■ It is important to salt the meat before grilling, as salt draws the meat's juices to the surface, where they caramelize and brown.

■ Use a wok or other domed lid to cover food on the grill without having to close the whole grill.

■ The warmer the meat starts out, the less time it takes to cook through and the less time the outer layers are exposed to high heat.

■ For hamburger and steak, if perfect grill marks are desired, then turn only once or twice. If texture and moistness are more important, then flip once a minute. Frequent turns prevent either side from absorbing or releasing large amounts of heat. The meat cooks faster and the outer layers are not overdone.

GRILLADE is French for the act of grilling or a dish of grilled meat. In French and Cajun cookery, this term is also used for a kind of meat stew usually made with beef steak.

GRIND is to reduce or crush into small pieces or particles by pounding, pulverizing, abrading, and also by chopping with metal blades. Most food can be ground to fine, medium, or coarse textures. Grind as a noun can describe the texture of something that is ground, as in a fine grind of coffee or a coarse grind of salt.

GRINDER has two meanings. The first is a kitchen appliance, often electric, that grinds a food such as coffee beans or meat. The second is a large sandwich on a long split roll filled with meats and cheese, and usually also lettuce, tomato, onion, and condiments. Though this sandwich is called a grinder in New England and northern California, it has different names in other parts of the United States: BLIMPIE, BOMBER, CUBAN SANDWICH, GARIBALDI, HERO, HOAGIE/HOAGY, ITALIAN SANDWICH, MUFFULETTA, POOR BOY, ROCKET, SPUCKIE, SUB, SUBMARINE, TORPEDO, WEDGE, and ZEPPELIN/ZEP. Most of these names are associated with a particular region of the country.

> **HINT** Some nuts and spices can also be ground in a coffee grinder. Remove odors from a grinder by running a few pieces of bread through it.

GRISSINI, also called BREADSTICKS, are long, thin sticks of crisply baked bread. It is the plural of the Italian *grissino*, "breadstick."

GRIST is grain that has been ground or is meant to be ground, especially corn. The word derives from an Old English word meaning "grinding."

GRITS or **GROATS**, also called HOMINY GRITS, are coarsely ground, dried, hulled corn kernels (hominy) that are boiled and sometimes then fried. It also refers to any coarsely ground hulled grain, such as oatmeal.

> **HINT** To make grits with a smooth texture, add the grits slowly, a little at a time, to the cooking liquid.

GROCER is an owner or manager of a store selling food and other household goods, or another term for GROCERY or GROCERY STORE. Grocer was originally a wholesaler and the food sold in retail amounts was called a spicer—so a wholesale dealer in these goods was called a *spicer en gross* or *grosser* (from the French *gros/grossus*, "great/large"). Grocer had appeared in English by 1321, and grocery had appeared by 1436 as the term for goods sold by a grocer.

GROG is rum diluted with water. It is named for E. Vernon (1684–1757), a British admiral who was nicknamed Old Grog (because he wore a grogram cloak) and ordered that the sailors' rum be diluted.

GROS SEL: see COARSE SALT.

GROUND CHERRY, also called HUSK TOMATO, MEXICAN GREEN TOMATO, and TOMATILLO is a plant (genus *Physalis*) that produces a small, round, orange fruit in an enlarged bladderlike enclosure (calyx) with a papery husk. The ground cherry has a pleasant, unique flavor that tastes like a blend of tomato and pineapple. The ground cherry is very similar to the cape gooseberry and it is used like a tomato.

GROUNDNUT or **GROUNDPEA**: see PEANUT.

GROUPER is any of various sea basses with lean white flesh, of the family Serranidae; the name comes from the Portuguese *garoupa*. Many groupers are important food fish, and some of them are now farmed. Unlike most other fish species, which are chilled or frozen, groupers are usually sold alive in markets.

GRUEL is a thin, watery porridge, usually made of oatmeal, barley, or cornmeal. In some cultures, gruel is considered a treat or delicacy.

GRUNT, also called SLUMP or COBBLER, is a New England dessert made of stewed fruit (usually sweetened and spiced apples, cherries, or peaches) topped with biscuit dough, which steams as the fruit cooks. The name may have come from the noise people made while eating it.

GRUYÈRE (pronounced groo-YEHR) is a firm, pale yellow, cow's milk Swiss cheese with small holes and a mild nutty-sweet flavor, named for a Swiss town. In France, Gruyère is a general term for three distinct cheeses: Beaufort, Comté, and Emmental. Gruyère is creamy and nutty when young, and becomes more assertive, earthy, and complex with age. When fully aged (five to twelve months), it tends to have small holes and cracks that impart a slightly grainy mouthfeel. Gruyère is generally known as one of the finest cheeses for baking, as it has a distinctive but not overpowering taste.

GUACAMOLE is a thick green paste made of mashed or puréed avocados with seasonings. The condiment is often mixed with lemon or lime juice, diced onion, tomatoes, chiles, and cilantro. The word guacamole is from the Nahuatl *ahuaca-molli*, "avocado sauce," and came into English from American Spanish around 1920.

> **HINTS** For making guacamole, select avocados that are firm yet yield to gentle pressure. Avoid those with soft spots or discoloration, signs that this tender fruit has been bruised. If planning to use avocados later in the week, buy firm avocados without give.
>
> ▌ Speed ripening of avocados by placing them in a paper bag and storing at room temperature. Use a sharp knife to slice the avocado in half, around the pit. Gently turn one side to separate the halves. Stab the pit with the sharp end of the knife and gently turn, and the pit will pop out. If making guacamole in advance, leave pits in the dip to prevent it from turning brown; oxygen is the enemy, so cover the bowl tightly with heavy-duty plastic wrap. Guacamole made in advance should be refrigerated.
>
> ▌ For chunky guacamole, use a knife to score or cut the fruit into small square pieces while still in the skin. Remove the skin and make guacamole with the chunks. Scoop avocado out of the halves with a spoon if making a cream-style dip. Cut other ingredients such as onion or peppers into uniform pieces for even flavor.

GUAVA is the cultivated round or pear-shaped tropical fruit of American shrubs or small trees (genus *Psidium*) of the myrtle family. The fruit is yellowish to deep red with sweet reddish or pinkish flesh. Guavas range from the size of a small egg to that of a medium apple, and are used in jam, jelly, and sauces. The word is from the Taino language.

> **HINT** Guavas should yield to gentle pressure. Avoid those with discolored, soft spots. When sniffed, they should smell floral. Guavas ripen fast at room temperature in a paper bag. Once ripe, keep in a plastic bag in the refrigerator for up to three to four days.

GUFFIN BEAN: see LIMA BEAN.

GUMBO is a stew made of fish, meat, or poultry and thickened with the pods of okra. The word gumbo is related to Umbundu *ochinggombo* and Luba *chinggombo*, both meaning "okra," and is from Louisiana French, probably ultimately from the Central Bantu dialect; it was first a colloquial name for the okra plant or pods. There is also a type of gumbo made with ground sassafras leaves, which are known as file or filé.

GUMDROP is a jellied candy coated with sugar crystals that is created in many colors and flavors. It is so named for being made with gum arabic (or gelatin). This U.S. term dates to 1860.

GYRO (pronounced YEE-roh or ZHIR-oh) is a type of sandwich consisting of pita bread filled with sliced meats, tomatoes, onions, and yogurt. This Greek specialty is authentically cooked on a spit and the term is from the Greek *gyros*, "turning."

HABA BEAN: see LIMA BEAN.

HABANERO is a small chile pepper (*Capsicum chinense*) that is light green to bright orange and extremely hot when ripe. The word is from the American Spanish (*chile*) *habanero*, literally meaning "Havanan chile." Habanero chile peppers are rated 100,000–350,000 on the Scoville scale. Habanero chiles accompany most dishes in Yucatán, either in solid or purée/salsa form. The Scotch bonnet is often compared to the habanero since they are two varieties of the same species but have different pod types. Habaneros are sometimes placed in tequila or mezcal bottles for a period ranging from several days to several weeks, to make a spiced version.

HACHOIR: see MEZZALUNA.

HADDOCK is an important food fish with lean white flesh, related to cod but smaller; it has a black lateral line and dark patch above the pectoral fin. The origin of the word is uncertain but it had appeared in English by 1307.

HAGGIS is a Scottish dish made of the heart, lungs, and liver (sometimes the tripe and chitterlings) of a sheep or calf that are mixed with suet and oatmeal; seasoned with salt, pepper, and onions; and boiled like a large sausage in a bag made from the animal's stomach. The origin of the term is unknown.

HAIXIAN SAUCE: see HOISIN SAUCE.

HALF-AND-HALF refers to a North American mixture of whole milk and cream, which is often used in coffee. The term dates to around 1890.

HALIBUT is a very large marine flatfish (flounder) of the North Atlantic and Pacific, with lean flesh. In Middle English any flatfish was called a *butte*, and fish was eaten on holy days, so *butte* was combined with *haly*, "holy," to form *halybutte*— now halibut. Halibut is typically broiled, deep-fried, or lightly grilled while fresh. Smoking is more difficult with halibut meat than it is with salmon, due to its very low fat content. Eaten fresh, the meat has a very clean taste and requires little seasoning. Halibut is also noted for its very dense and firm texture, akin to chicken.

HALVAH or **HALVA** (pronounced hahl-VAAH) is a sweet, candylike Turkish/Middle Eastern confection made with a flour of ground/crushed sesame seeds in a base of honey. The word is from the Arabic *halwa*, "sweetmeat."

HAM is the meat cut from the thigh of the hind leg of a hog, usually cured by salting and smoking. There are three typical ways of curing: dry-curing, sweet-pickle curing, or injection curing. Hams are sold boneless, partially boned, and bone-in. Country ham is dry-cured with salt and some sugar and saltpeter, and aged for months; Smithfield is a variety of country ham. Some hams are sugar coated. Curing hams by injection takes less time. They can be smoked by injection, too, and are juicier and more tender. Ham does not become gray-brown when cooked because a cured ham contains nitrite salt, which reacts with the myoglobin to create nitrous myoglobin, which stays rosy red even when exposed to high temperatures.

HAM ESSENTIALS

■ Avoid buying hams with these labels: "with natural juices," "water added," "ham and water product." Choose "no water added" or ham with no label. The phrase "water added" must appear on the label of a ham when the water content (total weight) is more than 8%. Up to that point it can be labeled as "ham with natural juices."

■ Fully cooked ham is labeled "ready to serve" or "heat and serve." On a ham, the label "cook before eating" means to heat it to an internal temperature of 160°F before eating.

- Bone-in hams tend to be more flavorful. Picnic ham is made from the picnic shoulder (front leg) and it is fattier and less expensive than hind-leg ham.

- Keep ham for no more than one week in the refrigerator. Freezing is not recommended because of the high salt content.

- Chill the ham for easier slicing. Country ham should be thinly sliced for serving because it is usually salted and this will reduce the level of saltiness in a mouthful.

- Cured ham should be soaked in milk for several hours before broiling or sautéing to improve tenderness and flavor.

- Ham rinds can be removed easily by slitting the rind before placing the ham in the oven. As it bakes, the rind will pull away and then can be easily removed.

- The best canned ham is put into large cans. The smaller ones are usually bits and pieces or small chunks of meat that have been pressed together. Generally, a canned ham that requires refrigeration is better than one that does not. In order to sterilize the ham in the can so that it doesn't require refrigeration it will be heated to a very high temperature, which negatively alters the flavor, aroma, texture, and nutritive value.

HAMBURGER or **HAMBURG STEAK**, also called BEEFBURGER or BURGER, is ground or chopped beef, usually cooked and part of a sandwich on a roll or bun, variously garnished. The word hamburger comes from the name of the German town, though it is disputed whether the hamburger steak originated there (the term hamburger had appeared by 1889, for a kind of sausage) and Hamburger originally meant "steak in Hamburg style" and it has spurred new forms such as cheeseburger, chiliburger, fishburger, and veggieburger. The term is also used for the ground beef itself, which is used as a base in many sauces, casseroles, and other dishes.

HINTS To cook hamburgers faster, make a few punctures in the patty before cooking.

▌ Don't press down a hamburger with the turner—doing so will cause it to lose its juices and be drier and less tender. To check the internal temperature of a hamburger, hold it with tongs and slide a thermometer through the side of the patty (125°F–130°F is medium-rare and 135°F–140°F is medium). The same method can be used to check the temperature for steak.

▌ Five ounces of ground meat make the perfect burger. Shape quickly because more handling makes a burger tougher, or line a Mason jar (or other large jar) lid with plastic wrap and then form the hamburger patty in the jar lid. Let the patties sit at room temperature for 5 minutes before cooking.

▌ Ground chuck is best for making hamburgers, at 80%–85% lean. Meat that is too lean produces burgers that are less flavorful, juicy, and tender. Store fresh ground meat in the coldest part of the refrigerator. Patties prepared ahead, wrapped well and stored in the refrigerator, should be used within eight hours or, if frozen, within two months. Defrost in the refrigerator, not at room temperature. Do not refreeze defrosted, uncooked ground meat. Cook as soon as possible after thawing.

HAND BLENDER: see Immersion blender.

HANDHELD JUICER: see Reamer.

HANGER STEAK or **HANGING TENDER**, also called Butcher's steak, Butcher's tenderloin, or Onglet, is a cut of beef similar to flank or skirt steak in texture and ribeye in flavor, cut from the diaphragm that "hangs" between the last rib and the loin. The hanger steak is not particularly tender, but has a lot of flavor, and is best marinated and cooked quickly over high heat (grilled or broiled) and served rare or medium-rare to avoid toughness.

HARD-BALL STAGE in candy making is 250°F–265°F. At this stage, the syrup will form thick, ropy threads as it drips from the spoon. The sugar concentration is rather high, which means there's less moisture in the sugar syrup. A little of this syrup dropped into cold water will form a hard ball. If you take the ball out of the water, it won't flatten. The ball will be hard, but you can still change its shape.

HARD-COOKED or **HARD-BOILED** describes an egg simmered (just below the boiling point) or boiled in the shell until the yolk and white solidify. The correct terminology is hard-cooked, not hard-boiled.

> **HINTS** When eggs are boiled, the sulfur present in the egg white combines with the iron in the egg yolk, producing ferrous sulfite, which creates a green film on the border between the white and the yolk. The presence of this line means the egg is overcooked. The egg isn't harmful to eat. Cooking water high in iron can also produce the green ring. So if your tap water is high in iron (ask your city water department), you might want to use bottled or filtered water to cook your eggs. Hard-cooked eggs can be stored in the refrigerator, well covered, for three to four days.

> For the best hard-cooked eggs, first make sure your eggs aren't brand-new. Buy a dozen and refrigerate them for five days, then use them. Newer eggs are harder to peel because the egg white is higher in acid when first laid, making the white adhere to the shell. The acidity of the egg white decreases over time, loosening its grip on the shell.

> Place the eggs in water that covers them by one inch. Bring to a boil over high heat. When the water boils vigorously, cover the pan and remove it from the heat. Let the pan stand, covered, for 15 minutes for large eggs (12 minutes for medium, 18 minutes for extra-large). Uncover the pan and place it in the sink. Run cold water into the pan for 7–8 minutes, until the eggs are cool to the touch. Then add

ice cubes to the pan and, leaving the eggs under the water, crack them gently against the sides of the pan. Let the eggs stand for another 5 minutes. This lets water seep between the shell and the egg, making peeling easier—or peel the eggs under water.

HARD-CRACK STAGE in candy making is 300°F–310°F. The hard-crack stage is the highest temperature specified in a candy recipe. At these temperatures, there is almost no water left in the syrup. Drop a little of the molten syrup in cold water and it will form hard, brittle threads that break when bent. Toffee, nut brittles, and lollipops are all cooked to the hard-crack stage.

HARD ROLL: see KAISER ROLL.

HARD SAUCE is a creamed mixture of butter and powdered sugar often with added cream and flavoring from brandy, rum, or vanilla. This sauce is often served chilled with fruitcake, gingerbread, or pudding. Hard sauce is not really a sauce at all, and could really more accurately be termed a spread.

HARDTACK is a very hard, thin unsalted biscuit or bread. This food was formerly eaten aboard ships or as military rations.

HARE is a term for the flesh of any of various wild or domesticated rabbits or hares, eaten as food.

HARICOT is any of several beans' ripe seeds or unripe pods, especially the kidney bean and the white varieties of the dried seeds. There is a second meaning of highly seasoned mutton or lamb stew with vegetables.

> **HINT** Like other dried beans, haricot beans will keep for a year or more when stored in a cool, dry place out of the sunlight. When selecting haricot beans in the market, avoid discolored beans, as they may have been poorly handled while they dried. When you are ready to use the beans, first rinse them and pick through the rinsed beans to remove small stones and organic material that may have been packaged with them.

HARVARD BEETS are cut-up beets cooked in vinegar, sugar, butter, cornstarch, and water. They are said to have been created by a Harvard student or to have been so named because the beets' color is the Harvard color. But there is also a theory that the term is a corruption of the name of a tavern in England named Harwood.

HASH is chopped food, especially chopped cooked meat and potatoes that are mixed and browned.

> **HINT** The crust in hash is formed on the bottom of the pan. The secret to getting a crust in hash is to stir the bottom after 10–15 minutes, so the crust comes up

into the meat. Then cook for 10–15 minutes more and repeat. The crust will end up throughout the hash. Some chefs believe that there should only be a crust on the bottom, so they don't stir.

HASH BROWNS is a North American dish made of cooked or boiled potatoes that are chopped and fried. The potatoes are sometimes browned with onions and seasonings and formed into small cakes or patties. The original name was *hashed brown potatoes*, from French the *hacher*, "chop up."

> **HINT** Grate potatoes just before making hash browns. Soak the grated potatoes in ice water, then strain well to remove starches. If you fry in butter, add some oil to raise the smoke point and reduce burning.

HASHI: see CHOPSTICKS.

HASTY PUDDING in the United Kingdom is a sweetened porridge made of tapioca, flour, or oatmeal cooked quickly in milk or water. In the United States hasty pudding is cornmeal mush served with maple syrup or brown sugar. It is also a synonym for INDIAN PUDDING.

HAUTE CUISINE is French for "high, elegant cooking" and it is used to describe classic French cooking or any elaborate and skillful manner of preparing food; it is also food preparation as an art.

HAVARTI is a mild, semisoft, pale yellow Danish cheese with a porous texture. The name comes from Havarthigård, the farm of Hanne Nielsen, a Danish cheese maker. Its taste is similar to Tilsit or Gouda, and it is often flavored with dill, caraway, cumin, or other spices.

HAWAIIAN PIZZA is a pizza topped with pineapple and ham or prosciutto. It is the most popular pizza in Australia. It was not a Hawaiian invention but may have been created in Germany.

HAZELNUT, also called FILBERT, is the edible nut of any of several shrubs or small hazel trees of the genus *Corylus*; the nuts have a hard, smooth shell.

> **CONFUSABLE** HAZELNUTS/FILBERTS. The difference between hazelnuts and filberts is that hazelnuts grow wild, while filberts are cultivated. Hazelnuts are the smaller of the two. Sometimes the names are used interchangeably.

HEART OF PALM or **HEARTS OF PALM**, also called PALM HEART, is the edible inner terminal bud of the cabbage palm. Hearts of palm look like white asparagus without tips and can be used in salads and in main dishes, or deep-fried. The cabbage palm is the state tree of Florida.

HINT When purchasing fresh hearts of palm, make sure the stalks are not dry or separated/split. Store for up to two days in a perforated plastic bag. Opened canned hearts of palm should be covered with water and refrigerated for up to one week. Soak canned hearts of palm for 10 minutes in water and a little lemon juice.

HEAVY CREAM is cream that contains a high percentage of butterfat, usually 36%–40%; it is called heavy whipping cream and sometimes DOUBLE CREAM in the United Kingdom. It also has 5% milk solids and more than 50% water.

CONFUSABLE HEAVY CREAM/BRITISH DOUBLE CREAM. British double cream has at least 48% butterfat, 8% higher than the highest-fat cream available in the United States. So even though the two types of cream are basically synonymous, heavy cream does have less butterfat.

HINT Heavy cream should be kept in the coldest part of the refrigerator. To substitute for 1 cup of heavy cream (for cooking only, not whipping), use ¾ cup of milk plus 1/3 cup of melted butter.

HEINZ 57 VARIETIES

The "Heinz 57 Varieties" slogan is synonymous with the name Heinz. In 1896 Henry John Heinz noticed an advertisement for "21 styles of shoes." He decided that his own products were not styles, but varieties. Although there were many more than 57 foods in production at the time, because the numbers 5 and 7 held a special significance for him and his wife, he adopted the slogan "57 Varieties." The following products constitute the original 57:

APPLE BUTTER	CHERRY PRESERVES	DISTILLED WHITE VINEGAR
APPLE JELLY	CHILI SAUCE	EVAPORATED HORSERADISH
BAKED BEANS IN TOMATO SAUCE WITHOUT MEAT	CHOW-CHOW PICKLES	FIG PUDDING
	COOKED MACARONI	GRAPE JELLY
BAKED BEANS WITHOUT TOMATO SAUCE WITH BOSTON-STYLE PORK	COOKED SPAGHETTI	GREEN PEPPER SAUCE
	CRAB-APPLE JELLY	INDIA RELISH
BAKED BEANS WITH PORK AND TOMATO SAUCE	CREAM OF CELERY SOUP	MANZANILLA OLIVES
	CREAM OF PEA SOUP	MAYONNAISE
BAKED RED KIDNEY BEANS	CREAM OF TOMATO SOUP	MINCEMEAT
BEEFSTEAK SAUCE	CURRANT JELLY	PEACH PRESERVES
BLACKBERRY PRESERVES	DAMSON PLUM PRESERVES	PEANUT BUTTER
BLACK RASPBERRY PRESERVES	DILL PICKLES	PLUM PUDDING

(continued)

PREPARED MUSTARD	QUINCE JELLY	SOUR SPICED GHERKINS
PRESERVED SWEET GHERKINS	RED PEPPER SAUCE	STRAWBERRY PRESERVES
PRESERVED SWEET MIXED PICKLES	RED RASPBERRY PRESERVES	STUFFED OLIVES
PURE CIDER VINEGAR	RIPE OLIVES	SWEET MIDGET GHERKINS
PURE MALT VINEGAR	SALAD DRESSING	SWEET MUSTARD PICKLES
PURE OLIVE OIL	SOUR MIDGET GHERKINS	TARRAGON VINEGAR
QUEEN OLIVES	SOUR MIXED PICKLES	TOMATO KETCHUP
	SOUR PICKLED ONIONS	WORCESTERSHIRE SAUCE

HEIRLOOM SEED is any seed handed down from one generation to another, usually by individual gardeners rather than by being sold in catalogs. An heirloom plant is a fruit or vegetable grown with these seeds. Many heirloom vegetables have kept their traits through open pollination, while fruit varieties such as apples have been propagated over the centuries through grafts and cuttings. The trend of growing heirloom plants in gardens has been growing in popularity in the United States and Europe.

HERB is, technically, any plant with aerial parts used for flavoring and garnishing foods, or any aromatic seed plant whose stem withers away to the ground after each season's growth. In other words, these plants do not develop persistent woody tissue. The word herb, derived from the Latin *herba*, "growing vegetation," can be pronounced with or without the *h*, though American English favors the silent *h*. A potherb is any plant with stalks and leaves that can be boiled as a vegetable or used in soups and stews. The chef James Beard had a "savory six," the herbs he could not cook without: basil, bay leaves, rosemary, savory, tarragon, and thyme.

HERB ESSENTIALS

CONFUSABLE HERB/SPICE. A spice (also called seasoning) is any substance used for seasoning foods; many herbs areused as spices, but not all. Herbs are usually the leaves or the whole of the plant, while spices are only part of the plant, commonly the seeds, or sometimes the roots or rhizomes.

■ Herbs, dried or fresh, may be bruised or crushed to release their aromatic oils so the flavor better infuses the dish. A small amount may be crushed with one thumb in the palm of the other, twisting the thumb. Large quantities should be crushed using a mortar and pestle.

■ Choose fresh herbs that are bright, fragrant, and healthy. Avoid wilting, blackening, yellowing, or moldy leaves or stems. Hothouse herbs will have less flavor than field-grown herbs. Leaves from plants without buds or flowers will have more flavor, too.

■ Wrap herbs in damp paper towels, put in a plastic bag, and refrigerate for three to five days. Long-stemmed herbs (basil, cilantro, parsley) may keep for up to ten days in a container of water (like a bouquet); trim the ends of the stems first. Put a plastic bag loosely over the herb-filled container, secure the bag around the top of the container, then put the container in the refrigerator. Rinse fresh herbs under cold running water or dunk in a bowl of water, but wait to do this until you need them. Put herbs in a large bowl of cool water and swish to loosen any dirt. Lift out the herbs and either spin in a salad spinner or blot dry with a towel, or put the herbs in a single layer between paper towels and microwave for 2 minutes to dry. Herbs that are chopped can be kept for twenty-four hours: place in an airtight container, cover with a damp paper towel, and put in the refrigerator. Fresh herbs can be frozen by blanching them in lightly salted water, draining, and plunging into ice water; then dry, chop, and put into a plastic bag with the air pushed out. When using frozen herbs, add them to the dish without thawing, and in extended cooking, add late in the process.

■ Dried herbs kept away from light and heat are good for four to six months. Dried herbs change as they age. They lose their volatile oils, so you will need a larger amount of them to achieve the desired level of seasoning. Dried herbs are best if used within about three months of the time the container is opened, but generally the jars should be replaced annually. Mark the date on a piece of tape when the jar is opened.

This means that economy-sized packages are really not economical unless you use herbs a lot. Roughly, to get the equivalent of 1 tablespoon of fresh herbs, use 1 teaspoon of dried herbs.

■ Tired herbs, dried or fresh, may be crushed, put in a nonreactive container, covered with a little warm vinegar, and refrigerated overnight. These herbs are good in a sauce or vinaigrette.

■ Fresh herbs are best when added toward the end of cooking. Dried herbs should be added early. Fresh herbs should be completely dry before mincing. Hold down the tip of a chef's knife so it does not leave the cutting board. Raise and lower the other part of the knife and push the herbs together to chop clumps. Scissors or a mezzaluna are good for mincing. Mincing by hand is preferable to using a food processor, which also bruises and crushes the herbs.

■ Don't boil an herb-seasoned dish, just simmer it, as the aromatic oils in the seasonings are volatile and will disappear into the air. For long cooking, add herbs during the last 20-30 minutes. For marinades or salad dressing, add herbs at the beginning.

■ To dry fresh herbs for storage, heat the herbs on a baking dish in a preheated 200°F oven until thoroughly dry. Store in sealed containers in a cool, dark place.

HERB AND SPICE MIXTURES

CLASSICS AND THEIR PLACE OF ORIGIN:

BOUQUET GARNI (FRANCE): Bay, parsley, thyme.

CHERMOULA (MOROCCO): Black pepper, chile, coriander, cumin, garlic, lemon, onion, saffron, salt.

CURRY POWDER (SOUTH ASIA): Six or more of the following—black pepper, caraway, cardamom, celery, chili powder/cayenne pepper, cinnamon, cloves, coriander, cumin, dill, fennel, fenugreek, ginger, mace, nutmeg, salt, turmeric.

FINES HERBES (FRANCE): Chervil, chive, parsley, tarragon, thyme.

FIVE-SPICE (CHINA): Cinnamon, cloves, fennel seed, star anise, Szechuan peppercorns.

(continued)

GARAM MASALA (INDIA): Allspice, anise, black pepper, cardamom, celery, cinnamon, cloves, coriander, cumin, mace, sea salt.

HERBES DE PROVENCE (FRANCE): Basil, fennel, lavender, marjoram, rosemary, thyme.

PANCH PHORAN (INDIA): Cumin, fennel, fenugreek, mustard seed, nigella.

PERI PERI (MOZAMBIQUE): Chile, citric acid, garlic, ginger, lemon peel, sea salt.

QUATRE-ÉPICES OR FOUR-SPICE (FRANCE): Cloves, ginger, nutmeg, white pepper; sometimes cinnamon.

RAS EL HANOUT (MOROCCO): Twenty ingredients including cardamom, cassia/cinnamon, chile, cloves, coriander, cumin,

fennel, ginger, mace, peppercorns, rose petals, sea salt.

RECADO ROJO OR ACHIOTE PASTE (MEXICO): Allspice, annatto, black pepper, cinnamon, cloves, cumin, garlic, Mexican oregano, salt.

SHICHIMI (JAPAN): Hemp seed, mandarin peel, mustard, nori or anori, poppy seed, sansho, sesame seed.

ZA'ATAR (MIDDLE EAST): Marjoram, oregano, salt, sesame seed, sumac berries, thyme.

ZHUG (MIDDLE EAST): Cardamon, chile, coriander, cumin, garlic.

HERB VARIETIES

Herbs are the fragrant leaves of plants used fresh or dried for flavoring food, as opposed to spices, which are any flavoring substances obtained from the seeds, fruits, or bark of a plant, especially one grown in warm places. Medieval monasteries were known for their cultivation of many different kinds of herbs. Aromatic plants such as bay, garlic, and rosemary were used to flavor the monasteries' food and to make medicines and ointments for healing the sick. The word herb comes via Old French from the Latin *herba*, which meant "growing vegetation/green plants/grass." Here is a sampling of herbs:

ABSCESS ROOT	BARBARA'S BUTTONS	CALIFORNIA BUTTERCUP
ACACIA BARK	BASIL	CAMAS
ADDER'S TONGUE	BAY LEAF	CARAWAY
AFRICAN DAISY	BELLADONNA	CARDAMOM
AFRICAN VALERIAN	BERGAMOT	CATNIP OR CATMINT
ALKALI MALLOW	BIRTHWORT	CENTELLA
ALPINE ANEMONE	BITTER ORANGE	CHAMOMILE
ALPINE ASTER	BITTERROOT	CHERVIL
AMERICAN MISTLETOE	BITTER RUBBERWEED	CHICORY
ANGELICA	BLOODROOT	CHIVE
ANISE	BLUE FLAG	CILANTRO
ANISE HYSSOP	BORAGE	CINNAMON
ARROW GRASS	BROOKWEED	CLARY
ARROWROOT	BUGLEWEED	CLIMBING ONION
AXSEED	BUTTERBUR	CLOVER
BALM	BUTTERWORT	COLTSFOOT
BAOBAB	CALENDULA	COMFREY

CORIANDER	JACKFRUIT	SAGE
COW PARSNIP	JOE-PYE WEED	SAINT JOHN'S WORT
CUMIN	KAPOK	SAVORY
DANDELION GREENS	LADY'S MANTLE	SESAME
DATURA	LADY'S SMOCK	SILVERWEED
DEADLY NIGHTSHADE	LAVENDER	SOAPWORT
DILL	LEMON BALM	SORREL
DITTANY	LEMONGRASS	SPEARMINT
DONG QUAI	LEMON MINT	SPIDERWORT
DROPWORT	LICORICE	STAR ANISE
ECHINACEA	LIVERWORT	STAR FRUIT
FENNEL	LOVAGE	SWEET BALM
FEVERROOT	LUPINE	SWEET BASIL
FIGWORT	MANDRAKE	SWEET BAY
FINOCCHIO	MARJORAM	SWEET CICELY
FRAXINELLA OR GAS PLANT	MINT	SWEET WOODRUFF
FUMEWORT	MONKSHOOD	TAMARACK
GARLIC	MOTHERWORT	TANSY
GINGER	MULLEIN	TARRAGON
GINKGO	MUSTARD	THYME
GINSENG	OREGANO	TINKER'S ROOT
GOAT'S RUE	PARSLEY	VERVAIN
GYPSYWORT	PEPPERMINT	WASABI
HAREBELL	PERIWINKLE	WATER HEMLOCK
HEMLOCK	POKEWEED	WILD GINGER
HEMP	PRIMROSE	WINTERGREEN
HENBANE	RATTLESNAKE WEED	WOODRUFF
HERB OF GRACE	ROSEMARY	WORMWOOD
HOREHOUND	RUE	YARROW
HORSEMINT	SACRED LOTUS	YELLOW BELLS
HYSSOP	SAFFLOWER	YERBA BUENA
	SAFFRON	

HERBES DE PROVENCE (pronounced EHRB duh proh-VAWNS) is a blend of herbs used for seasoning, such as basil, bay leaf, chervil, fennel, lavender, marjoram, mint, oregano, rosemary, sage, summer savory, tarragon, and thyme. It is a traditional blend of these herbs from the hills of southern France.

HERO SANDWICH is a variant name, used in certain regions, for a GRINDER, a large sandwich on a long split roll filled with meats and cheese, and usually also lettuce, tomato, onion, and condiments. The origin of the hero sandwich is much disputed.

HERRING is an important food fish (genus *Clupea*) of shallow waters of the North Atlantic and Pacific with valuable fatty flesh. Herring, small and silvery, is usually salted or pickled, or canned as a sardine. The herring family also includes the sprats, shads, and pilchards. Pilchard young are sardines. Kippers, bloaters, and red herrings are salted and smoked herrings; bucklings are hot-smoked herrings; gaffelbitar is semipreserved herring.

HIBACHI is a portable Japanese brazier, literally "fire bowl," consisting of a round, cylindrical, or box-shaped open-topped container, made from or lined with a heatproof material, with a grill over it. Traditionally, charcoal is used and it is an outdoor device. The term also refers to an iron hot plate or cooking surface in restaurants, also known as a TEPPAN.

HICKORY NUT is a small hard-shelled nut of the North American hickory tree. Some are edible nuts, each containing an edible seed and surrounded by a husk that splits into four valves. Pecan is a species of hickory nut.

HIGH-ALTITUDE COOKING/BAKING is the adjustment of cooking and baking temperatures, times, and methods for locations with air much thinner than at sea level. Foods take longer to cook because they are heating at a lower temperature. Water boils at 212°F at sea level, but at 198°F at 7,500 feet above sea level. Lower air pressure also causes quicker evaporation. Adjustments are crucial in candy making, canning, dough rising, and deep-fat frying. In general, for something that needs to be boiled, the cooking process will take longer at high altitudes than at sea level. For any baked goods that rise (yeast breads, or cakes or breads made with baking powder), it is important to adjust the recipe so that the rapid rise time doesn't make the resulting bread or cake too dry. Dough must be watched carefully and the rise time judged by the change in the dough's bulk, not by the amount of time it takes. For recipes using baking powder, one must be careful not to overbeat eggs (adding too much air), and one must be sure to raise the baking temperature slightly (to prevent overrising), decrease the amount of baking powder slightly (for the same reason), and grease baking pans thoroughly (because baked goods tend to stick more at high altitudes).

> **HINT** At high altitudes, there is decreased air density and pressure so water molecules turn to steam faster and boil at lower temperatures. Foods need to be cooked at a higher heat for a longer time. The amount of liquid should be increased in recipes. Baking powder, baking soda, and yeast produce gas more quickly—so leavening needs to be decreased.

HIGH-FRUCTOSE CORN SYRUP or **HIGH-FRUCTOSE SYRUP**, also called ISOGLUCOSE, is any of a group of corn syrups that has undergone enzymatic processing to convert its glucose into fructose and is then mixed with pure corn syrup (100% glucose) to produce a desired sweetness. In the United States high-fructose corn syrup is used as a sugar substitute and is ubiquitous in processed foods and beverages. The process used to create high-fructose corn syrup was invented in 1957.

HIGH TEA, also called MEAT TEA, is a cooked dish (often meat), bread and butter, and tea, served in the United Kingdom in the late afternoon or early evening. The term dates to 1831.

HOAGIE or **HOAGY** is a variant name, used in certain regions, for a GRINDER, a large sandwich on a long split roll filled with meats and cheese, and usually also lettuce, tomato, onion, and condiments. The hoagie is the official sandwich of Philadelphia, where it was introduced in 1936 by Al De Palma and originally spelled hoggie.

HOCK is the joint bending backward in the hind leg of a cow, horse, or other digitigrade quadruped, or the corresponding joint in the leg of a fowl. Mainly, in cooking, hock refers to a small cut of meat, especially ham, from the front or hind leg directly above the foot. Maryland end is the hock end of the ham, as opposed to the thick end or Virginia end.

HOECAKE: see JOHNNYCAKE.

HOISIN SAUCE, also called HAIXIAN SAUCE or PEKING SAUCE, is a thick sweet-and-sour sauce made of soybeans, chiles, vinegar, sugar, garlic, and various spices, and used as an ingredient and condiment in Chinese dishes. It is used in cooking shellfish, pork, and duck and eaten as a condiment with shrimp, pork, poultry, and Peking duck. The Cantonese term hoisin translates to "sea/fresh."

HOLD in cooking refers to keeping a cooked dish in a specified condition, such as warm or fresh, until served with other items being cooked.

HOLLANDAISE is a rich, creamy, emulsified sauce made of butter, egg yolks, salt, white pepper, water, and lemon juice, and cayenne pepper; it is the most celebrated emulsified sauce. Hollandaise sauce originated in Holland and the word means "Dutch sauce," which it was called as far back as the sixteenth century; the word hollandaise was not recorded until 1841. Hollandaise sauce will not properly emulsify during a thunderstorm because such storms are replete with both positive and negative charges that neutralize some of the emulsifying electrical charges of the sauce.

> **CONFUSABLE** HOLLANDAISE/BÉARNAISE. Both hollandaise and béarnaise are warm emulsion sauces, in which a lot of warm butter is emulsified with egg yolks into a small amount of acidified liquid. Hollandaise came first and is considered the mother of the warm emulsified sauces. Béarnaise is the best-known and certainly best-loved variation. Béarnaise sauce substitutes vinegar for the water used in hollandaise, and adds shallots, tarragon, chervil, and (sometimes) parsley, thyme, bay leaf, and cayenne pepper.

> **HINT** Hollandaise sauce can be made a couple of hours before serving. It can easily be overcooked when reheated and thus break or curdle. A good way to keep hollandaise sauce warm is to put it in a prewarmed small thermos.

HOME FRIES or **HOME FRIED POTATOES**, also called COTTAGE FRIED POTATOES, COTTAGE FRIES, or COUNTRY FRIES, are boiled, sliced or diced potatoes fried in butter or oil, sometimes with onions and seasonings. This North American dish dates to around 1950. Home fries are fried in a frying pan, as opposed to being deep-fried.

> **HINT** You can precook potatoes for home fries a day ahead of time. Simply cover the drained and cooled potatoes and refrigerate until you need them. Yukon Gold potatoes have a nice buttery flesh and they won't fall apart as baking/russets tend to.

HOMINY, also called NIXTAMAL, is hulled yellow or white corn (maize) with the bran and germ removed; it is often coarsely ground (into HOMINY GRITS or GRITS) and boiled with water or milk for dishes. Hominy is mild and sweet and is often produced by soaking hulled corn in a lye solution to remove the hulls. It is of American Indian origin and was mentioned by Captain John Smith in writing in 1629. American colonists used the words hominy and samp interchangeably to mean processed corn. Grits are a ground meal of yellow or white hominy that are cooked into a thick porridge. Samp is dried hominy that is made into a coarse meal. Hominy is boiled until cooked and served as either a cereal or as a vegetable. Hominy may also be pressed into patties and fried.

HOMINY GRITS: see HOMINY and GRITS.

HONEY is an ancient food, a sweet viscid fluid that is the nectar of flowers collected and made into food by certain insects, especially the honeybee. It is found in various shades from nearly white to deep golden and is sold in varieties with varying flavors, depending on the flowers from which it was made. In Old English it was *hunig*, from the Germanic **khunaga-*. Beekeeping was being practiced in Egypt at least as early as 3000 BC. A hive of bees must fly more than fifty-five thousand miles and visit two million flowers to make one pound of honey. Liquid honey is extracted by centrifugal force, gravity, or straining. Spun honey (also called granulated honey or crème honey) is crystallized. Comb honey, sold in chunks, also contains chunks of the honeycomb.

HONEY ESSENTIALS

- Honey keeps for more than a year in an airtight container at room temperature. Comb honey will keep for only six months. Honey should be stored tightly covered in a warm, dry area, not refrigerated, which will cause it to crystallize or become gray.

- Unfiltered honey may be cloudy and it may crystallize in storage. Reliquefy crystallized honey by setting an opened jar in a pan of very hot water for 10–20 minutes. Also, you can microwave it in 30-second intervals (stirring after each) until clear.

■ An easy way to measure honey by volume is to pour some oil or spray some nonstick cooking spray into a measuring cup or spoon and then pour the oil back into the bottle. Measure the honey by pouring it into the now oiled measuring cup or spoon. The thin oil film will let the honey slip out when poured. This procedure will also work for molasses or corn syrup.

■ Honey is sweeter than sugar, so use only 80% as much as you would sugar. Substitute 1 part honey for every 1¼ parts sugar. Honey is hygroscopic (water attracting) and thus keeps baked goods moister longer than sugar.

■ When microwaving honey, remove the lid. When the container has a tight cover, it is very likely to explode. If there is a metal band on the container, it may create electric sparks (arc), which will damage the microwave oven.

■ Use a heavy-duty rubber band to open a stuck honey jar.

■ Honey counterbalances a too-spicy food.

HONEY VARIETIES

The types of honey, based on processing technique, are blended honey, pasteurized honey, raw honey, strained or filtered honey, ultrafiltered honey, and varietal or monofloral honey. The forms of honey are comb honey, cut comb or chunk honey, liquid honey, naturally crystallized honey, and whipped/creamed honey. The type of flower that provided the nectar source determines the distinctive flavor of each variety of pure honey; these flower-based honey varieties are listed here. White honey is graded by color and not variety. It has a lighter flavor than darker forms of honey, like amber honey and clover honey. There are grades of white honey, from white to water-white.

ACACIA	CANOLA	ORANGE BLOSSOM
ALFALFA	CHESTNUT (DARK, STRONG)	POPLAR (DARK, STRONG)
APPLE BLOSSOM	CLOVER	ROSEMARY
ASTER	CRANBERRY	SAFFLOWER
AVOCADO (DARK, STRONG)	EUCALYPTUS (DARK, STRONG)	SAGE
BASSWOOD (STRONG)		SUNFLOWER
BLACK LOCUST (DARK, STRONG)	FIREWEED	TAWARI
	GALLBERRY (DARK, STRONG)	THYME
BLUEBERRY (DARK, STRONG)		TUPELO
	GOLDENROD	WHITE HONEY
BUCKWHEAT (DARK, STRONG)	LAVENDER	WILDFLOWER (DARK, STRONG)
	LINDEN	

HONEYBELL: see Tangelo.

HONEYBUN or **HONEY BUN**, also called Pinwheel roll or Sticky bun, is a sweet spiral-shaped bun, usually with cinnamon, raisins, and nuts and coated with honey or butter and brown sugar. It was created in the United States in the 1950s.

HONEYDEW is the large, smooth-skinned, greenish-white fruit of a variety of winter melon (*Cucumis melo*) with sweet greenish flesh. Honeydew melon was developed around 1916 and so named for its sweetness. Honeydew, casaba, and crenshaw are winter melons and their season peaks in autumn.

HONING STEEL: see STEEL.

HOOP CHEESE: see FARMER CHEESE.

HOREHOUND is any of various aromatic herbs (genus *Marrubium*) of the mint family. A bitter juice is extracted from its leaves, stem, or flowers and used in confections. Horehound is also the name of candy made with this juice. The word is from the Old English *harhume* and related to hoar, probably due to the plant's whitish flowers and white cottony leaves.

HORS D'OEUVRE is a hot or cold savory appetizer served before a meal—a food prepared to whet the appetite. It is French for "outside the work(s)" because appetizers are outside the principal task of preparing the meal. When capitalized, it is Hors d'Oeuvre. The term had been recorded in English by 1742. The rule of thumb for hors d'oeuvres served before dinner is to provide about five to six per person; twelve per person is what is generally provided for a cocktail party.

> **HINT** If the guest list has fewer than forty-five people, plan on serving roughly six different hors d'oeuvres; for more than forty-five guests, serve eight types. The rule of thumb for smaller gatherings is that three types are suitable for eight to ten guests; four or five types for fourteen to sixteen people. Having an equal number of hot and cold foods is also helpful so that while one appetizer is heating in the oven, a cold one can be circulating, keeping everyone nibbling happily.

HORSEBEAN: see BROAD BEAN.

HORSERADISH is a Eurasian plant (*Armoracia lapathifolia*) cultivated for its thick, white, pungent root, which is grated or ground for seasoning. Horseradish is also a pungent condiment made of the grated root. The "horse" in horseradish is an adjective used in the names of plants or fruits meaning "pertaining to a large, strong, or coarse kind."

> **HINT** Horseradish can be purchased fresh from late fall to early spring. The roots should not have mold, soft spots, or wrinkles. Wrap in a paper towel, then plastic, and refrigerate for up to three weeks. Horseradish can be frozen, too. Wash fresh roots, then peel and remove any green parts. Horseradish will turn brown once cut, so sprinkle it with lemon juice or vinegar to prevent discoloring.

HOT in cooking has three main meanings: (1) having a high temperature, capable of burning, searing, or scalding; (2) prepared by heating and served without cooling; and (3) producing a burning sensation in the mouth or throat (also called PEPPERY or PUNGENT). Do not add cold ingredients to hot foods, or vice versa.

BLOWING ON HOT FOOD TO COOL IT

When you blow on food to try to cool it, you are speeding up the evaporation of the liquid (just like blowing on nail polish makes it dry faster). Here's how it works:

1. The molecules in hot foods or hot beverages are fast-moving, high-energy molecules. Since they are moving so fast, as evaporation proceeds, more of these molecules leave than cool ones.

2. Blowing whisks away the newly evaporated molecules. Faster evaporation makes faster cooling.

3. The remaining food or beverage therefore becomes cooler than it was.

HOTCAKE: see GRIDDLECAKE and PANCAKE.

HOT CROSS BUN is a sweet yeast bun, sometimes containing dried fruit, with a cross made of frosting on it; it is baked and eaten during Lent. Hot cross buns, a traditional Good Friday food called cross buns until the early nineteenth century, became hot cross buns because of a popular vendors' rhyme. The first written account of a cross appearing on the bun, in remembrance of Christ's cross, appeared in *Poor Robin's Almanack* in 1733.

> **HINT** Hot cross buns are best eaten the day they are made; if you make them the day before, don't pipe the icing cross on the tops. Instead, warm the buns the next day in a 300°F oven, cool, and then decorate right before serving.

HOT DOG or **HOTDOG**, also called FRANKFURTER, RED HOT, or WIENER, is a smooth-textured smoked or cured sausage made of minced beef, pork, or turkey, often served on a bread roll with condiments. While Tad Dorgan did feature hot dogs in a few of his cartoons, he was not the originator of the term hot dog; the term, which dates to 1893, is simply an extension of the older use of "dog" to mean a sausage, with "hot" describing its temperature and sometimes spicy content. Hot dog was first a U.S. slang term. Charles Feltman is arguably credited with inventing the hot dog at Coney Island in Brooklyn, New York, in 1867.

> **CONFUSABLE** HOT DOG/FRANKFURTER/WIENER. Frankfurters and wieners become hot dogs when put on a bun.

> **HINT** Even though hot dogs are processed foods, they are not safe to eat without cooking. The FDA has recently announced that a large percentage of hot dogs

have pathogenic bacteria in them, and they should be cooked first. If the liquid in a package of hot dogs is cloudy, throw them out.

HOTEL PAN, also called STEAM TABLE PAN, is a large rectangular stainless steel pan used to cook, store, and serve large quantities of food and designed to fit in steam tables, racks, and chafers. A hotel pan is similar to a large metal roasting pan. A full-size pan is 20 x 12 inches and the standard depth is 2 inches, but there are other sizes available as well.

HOTEL STEAK: see NEW YORK STEAK.

HOT FUDGE is warm, rich chocolate used as a filling or topping for cakes or a sauce on ice cream.

HOT POT or **HOTPOT** or FIREPOT is a British stew of meat (beef, lamb, fish) and sliced potatoes slow-cooked in a covered pot. The word also denotes a small heated pot of boiling water or broth used to cook pieces of food at the table in East Asian cuisine. Originally, the word was used for a type of hot punch.

HOT SAUCE is a general term for a variety of pungent peppery sauces or condiments, often tomato-based and flavored with cayenne or chiles.

HOT TODDY: see TODDY.

HOWARD JOHNSON'S 28 ORIGINAL ICE-CREAM FLAVORS

Howard Johnson's opened its 351st restaurant in 1952 and became the world's largest food chain at the time. The first Dunkin' Donuts and the first Howard Johnson's were both in Quincy, Massachusetts. The orange-roofed buildings were as identifiable as McDonald's arches today; the slogan "28 Flavors" as familiar as Baskin-Robbins's 31.

BANANA	COFFEE	PEANUT BRITTLE
BLACK RASPBERRY	FROZEN PUDDING	PECAN BRITTLE
BURGUNDY CHERRY	FRUIT SALAD	PEPPERMINT STICK
BUTTERCRUNCH	FUDGE RIPPLE	PINEAPPLE
BUTTER PECAN	LEMON STICK	PISTACHIO
BUTTERSCOTCH	MACAROON	STRAWBERRY
CARAMEL FUDGE	MAPLE WALNUT	STRAWBERRY RIPPLE
CHOCOLATE	MOCHA CHIP	VANILLA
CHOCOLATE CHIP	ORANGE PINEAPPLE	
COCONUT	PEACH	

HUCKLEBERRY is a blue-black fruit from a low-growing eastern North American shrub (genus *Gaylussacia*). It is related to the blueberry (but has larger seeds) and bilberry and was first a dialect name for the bilberry. It is sometimes used as a synonym for Blueberry, which is of the genus *Vaccinium*.

ICE

> **CONFUSABLE** HUCKLEBERRY/BLUEBERRY. Usually the distinction is that blueberries have numerous tiny unnoticeable seeds, while huckleberries have ten larger seeds (making them more difficult to eat). The huckleberry has a thicker skin and a flavor that is slightly less sweet and more astringent than the blueberry.

HUEVOS RANCHEROS (pronounced WAY-vohs rah-CHEH-rohs) is a Mexican/Latin American dish of fried, poached, or occasionally scrambled eggs served with tomato salsa or chili and tortillas, cheese, refried beans, and sour cream. The term is American Spanish and literally means "ranchers' eggs" or "country-style eggs."

HUMMUS (pronounced HUM-uhs) is a thick spread made from mashed chickpeas, tahini, lemon juice, sesame or olive oil, and garlic; it is often served as a dip or filling for pita. Hummus is from the Turkish *humus*, "mashed chickpeas," and originated in the Middle East, entering English around 1955.

HUNDREDS and **THOUSANDS**: see Nonpareil.

HUSH PUPPY or **HUSHPUPPY**, also known as Corn dodger, is a small deep-fried ball of unsweetened cornmeal dough, sometimes flavored with scallions. This southern U.S. creation may have been so named because such cakes were fed to dogs to keep them from begging while food was being cooked.

HUSK is the outer cellulose covering of various seeds/nuts, fruits, and grains, such as barley, corn, filberts, and wheat.

HUSK TOMATO: see Ground cherry and Tomatillo.

ICE is frozen water and also a frozen dessert of water with fruit juice or flavoring, egg white, and sugar. American colonists farmed ice during the winter by cutting it from ponds, lakes, and rivers and then storing it in caves and underground cellars to last throughout the summer. In the late 1790s and early 1800s, ice became a commodity and the shipping and selling of ice began in earnest. By the 1850s, ice was inexpensive enough to make its way to the middle class of America, with ice wagons making daily deliveries to homes. During this time, thousands of Americans made their living in the ice business. Ice companies began to fade from the landscape in the mid-1910s. Electricity became available to more people in the 1930s, so that by the end of World War II, most Americans had refrigerators and freezers in their homes and did not need to have ice delivered anymore. The frozen dessert called ice is a mixture of ice and liquid, similar to sorbet. The liquid can be fruit juice, herbal infusion, coffee, or wine—but not milk or cream. However, in the United Kingdom, ice can refer to ice cream or water ice. Iced means chilled with ice, supplied with ice, or put on ice, but can also refer to something with icing/frosting.

HINT Use cardboard milk cartons for the mold when making large ice cubes.

ICE BATH or COLD-WATER BATH is basically a mixture of ice and water
used to chill a food or beverage rapidly. A technique in which food is immersed in cold water or ice water to immediately arrest a cooking process is called SHOCKING). The simplest cold-water bath is to pour cold water on foods like pasta or green beans while they are in a colander. This method can be used to minimize the cooking of food to retain a certain texture or firmness.

HINT For an ice bath, fill your sink (or a large bowl) with ice and cold water, and place a container of food in the ice bath. The container should be level with the ice. Stir the food every 10–15 minutes to distribute the heat to the cold areas so the food cools down evenly. As the ice melts, drain the water a little bit and add more ice. Monitor the food with a thermometer. Once your food has reached 40°F, it is safe to put it in the refrigerator or freezer.

ICEBERG LETTUCE is a round, tight, cabbagelike head of lettuce with crisp,
light green leaves. Iceberg lettuce got its name from the California growers who started shipping it covered with heaps of crushed ice in the 1920s; it had previously been called crisphead lettuce. Iceberg lettuce's leaves don't hold dressing well. It is the lowest in nutritive value of all lettuces and is low in vitamins A and C. While it is the least expensive type of lettuce, it also has the least flavor.

HINT Rap a head of iceberg lettuce on a counter to loosen the core, pull out the core, then fill the hole with water to rinse, separating the leaves. Iceberg lettuce keeps for weeks in the refrigerator. Wrap fresh, unwashed leaves in plastic warp and store in the refrigerator for a few days if necessary. Cooler temperature will keep lettuce fresh longer.

ICEBOX COOKIE, also called REFRIGERATOR COOKIE, is a type of cookie made by
forming and chilling dough, and then slicing if for baking.

HINT The dough for icebox cookies is usually formed into a log; wrapped in plastic wrap, parchment paper, or wax paper; and chilled. After it is chilled, the dough can be easily sliced into rounds and placed on a baking sheet and baked.

The freezing or cooling makes the dough stiffer, and ideally suited to slicing into thin rounds for baking. Icebox cookie dough can last a couple of months in the freezer when properly wrapped. Before freezing icebox cookie dough, wrap and seal it twice to prevent freezer burn and to keep the dough from absorbing any odd odors.

ICE CREAM is basically a frozen dessert containing cream or butterfat, egg yolks, sugar, and flavorings such as chocolate, nuts, and fruit. It has a minimum of 10% milk fat. Ice cream is an alteration of iced cream, meaning cream cooled by means of ice, but the *d* was dropped around 1744; ice cream is reputed to have been made in China as long ago as 3000 BC, but did not arrive in Europe (via Italy) until the thirteenth century. Premium ice cream is made with fresh cream, eggs, natural flavors, and little air. It and gelato require slightly lower serving temperatures, and should be served firm but not hard. The stemmed, wide-bowled dish used to serve ice-cream sundaes is called a coupe.

HINTS Homemade ice cream can be served when made, or frozen for 3 hours so it is the consistency of store-bought ice cream.

Ice cream in a partially empty container should be covered with plastic wrap pushed down onto its surface, and returned to the freezer. Avoid repeated softening and refreezing of ice cream. Ideally, ice cream should be stored in a freezer unit rather than in the freezer section of a refrigerator, because the freezer section in a refrigerator does not get as cold and does not maintain a consistent temperature. But if a freezer unit is not available, store ice cream in the main part of the freezer, not in the door, which is subject to greater fluctuations of temperature. The colder the temperature, the faster the ice cream will freeze. The best storage temperature range is −5°F–0°F, at which ice cream will hold its shape. The ideal serving range is 6°F–10°F.

ICE-CREAM MAKER is a manual or electric machine used to make small quantities of ice cream. The machine freezes the mixture, and must simultaneously stir or churn it to prevent the formation of ice crystals and aerate it to produce smooth and creamy ice cream.

HINTS After making ice cream in an ice-cream maker, allow it to freeze overnight in the freezer to improve taste and texture.

Generally speaking, you can store homemade ice cream for up to one month. Store in a container with a tightly sealed cover, and be sure there is at least ½ inch of headspace in the container to allow for expansion. Ice cream that has been stored needs to be tempered before it is served: after removing it from the freezer, leave it to slowly and gently soften at room temperature (usually this takes up to 20 minutes), or in the refrigerator if the room is warm. Be careful not to temper it too fast, though, or it will spoil the texture of the ice cream.

ICE-CREAM SODA, also called SODA, is a dessert/beverage of ice cream in any kind of soda or soda water, sometimes with the addition of a flavored syrup. This concoction dates to around 1886. The original ice-cream sodas did not contain ice cream. Ice cream was not added until around the early to mid 1870s, but had become hugely popular by the 1890s.

ICED: see GLACÉ.

ICED COFFEE or **ICE COFFEE** is strong coffee served over ice, often sweetened and sometimes with cream or flavoring.

ICED TEA or **ICE TEA** is strong tea served over ice as a beverage, often sweetened and with lemon. Iced tea is actually the correct spelling.

> **HINT** Fermented black teas, such as Darjeeling, Earl Grey, and English breakfast, are best for iced tea. Tea has to be brewed to a stronger level for iced tea than for hot tea.

ICE MILK is a sweet frozen dessert made like ice cream but with skim milk, so it contains less milk fat and milk solids. The result is a lower calorie count and a lighter, less creamy texture. Ice milk is around 3%–6% butterfat, 11%–14% nonfat milk solids, and 12%–15% sugar.

ICING, also called FROSTING, is a flavored sugar topping used to coat, fill, and decorate cakes, cookies, and other baked goods. It variously includes sugar, butter, flavoring, milk, water or other liquids, and egg whites. The main requirement is for icing to be thick enough to adhere to the item being coated, yet soft enough to spread easily; it is cooked or uncooked and can range from thick to thin.

> **CONFUSABLE** ICING/FROSTING. Frosting is thick and gooey with a cream or butter base. Icing may be thinner, often with just a sugar base, and slightly shinier. Frosting goes on cakes; icing goes on pastry or on cakes.

ICING SUGAR is the British term for CONFECTIONERS' SUGAR or POWDERED SUGAR.

IDAHO POTATO, also called BAKING POTATO or RUSSET POTATO, is a variety of russet potato, a long ovoid potato with thick brown skin. It is high in starch and low in moisture, so it bakes well and makes light, fluffy mashed potatoes. Idaho potatoes don't hold their shape after cooking, so they are not recommended for potato salads or scalloped potatoes.

> **HINTS** Small Idaho potatoes are best for use in salads, while medium-sized Idaho potatoes are quite versatile and can be baked, mashed, or fried. Large ones are ideal for French fries or baked potatoes.

⬛ The best way to open a baked Idaho potato is not to use a knife, which flattens the surface and alters the normal fluffy texture. Instead, pierce the potato with a fork, once lengthwise and once crosswise. Press the potato at both ends and it will "blossom."

⬛ Store Idaho potatoes in a cool, dark, well-ventilated place. A cellar is ideal, but any place where they won't be exposed to excessive heat or light will help prevent spoiling. It is best not to wash potatoes before storing. They will keep for about a week at room temperature and for several weeks at 45°F–50°F. However, refrigerator temperatures are too low, which converts the potato's starch into sugar, resulting in a sweet taste. The extra sugar also causes potatoes to darken prematurely while frying. (This process can sometimes be reversed by storing the potatoes at room temperature for seven to ten days.) If potatoes have green patches, cut them off, as these spots have been exposed too long to direct lighting and will have a faintly bitter taste. The rest of the potato will taste fine.

IMMERSE is to plunge, drop, or dip into, or as if into, a liquid, especially to cover completely.

IMMERSION BLENDER, also called HAND BLENDER, STICK BLENDER, or WAND BLENDER, is a long, narrow kitchen appliance that has a rotary blade at one end to blend ingredients or purée food in the container in which the food is being prepared. The immersion blender was invented in 1950 and is a good option for small tasks that do not require the heavy-duty capabilities of a food processor. It is built for the light- to medium-duty blending that is often required during the preparation of foods. Although immersion blenders take up less space in a kitchen and are easily portable, jobs with large batches of ingredients require a full-size food processor or stand mixer.

HINTS Use caution when blending any hot liquid. While immersion blenders are perfect for achieving a smooth consistency in soups, they can splatter and burn if you use them improperly. Don't turn on the blender attachment until the tool is submerged in the liquid, as a splatter may result. If your immersion blender has variable speeds, always begin at low speed, gradually increasing to high.

⬛ To clean an immersion blender, unplug it and hold the blade portion under hot running water; use a little soap if the surface is oily. Never submerge an immersion blender.

INDIAN FIG: see PRICKLY PEAR.

INDIAN PUDDING: see HASTY PUDDING.

INDUCTION COOKING is a method in which cookware is heated with electromagnetic energy, either by a special stove coil or through the use of specially designed cookware that uses an alternating magnetic field to generate heat rapidly. Induction cooking does not involve generating heat that is then transferred to the cooking vessel; instead, it makes the cooking vessel itself the original generator of the cooking heat.

INFUSE means to steep something, such as tea, herbs, or fruit, in liquid to extract the flavor. An infusion is a liquid that is made by infusing something like tea. Sauces that have been variously flavored, as with herbs, are also called infusions.

INGREDIENT denotes any food, herb, spice, or other substance that is an element in a cooking mixture or dish.

INSALATA (pronounced ihn-sah-LAH-tah) is Italian for "salad." Insalata verde is green salad or mixed green salad; insalata mista is mixed salad.

INSTANT is any foodstuff or beverage that is quick and easy to prepare; it is often premixed, precooked, or powdered. Examples are instant cocoa, instant coffee, and instant rice.

IODIZED SALT is common table salt with sodium or potassium iodide added for nutritional reasons. In regions where natural levels of iodine in the soil are low and the iodine is not taken up by vegetables, iodine added to salt provides the small but essential amount needed by humans.

> **HINT** The shelf life of iodized salt is about five years. The salt itself does not expire, but added ingredients such as iodine may reduce the shelf life. Iodized salt can yellow over time, but it is still good. Salt might cake under extreme humidity if there isn't an anticaking ingredient already in the salt. To avoid caking, store salt in an airtight plastic container or a zip-lock bag to prevent it from absorbing the moisture from the air. If caking has already happened, just dry the salt in the oven at 150°F for about an hour and break it up. It will still be perfectly usable.

IRISH COFFEE is hot coffee with sugar, Irish whiskey, and whipped cream. Irish coffee is usually served in a tall glass with a handle. The drink dates to 1950.

> **HINTS** When you make Irish coffee, it is always a good idea to heat the tall glass before adding ingredients to it, so it stays warm longer. You can run the glass under hot or warm water to warm it. Leave the hot water in the glass while you are making the coffee and preparing the cream. The thick mug-type glass is usually made of tempered glass, so it will not crack when you use it for

hot liquids. If you are using a stemmed glass, you need to be more careful so that it doesn't shatter from the hot water—use water with a lower temperature.

❚ Always add sugar to Irish coffee, even if you normally do not add sugar to your regular coffee. The sugar actually helps the cream to float above the coffee. The cream is added last and the drink is not stirred, because the coffee is drunk through the cream. You must pour heavy cream over the back of a spoon so that about ½ inch of cream floats on top of the coffee.

IRISH MOSS: see CARRAGEEN.

IRISH OATS are whole-grain groats that have been cut into only two or three pieces by steel rather than being rolled. They are also known as STEEL-CUT OATS, COARSE-CUT OATS, and PINHEAD OATS.

IRISH SODA BREAD, also called SODA BREAD, is a round loaf made from flour and whey or buttermilk, with sodium bicarbonate (soda) and acid in place of yeast, and often containing caraway seeds and raisins. It is traditionally served freshly baked and still warm. Usually, before baking, a cross is slashed in the top of the loaf. The purpose of the cross, legend says, is to scare away the devil. Placing a cross in the top of the loaf also helps with the cooking of the bread by allowing air circulation, which helps the bread rise.

IRISH STEW is a concoction of lamb or mutton with alternate layers of sliced potatoes and onions, covered with water and boiled or baked. The term dates to 1814.

> **HINT** Irish stew is best made the day before it is eaten, to allow the flavors to blend. If you want the lamb or mutton to be even more flavorful, season it with salt and brown it in oil before covering it with flour. Sauté the meat with some of the vegetables very briefly, then add some stout to the mix. This will help to tenderize the meat and bring out more of its natural flavor before it is immersed in the stew pot.

IRRADIATION is the application of ionizing radiation (gamma rays) for the sterilization or preservation of food. Irradiation improves the keeping quality of some foods, such as meats, making it possible to keep them longer and in better condition. Food is irradiated to provide the same benefits as when it is processed by heat, refrigeration, or freezing or treated with chemicals to destroy insects, fungi, or bacteria that cause food to spoil or cause human disease. Irradiation is an FDA-approved process. All irradiated foods must bear an international symbol, a plant within a broken circle. The only exceptions to this rule are irradiated foods, such as spices and herbs, that are used as an ingredient in other food products. Foods currently approved by the FDA for irradiation treatment are fruits, vegetables, dried spices, herbs, seasonings, teas, pork, white potatoes, wheat, and wheat flours.

ISOGLUCOSE: see HIGH-FRUCTOSE CORN SYRUP.

ITALIAN BREAD is a crusty yeast-raised bread made without shortening and usually baked in long, thick loaves with tapered ends, though sometimes the loaves are oblong or oval.

> **CONFUSABLE** ITALIAN BREAD/FRENCH BREAD. French bread is usually baked in long, thin loaves (baguettes), while Italian bread is baked in wider and sometimes shorter loaves.

> **HINT** Italian bread is best eaten the day it is baked. However, there are some ways to keep it fresh for one to two days. Store crispy-crusted Italian bread in paper. Keep it in a cool, dry place, such as a bread box. Do not store Italian bread in the refrigerator. This will dry it out and it will become stale faster. Italian bread can be freshened by quickly dipping it in cold water, draining it, and heating it in the oven.

ITALIAN BROWN MUSHROOM or **ITALIAN MUSHROOM**: see CREMINI.

ITALIAN DRESSING is an oil and vinegar concoction that is flavored, especially with garlic, oregano, basil, fennel, dill, and sometimes red pepper flakes. It dates to around 1900. American-style Italian dressing is unknown in Italy, where salad is normally dressed at the table with olive oil, vinegar, salt, and sometimes black pepper, and not with a premixed vinaigrette.

ITALIAN CRESS: see ARUGULA.

ITALIAN SANDWICH: see GRINDER.

ITALIAN SAUSAGE is a type of coarse pork sausage seasoned with garlic, fennel seed, and sometimes anise seed and made two ways: hot (with chiles) or sweet (without chiles).

> **HINT** Put Italian sausage in the refrigerator as soon as you get home from the store or after preparing your own. Use fresh sausage within two days of preparing or purchasing. If you are not going to cook your sausage immediately, it can be kept frozen in a zip-lock freezer bag or vacuum seal bag. Once you have cooked your sausage, eat it or freeze it within four days. Italian sausage must be well cooked before serving.

ITALIAN SCAMPI: see PRAWN.

JACK CHEESE or MONTEREY JACK is a mild, moist Cheddar made from whole, skimmed, or partially skimmed milk. Some types of jack cheese are aged, while others are not. Aged versions of jack cheese tend to take on a deeper yellow shade and develop a sharper taste. Versions that are not aged tend to be pale in color and retain a lighter taste.

JACKFRUIT is a very large East Indian fruit resembling breadfruit with edible pulp and seeds. One fruit can weigh up to one hundred pounds. The word is from the Portuguese *jaca*. Archaeological findings in India have revealed that jackfruit was cultivated in India three thousand to six thousand years ago. The flesh of the jackfruit is starchy and fibrous. Varieties of jackfruit are distinguished according to the characteristics of their flesh: *jaca-dura*, or "hard" variety, has firm flesh and the largest fruits; *jaca-mole*, or "soft" variety, bears smaller fruits with softer and sweeter flesh; and *jaca-manteiga*, or "butter" variety, bears sweet fruits whose flesh has a consistency intermediate between the hard and soft varieties.

JAGGING WHEEL: see PASTRY WHEEL.

JALAPEÑO or **JALAPEÑO PEPPER** is a plant bearing very hot and finely tapering long peppers, picked when green and sometimes orange-red; jalapeño gets its name from Jalapa, Mexico. The jalapeño is important in Mexican and southwestern U.S. cuisine. The term, pronounced hah-luh-PEYN-yoh, entered had English by 1949. Jalapeños are smooth and green or orange-red (scarlet red when ripe), hot to very hot (2,500–8,000 Scoville units), and easily seeded. They are available fresh and canned; in their dried or smoked form, jalapeños are known as CHIPOTLE.

> **HINT** Handling fresh jalapeños may cause mild skin irritation in some individuals. Some people choose to wear latex or vinyl gloves while cutting, skinning, or seeding jalapeños. When you prepare jalapeños, your hands should not come in contact with your eyes.

JAM is a spread or conserve made from fruit pulp boiled with sugar. The word was in English by the 1730s and is possibly derived from the word jam's meaning of "to bruise or crush by pressure."

> **CONFUSABLE** JAM/JELLY/PRESERVES/MARMALADE. Jam is a thick mixture made from fruit pulp and sugar, jelly is made from fruit juice boiled with sugar, preserves are fruit preserved whole or in large pieces and cooked with sugar, and marmalade is boiled fruit pulp, sugar, and fruit rinds. Jams contain the edible portion of the fruit in its entirety, and jellies have been strained to a smooth consistency. A hydrometer helps ensure proper consistency in jams and jellies.

JAMAICA PEPPER: see ALLSPICE.

JAMBALAYA (pronounced juhm-buh-LAHY-uh) is a spicy Creole dish of rice cooked with shrimp or other shellfish, oysters, ham, sausage, chicken, tomatoes, peppers, onions, celery, spices, and herbs. The word is from Louisiana French, from the Provençal *jambalaia*, "stewed mixture of rice and fowl," and the word's first printed appearance was in a Provençal poem published in 1837. Jambalaya is traditionally made in three parts: meats and vegetables, stock, then rice. The two main styles are called Creole jambalaya and Cajun jambalaya.

JAMBERRY: see TOMATILLO.

JAPANESE HORSERADISH: see WASABI.

JAPANESE KING CRAB: see KING CRAB.

JAPANESE MEDLAR: see LOQUAT.

JAPANESE RADISH: see DAIKON.

JARDINIÈRE is diced mixed vegetables stewed in a sauce or glaze with savory herbs, and used for garnishing meat or poultry or served as a soup. It is pronounced jahr-dn-EER and is a French term literally meaning "female gardener."

JARLSBERG or **JARLSBERG CHEESE** (pronounced YAHRLZ-burg) is a pale yellow, hard Norwegian cow's milk cheese with large irregular holes. The flavor is mild, buttery, nutty, and slightly sweet. The cheese is related to Emmental and other "Swiss" cheeses and melts well, so it is used for fondues, quiches, and sandwiches. In the 1830s Swiss cheese makers came to Norway to show Norwegian dairies how to make their classically nutty, sweet, holed cheeses. The Swiss-style cheese became very popular and was produced in large volume for several years before disappearing from the market altogether. In the 1950s scientists at the Agricultural University of Norway became curious about the cheese and attempted to recreate it, releasing Jarlsberg in 1956 and exporting the cheese in 1961. The cheese is named for the county in Norway where it was originally made in the 1830s. Jarlsberg was developed scientifically in a laboratory and is still made in a carefully controlled lab environment from a pooled milk supply in Norway. It is made from pasteurized milk, which is introduced to rennet and special cultures before being cut into curds and whey. The curds are pressed into cheese forms, salted, and allowed to age from one to fifteen months.

JASMINE RICE is an aromatic long-grain rice from Thailand with a nutty aroma. Jasmine rice is often compared to Indian basmati rice, another long-grain rice variety. However, basmati is aged before being sold, and has a different flavor. Both rice varieties tend to be less sticky than other forms of rice.

> **HINTS** Like many other kinds of rice, jasmine rice should be used within six months of purchase for optimal flavor and freshness.

> ▌ The trick to cooking jasmine rice well is using minimal water, so that the rice is steamed rather than boiled. Thai cooks actually wrap bundles of rinsed rice grains in muslin and suspend them in a steamer so that the rice cooks by steaming and never touches the water at all. Jasmine rice needs to be rinsed before cooking. To cook the rice by boiling, add the rice and water to the pot together. Keep the lid on the pot until the water comes to a boil, then remove and lower the temperature to a simmer until the rice is cooked all the way through. If the rice was presoaked, this will take about 10 minutes; if not, it will take around 20 minutes. When the rice is done, gently fluff it with a fork, cover, and let it rest for another 5 minutes before serving.

JASMINE TEA is black tea scented with jasmine blossoms.

JAVA was once the world's main producer of coffee beans, so coffee acquired the nickname of java.

JAVA PEPPER: see CUBEB.

JELLY is a fruit preserve that is made by boiling fruit juice, sugar, and sometimes pectin as the gelling agent and cooling until the mixture has a semisolid, smooth consistency. Jelly is a soft, resilient, partially transparent gelatinous food. The word jelly is based on words meaning freeze or frost, presumably because of its firm shape. Jelly has another meaning of a thickened meat stock made from gelatin boiled with meat stock. In the United States and Canada, the term jelly refers to a clear fruit spread made with pectin. In British English, these products are commonly referred to by the terms fruit spread or preserves, although jelly is also used in some instances, for example, mint jelly.

> **HINT** Jellies can be used as a glaze by melting them a little and adding liqueur if desired.

JELLY BEAN is a small bean-shaped fruit candy with a hard coating and a soft jelly center.

JELLY BELLY FLAVORS

Back in 1976, a Los Angeles candy distributor had an idea for a jelly bean made with natural flavorings. So he called up the candy makers at Jelly Belly (formerly known as the Herman Goelitz Candy Company), who had a reputation for making the very best candies. The candy

(continued)

makers cooked up a recipe for a new kind of jelly bean—intensely flavored throughout, with natural ingredients for flavoring whenever possible. In 1976 the first eight Jelly Belly flavors were born: cream soda, grape, green apple, lemon, licorice, root beer, tangerine, and very cherry. This is a list of most of the flavors offered now.

A&W CREAM SODA	GRAPE JELLY	PIÑA COLADA
A&W ROOT BEER	GREEN APPLE	PINK GRAPEFRUIT
BLUEBERRY	HAWAIIAN PUNCH	RASPBERRY
BUBBLE GUM	ISLAND PUNCH	ROOT BEER
BUTTERED POPCORN	JALAPEÑO	SIZZLING CINNAMON
CANTALOUPE	JUICY PEAR	STRAWBERRY CHEESECAKE
CAPPUCCINO	LEMON	STRAWBERRY DAIQUIRI
CHAMPAGNE PUNCH	LEMON-LIME	TANGERINE
CHOCOLATE PUDDING	LICORICE	TOASTED MARSHMALLOW
CINNAMON	MARGARITA	TOP BANANA
COCONUT	ORANGE JUICE	TUTTI-FRUTTI
COTTON CANDY	ORANGE SHERBET	VERY CHERRY
CREAM SODA	PEACH	WATERMELON
CRUSHED PINEAPPLE	PEANUT BUTTER	
GRAPE	PEPPERMINT STICK	

JELLY ROLL is a long cylindrical dessert made by rolling up a thin rectangle of light sponge cake spread with fruit jelly. Before jelly rolls got their name they were called jelly cakes, and in England they are called Swiss rolls. Known since the mid-nineteenth century, the jelly roll is a traditional German, Hungarian, and Austrian cake. A JELLY ROLL PAN is a baking sheet with one-inch-deep sides for making this cake.

JELLY ROLL PAN is a baking sheet with one-inch-deep sides for making a jelly roll.

JERKED BEEF: see BEEF JERKY.

JERKY or **JERKED MEAT** is an Americanism for meat, especially beef, that has been sliced into strips and dried. The term dates to around 1890 and is from the Spanish *charqui*, from the Quechua *c'arqui/ch'arki*.

JERUSALEM ARTICHOKE, also called SUNCHOKE, is not from Jerusalem nor is it an artichoke; it is a species of sunflower with an edible tuber from North America. The word comes from the Italian *girasole articiocco*, "sunflower artichoke," and was mistranslated into English as Jerusalem artichoke, partly because its flavor resembles that of a globe artichoke. It is eaten raw or boiled, or sliced thin and fried like potato chips. Jerusalem artichokes are high in iron content. Like beans, they have indigestible carbohydrates that can cause flatulence.

> **HINTS** Buy small, firm, smooth Jerusalem artichokes. Avoid those with sprouts or a green tinge. They will keep at room temperature for four days, or in paper towels covered with plastic wrap in the vegetable crisper of the refrigerator for up to two weeks.

> Jerusalem artichokes should be washed and scrubbed well. They will darken when exposed to air (or aluminum or cast iron), so sprinkle with lemon juice.

JICAMA, also called MEXICAN POTATO, MEXICAN TURNIP, or YAM BEAN, is a very firm, sweet, turnip-shaped root vegetable (*Pachyrhizus erosus*); it is brown on the outside with pearly white flesh. Jicama is used raw in salads and as crudités, or cooked in stews. It is pronounced HIC-uh-muh.

> **HINT** Choose firm, heavy jicama with thin, smooth skin. Uncut, it can be kept at room temperature for two to three days, or it can be kept, unwrapped, in the vegetable crisper of the refrigerator for three weeks. Wrap unused cut jicama in plastic wrap and refrigerate for up to one week. Cut pieces in water in the refrigerator can last for up to four days. Peel the skin off jicama before using; the flesh does not discolor.

JIMMIES: see SPRINKLES.

JOHANNISBERG RIESLING is a spicy white grape and the wine made from this grape. It gets its name from the castle and village on the Rhine in Germany where it was originally produced. It is considered the true Riesling. Riesling is an aromatic grape variety displaying flowery, almost perfumed, aromas as well as high acidity. It is used to make dry, semisweet, sweet, and sparkling white wines. Riesling wines are usually varietally pure and are seldom oaked.

JOHNNYCAKE, JOHNNY-CAKE, JONNYCAKE, or **JOURNEY CAKE** is corn bread usually fried or baked pancake-style on a griddle. The word was first recorded in 1739. It is a New England specialty, especially in Rhode Island, where it is celebrated by the Society for the Propagation of Johnny Cakes. The color of the cornmeal, the consistency of the batter, the size of the cake, and the cooking method can vary from region to region. Regional names are ASHCAKE, BATTER BREAD, BATTERCAKE, CORN CAKE, CORN PONE, HOECAKE, PONE, and SHAWNEE CAKE.

JORDAN ALMOND is a variety of large almond from Malaga. The Jordan almond is not related to Jordan but is from the Middle English *jardyne almaund*, "garden almond." The term also refers to a Jordan almond or other almond with a hard sugar coating.

JUICE is the liquid that can be extracted from fruits or vegetables, and also the liquid that comes from a piece of meat when it is roasted or otherwise cooked. The word is from the Latin *jus*, "broth/vegetable juice." Canned juices are usually enriched because the heat of processing destroys most of the naturally occurring vitamins.

> **HINT** Run a can of frozen juice concentrate under hot water to release it from the can. After adding water, you can use an immersion blender to blend the juice.

JUICE VARIETIES

APPLE JUICE	KIWI JUICE	PEAR JUICE
APRICOT JUICE	LEMON JUICE	PINEAPPLE JUICE
CARROT JUICE	LIME JUICE	PRUNE JUICE
CHERRY JUICE	LOGANBERRY JUICE	RASPBERRY JUICE
CRANBERRY JUICE	MANGO JUICE	STRAWBERRY JUICE
FRUIT JUICE	ORANGE JUICE	TOMATO JUICE
GRAPE JUICE	PAPAYA JUICE	VEGETABLE JUICE
GRAPEFRUIT JUICE	PEACH JUICE	WATERMELON JUICE

JUICER is an appliance or gadget for extracting juice from fruit and vegetables. Gadgets require hand or mechanical pressure, and appliances require electric power—but in each there is a conical ridged device that fits inside a cut half of a citrus fruit. Some larger models can make juice from larger vegetables. Varieties of juicer include the citrus juicer, juice press, mechanical citrus juicer, and reamer. The reamer is best for extracting the juice from a grapefruit.

JULEP, also called MINT JULEP, is a drink of bourbon, sugar, and mint over crushed ice. The word comes from French, ultimately from the Persian *gulab*, "rose water." The mint julep dates to around 1809 and is traditionally served in an iced silver or pewter mug at the running of the Kentucky Derby.

JULIENNE is an adjective for cut into very thin strips, like matchsticks, a verb for the act of creating them, and also is a noun for a soup made with vegetables cut this way. The word dates to 1841 is from a French word literally meaning "(soup made) in the manner of Julien," the proper name of an unknown cook.

> **HINT** Slice vegetables on the bias into ovals and then cut those into strips for julienne. This can be done with carrots, zucchini, and other cylindrical vegetables.

JUS or **AU JUS** is literally French for "with the juice" or "in broth" and should be pronounced ZHOO or oh-ZHOO. It is a sauce that consists primarily of the natural juices of the meat that are released when it is roasted.

KAFFIR LIME, also spelled/called KIEFFER LIME, LIMAU PURUT, or MAKRUD LIME, is the green fruit of an Asian citrus tree. It has wrinkly skin and aromatic leaves that are used in Thai and Indonesian cookery. The rind is used in curry paste, the leaves can be used fresh or dried, and the zest is also used.

KAISER PEAR: see BOSC PEAR.

KAISER ROLL, also called BULKIE ROLL, HARD ROLL, or VIENNA ROLL, is a large, rounded, crusty roll, usually formed by folding the corners of a square of dough toward the center and sometimes sprinkled with poppy seeds. It is often used for sandwiches. It was supposedly named for Emperor Franz Josef of Austria.

KALAMATA, also spelled CALAMATA, is a medium-sized, purplish black, almond-shaped olive with a fruity flavor and meaty texture. This type of olive is often split and cured in brine and packed in vinegar or olive oil. It is named for Kalamata, Greece, where the olives are grown.

KALE is a hardy cabbage with coarse, curly leaves; its name is a variant of cole, the archaic name. It is often dark green and has a mild cabbagelike flavor. Kale has an nutritional advantage over spinach because the human body absorbs only about 2% of the iron in spinach. Kale does not interfere with the body's absorption, so while kale has less iron, more is absorbed. It also has more than twice the vitamin C of spinach.

> **HINT** Select kale with leaves that are free of blemishes, yellow spots, and insect holes, and avoid heads with wilted or dried leaves. Kale keeps well in a plastic bag in the vegetable crisper of the refrigerator for up to five days. The longer it is stored, the more bitter its flavor becomes. Do not wash kale before storing because exposure to water encourages spoilage. Remove as much of the air from the bag as possible.

KANSAS CITY STRIP STEAK: see DELMONICO STEAK.

KEBAB, KEBOB, or **KABOB**, also called SHISH KEBAB, is a configuration of marinated cubes of meat cooked on a skewer, usually with vegetables. The word kebab dates to 1813 and shish kebab from 1914, from the Armenian *shish kabab*, from the Turkish *siskebap*, "skewered roast meat."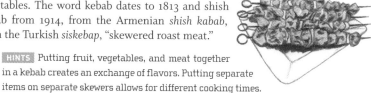

> **HINTS** Putting fruit, vegetables, and meat together in a kebab creates an exchange of flavors. Putting separate items on separate skewers allows for different cooking times.

> Coat skewers with cooking spray to prevent kebabs from sticking.

> Use a two-prong steel skewer with thin double blades to keep kebabs from spinning on the skewer.

KEDGEREE (pronounced kehj-uh-REE) is an Indian dish of fish, rice, lentils or other pulses, onions, and hard-cooked eggs, or a British dish of flaked smoked fish with hard-cooked eggs, rice, garam masala, and turmeric. It is from the Hindi *khichri*, from Sanskrit.

KEFIR, KEFYR, KEFIRS, KEEFIR, KEPHIR, or **KEWRA,** also called BÚLGAROS, MILKKEFIr, MUDU KEKIYA, or TALAI, is a creamy sour beverage of fermented cow's milk, usually containing a small amount of alcohol, originating in the Caucasus (Russia). It was first made from camel's milk and its taste and texture resemble liquid yogurt, and the grains look like cauliflower. The word kefir is purportedly derived from either the Turkish *keyif*, "joy/pleasure," or from the Persian *kef*, "foam," and *shir*, "milk."

KELP is a large brown seaweed occasionally used as food or a food ingredient. Today, seaweed is a staple in the diets of some people, as in Japan. Kombu and wakame are two popular types of kelp; kombu is used to make a broth, and wakame is used as an ingredient in soups and stir-fries. Sheets of wakame are used to prepare sushi. Powdered kelp can serve as a salt substitute, helping to flavor soups, salads, and tomato juice.

KETCHUP, also spelled CATCHUP or CATSUP, is a savory vinegar-and-tomato-based condiment. The word entered the English language at the end of the seventeenth century. The original spelling was catchup, with ketchup emerging around 1710, and catsup in the 1730s, possibly from some sort of erroneous or humorous association with cats supping. The spelling catsup was dropped by Del Monte in 1988 as they followed Heinz and Hunt's by using ketchup instead. The word is apparently originally from the Amoy dialect of Chinese *koe-chiap/ke-tsiap*, "brine of pickled fish or shellfish," which was borrowed into Malay as *kechap*, taken by the Dutch as *ketjap*, then adopted into English. In ancient times, tomatoes were an expensive rarity, and ketchups were vinegar-based sauces flavored with mushrooms, anchovies, onions, lemons, oysters, and pickled walnuts; the bonus was that these sauces kept for a long time. Some popular ketchups made from other ingredients include anchovy, banana, blueberry, celery, cranberry, cucumber, grape, kidney bean, lemon, lobster, mushroom, oyster, and walnut ketchup. Ketchup has been called a "perfect food" by some. It is inexpensive and is a condiment, not an ingredient, which means that it can be applied at the discretion of the food eater, not the food preparer. Elizabeth Rozin, a food theorist, said, "Ketchup may well be the only true culinary expression of the melting pot, and . . . its special and unprecedented ability to provide something for everyone makes it the Esperanto of cuisine."

HINTS Unopened bottles of ketchup can be stored for one year on a cool, dry, dark shelf. Tightly covered opened bottles will last a month in a cool, dry, dark place.

To release ketchup faster from the Heinz 57 glass bottle, apply a firm tap to the sweet spot on the neck of the bottle—the "57."

KETJAP IKAN: see FISH SAUCE.

KETTLE is a (usually metal) lidded pot for stewing or boiling, or another word for TEAKETTLE, a portable kettle with a cover, spout, and handle, used for boiling water. Kettle came through Old English from the Latin *catillus*, "deep pan or dish for cooking."

KEY LIME is a small, aromatic yellow-green lime of southern Florida, taking its name from Key West. KEY LIME PIE is made from thickened, sweetened condensed milk and eggs flavored with the juice of key limes, and served in a pastry shell, often with a meringue topping.

KIBBEH, KIBBE, or **KIBBI** is a Middle Eastern dish made of ground/chopped lamb or beef, bulgur, onions, and seasonings. It has many variations and is eaten raw, fried, or grilled. The word is from the Arabic kibbe, "ball/lump."

KIDNEY BEAN is the large, edible, strong-flavored, firm, reddish brown bean of the common bean plant. Kidney beans are popularly used in chili, refried beans, and marinated salads. White kidney beans are called CANNELLINI BEANS.

KIEFFER LIME: see KAFFIR LIME.

KIELBASA, also called POLISH SAUSAGE, is a highly seasoned (especially with garlic) pork or beef sausage, often smoked. It is mainly sold precooked in link form. Kielbasa is Polish for "sausage."

KILTED SAUSAGES: see PIGS IN BLANKETS.

KIMCHI or **KIMCHEE** is a vegetable pickle made of cabbage or white radish and seasoned with chiles, garlic, and ginger. Kimchi is salted, seasoned, and stored in sealed containers to undergo lactic acid fermentation. It is the national dish of Korea and references to kimchi can be found as early as three thousand years ago. Kimchi varieties include *baechu* (also known as Chinese cabbage); *ggakdugi*, made with cubed radishes; *pa-kimchi*, made with scallions; and *chonggak-kimchi* and *oiso-bagi*, made with cucumbers and hot and spicy seasoning.

HINT Kimchi will keep indefinitely in the refrigerator.

KING CRAB, also called ALASKA CRAB, ALASKAN KING CRAB, JAPANESE KING CRAB, and STONE CRAB, is a large edible arthropod of northern Pacific waters. It often weighs ten to fifteen pounds, and has delicately flavored white meat with red edges.

KING PINE: see PINEAPPLE.

KIPPER is salted, dried, and smoked herring or salmon.

KIR is an alcoholic beverage made of cassis and dry white wine, created in the twentieth century and named for Canon Félix Kir (1876–1968), mayor of Dijon, France. When it is made with Champagne instead of wine, it is called a Kir royale.

KITCHEN SHEARS or **KITCHEN SCISSORS** are scissors with the fulcrum located farther from the handles to provide more leverage and thus more cutting power; they are used for cutting items like poultry and other types of meat.

KIWI is the fruit of the kiwi plant, which has a greenish brown, fuzzy skin and sweet green pulp. The kiwi originated in China, was renamed CHINESE GOOSE-BERRY when exported to New Zealand, and was renamed for the New Zealand bird kiwi when imported to the United States.

> **HINTS** Choose heavy, unbruised kiwis that give to gentle pressure. Leave at room temperature until they soften. You can speed ripening by placing them in a paper bag with an apple or banana. Ripe kiwis can be kept in a plastic bag in the refrigerator for up to one week.

> ⫾ Peel off the fuzzy skin of a kiwi, or cut it in half and scoop out the flesh.

KNEAD (KNEADING) is to work dough into a uniform mass with the hands by pushing, stretching, and folding it. During kneading, the gluten in flour inter-locks to create a network that captures gases and stretches as the bread rises. The word is from the Old English *cnedan*, "to knead," from the Proto-Germanic *knedanan*.

> **HINTS** Kneading on a wooden surface helps the dough retain its warmth, which is important for its texture. A dough scraper is handy for moist dough. When kneading a sticky dough, coat your hands or the mixer's kneading attachment with oil. If you add too much flour when kneading, add warm water and continue kneading. Discard dry bits of flour and don't let them get back into the dough.

> ⫾ A test for kneading is to push your fingertips into the dough. If the indentations spring back, the dough is well kneaded.

KNIFE is a tool with a sharp blade and a handle used for cutting, slicing, or spreading. It was cnif in Old English and knif in Middle English, meaning "to pinch / to press together," from Germanic. The knife is the earliest-known implement, used as an eating utensil before it was a weapon. In prehistoric times knives were made of flint. Neolithic peoples used stone hammers to produce sharp-edged knives. Eventually, knives were created from metals and sharpened with whetstones. By the Middle Ages, the knife was used as a cutting implement, but the tip acted as a fork tine or was used to get salt from the salt cellar. The dinner knife originated in Italy in the sixteenth century. Table knives come in seven sizes; listed from largest to smallest, these are the dinner knife, steak knife, luncheon knife, fish knife, dessert knife, fruit knife, and butter spreader. Every knife has a tang (the end of the blade that extends into the handle) and a bolster (the thick band at the handle end).

KNIFE ESSENTIALS

■ A sharpening steel is the best tool for keeping knives sharp. Swipe each side of the cutting edge across and along the length of the steel, alternating sides and holding the blade at a fifteen-degree angle. A good kitchen knife will last a lifetime with proper maintenance. A good knife rarely needs sharpening if the blade is regularly maintained on a sharpening (or butcher's) steel. Dull knives are the most dangerous because people tend to be more careful with sharp knives. The duller the knife, the more apt it is to slip while cutting because it requires more downward pressure. Sharp knives are easier to work with and do the job quickly, making clean cuts and thin slices. Knives with serrated edges should be sharpened only by a professional.

■ A knife should be cleaned by wiping the handle and the blade with a soapy sponge or dishcloth. Rinse, and dry with a soft towel. Do not put a knife into a filled sink or full pot, as you might grab the sharp blade by mistake. Don't clean a knife in the dishwasher, as the blade can become nicked as it is jostled about, and the high heat can affect the tempering or split the handle. Do not soak a knife with a wooden handle. Store

knives in a knife block, not a drawer with other kitchen tools.

■ Always warn fellow cooks when carrying a knife. Always carry a knife with the pointed end down and the blade side away from you. Always place a knife on the work surface in such a way that the entire tool rests on the surface and no part extends beyond the edge; if it does, then it may be knocked off by someone passing by. Never place a knife where it can't be seen, such as in a pile with other utensils or in a sink covered with water. Always dry blades from the back spine to the cutting edge. When transferring a knife from one person to another, you should lay the knife on a counter so that the other person can pick it up.

■ The sharpness of a blade can be tested by holding a piece of paper in front of you and making a downward slice. The blade is sharp if the cut is smooth and the paper doesn't crumble.

■ When buying a kitchen knife, you should look for these features: a carbon steel or stainless blade; a high-quality manufacturer; a tang (the part of the metal enclosed in the handle) running the full length of the handle and well secured by at least three rivets or some other method; a handle that is

(continued)

easy to grasp and feels comfortable in your hand. Try the grip to see how it fits your hand. It should feel like an extension of your hand. Make sure the bulge in the handle put there by the manufacturer fits the way you like to hold the knife. The handle should be a poor conductor of heat, such as hardwood or modern plastic, but be careful of plastic hilts, as they may be made of cheap material that won't hold up.

■ Hold a kitchen knife with three fingers around the handle, and the thumb and forefinger pinching the blade. Hold the food to be cut with your fingers curled under, away from the blade. The position of your non-knife-holding hand is called the claw.

■ You can test the balance of a knife by pinching the blade at its base (next to the handle) and lifting it up. It should be balanced and not tilt up or down.

■ Make a knife-honing guide by folding a piece of paper to have a 20-degree angle. Start with a 90-degree angle, fold in half for 45 degrees, and then in half one more time for nearly 20 degrees. Use the paper as a guide when drawing a knife across a steel for sharpening.

■ Get a top-quality chef's knife, paring knife, and serrated knife.

■ With a paring knife you can peel toward you carefully, using your thumb to counter the pressure of the knife.

■ Use the dull side of a knife blade to move diced/sliced/chopped foods from the cutting board.

■ The many kinds of cutlery all have distinctive uses, the blade being the major determining factor. Cost is determined by the quality of the blade steel, workmanship, material used for the handle, and ornamentation.

KNISH is a small round or square of thin dough stuffed with a filling (such as potato, cheese, or chopped meat) and baked, grilled, or fried. The word's origin is Polish/Ukrainian and Yiddish. The pronunciation is with a hard *k*: kuh-NISH.

KNOCKWURST or **KNACKWURST** is short, thick, highly seasoned sausage. The word is from the German *knack*, "to make a sudden cracking sound," and *wurst*, "sausage"—it literally means "sausage that makes a crackling noise," as that is the sound it makes when it is bitten into. The word first appeared in English in 1939.

KNUCKLE is the knee or hock joint and nearby parts, or the carpal or tarsal joint, of a quadruped (such as a pig), used as food. The word is a diminutive of the Germanic *knoke*, "bone."

KOBE BEEF is a superior and extremely tender grade of beef from a breed of Wagyu cattle raised in Kobe, Japan, which are massaged in sake and given beer. Kobe beef in the United States is "Kobe-style" beef, from domestically raised Wagyu crossbred with Angus cattle.

KOHLRABI, also called CABBAGE TURNIP or STEM CABBAGE, is the fleshy, pale green or purple, turnip-shaped edible stem of the kohlrabi plant. Kohlrabi is a German translation of the Italian *cavolo rapa*, "cabbage turnip."

HINTS If the kohlrabi leaves are still attached to the bulb, trim them and store separately. If the leaves are firm and green, they can be cooked but will need to be used within a couple of days. The bulbs should be stored, unwashed, in a sealed zip-lock bag for about one week in the refrigerator. Smaller kohlrabi are the sweetest and most tender. Bulbs much bigger than the size of a tennis ball won't be as tasty and often have a pithy flesh.

Young kohlrabi leaves may be cooked like other greens. The bulbs can be eaten raw in salads or can be cooked like a turnip. Very young, tender bulbs can be used without peeling, but larger ones should be peeled. The bulbs can be hollowed out and stuffed with a vegetable or meat filling. The peeled flesh can be sliced, diced, or grated and used in recipes calling for radishes. If adding kohlrabi to slaw, lightly salt the kohlrabi first, let it stand for several minutes, and squeeze it to remove any excess water before adding dressing. When steaming or boiling kohlrabi, peel after cooking.

KOLACKEI, KOLACH, KOLACHY, or **KOLACKY** (pronounced kuh-LAH-chee) is a sweet yeast bun, usually with a fruit, cheese, or poppy seed center or filling. The word is from the Czech *kolace*, "wheel-shaped cake." Originally a sweet dessert from central Europe, it has become popular in parts of the United States.

KONA COFFEE is the market name for a variety of coffee (*Coffea arabica*) cultivated on the slopes of Mount Hualalai and Mauna Loa in the North and South Kona Districts of the Big Island of Hawaii. This coffee is expensive and sought after. The coffee plant was first brought to Kona in 1829 from Brazilian cuttings.

KOSHER refers to a variety of foods that have been prepared, grown, killed, and processed in accordance with Jewish laws. Some of the common requirements include restrictions from eating grapes grown by non-Jewish grape producers, restrictions from eating specified animals or specified parts of certain animals; removing blood by draining away or broiling food from animals containing blood, such as meats; restrictions on eating poultry, wild birds, and mammals in combination with dairy foods; and restrictions on reusing utensils used to eat hot kosher foods to eat nonkosher foods. The letter "K" on packaged foods means the food is kosher. It stands for "kosher," indicating that the food was produced under the supervision of a rabbi. However, in most states the "K" logo is not protected by law, so there is no guarantee that the product's preparation really was supervised. The letters "KD" stand for "kosher dairy product." The letter "U" in a circle indicates that the food has been certified kosher by the Union of Orthodox Jewish Congregations, under supervision of an individual rabbi or a regional certifying agent.

KOSHER SALT, also called PICKLING SALT, is a pure refined coarse-grained salt with no additives, used especially to draw blood from meat to make it kosher.

HINT Chefs like kosher salt because it is easy to grab a pinch and doesn't dissolve on their fingers.

KOURABIEDES (pronounced koo-rah-bee-YEH-thess) is a Greek butter cookie made with or without almonds and coated in confectioners' sugar.

KRULLER: see CRULLER.

KUCHEN is a type of coffee cake made of sweet yeast dough with spices, and often containing raisins or other fruit or cheese and nuts. The word is German for "cake" and is pronounced KOO-khuhn.

KUGEL is a crusty, baked, pudding-like casserole made of potatoes or noodles, eggs, and seasonings. It is a Yiddish word meaning "ball." The dish is traditionally eaten by Jews on the Sabbath. There are savory versions with meat, vegetables, and other ingredients, and also a sweet version with raisins and spices.

KUGELHOPF is a sweetened light yeast bread made in the shape of an inverted flowerpot with a hole; it is filled with raisins, currants, and almonds and dusted with confectioners' sugar. The word is from the German *Gugelhopf*, from *Gugel*, "a hood with a liripipe and partial covering for the shoulders" (a garment worn in the Middle Ages), and *hopf*, "skip/jump," apparently from the cake's tendency to overflow the pan in the shape of this hood. The cake is traditionally baked in a special fluted kugelhopf ring mold.

KÜMMEL is a colorless liqueur flavored with cumin and caraway seeds, and it is also the name for Leyden cheese containing caraway seeds. The word is from the German *kümel*, "cumin seed," and it is pronounced KIHM-uhl or KOO-muhl.

KUMQUAT, also spelled CUMQUAT, is small, oval, orange citrus fruit with a sweet rind and very sour pulp. It is especially used for preserves and confections. Kumquat, from the Cantonese *kum kwat*, is from the Mandarin Chinese *jin ju*, "golden orange." There are two main species of kumquat: oval and round.

> **HINT** Choose kumquats that are firm and blemish free, with smooth skin. Kumquats are at their peak in the winter.

KUNG PAO is a Szechuan dish of chicken in a sauce of peanuts or cashews, chiles, and peppercorns. In Westernized versions, other ingredients may be added such as green bell peppers, celery, Chinese cabbage, water chestnuts, carrots, sherry or rice wine, hoisin sauce, and oyster sauce. It is named after a late Qing (Manchu) dynasty official whose title was Gong Bao. The original Chinese version of the dish includes Szechuan peppercorns as an important ingredient, but the Western version does not.

LACTO-VEGETARIAN and **LACTO-OVO VEGETARIAN**, also called OVO-LACTO VEGETARIAN, are types of vegetarians. A lacto-vegetarian is a person who eats vegetables, grains, fruit, nuts, and milk products, but not meat or eggs. A lacto-ovo vegeterian or ovo-lacto vegetarian is a person who eats vegetables, grains, fruit, nuts, milk, and eggs, but not meat.

LADLE is a large spoon- or scoop-shaped utensil with a long handle, used to stir and transfer liquids, such as sauces, soups, and stews. Specialty ladles include the Chinese ladle, with a wide, shallow cup for wok cooking; pierced ladle; sauce or gravy ladle, with spouts on one or both ends; and soup ladle, with a deep cup.

> **HINT** Certain batters are best scooped with a ladle, such as crêpes, which are often made with 2 ounces of batter.

LADYFINGER is a small, finger-shaped sponge cake. Ladyfingers may be individual accompaniments to foods like ice cream, or parts of a dessert like a charlotte. Some tiramisu recipes call for ladyfingers. The term dates to 1818.

LAGER is a general term for beer made with slow fermentation (six weeks to six months) and matured with refrigeration. It is generally a light-colored beer made with a low proportion of hops. Lager is German for "storehouse." First called lager beer, the brew was popularly called lager by 1855. Bottom-fermented lagers have their origins in continental Europe. Brewers in the Czech Republic used local soft waters to produce the famous pilsner beer, which became the standard for highly hopped, pale-colored, dry lagers. The darker lagers' color comes from highly roasted malt, and other characteristic flavors arise during the decoction mashing process

LAKE TROUT: see CHAR.

LAMB is a sheep less than a year old or the flesh of a young domestic sheep eaten as food. There are five USDA grades for lamb based on proportion of fat to lean: Prime, Choice, Good, Utility, and Cull.

LAMB ESSENTIALS

- Lamb sold for cooking is Prime or Choice in grade, and spring lamb is supposed to be less than a year old, with baby lamb only six to ten weeks old. Avoid lamb cuts with any yellowed fat. Rack of lamb should have pale, slender bones.

- Store fresh lamb in the refrigerator for two to three days, or in the freezer for four to six months, well sealed in a zip-lock freezer bag. Ground or cooked lamb can only be frozen for up to three months.

(continued)

■ Cut off all but ¼ inch of fat on a lamb roast. Check the internal temperature with an instant-read meat thermometer, but remember that the meat continues to cook as it rests outside the oven. So when the lamb is within 5°F–10°F of the finishing temperature, go ahead and remove it from the oven. Fully cooked lamb should have these approximate temperatures: 115°F–140°F (rare), 140°F–150°F (medium), 160°F (well done).

■ A lamb roast should be sliced across the grain because when cut with the grain, the meat is tougher and chewier.

■ Butterflying lamb cuts the cooking time by almost two-thirds. Lamb chops should be 1⅓–1½ inches thick so they don't curl or dry out.

■ For a lamb shoulder, it is best if the blade bone is loosened from the flesh before roasting so that when it is done, the bone can be easily removed.

■ Lamb is cooked at a higher temperature than other meats so that it roasts more quickly, for if it is roasted slowly, the meat can become mushy.

■ The most tender cut of lamb is the double loin (saddle).

■ A frenched rack of lamb has the rib bones exposed.

LAMB CUTS

Lamb is young sheep that is killed and falls into three categories: milk lamb (killed at 30–40 days old), agneau blanc or laiton (70–150 days old), or broutart (6–9 months old).

The primal cuts are breast/brisket, flank, foreshank, hindshank, leg, loin, neck, rib, shoulder, and sirloin. These are some common lamb cuts:

ARM CHOP

BLADE CHOP

BONELESS LEG

BONELESS LOIN

BONELESS SHOULDER CHOP

BONELESS SIRLOIN

BREAST OR BRISKET (fatty and flavorful; for braising; yields riblets; used for ground lamb)

BUTTERFLIED LEG

CROWN ROAST

CUSHION ROAST

DENVER RIBS

DOUBLE LOIN CHOP

FLANK (flavorful; used for ground lamb)

FORESHANK

FRENCH RIB CHOP

FRENCH-STYLE LEG

HALF SHANK

LEG (flavorful; used whole or cut for kebabs and stew)

LOIN (yields tenderloin, loin chops, and loin roasts)

LOIN ROAST

MEDALLION

NECK SLICES (flavorful but tough; used for ground lamb)

PATTIES

RACK FOR ONE

RACK ROAST

RIB (tender; yields chops, rack of lamb, and crown roast)

RIB CHOP

RIBLETS

ROAST

ROLLED SHOULDER

ROUND LEG STEAK

SADDLE (tender, well-marbled sirloin chops and steaks; cut into cubes for shish kebab)

SARATOGA CHOP

SHANK (flavorful but tough; for braising and simmering)

SHISH KEBAB CUBES

SHOULDER (flavorful; yields chops, cubes, and rolled roasts; used for ground meat)

SHOULDER BLADE CHOP

SIRLOIN CHOP

SIRLOIN ROAST

SIRLOIN SHANK HALF

SIRLOIN STEAK

SQUARE-CUT SHOULDER ROAST

STEW MEAT

LAMBRUSCO, literally Italian for "grape of the wild vine," is a semisweet or dry red wine, often sparkling. There are also white and rosé versions. The name, which has been used in English only since 1934, also pertains to the grape from which the wine is made.

LAMB'S LETTUCE or **LAMB'S TONGUE**: see CORN SALAD.

LANGOUSTINE or **LANGOSTINO**, also called NORWAY LOBSTER, is a large prawn (or small lobster) of the North Atlantic. *Langouste* is French for SPINY LOBSTER and langoustine is the diminutive form of the word, pronounced lang-guh-STEEN.

LARD is soft, white, semisolid or solid fat obtained by rendering the fatty tissue of a hog's internal abdomen. Lard is usually melted and strained before use. To lard is to cover or insert with strips of fat. The word derives from the Latin *lardum*, "lard/bacon."

LASAGNA or **LASAGNE** is pasta in the form of broad, usually ruffled, ribbons. Lasagna is also the name of an Italian dish of cooked lasagna noodles layered with a tomato-based sauce, cheese(s), and ground meat or vegetables. The word goes back to the Latin *lasanum/lasania*, "cooking pot," and the Greek *lasana*, "trivet." The word had entered English by 1760. Thinner lasagna noodles are called lasagnette.

> **HINT** Rinse lasagna with cold water after cooking to remove the surface starch so they don't stick together during assembly. Pat dry before layering them.

LASSI is a salty or sweet Indian drink of flavored yogurt or buttermilk diluted with water. The word comes from Hindi and it has been used in English since 1894. Lassi may be the world's first smoothie and it dates to 1000 BC. It is prized across South Asia for its great taste and healing Ayurvedic properties. It is the beverage of choice with an Ayurvedic lunch because of its ability to enhance digestion. It can be enjoyed as a sweet beverage or as a spice- or herb-infused beverage.

LATKE is a flat, fried, grated-potato cake containing beaten egg and sometimes matzo meal, onions, and seasoning. It is an Eastern European and Jewish specialty; the word is Yiddish, from the Russian latka, "pastry" or literally "patch." Most people mispronounce this word; the correctly pronunciation is LAHT-kuh. Latkes are traditionally eaten during Hanukkah. The oil for cooking the latkes is reminiscent of the oil from the Hanukkah story that kept the Second Temple of ancient Israel lit with a long-lasting flame that is celebrated as a miracle. The word leviva, the Hebrew name for latke, has its origins in the second book of Samuel's description of the story of Amnon and Tamar.

LATTE, also called CAFFÈ LATTE, is espresso coffee mixed with steamed or foamed milk. Latte is an Italian word that by 1990 had been made into an Americanism for this drink; it comes from caffè latte, meaning "coffee [and] milk." Sometimes an incorrect accent mark is placed on the word caffè when it is misinterpreted as French. In some establishments, lattes are served in a glass on a saucer with a napkin that can be used to hold the (sometimes hot) glass. A latte is also sometimes served in a bowl. Latte art refers to patterns made in the foam topping on espresso drinks.

LAUREL LEAF: see BAY LEAF.

LAVASH, LAVOSH, LAHVOSH, LAWAASH, or **LAWASHA,** also called ARMENIAN CRACKER BREAD, CRACKER BREAD, or PARAKI, is a round, thin Middle Eastern bread that is soft like a tortilla or hard like a cracker. Traditionally, the dough is rolled out flat and slapped against the hot walls of a tandoor oven.

LAYER CAKE is any cake that is made in layers, with icing/frosting, cream, jam/jelly, or other filling between the layers.

> **HINTS** Bake a layer cake on the center rack of the oven. Do not open the oven door while baking. Heat escapes and if the oven door shuts hard, it can cause a cake to fall.

> It is best to freeze a layer cake unfrosted (the same goes for angel food, sponge, and chiffon cake). Put cooled layers on a baking sheet and freeze until firm, then transfer to zip-lock freezer bags or wrap and seal in freezer-weight plastic wrap and keep for up to four months, but only three months for angel food, sponge, and chiffon cake. Thaw at room temperature for several hours before frosting and serving.

LEAVENING is any substance, such as yeast, baking soda, or baking powder, that can be used to produce fermentation and release carbon dioxide, as in making dough rise. To leaven means to add such a substance, such as baking powder, to a dough or batter to produce gas and lighten the mixture. The term derives from the Latin *levamen*, "means of raising." The principle of leavening was discovered in the late eighteenth century when carbonate-rich wood ash caused quick breads to rise.

LEAVENING AND FERMENTING AGENTS

A leavening agent is a substance that causes expansion of doughs and batters by the release of gases within such mixtures, producing baked products with porous structure. Fermenting (or fermentation) is basically the changes brought about by yeasts and other microorganisms growing in the absence of air. Most fermentation processes begin with suitable microorganisms and specified conditions. Some leavening and fermenting agents are listed here:

AIR	CARBON DIOXIDE	POTASSIUM BICARBONATE
AMMONIUM CARBONATE	CREAM OF TARTAR	SODIUM BICARBONATE
BACTERIA	DIASTASE	SOURDOUGH
BAKING AMMONIA	EGG	SOUR MILK
BAKING POWDER	ENZYME	STEAM
BAKING SODA OR BICARBONATE OF SODA	INVERTASE	VINEGAR
	MALTASE	YEAST
BARM	PEPSIN	ZYMASE
BREWER'S YEAST	POTASH	ZYME
BUTTERMILK		

LEBKUCHEN is a type of gingerbread cookie, typically glazed or coated and containing honey, nuts, spices, and candied fruits. It is a traditional German Christmas baked good. *Kuchen* is the German word for "cake," but the origin of the initial element (leb) is uncertain, though it may derive from a word meaning "loaf."

LECHE is Spanish for "milk." Pronounced LEH-chay, the word appears in food terms such as dulce de leche, *arroz con leche*, and tres leches cake. Milk is a fairly recent addition to Mexican cuisine; the more common forms of dairy in Mexico are *crema*, cheese, and condensed milk.

LEEK is a plant bearing elongated cylindrical white bulbs with flat, overlapping, dark green leaves; it is related to the onion. The leek is eaten as a vegetable and used as an herb. The word leek goes back to Proto-Germanic and forms the second syllable of garlic. The leek is the mildest member of the onion family.

> **HINTS** Choose small, unblemished leeks with crisp, dark green leaves. The roots should be light colored and a little pliable. Keep leeks in a plastic bag in the refrigerator for up to five days.

> ▌ Choose leeks over onions when you want a milder, sweeter flavor and a texture that turns tender and silky when cooked.

LEGUME is the fruit or seed of plants of the legume family, such as beans, lentils, and peas, and refers to these as vegetables. Sometimes referred to as PULSE, these vegetables are the mature seeds that grow inside pods. The word is from the Latin *legere*, "to pick."

LEMON is a yellow thick-skinned citrus fruit (*Citrus limon*) that is said to have originated in the Indus Valley around 2500–1700 BC, and it got its name from the Arabic *limun/limah/laimun*, "citrus fruit" (also the source of the word lime)—reaching English via the French *limon*. MEYER LEMON is a small soft-skinned citrus fruit with a more orange color and a more orange-like flavor than a standard lemon. A medium lemon will yield about 3 tablespoons of juice.

LEMON ESSENTIALS

■ Add lemon juice or oil at the end of cooking for a fresher flavor.

■ Choose lemons that feel heavy for their size and are free of soft spots and blemishes. Lemons with smooth, glossy rinds make the most juice; ones with thick, bumpy skin are best for zest.

■ Frozen pure lemon juice can be thawed and stored in the refrigerator for up to a month. Lemons can be frozen: halve lemons, put in a plastic bag, and freeze. Defrost overnight before using for juice.

■ Lemons can be kept at room temperature for one week or in a plastic bag in the refrigerator for up to one month.

■ Lemons should be brought to room temperature before squeezing to increase the volume of juice extracted. To squeeze, first roll the lemon against a hard, flat surface or between your hands. You can also pierce the lemon with the tines of a fork and microwave for 10 seconds before extracting juice. Use a reamer but don't rub too hard. A fork rotated in the cut surface also works like a reamer. Extra juice from fresh lemons can be frozen in an ice cube tray.

■ To cut the acidity of lemon juice, add a pinch of salt or baking soda.

LEMONADE is a sweetened beverage of lemon juice mixed with water. In the United Kingdom it is generally made with carbonated water. Recipes for lemonade-type drinks found in Arabic cookbooks date back to the thirteenth century. In the nineteenth century, lemonade was used as a tonic to help the sick and frail.

LEMON CURD is a thick custardlike mixture made from lemon juice, sugar, butter, and egg yolks and used as a filling, conserve, or spread.

LEMONGRASS is a tropical grass (*Cymbopogon citratus*) native to India and Sri Lanka; its lemon-scented foliage is made into a seasoning and essential oil.

> HINT Look for firm stalks of lemongrass. Trim the leaves and refrigerate in a plastic bag for up to two weeks. Shredded lemongrass can be frozen for up to six months. Use only the pale bottom part of the stalk and crush it before chopping or mincing.

LEMON SOLE is any of various food flatfishes (English sole, winter flounder, blackback flounder) with a sweet white flesh. Lemon sole is not sole but flounder and has nothing to do with lemon other than its pale yellow color; the name dates to around 1876 and derives from French the *limande*, "flatfish." Lemon sole is often labeled as "fillet of sole" or "English sole." In London, lemon sole is the fishmonger's name for a kind of plaice somewhat resembling the true sole. In Australia and the United States, this name has been transferred through association to a flatfish of a pale yellow color, and in New Zealand it is applied to the turbot.

LEMON VERBENA is a shrub (*Aloysia triphylla*) with long, slender leaves that smell like lemon and are made into a flavoring.

LENTIL is a Eurasian herb grown for its small, flat, edible seeds. They are lens shaped (the word comes from the Latin *lens*, "lentil"), variously colored on the outside, and yellow/orange on the inside. The earliest written mention of lentils is in the book of Genesis; Esau sold his birthright in exchange for a dish of lentils. Lentils are high in fiber, vegetable proteins, and complex carbohydrates and fairly rich in iron and protein; they are low in sodium and fat-free.

LETTUCE is any of the plants of the genus *Lactuca* (especially *Lactuca sativa*) that are grown for their crisp, succulent, green leaves, which are used in salads. The word lettuce came into English around 1290 from the Latin *lactuca*, "milk," because of the white liquid that oozes from broken stalks.

> **HINTS** Select lettuce leaves that are free of blemishes, yellow spots, and insect holes, and avoid wilted or dried leaves. If buying greens in a bag or box, check the date and look at the bottom of the bag or box for discoloration or too much moisture. For heads, choose those that are heavy and densely packed. Some salad greens are fine stored in a plastic bag in the crisper. Romaine will keep for up to ten days. Most greens are available year-round.

> Lettuce should be dried after washing so that the dressing will cling to the leaves and won't become diluted. You can store cleaned lettuce in the salad spinner in the refrigerator for a couple of days or more. You can also store cleaned lettuce wrapped loosely in cloth or paper towels in a partly closed zip-lock bag. Putting a slice of bread in the bag with lettuce will absorb the moisture from the greens and keep them fresh longer.

LIAISON, also called BINDER, is a thickening agent such as egg yolks or flour, and also the name for the process of thickening a sauce, soup, or stew.

LICORICE is a European plant of the pea family with short, flat pods and a root that is dried to make an extract used as a flavoring. Candy flavored with this extract or imitating it is called licorice. The word came through French from Latin and ultimately from the Greek *glykyrrhiza*, "sweet root." Licorice root has been used for thousands of years as a remedy for ulcers, sore throats, and coughs. Its taste is so distinctive that its sweetness is detectable in water even when diluted to one part licorice to twenty thousand parts water. Licorice is fifty times sweeter than sugar. Licorice was discovered in the tomb of the Egyptian pharaoh Tutankhamen (1356–1339 BC).

LIEBFRAUMILCH, German for "milk of Our Lady," is a grape/wine that originated in the vineyards of the convent of the Church of Our Lady. The wine is slightly sweet and can be made from a blend of grapes that can include Muller-Thurgau, Silvaner, Kerner, and Riesling. It is pronounced LEEB-frou-milk.

LIGHT CREAM, also called COFFEE CREAM or TABLE CREAM is sweet cream with at least 18% butterfat (but no more than 30%), less than that of heavy cream. It cannot be whipped, as it does not have enough fat for the necessary emulsion, and is most commonly used in mixed drinks or as a cream for coffee.

> **HINTS** If you use light cream in a sauce, heat the sauce slowly and do not allow it to boil; the sauce may turn out thinner than expected because of the lower fat content, in which case it can be thickened with flour or cornstarch.
>
> ▌ Generally, light cream keeps for around ten days.

LIMA BEAN, also called BURMA BEAN, BUTTER BEAN, CIVET BEAN, DAU NGU, GUFFIN BEAN, HABA BEAN, HIBBERT BEAN, MADAGASCAR BEAN, PAIGA, PAIGYA, PALLAR BEAN, PROLIFIC BEAN, RANGOON BEAN, SIEVA BEAN, or SUGAR BEAN, is a tropical American plant (*Phaseolus limensis*) with broad, flat, edible, pale green or whitish seeds. The lima bean (pronounced LY-muh) is named for Lima, Peru, the region where it was found before being brought to Europe. Two separate domestication events are believed to have occurred. The first event was in the Andes around 2000 BC and it produced a large-seeded variety (lima type). The second event was in Mesoamerica around AD 800 and it produced a small-seeded variety (Sieva type). By 1301 cultivation had spread to North America, and in the sixteenth century the plant arrived in the Eastern Hemisphere and began to be cultivated there.

LIMAU PURUT: see KAFFIR LIME.

LIMBURGER, LIMBURGER CHEESE, or **LIMBURG** is a soft, very pungent, white cheese that is surface-ripened. It is named for the Duchy of Limburg, now divided between the Netherlands, Belgium, and Germany. The bacterium used to ferment Limburger cheese and other rind-washed cheeses is *Brevibacterium linens*; the same bacterium is found on human skin and is partially responsible for human body odor. In its first month, the cheese is firmer and more crumbly, similar to the texture of feta cheese. After about six weeks, the cheese becomes softer along the edges but is still firm on the inside and can be described as salty and chalky. After two months of its life, it is mostly creamy and much smoother. Once it reaches three months, the cheese produces its notorious odor.

LIME is the small, green citrus fruit of a small semitropical tree (*Citrus aurantifolia*) native to Asia. The fruit has a juicy, sour pulp and is rich in ascorbic acid; it is more acidic than lemon. The word came to English from French, from the Spanish *lima*, from the Arabic *limah*, "citrus fruit."

> **HINT** Persian limes are the grocery store variety and should have a dark green rind. Key limes have a yellowish rind when ripe. Buy smooth, glossy, plump limes. They can be kept at room temperature for three to five days, but will last longer in a plastic bag in the refrigerator.

LINGONBERRY, also called FOXBERRY, LOWBUSH CRANBERRY, MOUNTAIN BILBERRY, MOUNTAIN CRANBERRY, PARTRIDGEBERRY, QUAILBERRY, REDBERRY, and RED WHORTLEBERRY, and COWBERRY in the United Kingdom, is a shrub bearing edible, tart, dark red berries similar to but smaller than cranberries. The word is from the Swedish *lingon*, meaning "mountain cranberry." The berries are quite tart, so they are almost always cooked and sweetened before being eaten in the form of lingonberry jam, compote, juice, or syrup.

LINGUINE or **LINGUINI** is pasta in long, narrow strips and the word is Italian for "little tongues." A thinner version of linguine is called linguettine. While spaghetti traditionally accompanies meat and tomato dishes, linguine is often served with seafood or pesto.

LINZERTORTE or **LINZER TORTE** is a type of sweet pastry that includes powdered nuts; a filling of red jam, plum butter, or apricot jam; and a lattice crust. The dough is rolled out in very thin strips of pastry and arranged to form a crisscross design on top of the filling. The pastry is brushed with lightly beaten egg whites, baked, and sometimes decorated with sliced almonds. It is named for Linz, Austria, and Torte is German for tart; it was first mentioned in English in 1906 and is said to be the oldest-known torte in the world.

LIQUEFIER: see BLENDER.

LIQUEUR denotes a strong, sweet alcoholic beverage flavored with aromatic substances. When liqueur is served after a meal, it can be called AFTER-DINNER DRINK, COCKTAIL, or CORDIAL. Liqueur is the French word for "liquor."

> **CONFUSABLE** LIQUEUR/LIQUOR. Liqueur is essentially the same word as liquor (from Latin), though the words have different meanings—liqueur is a strong, highly flavored, often sweetened, alcoholic drink, while liquor is an

alcoholic beverage made by distillation, rather than fermentation as in the case of beer and wine.

LIQUIDIZE means to make a solid substance liquid, as by heating.

LIQUIDIZER: see BLENDER.

LIQUOR almost exclusively pertains to a beverage produced by distillation, rather than fermentation. Liquor, however, may contain a fermented mash of ingredients. Liquor comes from the Latin *liquere*, "to be fluid," and it originally meant any liquid or fluid. Liquor is also the liquid contained in oysters, and the term can also pertain to water in which meat has been boiled (also called BROTH or SAUCE) or the fat in which bacon or fish has been fried.

LITTLENECK CLAM or **LITTLENECK**, also known as STEAMER, is a young quahog clam that is suitable for eating raw. The round hard-shell clam is named for Little Neck Bay, off Long Island, New York. The smallest clams are called countnecks; next size up are littlenecks, then topnecks. Larger than that are the cherrystones, and the largest are called quahogs or chowder clams.

> HINTS When it comes to eating mollusks, smaller is often better, as smaller mollusks will be less chewy. When you are choosing littleneck clams to eat, look for medium-sized to small specimens, rather than going for the biggest clams you see. Clams should be alive at the time of purchase; this means that that their shells will snap shut when tapped. Ideally, you should store clams in the refrigerator in a colander or another device that drains readily into a plate or shallow bowl, allowing the bodily fluids of the clams to drain away rather than accumulating.
>
> ▌ Before eating a littleneck clam, remove the sheath from the "neck" or siphon.

LIVER is the liver of an animal used as meat; it is a glandular organ similar to the liver of a human.

> HINT Liver can be tenderized by soaking it in milk or tomato juice for several hours in the refrigerator.

LIVERWURST is a sausage containing ground cooked liver; it is usually eaten cold as a spread. The word is German for "liver sausage" and was first seen in English around 1852. Most liverwurst varieties are spreadable. The sausage is usually made with pork. Only about 10%–20% of the sausage is actually pork liver, which is enough to give it a distinctive liver taste. One very popular option for use of liverwurst is braunschweiger, a usually soft spreadable form of liver sausage mixture. This recipe calls for slicing or chopping the liverwurst sausage into sections or pinwheels and adding some other smoked meat into the pan, such as slabs of bacon. The two meat products are sautéed until both are browned and the flavors are thoroughly intermingled. Braunschweiger can be eaten as an entrée, or a sandwich spread, or the mixture can be served over pasta or a selection of cooked vegetables.

LOAF is a shaped mass of bread baked in one piece, or any mass of food shaped somewhat like a loaf of bread and baked, such as ground meat in meat loaf. A LOAF PAN is usually rectangular or oblong.

> **HINT** If you have only one loaf pan, but need two, start with a 13 x 9-inch baking dish and set your loaf pan inside, perpendicular to the length of the baking dish. You can then bake a loaf in the loaf pan, then another (or two) in a section of the baking pan.

LOBBIA: see BLACK-EYED PEA.

LOBSTER is any of several edible marine crustaceans/shellfish of the family Homaridae, with long antennae and five pairs of legs—one of which is the pincers. The lobster is valued for its succulent meat. The word is from the Old English *lopustre/ lopystre/loppestre*, from the Latin *locusta*, "locust," from the resemblance in shape. The male lobster has larger claws. The female lobster has a wider tail. A lobster can either be left- or right-handed, depending on which side has the larger claw. The larger claw has coarse teeth for heavy-duty crushing jobs. The smaller claw is for lighter ripping or tearing tasks. A wooden peg is usually placed in the hinge of a lobster claw, or a rubber band is placed around the claw, mainly to prevent the lobsters in a tank from destroying each other and to protect the human hands that have to handle them. The liver, called tomalley, is the green material inside a lobster. Although there are some who are afraid that it contains small amounts of dioxin, it is prized for eating by many and apparently imparts no harm.

> **HINTS** Choose a feisty live lobster. Hold it behind the claws and make sure it quickly snaps its tail under its body. You can subdue a live lobster by putting it in the freezer for 5–10 minutes before cooking. Cover a live lobster with a damp cloth or wet newspaper in a cardboard box or heavy paper bag in the refrigerator for up to two days. Lobster meat toughness doesn't vary with the size of the lobster; however, the smaller claw on a lobster is sweeter and more tender, thus superior. The larger claw has more meat and provides a taste contrast. A 1½-pound live lobster will yield 1¼ cups of cooked meat.
>
> Lobster shells can be simmered to make lobster stock or crushed and cooked with butter, then strained for lobster butter. A rolling pin can be used to pop the meat out of lobster legs.

❚ The pink material in a cooked female lobster is the roe or eggs (called coral). The roe is edible and is often used to color and flavor sauces. Coral is not like caviar and is not eaten raw. Cooking changes it from greenish black to pink and firms its structure, making it more edible.

❚ You can tell when the lobster is done cooking by pulling the feeler (the stem-like or needlelike protuberance in the head). The feeler will come off easily if cooking is complete and the shell will be red. Keep the tail straight with a stick or skewer.

LOBSTER NEWBURG, LOBSTER À LA NEWBURG, or LOBSTER À LA NEWBURGH is a dish of lobster meat cooked in a rich sherry or brandy sauce with butter and cream and usually served on small pieces of toast or croutons or in a pastry shell. The story is that lobster Wenburg was renamed lobster Newburg by Delmonico's restaurant after the patron for whom it was named got into a drunken brawl in the establishment and the management no longer wanted the dish named after that person.

LOGANBERRY is an acidic purple-red fruit of a bramble shrub (*Rubus loganobaccus*) of the rose family, a hybrid of the blackberry and red raspberry. It was named for J. H. Logan (1841–1928), a horticulturist who accidentally developed it in 1881. Loganberries may be eaten without preparation as well as used as an ingredient in jams, pies, crumbles, fruit syrups, and country wines. Loganberries, in common with other blackberry/raspberry hybrids, can be used interchangeably with raspberries or blackberries in most recipes.

LOIN describes either side of the backbone between the hip bone and the ribs in quadrupeds, especially a cut of meat taken from the side and back of an animal (such as a calf, lamb, or pig) between the ribs and the rump. Loin is a tender cut, as it is from parts of the animal that get less exercise.

LOIN TIP: see TOP SIRLOIN.

LOMBIA: see BLACK-EYED PEA.

LO MEIN is a Chinese dish of boiled thin wheat noodles (like spaghetti) stir-fried in a seasoned sauce and often including vegetables or meat or shrimp. The word is from the Chinese *lòu-mihn*, "stirred noodles." Often, lo mein noodles are labeled as such and can be found in grocery stores. If you cannot find them, use medium-sized egg noodles for lo mein, though some people prefer very thick noodles because they have more texture and are chewier.

LONDON BROIL is a boneless cut of beef from the flank or shoulder that is usually marinated, broiled, and sliced thin and diagonally across the grain.

Sometimes the term is applied to thick cuts of meat like sirloin tip and top round. The best cut for a London broil is the shoulder round; the second choice is top round.

LONGNECK CLAM: see SOFT-SHELL CLAM.

LOQUAT, also called JAPANESE MEDLAR, is the small, yellow, pear-shaped fruit of an evergreen of China and Japan; the fruit has a large freestone and very little flesh. The word is from the Chinese *luh kwat*, "rush orange."

> **HINT** The skin of a loquat, though thin, can be peeled off manually if the fruit is ripe. The fruits are the sweetest when soft and yellow. Loquats generally will keep for ten days at room temperature, and for sixty days in the refrigerator. After removal from cold storage, the shelf life may be only three days. Cold storage of loquats in plastic bags alters the flavor of the fruit and promotes internal browning and the development of fungi.

LOVAGE is a southern European herb of the carrot family cultivated for its edible stalks and seedlike fruit. The word is from the Latin *ligusticum*, "plant from Liguria" (in Italy). It passed through French into English, where in the fourteenth century the second syllable was mistaken to be *ache*, a term for parsley, and so the French *luve-sche* became *lovache* until the modern English spelling was adopted in the fifteenth century. The leaves and seeds or fruit of lovage are used to flavor food, especially in southern European cuisine. Lovage is similar to celery in flavor and appearance; the stalks are eaten like celery or candied. Typically, the young leaves are used in salad. Older leaves can be used in soup or stew and cooked slowly. The seeds are used as a garnish and in pickles.

> **HINT** Dry lovage leaves slowly and store them in an airtight container. Harvest the seeds after they have turned brown and dry them. Fresh lovage leaves can be stored in a plastic bag in the vegetable crisper of the refrigerator for four to five days.

LOWBUSH CRANBERRY: see LINGONBERRY.

LOW-FAT MILK is any milk from which some of the cream has been removed, leaving the milk around 2% or 1% butterfat. Low-fat milk still contains 5 grams of total fat and 3 grams of saturated fat per 1-cup serving.

LOW-SODIUM or **LOW-SALT** is defined as having less than 140 milligrams of sodium per serving of a food.

LOX is smoked salmon, usually brine-cured, salt-cured, or sugar-cured. It is known for being eaten with bagels and cream cheese. The word is from the Yiddish *laks*, "salmon." The process is to first cure with a salt or sugar rub, then put in a wet brine before smoking. Lox is different from basic smoked salmon, because it is cold smoked. The cold smoking does not cook the fish, resulting in its characteristic smooth texture similar to the raw product.

LUMPFISH is any of several sluggish marine percoid fishes, especially a large North Atlantic species; it has a heavy body with hard spines, lumps, and a powerful ventral sucker. Its roe is used for caviar.

LUNCH (short for **LUNCHEON**) is a light meal, especially one eaten at midday between breakfast and dinner, and also refers to the food prepared for this meal. The word lunch, in use from 1823, comes from the more formal luncheon (dating to around 1580), originally used for any meal that was inserted between more substantial meals.

LUNCHEON MEATS or **LUNCH MEATS**, also called COLD CUTS, are a type of precooked meats containing preservatives and served cold, such as sausages and molded loaf meats. The term has been used since 1945, though Spam, the first true luncheon meat, was introduced in 1937.

LUNCHROOM: see CAFÉ.

LUXURY CHOCOLATE: see DARK CHOCOLATE.

LYCHEE, LITCHI, or **LICHEE** is an oval Chinese fruit with a thin brittle shell, sweet whitish pulp, and a large central seed. Its seed/fruit is usually eaten as a dried or preserved nut called lychee nut, but is also sold fresh and canned. Its name comes from the Cantonese *lai ji* and first came into English as *lechia*.

> HINT   Buy fresh lychees with red or pink shells. They will keep in a plastic bag in the refrigerator for up to two weeks.

LYONNAISE, literally "in the manner of Lyon," means cooked with onion or in an onion sauce, especially referring to fried potatoes. The term dates to 1846 in English.

LYOPHILIZATION: see FREEZE-DRIED.

MACADAMIA NUT is the edible hard-shelled seed of an Australian evergreen tree. It was named for Dr. John Macadam (1827–1865), secretary of the Victoria Philosophical Institute in Australia. The nut has a mild, creamy flavor. Hawaii leads the world's commercial macadamia nut production. The first macadamia nut trees were brought to Hawaii in 1882 by William Purvis. Cracking a macadamia nut takes about three hundred pounds per square inch of pressure, which is roughly equivalent to six elephants standing on top of you. Other than humans, hyacinth macaws are the only animals that crack them for food.

MACARONI is any of various shaped dried pasta noodles made from flour and water, especially short, bent, hollow tubes. The word is from Italian, possibly from the Greek *makaria*, "food made from barley." Macaroni is often served in tomato, cheese, or meat sauce. The best-known tube shapes are elbow, ditalini (tiny, very short tubes), mostaccioli (large, two-inch diagonal tubes), penne (large, diagonal, straight tubes), rigatoni (short, grooved tubes), and ziti (long, thin tubes).

> **HINT** To measure macaroni, use these guidelines: 4 ounces uncooked pasta (elbow macaroni, shells, rotini, cavatelli, wheels, penne, or ziti) = 1 cup dried pasta = 2½ cups cooked pasta; 4 ounces uncooked pasta (spaghetti, angel hair, vermicelli, fettuccine, or linguine) = 1-inch-diameter bunch of dried pasta = 2 cups cooked pasta.

HOW DO THEY GET THE HOLE IN MACARONI?

1. Dough is made by hand or with a mixer.

2. The dough is kneaded until it reaches the correct consistency, and then it is pushed, or extruded, through a die, a metal disk with holes in it. To make hollow, dumpling-style pasta such as macaroni or penne, a special type of pasta maker is required that comes with die attachments.

3. The shape of the holes in the die governs the shape of the pasta. For spaghetti, the die has round holes; for macaroni wheels, the die pushes out the pasta, leaving a large hole in the middle and gaps left by the spokes. As the pasta emerges, the spokes join up in the center.

4. When the extruded pasta reaches the right length, it is cut with sharp blades that rotate beneath the die.

5. The pasta is then sent through large dryers that circulate hot, moist air to slowly dry the pasta. To be dried properly, pasta needs alternating heat and moisture.

MACARONI WHEAT: see DURUM WHEAT.

MACAROON is a type of small drop cookie usually made of egg whites, sugar, and ground coconut or almond paste. The word is from the Italian *maccarone*, "cake/biscuit made of ground almonds." Macaroons can be flavored with chocolate, maraschino cherries, or orange peel.

> **HINT** Use parchment paper under macaroons when baking, as it may help prevent them from spreading if the baking sheet is too warm for the dough.

MACE is an aromatic spice made from the dried fibrous covering of the nutmeg seed. The word, known from 1234, is from the Latin *macis*, "aril surrounding the nutmeg."

MACÉDOINE is a salad of small diced pieces of fruit, often in syrup or gelatin, or a mixture of diced vegetables served hot or cold. The term refers to Macedonia, an allusion to the many different peoples of the region governed by Alexander the Great. Vegetable macédoine is cut into small dice and used as a garnish for meats; fruit macédoine is cut into larger pieces and often marinated in sugar syrup with liqueur.

MACERATE is to soften, usually by steeping in liquid; it especially means to steep fruit or vegetables in wine or liqueur like brandy or rum.

MÂCHE: see Corn salad.

MADAGASCAR BEAN: see Lima bean.

MADEIRA is a fortified Portuguese wine made in the Madeira Islands.

MADEIRA CAKE is a rich, fine-textured plain sponge cake with no icing or filling, intended to be accompanied by a glass of Madeira wine. It is sprinkled with candied lemon peel halfway through baking or with Madeira wine after baking. Madeira cake can be cut into a shape as it is less likely to crumble than softer cakes.

MADEIRA SAUCE is a rich, peppery sauce traditionally made with Madeira wine and served with meats like roast beef and chicken. The key to a good Madeira sauce is a long reduction.

MADELEINE is a small, rich sponge cake baked in a fluted tin or ribbed mold. Madeleines are shaped like seashells and are usually decorated with coconut and jam. A génoise cake batter is used. The flavor is similar to, but somewhat lighter than, that of sponge cake. Traditional recipes include very finely ground nuts, usually almonds. This French cake was probably named for nineteenth-century French pastry chef Madeleine Paulmier, but is even better known from its literary description by the author Marcel Proust in *Remembrance of Things Past*, and the word now also has the meaning of "something that triggers memories or nostalgia."

MAIZE: see CORN.

MAKRUD LIME: see KAFFIR LIME.

MALBEC, also called AUXERROIS, CÔT, MÉDOC NOIR, or PRESSAC, is a variety of dark red grape from Bordeaux, France, that is used for making wine, especially in blends with Cabernet Sauvignon and Merlot.

MALT has several cooking meanings: a cereal grain that begins germination by soaking in water and then is kiln-dried and ground into a powder, and used especially in brewing and distilling; a fermented beverage of high alcohol content (more than lager or beer), more commonly called malt liquor; and a milkshake made with malt powder (also called malted milk, malted). In the United Kingdom, malt whiskey can be called malt, too. Malted milk powder, made from malted barley, wheat flour, and whole milk and evaporated to form a powder, was introduced in 1887 and was originally intended to be used as a health food for infants and invalids.

MALT VINEGAR is vinegar made from the fermentation of malt. Based on beer and widely used for preserving and pickling, malt vinegar is also available as a strong, colorless, distilled vinegar. People commonly use malt vinegar on fries (called chips in the United Kingdom), and it is similar to lemons in flavor.

MANDARIN ORANGE or **MANDARIN** is a flattened, globose citrus fruit of an Asian shrub or small tree, with very sweet pulp and a thin orange rind that is loose and easily removed. The color can be anywhere from orangish yellow to deep reddish orange. The mandarin orange is either named for the flowing orange robes of Chinese mandarin officials or the superiority implied by a mandarin; the term dates to around 1771. Mandarin is a family of fruits that includes clementines, tangerines, and satsumas. Some varieties of the mandarin are called TANGERINE.

> **HINT** Select deep-colored, heavy mandarin oranges without soft spots, bumps, or puffy parts. They keep at room temperature for up to one week, or in a plastic bag in the refrigerator for up to one month.

MANDOLINE is a kitchen utensil with a base that holds sliding blades for slicing and shredding fruits and vegetables. The word dates to 1951.

> **HINT** The time saved cutting something up with a mandoline may not make up for the time spent assembling and washing the tool and its parts. But the tool does offer the advantages of precision and regularity of cuts.

MANGO is a large, oval, smooth-skinned fruit of a tropical evergreen. It has a yellow-red rind; juicy, aromatic orange pulp; and a large, hard, flat seed. The word entered English around 1582 from the Portuguese *manga*, from the Malay *mangga*, from the Tamil *mankay*, "mango tree fruit." It is eaten ripe (yellow with a red blush) or used green for pickles or chutneys; the plural forms are mangoes (preferred) or mangos. More fresh mangoes are eaten every day than any other fruit.

> **HINTS** Choose a mango that gives off aroma at the stem end, and has smooth skin that gives a little to gentle pressure. Mangoes continue to ripen, so keep not-quite-ripe ones at room temperature for a few days. Refrigerate for two to three days once fully ripe.

> ▌Peel a mango by slitting the skin and pulling it off in strips. Be careful with the skin because some people are allergic to it, as it is related to poison ivy and poison oak.

MANGETOUT: see SUGAR SNAP PEA.

MANGOSTEEN

MANGOSTEEN (from a Malay word) is the edible fruit of an Asian evergreen, with a hard reddish brown rind when unripe and sweet, juicy white pulp. Although their names are similar, the appearance of a mangosteen and a mango are very different. Ripe mangosteen is roughly the size of a mandarin orange, with a reddish purple rind. There is always a scar at one end; this is a remnant of the flower, and the number of remnant flower parts contained in the scar will tell you precisely how many segments of fruit are inside. The fruit itself is sweet with a hint of acidity, and a texture that has been likened to a ripe plum. The seeds are partly or wholly lacking, and when present are very thin and small.

MANICOTTI

MANICOTTI is a dish of large, tubular noodles stuffed with cheese (like ricotta) or meat and baked in a tomato sauce. Manicotti means "little muffs/sleeves" in Italian.

> **HINT** Manicotti will keep for about twelve months in a cool, dry pantry. Cooked and stuffed tubes can be refrigerated for about five days. To freeze, prepare the manicotti, complete with stuffing, but withhold the sauce if possible. Traditional recipes call for a cheese and meat mixture, but manicotti is so flexible it can be stuffed with any type of filling.

MANIOC

MANIOC or **MANIOCA**, also called CASSAVA or YUCCA, is the long, tuberous, edible root of the *Manihot esculenta* plant. It is used to make TAPIOCA and manioc flour, which is gluten-free.

MAPLE SYRUP

MAPLE SYRUP is a sweet liquid made from boiling the sap of the sugar maple or from various other sugars and artificial flavoring. Real maple syrup is now considered a delicacy in the United States, but in colonial days it was used extensively as an ordinary sweetener. Maple sugar is the sugar made by evaporating maple syrup. Maple butter is the last stage that maple syrup goes through before it becomes maple sugar; the preceding stages are maple honey and maple cream. Good-quality maple syrup will taste of vanilla and caramel. It takes approximately thirty-two to forty gallons of maple tree sap to make one gallon of maple syrup.

HINTS Buy pure maple syrup, not maple-flavored, because the difference in flavor is significant. Once opened, maple syrup should be transferred to a glass jar and refrigerated. It can be frozen in the glass jar and will thicken but usually will not freeze solid.

▌ Bring maple syrup to room temperature for serving, or warm it in a microwave or a saucepan. Maple syrup should be served at room temperature, for otherwise it will not only prematurely cool the food but some of the maple flavor will be lost.

MAPLE SYRUP GRADES (USDA)

Grade A Light Amber (or Fancy) or Grade AA: Very light and has a mild, more delicate maple flavor. It is usually made earlier in the season when the weather is colder. This is the best grade for making maple candy and maple cream.

Grade A Medium Amber: Darker and has a bit more maple flavor. It is the most popular grade of table syrup, and is usually made after the sugaring season begins to warm, about midseason.

Grade A Dark Amber: Even darker and has a stronger maple flavor. It is usually made later in the season as the days get longer and warmer.

Grade B (Cooking Syrup): Very dark with a very strong maple flavor, as well as some caramel flavor. It is used as table syrup and for baking, cooking, and flavoring. This maple syrup is made late in the season and only in Vermont.

Grade C: Robust, molasseslike flavor. It is used mainly in making commercial table syrups.

MARASCHINO CHERRY or MARASCHINO is a bright red cherry preserved

in a sweet syrup flavored with maraschino or an imitation of it. Maraschino is a strong, sweet liqueur or cordial made from the fermented juice of the marasca. The marasca (from the Italian *amaro*, "bitter") cherry is pitted and fermented for maraschino (pronounced mair-uh-SKEE-no). Before all the processing starts, the maraschino is actually a sour cherry. Most North American maraschino cherries are made from Royal Ann (Napoleon) cherries. To make maraschino cherries, fresh cherries are soaked in brine to firm them up, then soaked in fresh water. After that, they are colored, flavored, and put into a sugar sauce. Almond flavoring is used for the cherries that have been colored red; mint is sometimes used for the green ones, though almond is used as well. The cherries are generally pasteurized to give them a shelf life of three to five years.

MARBLED refers to something patterned with veins or streaks or color resembling marble; meat with fat evenly distributed in narrow streaks is described this way. Marbling is the intermixture of fat and lean in a cut of meat, which contributes to flavor and tenderness. A marble cake has a streaked or mottled appearance achieved by mixing light and dark batter.

MARC is organic residue, such as skins and pulp, from a fruit that has been pressed or a brandy made from the residue of pressed wine grapes. Marc is from the French *marcher*, "trample." Pomace brandy (or marc brandy) is a liquor distilled from pomace wine. Marc is either fermented, semifermented, or unfermented.

MARCHPANE: see MARZIPAN.

MARENGO (often lowercased), also called À LA MARENGO, is an adjective for food sautéed in oil and cooked with tomatoes, garlic, mushrooms, and brandy or white wine, for example, chicken marengo or veal marengo. The dish is often served with scrambled eggs. It is named for the Battle of Marengo (1800). According to tradition, Napoleon demanded a quick meal after the battle and his chef was forced to work with a chicken and some eggs, tomatoes, onions, garlic, herbs, olive oil, and crayfish. The chef cut up the chicken (reportedly with a saber) and fried it in olive oil; made a sauce from the tomatoes, garlic, and onions (plus a bit of cognac from Napoleon's flask); cooked the crayfish; fried the eggs; and served the dish with the eggs as a garnish, with some of the soldiers' bread ration on the side. Napoleon reportedly liked the dish, and having won the battle, considered the dish lucky. He refused to have the ingredients altered on future occasions, even when his chef tried to omit the crayfish.

MARGARINE, also called OLEOMARGARINE, is a spread made chiefly from refined vegetable oils (sometimes with added animal fats), milk, and water and processed as a substitute for butter. The word comes from French, but ultimately the Greek *margaron*, "pearl," is the origin because of the luster of the crystals of esters from which the spread was first made. Margarine was developed by French chemist Hippolyte Mège Mouriès in the late 1860s and received an American patent in 1873. Softer tub margarine has 50%–80% less trans fat than the firmer stick margarine. Margarine has a higher melting point than butter, so it is good for browning and pan-frying, and for greasing cake pans.

MARGHERITA PIZZA, also called Pizza margherita, is pizza made with tomato, sliced mozzarella, basil, and extra-virgin olive oil. This authentic Italian pizza honors Margherita of Savoy (1851–1926), a queen of Italy. Pizza Margherita Extra is a version made with tomato, mozzarella from Campania in fillets, basil, and extra-virgin olive oil.

MARINADE is a savory mixture of vinegar or wine and oil with various spices and seasonings, used for soaking fish, meat, or vegetables before cooking, to add flavor or tenderness. The word marinade comes from the Spanish *marinar*, "to pickle in brine." To marinate is to soak a food in this acidic liquid. Originally, the term was for the pickling of fish (either raw or already cooked).

MARINADE ESSENTIALS

- The flavoring and tenderizing effects of marinade are actually small, as the acid in the acid-based mixture can only penetrate the surface of food. So marinade works best on small, thin cuts. For lean meats, make sure your marinade adds fats.

- Never use a meat/poultry marinade as a sauce without first boiling it in a separate pan for 5 minutes.

- Scoring thick meat cuts will help the penetration of the marinade. You can marinate at room temperature for up to 2 hours, but you should marinate in the refrigerator if marinating for a longer time period. Drain the marinade off the food before cooking.

- A few minutes in a marinade is fine for thin strips of beef. For larger cuts, an hour or less will do it. For tougher cuts, add more acid to the marinade. Marinade begins to work on fish in minutes.

- Use ½ cup of marinade for every pound of meat. Seal the food in a heavy-duty zip-lock bag with the marinade, squeezing out as much air as possible, and turn occasionally. This will reduce the amount of marinade needed.

- For vegetables like zucchini, eggplant, and mushrooms that absorb like sponges, marinate for 1–2 hours. For others such as asparagus or artichokes that don't absorb well, marination does little.

- When finished marinating, simply discard the bag and do not reuse the marinade unless you boil it first.

- Marinades that soften meat include yogurt, which breaks down the flesh of meat and fish; lemon and vinegar, which soften meat and impart a tangy flavor; green papaya, which digests protein; and tamarind, which tenderizes and seasons.

- Marinate chicken with the skin on for 24 hours for best results; longer won't bring much improvement. When marinating chicken with the skin off, the flavor intensification works in about 3 hours, while a longer time will dry out the meat.

MARINARA is a tomato-based pasta sauce usually containing onions, garlic, olive oil, spices, and herbs. Marinara's origin is the Italian *alla marinara*, "sailor-fashion," which refers to its being a sailor-style sauce—containing ingredients that would not spoil at sea and could be prepared with minimal use of fire. This red sauce tends to be a bit spicier than other standard tomato sauces, with large amounts of garlic, oregano, basil, and even chiles.

MARJORAM is an aromatic Eurasian plant (genus *Origanum*) with leaves used as an herb. Sweet marjoram is an herb for cooking; wild marjoram is another term for OREGANO. The origin of the word is unknown. All marjorams are oreganos, since the genus name for both is *origanum*, but not all oreganos are marjorams. Oregano is the genus, and marjoram or sweet marjoram (*Origanum majorana*) is only one variety of over fifty types of oregano.

> **HINT** Marjoram leaves are best fresh because of their mild flavor. The delicate flavor of marjoram may be lost if it is added too early in the cooking process, so add at the very end of cooking.

MARMALADE is a preserve made from citrus fruit, especially the peel of bitter orange. The name comes from the Portuguese *marmelada*, "quince jam" (which was the first marmalade), from the Latin *melomeli*, "honey flavored with quinces," and *melimela*, "sweet apple." The use of citrus fruits for marmalade seems to have begun in the seventeenth century; generally, only citrus marmalades are made now, with the exception of ginger marmalade. Scottish marmalade is made from oranges and contains more peel and zest than most other marmalades. Central European and California-style marmalades contain less peel and zest and so are less bitter. The traditional citrus fruit for marmalade production in the United Kingdom is the Seville orange, thus called because it was originally imported from Seville in Spain; it is higher in pectin than sweet oranges, and therefore sets well. Marmalade can be made from lemons, limes, grapefruits, oranges, or any combination.

MARMITE is the name of a French ceramic pot used for cooking soup, especially one with legs, or the soup made in such a pot. It is also the name of a British product that is a concentrated brewer's yeast paste.

MARRON, also called SPANISH CHESTNUT, is a large, sweet Mediterranean chestnut, often candied or preserved in syrup. It is also the name of a large Australian freshwater crayfish. Marrons (the crayfish) are very similar in taste to lobster and can be cooked just like lobster. Because they are a freshwater species, they are far less salty and provide an overall sweeter taste. They are distinct from other similar freshwater species in that they do not burrow and do not take on as much waste into their flesh. Even very large and old specimens maintain excellent eating quality and texture.

MARROW is the tissue that fills bone cavities; it is a culinary delicacy, especially marrow from long beef bones. Vegetable marrow is the flesh of any large, elongated, smooth-skinned, meaty varieties of summer squash.

MARSALA is a dark, fortified dry-to-sweet wine from the city of Marsala in Sicily that is used in cooking. Different Marsala wines are classified according to color, sweetness, and the duration of their aging. The three levels of sweetness are secco (with a maximum of 40 grams of residual sugar per liter), semisecco (41–100 grams per liter), and sweet (over 100 grams per liter). The wine produced for export is universally a fortified wine similar to port. Originally, Marsala wine was fortified with alcohol to ensure that it would last long ocean voyages.

MARSHMALLOW is a spongy white confection made of gelatin or gum arabic, sugar, and corn syrup; it is produced in regular and miniature sizes. Although marshmallows were originally made from the marsh mallow plant, which has a jellylike gum in its roots, marshmallows produced today contain no marsh mallow.

> **HINT** Put hardened marshmallows in a zip-lock bag with a couple slices of white bread for a few days to soften.

MARTINI is a cocktail made of gin or vodka and dry vermouth, usually served with a green olive or lemon twist. Martini became a proprietary name for Martini and Rossi vermouth in 1882, then a name for the cocktail using the vermouth. There are three types of martini: dry, medium, and sweet. While variations are many, a standard modern martini is an approximate four to one ratio, made by combining approximately two ounces of gin and approximately half an ounce of dry vermouth. While the standard martini may call for a four to one ratio of distilled spirits to vermouth, aficionados of the dry martini may reduce the proportion of vermouth drastically for a drier martini. A stirred martini will have a more potent, more "pure" taste, whereas a shaken martini will be somewhat watered down by the ice melting slightly during the vigorous shaking.

MARZIPAN, also called MARCHPANE, is a paste of almonds, sugar, and egg whites used to make confections shaped and colored realistically like small fruits and vegetables. Soft marzipan is used as a filling in a variety of pastries and candies; marzipan of firmer consistency is made into the shaped confections. The word is from the Italian *marzapane*, but beyond that the origin is unknown.

MARZIPAN/ALMOND PASTE. Marzipan is almond paste with added sugar and is often made with added egg whites. The two cannot be used interchangeably.

MASALA is an Indian mixture of ground spices (often garlic, ginger, onions), sometimes blended with water or vinegar to make a paste, used in a sauce to season a dish, and it is also the name of a dish made with this mixture, for example, chicken masala. The word is from Hindi and Urdu, a variant of a word meaning "spices/ingredients."

MASALA CHAI: see CHAI.

MASCARPONE is a soft, very mild Italian cow's milk cream cheese. The word is derived from the Italian *mascarpa/mascherpo*, which refers to a type of ricotta or cream cheese. Mascarpone is technically not a cheese, but a rich cream thickened by lactic fermentation, as though it were an Italian version of France's crème fraîche, or a smoother, milder take on Britain's clotted cream. Mascarpone is the proper cream cheese for tiramisu and is terrific for cheesecakes.

MASH means a mixture of mashed or ground malt or meal grains and hot water used in brewing beer. The verb means to change into a soft or uniform mass by beating or crushing.

MASHED POTATO, also called CREAMED POTATO or WHIPPED POTATO, is potato that has been boiled, peeled, and then mashed—though there are variations where some skin is included and herbs/spices added. Former names for the dish are DUTCH POTATOES and GERMAN POTATOES. Since potatoes are mainly starch and water, and the starch is in the form of granules in the starch cells, the higher the starch content of the potatoes, the fuller the cells (the space between the cells is mainly water). In high-starch potatoes, the cells are completely full; full cells are the most likely to maintain their integrity and stay separate during mashing, resulting in fluffy, full-textured mashed potatoes. Accordingly, the potatoes to use for mashed potatoes should be flaky, high-starch ones, such as Idaho or Yukon Gold, for they have the highest starch content, have similar texture, and are therefore fluffier when cooked.

MASHED POTATO ESSENTIALS

■ A food processor or blender should not be used for making mashed potatoes, as the high speed brings out too much starch, resulting in a gooey dish. A good tool to use for mashing potatoes is a potato masher in which the cooked potatoes are forced through a sieve-like cup. If not using a potato masher, always mash potatoes by hand or with a hand mixer, or they will get gluey.

■ If you overmash the potatoes, you rupture the cell walls, allowing starch granules to escape and cause gumminess. To prevent this, you could use the medium disk of a food mill or a potato ricer to get a smooth purée.

■ Mashed potatoes should be combined with warm milk only, not cold milk. Cold milk or cream lowers the temperature and makes them gummy. Also, make sure that the milk is not boiling hot. Boiling milk tends to make the mashed potatoes sticky.

■ Potatoes used for mashing should be peeled after cooking. If peeled or cut before being put into boiling water to cook, the potatoes will gain too much weight due to absorption of water and the results will be more watery.

■ Don't use low-starch, waxy reds or California whites for mashed potatoes, as they don't absorb cream or butter well.

■ To keep mashed potatoes warm once they are mashed, don't cover the pot or bowl with a lid, because the trapped steam will produce a soggy consistency. Instead, cover with a clean kitchen towel, which will absorb excess moisture and keep the heat in, or hold cooked mashed potatoes in a slow cooker on its lowest setting.

MASON JAR is a type of widemouthed glass jar with a lid that screws on and is hermetically sealed; it is used mainly for home canning and preserving. The jar is named for John L. Mason (1832–1902), the American inventor who patented it in 1858.

MATZO, MATZOH, or **MATZAH** is a kind of thin, crisp unleavened bread, especially eaten by Jews during Passover. The plural of this Yiddish word is matzos or matzoth. Matzo balls are small dumplings made with crushed matzo, often served in chicken broth. In the Passover meal, matzo is symbolic of the swift flight of the Jews from Egypt when they could not wait for their dough to rise. The dough is pricked in several places and not allowed to rise before or during baking, thereby producing a hard, flat bread. The five grains that may not be used during Passover in any form except for matzo are barley, oats, rye, spelt, and wheat. Eighteen minutes is the limit for making matzo that conforms to the Jewish standards for unleavened bread; after that time, the dough is considered leavened by fermentation.

MAYONNAISE is a simple emulsion of raw egg yolks, oil, lemon juice or vinegar, and spices. Mayonnaise may derive from a word meaning "native to Mahon," referring to Port Mahon, capital of Minorca, and was first written *mahonnaise*; the shortened mayo showed up in 1930. The sauce may have been created by the chef of the Duke of Richelieu, who captured Port Mahon in 1756. Mayonnaise is the best-known emulsified sauce, and one of the five foundation sauces in classical French cooking. Mayonnaise will not properly emulsify during a thunderstorm because such storms are replete with both positive and negative charges that neutralize some of the emulsifying electrical charges of the sauce.

CONFUSABLE MAYONNAISE/MIRACLE WHIP. The main difference between mayonnaise and Miracle Whip is the sweetener—high-fructose corn syrup and sugar are the fourth and fifth ingredients, respectively, of Miracle Whip. Miracle Whip is a whipped mayonnaise that has 64% less fat than regular mayonnaise. It got its name from the machine originally used to make it, called the miracle whip, which produced a mayonnaise that was more highly blended than competing products.

HINTS Mayonnaise-based salads should not be left unrefrigerated for more than two hours.

❙ Fix homemade broken (separated) mayonnaise by putting an egg yolk in a separate bowl and then gradually adding the broken mayonnaise, whisking steadily until it reforms. Some oil and seasonings can be added after that.

❙ To make your own mayonnaise most easily, start with a little bit of prepared mayonnaise and the emulsion will form readily. When making mayonnaise, be sure all of the ingredients are at room temperature.

MCINTOSH or **MCINTOSH RED** is a variety of red and green eating apple with tart flavor, grown in the northern United States. It was named for John McIntosh, a Canadian farmer on whose farm the cultivar was discovered around 1811. Every McIntosh apple has a direct lineage to a single tree in Dundela, Ontario. The Snow Apple, also known as Fameuse, is believed to be a parent of McIntosh. Offspring of the Mac include, among many others, the firmer Macoun (a Jersey Black cross), Spartan (recorded as a Newtown Pippin cross), Cortland, Empire, Jonamac, maybe Paula Red, and Jersey Mac.

MEAL is the edible part of a cereal crop (grain or pulse) that has been ground to a powder, or any other foodstuff ground to a fine or coarse powder. Its origin is the Indo-European *melu,* "crush/grind." The word also has the meanings of food served and eaten at one time, and the occasion of taking food by custom, habit, or plan at a fixed time of day. Its origin can be traced to the Old English *mael,* "mealtime/measure."

MEALS

A meal is any of the regular occasions in a day when a reasonably large amount of food is eaten. The word also refers to the food eaten on such an occasion. The earliest sense of meal involved a notion of fixed time. Here are some terms used today for different types of meals:

AFTERNOON TEA	BANQUET	BROWN-BAG LUNCH
AL DESKO OR DESKFAST	BARBECUE	BRUNCH
ANTIPASTO	BLUE-PLATE SPECIAL	BUFFET
APPETIZER	BREAKFAST	BURGOO

BUSINESS BREAKFAST	FORK SUPPER	POWER LUNCH
BUSINESS DINNER	FRY-UP	PRIX FIXE
BUSINESS LUNCH	HARVEST SUPPER	REFECTION
CLAMBAKE	HIGH TEA	REFRESHMENT
COFFEE BREAK	HORS D'OEUVRES	REPAST
COLLATION	LAST SUPPER	RERE-BANQUET
CONTINENTAL BREAKFAST	LOVE FEAST	SAFARI SUPPER
COOKOUT	LUNCH	SALAD BAR
CREAM TEA	LUNCHEON	SMORGASBORD
CRUDITÉS	MEALS-ON-WHEELS	SNACK
CUT LUNCH	MESS	SUPPER
DASHBOARD BREAKFAST OR CUPHOLDER MEAL	MIDDAY MEAL	TABLE D'HÔTE
	MIDNIGHT SNACK	TAKEAWAY
DINNER	MORNING	TAKEOUT
DINNER PARTY	NOONING	TAPAS
DOGGY BAG	NOSH	TEA
DRIVE-THROUGH MEAL	NOSH-UP	TEA PARTY
ELEVENSES	OSLO BREAKFAST	TIFFIN
ENTRÉE	PICNIC	TUCK-IN OR TUCK-OUT
EVENING MEAL	POTLUCK	TV DINNER
FAST-FOOD MEAL	POWER BREAKFAST	WEDDING BREAKFAST
FEAST		

MEASURE (MEASURING, MEASUREMENT) is the extent, dimensions, or capacity of anything, especially as determined by a standard—and the act or process of determining this. The word is based on the Latin *mensura*, "action or process of measuring" or "system of measurement."

HINTS Read the recipe carefully to see if items should be measured before or after some kind of preparation. Here's the difference: "1 cup nuts, chopped" means you measure the nuts before chopping. But "1 cup chopped nuts" means you measure the nuts after chopping. This can make a big difference.

▌ In measuring, the term rounded means slightly less than heaping.

▌ If you oil or butter a measuring cup first, a sticky liquid or ingredient will pour out more easily.

▌ To measure shortening, fill a large measuring cup with 1 cup of cold water, then add the shortening in spoonfuls until the water gets up to the desired amount of shortening plus 1 cup.

▌ Use metal cups for dry ingredients. Use glass (like Pyrex) cups for liquid ingredients. A clear material allows the cook to see the level of the liquid rise as it is poured and most liquid measuring cups also have pouring spouts. A 1-cup dry measure is exactly the same as a 1-cup liquid measure, but wet and dry ingredients have different volume measurements, so they require different measuring cups for accuracy.

MEAT was originally a general term for food or nourishment, especially solid food as opposed to drink. Meat is now a more specific term, referring to the flesh of animals used as food, especially mammals but also including fowl and fish. Meat inspectors stamp meat with a round purple mark: "U.S. INSP'D & P'S'D." Meat packaged in an inspection facility will have a stamp that identifies the plant. Grading is done only if the packer requests it. A USDA inspection stamp for meat wholesomeness is mandatory, unless there is a state stamp. However, when meat is cut for retail display and sale, the stamp won't be visible on most cuts. You do not need to cut off the meat, fat, or skin where the purple stamp of the inspection has been placed; it is a harmless purple vegetable dye. The criteria for grading meat are age, texture, appearance, and marbling. Meat is made of long strands of protein that run parallel to each other, producing long fibers. When meat is ground and mixed, these proteins get tangled in a weblike matrix that gives things like meatballs or hamburgers a cohesive structure. On a traditionally set dinner plate, the meat should be positioned at six o'clock.

MEAT ESSENTIALS

■ Break frozen ground meat into chunks for even defrosting in the microwave.

■ The reason not to let a thermometer touch the bone when inserted in meat is that bone conducts heat, which will skew the reading. A minimum temperature of 160°F is needed to destroy bacteria in cooked meat and poultry.

■ Meat always loses moisture when it cooks, so basting does not actually add moisture to the meat. Basting helps prevent the meat from drying out too quickly.

■ Do not buy meat in packages that are leaking in any way.

■ A resting period for roasts allows the juices to redistribute themselves in the meat, making the whole roast juicier. The meat's temperature will rise 5°F–10°F during resting.

■ A piece of meat toughens as it cools on the plate because as the meat cools, the gelatin (from the collagen) cools and thickens, causing the meat to lose some of its tenderness. You can minimize this process by using heated dinner plates.

■ According to the USDA, all meat, regardless of how the animal was raised, can be labeled "natural" if after slaughter no artificial ingredients or antibiotics were added and the meat has been minimally processed. If you want to buy meat that is truly natural, look for printed claims such as "raised without hormones or antibiotics" or "no antibiotics."

■ An animal's activity affects the meat's toughness. The more the animal exercises, the greater the connective tissue development, and therefore the tougher the meat. Thus, if the animal roams free instead of being confined, the meat will have more connective tissue and be tougher. Also, the older the animal, the less tender the meat will be.

■ Extra-lean meats by the USDA standard have less than 5 grams of fat per 100 grams of meat, less than 2 grams of saturated fat, and less than 95 milligrams of cholesterol.

■ It is dangerous to allow properly cooked meat to cool to room temperature because while the bacteria will have been killed by the cooking, if the cooked meat contains spores of the bacteria that survive and multiply, they will create a toxin that causes food poisoning. So if cooked meat has cooled down and is not being served immediately, refrigerate it, then reheat to 165°F for serving.

■ It is safe to refreeze frozen meat after a power failure even for fully cooked meats, but only if the temperature of the meat remains below 40°F. If it goes above that temperature for more than two hours, there is danger. Furthermore, even if the bacteria don't grow to a dangerous level, the fats in the meat may become rancid. If you have any question about the quality or safety of meat, throw it away.

■ Juices can be retained in meat when cooking by using tongs or a spatula instead of a fork to turn the meat, so that the juices won't ooze out of the fork holes. Quickly brown the meat over high heat, then finish cooking at moderate heat, turning only once.

■ Meat is pounded before cooking to increase the surface area for searing, improve caramelization of the surface, or tenderize it.

■ Older animals are more desirable for braising or stewing because slow, moist heat will tenderize even a somewhat tough meat by breaking down its connective tissue. The benefit is that the meat of the older animal has more flavor.

■ Slow-cooking of meat helps the collagen to shrink, and maintaining this low temperature promotes the conversion of collagen to gelatin. The goal is to cook the meat in such a way that the juice does not run out and the fat does not melt and run out.

■ The freezing and subsequent thawing of meat causes the meat to lose some of the internal juices that contribute to flavor, texture, and nutrition and that help keep the meat moist and tender as it cooks. Don't keep frozen steaks too long—a month at the most so that they retain good quality. However, they will be edible, possibly even good tasting, for several months if well wrapped.

■ The goal in handling tough meat is to tenderize it without drying so that the meat will not be stringy or fibrous. The resulting texture depends on the cooked meat's internal temperature, which should not exceed 160°F; the correct temperature should be reached by cooking the meat over very low heat over a relatively brief time.

■ The myoglobin (red) pigment of cooked beef undergoes chemical changes as the temperature rises. At rare (approximately 135°F) it retains most of its redness. At medium-rare (145°F) it is pink, and at well done (160°F) it has turned a drab brown.

■ The USDA says that you should leave meat out for warming up (from cold storage) for less than two hours. If the meat is in a marinade, the acidity of the vinegar or yogurt will inhibit, although not absolutely prevent, bacterial growth.

■ You can keep the foil on meat that is to be frozen from sticking to the meat by coating the foil with nonstick cooking spray before wrapping it for freezing.

■ Meat on the bone will be juicier and more flavorful.

(continued)

■ Add a little dark chocolate in meat dishes like chili to enrich the flavor.

■ Slice meat across, not with, the grain for a tender result.

■ Put meat to be sliced in the freezer for one to two hours for easier slicing.

■ Separate patties, chops, and steaks with pieces of parchment paper before putting in zip-lock freezer bags to freeze.

■ Cover a platter with foil before placing raw meat on it to be grilled, then remove the foil once the meat is on the grill so you can use the platter for the grilled food.

■ Try to turn meat only once. If you turn it over and over, meat will toughen. If meat is sticking, it is not ready to be turned.

■ Ask the butcher to score some cuts of meat such as brisket or flank and sirloin for London broil. These cuts must be sliced against the grain after cooking; the scoring will remind you which direction to slice.

■ For boneless or ground meat, buy ¼–½ pound per serving. For bone-in meat, buy at least ⅓–½ pound per serving, and for hearty meat eaters, buy 1 pound per serving.

■ Meat should be salted before cooking to help develop the meat's flavor. This is definitely true for ground meats, which should have salt and other seasonings mixed in before cooking.

■ This is the traditional way of testing meat for doneness: If you press on it and it feels soft, it is rare. If it feels hard, it is well done. Medium falls somewhere in between. Also, if juice comes out and it is pink, the meat is medium.

■ Thaw frozen meat in the refrigerator on a plate or in a pan.

MEAT CUTS AND JOINTS

In the Western world, meat usually refers to the flesh of cattle, pigs, sheep, and lamb. Beef, lamb, and mutton are generally classified as red meats, and veal and pork are white meats. The category of a cut of meat determines its culinary treatment. Some cuts are to be rapidly cooked (grilling, broiling, frying, roasting) and these generally come from the back part of the animal. Another category includes braising cuts, especially from around the legs. A third category consists of what is left (neck, knuckle, shin, breast, tail): these cuts need to be boiled or stewed for a long time. These are some common meat cuts and joints:

BACK RIB	BUTT	CUTLET
BARON OF BEEF	CENTER LOIN CHOP	ENTRECÔTE
BELLY	CHATEAUBRIAND	ESCALOPE
BELLY SLICE	CHINE	FILET MIGNON
BLADE	CHOP	FILLET OR TENDERLOIN
BRAIN	CHUCK	FLANK
BREAST	COLLAR	FORE RIB
BRISKET	CUBES	GIGOT

HOCK	RACK	SILVERSIDE
JOINT	RIB	SIRLOIN
KNUCKLE	RIBLET	SKIRT
LEG	ROUND	SPARERIB
LOIN	RUMP	STEAK
LOIN CHOP	SADDLE	T-BONE
MEDALLION	SHANK	TENDERLOIN
MIDDLE NECK	SHIN	TOPSIDE
NECK FILLET	SHOULDER	TOURNEDOS
NOISETTE	SHOULDER CHOP	UNDERCUT
PORTERHOUSE STEAK	SIDE	

TYPES OF MEAT, POULTRY, AND GAME

The flesh of cattle, pigs, sheep, and lamb is generally distinguished from that of domesticated birds and wild animals—such as chicken, duck, turkey, and rabbit—which is categorized as poultry or game. This list combines meat, poultry, and game to show all the common choices in a grocery store meat department or on a restaurant menu.

BACON	GOOSE	PHEASANT
BEEF	GROUSE	PORK
BEEFBURGER	GUINEA FOWL	POULTRY
BURGER	HAM	PROSCIUTTO
CAPON	HAMBURGER	QUAIL
CHICKEN	HARE	RABBIT
CHITTERLINGS	HORSEMEAT	REINDEER
COLD CUTS OR LUNCHEON MEATS	JERKY	RISSOLE
	KIDNEY	SALT PORK
CORNED BEEF	LAMB	SAUSAGE
CORNISH HEN	LIVER	SMOKED MEAT
DEVILED MEAT	MOOSE	STEAK
DRIED MEAT	MUTTON	SWEETBREADS
DUCK	OFFAL	TONGUE
DUCKLING	OXTAIL	TRIPE
ELK	PARMA HAM	TURKEY
FRANKFURTER OR HOT DOG	PARTRIDGE	TURTLE
FROG LEG	PÂTÉ	VEAL
GAME	PEA FOWL	VENISON
GOAT		

MEATBALL is ground meat formed into a ball and fried or simmered. The meat is usually combined with seasonings and a binder such as bread crumbs or egg.

HINTS To make meatballs of equal size, form the meat into a sheet that is thick enough to allow you to cut it into squares of the size desired. Cut into squares of uniform size. Roll the squares lightly with moist hands or use an ice-cream scoop to form the squares into balls.

❚ You can prevent meatballs from falling apart when cooking by refrigerating them for 20 minutes before cooking. Handle carefully when forming so you don't overcompact them. Add a little flour to the meat before shaping into meatballs. Once meatballs have browned on their two broader sides, use tongs to stand them on their edges to finish, leaning them against each other for balance.

❚ Wet your hands with cold water when making meatballs to keep the mixture from sticking to your hands. Handle the meat as little as possible. Dredge in flour before frying. Keep a bowl of water nearby to dip your fingers in to prevent the meatballs from sticking to them.

MEAT LOAF or **MEATLOAF** is a mounded/molded baked dish made of ground meat (beef, pork, veal, or a combination) and other ingredients, including a binder such as bread crumbs or egg. It is usually cooked in a loaf pan. The term dates to 1892.

HINTS Choose ground round meat for meat loaf because it has less fat, and the fat in meat loaf does not drain out as well as it does with burgers, as it is absorbed by bread crumbs and other ingredients. Ground round also has more flavor than ground sirloin. You can also use a mixture of meats to make a more flavorful meat loaf, such as beef with pork or veal, or beef with ground turkey or ground chicken. The meat you use should be coarsely ground rather than finely ground.

❚ You can avoid cracking in a meat loaf by not overmixing it. Form the loaf gently with your hands, so the result will not be dense and heavy.

❚ You can shorten the cooking time of meat loaf by making individual portions and baking them in a muffin tin. They will be ready in 15–30 minutes at 375°F.

MEAT TEA: see HIGH TEA.

MEDALLION or **MÉDALLION**, also called NOISETTE or TOURNEDOS, is a circular helping of food, especially a boneless round or oval cut of meat, such as beef or veal. It is so named because it is shaped like a medal/medallion.

MEDIUM refers to meat cooked until there is just a little pink meat inside and the meat is fairly firm (140°F–150°F); medium-rare is a warm red center (130°F–140°F); medium-well is only a small amount of pink in the center (150°F–155°F). RARE is a cold red center (125°F–130°F), and WELL DONE is gray-brown throughout (over 160°F).

The USDA recommends a temperature of at least 145°F for beef, veal, and lamb steaks and roasts, as well as fish, in order to prevent foodborne illness. The interior of a cut of meat may still increase in temperature by 5°F–10°F after being removed from the heat, and the meat is therefore allowed to "rest" before being served. Resting allows the temperature of the meat to stabilize and lets juices in the center return to the edges of the food.

MEDIUM RED SALMON: see COHO SALMON.

MEDLAR is the small, brown, crab apple–like fruit of a small Eurasian tree (*Mespilus germanica*) of the rose family, used for preserves and eaten, but not edible until the early stages of decay (bletted). Medlar fruits are very hard and acidic. They become edible after being softened by frost, or naturally in storage given sufficient time. Once softening begins, the skin rapidly takes on a wrinkled texture and turns dark brown, and the inside reduces to a consistency and flavor reminiscent of applesauce. They can then be eaten raw are often consumed with cheese as a dessert, although they are also used to make medlar jelly and wine.

MÉDOC NOIR: see MALBEC.

MELBA is a sauce made from puréed raspberries. French chef Auguste Escoffier named both MELBA TOAST and PEACH MELBA for Dame Nellie Melba (1861–1931), the famous Australian opera singer. The better known is peach Melba, created by Escoffier when he was chef at the Savoy in London to celebrate her visit to London in 1905, though the date is disputed. The original was an elaborate dish of a swan of ice with peaches on top of a bed of ice cream and topped with spun sugar. Today, the dessert consists of peach halves on a bed of vanilla ice cream topped with raspberry purée.

MELBA TOAST is thinly sliced bread, toasted, then cut into even thinner slices and toasted on the untoasted side. Melba toast is said to be derived from the crisp toast that was part of Dame Nellie Melba's diet during the year 1897, a year in which she was very ill. The hotel proprietor César Ritz supposedly named it in a conversation with French chef Auguste Escoffier but the date is disputed, though the *Oxford English Dictionary* puts it at 1924.

> **HINT** Melba toast is usually made by lightly toasting bread, then once the outside of the bread is slightly firm, it is removed from the toaster and each slice is cut laterally with a bread knife to make two slices. These two thin slices are then toasted again to make Melba toast.

MELLOWFRUIT: see PEPINO.

MELON is a general term for any of numerous fruits of the gourd family (*Cucumis melo* or *Citrullus lanatus*) with a hard rind and sweet, juicy flesh, such as cantaloupe, cucumber, muskmelon, and watermelon. The word melon comes from the Greek *melopepon*, "apple gourd."

> HINT For netted-skin melons, look for pronounced and even netting. Smooth melons should be smooth. An unripe melon (except for honeydew) will get a little sweeter if put in a paper bag at room temperature a few days. Ripe melons keep for up to five days in the refrigerator or in a cool, dark place. Wash melons in hot soapy water before cutting.

MELON VARIETIES

Melons are the roundish fruit of several types of trailing vine, climbing plants of the gourd family. All have a hard rind and sweet, juicy flesh, usually with a mass of seeds at the center. Melons originated in Asia and were known in China by 1000 BC. The three main groups are musk (or netted or nutmeg), cantaloupe, and winter melons.

CANTALOUPE	NETTED MELON OR NUTMEG MELON	POMEGRANATE MELON
CASABA	OGEN MELON	SNAKE MELON OR SERPENT MELON
CHARENTAIS	ORIENTAL PICKLING MELON	STINKING MELON
CRENSHAW		SUGAR MELON
GALIA	PEPINO MELON	SWEET MELON
HONEYDEW	PERSIAN MELON	WATERMELON
MANGO MELON	PICKLING MELON	WINTER MELON
MUSKMELON		

MELON BALLER is a kitchen utensil, usually with a small scoop of two sizes on either end, used to cut rounded pieces of melons or other foods.

> HINT Use a melon baller to core an apple for stuffed apples, but don't puncture the blossom end or the filling will leak out.

MELONGENE: see EGGPLANT.

MELON PEAR or **MELON SHRUB**: see PEPINO.

MERINGUE is a mixture of stiffly beaten egg whites and sugar that is baked; it is used as a topping for pies or made into shells or cookies. The word is from French and may be related to the Latin *meringa/merenda*, "afternoon meal."

> HINTS Older egg whites whip more easily and higher. Fresh egg whites hold air better and are more stable when whipped.

❚ Separate eggs while cold, but set egg whites out for 30 minutes before whipping. Make sure no yolk is in with the white. Use a copper bowl or add a little cream of tartar or lemon juice to increase the stability and volume of the whipped eggs.

❚ You can prevent weeping or cracking of meringue by leaving the meringue in the oven until it cools.

TYPES OF MERINGUE

DACQUOISE (ALSO CALLED JAPONAISE MERINGUE): Meringue with finely chopped almonds or hazelnuts.

FRENCH MERINGUE (ALSO CALLED COLD MERINGUE OR SIMPLE MERINGUE): Sugar beaten into egg whites until stiff and fluffy.

ITALIAN MERINGUE: Made by making a sugar syrup and beating the hot syrup into egg whites.

SWISS MERINGUE (ALSO CALLED WARM MERINGUE OR COOKED MERINGUE): Made by heating egg whites and sugar in a double boiler until 110°F–120°F, then beating the mixture until stiff.

MERLOT (pronounced mer-LOH) is a classic grape variety of Bordeaux, France, and elsewhere that makes a dark, dry red wine. Merlot is from the French *merle*, "young blackbird," for the dark color of the grapes. Merlot matures earlier than Cabernet Sauvignon and usually has medium body with hints of berry, plum, and currant. The wine produced is similar in flavor to Cabernet Sauvignon, but tends to be softer and mellower. Merlot is often used as a blending grape.

MESCAL is a colorless Mexican liquor distilled from fermented sap of certain desert plants of the genus *Agavaceae* (agave).

MESCLUN is French for "mixture" and pertains to a salad made from a number of different young lettuces/greens, such as arugula, chicory, dandelion, endive, and radicchio. The term arrived in English around 1970. In a spring mesclun mix, any variety of young greens will do: amaranth, arugula, endive, kale, mâche, mustards, perilla, radicchio, and so on.

MESQUITE is any of several small spiny trees or shrubs of the genus *Prosopis* found in the southwestern United States. The wood or charcoal of the mesquite is often used in grilling and barbecuing to impart a smoky flavor to food. The word is from the Nahuatl *mizquitl*. Mesquite wood adds a sweet, earthy flavor to meat and vegetables; acacia is also a wood from the mesquite family.

MEUNIÈRE, also called À LA MEUNIÈRE, is a term in French cuisine for food cooked by lightly coating in flour, frying in butter, and sprinkling with lemon juice, melted butter, and chopped parsley. The method is used mainly for fish, for example, sole meunière. This French term literally means "in the style of the miller's wife."

MEXICAN GREEN TOMATO: see Tomatillo.

MEXICAN POTATO or **MEXICAN TURNIP**: see Jicama.

MEYER LEMON is a citrus fruit thought to be a cross between a lemon and either a mandarin or orange, and the fruit is rounder and more yellow than a true lemon. Meyer lemon fruits have a sweeter, less acidic flavor than the more common lemon Lisbon or Eureka grocery store varieties. It originated in China and was brought to the United States in 1908 by USDA employee Frank Nicholas Meyer.

MEZE or **MEZZE** in Turkish, Greek, and Middle Eastern cookery indicates a selection of hot and cold dishes served as hors d'oeuvres. Examples are stuffed vine leaves, small pastries, or grilled sausages. The Turkish word literally means "appetizer" and comes from the Persian *maza*, "to relish." Meze is often served with anise-flavored liqueurs, such as arak, ouzo, or raki, or with a variety of wines.

MEZZALUNA, also called Hachoir, is a kitchen tool with a semicircular (half-moon) blade or two blades and a handle on each end, used for chopping food.

MICROPLANE is a long and very sharp steel-handled tool with small, fine edges used for grating various food items such as cheese and for zesting citrus fruit. The design is based on the rasp, a hand tool.

MICROWAVE or **MICROWAVE OVEN** is a kitchen appliance that cooks food by passing an electromagnetic wave through it. Internal heat is produced by the absorption of microwave energy by the water molecules in the food; this process cooks food quickly but does not brown it. The less moist a food is, the longer it will take to cook. The first commercial microwave cooker was introduced by the Raytheon Company of Waltham, Massachusetts, in 1947. Microwaves work at different speeds on different foods. Fats and sugars absorb microwave energy more efficiently than do water and other liquids. Thus foods with high sugar or fat content cook faster. The microwave is, therefore, good for softening such items as cream cheese, butter, and brown sugar (that has hardened), but heats water no faster than the stovetop. When a microwave oven has a turntable, the heat is more even.

■ When you cook large amounts of food, it becomes just as efficient to use a conventional oven as a microwave.

■ When preparing foods for the microwave, don't let plastic wrap touch the food it covers, and turn back a corner of the plastic wrap or make a small hole to vent. Pierce foods with skins or membranes with a fork or toothpick to vent.

■ Food continues cooking after it is removed from the microwave, so err on the side of undercooking.

■ To adapt a conventional recipe for the microwave, reduce the cooking time by about two-thirds.

■ A microwave may be damaged if it is empty when the power is turned on.

■ Microwaves penetrate food to a depth of up to 1–1½ inches, so if the food is thicker than that, be prepared to turn it over midway in the cooking.

■ There is an advantage to boning meat before microwaving. With the bone out, the cooking will be more regular.

■ Very little time is gained in cooking pasta or rice in the microwave, and, additionally, there is the possibility of it boiling over. For pasta and rice, it is best to use the microwave for reheating only.

■ When microwaving with the food covered with paper towels to prevent spattering, use only paper towels without any printed designs, as the printing ink might be transferred to the food.

■ You can tell if a container is safe for microwaving by placing the container next to a half-full cup of water in the microwave and heating on full power for 1 minute. If the container gets hot, don't use it. If it is warm or cold, the container is safe for microwaving.

■ Ingredients straight from the refrigerator or freezer will take longer to cook than those at room temperature.

THE MICROWAVE COOKING PROCESS

1. An electrical current is used to generate microwaves in a magnetron.

2. Electrons are emitted by a heated filament, forming a cloud that moves around in a circle due to the magnetic field.

3. As the electrons pass close to the vanes in the anode block, they induce rapidly changing positive and negative charges, creating an electromagnetic field oscillating at microwave frequency (2,450 megahertz) in the cavities between the vanes.

4. The electromagnetic field causes an antenna to emit microwaves at this frequency through a metal wave guide into the oven, where they are scattered by a rotating paddle or spinning fan.

5. Some of the microwaves penetrate the food directly, while others are reflected off the walls into the food, ensuring even cooking.

(continued)

6. Inside the food, water molecules rotate in time with the changing polarity of the electrical field. Each wave of energy causes the water molecules to align and then reverse alignment extremely rapidly.

7. Friction between rotating water molecules generates heat, cooking the food.

8. An electronic timer controls cooking time.

MIGNONETTE is a term for small cubes of beef and also for a type of sauce made typically with shallots, vinegar, pepper, and herbs and served with oysters. The term can also indicate a noisette or medallion. The word has yet another meaning of coarsely ground white pepper; this pepper is also called poivre mignonnette—the term comes from *mignonnette*, a French word for a small cloth sachet filled with peppercorns and cloves that is used to flavor soups and stews like a bouquet garni.

MILANESE, also called À LA MILANESE, literally means "made in the style of Milan" and pertains to meats coated with flour or bread crumbs and browned in hot oil or butter. The term also describes a pasta with a sauce of tomatoes, mushrooms, grated cheese, shredded meat, and truffles.

MILK is a liquid secreted by the mammary glands of female mammals for nourishment of their young, and the word is intimately connected to the action of milking a cow or similar animal. Milk commonly refers to cow's milk, which is available as whole milk, with at least 3.5% milk fat; lowfat milk, with 1%–2% fat; and skim or nonfat milk, with less than 0.5% fat. The word comes from the Proto-Indo-European *melg-*, "to stroke." The words for milk in the Romance languages, such as the French *lait*, Italian *latte*, and Spanish *leche*, come from the Latin *lac*, the source of the English words lactic and lactation. The flavor of milk comes from emulsified fats, the white color from casein protein, and the sweetness from lactose, a sugar found only in milk. One gallon of whole milk weighs 8.6 pounds.

CONFUSABLE MILK/CREAM. The difference between milk and cream is the amount of fat in each. Whole milk: 3% milk fat or more. Low-fat milk: 1%–2% fat. Skim milk: less than 0.1% fat. Heavy cream: 35% fat or more, up to 40%. Light cream: 16%–32% fat. Half-and-half: 10%–12% fat.

HINTS For making the froth topping for a latte, steaming alters the milk proteins in a different way than heating in a pot or in the microwave. Low-fat or skim milk makes a stiffer, more meringuelike froth than whole milk. Whichever milk you use, make sure you start with it cold. Prevent a boil-over when heating milk by rubbing butter along the top edge of the pan.

▌ The advantage of paper cartons for milk versus glass or clear plastic is that opaque paper blocks 98% of the harmful effects of light. In plastic or glass, just four hours of store light can destroy 44% of vitamin A in low-fat milk.

▌ If your mouth is on fire, get relief from a glass of milk.

MILK VARIETIES

Milk is a whitish nutritious liquid secreted by the mammary glands. Milking animals was originally a religious ritual among early human societies that raised livestock. Milk has always been a symbol of fertility and wealth: in the Bible, the Promised Land is described as flowing with milk and honey and Moses proclaimed that the milk of cows and ewes was a gift from God. The composition of milk varies according to the type and breed of animal, its state of health, and the diet on which it has been reared. In most Western countries, the word milk means cow's milk, which is a major source of calcium and protein. Some common varieties of milk are listed here:

ACIDOPHILUS MILK
BREAST MILK OR MOTHER'S MILK
BUTTERMILK
CHOCOLATE MILK
COCONUT MILK
CONDENSED MILK
COW'S MILK
DRIED MILK
EVAPORATED MILK
FILTERED MILK
FORTIFIED MILK
GOAT'S MILK OR GOATS' MILK
HALF-AND-HALF

HOMOGENIZED MILK
ICE MILK
LACTOSE-FREE MILK
LACTOSE-REDUCED MILK
LASSI
LOW-FAT MILK
MALTED MILK
NONFAT MILK
1% MILK
ORGANIC MILK
PASTEURIZED MILK
POWDERED MILK
RAW MILK
RICE MILK

SKIM MILK OR SKIMMED MILK
SOY MILK
STERILIZED MILK
STRAWBERRY MILK
SWEETENED CONDENSED MILK
2% MILK
ULTRA-HIGH-TEMPERATURE MILK, UHT MILK, ULTRA-HEAT-PASTEURIZED MILK, ULTRA-HEAT-TREATMENT MILK, OR LONG-LIFE MILK
ULTRAPASTEURIZED MILK
UNTREATED MILK
WHOLE MILK

MILK CHOCOLATE is chocolate made from chocolate liquor with sugar, cocoa butter, and vanilla, and enriched with powdered milk solids. The milk gives this chocolate a light brown color and sweet, creamy taste. The term was first recorded in 1723. Consuming milk chocolate or white chocolate, or drinking fat-containing milk with dark chocolate, appears largely to negate the health benefits of chocolate.

MILK GRAVY: see COUNTRY GRAVY.

MILKKEFIR: see KEFIR.

MILK POWDER: see DRIED MILK.

MILKSHAKE or **MILK SHAKE**, also called SHAKE, is a cold frothy drink of milk, ice cream, and flavoring made by shaking or whipping. The drink seems to have originated in the United States in the 1880s; regional names are CABINET, FRAPPÉ, and VELVET. In New England the term milkshake can be used for a frothy whipped drink made of just milk and flavored syrup. The original milkshakes did not include ice cream; they contained milk and flavoring and were shaken until frothy.

MILLE-FEUILLE (pronounced meel-FWEEH) is any puff pastry with many thin layers, filled with custard, whipped cream, fruit, or purée, or a savory pastry with a filling of seafood. The term often refers to a cream-filled rectangle of puff pastry or a NAPOLEON and is French for "a thousand leaves." Traditionally, a mille-feuille is made up of three layers of puff pastry, alternating with two layers of crème pâtissière (French pastry cream or custard), but sometimes whipped cream or jam. The top is usually glazed with icing or fondant in alternating white (icing) and brown (chocolate) strips, and combed.

MILLET is a type of cereal grass (*Panicum miliaceum*) whose small grains are sometimes used for food.

> **HINT** Toasting millet before cooking enhances its naturally bland flavor.

MILLING generally refers to the process or business of grinding grain into flour or meal, or the grinding or crushing of a foodstuff, spice, or herb in a mill, a usually small machine (for example, a coffee mill or pepper mill). Mills generally combine a crank or motor with a blade of some sort and yield a finer product than graters. Mills are also used on smaller, harder foods (grains, herbs, nuts, nutmeg, pepper). When buying a pepper mill, make sure it is adjustable for coarseness and has a superhardened or stainless-steel grinding mechanism.

MIMOSA is a cocktail of Champagne and orange juice, so called for its yellow color resembling the flowers of the mimosa shrub.

> **HINT** Make sure to chill both the Champagne and the orange juice at least an hour before serving mimosas, and prechill the glasses to help keep the mimosas cold. Make sure to serve your mimosas right after pouring them. If you wait too long, the carbonation from the Champagne will dissipate and you will have a flat cocktail. Serving the mimosa in a Champagne flute concentrates the carbonation. For a better mimosa, use freshly squeezed orange juice and high-quality dry Champagne.

MINCE is to cut meat or vegetables into very small pieces. The word is from the French *mincer/mincier*, "to cut up (food) into small pieces." The effect of mincing is to create a closely bonded mixture of ingredients and a soft or pasty texture.

MINCEMEAT was first an alteration of "minced meat," meaning meat cut up into very small pieces. By 1824 it was used for a baked loaf of currants, raisins, nuts, sugar, suet, apples, almonds, candied peel, and spices, originally with meat (beef), but later without meat, as in mince pies and other traditional Christmas dishes. Liquor or liqueur is sometimes added to the loaf.

MINERAL WATER is water naturally or artificially including mineral salts, elements, or gases and often effervescent. Mineral water from natural springs commonly has a high content of calcium carbonate, magnesium sulfate, potassium, and sodium sulfate. The mineral content of both natural and artificial mineral water varies greatly, and in some cases it may be less than that of ordinary tap water. The FDA classifies mineral water as water containing at least 250 parts per million total dissolved solids, and as also water coming from a source tapped at one or more bore holes or springs, originating from a geologically and physically protected underground water source; no minerals may be added to this water.

MINERALS IN FOOD

Minerals play a vital role in blood formation, blood clotting, regulation of heart rate, nerve and muscle activity, bone formation, and digestion. Soluble mineral salts also help to control the composition of body fluids. Several minerals, known as macrominerals, are needed in large amounts. Minerals required in very small amounts (milligrams or micrograms per day) are called trace elements or microminerals. The following minerals are found in food:

CALCIUM	IODINE	POTASSIUM
CHLORINE	IRON	SELENIUM
CHROMIUM	MAGNESIUM	SODIUM OR SODIUM CHLORIDE
COBALT	MANGANESE	
COPPER	MOLYBDENUM	SULFUR
FLUORINE OR FLUORIDE	PHOSPHORUS	ZINC

MINESTRONE is a thick vegetable soup usually containing dried beans and pasta. In Italy there are three versions of vegetable soup: *minestrina* (light and thin), minestrone (heavy and thick), and *minestra* (medium in consistency). Minestrone means "big soup" in Italian and comes from the Latin *minestrare*, "to serve/dish up." It was recorded in English in 1871 and is pronounced min-uh-STROH-nee, min-uh-STROHN, or mee-ne-STRAWN.

MINT is the leaves or oil of a mint plant (family Lamiaceae, genus *Mentha*) used as a flavoring, including spearmint, peppermint, basil, and bergamot. Peppermint has a sharp, pungent flavor, while spearmint is more delicate. The word is from the Latin *mentha/menta* and akin to the Greek *minthe*, "mint."

> **HINTS** Refrigerate mint in a covered jar with the stem ends sitting in a one-inch layer of water, or wrap the stem ends in a moist paper towel and seal in a plastic bag, then refrigerate.
>
> ▌ Since fresh mint bruises easily, chop or slice it with a sharp, dry knife.

MINT JULEP: see JULEP.

MIREPOIX or MIRE POIS (pronounced mir-PWAH) is a flavoring made from diced vegetables, seasonings, herbs, and sometimes meat (bacon, ham, salt pork), and often placed in a pan to cook with meat or fish. The term also can refer to such a mixture used as a bed for meat, poultry, or fish that is to be braised. It is named after the eighteenth-century French ambassador Charles de Lévis, Duke of Mirepoix, whose cooks may have created this. Each type of cuisine has its own variation, like Italian soffrito. A brown mirepoix (which will be browned in hot oil before being used) consists of two parts onion, one part carrot, and one part celery. A white mirepoix (generally added raw or lightly cooked in oil without browning) consists of one part onion and one part celery.

MIRIN: see RICE WINE.

MIRLITON: see CHAYOTE.

MISE EN PLACE (pronounced MEEZ ahn plahs) in professional cooking is proper planning of equipment and ingredients for a food preparation and assembly station. It is the setup of the ingredients, such as cuts of meat, relishes, sauces, partially cooked items, spices, freshly chopped vegetables, and other components that cooks require for the menu items that they expect to prepare during their shift. The term is also used in professional kitchens to refer to the ingredients themselves. Recipes are reviewed to check for necessary ingredients and equipment. Ingredients are measured out, washed, chopped, and placed in individual bowls. Equipment is prepared for use, while ovens are preheated. The term also refers to the preparation and layouts that are set up and used by line cooks at their stations in a commercial or restaurant kitchen.

MISO is a paste made from fermented soybeans, salt, and barley or rice malt, used in Japanese cookery. Miso soup is a stock called DASHI into which softened miso paste is mixed, and sometimes seaweed, vegetables, and tofu. The word miso is probably from the Korean *meju*, "soybean malt," and dates to 1615. Miso has many varieties including sweet, salty, white and red.

> **HINTS** It has been said that nibandashi (#2 dashi) or niboshidashi are more suitable for miso soup than ichibandashi (#1 dashi). The common ratio between

dashi and miso is 15 grams of miso per 1 cup of dashi. Overboiling causes flavor and aroma loss, so don't overboil after mixing miso into soup.

❚ When using root vegetables, cook them in dashi first, and when the vegetables are soft, add the miso, heat again, and stop heating just before the mixture comes to a boil. When using tofu, wakame, or green onions, add after mixing in the miso.

MIX is to bring together or combine ingredients, and mix (as a noun) is this act or process, as well as a mixture of ingredients, often a dry, commercially processed one.

MIXED DRINK is an alcoholic beverage combining two or more ingredients, such as liquor, a nonalcoholic mixer like juice or soda, and flavoring. The term dates to 1703. When creating a mixed drink, a bartender is looking to achieve two things: chilling the mixture and marrying the ingredients.

MIXED GRILL is a variety of broiled, fried, or grilled meats, and usually vegetables, served together. The dish originated in the United Kingdom by 1910.

MIXER is an electric appliance for mixing. It is also a nonalcoholic beverage, such as soda water or a soft drink, mixed with alcoholic liquor for a MIXED DRINK.

> **HINTS** Put a towel or cloth under a heavy stand mixer to make moving it easier. Drape a kitchen towel over a mixer when mixing to keep the mess under control.
>
> ❚ Put self-adhesive floor protector pads on the bottom of a heavy stand mixer (and other items like food processors and coffee machines).
>
> ❚ When using a mixer, start with a slow speed and build to a high speed to avoid splatters. If you add flour or confectioners' sugar, first mix in a little with a utensil before turning on the mixer.

MOCHA originally referred to a type of superior dark coffee named for Mocha, a seaport on the Red Sea in Yemen where it was grown and shipped. Today, the word more often denotes a coffee-and-chocolate flavoring or a drink made by combining or flavoring coffee with chocolate (also called MOCHA COFFEE or CAFÉ MOCHA). The world's oldest coffee blend, mocha-java, is traditionally a blend of Yemen Mocha and Java Arabica coffees, usually one part Yemen Mocha and two parts Java Arabica, and is distinguished by its winelike acidity and distinctively rich, intriguingly nuanced flavor.

MOCK TURTLE SOUP is made of meat such as calf's head or veal, wine, and spices. Mock turtle soup was an English soup created in the mid-eighteenth century as a cheap imitation of green turtle soup.

MOIST-HEAT COOKING is applying heat to food by submerging it in a hot liquid or by exposing it to steam. The four methods are poaching, simmering, boiling, and steaming. Slow, moist heat softens connective tissue in meat which is the protein collagen. In a hot, moist environment (boiling water, for instance), the collagen is partially transformed into gelatin and the tissue softens and dissolves, making the meat more tender.

MOLASSES is thick dark syrup produced by boiling down juice from sugar cane, especially during sugar refining. When the natural sugar crystallizes, the molasses is drawn off or "spun out." Columbus introduced molasses to the West Indies in 1493; the word comes from the Latin *mel*, "honey." Molasses is hygroscopic (water attracting) and thus keep baked goods moist longer.

> **CONFUSABLE** MOLASSES/SORGHUM. Molasses and sorghum are both sweeteners. Molasses comes from sugarcane or beets, while sorghum comes from the sorghum (sergo) plant. They can be used similarly, although sorghum has a considerably stronger flavor.

> **HINT** Molasses should be stored in a sealed container at room temperature.

MOLCAJETE: see MORTAR AND PESTLE.

MOLD is a container into which liquid is poured to create a given shape when it hardens, such as a gelatin mold. Molds are measured in terms of capacity and they tend to be deeper and come in more decorative shapes than regular cake pans. Examples are Bundt pan (fluted tube pan), cake cup, charlotte mold, fluted cake or aspic mold, kugelhopf pan, panettone pan, petit four mold, ring mold, ring cake mold, and savarin mold. To mold is to form by pouring into a mold. Mold is also a fungus that produces a superficial growth on various kinds of damp or decaying organic matter, such as on cheese. Spores may be added to the milk or the curds and/or the surface of a cheese to encourage mold growth as the cheese is formed; this type of surface mold is edible. Mold is also the undesirable growth that forms on the outside of old and/or poorly wrapped cheeses. This can often be cut away from the cheese so the remaining cheese can be eaten.

MOLE (pronounced MOH-lay) is the generic name for several sauces used in Mexican cuisine, as well as for dishes based on these sauces. The word is Mexican Spanish, from the Nahuatl *mulli/molli*, "sauce/concoction." MOLE POBLANO is what most people outside of Mexico call mole, and it is prepared with dried chiles, ground nuts and/or seeds, Mexican chocolate, salt, and spices and seasonings (onions, garlic, cumin, coriander, cinnamon). The word mole is also widely known in the combined form guacamole (an avocado concoction). Because of the labor-intensive nature of mole, when prepared at home it is most often made in large batches for special occasions, such as religious holidays, birthdays, or weddings.

MONKEY BREAD is the edible pulp of the baobab tree, so called because it is eaten by monkeys.

MONKEY NUT: see PEANUT.

MONOSODIUM GLUTAMATE, also called MSG, is a crystalline sodium salt derived from glutamic acid that has been used as a food additive to enhance flavor since 1929. This natural amino acid is found in seaweed, vegetables, cereal gluten, and the residue of sugar beets and was first discovered by Japanese scientists in the 1920s. Monosodium glutamate has the ability to intensify the flavor of savory foods, even though it has no flavor of its own. Many ingredients naturally contain MSG but are not required by the FDA to be labeled as such; examples are hydrolyzed plant protein, hydrolyzed vegetable protein, kombu extract, and natural flavoring.

MONTEPULCIANO (pronounced mawn-teh-pool-CHA-noh) is a type of full-bodied red wine made in Montepulciano, Italy, from the Sangiovese grape. Up to 10% Sangiovese is permitted to be added to the blend. It is typically a fruity, dry wine with soft tannins and is often consumed young.

MONTEREY JACK, also called JACK CHEESE, is a mild, moist Cheddar made from whole, skimmed, or partially skimmed milk; it was first made in Monterey County, California. Monterey jack is commonly sold by itself, or mixed with Colby to make a marbled cheese known as Colby jack. Monterey jack was made in its earliest form by Mexican Franciscan friars during the nineteenth century.

MOO GOO GAI PAN is a stir-fried Cantonese dish of chicken, mushrooms, assorted vegetables, and spices. The word literally means "mushroom chicken slice." Moo goo gai pan is different from other Chinese chicken dishes in that it eschews the traditional brown or soy sauce in favor of a light chicken-broth-based sauce.

MOOLI: see DAIKON.

MOO SHU, MOO-SHU, MOO SHOO, MO SHU, or **MU SHU** is a Chinese dish of stir-fried pork strips with vegetables, scallions, tiger lily buds, wood ears, scrambled eggs, and seasonings, rolled or folded into thin pancakes and served with a sauce. The term is from the Chinese *muxu*, meaning "dish containing scrambled egg." The small, thin pancakes are called moo shu pancakes or Peking doilies.

MOREL is any of various edible mushrooms (genus *Morchella*) with a brownish, spongelike, honeycombed, cone-shaped cap. The word is probably from the German *morchel*, "fungus." The morel is related to the truffle. Its cap ranges in height from two to four inches, and in color from a rich tan to an extremely dark brown. Generally, the darker the mushroom, the stronger the flavor. Dried morels have a more intense, smokier flavor than fresh ones.

MORELLO or **MORELLO CHERRY** is a sour, dark red cherry. The word is from the Latin *amarellum*, "sour cherry," from the Latin *amarus*, "bitter/sour." The morello is so sour that it is not eaten raw, but it is perfect for cooking.

MORNAY SAUCE is a béchamel (white sauce) containing cheese, especially Parmesan and Gruyère. The name dates to 1906, but it is disputed who it was named for: Philippe de Mornay, a French diplomat, or the son of a French chef. Mornay sauce is mainly used with fish, egg, and vegetable dishes that are browned in the oven or under the grill.

MORTADELLA is a smoked, fried, or steamed fatty Italian pork or beef sausage flavored with wine, garlic, and pepper. The word is derived from the Latin *murtatum*, "(sausage) seasoned with myrtle berries." It is a specialty of Bologna, in the Emilia-Romagna region of Italy. Mortadella is the original bologna, a delicate balance of fat, meat, and spice with a hint of pistachios and black peppercorns. It can be eaten alone, either sliced or cut into chunks.

MORTAR AND PESTLE is an ancient means of crushing or grinding grains, herbs, and spices. A mortar is a bowl-shaped container made of a hard wood, marble, pottery, or stone. A pestle is a bat-shaped tool that is used to grind the contents of the mortar. Crushing the fibers of herbs with a mortar and pestle releases the full range of essential oils. MOLCAJETE is the Mexican term for a mortar and pestle; SURIBACHI is the Japanese term.

> **HINTS** Crush the hardest ingredients first, then softer ingredients with the mortar and pestle. The proper technique for using a mortar and pestle effectively is a circular grinding motion instead of an up-and-down pounding one.

> ▌ A good way to season a mortar and pestle is to wash it with warm water, scrub it with a stiff brush, and let it air-dry. You could also put a handful of uncooked rice in the mortar and grind the rice with the pestle, repeating until the ground rice is white. Then rinse with warm, clear water and air-dry before storing.

MOSTACCIOLI, also called PENNE LISCE, is short tube-shaped pasta with angled ends, resembling a quill or pen point. The word means "little moustache" in Italian.

MOUNTAIN BERRY: see CLOUDBERRY.

MOUNTAIN BILBERRY or **MOUNTAIN CRANBERRY**: see LINGONBERRY.

MOUSSAKA or **MOUSAKA** is a Greek/Turkish dish made of sautéed sliced eggplant and ground lamb (or beef) layered with tomatoes, onions, potatoes, and cinnamon, and topped with a béchamel sauce and grated cheese before baking. Moussaka is ultimately from an Arabic word meaning "that which is fed liquid," referring to the added sauce.

MOUSSE (French for "froth/foam") is a light, airy mixture in which the main ingredient or flavoring is whipped with egg white or cream and can be sweet or savory.

> **CONFUSABLE** MOUSSE/SOUFFLÉ/PUDDING. Mousse is a light aerated dish made of ingredients beaten with whipped cream, gelatin, or egg whites; a soufflé is not made with cream or gelatin but with beaten egg white, and a pudding is made from milk, eggs, and other ingredients and flavorings.

MOUSSELINE SAUCE, also called Chantilly or Chantilly sauce, is any sauce lightened with whipped cream or beaten egg whites, such as hollandaise. This is also the term for an aspic lightened with whipping cream. The term is also applied to various meat, fish, and shellfish dishes or foie gras (usually puréed) to which whipped or beaten egg whites are added to lighten the texture.

MOUTHFEEL or **MOUTH FEEL** is a product's physical and chemical interaction in the mouth. The term is an Americanism dating to 1973. Mouthfeel is part of the testing and evaluating of foodstuffs, such as wine tasting and rheology. It is evaluated from initial perception on the palate, to first bite, through mastication, to swallowing and aftertaste.

MOZZARELLA is a soft/rubbery, mild white Italian cheese. It is made from cow's milk or water buffalo's milk and because of the way it is made, it is called a stretched-curd cheese. Mozzarella is the Italian diminutive of *mozza*, "kind of cheese," from *mozzare*, "cut off," so called because the cheese was shaped into a bundle and then chopped. Mozzarella is made by the pasta filata process in which the curd is given a hot whey bath, then stretched and kneaded to a pliable consistency. At one time, mozzarella was made only from the milk of water buffalo, but now the majority is made with cow's milk. Fresh mozzarella, which is usually packaged in whey or water, is often labeled "Italian-style" and is generally made from whole milk. Regular mozzarella is factory produced. Fresh mozzarella has a much softer texture and a sweet, delicate flavor.

MSG: see Monosodium glutamate.

MUDBUG: see Crayfish.

MUDDLE is to lightly mash or crush slices of a citrus or other fruit to release its essential oils. The technical name for a swizzle stick is muddler or mosser. You can muddle with a spoon or a muddler, which is a rod with a flattened end.

MUD FIZZ: see BLACK COW.

MUDU KEKIYA: see KEFIR.

MUENSTER or **MUNSTER** is a white or yellow, semisoft, strong-flavored or mild cheese made of whole milk that usually has an edible orange or red rind. It is named for a town in France. The highly prized European Muensters have red or orange rinds and a smooth yellow interior with small holes and range from mild to assertive depending on age. The American versions have an orange rind, a lighter yellow interior, and a bland flavor.

MUESLI is a mixture of rolled oats with dried fruit and nuts. It is often eaten at breakfast with milk. The word dates from 1926 and is from the German *Mus*, "stew/stewed fruit." Muesli was developed around 1900 by Swiss physician Maximilian Bircher-Benner for patients in his hospital, where a diet rich in fresh fruit and vegetables was an essential part of therapy. The original recipe calls for 1 tablespoon of rolled oats, soaked in 2–3 tablespoons of water; 1 tablespoon of lemon juice; 1 tablespoon of sweetened condensed milk; 1 large sour apple, finely grated; and 1 tablespoon of ground hazelnuts or almonds.

MUFFULETTA: see GRINDER.

MUFFIN is a sweet quick bread/sponge cake baked in a cup-shaped pan or mold. Muffin comes from the German *muffe*, "cake," and dates to 1835.

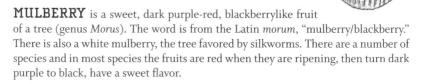

> **HINT** Inverted muffin tins work well as cooling racks. Let muffins cool and then put them in a zip-lock freezer bag to freeze.

MULBERRY is a sweet, dark purple-red, blackberrylike fruit of a tree (genus *Morus*). The word is from the Latin *morum*, "mulberry/blackberry." There is also a white mulberry, the tree favored by silkworms. There are a number of species and in most species the fruits are red when they are ripening, then turn dark purple to black, have a sweet flavor.

MULL is to heat with sugar and spices to make a hot drink, especially an alcoholic drink. Mulled wine is heated and infused or flavored with a spice or spices; beer, brandy, and cider may also be mulled and the practice was first recorded in 1607.

> **HINT** Mulling can be done in a slow cooker.

MULLIGATAWNY is a spicy Indian soup of chicken or lamb stock, vegetables, curry, other spices, and sometimes rice, coconut, or cream. The word is from the Tamil *milagu-tannir*, "pepper water," which partially describes the highly seasoned soup. The original mulligatawny soup can be traced back to the early days of the East India Company in Madras, and was more like a curry. Some recipes use apples or other fruits, nuts, or oatmeal along with meat and vegetables.

MUNG BEAN or **MUNG** (from Hindi and Sanskrit) is a plant of India, Indonesia, and the United States grown for its round green beans and bean sprouts used in Chinese cookery. Mung beans need no presoaking and when cooked have a tender texture and slightly sweet flavor. Dried mung beans are ground into flour, which is used to make noodles in China and a variety of dishes in India.

MUSCADET (pronounced muhs-kuh-DAY) is a type of white grape and dry white wine from the Loire Valley in France. Muscadet should be served chilled.

MUSCAT or **MUSCATEL** is any of several sweet aromatic grapes used for raisins and wine. The muscat grape is so named because of its musky taste and smell. Muscat is also a synonym for Muscatel, a sweet wine made from muscat grapes. Muscat is made from both the black and white varieties, so its color can be golden or amber to pale orange-red.

MUSHROOM is a general term for the fleshy body of any of numerous edible, fast-growing fungi; these were once called TOADSTOOL or FUNGE (from the Latin *fungus*) but the term mushroom has been in English since around 1400. A mushroom typically has a stalk capped with an umbrella-like top with gills. Small mushrooms are called buttons, medium-sized are cups, and the largest are flat or open mushrooms. There are cultivated and wild mushrooms. The most expensive and most highly esteemed mushroom is PORCINI, which sells for as much as thirty dollars a pound or even more.

MUSHROOM ESSENTIALS

■ Mushrooms should be firm and have smooth, unblemished caps. If the stems have dried gray ends or the caps are open with the gills exposed, they are too old or have been stored for too long. However, Portobello is a type where the gills are supposed to be exposed; in this type the gills should be unbroken.

■ Keep fresh mushrooms for three to four days in the refrigerator in a paper bag, or wrap loosely with slightly damp paper towels and place in the vegetable crisper of the refrigerator. Delicate mushrooms should be stored in a single layer on a tray and covered with a damp cloth. Plastic wrap turns them slimy and moldy. Don't store mushrooms in a closed container or a sealed bag, as they need a generous supply of cool, moist air to stay fresh.

■ Quickly rinse and dry mushrooms with paper towels. They can also be

(continued)

cleaned with a brush or damp cloth. White mushrooms can be tossed with lemon juice to prevent discoloring. A large quantity of mushrooms can be washed by plunging the caps into a bath of 2 quarts of water with ½ cup of vinegar and ¼ quarter cup of salt, briefly swirling the caps to dislodge the dirt, then lifting the caps out and draining. Morels and other wild mushrooms should never be peeled or washed, just brushed clean.

■ For the best flavor and texture, sauté mushrooms before adding to risotto, sauce, or soup.

■ Do not cook mushrooms in an aluminum pan, which may discolor them.

■ Use a melon baller to insert stuffing in mushroom caps. Make neat stuffed mushrooms by using a muffin tin, or a mini muffin tin.

MUSHROOM TYPES AND VARIETIES

BEECH	CULTIVATED	SHIITAKE
BEEFSTEAK	ENOKI	STRAW
BOLETUS	MAITAKE	TREE OR WOOD EAR
BUTTON	MATSUTAKE	TRUFFLE
CHANTERELLE	MOREL	WHITE
CHINESE BLACK	OYSTER	
CLOUD EAR	PORCINI	
CREMINI OR CRIMINI	PORTOBELLO (LARGE AND SMALL)	

MUSKMELON is any of several varieties of vine (*Cucumis melo*) of the gourd family whose fruit has a netted rind, sweet edible flesh, and a musky smell, especially cantaloupe and winter melon.

HINT Muskmelon will taste sweeter at room temperature or only slightly chilled.

MUSSEL is a type of edible marine or freshwater bivalve mollusk that lives attached to rocks; mussel gets its name from the Latin *musculus*, "little mouse," from the mussel's shape and color.

MUSSEL ESSENTIALS

■ Live mussels should have a fresh sea smell and no hint of ammonia. Tap the mussel and it should stay closed. To store, put in a bowl, cover with a damp kitchen towel, and refrigerate for up to one day. Dampen the towel if it dries out. If you want to freeze mussels, store them in a zip-lock freezer bag for up to three months. They can be defrosted slowly in the refrigerator.

■ A female mussel has orange-colored flesh. A male mussel has white-colored flesh.

■ Mussels are not poisonous, but they can absorb toxins from contaminated water or when the level of plankton in the water is high. Watch for public health warning signs (mainly May through October). Mussels offered commercially will be safe; most come from mussel farms and are not harmful.

■ The beard of a mussel is a small bundle of dark fibers the mussel uses to attach itself to its home base as it grows. They are not harmful but not tasty either. Remove the beard just before cooking with the aid of a small knife, stiff brush, or a pair of scissors under cold running water. Rinse again. If there is sand, soak them in cool salted water for 1 hour. If there is no beard, then it was probably removed by the processor in a way that didn't negatively affect the tissue.

MUSTARD is any of several cruciferous plants of the genus *Brassica* of the broccoli family, whose leaves are eaten as cooked greens and whose seeds are ground to make pungent powder or paste. Prepared (yellow) mustard is an American mixture generally made of powdered mustard, water, vinegar, sugar, and turmeric. The word had entered English by 1289 from the Anglo-Norman *mustarde/mustard/mostart/moustard* and the Old French *mostarde/moustarde*, so called because the condiment was originally prepared by making the ground seeds into a paste with must (grape juice before or during fermentation). Mustard greens are the leaves of these plants eaten as a cooked vegetable.

> **HINT** Mustard should not be cooked in aluminum pans because mustard and aluminum interact to produce an off-taste.

MUSTARD VARIETIES

Mustard is a herbaceous plant, originating in the Mediterranean, of which there are numerous species. Several have edible leaves, some produce edible oil, and a few provide seeds that are used to make the condiment of the same name. The seeds contain myronate and myrosin, which when crushed in the presence of water, release a volatile and piquant essence thath gives mustard its distinctive flavor. Mustard is a condiment that can be flavored with tarragon, garlic, mixed herbs, horseradish, honey, chile, paprika, or fruit. Some popular varieties of mustard are listed here:

AMERICAN MUSTARD	DIJON MUSTARD	POWDERED MUSTARD
BLACK MUSTARD	ENGLISH MUSTARD	PREPARED MUSTARD
BORDEAUX MUSTARD	EUROPEAN MUSTARD	TABLE MUSTARD
BROWN MUSTARD	GARLIC MUSTARD	WASABI MUSTARD
CHINESE MUSTARD	GERMAN MUSTARD	WHITE MUSTARD
CHIPOTLE MUSTARD	HONEY MUSTARD	YELLOW MUSTARD
CREOLE MUSTARD	ORIENTAL MUSTARD	

MUTTON is the flesh of mature domestic sheep eaten as food. Mutton is from a sheep over two years old and has a much stronger flavor and less tender flesh than lamb. The word is from the Latin *multo*, "ram/sheep."

MYSOST is sweet, semicaramelized hard cheese made from whey from cow's milk. Scandinavia's Mysost (or primost) tastes almost identical to GJETOST.

NAAN or **NAN** is a flat, round or oval, leavened white-flour bread traditionally cooked in a tandoor oven. It is important in Indian and South Asian cooking. Nigella seeds are commonly added to naan. The word is ultimately from the Persian *nagna* "naked/bare," probably from the bread's being baked uncovered, and it originally was a generic term for various flatbreads; it first appeared in English in 1780, during a travelogue by William Tooke.

NACHO is a Mexican dish/appetizer of tortilla chips topped with cheese, chiles, and various other foods and broiled. The term dates from around 1948 and may derive from a nickname for Ignacio Anaya, purportedly the name of the chef that created it, or it may come from a Spanish word for "flat-nosed." The original nachos consisted of fried corn tortillas covered with melted Cheddar cheese and pickled jalapeño peppers. Nachos sometimes appear on menus as "Mexican pizza," and may have additional toppings such as cooked ground chorizo, onions, and olives.

NAGE, also called À LA NAGE, in French cooking indicates that a shellfish dish is "swimming" in or served in aromatic poaching liquid, usually with a white wine base. Nage is also used for the aromatic court bouillon or stock itself.

NAM PLA: see FISH SAUCE.

NAPOLEON is a rectangular or oblong, layered puff pastry filled with custard cream, jelly, or pastry cream and either iced or dusted with confectioners' sugar. Some also call this MILLE-FEUILLE.

NASA CATEGORIES FOR SPACE FOOD

CONDIMENTS (ketchup, mustard)	REHYDRATABLE (macaroni and cheese, scrambled eggs, soup)
INTERMEDIATE MOISTURE (dried apricots and peaches)	THERMOSTABILIZED (beef, chicken, fruit, salmon, tuna)
IRRADIATED MEAT (beef)	
NATURAL FORM (cereal bars, cookies, nuts)	

NAVEL ORANGE is a large seedless orange with a pit at the apex where the fruit encloses a small secondary fruit, which is how it got its name. It has thick, easy-to-peel skin. A single mutation in 1820 in an orchard of sweet oranges planted at a monastery in Brazil yielded the navel orange, also known as the Bahia, Riverside, or Washington navel. Because the mutation left the fruit seedless, and therefore sterile, the only means available to cultivate more of this new variety is by cutting and grafting onto other varieties of citrus tree.

NAVY BEAN, also called YANKEE BEAN, is a type of small, white (haricot) kidney bean. The navy bean is so called because it was formerly a staple food of the U.S. Navy; this Americanism took hold around 1856. Navy beans require long, slow cooking are used in pork and beans and Boston baked beans. Navy bean varieties include Great Northern, Michelite, Rainy River, Robust, and Sanilac.

NEAPOLITAN ICE CREAM is ice cream in brick form with two to four layers of different colors and flavors; it is named for its layers' resemblance to the Italian flag. The word is an Americanism dating to 1868. The usual flavor combination is chocolate, vanilla, and strawberry. Spumoni was introduced to the United States in the 1870s as Neapolitan-style ice cream. Chocolate and pistachio are part of spumoni, and the fruit/nut layer often contains cherry bits.

NECTAR generally refers to undiluted fruit juice, a mixture of fruit juices, or a drink made from puréed fruit, but can also refer to any enjoyable drink. Nectar is further defined as the sweet liquid that flowering plants produce as a way of attracting the insects and small birds that assist in pollination. The word is from the Greek *nectar*, "drink of the gods." In the United States and the United Kingdom, the label "fruit juice" can only be used for beverages that are 100% pure juice, whereas "nectar" can appear on beverages diluted with sugar water and containing additives besides fruit juice, including sweeteners and preservatives.

NECTARINE is a smooth-skinned, mutated variety of the peach (*Prunus persica*). The word appeared in English in 1616 and comes from an adjective of the same spelling meaning "sweet as nectar." There are freestone and clingstone varieties.

> **HINTS** Nectarines, which never need peeling, can substitute for peaches in any recipe.
>
> ▌ Cut a nectarine in half at a ninety-degree angle to the crease; twist apart and remove the pit.
>
> ▌ Choose nectarines that give slightly to a little pressure, have a nice fragrance, and do not have blemishes. Avoid those with any green color. Keep nectarines at room temperature in a smooth bowl, as ridges can bruise them. If you need to hurry ripening, put them in a paper bag with an apple or banana. Once ripe, store in a plastic bag in the refrigerator for four to five days.

NESSELRODE is a cold mixture of candied fruits, nuts (often chestnuts), maraschino cherries, and liqueur (rum) used in nesselrode pudding, nesselrode pie, and nesselrode ice cream. The personal chef of Russian statesman Count Karl Nesselrode (1780–1862) created the pie/custard that bears his name. Other dishes were named after Count Nesselrode, including a game soup and a braised sweetbread dish, but none were as famous as Nesselrode pudding.

NEUCHÂTEL is a white or red wine produced in Neuchâtel, Switzerland.

NEUFCHÂTEL (pronounced noo-shuh-TELL or NOO-shuh-tell) is a soft white cheese similar to cream cheese made from whole or partly skimmed milk, originally from Neufchâtel, France. It is a slightly crumbly, mold-ripened cheese, and has an aroma and taste like those of mushrooms. The young version is delicate, mild, and a little salty and the ripened version is more pungent. The milk-fat content varies from 20% to 45%. Neufchâtel is available in a variety of shapes: square, rectangular, cylindrical, and the heart-shaped *Coeur de Bray*. American Neufchâtel (sometimes called FARMER CHEESE) is a lower-fat cream cheese product marketed as a healthier alternative to cream cheese.

NEW ENGLAND BOILED DINNER: see BOILED DINNER.

NEW POTATO is an immature potato, valued for its taste; a small potato taken from the ground early in the year.

NEW YORK STEAK, **NEW YORK STRIP**, **NEW YORK CUT**, or **NEW YORK SIRLOIN**, known by many other names, including CLUB STEAK, CONTREFILET, HOTEL STEAK, SHELL STEAK, STRIP LOIN STEAK, STRIP SIRLOIN STEAK, or TOP LOIN STEAK, is a porterhouse steak with the fillet removed, a steak cut from the upper part of the short loin.

> **CONFUSABLE** NEW YORK STRIP/STRIP STEAK. The difference between a New York strip and a strip steak is the name only. In the Midwest and West it is called a New York steak, but in New York it is called a strip steak. Both are porterhouse without the fillet. Other names include Delmonico, Kansas City, shell, boneless club, and sirloin strip.

NEWBURG when paired with a fish word means served in a rich sauce made of cream, egg yolks, butter, and sherry, for example, lobster Newburg or seafood Newburg. The origin of the word is unknown, but it first appeared in print in 1895. It is usually served over buttered toast points.

NIÇOISE, also called À LA NIÇOISE, refers to hot or cold dishes made with tomatoes, black olives, garlic, anchovies, and olive oil. A salad niçoise often includes capers, tuna, hard-cooked eggs, and green beans. The term is literally French for "pertaining to Nice" (the city). In addition, a niçoise olive is a small, oval olive that ranges in color from purple-brown to brown-black. It is originally from the Provence region of France and is cured in brine and packed in olive oil.

NGAN-PYA-YE: see FISH SAUCE.

NIXTAMAL: see HOMINY.

NOG was originally a strong variety of beer, but now is an abbreviation for EGGNOG.

NOISETTE, also called MEDALLION or TOURNEDOS, is a small, boneless, round or oval cut of meat, especially beef, lamb, pork, or veal. French for "little nut," the word also refers to a type of chocolate candy with hazelnuts, and is an adjective meaning made or flavored with hazelnuts.

NONDAIRY CREAMER or **NON-DAIRY CREAMER**, also called COFFEE WHITENER, is a powdered or liquid milk substitute for coffee or tea made from fat or casein, sweetener, preservatives, and emulsifiers; it is a creamer containing no dairy products. The adjective nondairy first appeared in print in 1933.

NONPAREIL, also called HUNDREDS AND THOUSANDS, is a colored bead of sugar used as a topping on cakes, candies, and cookies. It is also the name of a small, flat chocolate drop covered with white sugar beads. The word is pronounced non-puh-REL and was first applied to a kind of candy in 1697. The origin of nonpareils is uncertain, but they may have evolved out of the pharmaceutical use of sugar. The French name, which literally means "without equal," has been interpreted as meaning that these sugar beads were without equal for the intricate decoration of desserts.

NONSTICK PAN or **NON-STICK PAN** is a pan with a coating or surface allowing easy removal of cooked food. The best nonstick pans can brown food as well as a plain metal pan and are so tough that metal utensils can be carefully used in them. Most, though, require the use of wooden or plastic utensils to prevent scratching. Some of the best are anodized (electronically altered) prior to receiving their coatings, in order to create a harder surface and to actually incorporate the coating into the pan.

NOODLE is a general term for pasta, a food paste made usually with egg and shaped in various tube and ribbon forms. The word noodle came into English around 1779 and derives from the German *nudel*, probably a variant of *knödel*, "dumpling."

> **HINTS** Store fresh noodles in plastic in the refrigerator for up to three days; they can also be frozen. Cooked noodles can be coated with a little oil, wrapped, and kept in the refrigerator for one day.
>
> ▌ Uncooked spaghetti noodles work better than toothpicks to hold together stuffed chicken, such as chicken Kiev.

NORWAY LOBSTER: see LANGOUSTINE.

NOSE: see BOUQUET.

NOUGAT is a type of chewy or brittle confection made of sugar/honey paste with egg white and mixed with nuts (usually almonds) and sometimes pieces of fruit. Nougat derives from the Latin *nux*, "nut." The origin of nougat is in question. Most historians believe that nougat comes from ancient Rome, where a sweet made from honey, almonds, and eggs was made and reserved for special functions or as an offering to the gods. However, French historians think that nougat traces back to a Greek walnut confection. *The Oxford English Dictionary* records the word as dating to 1827.

NOUVELLE CUISINE is a new style/school of French cooking that avoids rich sauces and emphasizes freshness, bringing out the natural flavors of foods, as well as presentation. The style emphasizes using little flour or fat and stresses light sauces and the use of fresh seasonal produce. The term can be applied to other cuisines following this approach. Literally meaning "new cookery," the term was first recorded in 1975.

NUOC CHAM or **NUOC MAM PHA** is a Vietnamese dipping sauce/condiment made of lime/lemon juice, fish sauce (*nuoc mam*), sugar, and water. Sometimes minced garlic, chopped or minced Serrano peppers, and shredded carrot are added.

NUOC MAM: see FISH SAUCE.

NUT is the dry, one-seeded fruit of various trees or shrubs. It consists of a kernel or meat, often edible, in a hard and woody, or tough and leathery, shell, which is more or less separable from the seed itself. Familiar nuts are acorn, chestnut, pecan, and walnut. Other hard-shell fruits are also loosely called nuts, such as the almond and peanut. The word nut comes from the Indo-European root *kneu-, meaning "lump/nut." Ounce for ounce, peanuts and almonds have almost as much protein as red meat but without cholesterol. The nuts with the highest fat content are pecans, with more than 70% fat.

NUT ESSENTIALS

■ Nuts in the shell should not have cracks, holes, or mold. If you shake them, you should not hear rattling. They keep for six to twelve months if kept from heat, light, and moisture.

■ Shelled nuts should be plump. They should be kept in an airtight container at room temperature for one to two months or in the refrigerator for three to six months, or in a zip-lock freezer bag in the freezer for nine to twelve months. Pistachios and chestnuts cannot be kept that long.

■ One pound of unshelled nuts yields a half pound of nutmeats.

■ To aid in cracking, cover shells with boiling water for 15 minutes. Drain and dry before cracking. You can also bake at 350°F for 15–20 minutes to make the shells more brittle. Walnuts and pecans should be cracked along the seam. Pliers can be used to crack nuts.

■ It is better to chop nuts by hand than to use a food processor. If you want to use one, use the pulse setting. Nuts are best chopped when they are warm. Microwave or oven-warm them for a few minutes before chopping.

■ To use salted nuts when unsalted are called for in a recipe, put the salted nuts in boiling water for 2 minutes, then drain and dry on a baking sheet in a 250°F oven.

NUTS AND NUTLIKE FOODS

A nut is a dry, hard fruit that does not split open at maturity to release its single seed. A nut develops from more than one carpel (female reproductive structure) and has a tough, woody wall. Some things are called "nuts" that really are not: the peanut is a legume; the coconut, a drupe; and the Brazil nut, a seed. These are some nuts and nutlike foods:

ACORN	COCONUT	IVORY NUT
ALMOND	COFFEE NUT	KOLA NUT
ARECA NUT	COHUNE NUT	LYCHEE NUT
BEECHNUT	CONKER	MACADAMIA NUT
BEN NUT	COQUILLA NUT	MONKEY NUT
BETEL NUT	COROZO	PALM NUT
BITTERNUT	CUMARA NUT	PEANUT
BLACK WALNUT	DIKA NUT	PECAN
BONDUC NUT	EARTHNUT	PHYSIC NUT
BRAZIL NUT	ENGLISH WALNUT	PINE NUT, PIGNOLI, OR PIÑON
BREADNUT	FILBERT	PISTACHIO
BUTTERNUT	GROUNDNUT	QUANDONG
CANDLENUT	GRUGRU	QUINOA
CASHEW	GUM NUT	SAL NUT
CHESTNUT	HAZELNUT	SASSAFRAS NUT
CHINQUAPIN	HICKORY NUT	SOUARI NUT
CIKA	HOGNUT	WALNUT
COBNUT	HORSE CHESTNUT	WATER CHESTNUT

NUTMEG is an East Indian evergreen tree widely cultivated for its aromatic seed that yields two spices, nutmeg and mace. (Mace comes from the outer covering of the seed.) Etymologically, nutmeg means "nut that smells of musk," probably from the Latin *nux muscata/muga*, "musky or musk-scented nut." Nutmeg was not used for cooking until the sixteenth century.

HINTS Nutmeg you grind yourself is far superior to the powdered version. Add it at the start of cooking so its flavor mellows and combines with other ingredients.

▌Nutmeg should be stored in an airtight container if ground ahead of time but is best if ground as you need it. It is more delicate in flavor and aroma than mace.

OAKY is a taste in a wine or liquor derived from aging in oak casks and barrels. Many of the world's best red and white wines are aged in wood before bottling. This taste usually has a smokiness and flavoring of vanilla, cloves, or other spices. New oak barrels contribute stronger flavor to a wine than older storage barrels. The characteristic flavorings derive from the "charring" of the barrel, which occurs from heating the iron stave-rings that hold the barrel staves in place after contraction and the flaming of the interior.

OAT (OATS) is a hardy cereal grass and its grains used as food. The *Oxford English Dictionary* says that the word oat differs from other names of cereals (like wheat and rye) in that, while these are mass nouns, the collective form of which is singular, and with no plural form in ordinary language, oat is an individual singular, the collective or mass sense of which has to be expressed by the plural, for example, "Is the crop rye or oats?" Wheat, barley, and oats are cereals. The *Oxford English Dictionary* says it seems likely that the word originally denoted not the plant or its produce, but an individual grain. Oats are the most nutritious of the cereal grasses, and are also the grain with the highest fat content. Oats contain two to five times the amount of fat as wheat.

OATCAKE is a flat, unleavened cake of baked oatmeal, usually thin and unsweetened. It was first recorded in English around 1400.

OATMEAL is a word for porridge or meal made from rolled or ground oats. The porridge is also called ROLLED OATS. Quick-cooking rolled oats are hulled groats that have been cut into several pieces before being steamed and rolled into thinner flakes. Steel-cut oats (or IRISH OATMEAL) are groats that have been cut into two to three pieces and not rolled. They take considerably longer to cook than rolled oats and are chewy. Oatmeal's high level of soluble fiber slows down the digestive process, making you feel full longer. Oatmeal traveled to the North Pole with Admiral Richard Byrd, to the South Pole with Roald Amundsen, and to Mount Everest with Sir Edmund Hillary. It also has orbited the Earth with the astronauts.

HINT If you cook oatmeal in milk rather than water, the oatmeal will taste creamier.

OBENTO: see BENTO BOX.

O'BRIEN POTATOES is a dish of diced potatoes fried with chopped onions and pimientos or red and green sweet peppers. The name seems to come from the longtime association between the Irish and potatoes.

OENOLOGY, also spelled ENOLOGY, is the art and science of winemaking, or the knowledge of or expertise in wines and winemaking. The term dates to 1814 and comes from French.

OFFAL are viscera/entrails, internal organs, and trimmings of a butchered animal, often considered inedible or worthless. However, many do consider the heart, liver, brains, tongue, feet and ankles, kidneys, sweetbreads, and tripe of some animals to be edible; these are also called VARIETY MEATS. The term offal may derive from Middle Dutch and German and was first recorded in English around 1425 in this sense.

OFFSET SPATULA, also called TURNER or FLIPPER, has a blade that does not come straight (parallel) out of the handle, but angles down. This style of utensil aids in trying to get around or under certain items that are cooking in a frying pan or on a griddle without disturbing other items.

OIL is basically any of a group of liquid edible fats that are obtained from animals and plants, and are generally slippery, combustible, viscous, liquid, or liquefiable at room temperatures. Olive and canola oils lower blood cholesterol and resist oxidation, making them the healthiest choices.

OIL ESSENTIALS

■ When oil is being heated, it is hot and ready to cook with when it becomes fragrant and shimmers. The minimum smoke point of an oil to be used for frying is 375°F or more. An oil going beyond the smoke point is at the flash point, where it will burst into flames.

■ Store any oil in airtight containers away from light and heat. Store cooking oils in a tray that can be cleaned; this also keeps the bottles from getting knocked over.

■ Do not drop food into hot oil or fat (or even boiling water). Gently slip it in using a slotted utensil or long-handled tongs.

■ If you keep the oil for reuse when frying, make sure you strain the oil after each use through cheesecloth or paper towels and refrigerate the oil to preserve it. Discard the oil after five to six uses, for it develops fatty acids that will result in bad flavors. Also, use the oil only for frying the same food, which will prevent the transfer of flavors from one food to another.

■ Clean up spilled oil with flour, then spray with window cleaner.

■ Butter and extra-virgin olive oil have low smoke points. But combining another vegetable oil with butter raises the smoke point. Canola, corn, peanut, and safflower oils have high smoke points. Unrefined oils are best for adding flavor to dressings but are not good for cooking due to their low smoke points.

OIL

389

OKRA are the long, green, edible pods of a tall, coarse tropical plant. These slender, ribbed, sticky, pods are cooked as a vegetable and used as the base for soups and stews, as cooked okra releases a viscous substance that can serve as a thickening agent. The word is from a West African language.

> **HINTS** Choose okra that has bright color and no soft spots or bruises, especially pods no longer than four inches. Large pods are tougher and more fibrous.

> ▌Keep pods in a paper towel in a perforated plastic bag in the refrigerator for up to three days. Blanched, they can be frozen for up to eight months.

OLEOMARGARINE: see MARGARINE.

OLIVE is an evergreen tree (*Olea europaea*) long cultivated in the Mediterranean region for its one-seeded fruit and its oil. The word olive comes from the Latin *oliva*, "oil." Fresh, unprocessed olives are inedible because of their extreme bitterness, resulting from a glucoside that can be neutralized by treatments with a dilute alkali, such as lye or salt, that dispels some of the bitterness. The fruit is eaten green, ripe, or pickled, or pressed to extract olive oil. The edible olive was grown on the island of Crete about 3500 BC. Olive oil was prized in Greece during the time of Homer. The olive tree is a very hardy plant and can live for a long time, up to fifteen hundred years or more. Some plants are said to be over two thousand years old and still producing olives.

> **HINTS** The color of an olive depends on when it is picked; green are those picked before ripe; black are completely ripe when picked. Choose evenly colored olives without white spots.

> ▌Olives do not lose their flavor with high-cooking temperatures. The flavors are quite stable and heat resistant.

OLIVE VARIETIES

The only difference between green olives and black olives is ripeness. Unripe olives are green, whereas fully ripe olives are black. Olives are cured or pickled before consumption, using various methods; they may be oil-cured, water-cured, brine-cured, dry-cured, or lye-cured. Some varieties of olives are listed here:

ALPHONSO	LIGURIA	PICHOLINE
ARBEQUINA	LUGANO	PONENTINE
CERIGNOLA	MANZANILLA	SEVILLANO
GAETA	MOROCCAN	SICILIAN
KALAMATA OR GREEK	NIÇOISE	SPANISH
LA CATALAN	NYON	

OLIVE OIL is oil pressed from the fruit of the olive tree. Olive oil is classified into five grades: (1) virgin, from first pressings that meet defined standards; (2) pure, or edible, a mixture of refined and virgin; (3) refined, or commercial, consisting of lampante from which acid, color, and odor have been removed; (4) lampante, high-acid oil, obtained from a second pressing of residual pulp with hot water (some inferior virgin oils are classed as lampante); (5) sulfide, extracted with solvents and refined repeatedly. In the United States olive oil is graded differently than it is in the rest of the world, as the nation is not part of the International Olive Oil Council, which defines the standards and monitors production of olive oil. In Europe the source on an olive oil label means only the country in which it was bottled, not where the olives were grown, unless the specific estate from which the olives came is given. The best Italian olive oils are labeled "*produtto e imbottigliato*," which means "produced and bottled by," but if only one of these words is on the label, the olive oil could have come from anywhere, even another country. Olive oil does not improve with aging. It is probably at its best soon after pressed, but the diminution of quality, with good storage, is quite slow. Color is also not a gauge as to the quality of olive oil. You can determine which olive oil is best by tasting it like wine (taking a sip and swishing it around your mouth and tongue), or dipping a piece of bread into it and tasting it (this is the traditional way). Olive oil does not prevent sticking in cooking if it is heated to its smoke point (around 400°F).

OLLA PODRIDA (pronounced ol-uh puh-DREE-duh) is a highly seasoned Spanish and Latin American stew made of meat and vegetables like tomatoes, as well as sausage and chickpeas. Olla podrida (Spanish for "rotten pot") also describes any dish containing a great variety of ingredients.

OMEGA-3 FATTY ACID or **OMEGA-3** is a type of polyunsaturated fatty acid that is found especially in fish, fish oils, green leafy vegetables, and some nuts and vegetable oils. This fatty acid has received much attention for its contribution in reducing the risk of heart disease and stroke. Although omega-3 fatty acids have been known as essential to normal growth and health since the 1930s, awareness of their health benefits has dramatically increased in the past few years. Six times richer than most fish oils in omega-3, flax (or linseed) and its oil is the most widely available botanical source of omega-3. Eggs from chickens fed greens and insects, milk and cheese from grass-fed cows, and grass-fed beef are also good sources.

OMELET or **OMELETTE** is a dish of beaten eggs or an egg mixture cooked until just set, often with seasonings and fillings and folded in half. Omelet's root sense is "thin layer/crêpe," and it was first described in English as a "pancake of eggs." Rolled omelets are called French omelets. French and American omelets are folded differently. The American way is once over. The French way is to fold it in thirds, with each side folded toward the middle. Some cooks use a special omelet pan for making this dish: a shallow frying pan, often with nonstick coating. A Japanese *tamago* is a square omelet cooked in a pan called a *makiyakinabe*.

OMELET/FRITTATA. There is a difference between an omelet and a frittata. In an omelet, the filling is spooned on top of partially set eggs, then the omelet is cooked a few seconds more, folded, and turned onto the plate and served warm. An omelet can also be made without a filling. In a frittata, the filling is prepared in the pan, and the egg mixture is poured over it and then cooked until the eggs are set. A frittata can be finished on the stovetop or in the oven; it can be served hot, warm, or at room temperature.

HINT Use a nonstick or well-seasoned pan with sloped sides so you can easily slide out a finished omelet. Use unsalted (not salted) butter in the pan. Do not add fillings until the eggs have started to set.

ONGLET: see HANGER STEAK.

ONION is a plant (*Allium cepa*) cultivated for its rounded aromatic/pungent edible bulb. Onions are one of the most versatile vegetables and can be eaten raw, cooked, or pickled, and used as a flavoring or seasoning. Onion comes from the Latin word *unio*, "oneness," as it consists of a single bulb. There are two basic types of onion: fresh/spring onions and dried/storage onions. Fresh includes green onions, Vidalia onion, Maui onion, and Walla Walla onion. Dried includes pearl onion, red onion, shallot, Spanish onion, white onion, and yellow onion. Onions, scallions, shallots, leeks and others in the onion family are widely used in cooking because they do more than add flavor. The volatile oils irritate your eyes, taste buds and olfactory cells. This is a plus if kept in bounds, because if the taste buds and olfactory cells are slightly teased, you are better able to taste and smell the food. Some onions are sweeter than others because they have a higher water and sugar content and a lower level of sulfuric compounds. Sweetness depends on the type of onion, the climate, and the soil they were grown in. The accepted standard for a sweet onion is at least 6% sugar, and it sometimes exceeds 10%, depending on the particular growing season. The water content of sweet onions is higher than that of regular onions, which further dilutes the sulfur.

ONION ESSENTIALS

■ French onion soup sometimes turns blue or blue-gray because red onions have a pigment that turns the soup alkaline, which causes the blueness. To overcome or prevent this, add an oxidative agent, such as lemon juice or wine.

■ Choose firm dry onions with shiny, tissue-thin skins. "Necks" should be tight and dry. If they look too dry or discolored or have soft, wet spots, they aren't fresh. Avoid those with green shoots.

■ Choose green onions with green shoots and white bulbs.

■ Green onions can be kept in the refrigerator in a perforated plastic bag for up to two weeks. Keep other onions in a basket or crate in a cool, dark, well-ventilated place, away from other vegetables.

■ To mellow an onion, slice or cut it as the recipe directs, then soak in cold water for 30–60 minutes, changing the water a few times. Drain and pat dry. Another way is to rinse the onion in a colander and then squeeze off the moisture with a towel. To make onions milder before further cooking, blanch them for 3–5 minutes in boiling liquid.

■ Using a food processor to chop an onion is not a good idea, as it actually crushes the onion. You want to avoid crushing the onion cells and releasing their gas.

■ To remove onion odors, rub your hands and utensils with lemon juice or with a mixture of vinegar and salt, or rub your fingers on the bowl of a stainless-steel spoon under warm water.

■ Don't throw the paperlike onion skin into the garbage disposal, as it might clog the disposal. Instead, throw it into a wastebasket.

■ To minimize tearing when peeling or cutting onions, try putting them in the freezer for 20–30 minutes or refrigerating for a couple of hours before slicing. Using a sharp knife also reduces the amount of juice, and the sharper the knife, the cleaner the cut, and thus the faster the job is done. Cut off the stem end first and the root end last, or peel under cold water, which will prevent the volatile oils from rising.

■ Onions cooked in butter are more flavorful than those cooked in water because not only does the butter contributes its own distinctive flavor, but its fat content (about 80%) captures the desirable onion essence that would otherwise partially dissipate into the air.

■ Sometimes the inside of a whole onion pops out when boiled, because

of the force of pent-up steam. To avoid this, pierce the onion a couple of times with a thin skewer or make a ¼-inch X-shaped incision into the root end. Onions should be simmered and not boiled—boiling increases the chance of pop-out, because the bulb bounces around in the pot.

■ Sweet onions can be used to make wonderful onion rings. Turn the onion so that the tapered side sits to your right. Chop off the right and left ends (this is a vertical cut). Set the onion on one of the flat sides. Cut it in half vertically. Take one half and set it on the big flat side so that it arches upward. Make vertical cuts about ¼ inch apart. Repeat with the other half.

■ To eliminate onion cooking odor, boil 6 cups of water, 1 cup of vinegar, and 1 teaspoon of cloves for 5 minutes.

■ Hang onions in a nylon stocking in a dry place. Store onions at cool room temperature (not in the refrigerator) and out of the light.

■ Cut onions into thick slices for the grill and skewer them edgewise through the layers.

■ Stick a corncob holder in one end of an onion to hold it for slicing, or leave the root end on and hold it during slicing.

■ Make raw onions taste sweeter by soaking them in several changes of cold water. Use vinegar to rinse them and they will seem even sweeter. For salads, put raw onion slices on a plate, cover with plastic wrap, and microwave for 15–20 seconds to sweeten. When they are cool, add to the salad.

■ Chop an onion small and it will blend in with other ingredients; chop it large if you want both texture and flavor to retain their bite.

(continued)

■ Sliced with the grain, pole to pole, onions retain their shape when cooked.

■ A 2-inch-diameter onion = ½ cup chopped onion; a 2½–3-inch onion = 1 cup chopped onion; a 4-inch onion = 2 cups chopped onion.

■ Place a burning candle next to where you are cutting onions and the candle will burn off the onion fumes before they reach your eyes. A small fan will also work. Running water while you cut onions also helps.

ONION FAMILY MEMBERS

CHIVE	GREEN ONION OR SCALLION	ONION
EGYPTIAN LEEK	JAPANESE BUNCHING ONION	RAKKYO
ELEPHANT GARLIC		RAMP
GARLIC	JAPANESE LONG ONION	RAMSON
GARLIC CHIVE OR CHINESE CHIVE	LEEK (Cultivated or wild)	SHALLOT

ON THE HALF SHELL refers to raw shellfish served in the bottom shell, chilled and with condiments. The term dates to around 1860.

> **HINT** For easier shucking, place raw oysters in the freezer for 15–20 minutes to weaken the oysters and cause them to release their grips on their shells slightly.

OOLONG is dark Chinese tea leaves that have been partly fermented before being dried. Recorded in English in 1845, the word is from a Chinese word meaning "black dragon." Oolong is a mix of black and green tea leaves from Japan or Taiwan. The leaves are only partially fermented, which results in the development of some good-tasting oils while not changing naturally occurring oils. The result is a medium-flavored tea.

OPEN-FACE SANDWICH or **OPEN-FACED SANDWICH** is a sandwich made on top of a piece of bread, but not covered with a piece of bread. This term can also be applied to a pie without a top crust.

OPEN FRY PAN: see SAUTÉ PAN.

ORANGE is any of several species of small trees or shrubs (family Rutaceae, genus *Citrus*) with nearly round, orange fruits that have leathery, oily rinds and edible, juicy inner flesh. Orange comes from the Sanskrit word *naranga*; the name of the fruit orange came first, then the color by association. Up until 1920 the orange was mainly considered a dessert fruit. The spread of orange juice drinking significantly increased the per capita consumption of oranges. Essential oils, pectin, candied peel, and orange marmalade are among the important by-products. Sweet oranges are Valencia, navel, and blood. Mandarin oranges grown in Florida, where they were introduced from Tangier, Morocco, generally are called tangerines. Oranges only turn orange when they are exposed to cold weather while still on the vine.

> **HINTS** Choose oranges heavy for their size, with smooth skins. Brown patches are fine; color is not the best indicator. Keep oranges at room temperature for up to one week or in the refrigerator for up to three weeks.

> ▌ Before peeling, squeeze an orange between your hands or roll it on a counter-top. It will be easier to peel and juicier. Or you can soak it in boiling water for 5–6 minutes, which also shrinks the white pulp.

> ▌ Run a can of frozen orange concentrate under hot water to release it. Use an immersion blender to mix the juice with water.

ORANGE PEKOE is a superior grade of black tea grown in South Asia. It is made using only the small, young, tender leaves growing at the tips of the stems. Orange pekoe indicates that the leaves were picked from the top of the plant and are the smallest-sized leaves. There are a number of theories regarding the origin of the epithet orange: perhaps it referred to the color of the leaf buds or of the infusion, or originally there may have been some orange bush in the mixture, or the tea may have been named for the Dutch House of Orange, which first imported it in the seventeenth century. Orange pekoe is now simply a grade based on the size and age of the leaves used.

ORANGEADE is a sweetened beverage of orange juice and water.

ORECCHIETTE, also called CHIANCARELLE, is a type of pasta shaped like little ears, its literal meaning in Italian. A nondomed version is called STRASCINATE. Orecchiette probably originated in the Provence region of France, where a similar type of pasta has been made since medieval times and was likely brought to Italy by the Anjous, the French dynasty that dominated Apulia in 1200.

OREGANO, also called WILD MARJORAM, is a plant of the mint family whose aromatic leaves are used as an herb. Oregano is sold as fresh sprigs or chopped dried leaves. Wild marjoram is another term for oregano, and the word oregano derives from the Latin *origanum*, "wild marjoram," and Greek *oreiganon*, meaning "joy of the mountain." Oregano was introduced to America by soldiers returning from Italy after World War II.

> **HINT** Choose bright green, fresh-looking bunches of oregano with no signs of wilting or yellowing. Refrigerate in a plastic bag for up to three days. Dried oregano may be stored in a cool, dark place for up to six months.

ORGANIC in relation to food means grown with only animal or vegetable fertilizers, such as manure, bonemeal, or compost. Organic farming originated in the 1930s. Organic vegetables have no pesticides or other harmful chemicals and probably arrive at the market fresher. However, organic vegetables are more expensive and sometimes more difficult to find. It is hard to tell the difference in flavor between organic and nonorganic products. The amount of pesticides or other chemicals in nonorganic products is minimal.

ORGANIC FOODS AND PESTICIDES

According to the Environmental Working Group, a nonprofit organization, these foods have the least pesticide used on them:

AVOCADOS	CAULIFLOWER	ONIONS
BANANAS	CORN	PLUMS
BROCCOLI	GRAPES	SWEET POTATOES
BRUSSELS SPROUTS	GREEN ONIONS	WATERMELON

According to the same source, these foods have the most pesticide used on them, thereby making it more desirable to buy organic versions:

APPLES	CELERY	GREEN BEANS
APRICOTS	CHERRIES	PEACHES
BELL PEPPERS	CUCUMBERS	SPINACH
CANTALOUPE (FROM MEXICO)	GRAPES (FROM CHILE)	STRAWBERRIES

ORIENTAL BLACK MUSHROOM: see SHIITAKE.

ORIENTAL RADISH: see DAIKON.

ORVIETO is a light blended white wine, usually dry, from central Italy and named for a town there.

ORZO is tiny pasta shaped like rice or pearls of barley. The name literally means "barley" in Italian. Orzo is ideal for soups and wonderful when served as a substitute for rice.

OSSO BUCO, OSSO BUCCO, or **OSSOBUCO** is a dish of veal shanks and vegetables braised in a white wine–seasoned stock. The term is Italian, literally meaning "bone with a hole/marrow bone." More specifically, it is sliced veal knuckle or shin bone cooked with olive oil, white wine, and tomatoes and served with rice, risotto, or vegetables and garnished with gremolata (finely chopped garlic, parsley, and lemon zest).

OSWEGO TEA: see BERGAMOT.

OUZO is a colorless anise-flavored Greek liqueur with a taste similar to arak/raki, pastis, absinthe, sambuca, and mastika. It is possible the word derives from the Turkish *üzüm*, grapes. It is considered poor form to drink ouzo without eating something. Ouzo is often referred to as a particularly strong drink, although its alcohol content is not especially high compared to those other liquors. The reason mainly has to do with its sugar content. Sugar delays ethanol absorption in the stomach, and may thus mislead drinkers into thinking that they can drink more, as they do not feel tipsy early on. Then the cumulative effect of ethanol appears and drinkers become inebriated rather quickly.

OVEN is a general term for a kitchen appliance used for baking or roasting. The ancient Greeks are credited with developing the oven for the art of bread baking. The word goes back to Old English.

> **HINTS** It is important to have a clean oven because small pieces of residue can start smoking at high temperatures and set off the smoke alarm. Clean the oven with a paste of baking soda and water.

> Many ovens give false readings by as much as 25°F or even as much as 75°F, which is enough to cause trouble. Test the oven at least twice a year (or more often) with a reliable thermometer. An oven takes about 20 minutes to preheat. Don't rely on an oven's preheating timer/signal; always allow at least 20 minutes before baking or roasting.

> For ovens that need to be open for broiling, first heat the oven to its highest setting with the door closed, then switch to broil and open the door a crack.

> You should not buy a restaurant-style oven/stove for your home unless you have sufficient ventilation (because it generates considerable heat and fumes, which may scorch wood walls and shelves) and a sufficient energy source (it demands more). There are two types of oven hoods. One sucks air out of the kitchen and releases it outside. The other only filters and recycles the air and is therefore less efficient. A hood should cover both the front and rear burners and be big enough to extend over the edges of the stove by at least three inches. It should also be no more than twenty inches above the burners; at a greater distance it becomes less effective.

OVENWARE: see BAKEWARE.

OVER EASY pertains to an egg that is flipped over gently when the white is nearly cooked, and fried on the other side, with the yolk still being somewhat liquid. The cookery term is dated to 1930.

OVO-LACTO VEGETARIAN: see LACTO-OVO VEGETARIAN.

OXTAIL is the skinned and chopped tail of cattle, used especially for soup. It can be very tough and is braised or simmered for a long time to make oxtail soup. Oxtail originally came from ox but now generally comes from beef or veal tail. Mentioned as an ingredient in Old English, the soup was first recorded in 1834, though it may have been introduced into Britain by refugees from the French Revolution. The clear soup is flavored with basil, marjoram, savory, and thyme, although these are often replaced by the braising vegetables of carrots, leeks, and onions.

OX TONGUE: see BEEFSTEAK MUSHROOM.

OYSTER is a type of marine mollusk with a rough, irregular shell, found on the sea bed of temperate coastal waters. Oysters have been cultivated as food for more than two thousand years; they are shucked and eaten raw, cooked, or smoked. The Greek word for oyster, *ostreon*, etymologically an allusion to its shell, is from the Indo-European base *ost-*, "bone." The top of an oyster tends to be flatter; the bottom is more bowl shaped. On-the-half-shell oysters are left in the bottom half. A Chesapeake stabber is an oyster-shucking knife. The flavor of an oyster is determined by the species and by its home waters.

HINTS Fresh live oysters have a sweet, mild smell. The shells should be tightly closed and feel heavy. If an oyster stays open when touched, do not buy it. If you are eating them raw, the oysters should be fresh and shucked within a few hours before serving. Only buy shucked-for-you oysters that are plump with totally clear liquor.

▌ Put live oysters out on a large tray and cover with a damp cloth. You can keep them in the refrigerator for one to two days, but make sure the cloth stays damp. Refrigerate shucked oysters in their liquor in an airtight container for up to two days. Frozen oysters can be kept for three to four months.

▌ Scrub oysters with a stiff brush and rinse well before opening. Reserve the liquor. If you soak oysters in club soda for about 5 minutes, the oysters will usually be easier to remove from the shells.

OYSTER TYPES

ATLANTIC OR EASTERN OYSTER (Blue Point, Cape Cod, Chesapeake, Kent Island, Long Island, Malpeque, Wellfleet)	OLYMPIA OYSTER
	PACIFIC OR JAPANESE OYSTER (Hama Hama, Hog Island, Kumamoto, Quilcene, Tomales Bay)
FLAT OR BELON OYSTER	

OYSTER CRACKER is a small, round, salty cracker served with soup and chowder. The oyster cracker was invented by Adam Exton, a baker in Trenton, New Jersey, in the mid-nineteenth century. The origin of the name is unclear, but it may be that the crackers were originally served with oyster stew or clam chowder, or merely that their form (a vaguely round "shell" that splits evenly into two parts) was suggestive of the shape of an oyster in its shell.

OYSTERS ROCKEFELLER are oysters baked in a sauce of butter, spinach, watercress, shallots, celery, and seasonings and served on the half shell. This dish was created at Antoine's in New Orleans around the turn of the twentieth century and was named for U.S. industrial magnate John D. Rockefeller due to the richness of the sauce. Antoine's, where the dish was invented, is the country's oldest family-run restaurant. Their recipe for this dish is a secret.

PADDLE is a small, flat, wooden instrument for shaping, stirring, or beating; it is used for tasks such as working butter.

PAD THAI is a Thai dish of stir-fried rice noodles with eggs, fish sauce, tamarind juice, and red chiles, plus any combination of bean sprouts, shrimp, chicken, or tofu, and garnished with crushed peanuts and coriander. Pad thai, which literally means "fried dish," is one of the best-known Thai dishes outside of Thailand. It was first recorded in English in 1978 and is pronounced path-TIE or pad-TIE.

PAELLA (pronounced pi-AY-yuh or pa-AY-ya) is a Spanish dish made of saffron-flavored rice with tomatoes and a variety of other ingredients such as chicken, shellfish, mussels, and peppers. Paella was born in Valencia, a rice-producing area on Spain's eastern coastline. Early paellas were cooked outdoors over wood-burning fires for farm workers. They were made with rabbit, snails, and beans, and traditionally eaten straight from the pan. The pan used to make paella—a *paellera*—gave the dish its name. Paella is Spanish for "frying pan," from the Latin *patella*, "little pan." Special paella pans are large, anywhere from twelve to thirty-two inches in diameter, with two handles, and paella is traditionally cooked outdoors over a fire in this pan. The pan is shallow, wide, and round with slightly sloping sides that ensure that the rice cooks evenly in one layer. Paella experts like the thin carbon-steel pans that heat fast and don't retain too much heat. You can substitute a stainless-steel or aluminum skillet, but cast-iron and nonstick pans are discouraged. Bomba and other Spanish short-grain rice are the best for paella. Arborio can also be used.

PAIGA or **PAIGYA**: see LIMA BEAN.

PAIN PERDU: see FRENCH TOAST.

PAK CHOI or **PAK CHOY**: see BOK CHOY.

PAKORA is an Indian/South Asian fritter, a piece of battered and deep-fried vegetable, fish, or meat. It is coated in a spicy batter made from chickpea flour (also called gram flour). The word is from Hindi and appeared in English in 1932. Pakoras are usually served as snacks or appetizers. They are created by taking one or two ingredients, such as chicken, onion, eggplant, potato, spinach, cauliflower, tomato, or chiles; dipping them in a batter of chickpea flour; and then deep-frying them.

PALLAR BEAN: see LIMA BEAN.

PALM HEART: see HEART OF PALM.

PAN is a metal cooking vessel that is usually wide and often has a lid and handle(s).

CONFUSABLE PAN/POT. Pots are deeper, with high sides that tend to go straight up from a circular base. A pan, on the other hand, is fairly shallow. Empty clamshells were among the early forms of pot and pan scrapers.

PAN ESSENTIALS

■ To clean pans used for starchy foods (pasta, potatoes, rice), soak in cold soapy water. Hot water makes the starch gluey. Soak a pan coated with a sugary substance in hot soapy water.

■ Grease a pan by putting your hand in a plastic sandwich bag and use that to apply the butter or shortening to the pan.

■ Nonreactive pans are those unaffected by acid, such as ones made of glass, plastic, and stainless steel. Metals that chemically react with acidic food include aluminum and copper, as well as cast iron.

■ A dark-colored pan absorbs heat more quickly than a light-colored one and should be watched so there is no overbrowning.

■ A baking sheet placed under cake pans or a soufflé dish can help the contents rise higher by conducting heat to the dishes and helping to retain it.

■ To clean a burnt pan, put 2 tablespoons of dishwashing liquid in it, add hot water to cover, and boil on the stovetop. You can also soak the pan in baking soda and water for 10 minutes.

■ Use plastic or wooden utensils in nonstick pans. Place cloth, paper plates, or paper towels between pans and cookware that are stacked to prevent scratching.

■ A roasting pan should have sides no higher than two to three inches so the steam will not be retained.

■ To test a pan for hot spots, pour a uniform layer of 4–5 tablespoons of sugar mixed with a couple of tablespoons of water into the pan, then turn the heat to low to medium and wait for the mixture to start to caramelize. If it caramelizes evenly, there are no hot spots.

■ Choose a frying pan or pot that is larger than the burner you are cooking on.

■ Always open a pan or pot lid away from you for safety.

■ It is smart to work with two burners at the same time, one on lower heat than the other. A pan retains heat, so you can move it from the higher burner to the lower burner if the heat gets too high.

■ To prepare a baking pan, grease it evenly with shortening, butter, or oil and make sure there are no uncovered spots. Dust lightly with flour. Chill the pan in the freezer for 5–10 minutes before adding the dough.

■ To avoid carbonized oil buildup in a nonstick pan, use refined vegetable oils that tolerate higher degrees of heat. This includes canola, corn, safflower, soy, and sunflower oil.

■ To coat a regular pan so it is like a nonstick one, coat with butter and freeze the pan for a few minutes. Then coat the pan with vegetable oil.

■ Set a saucepan inside a cast-iron skillet to buffer the saucepan from the heat when making a delicate sauce.

■ Water spots can be removed from stainless steel by putting alcohol or white vinegar on a cloth and rubbing the spot.

PANADA or **PANADE** is a dish of bread boiled to a pulp in water, sometimes flavored with sugar, currants, or nutmeg. The word is from the French *panade*, "dish of bread boiled in water." One version of panada was a concoction of crumbled hardtack and medicinal whiskey or water that was popular in Mexican War field hospitals, where it was given to weak patients; the dish made its way into the Civil War based on veterans' recommendations. The term panada is also used for a thick paste of fat, flour, and liquid (stock or milk) that is used as a base for sauce or a binder for forcemeat or stuffing.

PANCAKE, also called Flapjack, Griddlecake, Hotcake or Johnnycake, is a flat cake of thin batter fried on both sides on a griddle. The word first appeared in English around 1400.

> **HINTS** Whisk pancake batter only until the ingredients are moistened; the batter can have lumps. Too much stirring makes tough pancakes.

> ▌ Heat the pan for pancakes thoroughly before putting in any batter. Turn the pancake when there are bubbles on top. Use a little butter or grapeseed or corn oil each time you add batter, unless the skillet is truly nonstick. Don't smash or push down on the pancakes while they are cooking or they will get dense.

> ▌ If you are holding pancakes for serving, do not stack them more than two or three high.

PANCETTA is a mild, spicy-sweet, Italian-style bacon cured with salt and usually unsmoked. Pancetta is an Italian diminutive for "belly," and it is the cured belly of pork.

> **HINT** Pancetta can be kept wrapped in plastic wrap in the refrigerator for up to two weeks.

PANDOWDY, also called Cobbler among other names, is a deep-dish fruit pie sweetened with sugar, molasses, or maple syrup, with a rich top crust but no bottom crust. The origin is unknown but probably alludes to the dessert's plain appearance. Pandowdy can be made with a variety of fruit, though Apple pandowdy is the most common. The topping is a crumbly type of biscuit, except the crust is broken up during baking and pushed down into the fruit to allow the juices to come through. Sometimes the crust is on the bottom and the desert is inverted before serving.

PANEER (Hindi for "cheese") is a type of curd cheese used in Indian and South Asian cooking. It is an unaged, acid-set, nonmelting cheese made by curdling heated milk with lemon juice or other acidic liquid. Paneer is the most common South

Asian cheese and its consistency is like firm tofu. Most varieties of paneer are simply pressed into a cube and then sliced or chopped, but *chhana* (curd cheese) is beaten or kneaded like mozzarella, and crumbles more easily.

PANETTONE (pronounced pan-uh-TOH-nee) is a tall, dome-shaped, Italian yeast-leavened bread/cake flavored with vanilla, dried and candied fruits and peels, raisins, almonds, and brandy, and traditionally given and eaten at Christmas and Easter. The word is Italian for "big loaf." Panettone is baked in a special tubular mold to give it height. It is beautifully packaged in tall decorated boxes and available from Italian delis and some larger supermarkets.

PAN-FRY (PAN-FRYING), also called SAUTÉ, is to fry in a small amount of fat, as in a skillet or shallow pan.

> **CONFUSABLE** PAN-FRYING/SAUTÉING. There is no difference between pan-frying and sautéing. Sauté is the French word for pan-frying; it comes from the verb form meaning "to jump." Pan-frying can also be called shallow frying, which is the same as sautéing but with more fat, such as ¼ inch of oil in a large, deep skillet over medium-high heat.

> **HINT** When browning meat or vegetables, don't keep moving or shaking the pieces of food, because this prevents them from browning.

PAN GRAVY is gravy made from meat juices, such as from a roast, that are seasoned but not thickened.

> **HINTS** Pour lumpy gravy into a blender and blend for no more than 30–60 seconds. Do not overblend. Pour back into the pot and reheat.

> ▌ Avoid making gravy in an aluminum pan (anodized is okay), as it can turn the gravy gray. Liquid gravy browner can be added to gravy to improve color. Adding 1 teaspoon of instant coffee granules or cocoa per 2 cups of gravy enriches the flavor, as well as adding color.

PANINI are traditional small Italian sandwiches filled with meat, cheese, and grilled vegetables, and usually toasted with grill marks. Panini are made from small loaves of bread, typically ciabatta. The word is an Italian diminutive meaning "little breads," from the Italian *panino (imbottito)*, "stuffed bread/sandwich." Panini is plural and the correct usage for one sandwich is panino, but the usage of panini for a single sandwich is common outside of Italy.

> **HINTS** For panini, buy crusty, unsliced artisan loaves with neutral flavors like wheat or white sourdough that won't clash with or mask the flavors of the fillings. Limit your filling to four or five flavors. For richness, make at least one of the fillings a meat or cheese. Less is more when it comes to filling volume, too. The filling should be thin enough that the halves of bread almost touch at the edges.

Once the panini is filled, press it down with your palm before placing it on the grill or pan so it doesn't slide apart. Toast the sandwich over medium heat so the bread doesn't burn before the filling heats. If using a grill pan or skillet, weigh down the sandwich with a heavy smaller pan, such as a cast-iron skillet. (Cover the bottom of the smaller pan with foil if you wish.) If you don't have a smaller pan that is heavy enough, pull a can or two from your pantry shelf and put inside a smaller pan.

PAN JUICES: see DRIPPINGS.

PANNA COTTA (Italian for "cooked cream") is a type of crème caramel, a cold, light, molded eggless custard flavored with caramel and sometimes served with caramel or raspberry syrup. It is not known exactly how or when this dessert came to be, but some theories suggest that cream, for which mountainous northern Italy is famous, was historically eaten plain or sweetened with fruit or hazelnuts.

HINT If you want to cut the richness of panna cotta, you can swap out half-and-half for some or all of the heavy cream.

PANOCHA: see PENUCHE.

PANTRY is either a small room or closet off the kitchen for cooking ingredients, or a small room between the kitchen and dining room for storing tableware and for serving. The Latin *panis*, "bread," is the base of the word and it originally referred to a room where bread was kept. The pantry dates from at least medieval times and there were similar rooms for storage of bacon and other meats (larder), storage of alcoholic beverages (buttery, named for the "butts" of the barrels stored there), and cooking (kitchen).

PANTRY CHEF: see GARDE MANGER.

PAPAYA is a large oval/oblong tropical fruit of a large tropical American shrub/tree (*Carica papaya*); it has deep yellow pulp and numerous seeds.

HINTS Buy papayas that give slightly when pressed. The skin should be smooth and starting to turn yellow. Let papayas ripen at room temperature. Ripe, cut papayas can be stored in an airtight container in the refrigerator for up to two days.

To ripen a papaya quickly, score the skin the length of the fruit, exposing some flesh. Put the papaya, stem down, in a large jar or glass at room temperature for a day.

PAPILLOTE is a greased, usually paper wrapper (parchment paper) in which food (meat, fish, vegetables) is cooked and served in French cuisine. The word comes

from the French *papillon*, "butterfly." En papillote means cooked in a paper wrapper. Papillote is pronounced PAP-uh-loht or pa-pee-YAWT.

PAPPARDELLE is a type of pasta in broad, flat, 1¼-inch wide, ripple-edged ribbons; it is wider than tagliatelle and often served with a sauce made of game or other meat. The word came to English around 1899 and is Italian from the verb *pappare*, "eat hungrily."

PAPRIKA is a mild powdered spice made from dried pimientos, and it is also the name of the sweet red pepper and the plant on which it grows. The word entered English around 1830 and is derived from the Hungarian/Serbo-Croatian *papar*, "pepper." The best paprika comes from Hungary rather than from Spain or California. The spice originated in the New World and was brought back to Europe by Christopher Columbus. It reached Hungary in the sixteenth century. Paprika had always been fiery hot until Hungarian millers in the nineteenth century discovered a method of removing the seeds and veins in which the fiery quality lies. Now almost all paprika is sweet and is made from a mild hybrid of the plant.

PARAKI: see Lavash.

PARANUT: see Brazil nut.

PARBOIL is to boil briefly and partially cook, especially vegetables. Parboil actually comes from a Latin word meaning "boil thoroughly," but the prefix became confused with one that means "partially."

PARCHMENT PAPER is strong, tough, and often somewhat translucent paper made to resemble parchment; this waterproof, grease-resistant, cellulose-based paper is used as a disposable nonstick surface in baking. Parchment paper is sold in rolls, in folded sheets, and also in precut circles and triangles. Some types may even have silicone added for enhanced nonstick performance. The sheets are used to make envelopes for baking seafood dishes en papillote. Parchment paper is also useful for covering dishes during microwaving.

PARE, also called Peel or Skin, is to remove the skin or outer layer of something such as a vegetable or fruit thinly and neatly, usually with a special short-bladed paring knife. The word dates to around 1415.

PARING KNIFE or **PARER**, also called Couteau d'office or Utility knife, is a short-bladed knife with a tapered 3- to 4-inch blade. It is used for paring, chopping, and slicing, and is one of the most frequently used kitchen knives. Types of paring knife include bird's beak, chef's paring knife, clip-point parer, miniature boning knife, sheep's foot, and slim jim. The balance point should be behind the bolster, about 1–1½ inches into the handle. The main advantage of this knife is the control it offers for precise work.

PARFAIT has two meanings: a dessert made of rich cream, eggs, and syrup that are frozen together and served with whipped cream and syrup in a tall, slender glass; and a dessert of layers of ice cream, fruit, syrup, and whipped cream in such a glass. Parfait is French for "perfect" and was originally a frozen dessert made with cream and mocha; the word first appeared in English in 1884. The parfait glass is a tall, narrow glass with a short stem, and this term came into English around 1907. A parfait mold is usually an aluminum, rounded, cone-shaped mold with a tight-fitting lid, used for molding ice cream for a parfait.

PARKER HOUSE ROLL is a soft yeast-leavened dinner roll made by folding a round, flat piece of dough in half. The word is an Americanism dating to around 1873; the roll is named for the Parker House, the hotel in Boston where it was first made.

> **HINT** As you shape Parker House rolls, you want to stretch the top of the dough ball while simultaneously sealing the bottom. The stretching helps the dough hold up to the expansion that occurs in the oven, while the sealing prevents the rolls from opening up while baking and becoming wrinkled and doughy on the bottom. Roll out the dough into an oblong shape, about ¼ inch thick. Cut into 3-inch circles and brush with melted butter. Make a crease across each circle; fold so the top half overlaps slightly. Press the edges together. Place the rolls close together on a greased baking pan and brush with butter.

PARMA HAM, also called PROSCIUTTO, is a seasoned, salt-cured, unsmoked ham with dense reddish brown flesh, originally from Parma, Italy. It is eaten uncooked. The term dates to 1954 in English. The most prized prosciutto comes from the hams produced in Parma, Friuli-Venezia Giulia, Emilia, and San Daniele.

PARMESAN or **PARMESAN CHEESE** is a hard, dry, pale yellow cheese made with pasteurized or heat-treated milk and usually grated. The curds are cooked and the salt is either added to the curds, or the pressed cheese is placed in a salt-water brine. The word Parmesan is French and comes from the Italian *parmigiano*, "of Parma." PARMIGIANO is an adjective meaning "made or covered with Parmesan cheese." PARMIGIANO-REGGIANO is a premium aged, hard, sharp, dry cow's milk cheese produced in Italy. The trademark name Parmigiano-Reggiano stenciled vertically on the rind indicates true Parmesan from Italy.

> **HINT** Buy Parmesan whole and keep it tightly wrapped in plastic wrap or foil in the refrigerator for up to two weeks. If it starts to dry out, wrap it in a damp cloth covered with foil for a day, then remove and reseal in plastic or foil.

PARSLEY is an herb of the umbel family with aromatic finely cut flat or curly leaves; the Greek root of parsley is *petroselinon*, "rock parsley." Parsley is used to flavor and garnish foods. Flat-leaf or Italian parsley has a milder flavor than the curly-leaf variety. Parsley is often the principal ingredient of bouquet garni and fines herbes.

> **HINT** Refrigerate parsley in a covered jar with the stem ends sitting in a one-inch layer of water, or wrap the stem ends in a moist paper towel and seal in a plastic bag, then refrigerate. The stems of parsley are soft and can be used if chopped.

PARSNIP is a strong-scented plant of the umbel family cultivated for its edible, thick, sweet whitish root. Parsnip comes from the Latin *pastinare*, "to dig or trench the ground," and *napus*, "turnip."

> **HINTS** Choose small or medium parsnips that are firm and not blemished.
>
> ▌ Store parsnips in a perforated bag in the refrigerator for up to one month.
>
> ▌ Waxed parsnips should be peeled. Unwaxed parsnips can be scrubbed with a brush. Cut parsnips can be sprinkled with lemon juice to slow discoloration.

PARTRIDGE is a short-tailed game bird related to pheasants and grouse. The word dates to around 1300 and comes from Latin and Greek words meaning "to break wind," probably from the noise made by the bird as it flies away.

PARTRIDGEBERRY: see Lingonberry.

PASSION FRUIT, also known as Granadilla, is an edible, egg-shaped, purple tropical fruit of certain passionflower vines.

> **HINTS** Buy wrinkled, even moldy, passion fruit and eat within a day. If you buy one that is smooth skinned, it will need three to five days to ripen.
>
> ▌ Keep passion fruit at room temperature until wrinkled. Ripe fruits should be refrigerated for one to two days or frozen whole for up to six months.

PASSOVER MEAL OR SEDER

The seder (Hebrew for "order") is a religious meal served in Jewish homes on the fifteenth and sixteenth of the month of Nisan to commence the festival of Passover (Pesach). Some items on this list are symbolic, and some are actually eaten.

AFIKOMEN	KARPAS	SALTWATER
BETZA/EGG	KISHKE	WINE
BITTER HERBS	MAROR	ZEROAH/LAMB SHANK BONE
CHICKEN SOUP	MATZO, MATZOH, OR MATZAH	
GEFILTE FISH	PARSLEY	
HAROSET OR CHAROSET		

PASTA, dough made from ground wheat and water and formed into various shapes to be cooked, literally means "dough" or "paste" in Italian. Pasta is also the name of any dish consisting of this, typically served with a sauce. The word spaghetti was first recorded in English in the nineteenth century and macaroni as early as the sixteenth century. Pasta as a term for the general concept did not become well known until after World War II. A pasta pot is usually a two-in-one stainless-steel cooking pot with an interior basket with holes for removing and draining cooked pasta.

PASTA ESSENTIALS

- Boiling dried pasta in a large pot can disperse the starch that naturally comes off pasta as it cooks, leaving it neither gummy nor sticky. Use a pot big enough to allow 5 quarts of water for 1–1¼ pounds of dried pasta or 1 pound of fresh pasta.

- Bring the water to a boil, salt it, then add the pasta. When the water returns to a boil, start timing.

- Adding a tablespoon of vegetable oil to the cooking water when boiling pasta helps keep pasta from sticking together but acts mainly to keep the water from frothing. However, if the pasta is served with a thin sauce, the oil will prevent the sauce from adhering, and therefore adding oil is not recommended in this case. Besides adding oil to the cooking water to keep pasta from sticking together, make sure there is enough water and stir the pasta after adding it to the boiling water. For lasagna noodles, cook only a few at a time and remove them with tongs when done.

- It is not necessary to break pasta to fit the pot. As you add the pasta it will quickly soften and fit. But you may find it easier to serve or eat if the strands aren't so long. The longer the strands of the pasta, the more difficult it is for the diner to lift the pasta off the plate. Breaking pasta, however, is contrary to Italian practice.

- Have the sauce hot before cooking the pasta. Toss the sauce and pasta together immediately or do it at the table, letting diners add as much sauce as desired, as they do with the grated cheese.

- Pasta should not be rinsed after it is drained, except when making pasta for a cold salad, because this will lower the pasta's quality and cool it. If rinsing pasta for a salad, rinse only briefly in cold running water.

- Semolina is the best flour for making pasta or noodles because it is made from the durum wheat berry, so it has lots of protein and cellulose and is high in gluten. Pasta made from it keeps firm and doesn't get mushy, for the pasta absorbs less water. It isn't necessary to wash the pasta before cooking. Semolina products are usually more expensive, but they are worth it because they taste better and hold their shape better.

- Undercook pasta that will be baked with a sauce so that it just softens but is quite flexible.

- When draining pasta in a colander, do not drain it so much that it becomes absolutely dry—it should be shaken only a couple of times. The warmth of the cooked pasta will continue to cook it, and and the small amount of water remaining will also help spread the sauce.

- For serving a large bowl of pasta, heat the bowl in a 200ºF oven.

(continued)

■ With pasta (and rice), heating the cooked pasta along with the sauce, even if only briefly, allows the flavors to penetrate the noodles.

■ Use the starch from pasta to thicken the sauce by ladling some of the cooking water into the sauce.

PASTA AND NOODLES: SHAPES AND TYPES

There are many forms of pasta, most of which can be categorized as Italian-style or Asian. Italian-style pasta is primarily wheat based and comes in a huge number of shapes. Asian pastas are prepared from a variety of flours and starches, and they often take the form of long strands or strips. The first known reference to pasta can be traced to Sicily in the Middle Ages. A variety of shapes and types of pasta and noodles are listed here:

ACINI DI PEPE
AGNOLOTTI OR AGNELLOTTI
ALPHABET NOODLE
AMORI
ANGEL HAIR
ANNELLINI
BAVETTE
BIGOLI
BUCATINI
BUCKWHEAT NOODLES
CAMPANELLE
CANNELLONI
CAPELLI
CAPELLINI OR CAPELLI D'ANGELO
CAPPELLETTI
CASARECCIA OR CASARECCIE
CHIFFERONI
CHITARRA
CHOW MEIN NOODLES
CONCHIGLIE
CONCHIGLIETTE
CRAVATTINE
DITALI
DITALINI
DITALONI
DUMPLING WRAPPERS
EGG NOODLES
ELICHE
FARFALLE

FARFALLINE
FEDELINI
FETTUCCE
FETTUCCINE OR FETTUCCINI
FETTUCELLE
FIDELINI
FILINI
FUSILLI
FUSILLI COL BUCO
GELATIN NOODLES
GEMELLI
GENOVESINI
GLASS NOODLES
GNOCCHI
GRAMIGNA
KNODEL
KREPLACH
LASAGNA OR LASAGNE
LASAGNETTE
LINGUINE OR LINGUINI
LO MEIN NOODLES
LUMACHE
MACARONI
MACCHERONCINI
MAFALDE
MANICOTTI
MARUZZE
MEZZA
MEZZE PENNE
MEZZANI

MIE OR MIEN
MOSTACCIOLI
MUNG BEAN NOODLES
NIDI
NOODLES
ORECCHIETTE
ORZO
PAGLIA E FIENO
PAPPARDELLE
PASTA
PASTINA
PENNE
PENNE RIGATE
PERCIATELLI
PIPE
PIPETTE
QUENTELLE
RADIATORE
RAVIOLI
RICE PASTA OR RICE NOODLES
RICE VERMICELLI
RIGATONI
RISONI
ROTELLE OR ROTELLI
ROTINI
RUOTI OR RUOTE
SEDANI
SEDANINI
SEMI DI MELONE
SHELLS

SOBA NOODLE	TAGLIOLINI	TUFFOLI
SOMEN NOODLES	TAGLIONI	TUFFOLONI
SPÄETZLE	TEMPESTA	UDON NOODLES
SPAGHETTI	TORTELLI	VERMICELLI
SPAGHETTINI	TORTELLINI	VERMICELLINI
SPAGHETTONE	TORTELLONI	WHEAT NOODLES
STELLINE	TORTIGLIONI	WONTON WRAPPER
TAGLIARINI	TRENETTE	ZITI
TAGLIATELLE	TUBETTI	

PASTA AND SAUCE PAIRINGS

LONG, THIN STRAND PASTA (angel hair, capellini, thin spaghetti, vermicelli) in oil-based sauce, light thin broth, or light thin sauce	SHORT, CHUNKY SHAPED PASTA WITH HOLES OR RIDGES (farfalle, fusilli, penne, rigatoni, shells, ziti) in chunky sauce, meat sauce, primavera, pasta casserole, or pasta salad
LONG, WIDE STRAND PASTA (fettuccine, linguine, pappardelle, perciatelli, spaghetti) in light cream sauce, Alfredo sauce, light tomato sauce	TINY SHAPED PASTA (alphabet, ditalini, orzo, pastina, small shells, tubetti) in salad, soup, stew

PASTA E FAGIOLI is an Italian cannellini bean and pasta soup served with sausage. Pasta fagioli is considered a peasant soup dish; it was originally made by those who could not afford fancy food, much less meat, and had to make do with cheaply available beans and pasta. Fagioli (pronounced fa-ZHOOL) refers to the cannellini beans themselves.

PASTA WHEEL is a handled tool with a flute-edged wheel, used for marking and cutting rolled-out dough and cuts a jagged or wavy edge.

PASTE has several meanings: a soft food product that can be spread on something such as bread, any soft food mass or mixture with a consistency between a liquid and a solid, and pastry dough usually made with shortening. Paste, from Latin, first meant "dough/pastry."

PASTE TOMATO: see PLUM TOMATO.

PASTEURIZATION is the heating of milk to destroy pathogenic bacteria. This partial sterilization is done at a temperature that destroys harmful microorganisms without major changes in the chemistry of the food. Louis Pasteur (1822–1895) discovered the process in 1886. Milk is also homogenized, which means that it is processed so that the fat globules have been broken up and distributed throughout.

Pasteurization of milk requires temperatures of about 145°F maintained for 30 minutes or, alternatively, heating to a higher temperature, 162°F, for shorter periods of time. The times and temperatures are those determined to be necessary to destroy *Mycobacterium tuberculosis* and other more heat-resistant, non–spore-forming, disease-causing microorganisms found in milk. The treatment also destroys most of the microorganisms that cause spoilage and so prolongs the storage time of food. Ultra-high-temperature (UHT) pasteurization involves heating milk or cream to 280°F–302°F for one to two seconds. Packaged in sterile, hermetically sealed containers, UHT milk may be stored without refrigeration for months. Pasteurization of some solid foods involves a mild heat treatment, the exact definition of which depends on the food. Radiation pasteurization refers to the application of small amounts of beta or gamma rays to foods to increase their storage time.

PASTRAMI is a brisket or other cut of beef (or even turkey) that has been cured in a brine and coated with a mixture of spices such as garlic, black peppercorns, paprika, cloves, allspice, mustard seed, sugar, and coriander, then smoked before cooking. Pastrami is a Yiddish word, from the Romanian *pastra*, "preserve"; it appeared in English around 1914. Both the dish and the word pastrami were brought to the United States in a wave of Jewish immigration in the second half of the nineteenth century. Early references in English used the spelling pastrama and it is likely that the modified spelling imitated the Italian word salami. Pastrami, like corned beef, was created as a method for preserving meat before modern refrigeration. It is often served in thin slices. Traditional New York pastrami is made from the navel end of the brisket.

PASTRY generally refers to sweet baked goods made of dough having a high fat content, and to a dough that contains a considerable proportion of fat and is used for making these baked goods. The word pastry is a derivative of paste, ultimately from the Latin *pasteria*, "pastry," and was coined in the fifteenth century.

PASTRY ESSENTIALS

■ If you don't have a pastry blender, you can use a fork, two table knives, or a food processor to cut in the butter or shortening.

■ Cover short-crust pastry with plastic wrap and put in the refrigerator for 30 minutes so it can rest before being rolled out. This may prevent shrinking during baking.

■ To avoid dark spots on the bottom of pastries, loosen them from the baking sheet using a metal spatula about halfway through the baking; this allows heat to be distributed evenly to the top and bottom.

■ Use ice packs to cool your countertop before making pastry dough. Also, chill the cutting board and rolling pin in the freezer or refrigerator.

■ Roll "around the clock" to flatten dough evenly, instead of rolling back and forth. Think of the dough as a clock face and roll in four directions, then "hourly."

■ A tool called a roller docker or docker, basically a roller with spikes, can be used to prick dough for more even baking.

PASTRY STYLES

CRUMBLY (such as short pastry) FLAKY (such as pie crust) LAMINATED (such as phyllo, puff pastry, strudel)	LAMINATED BREAD (such as croissant, Danish pastry)

PASTRY TYPES

Pastry is a mixture of flour and liquid, usually enriched with fat, forming a light dough. Pastry is used in recipes to encase a filling, or it may be baked and filled or topped after cooking. Most pastry is leavened only by the action of steam, but Danish pastry is raised with yeast. Pastry is the term used not just for the dough itself but for sweet baked goods made of dough having a high fat content. These are some common types of pastry:

BAKED PASTRY	FINE-LAYERED PASTRY	SCONE
CANNOLI	HOT-WATER-CRUST PASTRY	SHORT PASTRY OR SHORTCRUST PASTRY
CHOUX PASTRY	LAYERED FLAKY PASTRY	STRUDEL
CREAM PUFF	NAPOLEON	SUET PASTRY
CROISSANT	PHYLLO PASTRY OR FILO PASTRY	SWEET ROLL
CRUMPET		TART
DANISH PASTRY	PIE	TARTLET
DOUGHNUT	PUFF PASTRY	TURNOVER
ÉCLAIR		

PASTRY BAG is a cloth or paper, cone-shaped bag with one or more nozzles (pastry tip), through which pastry, icing, or a similar food may be squeezed, especially for decorating.

> **HINT** To make a substitute for a pastry bag, cut off a small piece of one corner of a plastic bag. You can even insert a metal decorating tip.

PASTRY BLENDER is a kitchen utensil constructed of several parallel wires bent in a semicircle and secured by a handle, used especially for mixing pastry dough. A pastry blender is used to mix the fat into the flour by pressing down on the items to be mixed (this process is called "cutting in").

PASTRY BRUSH is a small flat brush used for coating pastry with butter, oil, egg wash, or glaze.

> **HINT** A good pastry brush has a comfortable handle that's easy to control at all angles. To clean and dry a pastry brush, rinse the brush in hot water, then squeeze out as much of the water as possible and dip it into salt, which will absorb the moisture. Many pastry brushes are dishwasher-safe.

PASTRY WHEEL or **PASTRY CUTTER** is a handled tool with a thin, sharp wheel, used for marking and cutting rolled-out dough. It cuts a straight edge, while a *pasta wheel* (with which it is sometimes confused) cuts a jagged or wavy edge.

PASTY (pronounced PASS-tee) is a British term for a small savory meat or fish pie or turnover. The Cornish pasty is named after Cornwall, England, and is a short-crust pastry enfolding a chopped meat-and-potato filling. In the eighteenth and nineteenth centuries, pasties were the standard lunch of tin miners in Cornwall, hence the term Cornish pasty. A savory mixture was placed in one end and an apple mixture in the other so meat and dessert could be eaten together.

PÂTÉ is a paste spread of finely chopped or puréed seasoned meat (liver, meat, fish, game). Pâté de foie gras (pronounced pah-TAY duh fwah grah) is a pâté of fat goose liver and truffles, sometimes with pork fat and onions.

> **CONFUSABLE** PÂTÉ/TERRINE. Pâté (French for "paste") was originally baked in a crust, and terrine (French for "made in earthenware") was baked in a dish without a crust. In addition, a pâté usually has a finer consistency than a terrine. When pâté is served in a terrine, it is called a terrine.

> **HINT** Before serving, let pâté sit at room temperature for 30 minutes.

PATIS: see FISH SAUCE.

PÂTISSERIE is a bakery that specializes in pastries and cakes, and the word can also refer to pastries and cakes collectively, as well as to the art of pastry making. The word appeared in English around 1594 and derives from a French word meaning "make pastry," ultimately from the same Latin root shared by pasta.

PATTY is a small, flat, formed mass of chopped food, such as a hamburger. Patty is also used to denote a small pie, small pie shell (patty shell), or a small flat candy.

> **HINT** One way to make patties is to use an ice-cream scoop; another is to make a ball in the palm of one hand, using the other palm in a circular motion to form

the ball. Then put the ball between sheets of wax paper and flatten. Another way is to use the top of a Mason jar.

PATTYPAN SQUASH, also called CUSTARD MARROW, CYMLING, or SCALLOP SQUASH, is a variety of round, flattened, pale green summer squash (*Cucurbita pepo*) with a scalloped edge. It is so named because it is flattened like a patty.

> **HINTS** Pattypan squash is excellent when it is small, smooth, and firm, and has nice color. As it gets older, the flesh whitens and toughens. Buy young spring pattypans picked when half-ripe or mini pattypans.

> Since pattypans are picked when immature, they should be eaten as soon as possible. Keep in a cool place without any plastic wrapping.

> To test cooked pattypan squash for doneness, poke it with a knife as you would a potato. Its tender flesh can be scooped out with a spoon.

PAUPIETTE: see ROULADE.

PEA is a leguminous plant (genus *Pisum*) bearing long green pods containing edible green seeds. *Pisum sativum* is the common garden pea of the Western world; it is one of the oldest of cultivated crops. Pea comes from the Greek *pison*, "pulse/pease/pea."

> **HINTS** Choose peas with smooth, glossy, bright green pods. If you must, they can be stored in a plastic bag in the refrigerator for three to four days. A pound of peas in the pod will yield about 1 cup. Plan on about a half pound of unshelled peas per serving.

> To revive snow peas, soak them in cold water for 10–15 minutes.

PEACH is the round, fuzzy-skinned fruit of a small tree (*Prunus persica*); the juicy, orange-yellow or pinkish yellow fruits have a single, rough pit. The word peach derives from the Latin *persicum malum*, "Persian fruit." The Spanish brought peaches to the New World in the sixteenth century.

> **HINTS** Choose peaches that give slightly to a little pressure, have a nice fragrance, and do not have blemishes. Avoid those with any green. Keep peaches at room temperature in a smooth bowl, as ridges can bruise them. If you need to hurry ripening, put them in a paper bag with an apple or banana. Once ripe, store in a plastic bag in the refrigerator for four to five days. Wash before serving or cutting. Pour citrus juice or a liqueur on cut peaches to slow discoloring.

> Peaches should be peeled before cooking unless you are poaching them. Peaches should be peeled before puréeing if the skin is thick, but not necessarily if the skin is thin. However, a thin skin left on will result in some color flecks in the purée.

> Cut peaches at a ninety-degree angle to the crease, cutting pole to pole. You can twist the two halves of the peach apart and easily remove the pit. Freeze soft peaches partially for 20 minutes to make it easier to slice them.

PEACH TYPES AND VARIETIES

The fruit of the peach tree has a velvety skin, juicy sweet flesh, and a single stone (pit). The peach tree originated in China around the fifth century BC. It was introduced to Japan and then to Persia, where it was discovered by Alexander the Great. Some well-known peach types and varieties are listed here:

AUTUMN RED	LORING	RED HAVEN
CARDINAL	LOVELL	REDWING
CHARLES-ROU	MELOCOTOON	RIBET
DIXIRED	MERRILL GEMFREE	ROBIN
ELBERTA	MICHELINI	SPRINGTIME
FLAMEPRINCE	MOUNTAIN ROSE	SUNCREST
FLAVORCREST	MUIR	SUSQUEHANNA
GREENSBORO	NECTARINE	TRIUMPH
HEATH	PAVIE	WHITE PEACH
LATE CRAWFORD	PHILLIPS	YELLOW PEACH

PEACH MELBA is a dessert of peach halves served with vanilla ice cream and raspberry sauce (called Melba sauce). It was named after the singer, Dame Nellie Melba, by the French chef Auguste Escoffier.

PEANUT, also called EARTHNUT, GOOBER, GROUNDNUT, GROUND PEA, MONKEY NUT, or PINDA, is a vine (*Arachis hypogaea*) of the pea family with brittle pods ripening underground and containing one to three edible seeds. The peanut takes its name from its resemblance to peas in a pod. The word peanut appeared in the early nineteenth century, but the peanut is not a nut but a legume (pea). The peanut plant is unique in that its flower stalks, after fertilizing themselves, each grow a stem that plants itself in the soil. The seedpods develop and mature underground.

> **HINTS** A recipe calling for 1 pound of shelled peanuts means you need 1½ pounds of peanuts in the shell.
>
> ▌ When purchasing unshelled peanuts, shake them in their shell; they should not rattle. Store unshelled peanuts in a plastic bag in the refrigerator for up to six months.
>
> ▌ Press your thumb lengthwise on a peanut shell to shell it.

PEANUT BUTTER is a paste of shelled, dry-roasted, ground peanuts, vegetable oil, and salt, and was created by Dr. Ambrose Straub of St. Louis in 1903 to nourish elderly patients and invalids. Vegetarian John Harvey Kellogg (brother of the cornflake maker) was a big promoter of peanut butter. About 75% of the calories in peanut butter come from fat. Beginning in the 1890s, peanut butter was promoted as a health food for people with poor teeth and as a source of protein for vegetarians. Arachibutyrophobia is the fear of peanut butter sticking to the roof of your mouth.

PEAR is the sweet, juicy fruit, usually with green, yellow, or brown skin and firm white flesh, of a cultivated tree (*Pyrus communis*) of the rose family. The fruit is rounded and elongated and gets narrower toward the stem. The word is from the Latin *pirum*, "pear." Pears are generally sweeter and of softer texture than apples.

HINTS Buy smooth, unblemished pears with stems attached, that are just starting to soften near the stem. Pears must be ripened off the tree. Pears will ripen at home, slowly, if placed in a perforated brown paper bag, preferably with a ripe apple. Place the bag in a cool, dark place. When fully ripened, refrigerate the pears (without the apple). They can be refrigerated in a plastic bag for three to five days. They will usually also ripen, but much more slowly, on a plate at room temperature.

▌ Use a melon baller to core a pear. Toss cut pears with a little lemon juice to prevent discoloring.

▌ A pear should be tested to see if it is the right ripeness for baking by pressing the stem end; if there is a slight give, it is ripe enough. Don't use fully ripened pears for baking, as they will be mushy.

▌ For best results when canning pears, cut them in half (lengthwise), for the core is then visible and less of the pear will be lost when it is removed.

PEAR TYPES AND VARIETIES

The pear has yellow, brown, or green skin; fine white granular flesh; and a central core. The tree is native to Asia Minor and grew wild in prehistoric times. A distinction is made between summer, autumn, and winter pears, and there are dessert and cooking varieties. Some popular pear types and varieties are listed here:

ANJOU	DESSERT PEAR	PASSE CRASSANE
BARTLETT	DOCTEUR JULES GUYOT	SAND PEAR
BEURRE HARDY	DOYENNE DU COMICE	SECKEL
BOSC	GENERAL LECLERC	SHELDON
CHINESE PEAR	JAPANESE SAND PEAR	SNOW PEAR
CHOKE PEAR	KIEFFER	SUGAR PEAR
CLAPP FAVORITE	LE CONTE	WILDER EARLY
COMICE	LOUISE BONNE OF JERSEY	WILLIAMS' BON CHRETIEN
CONFERENCE	NATIVE PEAR	WINTER NELLIS
COOKING PEAR		WINTER PEAR

PEARL ONION is a tiny mild-flavored onion, often pickled and used as a condiment.

> **HINT** An easy way to peel pearl onions is to drop them into boiling water, bring the water back to a boil, and boil for 1–2 minutes. Transfer the onions to a colander and run cold water over them to stop the cooking. Trim the root ends, keeping the base intact. Squeeze each onion gently from its skin.

PEARL RICE: see GLUTINOUS RICE.

PEA SOUP is a thick soup of cooked dried peas, fresh peas, or split peas. Pea soup can be eaten chilled with crème fraîche.

PECAN is a large hickory tree that bears an edible smooth-shelled nut. The pecan has one of the highest fat contents of any vegetable product and a caloric value close to that of butter. The word pecan is borrowed from the Illinois *pakani*, "nut that is cracked," and it was first spelled paccan. Although pecans have a fat content of more than 70%, almost 90% of the fats are heart-healthy. Pecans also contain protein; vitamins A, B, and E; folic acid; and a number of minerals.

> **HINTS** To crack pecans, cover them with water, bring to a boil, cover the pot, and let cool. Dry and crack.
>
> ▌ Keep unshelled pecans tightly wrapped in a cool, dry place for up to six months. Store shelled pecans in an airtight container in the refrigerator for up to three months and in the freezer for up to six months.

PECORINO is a family of hard, pungent Italian sheep's milk cheeses; *pecora* is Italian for "sheep." The most common type is Pecorino Romano, which is salty and usually served grated. Pecorino without a modifier applies to a delicate, walnut-flavored cheese that is mild when young and becomes firmer and sharper with age, while gaining a flaky texture. Pecorino Romano cheese, whose method of production was first described by Latin authors like Varro and Pliny the Elder about two thousand years ago, was originally created in the countryside around Rome.

> **HINT** Forms of Pecorino Romano are barrel shaped and weigh between forty and ninety-five pounds; before release, the cheese is marked with an archaic sheep's head inside a diamond. Select a wedge from the middle of the form, which will not have the bottom rind. The body of the cheese should be white with faint straw yellow overtones, and the cheese should break like granite but should not look too dry. Store in the cheese box of the refrigerator, wrapped in either plastic wrap or foil to keep it from drying out.

PEEL, also called BAKER'S PEEL or PIZZA PEEL, is a flat, shovel-like, usually hardwood implement used to move pizzas and breads in an oven. Peel also refers to the outer layer (rind) of a fruit or vegetable, and to peel is to remove this from a fruit or vegetable. These words date to around 1450 in cookery. A peeler is a utensil for peeling fruits and vegetables and it existed by 1883.

> **HINTS** Before you put anything on a peel, you can cover the peel with parchment paper or dust it with flour or cornmeal so that when you go to slide off your prepared item to be baked, it actually will slide off.
>
> ▌ Try using a swivel-blade peeler for vegetables with thin skin like asparagus and carrots. Use a fixed-blade peeler for thicker-skinned produce like apples, eggplants, and potatoes.

PEKING DUCK is a Chinese dish of strips of crisp duck skin, duck meat, cucumber, scallions, and hoisin or sweet noodle sauce rolled inside thin pancakes. This dish has been made since the imperial era, and is now considered one of China's national foods. Though it did not move into English-speaking territory until around 1874, it was mentioned in a Chinese cooking manual dated 1330. Ducks bred specially for the dish, known since the Ming dynasty, are slaughtered after sixty-five days and seasoned before being roasted in a closed or hung oven. The cooked Peking duck is traditionally carved in front of the diners and served in three stages. First, the skin is served dipped in sugar and garlic sauce. The meat is then served with steamed pancakes, scallions, and sweet bean sauce. Several vegetable dishes are provided to accompany the meat, typically cucumber and carrot sticks. The diners then spread sauce, and optionally sugar, over the pancake—which is wrapped around the meat and vegetables and eaten by hand.

PEKING SAUCE: see HOISIN SAUCE.

PEKOE is a superior grade of black tea, picked so young that its leaves still have a coating of white down; hence the term comes from the Chinese *pek ho*, "white down." The tea is made from the small leaves at the tips of the stem. Pekoe's leaves are slightly larger than those of orange pekoe.

PENNE is a type of pasta in short tubes that are cut diagonally at the ends like an old-fashioned quill pen. The name is the Italian plural of *penna*, "quill/pen." It dates to 1919 in English and is pronounced PEN-ehy. The term is also applied to a dish of this pasta, usually served with sauce.

PENNE LISCE: see MOSTACCIOLI.

PENUCHE, also called PANOCHA, is a type of fudge made of brown sugar, butter, milk or cream, and sometimes nuts. The word is pronounced puh-NOO-chee and is from the Mexican Spanish *panoche*, "(lump or slab of) coarse brown sugar." Penuche was once very popular in Hawaii, where the name was localized as panocha or panuche. The word also refers to a frosting/icing made of this.

PEPINO or **PEPINO DULCE**, also called Mellowfruit, Melon pear, Melon shrub, or Sweet pepino, is a plant bearing an ovoid, purple-streaked yellow fruit with melon-flavored yellow flesh. The name comes from the Latin *pepo*, "melon." Pepino is also the Spanish word for "cucumber."

> **HINT** Pepinos are great served peeled and cubed or sliced. Good-quality pepino melon is smooth skinned and has a sweet smell on the stem end. The coloring of ripe fruit is pale yellow with purple stripes. Avoid fruit that is soft, dented, or light for its size. Ripen pepinos at room temperature until they are as firm as a slightly ripe plum, then refrigerate ripe fruit for up to three days.

PEPPER is a climbing vine (genus *Piper*) with red berries that are dried as peppercorns and also ground as a spice or condiment. Black pepper is made from berries that are dried before they ripen, and white pepper from berries that ripen before being dried. Pepper contains up to 3% essential oil that has the aromatic flavor of pepper but not the pungency. One of the earliest spices known, pepper is probably the most widely used spice in the world today. Pepper is also the name of a plant of the genus *Capsicum*, of which some varieties yield sweet peppers and others yield hot-tasting peppers that can be made into spice/seasoning. The fruit is green, red, or yellow; is hollow with firm walls containing seeds; and has mild or pungent flesh. Peppers that are pungent contain more of the compound capsaicin. The word pepper is ultimately derived from the Sanskrit *pippali*, "berry/peppercorn/long pepper"; application of this word to fruits of the *Capsicum* genus (an unrelated genus native to tropical America) occurred in the sixteenth century. Red, yellow, and orange peppers are sweeter, more mature, and easier to digest than green peppers.

> **HINTS** Help stuffed peppers to keep their shape when baked by placing them in the cups of a well-greased muffin tin.
>
> Don't add black pepper until just before serving or just before browning.
>
> Buy firm, smooth, and bright-colored peppers. Refrigerate immediately in a perforated plastic bag. All kinds keep for a week or less. Remove the white membranes inside a sweet pepper with a melon baller.

PEPPERCORN is the dried berry of any plant of the pepper family. Peppercorns are used whole as a spice or crushed or ground to make pepper. Black pepper is made from sun-dried, unripe peppercorns when the red outer skin turns black. White pepper is made by soaking ripe berries and rubbing off the outer skin. Black and white pepper are both usually ground as a condiment. White pepper is milder and can be used in light-colored sauces because it isn't so visible. It can also be used with grilled meats and potato salads, but it has less flavor and less bite than the black. Green peppercorns are dried or pickled unripe fruit. Pepper's pungency is due to the alkaloids piperine, piperidine, chavicine, and piperettine.

PEPPERMINT is an herb (*Mentha piperita*) that yields a pungent oil used as a flavoring. Peppermint is also a candy flavored with peppermint or a reference to the flavoring itself. Oil of peppermint, a volatile essential oil distilled with steam from the herb, is widely used for flavoring; it consists mainly of menthol and menthone. Indigenous to Europe and Asia, peppermint has been naturalized in North America and is found near streams and in other wet sites. It is cultivated in Europe, Asia, and North America for its essential oil.

PEPPERONCINI or **PEPERONCINO**, also called FRIGGITELLO, GOLDEN GREEK PEPPER, SWEET ITALIAN PEPPER, or TUSCAN PEPPER, is a small, slightly sweet, medium-hot chile. Pepperoncini are typically used in sandwiches, in salads (particularly Greek salads, tossed salads served in pizzerias, and antipasto platters), and as a garnish to lend dishes a crunchy texture and a salty taste.

> **HINT** Pepperoncini are sometimes briefly rinsed in cold water before serving to reduce the effects of the pickling brine on the taste.

PEPPERONI is a type of highly peppered Italian salami (pork and beef sausage). The name is an adaptation of the Italian *peperone*, "chile/red pepper," as salami is seasoned with this. Pepperoni can be traced back to ancient Roman times, when it was easy for soldiers to eat it while marching.

PEPPER POT, also called PHILADELPHIA PEPPER POT, is a highly peppered and seasoned soup made with vegetables, meat, tripe, and dumplings. There is also an Indian version of this soup with vegetables and meat or fish, flavored with cassareep (flavoring from cassava). Pepper pot is also a variant name for a pepper shaker (pepperbox) in the United Kingdom.

PEPPER STEAK, also called STEAK AU POIVRE, is steak covered with crushed peppercorns that is pan-broiled and usually served with a sauce (often made with butter and brandy or cognac). It is also the name of another dish (also called GREEN PEPPER STEAK) of beefsteak strips stir-fried/sautéed with green pepper and onion, and flavored with soy sauce and ginger.

PEPPERY: see HOT.

PERCH is any of numerous bony food fishes (families Percidae, Centrarchidae, and Serranidae) of America and Europe. The derivation is Latin and Greek words meaning "speckled" or "dark-colored."

PERCOLATE is to pass a liquid, like coffee, gradually through small holes or a porous substance. In percolation, water is brought to the boil in an urn and fed up a tube to a basket holding the coffee. After filtering through the coffee, the water drips back to the urn, where it is forced back up the tube and recirculated until the brew reaches the desired strength. It is now known that since this method involves recirculation and reboiling of extracted coffee solution to brew the coffee grounds, the high temperature and reboiling of the coffee actually ruin it.

PERFORATED SPOON, also called SLOTTED SPOON, is a long-handled spoon with a pattern of holes in the bowl. It is used for straining and draining liquids and fats.

PEROGI: see PIEROGI.

PERSIMMON is the orange fruit of a North American tree and a tree of Japan and China, bearing soft, red or orange fruit; the plumlike fruit is edible only when ripe. Recorded in 1612, the word is from the Powhatan (Algonquian) *pasimenan*, "fruit dried artificially," from *pasimeneu* "he dries fruit." The Hachiya persimmon is large, deep orange, and acorn shaped with a pointed end. The Fuyu persimmon is smaller, lighter in color, and rounder.

> **HINT** Choose smooth, shiny, plump persimmons with no yellow. The stem caps should be green. Persimmons must be handled carefully; place them stem down on a plate or in a bowl and allow them to ripen at room temperature for one to two weeks, until very soft. You can speed ripening by placing them in a paper bag with an apple or banana. Once ripe, persimmons can be refrigerated in a plastic bag for up to two days.

PESCE is Italian for "fish."

PESTO is an herb-based Italian green sauce, a purée of fresh basil, garlic, pine nuts, and grated Parmesan cheese in olive oil. The word dates to around 1848 and comes from the Italian *pestare*, "crushed/pounded." Pesto is served with pasta and soup. The Genoese are known for dropping the ends of words and that may be how *pesto al basilico* (pesto with basil) became shortened to pesto. Tradition says that pesto must be pounded with a marble pestle in a marble mortar, using Genoese basil. The purest versions contain nothing but basil, cheese, garlic, and olive oil. The classic pesto contains two kinds of cheese—a little Parmesan and young, sharp pecorino or Pecorino Romano—along with pine nuts. Today, the word pesto is also used to refer to similar mixtures of any herbs, nuts, and other ingredients, and some recipes called pesto don't include basil at all. Pesto and the other green sauces of Italy all predate the tomato; many had their origin in Roman times.

> **HINTS** To prevent the discoloration of basil pesto, be sure that the basil leaves are dry before you purée them, and pour a thin layer of oil over the top of the pesto to keep the air out. Add about 1 teaspoon of lemon juice for every pint of pesto to counteract the browning.
>
> ▌ Often in Italy the pesto is thinned by adding 1 or 2 tablespoons of the hot spaghetti water to it before mixing it with the pasta.

▌Although you can prepare pesto in advance and store it in the refrigerator, it is preferable to eat it freshly made. Sun-dried tomato and olive pesto can be stored in the refrigerator for up to one week. Freezing pesto is not recommended because the texture gets mushy.

PETIT-CABERNET: see CABERNET.

PETIT FOUR (pronounced PET-ee FOHR) is a small, square or rectangular, frosted and decorated piece of pound cake or sponge cake. It may also refer to small, fancy cookies. The term is French for "little oven" and may have come from the practice of cooking these tiny cakes in a low oven at a low temperature. Petits fours can be made with cake of any flavor, though vanilla and chocolate are the most common.

PFEFFERNÜESSE is a tiny, round, spicy Christmas cookie flavored with ginger, cinnamon, honey, nutmeg, nuts, and black pepper (for which it is named). The name is German for "peppernuts/gingerbread nuts."

PHEASANT is a large, long-tailed gallinaceous bird (family Phasianidae), a game bird often braised or roasted. Wild birds have a different flavor from farm-raised pheasants and speciality shops often carry dressed frozen pheasant.

> **HINT** Very young pheasants may be roasted as is, but older pheasants should be barded or cooked with moist heat because their flesh is lean and dry. Meat from wild birds tends to be reddish, while farmed birds have white flesh with yellow fat around the wing joints. Though the hens are more tender, the males have more flavor.

PHILADELPHIA CHEESESTEAK or PHILLY CHEESESTEAK: see CHEESESTEAK.

PHILADELPHIA PEPPER POT: see PEPPER POT.

PHYLLO or FILO is dough in extremely thin sheets that are layered and become very flaky when baked; this dough is very important in Greek cooking. The word derives from the Greek *phullon*, "leaf," as the pastry is thin and leaflike. These tissue-thin sheets of flour-and-water dough are made and sold in 10 x 14-inch sheets as wrappers for savory or sweet fillings for appetizers and desserts.

PHYLLO ESSENTIALS

■ Wrapped well, phyllo can be frozen for up to six months. Defrosted, it will keep for up to three weeks in the refrigerator. Thaw overnight in the refrigerator, and keep the phyllo package closed when thawing. As a last resort only, thaw at room temperature for 5 hours and use immediately. Prepare all ingredients for your recipe before opening the thawed phyllo.

(continued)

- The filling should be cool and it is important to keep the phyllo layers dry and crisp—which can be done by sprinkling bread or cookie crumbs on top of the layers after spreading with butter or oil.

- Your hands should be as dry as possible when handling phyllo. Bring the phyllo to room temperature, work quickly, and cover the unrolled phyllo with plastic wrap or a sheet of wax paper covered by a damp towel to keep it moist. It dries out very quickly. As you remove one sheet at a time, cover the remainder.

- If you tear a piece of phyllo by mistake, don't worry. You can patch pieces together to use in a middle layer of the pastry, and this will rarely, if ever, show in the final product. If you need to cut it, use scissors.

- As soon as you use the quantity of phyllo dough you need, roll up any remaining sheets with the original protective paper, and cover them carefully with wax paper and plastic wrap to keep air out. The unused phyllo can be stored this way in the refrigerator for about one week; you can also refreeze it.

PIAZELLE or **PIAZELLA**: see PIZZELLE.

PICANTE or **PICCANTE** is any of various spicy, hot sauces or dishes of Spanish or Latin American cuisine, typically containing tomatoes, onions, peppers, and vinegar. As an adjective, it means hot and spicy; accordingly, the word comes from the Italian *piccante*, "to sting."

PICCALILLI is a relish of chopped pickled cucumbers, green peppers, onion, mustard, and other hot spices. The plural is either piccalillies or piccalillis. It is of East Indian origin and was formerly called INDIAN PICKLE.

PICCATA is an adjective meaning sliced, sautéed, and served in lemon, parsley, butter, white wine, and spices; thin, breaded slices of veal or chicken are often cooked this way. The word is from the French *piqué/piquer*, "to prick."

PICKEREL is any of several North American species of small pike and the flesh of young or small pike (the word is a diminutive form of pike).

PICKLE (or BRINE) is a vegetable, usually the cucumber, preserved in a brine, vinegar, mustard, or other solution including dill and other spices; the word also refers to the liquid solution itself, and as a verb refers to the act of preserving vegetables in this solution. It is of Indian origin but came into English from the Dutch *pekel*, "brine/pickle," and the German *pökel*, "brine/pickle." Pickle's original meaning was a spicy sauce served with meat. Vegetables immersed in a 5%–10% salt solution (brine) undergo lactic acid fermentation, while the salt prevents the growth of undesirable organisms. The sugars in the vegetables are converted to lactic acid. Pickling is also called BRINING. It takes at least six weeks for pickled food to develop its full flavor.

> **HINTS** Before pickling cucumbers, cut off ¼ inch from each end of the cucumber because the end has an enzyme that may cause the pickles to soften.

> While any vinegar with enough acidic acid (most commercial ones have 4%–6%) will work for pickling, distilled white vinegar is good because it won't compete with the flavor of the vegetable or fruit being pickled.

> Iodized salt should not be used for pickling because it creates a film.

PICKLES AND RELISHES

A pickle is a condiment of vegetables or fruits (or both) preserved in spiced vinegar, brine, or mustard. A relish is a highly flavored condiment that is served to spice up plain foods—or a thin sauce with a strong mustard flavor combined with sweet or fruity content and a vinegar base. Some popular pickles and relishes are listed here:

ASPIC	FRUIT RELISH	PICCALILLI
BEET RELISH	GHERKIN	PICKLED ONION
BRANDIED FRUIT	HAMBURGER RELISH	PICKLED VEGETABLE
BREAD-AND-BUTTER PICKLE	HORSERADISH RELISH	PICKLE RELISH
CAPONATA	HOT DOG RELISH	PRESERVES
CHILI SAUCE	INDIAN RELISH	SALSA
CHOW-CHOW	JAM	SPICED APPLES
CHUTNEY	JELLY	SWEET AND SOUR PURÉE
CONSERVE	KETCHUP OR CATSUP	SWEET PICKLE
CORN RELISH	KOSHER PICKLE	TOMATO PICKLE
CRANBERRY RELISH	MARMALADE	VEGETABLE RELISH
DILL PICKLE	MUSTARD PICKLE	WATERMELON PICKLE
	PEPPER RELISH	

PICKLING SALT: see KOSHER SALT.

PICNIC is any informal meal eaten outside or on an excursion. The word picnic had entered English by 1748 and was borrowed from the French *piquenique* (from the French *piquer*, "to pick at food," and *nique*, "something small of no value"), which originally denoted a sort of fashionable party to which everyone brought some food, and evolved in the nineteenth century to mean an outdoor meal. Food historians tell us that picnics evolved from the elaborate traditions of movable outdoor feasts enjoyed by the wealthy. Medieval hunting feasts, Renaissance-era country banquets, and Victorian garden parties lay the foundation for today's leisurely repast. Picnics, as we Americans know them today, date to the middle of the nineteenth century. Although the "grand picnic" is generally considered a European concept, culinary evidence confirms that people from other parts of the world engage in similar practices.

PICNIC HAM or **PICNIC SHOULDER** is a cut of pork from the upper portion of the foreleg extending into the shoulder; it is not a true ham, as true ham is just from the back leg. It is slightly tougher and requires longer cooking, but is a good, inexpensive substitute for regular ham. Picnic ham is usually boned and smoked, and weighs four to six pounds. This Americanism was coined around 1890.

PICO DE GALLO, also called SALSA MEXICANA, is a relish of finely chopped jicama, jalapeños, cucumbers, radishes, onions, tomatoes, bell peppers, and various other ingredients like oranges and lemon or lime juice;. The term is Spanish for "rooster's beak," possibly because the condiment was once eaten with the thumb and forefinger, in a motion similar to the pecking of a rooster beak.

PIE is simply a dish baked in a pastry-lined pan, often with a pastry top. Pie can be sweet (apple pie) or savory (chicken pot pie). Pies were originally filled with a number of ingredients, so this word may be connected to magpies, a bird that steals miscellaneous objects. In colonial America, pie was eaten three times a day. Apple pies were first served with ice cream on top (à la mode) around the 1890s. The original pumpkin pies made by American settlers beginning in the early 1620s consisted of a hollowed-out pumpkin shell filled with milk, spices, and honey and then baked in hot ashes.

PIE ESSENTIALS

■ Put a couple of large uncooked penne or ziti in a fruit pie's center to prevent the filling from spilling over. Put a baking sheet covered with foil or parchment paper on the rack beneath a baking pie to catch pie juices that spill.

■ Small cracks in pie pastry can be repaired by pressing them together with your fingers; if this does not work, cover with a damp towel and chill in the refrigerator for 30 minutes and try again.

■ You can use a crust-edge shield, or create one with strips of foil with the shiny side placed on the inside, to prevent a pie crust's edge from browning too fast. You can also protect a pie crust's edge from overbrowning by inverting a disposable aluminum pie pan over it, with the center cut out.

■ You should use a high-grade ice cream when topping a slice of hot pie because a mediocre (cheap) ice cream will melt too quickly and waterlog the pie crust because it has so much air whipped into it.

■ Grease and flour a pie pan before putting in the pastry to prevent it from sticking to the pan. You can also butter the pie pan and rim before lining it with pastry to hold the pastry in place, decrease shrinkage, and promote browning.

■ Cover a fruit pie with plastic wrap and store at room temperature for up to three days.

- Cold butter and cold water are key for making pie dough.

- Cooking the filling before it goes in the pie keeps the crust crisp.

- Rotate the pie during baking for even browning.

- A pie will hold its shape best if it is chilled for 30 minutes before baking.

- To store a meringue-topped cream pie, let it cool for 1 hour, then refrigerate. Chill it for 3–6 hours before serving. For longer storage of a cream pie with meringue, insert wooden toothpicks and loosely drape plastic wrap over it and refrigerate for up to two days. Do not freeze cream pies.

- Dip the knife in water before cutting a meringue-topped cream pie, to prevent the meringue from clinging to the knife.

- Fruit pies should bubble in the center, indicating that they are properly cooked. A double-crust pie should bubble around the slits of the top crust.

- To freeze a baked fruit pie, let it cool completely, place it in a freezer bag, and store in the freezer for up to four months. To serve, thaw the pie, covered, at room temperature. It can be heated in a 325°F oven until warm.

PIE VARIETIES

APPLE PIE	FISH PIE	PRUNE PIE
BANANA CREAM PIE	FRUIT PIE	PUDDING PIE
BANOFFI PIE	GAME PIE	PUMPKIN PIE
BLACKBERRY PIE	HUCKLEBERRY PIE	RASPBERRY PIE
BLUEBERRY PIE	KEY LIME PIE	RHUBARB PIE
BOSTON CREAM PIE	LATTICE-TOP PIE	SCOTCH PIE
BUTTERSCOTCH PIE	LEMON MERINGUE PIE	SHEPHERD'S PIE
CHERRY PIE	MEAT PIE	SHOOFLY PIE
CHICKEN POT PIE	MINCE PIE	SOUR CREAM–RAISIN PIE
CHIFFON PIE	MISSISSIPPI MUD PIE OR MUD PIE	SQUASH PIE
CHOCOLATE CREAM PIE		STEAK AND KIDNEY PIE
COTTAGE PIE	OPEN-FACED PIE	STRAWBERRY PIE
CREAM PIE	PEACH PIE	STRAWBERRY-RHUBARB PIE
CUSTARD PIE	PECAN PIE	TOURTIÈRE
DEEP-DISH PIE	PIROG	VEGETABLE PIE
	POT PIE	

PIE CRUST or **PIE DOUGH** is pastry used to hold pie fillings. The basic pie dough is called 3-2-1 dough because it is composed of three parts flour, two parts fat, and one part water (by weight), and when properly made it should be flaky and crisp.

CONFUSABLE FLAKY CRUST/TENDER CRUST. Flaky pie crust is made by not mixing the fat and flour thoroughly in the dough. The fat melts during baking, creating steam that lifts the pastry and forms air pockets and flakes. In tender crust, the fat and flour are mixed so the fat cuts the gluten strands in the flour, making them short and crumbly.

HINTS For a flaky pie crust, keep all the equipment and ingredients cold; for tender crust, keep them at room temperature.

❚ Pie dough should rest in the refrigerator for at least 30 minutes. This firms the fat and lets moisture distribute evenly.

❚ Baking a pie crust "blind" means baking without any filling to avoid having a soggy crust when a moist filling, such as a custard, is added later.

PIE PAN is a pan for holding and shaping the dough and filling of a pie. There are pie pans with juice-saver rims to capture juices and also prevent them from dribbling onto the oven floor.

HINT The advantages of using a glass pie pan are that the glass-type (Pyrex) pans give a beautiful color to the crust and allow it to brown rather quickly.

PIERCED SPOON: see SLOTTED SPOON.

PIEROGI, also spelled PEROGI, is a semicircular dumpling with any of various fillings, such as cheese, chopped meat, mashed potato, or vegetables. The edges are sealed and crimped, then the pierogi are boiled and sautéed/pan-fried and served with onions or sour cream. The word is from the Polish *pierogi*, "dumpling/large piece of ravioli," from the Russian *pirog*, "large pie." The plural is pierogi or pierogies. In English the word pierogi and its variants (perogi, perogy, pierogi, pierogie, pierogy, pirogen, piroghi, pirogi, pirohi, pirohy, pyrohy) are pronounced with a stress on the letter *o*. Pierogi are small enough to be served several or many at a time, so the plural form of the word is usually used when referring to this dish.

PIE WEIGHTS are small ceramic or metal pieces used inside a pie shell to keep it from shrinking, curling, or puffing while prebaking (to prebake in such a way is to BAKE BLIND); the pie weights are removed before final baking.

HINT Raw rice or dried beans can substitute for pie weights.

PIGNOLI or **PIGNON SEED**: see PINE NUT.

PIGS IN BLANKETS also called COCKTAIL FRANKS IN PASTRY, KILTED SAUSAGES, WIENER WINKS, WILD WILLIES, or WORSTJES IN DEEG, are frankfurters or small sausages wrapped in biscuit dough and baked or broiled.

PIKE is any of several elongate, long-snouted, bony freshwater game and food fishes (genus *Esox*) of the Northern Hemisphere. The fish is probably so called because of its snout and long teeth, which resemble a pike (the weapon), and the word is also applied to related fishes of other families, such as the pickerel and muskellunge.

PIKELET is a thin type of crumpet or small, thick pancake in Australia and New Zealand.

PILAF, PILAFF, PILAU, PILAW, or **PILAV** is a dish made of rice boiled in a seasoned broth with onions and celery, and usually containing meat, poultry, or shellfish. The word is from the Turkish *pilâv*, "cooked rice," from the Persian *pilaw*, "cooked rice and meat." Some pilaf is made with bulgur wheat instead of rice.

PILCHARD is a small, edible, commercially valuable marine fish of the herring family.

PILSNER or **PILSENER** is a pale lager with a strong flavor of hops, first brewed in the town of Pilsen, Czech Republic, where the water gave it its distinctive flavor. It is also the name of the tall glass that tapers from mouth to foot and is used for the lager.

PIMIENTO or **PIMENTO** is a plant (*Capsicum annuum*) bearing large, red, mild, thick-walled, bell-shaped fruits. They are used especially as a garnish and a stuffing for olives, and to make paprika. Pimento (spelled without the second i) is also a synonym for ALLSPICE. The plural of pimiento is pimientos or pimiento. The word dates to around 1690 and is Spanish for "green or red pepper," from the Latin *pigmentum*, "pigment/spice."

> **HINT** Choose firm, smooth pimientos with no soft spots. Wrap in a paper towel, put in a plastic bag, and store in the refrigerator for up to one week.

PINCH in cooking is the quantity that may be grasped between the finger and thumb.

PINDA: see PEANUT.

PINEAPPLE, also called KING PINE, is large, sweet, yellow, fleshy fruit with bumpy skin and a tuft of stiff, pointy leaves from a tropical plant (*Ananas comosus*). Originally, pineapple was the word for pinecone, since the cone is the fruit of the pine and apple formerly had the general meaning of "fruit." However, pineapple is neither pine nor apple, but rather a very big berry. The pineapple is classified as a multiple fruit because it is not a single fruit, but the fruits of a hundred or more separate flowers that grow on a central plant spike and fuse together, forming what appears to be a single fruit.

> **HINTS** A pineapple must be ripe when taken from the field. Pineapples do not ripen once they are picked, although they will soften. A pineapple that

shows no signs of ripeness cannot be rescued. Select a pineapple that gives slightly when pressed. It should have deep green, healthy leaves. The eyes should be dry, pale, and mold free. On a ripe pineapple, the center leaf will pull out easily.

▌ If a pineapple is not quite ripe, you can still salvage it: you can increase the sweetness and decrease the tartness by storing it in a perforated plastic bag at room temperature for a couple of days.

▌ Peeled, cut pineapple can be kept in an airtight container in the refrigerator for up to four days.

▌ Pineapple's enzyme, bromelin, breaks down protein, so it can be a problem in gelatin or a meat marinade. Pineapple cannot be mixed with cream because it will cause the cream to curdle.

PINE NUT or **PIÑON**, also called PIGNOLI or PIGNON SEED, is the edible seed of any of several nut pines especially some piñons. These are eaten roasted or salted, or used in making candy or pastry, pesto, and other dishes after the hard seed coat has been removed. Pignoli is Italian and piñon is Spanish. The plurals of pignoli are pignoli, pignolis, pignolia, and pignolias.

> **HINT** Pine nuts are most commonly sold already shelled. The high oil content makes pine nuts quickly turn rancid if not stored properly. Both shelled and unshelled pine nuts can be kept in an airtight container in the refrigerator for up to one month or in the freezer for up to three months.

PINOT is any of several purple/black or white wine grapes used especially for Burgundies and Champagnes. PINOT NOIR means "black," Pinot Gris or Pinot Grigio "gray," and PINOT BLANC is "white." The grape gets its name from the shape of the grape cluster, which resembles a pinecone; the name dates to around 1854.

PINOT BLANC: see CHENIN BLANC.

PINTO BEAN, also called RED MEXICAN BEAN, is a medium-sized speckled/mottled variety of kidney bean; its name comes from the Spanish *pinto*, "spotted/painted." Pinto beans are often served with rice, used in soups and stews such as chili con carne, or used for refried beans.

PINWHEEL ROLL: see HONEYBUN.

PIPÉRADE (pronounced pee-pay-RAHD) is a French dish of the Basque region of eggs scrambled with tomatoes, onions, and sweet peppers, though there are many variations involving other ingredients. It was first mentioned in 1931 in English.

PIPING is ribbons or tubular lines of icing/frosting or cream used to decorate cakes, pastry, and desserts. To pipe is to trim a foodstuff with piping.

PIPPIN is any of numerous eating or dessert apples with yellow or greenish yellow skin flushed with red. Pippins are sweet, typically ripen late, and have good keeping qualities.

PIQUANT means agreeably or pleasantly pungent, biting, tart, or sharp in taste or flavor; it can also mean spicy.

PISSALADIÈRE in Provençal cuisine is an open tart similar to pizza, usually made with onions, anchovies, and black olives. The word is from the French *pissalat*, "anchovy."

PISTACHIO is the edible green kernel/nut of a tree (*Pistacia vera*) of the cashew family. It is sold slightly open and made into a flavoring and coloring. The word originated as the French *pistace*, Persian *pistah*, and Greek *pistákion*. Pistachio shells are naturally beige in color, but were originally dyed red (sometimes green) by importers to hide the blemishes and stains on the shells caused by the harvesting method. Since modern-day harvesting techniques have improved and no longer cause a blemish or stain on the shell, pistachios are dyed only to meet consumer expectations.

PIT designates the hard inner layer of the pericarp of some drupaceous fruits (cherries, peaches, plums, olives) that contains the single seed.

PITA, PITA BREAD, or **PITTA** is a flat unleavened bread made from wheat flour; the rounds are cut in half, and may be split into two layers or cut crosswise to form a pocket for a filling or dip. The word pita traces back to the Greek *petta*, "bread," from *pessein*, "bake/cook."

> **HINT** After you have let the dough rise, punched it down, and shaped it into individual pitas (rolled thin), you can place the pitas on a clean kitchen towel to sit for 30 minutes, covered with another towel. Then place them on an ungreased baking sheet upside down to bake. Turning them upside down immediately before putting them in the oven helps them to puff up.

PIZZA is an Italian open pie made of thin bread dough spread with a mixture of, usually, tomato sauce, cheese, and spices, but there are many variations. Pizza is literally "pie" in Italian and *pizze* is the plural of pizza; pizza pie is redundant. Pizza bone refers to the thick, generally curved, end piece (crust) of a slice of pizza. Pizza was invented in the sixteenth century, and the first U.S. pizzeria opened in 1895. Ultimately, the word is either from the Latin **picea*, a derivative of the Latin *pix*, "pitch," probably for the color of the bottom of the crust after baking, or the Latin *piza/pizza*, "flatbread."

PIZZA ESSENTIALS

■ Cut pizza with a wheel from the center to the crust edge, so you do not drag the toppings out of place. You can also cut a pizza with kitchen shears, which may be neater than using a knife or pizza cutter.

■ Preheat the oven completely for pizza about 30 minutes before baking, as pizza cooks best in a very hot oven at 500°F or higher (professional pizza ovens are around 700°F). A pizza stone, baking stone, or tile placed on the lowest oven rack will mimic the radiant heat of a baker's oven. A pizza cooked on one of these will have a crisp crust, as the stone/tile absorbs moisture from the dough.

■ A crisp crust can be obtained in a cheese pizza by putting a thin layer of cheese on the crust first, then adding the sauce, then any topping, then more cheese, if desired; or by using some cornmeal in making the dough, about ⅓ cup per cup of all-purpose flour.

■ Dust the peel or baking sheet for pizza with cornmeal before putting down the dough.

■ Enrich mozzarella cheese by combining 1½ tablespoons of olive oil and ¼ teaspoon of ground black pepper with ½ pound of mozzarella cheese and letting it sit for a bit before using on pizza.

■ Reheat leftover pizza in a large non-stick skillet over medium heat. Add some oregano, cover, and heat for 5 minutes.

■ For grilling pizza, hold your hand a few inches above the fire—if you can hold your hand in place for only 3–4 seconds, the grill is hot enough to brown the dough but not so hot that the dough will scorch before the inside cooks. Set one side of the grill to high and the other to low, and grill the pizza, then flip and add toppings. To make the toppings hot, close the grill.

PIZZA TOPPINGS

After World War II, pizza's popularity soared. According to a survey, about 62% of Americans prefer meat toppings on their pizza, while 38% prefer vegetables. Some favorite pizza toppings are listed here:

ANCHOVY	EGGPLANT	MEATBALL
ASPARAGUS	EUROPEAN BACON	MOZZARELLA CHEESE
BACON	FETA CHEESE	MUSHROOM
BARBECUE SAUCE	FOUR CHEESE	ONION
BASIL	GARLIC	PARMESAN CHEESE
BLACK OLIVE	GORGONZOLA CHEESE	PASTRAMI
BROCCOLI	GREEN PEPPER	PEPPERONCINI
BUFFALO CHICKEN	HAM	PEPPERONI
CANADIAN BACON	HAMBURGER	PINEAPPLE
CHEESE	HAWAIIAN OR HAM AND PINEAPPLE	PLUM TOMATO
CHICKEN	JALAPEÑO	PROSCIUTTO
CLAM		

PROVOLONE CHEESE	SAUSAGE	THAI CHICKEN
RICOTTA CHEESE	SHRIMP	THYME
ROMANO CHEESE	SPINACH	VEGETABLE OR VEGETARIAN
SALAD	SUN-DRIED TOMATO	WHITE
SALAMI	TACO	

PIZZAIOLA means prepared with an Italian sauce made from tomato and oregano. Pizzaiolo is also the name for a professional pizza maker who is male; a pizzaiola is the female professional.

PIZZA MARGHERITA: see MARGHERITA PIZZA.

PIZZA PEEL: see PEEL.

PIZZELLE, PIZZELE, or **PIZELLE**, also spelled PIAZELLE or PIAZELLA, is a thin Italian wafer cookie. The batter is cooked in a pizzelle iron, similar to a waffle iron, which has an intricately carved surface that imprints a floral design onto the cookie. The pizzelles are usually dusted with powdered sugar and served as a cookie or part of a dessert. The word is a diminutive of the Italian plural of *pizzella*, "small pizza or pie/fritter." A small pizza can also be called a pizzelle.

PLACE SETTING is the group of dishes, silverware, glasses, etc., set at the place of each person at a meal; also, a single group of such dishes or eating utensils sold as a unit.

PLAIN CHOCOLATE: see DARK CHOCOLATE.

PLANK is a length of sawn timber, and to plank is to cook and serve on a plank. This method is used to prepare foods such as shad, salmon, and steak.

PLANTAIN, also called ADAM'S FIG or COOKING BANANA, is a starchy banana-like fruit from a tree (*Plantago*) bearing hanging clusters of these, which are eaten (always cooked) as a staple vegetable throughout the tropics. It is usually cooked while green, before the starch has converted into sugar. The word is from the Spanish *plá(n)tano*, "plane tree."

> **HINTS** Select plantains that are firm and have unbroken skin. Ripe plantains have soft black skin. For a recipe in which plantains are to be cooked by deep-frying, sautéing, or stewing, select yellow-green plantains or yellow ones with black spots.
>
> Keep plantains at room temperature while ripening. Once ripe, refrigerate for up to one week. You can also freeze them tightly wrapped in freezer-weight plastic for two to three weeks.

PLAT À SAUTER: see SAUTÉ PAN.

PLAT DU JOUR (literally "dish of the day" in French) is a dish prepared as a special at a restaurant, in addition to the regular menu. The plural is plats du jour.

PLATE is a dish on which food is served or from which food is eaten, or the contents of such a dish, i.e., the amount of food on a plate. The tableware meaning had appeared in written English by 1545. To plate is to arrange food on a plate, as for serving. The word is from the French *plat*, "platter/large dish," from the Greek *platus*, "flat." Plate is also a cut of meat that produces the skirt steak and hanger steak. Plating is also the act of arranging the meal on the individual plate immediately before it is served. In antiquity, food was placed directly on the table or served in bowls, though there are records of banquets where food was served on platters. Bas reliefs on Assyrian buildings show noblemen eating from individual trays, and archaeologists have found Assyrian plates made of alabaster, bronze, and stone. When the Dark Ages arrived, the plate disappeared and did not reappear until the sixteenth century. However, it was the boule, a round bread loaf popular in the Middle Ages, that evolved into the trencher (at first a slice from the boule), which evolved into the rim-shape plate.

PLUM is any of numerous varieties of small to medium-sized, round or oval, smooth-skinned fruits with a single pit from a tree (genus *Prunus*). Plum and PRUNE are ultimately the same word, coming from the Latin *prunum* and Greek *proumnon*. Plums are grown and cultivated on every continent in the world except Antarctica.

> **HINTS** Ripe plums have some give on the blossom end. Put unripe or hard plums in a paper bag at room temperature for a few days. Ripe plums can be kept in the refrigerator for three to five days.

> Plum skins can be removed by blanching the plums for 1–2 minutes after cutting an X in the skin.

PLUM TYPES AND VARIETIES

The plum is a stone (pit) fruit like the cherry and peach. It originated in Asia and was particularly prized after the Renaissance. Some varieties are used for jams, preserves, and distillation, and others are cooked or eaten as dessert fruits. Plum varieties that can be or have been dried without resulting in fermentation are called prunes. A number of plum types and varieties are listed here:

ALLEGHENY PLUM	BONNE DE BRY PLUM	CHERRY PLUM
AMERICAN RED PLUM	BRIGNOLE PLUM	COMMON PLUM
AUGUST PLUM	BROWN PLUM	CZAR PLUM
BEACH PLUM	CANADA PLUM	

DAMSON PLUM OR DAMASK PLUM	HOG PLUM	PURPLE PLUM
DATE PLUM	JAPANESE PLUM	RED PLUM
DRIED PLUM	KIRKE BLUE PLUM	SIERRA PLUM
GOOSE PLUM	MARMALADE PLUM	VICTORIA PLUM
GREENGAGE PLUM	MYROBALAN PLUM	VIOLET PLUM
GREEN PLUM	PACIFIC PLUM	WILD PLUM
GROUND PLUM	PERSHORE PLUM	YELLOW PLUM

PLUM PUDDING is a rich boiled or steamed pudding containing fruits and spices, made from flour and suet and often flavored with brandy or rum. Plum pudding was so named because it was originally made with plums, and the word plum was retained to denote raisins, which became the main ingredient; the term dates to around 1711. CHRISTMAS PUDDING is a plum pudding rich with raisins, currants, and dried fruit; SUET PUDDING has just raisins.

PLUM SAUCE: see DUCK SAUCE.

PLUM TOMATO, also called PASTE TOMATO or PROCESSING TOMATO, is a kind of small, firm, oblong, or plum-shaped tomato. The word dates to 1879 in English. The plum tomato is a type of tomato bred for sauce and packing purposes. Plum tomatoes have significantly fewer seed compartments than standard round tomatoes and a generally higher solid content, making them more suitable for processing. Plum tomatoes are also sometimes favored by cooks for use during the tomato off-season, as they are generally considered more amenable to handling and are therefore available in a state closer to ripe than other supermarket tomatoes.

PLUOT or **PLUMCOT** is a plum and apricot hybrid. A pluot is about two-thirds plum and one-third apricot in parentage. The pluot was introduced and patented by Californian Floyd Zaiger.

> **HINT** Pluots should be plump with consistent skin color and firm texture. Avoid those with soft spots or that are green in color. To ripen, put pluots in a closed paper bag at room temperature. Store ripe fruit in the vegetable crisper of the refrigerator for one to two days.

PLUTO PUP: see CORN DOG.

POACH is to cook in a simmering liquid, usually referring to fish or an egg without its shell cooked in water or other liquid near the boiling point, or to cook in a small receptacle placed over boiling water. Poach, the cooking term, is from the French *pocher*, "to enclose in a bag," as the food is cooking while submerged in a special pan, and in the case of an egg, the yolk is enclosed in the white as in a bag. A poacher is a cooking vessel designed to poach food.

> **HINT** To ensure even cooking, bring food to room temperature before poaching.

POBLANO, also called CHILE POBLANO, is a long, wide, dark green, thick-skinned, slightly hot chile pepper (*Capsicum annum*), used especially in Mexican cooking; it appears in dishes such as chile rellenos. Chile poblano literally means "chile from Puebla." Dried, the poblano is called an ANCHO CHILE.

POGO: see CORN DOG.

POIVRE is French for "pepper."

POLENTA is an Italian dish of thick mush made of cornmeal and water that is boiled and then fried or baked; there is usually added butter and cheese, and sometimes other ingredients. Basically, polenta is Italian-style cornmeal cooked until porridgelike. Known since Old English, the word is ultimately from the Latin *polenta/polenta*, "hulled and crushed grain, especially barley meal."

> **HINT** For the best consistency, instant polenta should be cooked for about 15 minutes. This is longer than most packages' instructions suggest. Polenta should be cooked in a copper pot or a very heavy pot.

POLISH SAUSAGE is another term for KIELBASA, the Polish word for "sausage." Sausage is a staple of Polish cuisine and comes in smoked and fresh varieties, almost always based on pork but sometimes made with beef, turkey, horse, lamb, veal, or bison; every region has its own specialty.

POLLO is the Italian word for "chicken."

POLLOCK, also called SAITHE, is an important food and game fish (*Pollachius virens*) of northern seas of the North Atlantic, related to cod and having lean white flesh. It is pronounced POL-uhk.

POLONAISE, also called À LA POLONAISE, is an adjective indicating a dish, such as a boiled or steamed vegetable, is garnished with chopped hard-cooked egg yolk, bread crumbs fried in butter, and parsley. This is a Polish-style dish.

POLONY: see BOLOGNA.

POME is any fruit consisting of a fleshy, enlarged receptacle and a tough central core containing the seed. The flesh of the fruit develops from the receptacle of the flower, which completely encloses the fused carpels. After fertilization, the carpels form the core of the fruit, which contains the seeds.

POME FRUITS

APPLE	JUNEBERRY	ROSE HIP
CHOKEBERRY	LOQUAT	ROWAN
CRAB APPLE	MEDLAR	SERVICEBERRY
HAWTHORN	PEAR	
JAPANESE PLUM	QUINCE	

POMEGRANATE is a large, many-seeded, round fruit (*Punica granatum*) native to tropical Asia, with tart, juicy, red pulp in a tough, brownish red rind. The word is from the French *pome grenate*, "seedy apple." The fruit is eaten fresh, and the juice is the source of grenadine syrup, which is used in flavorings and liqueurs.

> **HINT** Pomegranates should be large and deep colored. They can be kept at room temperature for three to five days or in the refrigerator in a plastic bag for up to three weeks.

POMELO or **POMMELO**, also spelled/called PUMELO, PUMMELO, or SHADDOCK, is a large round or pear-shaped fruit (*Citrus maxima*) native to Southeast Asia, descended from and similar to grapefruit, but with coarse-grained pulp and a thick rind. In the United States, sometimes pomelo is a synonym for GRAPEFRUIT.

> **HINT** Pomelos may be used just like grapefruits. Choose fruit that is heavy for its size, blemish free, and sweetly fragrant. Store in the refrigerator for up to one week.

POMME is French for "apple."

POMMES DUCHESSE: see DUCHESS POTATOES.

POMMES FRITES, also called FRITES, is French for "French-fried potatoes." It is pronounced pom FREET and is short for *pommes de terre frites* (*pomme de terre* means "potato").

POMODORO is Italian for "tomato." Dishes described as *al pomodoro* are served with a tomato sauce.

PONE: see JOHNNYCAKE.

POOR BOY: see GRINDER.

POORI or **PURI** is a light, unleavened Indian wheat bread usually fried in deep fat (ghee or oil), in which the flat round of dough puffs out when fried.

POOR MAN'S LOBSTER or SMALL CAPS MONKFISH is a large bottom-dwelling anglerfish native to Atlantic waters. It is firm textured and has a mild sweet flavor, often compared to lobster. The edible tail (loin) is what is usually prepared.

POOR MAN'S PEA: see BLACK-EYED PEA.

POP: see SODA and SOFT DRINK.

POPCORN is the popped grains of a variety of Indian corn with small ears. The hard, pointed grain pops open into a white, puffy mass when heated. Popcorn is usually served as a snack with butter and salt. It has also been called popped corn, parching corn, pot corn, cup corn, dry corn, and buckshot. Most of the world's popcorn is grown in the U.S. Midwest. The term was first recorded in 1819; the oldest ears of popcorn ever found by scientists were discovered in the Bat Cave, an archaeological site in New Mexico, dating back to more than 5,600 years ago. There is very little difference or no difference between the nutritional value of regular popcorn and gourmet popcorn. The gourmet type makes the largest blossoms, but usually they are slightly tougher and less crisp.

> **HINTS** The advantage of air-popped popcorn over microwave popcorn is that it makes larger blossoms, but usually air-popped popcorn is tougher and less crisp.
>
> ❚ Put melted butter in a bowl, then add popcorn and toss before adding salt.

POPPING POPCORN

Popcorn, a kind of flint corn, has harder kernels than other types of corn. Its outer shell surrounds a small amount (11%–14%) of moist, starchy material. Here's how the popping process works:

1. When the kernels are heated, the moisture inside them turns to steam.

2. The kernels have a tough, elastic layer called the endosperm, which resists the buildup of steam pressure within the heated kernels.

3. When the temperature reaches around 400°F, the steam builds up enough pressure and it inflates the starch granules to thirty-five times the kernel's original size.

4. The endosperm of the kernels then bursts and the kernels are turned inside out into light, fluffy masses.

POPOVER is a light, puffy, hollow muffin made of eggs, flour, salt, and milk that rises well over the rim of a muffin cup; it is sometimes also called YORKSHIRE PUDDING, though popover is a strictly North American term, dating to around 1850. Popover pans have deep muffin cups. A popover's dramatic rise demonstrates the power of steam generated by evaporating liquid.

Popover batter must be cold; it should be refrigerated for at least 1 hour and up to 1 day. The cups must be buttered. Take the batter out of the refrigerator 1 hour before baking and stir just before using.

When baking popovers, do not open the oven door during the first 30 minutes of baking. After 30 minutes, pierce the side of each popover with a sharp knife to release steam so they won't be soggy. After baking, pierce again and remove from the cups quickly.

POPPY SEED is the small gray/black seed of a poppy flower, used whole or ground in or on baked goods. Poppy seed is an ancient spice; the seed capsules have been found in Switzerland in the remains of prehistoric lake dwellings. It takes approximately nine hundred thousand poppy seeds to make one pound.

HINT Poppy seeds should be stored in a tightly closed container in the refrigerator to prevent rancidity.

PORCINI or **PORCINI MUSHROOM**, also called BOLETES, CEP, CÈPES, FUNGO PORCINO, or STEINPILZE, is a large edible mushroom (*Boletus edulis*) with a thick, rounded brown cap.

HINT Choose porcini with firm, large (about six-inch) caps and pale undersides. The dried form of this mushroom is more readily available: choose those that are tan to pale brown in color and avoid those that are crumbly. Dried porcini must be softened in hot water for about 20 minutes before using.

PORK is meat from a domestic hog or pig, especially when fresh or uncured. Cured pig meat is HAM. Common pork cuts include shank, tenderloin, loin, bacon, back, spareribs, back ribs, baby back ribs, side meat, shoulder, loin roast, crown roast, loin chops, shoulder chops, hock, Boston butt, plate, jowl, pig's feet, fatback, and ham. Pork marketed today is different from that sold a decade or more ago. Modern pork is higher in protein and has 32.5% less fat and 14% fewer calories; it should be cooked slowly because it is quite lean. There are only two USDA levels of quality for pork: acceptable and unacceptable.

PORK ESSENTIALS

■ Choose pork with a clean smell, rosy to dark pink flesh, and white fat. The leanest cut of pork is the tenderloin, with only four grams of fat in a three-ounce serving of roasted meat.

Good-quality pork is identified by firm pink flesh that shows no trace of moisture. If it is whitish and damp, the meat will be bland.

(continued)

■ Keep pork in the coldest part of the refrigerator for two to three days. Wrap in plastic or wax paper and put on a plate. Bacon, ham, and sausage should be stored in the refrigerator for up to one week.

■ Pork to be frozen should be in freezer-weight bags or wrap. Large cuts can be frozen for up to six months. Smaller cuts and ground pork can be frozen for up to three months. Freezing pork is more damaging than freezing other meats because the flesh is so lean it will become unnecessarily dry when cooked.

■ If you marinade pork, do not serve the marinade unless you first boil it on its own for 5 minutes after separating it from the meat.

■ When cooking pork, the temperature must reach at least 137°F because at that temperature the trichinosis-causing organism dies. But pork tastes better at 160°F–165°F, and should not be tasted until it reaches 160°F internal temperature. All traces of pink do not have to disappear. The meat is safe when the color of the interior changes from a rose pink to a blush of pink. Further cooking toughens the pork. Cook to 145°F and let the roast stand for 20 minutes before slicing, and the temperature will rise to 160°F and the pork will therefore be safe.

PORK CUTS

Pork is eaten fresh, slightly salted, cured, or smoked. There is an old French saying that all parts of a pig can be eaten, and an English saying that all parts can be eaten except the squeak. Pork cuts are listed here, with further descriptions included for the five primal cuts.

ARM SHOULDER	FEET (trotters, pig's feet)	RIBLET
BACON	HAM	RIB ROAST
BACK	HOCK	ROAST
BLADE SHOULDER OR BLADE BONE	JOWL	SHOULDER (pork shoulder, pork butt, Boston shoulder, picnic shoulder)
BONELESS CHOP	KNUCKLE	
BOSTON BUTT	LEG (HAM)	SIDE AND BELLY (spareribs, fresh side pork)
CHOP	LOIN (blade, center loin, blade roast, blade chop, tenderloin, baby back ribs, sirloin)	SPARERIB
CLEAR PLATE		TENDERLOIN
CROWN ROAST		
CUMBERLAND	PICNIC HAM, PICNIC SHOULDER, OR HAND	
ENGLISH-STYLE	PIG'S FEET	
FATBACK		

PORK CHOP is a cut of pork that is cut perpendicularly to the pig's spine and usually contains a rib or part of a vertebra. The center cut or pork loin chop includes a large T-shaped bone. Rib chops come from the rib portion of the loin. Blade or shoulder chops are cut from the shoulder end of the loin. The sirloin chop is taken from the rear leg end.

HINTS A pork chop should be about one inch thick; otherwise, it is likely to dry out when cooked. When broiling or sautéing a pork chop, leave the bone in it to reduce shrinkage.

▌ Besides using a meat thermometer to tell when pork chops are done, press the chop. If it is firm but not hard, it will be medium-rare. At this point, the temperature will be about 137°F, which will kill any trichinosis-causing parasites. Above 165°F, the meat will be harsh and dry.

▌ The shoulder-end pork chop (also called a rib chop or center-cut rib chop), a one-sided, curved, boned chop, has more flavor from fat than a chop with meat on both sides of the bone from the sirloin end.

PORK LOIN is a cut of pork from along the top of the pig's rib cage. The loin has the leanest and most tender pork cuts. Since they're lean, these cuts tend to dry out if overcooked. There are three main parts of the loin: the blade end, which is closest to the shoulder and tends to be fatty; the sirloin end, which is closest to the rump and tends to be bony; and the center portion in the middle, which is lean, tender, and expensive.

PORK RINDS or **PORK SCRATCHINGS** are a snack food made from cured pork skin. Chunks of cured pork skins are deep-fried and puffed into light, irregular curls, and often seasoned with hot pepper or barbecue flavoring.

PORRIDGE is a soft food made of cereal or meal (like oats) boiled in water or milk until thick. The word porridge started out as pottage, which was a beef and vegetable stew.

PORT is a sweet, dark red, fortified dessert wine originally made in Portugal.

PORTER (short for porter's beer) is a very dark, bitter, heavy beer brewed from partly browned or charred malt. It is higher in alcohol than other beers. There is also a sweet, very dark ale of this same name.

PORTERHOUSE or **PORTERHOUSE STEAK** is a choice cut of beef from between the prime ribs and the sirloin, from the thick end of the short loin, containing a T-bone and a sizable piece of tenderloin. The USDA's Institutional Meat Purchase Specifications state that the tenderloin must be at least 1¼ inches thick at its thickest to be classified as a porterhouse. The origin of the name is uncertain, but the name may derive from Zachariah B. Porter, a stockman and the proprietor of the Porter House hotel of Cambridge, Massachusetts, or from a New York City porterhouse proprietor, Martin Morrison. Yet another theory is that the name arose from the Porter House Hotel in Georgia, just northeast of Atlanta. Porterhouse steaks are even more highly valued than T-bone steaks due to their larger tenderloin.

PORTOBELLO MUSHROOM, PORTABELLA MUSHROOM, or **PORTABELLO MUSHROOM** is a very large, rich-flavored, mature, dark cremini mushroom known for its meaty texture, open flat cap, and musky smell. Portobellos are often grilled, broiled, or sautéed. Baby portobello mushrooms are CREMINI MUSHROOMS.

> **HINT** Check that the gills of Portobello mushroom caps are unbroken. Refrigerate Portobello mushrooms for three to four days in a paper bag. The stems should be removed before cooking or eating.

PORT-SALUT or **PORT DU SALUT** is a flat, round, mild whole-milk French cheese that is yellowish and creamy with an orange/brown rind. It is named for Notre Dame de Port-du-Salut, a Trappist monastery in France.

POT is a metal or earthenware cooking vessel that is usually round and deep, often with a lid and handle(s).

> **HINTS** The value of first soaking a clay pot in water is that when the pot is submerged in cold water for 15 minutes, it will absorb water, which will then be released as it heats in the oven. This creates a steaming effect in the food.
>
> ▌ If a pot to be put in the oven does not have a lid, you can cut a piece of parchment paper slightly smaller than the top and put it onto the food. Then cover the top with foil. This is not as good as a metal top, but is second-best.

POTAGE (French for "what is put in a pot") is thick, usually cream, soup.

POTASSIUM HYDROGEN TARTRATE: see CREAM OF TARTAR.

POTATO, also called SPUD, is the edible, oval, tuberous root of a plant (*Solanum tuberosum*) with sweetish orange or white flesh. The potato (common potato, white potato, or Irish potato) is one of the world's main food crops. The edible part of the plant is a tuber. The word potato was first recorded in English in 1565. *Batata* in Taino was changed to Spanish *patata* and became potato in English, and batata still means "sweet potato," though. The potato was once called an earth apple. Baked potatoes are fluffy because they are high in starch and the starch cells, when heated, separate from one another.

POTATO ESSENTIALS

- Select potatoes that are firm, not tinged with green, and without blemishes, cracks, or wrinkles. The buds/eyes should not have sprouted.

- Keep potatoes in a cool, dark, well-ventilated place for up to two weeks. New potatoes should be used within two to three days.

■ Slices of potato can be put in a soup or stew that has been oversalted. In 5–10 minutes, the potato will absorb the salt.

■ Scrub all potatoes with a stiff brush, exfoliating glove, or clean pan-scrubbing sponge under cold running water to clean them.

■ Prick baking potatoes before baking. Foil covering a potato when baking produces more of a steamed potato than a baked potato because the foil traps the heat. So don't use foil if you want the best flavor and texture. If you do use foil, then after the first half of the baking time, uncover the potatoes so that the skin will dry and crisp during the rest of the baking. To retain more nutrients in the skin of a baked potato, shorten the baking time; to prevent the skin from cracking, rub the skin with butter or oil before baking.

■ Put cut and peeled potatoes in cold water to keep them from discoloring while waiting to cook—unless a recipe says specifically not to do this. You can also put raw cut potatoes in acidulated water (4 cups of water and 4 tablespoons of lemon juice or 2 teaspoons of vinegar).

■ Do not buy or use green-tinged potatoes. Green surface color/blemishes are caused by overexposure to light. The tainted areas will taste bitter and contain some level of a toxic alkaloid, solanine—not enough to kill, but it can make you sick. Potato sprouts contain solanine so discard these, too. Brown areas on sliced potatoes mean that the vitamin C has been destroyed.

■ Do not store a raw, whole potato in the refrigerator. The cold environment encourages the conversion of too much of the starch into sugar. If you want sweet potatoes, then buy sweet potatoes. However, the sugar will revert back to starch if refrigerated potatoes

are left at room temperature for several days.

■ Do not store potatoes and onions together because they both emit gases that have negative effects on the flavor of the other and also speed up the rotting process.

■ Processing or cooking a potato and reheating it a few hours later will reduce its vitamin content.

■ To prevent potatoes from sprouting when in storage, store them in a brown paper bag at room temperature. For even better results, put an apple in the bag.

■ To shorten the time for baking a potato, oil the skin before baking or boil in salted water for about 10 minutes or microwave until just beginning to soften. Then place the potato in a very hot oven.

■ Add a few teaspoons of lemon juice to the cooking water to keep potatoes white, or whiten cut potatoes by simmering in milk.

■ Peel a strip around the center of new potatoes before boiling them to keep the skin from splitting.

■ Open a baked potato by first making a dotted X on the top with a fork. Press in at the ends to push the flesh up and out.

■ Dry grated potatoes with a salad spinner before browning them.

■ High-starch, low-moisture potatoes such as russets and Idahos are best for French fries, roasted potatoes, and mashed potatoes.

■ Medium-starch potatoes such as Yukon Golds, Yellow Finns, and Purple Peruvians hold their shape but also have traits of high starch.

■ Low-starch, high-moisture potatoes such as all red-skinned potatoes and new potatoes hold their shape better

(continued)

for soup, stew, and salad, though russets are great for potato salad.

■ Use waxy (new/boiling) potatoes for home fries.

■ If you microwave a baked potato, pierce all sides with a fork and turn over once during the 4–5 minutes of baking

time. Cover the potato with a kitchen towel and let it stand for 5 minutes before serving.

■ Cook baked potatoes for 60–75 minutes at 375°F, for 75–90 minutes at 350°F, and for 90 minutes at 325°F.

POTATO DISHES AND VARIETIES

The potato is one of the world's main food crops, differing from others in that the edible part of the plant is a tuber, the swollen end of an underground stem. It is native to the Americas and was originally grown by the Incas. The potato was discovered in Peru by Francisco Pizarro and brought to Europe in 1534. Fifty years later, Sir Walter Raleigh made the same discovery in Virginia and brought the potato to England. It is always cooked and is also processed in a wide variety of ways, including distilling. For cooking, there are high-starch potatoes (russet, Idaho, purple), medium-starch potatoes (Yukon Golds, round whites, long whites, yellow), and low-starch potatoes (round red, new potatoes).

POTATO DISHES

AU GRATIN POTATO	HASH BROWNS	POTATO STICKS
BAKED POTATO	HOME-FRIED POTATO OR HOME FRIES	POTATO STRAW NEST
BOILED POTATO		RICED POTATO
CANDIED POTATO	JULIENNE POTATO	SCALLOPED POTATO
DUCHESS POTATOES	LYONNAISE POTATO	SHOESTRING POTATO
FRENCH-FRIED POTATO, FRENCH FRY, OR CHIP	MASHED POTATO	SOUFFLÉ POTATO
	O'BRIEN POTATO	TWICE-BAKED POTATO OR STUFFED POTATO
GERMAN-FRIED POTATO	POTATO SALAD	

POTATO TYPES AND VARIETIES

BAKING POTATO	NEW POTATO	SPUD
BLUE POTATO OR PURPLE POTATO	PURPLE PERUVIAN	SWEET POTATO
	RED BLISS	WHITE POTATO
COMMON POTATO	RED POTATO OR RED-SKINNED POTATO	WHITE ROUND POTATO
FINGERLING POTATO		YELLOW FINN
IDAHO POTATO	ROUND RED POTATO	YELLOW POTATO
IRISH POTATO	ROUND WHITE POTATO	YUKON GOLD POTATO
LONG WHITE POTATO	RUSSET POTATO	

POTATO CHIP is a thin slice of potato fried in deep fat (though some are baked) until crisp and then usually salted or otherwise seasoned; there are many variations. The potato chip is also called the Saratoga chip, since it was supposedly invented by a Native American chief in Saratoga, New York. The term was first recorded in 1854. Potato chips are called potato crisps in the United Kingdom and Australia. Before the potato chip bag was invented in 1926 by Laura Scudder of Scudder's Potato Chips in Monterey, California, when she ironed two pieces of wax paper together, potato chips were stored in glass bins and sold fresh or sold in five-gallon metal tins that when empty were returned to the store to be refilled.

> **HINT** Restore stale potato or tortilla chips by spreading them on a glass (Pyrex) plate and microwaving on high for 1 minute. Transfer them to a double layer of paper towels to cool to room temperature.

POTATO FLOUR is a gluten-free flour made from cooked, dried, and ground potatoes that is used in baking and as a thickener for sauces. Potato bread is a type of bread made with this.

POTATO PANCAKE or **POTATO LATKE** also called LATKE, is made of coarsely grated potato and egg, flour, onion, and seasonings. It is often eaten with applesauce and sour cream.

POTATO SALAD is a salad of pieces of cold cooked potato cubes mixed with mayonnaise or salad dressing and other ingredients such as hard-cooked egg, onion, celery, and seasonings. The term was recorded in English in 1796.

> **HINT** The best potatoes to use for potato salad are low-starch ones, such as new potatoes or Red Bliss. Boil the potatoes in salted water. The potatoes should not be skinned before they are boiled. Skinning potatoes offers no advantage in flavor but usually results in a loss of texture. When you make potato salad, the potatoes should be peeled, cut, and seasoned while still hot, because hot potatoes will absorb flavors easily and cold ones won't.

POT-AU-FEU is literally "pot on the fire," a French stew of boiled vegetables and beef with the stock served first as a soup and the meat and vegetables served separately. It is pronounced paw-toh-FEY and is also the name of the pot used to cook this dish. The dish is often served with coarse salt and strong Dijon mustard, and sometimes also with gherkins and samphire (a leaf vegetable) pickled in vinegar.

POT CHEESE is a type of soft, crumbly, unaged cheese made with sour milk and buttermilk—the midway stage between cottage cheese and farmer cheese. Pot cheese is also used as a synonym for COTTAGE CHEESE, although they are not the same cheese. The word is an Americanism dating to 1810.

POTLUCK is mainly thought of as a communal meal to which people bring food to share, sometimes without arranging beforehand which dish to bring; this meaning of the word dates to around 1867. It is also a term for the regular meal of a family made available to a guest. The original meaning of the word potluck dates to around 1592 and comes from the practice of throwing leftovers in a pot and the luck involved in how good this stew would taste.

POTPIE, POT PIE, or **POT-PIE** is a meat (usually cubed, often poultry) and vegetable pie made in a pot or deep dish, usually with only a top crust. The term dates to 1702.

> **HINT** Change the shape of potpies by using rectangular, square, or oval dishes. Use puff pastry, pie crust (upper or lower or both), corn bread, biscuits, or mashed potatoes for the crust.

POT ROAST is a large piece of beef braised slowly in a covered dish in the oven or on the stove. It is also the term for a cut of beef suitable for simmering in liquid in a closed pot.

> **HINT** The best meat for pot-roasting is well-exercised muscles that contain a good deal of connective tissue. Even though these muscles contain considerable collagen (connective tissue protein), which is a major factor in toughness, they can be pot-roasted to change the collagen to gelatin. The best beef cuts for pot-roasting are chuck, boneless shoulder, eye of round, and rump. Chuck is the most tender and flavorful. Chuck cuts can also be called beef chuck, mock tender roast, top chuck roast, chuck shoulder, or boneless roast.

POT STICKER or **POTSTICKER** is a type of Chinese dumpling filled with ground meat and vegetables, and fried, steamed, or both. It is served with a dipping sauce. The Chinese have been enjoying potstickers since the Song dynasty (AD 960–1280). The legend goes that they were invented by a chef in China's imperial court, who accidentally burnt a batch of dumplings. The overcooked dumplings were burnt on the bottom only, and not on top. With no time to prepare a new batch, the chef served the dumplings with the burnt side on top, announcing that they were his own special creation. Their Chinese name is *wortip* (roughly translated as "pot stick").

> **HINT** Properly made, potstickers are crisp and browned on the bottom, sticking lightly to the pan but easy to remove with a spatula. The trick to making potstickers is not to overcook them.

POTTED in cooking means cooked or preserved in a pot.

POUILLY-FUISSÉ is a dry white wine from Burgundy, France, named for Mont de Pouilly and the commune of Fuissé.

POULTRY is any domesticated gallinaceous bird such as chicken, duck, geese, or turkey—especially one raised for food; it is synonymous with FOWL, The word poultry first came into English around 1345 to describe a place where fowl was sold, but by 1387 it meant birds reared for their flesh and eggs as food.

POULTRY ESSENTIALS

■ Deboning leftover cooked poultry will help it hold its flavor longer.

■ It is dangerous to allow properly cooked poultry to cool to room temperature, because while the bacteria will have been killed by the cooking, if the cooked poultry contains spores of the bacteria that survive and multiply, they can create a toxin that causes food poisoning. So when the product has cooled down and is not going to be served immediately, refrigerate it, then reheat to 165°F for serving. Refrigerate or freeze any leftovers within two hours.

■ You can tell a bird's age in pre-packaged poultry by the weight and the appearance of the skin. The heavier the package, the older the bird. The smoother the skin, if visible, the younger the bird. Buy ½–¾ pound per serving.

■ Allow poultry to rest for about 20 minutes after roasting. Turn the oven off and leave the roast inside the oven, or remove from the oven and cover with foil.

■ Poultry should be cooked to 160°F–165°F.

POUND CAKE is a rich, dense yellow cake that got its name from the one-pound quantities of the key ingredients—sugar, butter, flour, and eggs—in the original recipe. The British call it MADEIRA CAKE. Pound cake is also the American English name for a type of British fruitcake.

POWDERED MILK: see DRIED MILK.

POWDERED SUGAR, also called CONFECTIONERS' SUGAR, is finely ground and sifted sugar with added cornstarch to prevent clumping. It is called ICING SUGAR in the United Kingdom and *sucre glace* in France. Because it dissolves so readily, confectioners' sugar is often used to make icings and candy, and as a fine dusting on desserts.

> **HINT** Powdered sugar labeled XXXX is slightly finer than that labeled XXX, but they can be used interchangeably and both may need to be sifted before using. Keep in mind that 1¾ (packed) cups of confectioners' sugar equals 1 cup of granulated sugar.

PRAIRIE OYSTER is a drink made of a raw egg, Worcestershire sauce, hot sauce, salt, and pepper, taken by some people as a hangover cure. Prairie oyster(s) is also the name for fried calf or pig testicle, which is eaten as a delicacy in the U.S. Midwest (they are also known as CALF FRIES or ROCKY MOUNTAIN OYSTERS).

PRALINE is a bite-sized candy made of brown sugar, butter, and pecans (or almonds), a specialty of New Orleans. It was based on a French confection of the same name made with ground caramelized almonds or hazelnuts. Praline is also the name of a brittle confection made of almonds and caramelized sugar eaten as candy or ground and used as an ingredient or garnish. The praline is named for a French field marshal and diplomat, César du Plessis-Praslin (1598–1675), whose chef created this sweet. There are variations using nuts mixed or covered with chocolate, coconut, or maple sugar or syrup. Praliné [pronounced pra-lee-NAY] describes any food that is garnished, coated, or made with praline or almonds.

PRAWN is any of various edible, shrimplike decapod crustaceans with two pairs of pincers and it is larger than shrimp, though the word is sometimes used to describe any large shrimp. The prawn of the lobster family also goes by these names: CARIBBEAN LOBSTERETTE, DANISH LOBSTER, DUBLIN BAY PRAWN, FLORIDA LOBSTERETTE, ITALIAN SCAMPI, LANGOUSTINE, and LANGOSTINO. Prawns are six to eight inches long and have pale red bodies deepening to dark red tails. Freshwater prawns migrate from saltwater to freshwater to spawn, like salmon, and look like a cross between lobster and shrimp, with narrower abdomens and longer legs than shrimp.

PRECOOK means to cook partly or completely ahead of time so that the actual preparation—final cooking or reheating—will not take as long.

PREHEAT is to heat an oven before the cooking begins. Before something is cooked in an oven, the oven needs to be heated to the proper temperature.

> **HINTS** An oven should be preheated for 15–20 minutes, no matter what the oven directions say for how long it takes to preheat. When using baking stones or tiles, you need to preheat for at least 45 minutes.
>
> ▌ Preheat pans and skillets before pan-broiling, sautéing, or stir-frying to prevent the food from sticking.
>
> ▌ Electric broilers only need 5 minutes to preheat, and preheating is unnecessary for gas broilers.

PREP is short for prepare and means to make ready for cooking or serving. Prepped means ready for cooking or serving.

> **HINT** Use an artist's watercolor palette to hold seasonings and garnishes when cooking.

PREPRANDIAL LIBATION: see APERITIF.

PRESENTATION is the art and practice of presenting cooked food to diners. To PLATE is to arrange the meal on the individual plate immediately before it's served. Many chefs use artistic framing strategies for food's presentation, including combining foods with different shapes, colors, and textures on the same plate. Garnishes are also an important part of presentation in restaurants.

PRESERVATIVE is a chemical substance used to preserve foods from decomposition, discoloration, or spoilage. Along with emulsifying and stabilizing agents, preservatives also help to maintain freshness of appearance and consistency. Some preservatives improve the appearance of the product. Preservatives are also used to maintain moisture and softness in baked goods.

PRESERVE or **PRESERVES** is fruit preserved whole or in large pieces by cooking with sugar or syrup, then canned or made into marmalades, jams, or jellies. This method of cooking is done to let the fruits keep their shape. To preserve is to cook fruit by this method. Preserves differ from jam, which is made from fruit pulp; jelly, which is made from fruit juice; and marmalade, which includes pulp and rind.

PRESS is to extract, express, or squeeze out juice, sugar, oil, or other substances by pressure.

PRESSAC: see MALBEC.

PRESSED CHEESE: see FARMER CHEESE.

PRESSURE COOKER is an airtight metal pot that uses steam under pressure at high temperature to cook food quickly; it has a removable safety valve (on older models) that attaches to the lid or a built-in value with easy-to-read pressure markings (on newer models). The device dates to 1914. When the pressure cooker is over high heat and the pressure builds, the temperature will be at about 250°F instead of the 212°F of boiling water; thus, the pressure cooker works faster.

> **HINT** It is best to use at least a six-quart pressure cooker so that it is safe. A pressure cooker should not be more than two-thirds full for soups and high-liquid dishes, half full for beans and grains, and three-quarters full for other foods, so that there is room for the steam pressure to build.

THE PRESSURE-COOKING PROCESS

All pressure cookers have a lock-on lid and a vent or pressure-relief valve. Water boils at 212°F, and no matter how long you boil it, the water and its steam do not get hotter than that. The only way to make steam hotter is to put it under pressure. Steam has six times the heat potential when it condenses on a cool food product. This increased heat transfer potential is why steam is

(continued)

such an effective cooking medium. Here's how a pressure cooker works:

1. Water and food are put in the pressure cooker.

2. When the tightly sealed cooker is set over high heat, steam pressure builds and the internal temperature rises. The steam will remain trapped and pressure will build, raising the temperature at which the liquid will boil. So at fifteen pounds per square inch of pressure, the food is cooking at about 250°F instead of 212°F.

This reduces the time needed to cook the food. This high temperature is made possible by raising the pressure to a point greater than atmospheric pressure.

3. Under high pressure, the fiber in food is tenderized and flavors mingle in record time. Also, fewer nutrients are lost because cooking is so speedy and because nutrient-rich steam condenses in the pot instead of being lost in the air.

PRETZEL, a soft or hard, salt-sprinkled bread cooked into a knot shape, descends from the Latin *bracellus*, "bracelet," or *bracchioli*, "arms," coming to English as *bretzel* from German, meaning "biscuit baked in the shape of folded arms."

PRICKLY PEAR is a pulpy, often edible, round or pear-shaped, spiny fruit of any of various prickly pear cacti. The fruit of prickly pears, commonly called CACTUS FIG, INDIAN FIG, or CHUMBO FIG, is edible, although it has to be peeled carefully to remove the small spines on the outer skin before consumption. If the outer layer is not properly removed, glochids can be ingested, causing discomfort of the throat, lips, and tongue as the small spines are easily lodged in the skin.

PRIMAL CUT is a piece of meat initially separated from the carcass during butchering. Different countries and cultures make these cuts in different ways. An example is the American primal cuts for beef, listed in order from front to back, then top to bottom: Upper half: chuck, rib, short loin, sirloin, round. Lower half: brisket, shank, plate, flank, hoof.

PRIMAVERA describes a dish made with an assortment of fresh spring vegetables in a light cream sauce, especially an accompaniment to pasta, meat, or seafood. The Spanish word primavera literally means "spring" (the season) and first referred to a tree native to Mexico and Central America, so called for its early flowering; the word ultimately derives from the Latin *primus*, "first," and *ver*, "spring," and the Italian culinary term primavera is short for alla primavera, literally meaning "in the style of springtime," which denotes anything served with a mix of fresh spring vegetables, such as asparagus, broccoli, carrots, peas, peppers, or zucchini.

PRIME grade is produced from young, well-fed beef cattle and has abundant marbling. Prime roasts and steaks are excellent for dry-heat cooking methods such as broiling, roasting, or grilling. Prime meat is generally sold in restaurants and hotels. Beef with the USDA's Prime designation is usually sold only to the food service industry, while Choice is the best grade available to retail sources.

PRIME RIB, also called RIB ROAST or STANDING RIB ROAST, is a cut of beef taken from the loin area of cattle, some of the least-used muscles, and this cut is richly marbled with fat. It therefore lends itself to dry-heat cooking methods such as roasting. A full prime rib is seven ribs. Most butchers recommend that you request a prime rib from the small end toward the back of the rib section, which is leaner and gives you more meat for your dollar. This cut is referred to as the first cut, the loin end, or sometimes the small end, because the meat and ribs get larger as they move up toward the shoulder.

> **HINTS** Trim prime rib of excess fat, but not the thin layer of fat the butcher leaves on the roast to protect and baste it while it cooks. Excess fat means any fat more than one inch thick. It is important to tie the prime rib before roasting. If left untied, the outer layer of meat will pull away from the ribeye muscle and overcook. To prevent this problem, tie the roast at both ends, running the cooking twine parallel to the bone. Most butchers will tie your prime rib for you. Do not salt the outside of a prime rib roast, as salt draws out moisture from the meat while cooking.

> To cook evenly, the prime rib must not be cold—let it stand at room temperature, loosely covered, for about 2–4 hours before cooking.

PRIX FIXE, also called TABLE D'HÔTE, is a fixed-price charge for a complete meal of several courses at a restaurant or hotel, sometimes with choices permitted. It is also the term for such a meal with a fixed price. The term is pronounced PREE-FIKS and dates to 1851.

PROCESSED refers to food that has been transformed from raw ingredients into food, either in the home or by the food processing industry. Food processing typically takes clean, harvested crops or slaughtered and butchered animal products and uses these to produce attractive, marketable products, often with a long shelf life. On the labels of processed foods, ingredients are listed in descending order, according to the amount in the food.

PROCESSED CHEESE or **PROCESS CHEESE** is a product made of one or more types of cheeses that have been heated and mixed with emulsifiers, gums, stabilizers, colorings, and flavorings. This is done to make the cheese spreadable and to delay or prevent its spoilage. The processes improve shelf life but compromise flavor and texture. Pasteurized processed cheese is a blend of fresh and aged natural cheeses that have been shredded, mixed, and heated with the addition of an emulsifier salt, after which no further ripening occurs. The term processed cheese dates to 1918. Products labeled "cheese spreads" or "cheese foods" contain added liquid for a softer, more spreadable mixture. According to U.S. government standards, only 51% of the final weight needs to be cheese.

PROCESSING TOMATO: see PLUM TOMATO.

PRODUCE is a term for fresh fruits and vegetables grown for market.

PROFITEROLE is small, hollow ball of soft, sweet choux pastry with a cream filling or vanilla ice cream filling and served with chocolate sauce. It is basically a miniature cream puff with a sweet filling, though there are also savory profiteroles with a creamy fish filling. The word is pronounced pruh-FIT-uh-rohl and is literally French for "small profit"; its use in English dates to around 1521. A CROQUEMBOUCHE is a traditional French wedding cake consisting of a cone-shaped tower of profiteroles glazed in caramel. GOUGÈRE is the savory equivalent of a profiterole and may be filled with a cheese mixture or game purée.

PROLIFIC BEAN: see LIMA BEAN.

PROOF or **PROVE** is to cause bread dough to rise due to the addition of baker's yeast or other leavening, and to test the effectiveness of yeast, often by combining with warm water so that a bubbling action occurs. Proof as a noun is the strength of distilled alcoholic liquor based on an arbitrary standard of 100, with 1 degree proof equal to 0.5% alcohol, and 100 degrees proof equal to 50% alcohol.

> **HINT** To create a proofing box for dough, heat a measuring cup filled with water in the microwave until boiling. Cover the bowl of dough with plastic wrap, place the bowl inside the microwave along with the cup of water, and close the door.

PROSCIUTTO, PROSCIUTTO HAM, PROSCIUTTO COTTO, or **PROSCIUTTO CRUDO**, also called PARMA HAM, is a seasoned, salt-cured, unsmoked Italian ham with dense reddish brown flesh and a delicate flavor. Prosciutto is Italian for "cured ham." Parma proscuitto's process for curing is dictated by law. It will have the five-pointed Parma crown seared into the side.

> **HINT** Prosciutto should be rosy pink, and under the rind there should be a thick layer of white fat. Proscuitto is best sliced by the butcher. Store, wrapped, in the refrigerator. Bring to room temperature for 1 hour before serving.

PROTEIN is technically any of a large class of complex polymers consisting of long chains of polypeptides often bonded with nucleic acids and lipids. Protein is essential to the diet of animals and humans. Humans obtain proteins principally from animals and their products, such as meat, milk, and eggs. The seeds of legumes are increasingly being used to prepare inexpensive protein-rich food.

PROVENÇAL, also called **PROVENÇALE**, À LA PROVENÇAL, describes a dish prepared with a thick sauce (Provençale sauce) of olive oil, garlic, herbs, and tomatoes. The term is French for "in the Provençal style," referring to Provence, a region on France.

PROVOLONE (pronounced proh-voh-LOH-nee) is a firm, light-colored, usually smoked, salty Italian cow's milk cheese that is often molded into a pear shape. It is mild when young and becomes more potent with age. The rind is golden brown. The word dates from aroun 1904 and comes from the Italian *provola*, "buffalo or cow's milk cheese." Most provolone is aged for two to three months and has a pale yellow color, though some is aged for six to twelve months. As the cheese ripens, the color becomes a richer yellow and the flavor becomes more pronounced.

PRUNE is any of various varieties of plum that can be dried for eating without spoiling. It comes from the Latin wortd *prunum,* "plum."

> **HINTS** Pick large, plump, blackish purple prunes.
>
> ▌Store prunes in a container in a cool, dry place for up to one month or in the refrigerator for up to six months.
>
> ▌Remove crystals from prunes by dipping them in boiling water and then drying them. If prunes are too dry, plump them in hot water for 15–20 minutes.

PUDDING is any of various soft, sweet desserts that are thickened and baked, boiled, or steamed. Pudding usually has flour or some other thickener, milk, eggs, a flavoring, and sweetener. The usage of the word for the sweetened dish dates to around 1543. The word may also refer to a similar dish that is unsweetened, such as corn pudding. Originally (around 1287), pudding referred to a sausage consisting of the stomach or intestine of a pig or sheep stuffed with minced meat and other ingredients. In the United Kingdom, the dessert course of a meal may be called pudding.

> **HINT** To speed the cooling of pudding, move it to a bowl or spread it on a rimmed baking sheet.

PUFF PASTRY is a light, flaky pastry dough made of many layers of butter/fat alternating with dough; the term also refers to any light, flaky pastry made with this dough. The dough itself is also called puff paste. Puff pastry is a term dating to 1788.

> **HINTS** Store premade puff pastry by wrapping well in plastic wrap and foil. Refrigerate for up to three days or freeze for up to three months.

▌ Commercially prepared frozen puff pastry should be defrosted for 2 hours in the refrigerator before using.

PULLET is a young domestic hen up to a year old and its flesh.

PULP is the soft, juicy part of a fruit or vegetable; it is also the pith or soft fleshy inside of the stem of a plant.

PULSE is the edible seeds of various leguminous pod-bearing plants, such as peas, beans, or lentils.

PUMELO or **PUMMELO**: see POMELO.

PUMPERNICKEL is a dark, coarse unleavened bread with a high proportion of rye flour and molasses. Pumpernickel may get its name, which dates to around 1738, from the German words *pumpern*, "breaking wind," and *nickel*, "demon/goblin," probably from the bread's purported tendency to cause flatulence, though there is also a story that pumpernickel got its name from a German baker named Pumpernickel.

PUMPKIN is the large fruit of a vine (*Cucurbita Pepo*), with a thick orange rind; it is cooked as a vegetable or made into a sweet filling. The word dates to around 1647 and evolved from the original English spelling of *pompeon*, *pumpion*, or *pompion* to pumkin and finally to pumpkin. The word *pumpion* came from *pompion*, from the Latin *pepon/peponem*, from the Greek *pepon*, "large melon/edible gourd," from an earlier meaning of *pepon*, "cooked by the sun/ripe." Another spelling variant is punkin. Only 1% of pumpkins are sold as food; the other 99% are sold as decorations.

> **HINTS** Select solid, heavy pumpkins with no soft spots or blemishes. Keep for up to one month in a cool, dry place. Wrapped in plastic, cut pumpkin can be kept in the refrigerator for three to four days.
>
> ▌ Use a metal spoon to scrape out the seeds and strings inside a pumpkin.
>
> ▌ Canned pumpkin can be used for making good pies. Pumpkin is one of the best of the canned vegetables. To temper the flavor of pumpkin that is being cooked, add 1 tablespoon of orange or lemon juice.

PUNCH is a sweetened drink made with fruit juices, carbonated beverages, and sherbet, and sometimes mixed with wine or liquor, and served in cups from a large bowl (punch bowl). The word punch is ultimately from the Sanskrit *panca*, "five/five kinds of," as the original version had five ingredients.

PUNGENT means strong/intense and sharp in taste/flavor or smell/odor. Synonyms include biting, bitter, spicy, tangy, and tart. The word is derived from the Latin *pungere*, "to pierce/prick/sting."

PURÉE is to rub or run food such as fruits or vegetables through a strainer or process in a sieve or blender to liquidize it. The noun purée refers to food liquidized by straining or blending; it originally meant a broth or soup made of fruit, vegetables, fish, or meat boiled to a pulp and put through a sieve. The word is from the French *purer*, "to strain/cleanse," from the Latin *purare*, "purify." The noun came into English almost two centuries before the verb.

> **HINT** To purée small quantities of food, use a mortar and pestle. To make chunky purée, use a wire masher. To make a purée that eliminates seeds and skins, use a food mill. To purée very liquid mixtures, use a blender or food processor. To make the smoothest purée, strain with a sieve.

PURPLE ONION: see RED ONION.

PURSLANE is a plant (family *Portulacaceae*) with fleshy succulent leaves; it is often grown as a potherb and used raw or cooked in salads.

> **HINT** Store purslane loosely in a plastic bag in the refrigerator for three to four days.

PUTTANESCA is an adjective denoting a dish served with a sauce of tomatoes, garlic, black olives, anchovies, capers, and chiles. Puttanesca is an Italian word and comes from *puttana*, "prostitute," as the sauce was said to have been created by prostitutes because it could be cooked quickly between clients' visits.

QUAHOG or **QUAHAUG**, also called AMERICAN QUAHOG, HARD-SHELL CLAM, or ROUND CLAM, is an edible clam (*Mercenaria mercenaria*) of the eastern coast of North America, with a large, thick, hard shell, often three or more inches in diameter. The word describes the largest of the hard-shell clams, which are used for chowders and other dishes. The word quahog, pronounced COE-hog, is from the Narragansett *poquauhock*.

QUAIL is any of a number of small, short-tailed gallinaceous game birds (family Phasianidae). American quail are known by various names depending on the region—bobwhite in the East, PARTRIDGE in the South, quail in the North, and blue quail in the Southwest. The plural is quail or quails.

Packages of frozen quail should not contain pink-tinged ice. Fresh quail should be plump with even color. Provide two or more quail per person for an entrée.

QUAILBERRY: see LINGONBERRY.

QUATRE FROMAGE, QUATTRO FORMAGGI, or **QUATTRO FROMAGE** describes a dish using four different cheeses (the first term listed is French, the second is Italian, and the third combines Italian and French). Often the four cheeses are cottage, ricotta, Parmesan, and mozzarella.

QUENELLE is a delicate, poached oval dumpling of puréed and seasoned fish, meat, or vegetables bound with eggs and cheese and then served in a rich cream sauce. Quenelle is a French word derived from the German *knödel*, "dumpling." It is pronounced kuh-NEHL.

QUESADILLA (pronounced keh-sah-DEE-yah) is a Mexican dish of a flour tortilla filled with cheese, chiles, and chopped tomatoes, then folded and deep-fried, baked, or broiled. Filling variations are many, including meat that is ground or in strips, and refried beans. Quesadilla is literally Mexican Spanish for "little cheese pastry," and the word was first recorded in English in 1857. Quesadillas are often cut into strips or triangles and served as an appetizer.

> **HINT** The tortillas for quesadillas can be flour, corn, blue corn, or gorditas. Use a round skillet that is big enough for grilling and flipping the tortillas without losing the filling. Lightly oil or butter the outside of the tortillas and place them in the hot pan, one at a time, greased side down. Put the filling in the middle and cover with another tortilla, greased side up. Place your hand on the top of the quesadilla and help flip it with the turner.

QUESO is "cheese" in Spanish.

QUICHE is a tart or pie filled with a rich egg-and-cream mixture and sometimes various meat or vegetable ingredients, then baked to a custard consistency. The word quiche may derive from the German *kuchen*, "cake," though the dish originated in France around 1925. Quiche Lorraine has bacon bits and Gruyère cheese added to the custard filling.

> **HINT** To avoid a soggy crust, prebake the pastry. Sprinkle grated cheese or brush egg white inside the prebaked pastry while it is hot, to seal the pastry. Also, parboil watery vegetables and then thoroughly drain them before adding to the quiche mixture.

QUICK BREAD is any bread leavened with baking soda or powder instead of yeast and baked immediately, such as muffins or biscuits; in other words, it is a bread prepared with a batter instead of a dough.

HINTS Check quick bread 10–15 minutes before the minimum baking time is reached. Cover with foil if the bread is browning too fast. To test a quick bread for doneness, insert a toothpick in the center; it will come out clean or very close to clean when the bread is done. Do not be concerned about a crack down the top of the loaf; this is typical for quick breads. Allow quick breads to cool in the pan for 10 minutes, which lets them firm up. Then transfer to a wire rack so the crust does not become soggy. Once cool, wrap in foil or plastic wrap and store at room temperature. If you store the bread overnight before slicing and eating, it allows the flavors time to mellow.

▌ Do not overmix quick bread batter; instead, combine the ingredients gently and leave the batter slightly lumpy. Bake as soon as possible so the leavener does not dissipate.

▌ To make quick bread ahead, combine the dry ingredients in one bowl and the wet ingredients in another. Then combine and bake the next day.

QUICK-FROZEN: see FLASH-FROZEN.

QUINCE is an aromatic, acid-tasting, pear- or apple-shaped Asian fruit used especially in preserves. The word is from the Latin *cotoneum malum*, "quince fruit," from the Greek *kydonion*, "apple of Kydonia."

HINT Buy firm quinces with green skin starting to turn gold. Store at room temperature for one week or more. Ripe quinces can be refrigerated in a plastic bag for up to two weeks.

QUINOA (pronounced KEEN-wah) is the high-protein dried fruits and seeds of a goosefoot plant (*Chenopodium quinoa*); these are used as a food staple and ground into flour. Quinoa is washed before cooking to remove a bitter residue from the spherical seeds. It is treated like a grain, but it is actually the fruit of an herb and it cooks twice as fast as rice. Quinoa produces its own natural insect repellent.

RABBIT in cooking generally refers to the meat of any of various wild or domesticated rabbits or hares. It is almost totally white meat.

CONFUSABLE RABBIT/HARE. Rabbits are smaller than hares and their meat is all white; hares have dark meat.

RACK is the rib section of a forequarter of veal or pork or especially lamb or mutton; rack of lamb is a roast of the rib section of lamb. Rack is also a metal frame or shelf in an oven, or a separately sold item used in the kitchen for cooling baked goods. Cooling on a rack allows air to circulate around cookies and cakes so they cool faster and more evenly.

RACLETTE is a Swiss dish of melted cheese scraped onto boiled potatoes or dark bread and small sour pickles. Raclette is also the name of the semifirm cow's milk cheese used in making this dish. The French term means "small scraper," from the practice of scraping the melted cheese onto the plate.

RADICCHIO (pronounced rah-DEE-kee-oh) is Italian for red-leafed chicory, an herb with crisp, spiky leaves that have a somewhat bitter taste and are used in salads.

> **HINT** Buy a head of radicchio with a firm white core without blemishes. The leaves should not be moist. Store in the refrigerator in a perforated plastic bag for up to one week.

RADISH is the pungent edible fleshy root of any of various cultivated radish plants (*Raphanus sativus*) of the mustard family; it is usually eaten raw. The easy-to-grow radish takes its name from the Latin *radix*, "root." Its skin can vary in color from white to red to purple to black.

> **HINTS** Choose small round radishes in spring and more elongated ones in summer. They should be firm with smooth skins and unwilted leaves.
>
> ▌ If storing radishes, remove the leaves, scrub the radishes clean, and trim off the ends. Store in a perforated plastic bag in the refrigerator for up to one week, though large varieties keep for up to two weeks.
>
> ▌ Make radishes crisper by covering them with ice water in the refrigerator for 2–3 hours.

RAGOUT (from French) is a term for any highly seasoned stew of meat and vegetables in a thick sauce.

RAGU or **RAGU BOLOGNESE**, also called Bolognese or Alla bolognese, is a meat sauce that is typically served with pasta, usually containing ground beef, tomatoes, onions, celery, carrots, white wine, and seasonings. The word is from the French *ragoûter*, "to stimulate the appetite."

RAINBOW TROUT is a large, stout salmonid food and game fish of western North America that is related to the Pacific salmon. It is usually greenish on top and white on the belly, with black dots all over and a pink, red, or lavender stripe along each side of the bod.

RAISE means to cause to puff up with a leavener; RISE is to increase in volume due to leavening.

RAISIN refers to any of various kinds of sweet grapes, usually seedless, that are dried for eating. The word comes from *racemus*, Latin for "cluster of grapes." Raisin grapes were grown as early as 2000 BC in Persia and Egypt, and dried grapes are mentioned in the Bible. Thompson seedless, Muscat, and Black Corinth grapes are the varieties dried for raisins.

> **HINTS** Plump, moist raisins are the freshest. Raisins can be refrigerated for up to six months.

> ▌ Revive raisins that are hard and dry in hot water for 20 minutes.

HOW GRAPES TURN INTO RAISINS

Here's how grapes become raisins:

1. About 6% of the grapes grown are taken off the vine and transported to raisin manufacturing plants for immediate processing. Alternatively, seedless grapes taken from the vines may be placed on paper trays to sun-dry, which takes about two to three weeks for the raisins to reach the correct degree of moisture (raisins have 15% water; grapes have 78%).

2. Muscat seeded grapes are also used for raisins, but must undergo the additional step of being puffed with steam and passed between rollers that force the seeds out.

3. The grapes are cured with sulfur dioxide to preserve their color and then further dried in ovens. Four to five pounds of grapes yield one pound of raisins. At this stage, they are golden seedless raisins.

4. All raisins are washed in tanks of hot water, which opens up the wrinkles and ensures that the raisins are clean.

RAITA is a cooling Indian side dish of yogurt and chopped cucumbers or other vegetables and spices. Bananas or tomatoes may also be used. It is variously seasoned with black mustard seed, garam masala, and herbs such as chervil, coriander, cumin, dill, mint, parsley, or tarragon.

RAMBUTAN is an acidic, bright red, oval Malayan fruit covered with soft spines. The term means "hairy fruit" in Malay. The best-quality rambutans are generally those that are harvested and sold when still attached to the branch; they are less susceptible to rot, damage, and pests, and remain fresh and flavorful for a much longer time than those sold as individually picked fruits.

RAMEKIN is a small, lidless, ceramic individual-portion baking dish used for foods like crème brûlée. It is also the name of a cheese dish made with eggs and bread crumbs or unsweetened puff pastry that is baked and served in this type of dish. The French word may have derived from the Dutch *rammeken*, "toasted bread." A wide, shallow ramekin is also known as a CUSTARD CUP or crème brûlée ramekin.

RAMEN is a Japanese dish of wheat-flour noodles served in a broth with garnishes such as meat, seaweed, and vegetables. It also refers to instant-style deep-fried noodles that are usually sold in packages, sometimes with bits of dehydrated vegetables and broth mix. The word dates to around 1966 and is from a Chinese word meaning "hand-pulled wheat-flour noodles."

RAMP, also called WILD LEEK, is a wild onion (*Allium tricoccum*) of North America that is eaten raw or used as a flavoring. Its garlicky flavor is a bit stronger than that of leeks, scallions, or onions.

> **HINT** Choose ramps that are firm with bright-colored greenery. Wrap tightly in a plastic bag and refrigerate for up to one week. Trim the root ends just before using.

RANGOON BEAN: see LIMA BEAN.

RAPINI: see BROCCOLI RABE.

RARE refers to meat cooked for a short time and still red inside.

RASHER denotes a thin slice of bacon or a serving of three to four thin slices of bacon. This term can also refer to ham. The word, dating to around 1584, has an uncertain origin, but its original meaning was one slice of meat.

RASPBERRY is the small red (or black or purple) edible fruit of a woody bramble; it is rounder and smaller than a blackberry and has clusters of drupelets. The raspberry probably takes its name from the English word *rasp*, "to scrape roughly," from the thorned canes bearing the berries. The berry was first called the raspis-berry and has also been called a hindberry. Black raspberries are nearly as common as red.

> **HINT** Raspberries are extremely delicate and have hollow centers. Do not buy a leaking or wet carton or one with any visible mold. Raspberries require refrigeration and should be washed right before you use them. They should be eaten immediately after purchase, or they can be rinsed, dried, and frozen for eight to ten months.

RATATOUILLE (pronounced rat-uh-TWEE) is a Provençal vegetable stew of eggplant, zucchini, onions, peppers, tomatoes, and seasonings such as garlic and basil. Ratatouille ingredients are stewed together (sometimes after an initial sauté to better develop their flavors) until the mixture is very soft and the flavors have blended together. The word is from the French *touiller*, "to stir up." This dish is served hot, cold, or room temperature as a side dish or appetizer.

RAVIGOTE or **RAVIGOTTE** is a velouté (white wine) sauce made with herbs, shallots, capers, and mushrooms. The term can also refer to a thick, hot vinaigrette sauce (or a cold mayonnaise) with capers, parsley, chervil, tarragon, and onion, served cold with vegetables or warm with meat or fish. Ravigote is French for "invigorate" and is pronounced ra-vee-GAWT.

RAVIOLI is pasta in the form of small, often square, casings of dough that are filled with seasoned ground meat, cheese, or vegetables, boiled, and served with a sauce. There are variations with lobster and other ingredients. The word ravioli (the plural of *raviolo*) derives from the Italian *raviolo*, "little turnip." The earliest mention of ravioli appeared in the writings of Francesco di Marco, a merchant of Prato in the fourteenth century. The *Oxford English Dictionary* also notes the Latin *raviolus*, "meatball," and from 1284 in Italian sources, *raviolus sine crusta de pasta*, "meatball without a pastry crust."

RAW describes a food that is not cooked or treated with heat to prepare it for eating. Raw foodism is the consumption of uncooked, unprocessed, and often organic raw food as a large percentage of the diet.

RAW SUGAR is light brown, coarse sugar, containing the natural molasses present in sugarcane; it is not true raw sugar. Raw sugar is the product of the first stage of the cane sugar–refining process. Because raw sugar is not heavily refined, it has a higher molasses content than table sugar, which lends the raw sugar a rich, complex flavor. There are some cautions involved in using raw sugar in cooking, as it has a higher moisture content than regular sugar. It can also dry out, causing it to harden, so raw sugar should be kept in an airtight container.

REAMER, also called HANDHELD JUICER, is a small kitchen utensil with a conical, ridged center and fluted point and is used for squeezing juice from citrus fruit. The fruit is cut in half and placed on the cone and twisted over a bowl or glass. A reamer is particularly useful for extracting juice from a grapefruit.

REBLOCHON is a semisoft, mild, creamy washed-rind cow's milk cheese with a pale, pinkish skin. The word comes from a French word for "milk for a second time."

RÉCHAUFFÉ is a lovely French term (literally meaning "warm again") for a dish of reheated leftovers.

RECIPE is a list of ingredients, utensils and gear, and instructions for preparing a food dish or drink. The term in this sense dates to 1631 and first appeared in Middle English from the Latin word *recipe*, literally a command to "receive!" It was first used in English as an instruction in medical prescriptions.

> **HINT** Always read the whole recipe first, before doing anything. Then make a shopping list for ingredients or equipment you don't have. Assemble all the ingredients. Measure or prepare each ingredient and put into small bowls or other containers. Assemble all the equipment and utensils. Prepare any pans.

RECOOK: see REHEAT.

REDBERRY: see LINGONBERRY.

RED DELICIOUS is a bright red (sometimes streaked with green), sweet eating apple with an elongated shape and five distinctive knobs at its base. It is not genetically related to the Golden Delicious apple. This cultivar was recognized in Wellsburg, Iowa, in 1880. The Red Delicious is more of an eating apple than a cooking apple. It is juicy and sweet but lacks any distinguishing tartness.

REDEYE GRAVY or **RED-EYE GRAVY** is a gravy made by thickening the juices of cooked ham with flour, then frying the juices in coffee or red wine and water. It is named either for the small bubbles of ham fat that form in it while cooking, or for its appearance before the fat and water are combined; the term dates to around 1931.

RED FLANNEL HASH is made with beets, coarsely grated red-skinned potatoes, and chopped meat. This New England specialty is so named for the mixture of colors; the name dates to around 1902. The hash is often served with corn bread.

RED HOT: see HOT DOG.

RED MEAT is meat that is dark in color before cooking, namely beef, lamb, and venison. Modern slimmed-down cows and pigs have cuts that are lower in fat than the dark meat of chicken. On average, red meat has less than 4% saturated fat.

RED MEXICAN BEAN: see PINTO BEAN.

RED ONION, also called PURPLE ONION, is a medium to large onion with reddish-purplish skin and a mild to sweet flavor.

> **HINT** The red color in red onions comes from anthocyanidins such as cyanidin; red onions are also high in flavonoids. They can be stored for three to four months at room temperature.

RED PEPPER: see CAYENNE.

RED POTATO is any kind of potato with a red skin. Red potatoes are waxy potatoes that hold their shape after they are cooked; they are good for salads and scalloped potato dishes. NEW POTATO is a young potato of any variety, especially small early red potatoes.

> **HINTS** Good-quality red potatoes are firm and have smooth skin and bright red coloring. They should have few eyes, and those few eyes should be shallow. Avoid any that are soft, wrinkled, or green tinted, or have cuts in the skin.

> ▌ Red potatoes should not be mashed as they will be sticky and gooey.

RED SNAPPER is an important lean saltwater food fish with a pinkish red head and body. It has mild-flavored flaky white flesh.

REDUCE (REDUCTION) is to boil down or simmer a liquid to decrease its volume through evaporation, which thickens its consistency and concentrates its flavor.

> **CONFUSABLE** REDUCE/COOK DOWN: Reduce and cook down are synonymous. Stocks, wine, braising liquids, cream, and vinegar are candidates for reduction. If a food is labeled "reduced," it means that the calories, fat, cholesterol, or sugar content is 25% lower than in the product's normal form. Through reduction, the flavor of a wine may be intensified and its consistency thickened, delivering a pleasing fruity taste and rich body to a finished dish.

> **HINTS** Use reduced-sodium broth if you are using a commercial product in making a reduced sauce. All reduction sauces are best when seasoned after reaching their desired consistency.

> ▌ Use a wide, heavy saucepan for making a reduction sauce.

RED WHORTLEBERRY: see LINGONBERRY.

REFINED means a food has been freed from impurities by processing. In winemaking, it means well-balanced, especially applied to red wine.

REFRESH: see SHOCK.

REFRIED BEANS or **REFRITOS** is a Mexican/Spanish dish of red or pinto beans cooked and mashed, then fried in fat with various seasonings. "Refried beans" is a translation of the Spanish *frijoles refritos*—but *refritos* actually means "well fried" not "refried."

REFRIGERATOR is a machine or room in which food and drink are kept cool, either by ice or mechanical cooling. The word dates to around 1611.

Hot food should be cooled to room temperature before refrigerating. Refrigerate within 2 hours.

❙ A packed refrigerator is not good because air needs to circulate around food to keep it the right temperature. But an empty refrigerator is not efficient either, as a good amount of food helps maintain the temperature.

REFRIGERATOR COOKIE: see ICEBOX COOKIE.

REHEAT, also called RECOOK or REWARM, is to heat again.

HINTS Reheat at a high temperature. Heat prepared foods at 425°F–475°F for a few minutes before serving.

❙ A method of easily reheating slices of cooked meat is to place the pieces of meat in a casserole dish with a lettuce leaf in between slices. Then heat in the oven or microwave. This will retain the tenderness and moistness of the meat.

REHYDRATE is to restore water or other liquid to something that has been dehydrated.

RELISH is any of a variety of foods, such as pickles, olives, piccalilli, or raw vegetables, served as an appetizer or hors d'oeuvre. Relish is also a piquant or spicy condiment usually made with finely chopped pickled cucumbers and spices, sugar, and vinegar, and used on hot dogs and hamburgers as well as in various recipes. The term in this sense is an Americanism dating to 1826.

RELLENO is a Spanish adjective meaning "stuffed or filled," as in *chile relleno*.

RÉMOULADE (pronounced ray-muh-LAHD) is a chilled mayonnaise sauce with herbs, mustard, capers, anchovies, and pickles (gherkins) and sometimes chopped hard-cooked egg. The word seems to derive from the French *rémola*, "horseradish," which came from the Latin *armoracia*, "horseradish." Rémoulade is often served with cold meat or fish.

RENDER in cooking means to melt fat (such as lard) to separate out impurities, or to purify or extract something by melting, especially to heat solid fat slowly until as much liquid fat as possible has been extracted from it, leaving crisp remains.

RESERVE in cooking means to hold back or set aside, especially for future use in a recipe.

CONFUSABLE SET ASIDE/RESERVE. Set aside means to put a component of a dish to the side while preparing other parts. Reserve means that a component of a recipe is prepared and reserved for a later stage, while an ingredient to be set aside is used sooner. A reserved component may not be used in the recipe at all, but saved for a different recipe.

REST is to remove meat, such as a roast or meat loaf, from the heat and let it sit for a short time before being served. Resting allows the temperature of the meat to stabilize and lets juices in the center return to the edges of the food.

RESTAURANT is a business where food is cooked and served, purchased and eaten. Restaurant owners are restaurateurs (no *n* is involved), a word taken directly from the French *restaurer*, "restore." The word restaurant appeared in the sixteenth century and first meant "a food which restores"—specifically a rich soup thought capable of restoring health. Later, the eighteenth-century gastronome Jean Anthelme Brillat-Savarin referred to chocolate, red meat, and consommé as "restaurants." The word did not develop the meaning of "an establishment specializing in the sale of restorative foods" until the nineteenth century. The first restaurant worthy of the name was founded by Antoine Beauvilliers in 1782, and called Grande Taverne de Londres. He introduced the novelties of listing the dishes available on a menu and serving them at small individual tables during fixed hours.

RESTAURANT SLANG

ADAM AND EVE ON A RAFT: Two poached eggs on toast.

ADAM'S ALE: Plain water.

AXLE GREASE OR SKID GREASE: Butter.

BABY, MOO JUICE, SWEET ALICE, OR COW JUICE: Milk.

BELCH WATER: Seltzer or soda water.

BIRDSEED: Cereal.

BLUE-PLATE SPECIAL: A dish of meat, potato, and vegetable served on a plate (usually blue) sectioned in three parts.

BOSSY IN A BOWL: Beef stew.

BOWL OF RED: A bowl of chili con carne.

BOWWOW: A hot dog.

BREATH: An onion.

BRIDGE OR BRIDGE PARTY: Four of anything.

BULLETS: Baked beans.

BUN PUP: A hot dog.

BURN ONE: Put a hamburger on the grill.

BURN THE BRITISH: A toasted English muffin.

CAT'S EYES OR FISH EYES: Tapioca.

CHINA: Rice pudding.

CHOPPER: A table knife.

CITY JUICE: Water.

CLEAN UP THE KITCHEN: Hash or hamburger.

CONEY ISLAND CHICKEN OR CONEY ISLAND: A hot dog.

COWBOY: A western omelet or sandwich.

COW FEED: A salad.

CREEP: Draft beer.

CROWD: Three of anything.

DEADEYE: Poached egg.

DOG AND MAGGOT: Cracker and cheese.

DOG BISCUIT: Cracker.

DOUGH WELL-DONE WITH COW TO COVER: Buttered toast.

EVE WITH A LID ON: Apple pie.

FIFTY-FIVE: A glass of root beer.

FIRST LADY: Spareribs.

FOUR-TOP: Table that seats four people.

FRENCHMAN'S DELIGHT: Pea soup.

GAC: Grilled American cheese sandwich.

GENTLEMAN WILL TAKE A CHANCE: Hash.

GO FOR A WALK: An order to be packed and taken out.

GRAVEL TRAIN: Sugar bowl.

GRAVEYARD STEW: Milk toast.

GROUNDHOG: A hot dog.

HEMORRHAGE: Ketchup.

HIGH AND DRY: A plain sandwich without butter, mayonnaise, or lettuce.

HOUSEBOAT: A banana split made with ice cream and sliced bananas.

IN THE ALLEY: Serve as a side dish.

(continued)

IRISH TURKEY: Corned beef and cabbage.

JAVA OR JOE: Coffee.

LUMBER: A toothpick.

MAIDEN'S DELIGHT: Cherries.

MIKE AND IKE OR THE TWINS: Salt and pepper shakers.

MUD OR OMURK: Black coffee.

MURPHY: Potatoes.

NOAH'S BOY: A slice of ham.

NO COW: Without milk.

ON THE HOOF: Meat done rare.

ON WHEELS: An order to be packed and taken out.

PAIR OF DRAWERS: Two cups of coffee.

PITTSBURGH: Toast or something burning.

PUT OUT THE LIGHTS AND CRY: Liver and onions.

RADIO: A tuna-fish-salad sandwich on toast.

SAND: Augar.

SEA DUST: Salt.

SINKERS AND SUDS: Doughnuts and coffee.

TWO-TOP: Table that seats two people.

VERMONT: Maple syrup.

WARTS: Olives.

WREATH: Cabbage.

WRECK 'EM: Scramble the eggs.

YUM-YUM: Sugar.

ZEPPELINS IN A FOG: Sausages in mashed potatoes.

RESTAURANT TYPES

The public dining room that ultimately became known as the restaurant originated in France. The first restaurant proprietor was A. Boulanger, a soup vendor who opened his business in Paris in 1765. The sign above his door advertised "*restoratives*" or "*restaurants*," referring to the soups and broths available within. The institution took its name from that sign, and the word restaurant now denotes a public eating place in English, Danish, Dutch, French, Norwegian, Romanian, and many other languages. The specialty restaurant (serving one or two kinds of food, such as seafood or steak), the cafeteria, and fast-food establishments are types of restaurants originating in the United States. Here is a sampling of the wide variety of restaurants available to today's diners:

À LA CARTE RESTAURANT
ALTERNATE
AUTOMAT
BARBECUE
BEANERY
BISTRO
BRASSERIE
BREWPUB
BUFFET
CAFÉ
CAFETERIA
CANTEEN
CARRYOUT
CARVERY

CHOPHOUSE
COFFEE SHOP OR COFFEEHOUSE
COMMISSARY
CRÊPERIE
DAIRY BAR
DINER
DRIVE-IN
DRIVE-THROUGH
FAST CASUAL RESTAURANT
FAST-FOOD RESTAURANT
GASTROPUB
GREASY SPOON
GRILLROOM

LUNCHEONETTE
LUNCHROOM
MESS
MILK BAR
MOBILE CANTEEN
NOSHERY
OYSTER BAR
PIZZERIA
PRIX FIXE RESTAURANT
RISTORANTE
ROADHOUSE
ROTISSERIE
SIT-DOWN RESTAURANT
SNACK BAR

SPECIALTY	TANDOORI	TRATTORIA
STEAK HOUSE	TAQUERIA	TRUCK STOP
SUPPER CLUB	TAVERNA	WHITE-TABLECLOTH RESTAURANT
SUSHI BAR	TEAROOM OR TEAHOUSE	WINE BAR
TAKEAWAY	THEME RESTAURANT	

R

RIB ROAST

RETSINA is a resin-flavored Greek wine, so named because it includes pine resin.

REUBEN SANDWICH is corned beef, Swiss cheese, sauerkraut, and either Russian or Thousand Island dressing, served hot on toasted rye bread. It likely takes its name from Arnold Reuben (1883–1970), a restaurateur; the term was first recorded in 1956.

REWARM: see REHEAT.

RHUBARB is any of several species of the genus *Rheum* grown for its large, succulent leafstalks, which are edible. The tart leafstalks are used in pies (it is also called the pie plant), often with strawberries; in compotes and preserves; and sometimes as the base of a wine or an aperitif. Rhubarb appears to come from the Latin *rha*, "rhubarb root," and *barbarum*, "foreign."

> **HINTS** Rhubarb can be tested for freshness by snapping the base of the stalk; there should be a slight resistance. The stalks should be crisp and firm, with no blemishes or cuts, and the leaves should be fresh, not wilted. Peel any brown spots or strings on rhubarb. The stalks should not be turning green. Rhubarb leaves are mildly toxic, so you should throw them away.
>
> Refrigerate whole stalks of rhubarb for up to three days in perforated plastic bags in the vegetable crisper. Freeze cut-up rhubarb for up to eight months.

RIB (RIBS) is a supporting or strengthening part of an animal or plant. Rib or ribs also refers to a cut of meat that contains ribs.

RIBEYE STEAK, RIB EYE, RIB-EYE STEAK, RIB EYE STEAK, or **RIB STEAK**, also called DELMONICO STEAK, is a tender beefsteak cut from the center (eye) of the rib or outer side of the rib section of a cow. It is so named because it comes from the "eye" of the prime rib. The ribeye can be cut boneless or bone-in; a bone-in ribeye (sometimes called a cowboy ribeye) is synonymous with a rib steak.

RIB ROAST, also called STANDING RIB ROAST, is a cut of beef taken from the small end of the ribs and containing a large ribeye and two or more ribs; it is also defined as a cut of beef containing the large piece that lies along the outer side of the rib.

RICE is a cereal grass (*Oryza sativa*) grown widely in warm, wet climates and the starchy seeds/grains of this grass used as food. The word rice derives from the Greek *oryza*, but is ultimately from the Sanskrit *vrihi-s*, "rice." To rice means to push cooked food through a perforated kitchen tool called a RICER. Archaeological evidence shows rice cultivation dating to 7000 BC. Roughly half of the world population, including virtually all of East and Southeast Asia, is wholly dependent upon rice as a staple food; 95% of the world's rice crop is eaten by humans. Short-grain rice is stickier than long-grain rice because the starch amylase produces a less sticky rice, and amylase is dominant in the long-grain varieties, while amyloperctin, which increases water absorption by the starch, is dominant in the short-grain type. This stickiness makes short-grain rice the selection for dishes to be eaten with chopsticks, and for risotto, puddings, and sushi. There are over eight thousand different varieties of rice worldwide that can be classified by the length of the grain into short-, medium-, and long-grain, plus sticky rice.

RICE ESSENTIALS

■ To remove excess starch that can make rice gummy, rinse rice in a large pot before cooking until the water runs clear. However, white rice should not be rinsed before cooking, because it will wash away the nutrients that have been added to it during processing.

■ Allow extra cooking time if rice has been stored for a long time, because it will have lost its moisture.

■ Brown rice has some nutritive advantages over white rice. It has twice the fiber of white (but still only about a half gram of fiber per cup of cooked rice); slightly more protein; two to three times more vitamin E, magnesium, potassium, and phosphorus; and volatile bran oils, which have been linked to cholesterol reduction in humans. Both instant rice and quick-cooking are the lowest in nutritional content of any rice.

■ Brown rice takes approximately three times longer to cook than white rice because the bran covering of brown rice hinders the absorption of water by the starchy interior. One and a half times more water is also required to steam brown rice, partly because of the longer cooking period. While cooking brown rice in a microwave may save a little time, the rice tends to be sticky. There is very little difference between the nutritional value of regular, instant, or precooked brown rice.

■ Cooking rice with 1–2 teaspoons of butter or oil per cup of raw rice produces a moister, softer, and slightly more flavorful rice.

■ Leftover cooked rice can be put in a sealed container and stored for three to five days in the refrigerator, or in the freezer for up to a month. To reheat leftover rice, put it in a saucepan with a few tablespoons of water and heat over low heat for 3–5 minutes, stirring occasionally. Add more water as needed or sprinkle with water and cover. You can also microwave the rice on high power for 1–2 minutes.

■ Rice is perishable. It should be stored in airtight containers. It will last for several months in a cool, dark place without deterioration. Brown rice should be refrigerated, since it contains the nutritious germs, which become rancid easily at room temperature.

- For fluffy rice, remove a saucepan of rice from the heat once tender, remove the lid, put a folded kitchen towel over the pan, put the lid back on, and let sit for 5–10 minutes.

- The best kind of rice for salads is long-grain that is cooked to be fluffy and firm. The best way to season rice salad is to season it while still warm, just after draining.

- Without salt, rice tends to be softer, almost mushy, since the salt slows down the absorption of water, because water is attracted to the salt and resists penetrating the rice. Slowing water absorption increases cooking time. You should use about ½ teaspoon of salt per cup of raw rice.

- To prevent rice from boiling over as it cooks, add 1 teaspoon of oil or butter to the cooking water.

RICE VARIETIES

ARBORIO RICE	GLUTINOUS RICE, STICKY RICE, WAXY RICE, OR SWEET RICE	PECAN RICE
AROMATIC RICE		PIGMENTED RICE
BASMATI RICE	INSTANT RICE OR QUICK-COOKING RICE	RED RICE
BLACK RICE		SHORT-GRAIN RICE
BROWN RICE	JASMINE RICE	SUSHI RICE
CONVERTED RICE	LONG-GRAIN RICE	WHITE RICE
DELLA RICE	MEDIUM-GRAIN RICE	WILD RICE

RICE CAKE is a usually circular, palm-sized patty made from congealed puffed rice. The term dates to 1683. Soft forms of rice cakes have been popular in Japan for hundreds of years. The rice cake called *mochi* was a sweet confection eaten by the nobility during the Nara period from AD 710–794. The popularity of rice cakes blossomed during the Kamakura shogunate from 1192–1333 and the variety of cakes included *botamochi*, *yakimochi*, and *chimaki*. During the Edo period (1601–1868), rice cakes became even more popular as treats for festivals and as local specialties. Rice cakes were commonly sold by roadside vendors, a tradition which continues in most of Asia. Rice cakes have only two critical ingredients: rice and water. The rice itself needs certain characteristics to produce the best-quality cake and limit breakage. Sticky rice, whether white or brown, tends to work best. Other ingredients like salt and various flavorings are important considerations to taste- and nutrition-conscious consumers but are not significant to the production process.

RICE FLOUR is powdery, finely ground white or brown rice and is used for baking, for making rice noodles and some pancakes, and as a thickener. Rice-flour noodles are thin Chinese noodles that explode into crunchy strands when deep-fried.

RICE PUDDING is a milk custard made from rice, milk, sugar, and nutmeg. Originally used to sustain malnourished people, rice pudding was first made in Asia.

Rice puddings are found in nearly every area of the world, and recipes can vary greatly even within a single country. The dessert can be boiled or baked.

RICER, also called POTATO RICER, is a kitchen utensil used for extruding soft foods through small holes to produce bits or particles about the size of grains of rice, or long strings. Ricers are handy for making smooth mashed potatoes or preparing other root vegetables. Ricers come in a variety of shapes, are usually made of aluminum or steel, and have a three- to four-inch round basket or a V-shaped bucket.

RICE VINEGAR is a type of vinegar made from rice and is milder and sweeter than vinegars made from grapes.

RICE WINE, also called SAKE or MIRIN, is a sweet low-alcohol beverage made from fermented glutinous rice.

RICOTTA (pronounced ri-KOT-uh) is a soft, dry, or moist Italian cheese made from whey, but is also a U.S. cheese resembling cottage cheese and made from whole milk or whey and whole cow's milk. Ricotta literally means "recooked" in Italian, from the fact that the cheese is made by heating the whey from another cooked cheese. Ricotta is slightly grainy but smoother than cottage cheese. It is a favorite component of many Italian desserts, such as cheesecakes and cannoli, as well as savory dishes, such as pasta, calzones, pizza, manicotti, lasagna, and ravioli.

RIESLING, also called JOHANNISBERG RIESLING, is a fragrant white wine from Germany and Austria or a similar wine from elsewhere. Riesling can be dry to very sweet, and is crisp and more acidic than other white wines.

RIGATONI is chubby tubular pasta in short ribbed pieces. The word comes from the Italian *rigare*, "to mark with lines/to make fluting." Rigatoni's ridges and holes are perfect with any sauce, from cream or cheese to the chunkiest meat sauces.

RILLETTES or **RILLETTES D'OIE** is seasoned minced pork or goose cooked in its own seasoned fat until very tender, pounded into a paste, potted, and sealed with a layer of fat as a type of pâté. Rillettes (pronounced ree-YEHT) is a French word meaning "small pieces of pork," from *rille*, "piece of pork." Rillettes can also be made with duck, fish, or rabbit. It is a cold appetizer served with bread or toast.

RIND is the hard or tough covering/skin on fruits such as oranges, grapefruit, and watermelon; once removed, skin or rind is usually known as peel. The rind of fruit is usually the botanical exocarp. Rind is also any outer layer or skinlike covering, as on a cheese. Rind on a cheese can be either natural or artificial, and it protects the interior of the cheese and often imparts a flavor of its own. Pork rind or crackling is the fried or roasted skin (rind) of a pig.

RIOJA (pronounced ree-OH-hah) is the name of various dry rich and fruity red wines from the Tempranillo grape, produced in La Rioja, a region of northern Spain. There are also white Rioja wines.

RIPE means fully developed or matured and ready to be eaten or used. This adjective is used for cheese, too: a ripe cheese is one that has has arrived at peak flavor through aging. The time of ripeness varies widely for all foods.

> **HINT** Hasten fruit's ripening by putting it in a paper bag with a few holes punched in the bag.

RISE: see RAISE.

RISOTTO is a dish of medium-grain rice (like Arborio) lightly sautéed in butter or oil, with chopped onion and stock. There are many variations on the dish. Risotto is Italian for "little rice" and the dish originated in Lombardy and Emilia-Romagna. In the United States medium-grain rice is used for risotto, but in Italy the same rice is called short-grain. Arborio from Italy is by far the first choice; Japanese short-grain or California medium-grain can be used with somewhat inferior results.

> **HINTS** Cook risotto in a pan allowing one-quart capacity for each serving, for example, a four-quart pan for four servings. Risotto needs to be stirred frequently—almost constantly—to prevent the rice from burning and to liberate the amylopectin (rice starch) that will swell and help make the sauce. Gradual release of this starch gives the dish the desired creamy texture. Add liquid a little at a time, stirring constantly, to release as much starch as possible into the liquid to make a creamy risotto.
>
> ▌ Risotto can be cooked to a point, stopped, and finished later. Cook until half of the liquid has been added. Spread the risotto on a baking pan to arrest the cooking. Return it to the pot to finish, and add a little more butter and/or cheese than called for in the recipe.
>
> ▌ Finish risotto by beating some butter or grated cheese in to release even more starch. Risotto continues to cook after you take it off the heat.

RISSOLÉ is a small cake made of minced, cooked meat or fish coated in egg and bread crumbs and fried in deep fat. The word is from the Latin *russeolus*, "reddish." Rissolé is an adjective meaning browned and crisped by frying; rissolé is variously pronounced as RIHS-uh-lee, rihs-uh-LAY, or ree-saw-LAY.

ROAST is to cook by dry heat in an oven, and a roast is a piece of meat roasted or for roasting, usually two or more portions in size (such as roast beef). For coffee, roast means to dry and parch by exposure to heat, and a roast is a coffee roasted in a particular way. For example, in lighter roasts, the bean will exhibit more of its origin flavor—the flavors created in the bean by the soil and weather conditions in the location where it was grown. For darker roasts, the roast flavor is so dominant that it can be difficult to distinguish the origin of the beans used in the roast. Roast originally meant "cook before a fire" before it meant "cook in an oven." The tender parts of the animal make the best cuts for roasting. The neck, shoulder, and hips are tougher because they are the most active. The loin or tenderloin are the best. Young animals, such as lambs or calves (veal), are good for roasting. The closer the cuts are to the head, horn, or tail, the less tender they are.

ROASTING ESSENTIALS

CONFUSABLE ROASTING/BAKING. There is no difference between oven roasting and baking. The term baking is usually used for bread, pies, cakes, and so on, while roasting is used for meats.

■ Large roasts should be cooked at 325ºF–350ºF so the outside does not get overcooked before the inside is done. Smaller roasts cook better at higher temperatures for a shorter time.

■ A boned roast will be easier to carve, but will be less flavorful, since the bone adds flavor. Use a bone-in roast to add flavor to the meat and help it cook faster.

■ A fatty cooked roast can be made to look better by refrigerating it until the fat solidifies, then cutting off the fat and cooking, basting periodically, until hot.

■ A roast is tied to ensure that it cooks evenly and retains its shape. A roast should be at or near room temperature before cooking, mainly as a precautionary measure so that the roast's outside doesn't overcook and dry out before the inside is warmed and cooked, and to save time and energy since a room-temperature roast cooks more quickly than a colder one. If you do not have time to bring the roast to room temperature before cooking it, set the oven temperature slightly lower and roast slightly longer.

■ An oven rack is important for a roast because if the roast is elevated on a rack in a roasting pan, hot air gets to all surfaces. Without it, the bottom will be sautéed instead of roasted. Without air circulation all around the roast, steam can accumulate, forming a liquid pool, which will prevent browning.

■ If you add tomatoes to a roast, the acidity from the tomatoes will help to tenderize the roast.

■ Meat should not be roasted in the same pan with vegetables, such as potatoes or corn. The vegetables will yield moisture that will partially steam the meat, which should be cooking in dry heat.

■ Preheat the oven before roasting. Cook the roast fat side up, so that the melting fat will baste the meat. Turning the roast once or twice will help brown it evenly. Baste frequently. Don't use a covered pan, as uncovered means dry heat. When the meat is covered, the steam is trapped and this results in a mushy rather than a crisp surface, and a pale brown color rather than deep brown. Let the roast stand for 10–15 minutes before carving. When the roast is first removed from the oven, the surface has less juice than the meat at the core. If you carve the roast immediately, the edges of the slices will be unnecessarily dry and the meat's juices will seep out, because the saturated muscle tissue in the interior cannot absorb and hold the excess liquid. The resting period gives the liquid a chance to redistribute and settle throughout. The meat also becomes firmer, making it easier to cut thin slices. Cover the resting meat with a foil tent if the kitchen is cold or cool.

■ The advantages of slow roasting are less shrinkage, a uniform doneness, and better flavors. The advantages of using a high-temperature oven for roasting are quicker cooking, a better crust, and juicier meat.

■ The internal temperature of a roast will increase by about 5°F after it is removed from the oven. Therefore, remove it when the internal temperature is just under the desired temperature (as measured by a meat thermometer).

■ When you cook meat with dry heat, it should be salted before roasting. Unless the meat is salted before cooking begins, the salt will not have a chance to infuse it and trigger flavor-enhancing chemical reactions.

■ When roasting, the meat or fish should be three to five inches away from the burner flame or electric coil.

■ Some cooks prefer to start roasting at 500°F, then reduce to 325°F after the meat is seared and has browned. But at 325°F, the roast cooks consistently and this reduces shrinkage, so it is better to roast at 500°F for the entire time. Either way, the fat side should be up, as the fat bastes the meat as it cooks.

ROASTER or **ROASTING PAN** is a special cooking pan for roasting. A roaster is often accompanied by a roasting rack that holds the roast up out of the pan bottom and the roast's juices/drippings. A roaster is used for holding large cuts of meat for roasting or for cooking custards in a hot-water bath. Using a rack allows for poaching or steaming. A double roaster has a lid that is the same as the bottom, so you have two open roasters or one covered roaster. A French-style roaster is a large, rectangular, covered roasting pan. The deepest roaster is called a brazier—it is about six inches deep and very long and wide. Lasagna pans are also considered a type of roasting pan. Such a pan should be heavy and about three inches deep to prevent overflow. Roaster is also the term for the meat of a large young chicken over 3½ pounds, or a joint of meat suitable or intended for roasting.

ROBUSTA is a species of coffee bush (*Coffea canephora*) that produces beans of this name. It is native to West Africa but widely cultivated. The word is from the Latin *robustus*, "robust." Robusta beans are of lesser quality than Arabica beans.

ROCK CANDY is sugar in large, hard, clear crystals on a string or stick, made by boiling sugar and then letting it form large crystals. Named for its resemblance to rock, the name was first recorded in 1723.

ROCKET or **ROQUETTE**, is another name for ARUGULA, is an erect plant (*Eruca vesicaria sativa*) of the crucifer family whose young tender leaves are harvested for salad. The English word dates to around 1530 and is from the French *roquette,* from an Italian diminutive form, ultimately from the Latin *eruca,* "kind of cabbage."

ROCKFISH: see STRIPED BASS.

ROCK SALT is coarsely ground or granulated common salt, or salt artificially prepared in large crystals.

ROCKY MOUNTAIN OYSTERS: see PRAIRIE OYSTER.

ROE generally is fish eggs or egg-filled ovaries, specifically female fish eggs (hard roe), or the egg-laden ovary of a fish and that of certain crustaceans such as lobster. However, it also refers to the milt or sperm of male fish (soft roe). Popular roes come from carp, herring, lumpfish, mackerel, perch, salmon, sturgeon, and whitefish. The word roe dates to the fifteenth century. The pale pink roe of scallops, red-orange roe of crabs, and coral-colored roe of lobsters are quite good for eating.

ROLL refers to any of various foods that are rolled during preparation, for example, a small portion of bread, variously shaped; a cake covered with fruit and nuts and rolled (such as a jelly roll); or beef or veal rolled and cooked (such as rolled roast).

> **HINT** For soft crust on bread rolls, dust the top of the dough with flour before baking. Cover with a clean kitchen towel when cooking. Brush with warmed honey or maple syrup if you want a glossy, sweet glaze.

ROLLED OATS are oats that have had the husks removed and been flattened and are used in making oatmeal.

ROLLED ROAST or **ROLLED RIB ROAST** is a meat roast with the ribs removed that is rolled and tied into a cylinder.

ROLLING PIN is a cylindrical utensil (usually wood), sometimes with a handle at each end and sometimes without handles, that is used to roll out dough. American rolling pins have handles, while French-style pins do not have handles.

> **HINT** A clean wine bottle can substitute for a rolling pin.

ROMAINE, also called COS or COS LETTUCE, is a lettuce (*Lactuca sativa*) with long green leaves in a loosely packed, elongated head. The sturdy leaves have a firm rib down their centers. Romaine is the classic lettuce for Caesar salad. The name comes from the Latin *laitue Romaine,* "Roman lettuce," so called because it was used as a leafy vegetable in ancient Rome, through which it was shipped to other places.

> **HINT** Avoid heads of romaine with any signs of rust, as well as older plants with large, strong, milky ribs. Ideally, romaine should be stored at 33°F–35°F. Store the unwashed whole heads in plastic bags to retain natural moisture, and keep in the vegetable crisper of the refrigerator. Uncut, whole heads of lettuce retain nutrients best. Surface water from washing encourages bacterial growth. Romaine will keep for seven to ten days this way. Keep it away from apples, as ethylene gas will turn the romaine brown.

ROMAN CUMIN: see Cumin.

ROMANO or **ROMANO CHEESE** is a dry, sharp, salty, very hard sheep's, cow's, or goat's milk cheese, usually grated. The Italian word *Romano* is short for Pecorino Romano, Roman sheep's milk cheese. This cheese is named after Rome, where it has been made for more than two thousand years, originally in the region of Latium; it is one of the oldest Italian cheeses. Romano cheese is made by a special method called rummaging curd, which involves draining the curd quickly after molding. The surface is then pierced slightly before the cheese is salted. The cheese is then aged for five months. Romano cheese has a fat content of 27% and a water content of 32%. It is different from other cheeses because it requires more milk per pound, most water being lost in processing.

ROMANOFF or **ROMANOV** describes fruit, often strawberries, macerated in liqueur and topped with whipped cream.

ROOT is the part of a plant, usually below the ground, that lacks nodes, shoots, and leaves; holds the plant in position; draws water and nourishment from the soil; and stores food.

ROOT BEER is a sweet carbonated soft drink made from the extracts of various roots and herbs. It is American in origin and dates to 1843. Pharmacist Charles E. Hires introduced Hires Root Beer in 1876 after experimenting with a recipe for herbal tea made of roots, berries, and herbs. Originally, the root beer was sold as a dry extract that was brewed at home by adding water, sugar, and yeast, and was promoted as a healthy beverage.

ROOT VEGETABLE is any of various underground roots or tubers, including the beet, carrot, potato, rutabaga, sweet potato, turnip, and yam, grown for their fleshy, edible underground parts. Botany distinguishes true roots such as tuberous roots and taproots from nonroots such as tubers, rhizomes, corms, and bulbs. The term "root and tuber crops" is a catchall term for subterranean storage organs of which there are approximately 38 root, 23 tuber, 14 rhizome, 11 corm, and 10 bulb crops. Roots and tubers were critical components in the diet during the early evolution of mankind.

ROQUEFORT is strongly flavored, semisoft French blue-veined cheese made from sheep's milk and matured in limestone caves; Roquefort-sur-Soulzon is the name of the village where it was created. The term appeared in English around 1766; Roquefort dressing arrived in 1943. Roquefort, or similar-style cheese, is mentioned in literature as far back as AD 79, when Pliny the Elder remarked upon its rich flavor. Roquefort is sold in foil-wrapped cylinders; true Roquefort is known by a red sheep on the wrapper's emblem. The name Roquefort is protected by law from imitators; only those cheeses aged in the natural Combalou caves of Roquefort-sur-Soulzon may bear the name Roquefort. Roquefort has the highest level of glutamates of any naturally produced food, containing as much as 1,280 milligrams of glutamate per 100 grams of cheese.

ROSÉ is a pinkish table wine from red/purple grapes whose skins were removed after fermentation began. The word is short for the French *vin rosé*, literally meaning "pink wine."

ROSEMARY is the extremely pungent gray-green leaves of a plant (*Rosmarinus officinalis*) of the mint family that are used fresh or dried as an herb for meat, poultry, and vegetables. The flavor is described as pinelike. It is native to the Mediterranean region. Fresh rosemary is preferable to dried because it is more aromatic and flavorful. Of the dried rosemary, the whole leaf is better than the ground. The stems of rosemary cannot be used.

ROSETTE is a food decoration or garnish in the shape of a rose, often made from icing, but some vegetables like carrots and radishes can also be shaped like this.

RÖSTI is a fried potato cake made from thinly grated potatoes, sometimes with onions and bacon, butter or fat, salt and pepper, and topped with cheese; it is a Swiss term meaning "crisp and golden." Rösti is very similar to HASH BROWNS. It was originally a common breakfast eaten by farmers in the canton of Bern, Switzerland.

ROTI (Hindi for "bread") is a round, soft unleavened Indian bread made from wheat flour and cooked on a griddle (*tawa*). It is also the term for this bread with a filling, eaten as a sandwich. When roti is cooked over an open flame, it fills with steam and puffs up.

ROTINI is short corkscrew-shaped pasta; it is Italian for "twists."

ROTISSERIE is a type of oven or broiler with a rotating spit on which meat cooks as it turns. Rotisserie first meant a restaurant or shop specializing in roasted or barbecued meat. The word is from the French *rôtir*, "to roast." Rotisserie often refers to an attachment for a grill with a spit rod and spit forks to hold the food. The spit rotates at a slow speed over a heat source, allowing the food to baste itself.

ROUGHY is a small marine food fish similar to perch, named for its rough scales.

ROULADE or **ROULADEN**, also called BIRD, BRACIOLA, or PAUPIETTE, is a piece of meat or fish spread with a savory filling and rolled up, then cooked (braised or steamed). The rolled package is usually secured with string or a wooden pick, and it is browned before being baked or braised in wine or stock. The word roulade comes from the French *rouler*, "to roll." This term can also be applied to sweet foods, such as a soufflélike mixture or sponge cake baked in a flat pan rolled around a filling.

ROUND or **ROUND OF BEEF** is a cut of the thigh of beef below the rump and above the leg. Round is also a synonym for ROUND STEAK.

ROUND STEAK is a lean but somewhat tough, oval cut of beef from between the rump and shank. Specifically, a round steak is the eye of round, bottom round, and top round still connected together, with or without the "round" bone (femur), and may include the knuckle (sirloin tip), depending on how the round is separated from the loin. Round steak is commonly prepared with slow moist-heat methods including braising, to tenderize the meat and maintain moisture.

ROUX (French for "browned butter") is a mixture of flour and fat used to thicken sauces, and used as the basis for sauces, gravies, and soups.

> **HINT** When you add liquid to a roux, it is better to have the liquid cold or at room temperature.

RUB is a spice and/or herb mixture that is applied to the surface of food before cooking, especially meat to be grilled/barbecued.

RUM is an alcoholic liquor/spirit distilled from molasses or some other fermented sugarcane product. Rums originated in the West Indies and were first mentioned in records from Barbados in about 1650; they were called kill-devil or rumbullion and by 1667 were simply called rum. The light-bodied rums tend to be from Cuba and Puerto Rico, and the heavier and fuller-flavored rums from Jamaica. Rum, the major liquor distilled during the early history of the United States, was sometimes mixed with molasses and called blackstrap, or mixed with cider to produce a beverage called stonewall.

RUMAKI is an appetizer of Japanese/Polynesian/Hawaiian origin made of a marinated piece of chicken liver and a water chestnut wrapped in a slice of bacon and grilled or broiled. The marinade is usually soy sauce and either ginger or brown sugar. The English use of the word rumaki dates to around 1965; it may be an alteration of the Japanese *harumaki*, "spring roll." There is a theory that rumaki was invented by Victor Bergeron, known as Trader Vic.

RUMP or **RUMP ROAST** is a cut of meat from the fleshy hindquarters, behind the loin and above the round.

RUSSET POTATO, also called BAKING POTATO or IDAHO POTATO, is a long ovoid potato with brown skin and white flesh that is high in starch and low in moisture.

> **HINT** Russet potatoes bake well and yield light, fluffy mashed potatoes. They don't hold their shape after cooking, so don't use them to make potato salads or scalloped potatoes. Don't wrap them in foil while baking them; the foil traps moisture and makes the potato mushy.

RUSSIAN DRESSING is a salad dressing with a mayonnaise base, with chili sauce or ketchup, chopped pickles, and sometimes onions, pimientos, or horseradish. Russian dressing originated not in Russia but in the United States. The name is from one of the original ingredients, red or black Russian caviar. The dressing is known as Marie Rose sauce in Europe.

RUTABAGA, also called SWEDE or SWEDISH TURNIP, is the large edible root of a turniplike plant (*Brassica napobrassica*) of the crucifer family. The word is from the Swedish *rotabagge*, "root bag." The vegetable is thought to be a cross between cabbage and turnip.

> **HINTS** Rutabagas are at their peak in cool weather. Choose firm ones that are heavy for their size; small ones are sweeter. Keep rutabagas for up to ten days in a cool, dark place, or in a plastic bag in the refrigerator for up to one month.
>
> ▌ Cut rutabaga can be sprinkled with lemon juice to stop discoloration.

RYE is a hardy annual cereal grass (*Secale cereale*) and the flour made from it. Rye is also whiskey distilled from rye or rye and malt.

RYE BREAD is a dense, dark or light bread made using rye flour, often flavored with caraway seeds. The nutrients in rye are calcium, phosphorus, riboflavin, iron, thiamine, potassium, and niacin, but their quantities are greatly diminished if the flour is made from rye that has had the bran removed.

SABAYON: see ZABAGLIONE.

SACHER TORTE or **SACHERTORTE** is a chocolate three-layered gateau with glossy, dark chocolate icing and an apricot jam filling; it is traditionally served with whipped cream without any sugar in it. The cake was created in Vienna by Franz Sacher (from a family of restaurateurs and hoteliers) in 1832. The Original Sacher

Torte is made only in Vienna and Salzburg. The only place where the Original Sacher Torte is available outside of Austria is in the Sacher shop of Bolzano, Italy.

SADDLE is a meat cut, often lamb, veal, or venison, that is a joint of meat consisting of the two loins (unseparated loin from two sides) of an animal.

SAFFLOWER OIL is a colorless, flavorless oil from seeds of the safflower plant. It contains more polyunsaturates than any other oil, and has a high smoke point, so it is favored for deep-frying. Safflower is a combination of the words saffron and flower, as the petals are an orangish yellow color. There are two types of safflower that produce different kinds of oil: one is high in monounsaturated fatty acid (oleic acid) and the other is high in polyunsaturated fatty acid (linoleic acid). The former is actually lower in saturates than olive oil.

> **HINT** Safflower oil is great for salad dressings because it doesn't solidify when chilled.

SAFFRON is an Old World plant (*Crocus sativus*) of the iris family with funnel-shaped flowers containing aromatic orange-yellow stigmas from which flavoring and coloring are made. The word is Arabic and has been used in English since around 1200. Saffron is the world's most expensive spice, with one pound requiring at least 225,000 stigmas. The best saffron comes from Kasmir in India and is labeled "Magro Cream." The next best is Spanish. Avoid saffron from Mexico, even though it is the least expensive, for it usually is not genuine saffron. Real saffron is the stigmas (threads) of a purple crocus flower. One acre produces 70,000 crocuses, each of which yields, hand-harvested, three threads. It takes 14,000 threads to make one ounce. An acre will yield only one pound of saffron. There are quality grades that differ in intensity of flavor, and therefore varying amounts are required to obtain the desired flavor.

SAGE is an herb of the mint family (*Salvia officinalis*) with aromatic fresh or dried gray-green leaves used for seasoning. Sage is a subtly bitter, musty, mintlike herb. Coming through French, the word is ultimately from the Latin *salvia*, "healing plant."

> **HINTS** It is best to add sage about a half hour before the finish of the cooking process.
>
> ▌ Dried sage can be kept no longer than six months.

SAITHE: see POLLOCK.

SAKE or **SAKÉ**, also called RICE WINE or MIRIN, is a fermented, mildly alcoholic Japanese beverage made from rice. The word possibly derives from *saka mizu*, "prosperous waters." Sake was mentioned in Japanese texts as long ago as the third century, but was not mentioned in English until 1687. In Japanese, *saké* or *o-saké* refers to alcoholic drinks in general. The Japanese term for this specific beverage is *nihonshu*.

SALAD is a dish, usually cold, of raw or sometimes cooked vegetables or fruits in various combinations, served with a dressing, or molded in gelatin, and sometimes with seafood, poultry, or eggs added. We mainly think of lettuce and other greens as the basis of salad. Another main meaning is a chopped or ground food mixed with mayonnaise and seasonings and often served on greens or in a sandwich, such as chicken salad, tuna salad, and egg salad. The English word salad dates to the late fifteenth century and is a shortened version of the Latin *herba salata*, "salted vegetables," from the Latin *sal*, "salt." In a composed salad, such as chef's salad, all the ingredients are placed on a plate, then dressing is drizzled on top. The salad plate is to the left of the forks in a place setting.

HINTS Toss a salad lightly, mixing with only a small amount of dressing (that's what "dress" means). You can put the dressing in the bottom of the bowl with the greens on top, cover and refrigerate, and toss just before serving. Dress a salad just before serving, especially when using a vinaigrette. If the salad gets overdressed, add more greens and retoss.

▌When transporting salad ingredients for a picnic, wrap salad greens in a moist towel and add the dressing when ready to serve.

▌Refresh wilted salad greens by putting them in ice water with 2 tablespoons of lemon juice and refrigerating for 1 hour. Drain the greens, wrap them in towels, and keep them bagged in the refrigerator for at least 4 hours before serving.

TYPES OF SALADS

Salad has a number of categories: green salad; vegetable salad; pasta or bean salad; mixed salad incorporating meat, poultry, or seafood; and fruit salad. Most salads are traditionally served cold, although some, such as German potato salad, are served hot. The restorative powers of green salad have been celebrated since antiquity: "Eat cress and gain wit" is a Greek proverb. The earliest salads were wild greens and herbs seasoned with salt; these were the first vegetable foods available in spring and were considered a tonic after a dull winter diet. Salad can be served as a side dish, as a separate course, or as the main course of a meal. Some popular salads are listed here:

ARTICHOKE SALAD	CHICKEN SALAD	CUCUMBER SALAD
ARUGULA SALAD	CHOPPED SALAD	DINNER SALAD
AVOCADO SALAD	COBB SALAD	EGG SALAD
BEAN SALAD	COLESLAW	FRUIT SALAD
BEET SALAD	COMBINATION SALAD	GARDEN SALAD
CABBAGE SALAD	CONGEALED SALAD	GERMAN POTATO SALAD
CAESAR SALAD	CORN SALAD	GREEK SALAD
CHEF'S SALAD	CRABMEAT SALAD	GREEN SALAD

GREEN GODDESS SALAD	MESCLUN SALAD	SPINACH SALAD
HOT SALAD	MOLDED SALAD	TABBOULEH
HOUSE SALAD	PASTA SALAD OR MACARONI SALAD	TACO SALAD
ICEBERG LETTUCE SALAD		TOSSED SALAD
INSALATA VERDE	POTATO SALAD	TUNA SALAD
LOBSTER SALAD	SALAD NIÇOISE	VEGETABLE SALAD
MEAT SALAD	SEAFOOD SALAD	WALDORF SALAD

SALAD DRESSING is a sauce for a salad usually based on vinaigrette, mayonnaise, or another emulsified mixture. Salad dressing was first mentioned by Charles Dickens in 1836. The Association for Salad Dressings and Sauces lists these as the most popular (in descending order): ranch, Italian, blue cheese, Caesar, Thousand Island, balsamic vinaigrette, French, Asian, honey-Dijon/mustard, and red wine vinaigrette.

SALAD DRESSINGS

The simplest salad dressings are mixtures of oil and vinegar with salt and pepper, herbs, and other ingredients like mustard. Creamy dressings have a base of mayonnaise (egg and oil emulsion), sweet cream, or sour cream and can be a cooked sauce containing eggs, flour, milk, or cream. These dressings are often highly seasoned and may include ingredients such as anchovy paste, cheese, egg, garlic, ketchup, olives, onion, parsley, or tarragon. Salad dressings, or sauces as they are also known, have evolved into many different types and varieties. Historically, dressings such as Thousand Island, vinaigrette, French, Russian, and Green Goddess have been made from well-known recipes handed down through generations. However, new versions of old recipes continue to be created, using a variety of ingredients to enhance the foods being dressed and draw out their flavors. Salad dressings are available as prepared dressings sold commercially, or can be made by hand. These are some of the dressings that appear on salads:

AIOLI	CREAMY PARMESAN DRESSING	ORANGE GINGER DRESSING
ANCHOVY DRESSING		POTATO SALAD DRESSING
BALSAMIC VINAIGRETTE	FRENCH DRESSING	RANCH DRESSING
BLUE CHEESE (OR BLEU CHEESE) DRESSING	GORGONZOLA DRESSING	RASPBERRY VINAIGRETTE
	GREEN GODDESS DRESSING	RÉMOULADE
CAESAR SALAD DRESSING		ROQUEFORT DRESSING
CHIPOTLE DRESSING	HERB DRESSING	RUSSIAN DRESSING
COLESLAW DRESSING	HONEY-DIJON DRESSING	SALAD CREAM
CREAMY DILL DRESSING	HONEY-MUSTARD DRESSING	THOUSAND ISLAND DRESSING
CREAMY GARLIC DRESSING	ITALIAN DRESSING	VINAIGRETTE
CREAMY ITALIAN DRESSING	MAYONNAISE	YOGURT DRESSING
	OIL AND VINEGAR	

SALAD FORK is smaller than a dinner fork, usually small and broad and part of a service. It is used for salads and also desserts and hors d'oeuvres. The salad fork is placed to the left of the dinner fork in a place setting.

SALAD SPINNER is a kitchen utensil for cleaning greens, consisting of a perforated basket inside another container and turned by a button or handle so that the basket revolves, throwing off water into the larger container. It is sometimes useful for cleaning or draining other foods.

> HINT Many salad spinners are large enough to hold an entire head of lettuce. Be sure to dry the outer container thoroughly before putting the spinner away. The salad spinner can be used to remove moisture from other foods, too.

SALAMI is a very spicy, salted Italian sausage, made of pork and beef or just beef. Salami is the plural of the Italian *salame*, "spiced salt pork," from the Latin *sal*, "salt"; the word first appeared in English around 1852. Salami is often flavored with garlic and sliced cold. It is from a family of sausages called cervelats, which are safe to eat without heating because they have been preserved by curing. Salamis are usually air-dried and vary in size, shape, seasoning, and curing process. Italian salamis include Genoa, cotto, and pepperoni. Kosher beef salamis are cooked and semisoft.

> HINT With the casing intact, salami can keep for years. Once cut, it should be tightly wrapped and stored in the refrigerator, where it will keep for up to two weeks. Salami is best served at room temperature.

SALISBURY STEAK is a patty of ground beef mixed with eggs, milk, onions, and various seasonings and broiled, fried, or baked; it is usually served with gravy. The dish was named in 1897 for a Civil War doctor, J. H. Salisbury (1823–1905), who promoted eating shredded beef three times a day. The USDA standard for Salisbury steak requires a minimum content of 65% meat, of which up to 25% can be pork; the remainder must be beef.

SALLY LUNN is a sweet, light yeast bread baked in a tube pan and served warm in slices with butter. It was probably named for a woman who sold these cakes in Bath, England, around 1800.

SALMAGUNDI is a dish of cooked meats, anchovies, onions, eggs, and vegetables, usually arranged on a plate of lettuce and dressed with a vinaigrette. The word is from the French *salmigondis*, "seasoned salt meats," probably related to *salomene*, "hodgepodge of meats or fish cooked in wine."

SALMON is any of various large food and game fishes of northern waters that usually migrate from saltwater to freshwater to spawn. The flesh is yellowish pink to pale red when cooked. The Indo-European ancestor of the word salmon is *lax*, also the source of the English word *lox*, "salmon."

HINTS There is a difference between wild and farmed salmon. Wild salmon is more complex in flavor and has a meaty texture. Farmed salmon has slightly more fat.

Salmon should be cooked the day of its purchase or within twenty-four hours. Keep in the refrigerator in plastic on a bed of ice.

SALPICON is a mixture of chopped meat, fish, or vegetables, bound by a thick sauce and used as a stuffing for croquettes, vol-au-vents, or pastries. The word came through French from the Spanish *salpicar*, "sprinkle with salt."

SALSA is a spicy/hot sauce of finely chopped vegetables including tomatoes, onions, and chiles, eaten as a condiment with tortilla chips and other Mexican foods. Salsa is Spanish/Mexican and Italian for "sauce" and it was first recorded in English in 1846. Salsa cruda or pico de gallo is uncooked salsa that is like a relish of chunky tomatoes, chiles, and onions. Salsa verde is a cooked "green salsa," of tomatillos, green chiles, and cilantro. There are also bean, corn, and fruit salsas.

HINT Unopened cooked salsas can be stored at room temperature for six months. Opened salsa can be refrigerated for up to one month.

SALSA MEXICANA: see PICO DE GALLO.

SALT is a white crystalline form of sodium chloride used to season and preserve food. Table salt usually contains added iodine and additives that keep it from clumping. Kosher salt, a coarse-grained salt without additives, is less salty than table salt. Sea salt, in coarse and fine grinds, is extracted from seawater and has a stronger flavor than table salt; it has no additives but has more minerals than table salt. The word salt is from the Latin *sal*, "salt." Fleur de sel is grayish ivory sea salt hand-gathered from the salt beds of Brittany in France. Rock salt is used for making ice cream and as a bed for roasting oysters on the half shell. Pickling salt is finely ground, has no additives, and dissolves quickly.

SALT ESSENTIALS

■ Salt is added to the water when cooking pasta or vegetables because salt is leached from the food during boiling. Add the salt after the water comes to a boil, not before.

■ It is generally best to salt food toward the end of cooking, especially for anything that cooks a long time. A pinch of salt at the beginning is good, though, to develop the flavor of the food.

■ To fix food that is oversalted, add more of an unsalted liquid, starch, or vegetable to dilute and/or correct the flavor. Another rescue is to add a little brown sugar and/or vinegar.

■ Salt raises the boiling point of water above the 212°F level. Sugar and other soluble substances will also raise the temperature, but by only a tiny amount. Also, hard water (containing dissolved

(continued)

mineral salts) will raise the temperature a degree or two.

■ Add raw rice grains to a salt shaker to prevent the salt from clumping. You can also put rice in a bag or filter if salt is kept in a canister. Mixing 1 tablespoon of cornstarch into a 1-pound container of salt will work too.

■ Kosher salt is best for salting large amounts of water for boiling vegetables or pasta.

■ You can salt meat or fish a couple hours or more before cooking to let

it penetrate the food, then pat dry because salt draws water out. Salt again just before serving.

■ In yeast doughs and breads, salt helps strengthen the gluten so it can bond in a tighter fashion, and traps the gases from yeast, making a higher rise.

■ Whether you use regular, kosher, or sea salt, the same amount is used in recipes.

■ Salt and pepper are always supposed to be passed as a pair, regardless of the request.

SALT COD is salted and dried cod that must be reconstituted and soaked to remove some of its saltiness before using in recipes.

SALT-CURED indicates a food was preserved in salt; bacon and kippered herring are examples of meat or fish preserved or cured with salt. Salt inhibits the growth of microorganisms by drawing water out of microbial cells through osmosis. Concentrations of salt up to 20% are required to kill most species of unwanted bacteria. Salt-curing was first mentioned in writing in 1883.

SALTIMBOCCA is an Italian dish of thin slices of veal (or poultry) and prosciutto ham rolled up with fresh sage leaves, herbs, and bacon; sautéed; and braised in white wine. The word is Italian for "leap into the mouth."

SALT PORK is fat cut from pork belly, back, or sides, then cured by salting. Salt pork is often used for flavoring.

SALTWATER TAFFY is a type of candy made chiefly from corn syrup and sugar, originally at seaside resorts of the northeastern United States; the term dates to around 1894. Saltwater taffy is sometimes made with seawater but more generally made with salted fresh water.

SAMBUCA is an Italian liqueur made with elderberries and flavored with anise or licorice. The word is from the Italian *sambucus*, "elder tree"; it was first recorded in English in 1971.

SAMOSA is a small, triangular Indian turnover filled with spicy vegetables (peas, potatoes) or meat and fried. The word is from Hindi and dates to 1955 in English. The samosa has been a popular snack in South Asia for centuries, and it probably originated in Central Asia prior to the tenth century.

SAMOVAR is a metal urn with a spigot at the base used in Russia to boil water for tea; the word is from Russian and literally means "self-boiler." This teakettle has two handles and a chimney and is a traditional Russian wedding gift.

SANDWICH is two (or more) slices of bread with a filling. The sandwich was named around 1762 for the fourth Earl of Sandwich, a gambling man who wanted a handheld lunch brought to him so he did not have to leave the gaming table. A sandwich is usually a light meal or snack.

> **HINT** To keep sandwiches made in advance fresh, store them in plastic wrap or a zip-lock bag in the refrigerator. To prevent bread from becoming soggy, spread it with softened butter or margarine rather than salad dressing or mayonnaise. (Alternatively, spread the mayonnaise or dressing between the layers of ingredients rather than directly onto the bread.) It is a good idea to keep moist ingredients—such as tomato and cucumber slices, lettuce, and pickles—in separate containers or bags and add them to the sandwiches at the last minute.

SANGIOVESE (pronounced sahn-joe-VEEZ or sahn-joe-veh-ZEH) is a variety of grape from Italy that is used to make medium-bodied red wine such as Chianti.

SANGRIA or **SANGAREE** is a mixed drink of red wine diluted and sweetened with fruit juice and/or soda water, and garnished with various fruits. Sangria is Spanish for "bleeding," as the drink is dark red. It may be sweetened with orange juice or lemonade, or made with brandy instead of wine.

SARDINE is any of various small, fatty, edible herring or related food fishes (pilchard, sprat) that are salted, smoked, or canned, either in oil or a sauce. The process of canning small herrings was invented on the island of Sardinia, hence the name sardines. A large sardines is called a PILCHARD.

SASHIMI is a Japanese dish of thinly sliced raw fish served with soy sauce. The word is a compound formed from the Japanese *sashi*, "pierce," and *mi*, "flesh."

SASSAFRAS is a yellowwood tree with aromatic leaves and bark that is dried for seasoning; it is also the source of sassafras oil (safrole). The tree is native to North America and was discovered by the Spanish, who named it *sasafras*, possibly from the Latin *saxifraga*. In 1960 the FDA banned sassafras oil from food and drugs because it is a proven carcinogenic substance.

SATAY (pronounced sah-TAY) is a Malaysian/Indonesian dish of marinated chunks of meat, poultry, or shrimp broiled or grilled on skewers and dipped in a spicy peanut sauce.

483

SATURATED FAT is a fat mainly from animals but also from vegetable products in which the carbon atoms are fully hydrogenated. Most are solid enough to hold their shape at room temperature. Saturated fat is found in butter, lard, margarine, vegetable shortening, meat, egg yolks, and coconut or palm oil, and in humans it tends to increase cholesterol levels in the blood. Butter is actually higher in saturated fat than lard (processed pork fat).

SAUCE is a general word for a thick liquid served with food to add flavor or moistness. The word is from the Latin *salsus*, "salted food." The five mother sauces of French cuisine are béchamel (basic white sauce), velouté (stock-based light sauce), espagnole (stock-based brown sauce), emulsions (mayonnaise, hollandaise), and vinaigrettes (oil and vinegar).

SAUCE ESSENTIALS

■ Unheated raw egg yolks should never be added to a hot sauce, because the sudden change in temperature will curdle the yolks and thus prevent them from being evenly distributed throughout the sauce, which is necessary for optimum thickening. Instead, gradually raise the temperature of the yolks with small amounts of the heated sauce and then the yolks can be safely blended.

■ Sauces can be defatted by reducing the heat to low so that the fat will rise to the surface. Add a few drops of cold water and the fat can then be spooned off. Alternatively, chill the sauce and lift off the hardened fat.

■ To strain sauces, rinse several layers of cheesecloth in hot water and then in cold water to remove any loose fibers. Drape the cheesecloth over a bowl and pour the sauce in. Close the cloth and twist, holding the cloth at two ends and tightening until all the sauce is in the bowl. This procedure works best with two people.

■ Sauces can be thickened by raising the ratio of solids to liquid by adding more solids such as puréed vegetables. The more absorbent these food particles are, the thicker the sauce. In addition, reduction can be used to evaporate some of the liquid. Sauces are also thickened by cooling.

■ You can thicken sauce without adding more fat by adding arrowroot. Make the arrowroot into a paste by adding 1 tablespoon of arrowroot and 2 tablespoons of water per cup of liquid to be thickened, then stir in some of the hot liquid from the pan. Return the mixture to the pan and cook for 1–2 minutes, stirring until thickened. Cornstarch can be added to a sauce in the same way. You can also use a children's lidded cup, filling it with equal parts cold water and cornstarch. Put the lid on, cover the spout, and shake vigorously. Then add the mixture to the sauce little by little until the thickener does its job. Potato flour (or instant mashed potato flakes) can also be used to thicken a sauce, without boiling. Once a sauce has thickened, keep the stirring to a minimum. Keep starch-thickened sauces warm over low heat.

■ Reheat a sauce slowly over low heat.

■ Rub the surface of a starch-based sauce with a piece of butter to keep it from drying out and forming a skin.

SAUCES AND DIPS

A sauce is a liquid or semiliquid mixture that is added to a food as it cooks or that is served with it. Sauces provide flavor, moisture, and a contrast in texture and color. They may also serve as a medium in which food is contained, for example, the velouté sauce of creamed chicken. Seasoning liquids (soy sauce, hot pepper sauce, fish sauce, Worcestershire sauce) are used both as ingredients in cooking and at table as condiments. Many sauces begin with a roux, which is a mixture of flour and fat that is cooked for a few minutes to eliminate the raw taste from the flour and to enable the flour to absorb a maximum amount of liquid. Other sauces may be thickened with egg yolks, including mayonnaise and its variations, which are cold emulsions of egg yolks and vegetable oil, and hollandaise and its variations, which are hot emulsions of egg yolks and butter. There are also oil and vinegar sauces, tomato sauces, fruit purées, and dessert sauces. In the days before refrigeration, sauces were most often used to smother the taste of foods that had begun to go bad. The French are credited with refining the sophisticated art of sauce making. In the nineteenth century, French chef Marie-Antoine Carême developed an intricate methodology by which hundreds of sauces were classified under one of five "mother sauces": espagnole, velouté, béchamel, hollandaise and mayonnaise, and vinaigrette. A dip, by contrast, is a creamy mixture created to be scooped by food such as crackers, chips, or vegetables and is often served as an hors d'oeuvre. Some well-known sauces and dips are listed here:

AIOLI
ALLEMANDE
A.1. SAUCE
APPLESAUCE
BABA GHANOUSH
BARBECUE SAUCE
BÉARNAISE
BÉCHAMEL
BERCY
BOLOGNESE SAUCE
BORDELAISE SAUCE
BOURGUIGNONNE
BROWN GRAVY
BROWN SAUCE
BURGUNDY SAUCE
CAPER SAUCE
CARBONARA SAUCE
CHASSEUR SAUCE
CHAUD-FROID
CHEESE SAUCE

CHILI SAUCE
CHIP DIP
CLAM DIP
COCKTAIL SAUCE
CRANBERRY SAUCE
CREAM SAUCE
CUMBERLAND SAUCE
CURRY OR CURRY SAUCE
DEMI-GLACE
DIABLE SAUCE OR SAUCE DIABLE
DILL SAUCE
DUCK SAUCE
ENCHILADA SAUCE
ESPAGNOLE
GIBLET GRAVY
GRAVY
GUACAMOLE
HARISSA
HOISIN SAUCE

HOLLANDAISE SAUCE
HORSERADISH SAUCE
HOT SAUCE
HUMMUS
KETCHUP OR CATSUP
LOUIS SAUCE
MARIE ROSE SAUCE
MARINARA
MATELOTE
MAYONNAISE
MILANESE SAUCE
MINT SAUCE
MOLMORNAY SAUCE
MOUSSELINE SAUCE
MUSHROOM SAUCE
MUSTARD SAUCE
NANTUA SAUCE
ONION DIP
ONION SAUCE
OYSTER SAUCE

(continued)

PAN GRAVY	SALSA VERDE	TACO SAUCE
PEPPER SAUCE	SAMBAL	TAHINI
PESTO	SATAY SAUCE	TAMARI
PISTOU	SHALLOT SAUCE	TARTAR SAUCE OR TARTARE SAUCE
PIZZAIOLA SAUCE	SOUBISE	
RAGU	SOY SAUCE	TERIYAKI SAUCE
RAVIGOTE	SPAGHETTI SAUCE	TOMATO SAUCE
REDEYE GRAVY	STEAK SAUCE	VELOUTÉ
REFORM SAUCE	SUPRÊME	VINAIGRETTE
RÉMOULADE	SWEET-AND-SOUR SAUCE, SWEET AND SOUR SAUCE	WHITE SAUCE
ROUX		WINE SAUCE
SALSA	TABASCO	WORCESTERSHIRE SAUCE

SAUCE ALBERT: see ALBERT SAUCE.

SAUCE BOAT: see GRAVY BOAT.

SAUCEPAN or **SAUCE PAN** is a (usually) small, deep cooking pan with a handle and a lid for making sauces. A saucier pan is a short and differently shaped version of a sauce pan—often used for preparations requiring more repetitive motions such as whisking or stirring. The thickness of the sides and the heaviness of the saucepan do not matter, only how well the bottom of the saucepan is made—particularly, of a material that heats very well and evenly.

SAUCE SUPRÊME: see SUPRÊME.

SAUCISSON is a large, air-dried, cured, garlic-flavored French ground pork sausage, like salami, eaten as a cold cut. Saucisson is from the French *saucisse*, "sausage."

SAUERBRATEN is pot roast marinated in seasoned vinegar, sugar, and seasonings before cooking; it is traditionally served with potato dumplings, boiled potatoes, or noodles. Sauerbraten is literally German for "sour roast meat." A solid cut from the round or rump is usually marinated for two to four days. After being dried and browned, the beef is braised in the strained marinade, which may then be thickened with gingersnap crumbs.

SAUERKRAUT is shredded cabbage fermented in a brine of its own juice with salt. Sauerkraut is literally German for "sour cabbage"; though *kraut* generally means "leafy plant," it is a dialect word for "cabbage." During World War I, the term "liberty cabbage" was used to refer to sauerkraut in the United States to avoid using a German word.

SAUSAGE is a tube-shaped skin or casing stuffed with highly seasoned, finely chopped pork, beef, or other meat. Sausage is grilled or fried before eating, though some are cooked or preserved and eaten cold in slices. The word often refers to a link or patty of sausage. Sausage's name goes back to the Latin *salsus,* "salted."

> **HINTS** Store uncooked fresh sausage for two to three days in the refrigerator or for up to two months in the freezer. Smoked fresh sausage can be kept in the refrigerator for up to one week, as can cooked sausage.

> ▌ Semidry sausage can be kept at room temperature for up to three days or in the refrigerator for up to three weeks. Unsliced dry sausage keeps at room temperature for up to six weeks. Sliced dry sausage can be refrigerated for up to two weeks.

> ▌ Prick sausages several times with a fork and cook in ¼ cup of water, turning often. You can minimize shrinkage and/or splitting of sausages by making a few skin punctures before cooking; by boiling in oil for 3-5 minutes before frying; by rolling in flour; and for link sausages, by precooking at a simmer until the juices run clear. As a general rule, link sausages should have their casings removed.

SAUSAGE VARIETIES

Sausages can be fresh/uncooked, uncooked and smoked, cooked, cooked and smoked, or dry and semidry (cured). The sausage casing or skin can be made from natural material, such as pig or sheep intestine, or artificial material, such as cellulose or synthetic material. These are some well-known varieties of sausage:

AIR-DRIED SAUSAGE	CHORIZO	KNOCKWURST OR KNACKWURST
ANDOUILLE OR ANDOUILLETTE	CRÉPINETTE	KOSHER SALAMI
BANGER	CUMBERLAND SAUSAGE	LINGUICA
BEEF SAUSAGE	CURED SAUSAGE	LIVER PÂTÉ
BLACK PUDDING	DUCK SAUSAGE	LIVER SAUSAGE
BLOOD PUDDING	FISH SAUSAGE	LIVERWURST
BLOOD SAUSAGE	FOIE GRAS	MERGUEZ
BOCKWURST	FORCEMEAT	MORTADELLA
BOEREWORS	FRANKFURTER OR FRANK	MULLIATELLE
BOLOGNA OR BALONEY	FRESH RAW SAUSAGE	PÂTÉ
BOUDIN BLANC	GALANTINE	PÂTÉ DE CAMPAGNE
BOUDIN NOIR	GENOA SALAMI	PÂTÉ DE FOIE GRAS
BRATWURST	GERMAN SAUSAGE	PÂTÉ EN CROÛTE
BRAUNSCHWEIGER	HEADCHEESE	PEPPERONI
CERVELAT	HOT DOG	POLISH SAUSAGE
CHICKEN LIVER PÂTÉ	HOT LINK	PORK SAUSAGE
CHIPOLATA	ITALIAN SAUSAGE	PRECOOKED SAUSAGE
	KIELBASA	

(continued)

SALAMI	SMOKED SAUSAGE	WHITE PUDDING
SAUCISSE	SUMMER SAUSAGE	WIENER OR WEINER
SAUCISSON	TERRINE	WURST
SCRAPPLE	VIENNA SAUSAGE	ZAMPONE
SLIM JIM	WEENIE	

SAUTÉ (SAUTÉING) is a verb meaning to fry briefly in some fat. Sautéed is an adjective meaning fried quickly in a little fat (butter, oil). Sauté is also a noun for a dish of food so prepared. Sauté is from the French *sauter*, "to leap" or "to cause to toss."

HINTS Sautéing is a quick-cooking method that requires food to be in thin or small slices or pieces. Food should be dried before being fried to avoid spattering the fat and to avoid steaming the food.

For butter flavor in sautéed food, add half butter and half oil to the pan, as butter alone will burn, and set the heat to medium-high. When the butter bubbles or the oil shimmers, add the food. Don't crowd the pan or move the food around until the pieces start to brown and release naturally and easily from the pan.

There are several ways to avoid burnt particles when sautéing. Shake floured food before sautéing it to rid it of excess flour. Sauté in oil, oil and butter, or in clarified butter. Add food in batches. Keep adjusting the heat as needed so the food doesn't scorch. If there are any burnt bits, quickly remove them from the pan with a moistened paper towel.

Spices should be added toward the end when sautéing. It is not wise to add chili powder, black pepper, or similar seasonings at the beginning as they may either become bitter or lose their bite.

SAUTÉ PAN, **SAUTEUSE**, or **SAUTOIR**, also called DEEP-FRYING PAN, OPEN FRY PAN, or PLAT À SAUTER, is a wide pan with sloping or straight sides and a single long handle, for cooking foods quickly in a small amount of fat; it is also a straight-sided saucepan. A sauté pan is 8–14 inches in diameter and the sides are 2½–4½ inches high. Sauté pans are used for sautéing and frying in fat, cooking liquids or sauces, browning vegetables, poaching, and stir-frying. Food in the pan can be stirred by shaking the pan while holding the long handle.

SAUTERNES is a semisweet to sweet, golden-colored, table or dessert white wine originally from the region around Bordeaux, France.

SAUVIGNON BLANC is a white grape grown primarily in France and California and the wine made from this grape.

SAUVIGNON ROUGE: see CABERNET.

SAVORY in cooking means salty, pungent, or sharp-tasting rather than sweet. It is also the name of either of two aromatic herbs of the mint family: SUMMER SAVORY and WINTER SAVORY. Winter savory (*Satureja montana*) has a heavier aroma, while summer savory (*Satureja hortensis*) has a sweeter, more delicate scent. Most commonly used as a seasoning for green vegetables, savory has a special affinity for beans. Both summer and winter savory have a peppery bite to them, although the summer savory is milder.

SCALD means to heat to the boiling point (especially milk), or to treat with or dip in boiling water. The latter is done mainly to fruits, vegetables, or nuts to facilitate removing the skin or shell.

SCALE is any flattened rigid plate forming part of the body covering of many animals, such as fish. As a verb, to scale is to remove the scales from fish with a knife or a fish scaler. A scale is also a measuring instrument for weighing.

SCALLION, also called GREEN ONION, LEEK, SHALLOT, and sometimes BUNCHING ONION, is basically a young onion before the bulb has enlarged, with a small bulb and long green leaves. Scallions get their name from the ancient Palestinian seaport of Ascalon and were originally called *caepa Ascolonia*, "Ascalonian onions."

> **CONFUSABLE** SCALLION/GREEN ONION. True scallions are identified by the fact that the sides of the base are straight, whereas the green onion is usually slightly curved, showing the beginnings of a bulb.

> **HINTS** About nine to ten scallions are required if a recipe calls for 1 cup of chopped scallions.

> ▮ Use a scallion instead of a larger onion when you just need a little onion.

> ▮ Scallions should have green shoots and white bulb ends. Store in a perforated plastic bag for up to two weeks in the refrigerator.

SCALLOP has several cooking meanings: (1) an edible marine bivalve with a fluted fan-shaped shell, often served broiled or poached, especially in cream sauce; (2) a thin boneless slice of meat (especially veal), usually fried or broiled, also called ESCALOPE; and (3) to bake food in a cream sauce, usually with bread crumbs on top. The latter usually involves baking in a shell (for example, oysters) or in a similar-shaped pan or plate, with bread crumbs, cream, butter, and condiments. The word is from the French *escalope*, "shell."

> **HINTS** Select creamy white or slightly pink scallops, though bay scallops should be pale pink to light orange. Scallops that have not been soaked in preservative are pale ivory to pale coral and clump together. Pick those with

the mildest scent. Buy scallops in the shell if possible; the shells should gape and close a little when pinched. Quick-frozen scallops (unshelled) are a good choice.

❚ Put scallops in the shell in a bowl covered with a damp cloth. Shelled scallops should be refrigerated. Unlike clams, oysters, or mussels, which can remain alive and healthy out of the water, scallops die quickly when harvested, so they are usually sold out of the shell.

SCALLOP TYPES

BAY SCALLOP	SEA SCALLOP
CALICO SCALLOP	SINGING PINK SCALLOP

SCALLOPINI, SCALLOPINA, SCALOPPINI, or **SCALLOPINE** is a dish of veal or poultry cutlets that have been pounded thin and coated with flour or bread crumbs, then sautéed. Scallopini is a diminutive of the Italian *scallapo*, "thin slice."

SCALLOP SQUASH: see PATTYPAN SQUASH.

SCAMORZA, SCAMORZE CHEESE, or **SCAMORZO**, also called FIOR DI LATTE, is a firm, oval, slightly salty, white Italian cow's milk cheese. Scamorza can be substituted for mozzarella in most dishes; it is reputed to melt better in baking.

SCAMPI is a dish of a very large shrimp (actually Norway lobster or Dublin Bay prawn) that are split and sautéed in oil or butter and garlic. Scampi is actually the plural of the Italian *scampo*, "shrimp/prawn," and ultimately from a Greek word meaning "a bending." The term shrimp scampi is redundant.

SCHNAPPS is a generic term for a strong, colorless alcoholic beverage distilled from grains or potatoes and variously flavored. It comes from a Dutch word meaning "mouthful." Specifically, schnapps applies to Hollands or Holland gin, a strongly flavored gin with the flavorings distilled in.

SCHNITZEL is deep-fried breaded meat; WIENER SCHNITZEL is veal cutlet made like this. Schnitzel is a diminutive of the German *sniz*, "slice," and also means escalope. The word was recorded in English in 1854, but the dish may have existed since the fifteenth or sixteenth centuries. In Austria the dish is traditionally served with a lemon slice, lingonberry jam, and either potato salad or potatoes with parsley and butter.

SCONE is a small rich biscuit baked on a griddle or in an oven. Plain scones are served with jam and clotted cream as part of the traditional British cream tea.

The word dates to around 1513 and is a Scottish contraction of the Middle Dutch *schoonbrot*, "beautiful/fine bread."

> **HINT** It is important to be very quick and limit the handling of dough when making scones, because the longer the handling, the tougher the scones will be.

SCOTCH EGG is a hard-cooked egg wrapped in sausage meat, covered with bread crumbs, and then deep-fried.

SCOVILLE scale measures the hotness or piquancy of a chile, as defined by the amount of capsaicin (a chemical compound that stimulates nerve endings in the skin) present. Some hot sauces use their Scoville rating as a selling point in advertising. The scale is named after its creator, American chemist Wilbur Scoville, who developed a test for rating the pungency of chiles in 1912.

SCRAMBLED EGG is an egg or eggs beaten (whites and yolks) and cooked to a soft, firm consistency (coagulating, forming curds) while stirring.

> **HINTS** When making scrambled eggs, you can create a softer texture by adding liquids such as stock, cream, butter, milk, water, or oil while whisking the eggs; add about 1 teaspoon of liquid per egg. Add salt, pepper, or other seasonings to taste. Pour the whisked eggs into a medium-hot, greased nonstick pan and they will coagulate almost immediately. Turn down the heat to low and stir the eggs constantly as they cook. If you keep the pan and the stirring implement in constant motion, small, soft curds will form. The lower the heat and the more constant the movement, the creamier the scrambled eggs will be.

> ▌Scrambled eggs should be slightly undercooked when removed from the heat, since the eggs will continue to set. If this technique is followed, the eggs should be moist in texture with a creamy consistency. If any liquid is seeping from the eggs, this is a sign of undercooking or adding overcooked high-moisture ingredients. If you add 1 tablespoon of heavy cream at the very end of the cooking, the cool liquid stops the cooking.

SCRAPPLE is scraps of pork mixed with cornmeal, pork broth, and seasonings, formed into a mushy loaf and cooked or just cooled. It is allowed to set, then sliced and fried in butter. This is a Pennsylvania Dutch concoction served for breakfast or brunch.

SCROD is young Atlantic cod or haddock (or pollack, whiting, or hake), especially one split and boned for cooking and weighing less than three pounds, or a fillet from one of these fish. In New England, scrod is loosely defined as "catch of the day" in restaurants. The word may come from the Dutch *schrode*, "piece cut off."

SEA BASS is any of various elongated food and sport fishes of the Atlantic coast with moderately oily white flesh, but most are not actually of the bass family. Sea bass flesh is lean to moderately fat.

SEA CUCUMBER is an invertebrate echinoderm (not a plant) with a long, tough, cucumber-shaped muscular body. Sea cucumber is a slimy relative of the sea urchin, and it is boiled, dried, and smoked to make *beche-de-mer* (literally "worm of the sea"), which is used for soups in China.

SEAFOOD is a very broad (collective) term for edible fish or shellfish, sometimes even including freshwater fish.

SEAFOOD DISHES AND ENTREES

BAKED FISH	FISH SALAD	SEAFOOD CASSEROLE
BARRACUDA	FISH STEW	SEAFOOD SALAD
BASS	FLOUNDER	SEAFOOD STIR-FRY
BONITO	GRILLED FISH	SHAD OR SHAD ROE
BROILED FISH	HADDOCK	SHARK
CALAMARI	LOBSTER	SHELLFISH
CARP	MACKEREL	SHRIMP
CATFISH	MAHI MAHI	SKATE
CAVIAR	MARLIN	SNAPPER
CHOWDER	MUSSEL	SOLE
CLAM	OCTOPUS	SQUID
COD	OYSTER	STEAMED FISH
CRAB	PERCH	SURF AND TURF
CRAB CAKES	PORPOISE	SWORDFISH
CRAYFISH	PRAWN	TILAPIA
CUTTLEFISH	PUFFER	TROUT
EEL	ROCKFISH	TUNA
FISH FILLET	SALMON	WHALE
FISH KEBAB	SCALLOP	WHITEFISH

SEA KALE or **SEA-KALE** is a coastal plant of the mustard family cultivated for its young blue-green shoots, which are used as potherbs or eaten like asparagus.

SEA SALT is table salt obtained from letting seawater evaporate. It is grayish in color and contains traces of minerals. Sea salt and table salt have the same basic nutritional value; both mostly consist of two minerals—sodium and chloride. However, sea salt is often marketed as a healthier and more natural alternative. The real differences between sea salt and table salt are in their taste, texture, and processing, not their chemical makeup.

SEAR (SEARING) is to brown meat quickly with intense heat, sometimes in a little fat, before grilling or roasting. Searing usually burns or chars the surface of the meat. The word derives from a Proto-Germanic root *saurajan*, "dried up/withered."

> **HINT** When searing, make sure the food is blotted dry on paper towels, then add it to hot oil without crowding the pan; do not stir too often. Contrary to popular belief, searing meat does not seal in the juice—the juice still comes out.

SEASON is to make food better tasting or to make it acquire a certain taste by adding salt, pepper, herbs, or spices.

SEASONED SALT is any of various combinations of salt with vegetable extracts, spices or herbs, and a preservative like monosodium glutamate.

SEASONING is salt, pepper, herbs, and/or spices used to enhance the flavor of food or to make it acquire a specific taste. Seasoning usually adds zest and makes food taste better. Seasoning is also the act or process of adding seasoning to food.

> **HINTS** Don't add seasonings until 30 minutes or less before the end of the cooking process.
>
> ▌ If you plan to freeze the dish, add all, or at least most, of the seasoning after you thaw the food. Seasonings lose much of their aromatic and flavoring strength when they are frozen.
>
> ▌ Before adding herbs or spices to soups, stews, or sauces, place them in the palm of your hand and crush them with the thumb of your other hand. This not only enhances the seasoning by releasing the aromatic oils, but also helps you to spot and discard unwanted stems.

SEAWEED is a general term for plants that grow in the ocean, such as algae and kelp; it is any of various marine plants. Edible seaweed is a marine algae that can come in many forms, including kombu, wakame, and nori seaweeds. Seaweed has many nutritional benefits and relatively low pollutant levels.

SEED is the part of a flowering plant that contains the embryo with its protective coat and stored food; in other words, it is the fertilized and mature ovule of that plant. Seed also refers to a bulb, tuber, or spore from which a new plant can grow. Seed is the term, too, for the small, dry, hard fruit produced by cereal plants or grasses. Finally, seed is applied to any small seedlike fruit.

> **CONFUSABLE** NUT/SEED. A nut is a seed, but not all seeds are nuts. A seed comes from fruit and can be removed from the fruit. A nut is a type of seed that is also a fruit. Technically, *all* nuts are seeds of a plant, and sunflower, sesame, and pumpkin seeds are simply seeds in the truest sense because they originate at

the center of the plant. A fruit is the part of a plant that contains the seeds. So the nutshell is the fruit, and the nut is the seed. In botany, a nut is a dry, one-seeded, usually oily fruit. True nuts include the acorn, chestnut, and hazelnut. The term nut also refers to any seed or fruit with a hard, brittle covering around an edible kernel, like the peanut, which is really a legume.

SEEGOO: see ARROWROOT.

SEITAN is a protein-rich food made from wheat gluten, with a meatlike texture and a neutral flavor. It is made by washing wheat-flour dough with water until all the starch dissolves, leaving insoluble gluten as an elastic mass, which is then cooked before being eaten. Seitan is used as a meat substitute in vegetarian dishes; it is an alternative to soybean-based meat substitutes such as tofu. The term seitan is said to have been coined in the early 1960s by the Japanese founder of macrobiotics, Nyoichi (or Nyoiti) Sakurazawa (1893–1966), known in the West as George(s) Ohsawa; the term possibly derives from Japanese words meaning "having the nature of a vegetable protein." Although it is made from wheat, seitan has little in common with flour or bread. Also called WHEAT MEAT, WHEAT GLUTEN, or simply GLUTEN, seitan becomes surprisingly similar to the look and texture of meat when cooked.

SELECT is a grade of meat that is very uniform in quality and normally leaner than the higher grades. It is fairly tender but has less marbling, so it may be less juicy and flavorful than the higher grades. Tender cuts (loin, rib, sirloin) can be cooked with dry heat, but other cuts should be marinated before cooking or braised to obtain maximum tenderness and flavor.

SELF-RISING FLOUR is a mix of all-purpose flour, salt, and a leavening agent, such as baking soda. Cake mixes and pancake mixes contain self-rising flour. The term dates to 1865.

> **HINT** You can make your own self-rising flour: for each cup of all-purpose flour, add 1½ teaspoons of baking powder and ½ teaspoon of salt.

SELTZER or **SELTZER WATER** is naturally effervescent mineral water. The term is also used for tap water that has been commercially filtered, carbonated, and bottled but with no minerals or mineral salts added; this type of water is also called CARBONATED MINERAL WATER, CARBONATED WATER, CLUB SODA, or SODA WATER. The word is from the German *selterser*, from Niederselters in Germany, where the first medicinal mineral springs were recognized.

SEMIFREDDO or **SEMIFRIO** is a chilled or partly frozen dessert of gelato, spumoni, mousse, or Neapolitan ice cream layered with whipped cream or meringue and sometimes sponge cake. The word is Italian and means "half frozen/half cold."

SEMISOFT CHEESE is any type of cheese that is soft but firm and easily cut/sliced, such as as Edam or Roquefort. Other semisoft cheeses include asadero, Beaumont, bierkase, Bel Paese, brick cheese, buffalo milk mozzarella, caciocavallo, casero, Chaubier, Danish Port Salut, Gouda, Haloumi, Havarti, jack cheese, laguiole, lappi, Limburger, Morbier, mozzarella, Muenster, oka, Ossau-Iraty, pasta filata, Port du Salut, provolone, Saint Paulin, Samsoe, Scamorza, string cheese, taleggio, Tilsit, tomme de savoie, tybo, urgelia, and Vacherin.

> **HINT** Semisoft cheeses are great for snacking or desserts, and a few are heat tolerant enough to be good cooking cheeses. Many semisoft cheeses can be frozen and thawed without losing too much flavor, though some become crumbly. For best results, first cut the cheese into small (half-pound) chunks, and wrap each chunk in an airtight package. Thaw in the refrigerator, and use the cheese soon after it's thawed.

SEMISWEET CHOCOLATE or **SEMI-SWEET CHOCOLATE** is a dark chocolate with a low sugar content; it is slightly sweetened during processing. It is a little sweeter than bittersweet chocolate and is good for eating and baking. Semisweet is around 35% chocolate liquor, with cocoa butter and small amounts of sugar and vanilla; lecithin is usually added. Bittersweet, semisweet, and sweet chocolate may be used interchangeably in some recipes with little textural change.

SEMOLINA is the yellow milled product of durum wheat (or other hard wheat) used in making pasta and cereal. It is the gritty coarse particles of wheat left after the finer flour has passed through a milling machine. The word semolina is the diminutive of the Italian *semola*, "bran," from the Latin *simila*, "finest flour."

SERRANO or **SERRANO CHILE** is a small, slender, green, very hot chile pepper that is red when mature. Its flavor is crisp, bright, and biting; it is notably hotter than the jalapeño pepper it resembles; and it is typically eaten raw. Its Scoville rating is 10,000 to 23,000. The word is Spanish meaning "mountainous, highland."

SERRATED is notched like a saw with teeth; the term is mainly used in cooking to describe knives. The word is from the Latin *serrare*, "to saw." A serrated knife is designed to cut soft foods such as breads, cakes, and tomatoes.

SERVEWARE comprises the dishes, platters, and bowls that hold the food to be served at a meal. The first serveware was made from hollowed-out rocks and tree barks, which evolved into the forms we use today. The word serveware comes from the Latin *servire*, "to serve," and the Anglo-Saxon *waru*, "special merchandise." Serveware made with height, depth, and a hollow center is also called holloware.

SERVICE PLATE: see CHARGER.

SESAME is a tropical and subtropical Asian herb (*Sesamum indicum*) that is the source of the small, oval sesame seed and sesame oil. The word dates to around 1440 and derives from the Greek *sesamon*, "sesame."

> **HINT** Sesame seeds easily turn rancid so smell or taste them when grating or grinding to check for freshness. Sesame seeds taste better when pretoasted, but toasting is not necessary when they are used in baking.

SEVICHE: see CEVICHE.

SEVILLE ORANGE, also called SOUR ORANGE or BITTER ORANGE, is a highly acidic, bitter-tasting orange (*Citrus aurantium*) with a flattened appearance and rough skin, used mainly in marmalade. This orange was reported to be growing in Sicily in AD 1002, and it was cultivated around Seville, Spain, at the end of the twelfth century. For five hundred years it was the only orange in Europe, and it was the first orange to reach the New World. It was naturalized in Mexico by 1568 and in Brazil by 1587, and not long after, it was running wild in the Cape Verde Islands, Bermuda, Jamaica, Puerto Rico, and Barbados. Sir Walter Raleigh took sour orange seeds to England; they were planted in Surrey and the trees began bearing regular crops in 1595, but were killed by cold in 1739. Spaniards introduced the sour orange into St. Augustine, Florida. It was quickly adopted by the early settlers and local Native Americans, and by 1763 sour oranges were being exported from St. Augustine to England.

SHAD is any of several bony, herringlike food fishes that migrate from the sea to freshwater to spawn. It weighs three to five pounds and is prized for its eggs, the delicacy known as shad roe. The American or Atlantic shad was an especially valuable food fish in the eighteenth century; however, many of the rivers where it was common now suffer from pollution. Traditionally it was caught along with salmon in set nets, which were suspended from poles driven into the river bed reasonably close to shore in tidal water. Shad are richly flavored thanks to omega-3 fatty acids, but they are among the boniest fish in the world. An old Native American legend says that a porcupine fled into the water and was turned inside out to become the shad. Shad is eaten with one hand and the bones are picked away with the other. Shad were George Washington's favorite fish.

SHADDOCK: see POMELO.

SHAKE: see MILKSHAKE.

SHALLOT is a small onion (*Allium ascalonicum*) whose clustered bulbs are used for flavoring; it is sometimes called GREEN ONION, LEEK, or SCALLION. It has a long, pointed, pear-shaped, divided bulb and looks more like garlic than an onion. The taste is more subtle than that of the onion and less pungent than that of garlic. Shallot is etymologically "the onion from Ascalon," an ancient port in Palestine.

HINTS Choose shallots over onions for a milder, more delicate flavor. Use them when you want both a silky texture and an onion flavor in a dish.

❚ To make shallots milder before further cooking, blanch them for 3–5 minutes in boiling liquid.

SHANDY is a mixed drink of beer and lemonade or lemon-lime soda. It is also a drink of beer and ginger beer, which is sometimes called shandygaff.

SHANK is a cut of meat (beef, pork, lamb/mutton, veal) from the upper part of the leg of an animal. The top part of the front leg is the foreshank and the hind shank is the top part of the back leg. The word goes back to a Latin form meaning "tibia." Shank has much connective tissue and is some of the toughest meat on an animal, though it is flavorful. It requires a long, slow cooking method.

SHARPENING STEEL: see STEEL.

SHAWNEE CAKE: see JOHNNYCAKE.

SHEET PAN is a type of flat, rectangular metal pan used in an oven. A sheet pan that has a continuous lip around all four sides may be called a JELLY ROLL PAN. A pan that has at least one side flat, so that it is easy to slide the baked product off the end, may be called a BAKING SHEET or COOKIE SHEET. Materials range in weight from very light to very heavy, including insulated aluminum, plain aluminum, anodized aluminum, nonstick aluminum, aluminum foil, and stainless steel. The typical size is 14 x 12 inches.

HINT Make sure there is a gap of at least two inches between the edges of the sheet pan and the oven walls for the best baking. Sheet pans with two or three edges turned up are less likely to warp. If you have two sheet pans, you can fill one while the other is in the oven.

SHELF LIFE is the length of time a packaged or processed food should be usable or edible without having deteriorated, or the length of time a product may be stored before it begins to lose its freshness or effectiveness. Shelf life is different from expiration date; the former relates to food quality, the latter to food safety. A product that has passed its shelf life might still be safe, but quality is no longer guaranteed. In most food stores, shelf life is maximized by using stock rotation, which involves moving products with the earliest sell-by date to the front of the shelf, making shoppers more likely to pick them up first. Terms used on packaging include "best before," "use by," "sell by," and "display until." Open dating is the use of a date or code stamped on the package of a food product to help determine how long to display the product for sale.

SHELL is a hard outer covering, such as the shell of a bird's egg, fruit, mollusk, nut, turtle, or seed. To shell is to remove the shell or covering from an item; foods that are shelled include peas, walnuts, and oysters. To shell is also to separate kernels or grains from a cob or hull, as is done with corn or wheat.

SHELLFISH is any invertebrate, such as crustaceans (lobster) or mollusks (oyster), having a soft, unsegmented body usually enclosed in a shell or shell-like exoskeleton, especially the edible meat of these.

> **CONFUSABLE** CRUSTACEAN/MOLLUSK. Crustaceans have a tough external skeleton and include crabs, crayfish, lobster, and shrimp. They scurry or swim. Mollusks can be bivalves with hinged shells, such as clams, mussels, and oysters; or cephalopods with penlike bones, such as octopus and squid. Another type of mollusk is the gastropod or univalve, which has one shell, such as abalone, conch, and snails.

> **HINT** Not all shellfish are cholesterol builders and therefore bad for the heart. Some shellfish, such as squid and shrimp, are high in cholesterol, but those that primarily feed on microscopic plant life, such as the bivalves (mussels, scallops, clams, oysters), are not. More importantly, all shellfish are very low in both total fat and saturated fat.

SHELL STEAK: see Club steak, New York steak, and Strip steak.

SHEPHERD'S PIE, also called Cottage pie, is a meat pie of ground or diced meat in gravy with a crust or topping of mashed potatoes. The term cottage pie is often used for the beef version; this term was used in England and Scotland by 1791, when the potato was being introduced as an edible crop ("cottage" referred to a modest dwelling). The term shepherd's pie, used more often for the lamb or mutton version, did not appear until the 1870s.

SHERBET is a frozen dessert made with fruit syrup, milk, gelatin, and egg white, which are whisked until smooth and opaque; it is sometimes called Water ice or Sorbet, although these are different dishes. Sherbet was originally a drink of sweetened, diluted fruit juice (a sense still used in the United Kingdom); the word comes from the Arabic *sharbah*, "drink." Sherbet should be pronounced SHUR-buht or SHUR-bit.

> **CONFUSABLE** SHERBET/SORBET. Sherbet and sorbet are often used interchangeably, but a sherbet has milk products, while a sorbet does not.

SHERRY is a dry to sweet, amber to brown wine/aperitif from the Jerez region of Spain or made elsewhere. Sherry is fortified with brandy and has a high alcohol content; it ranges from very sweet to very dry. The word is a mistaken singular of the Spanish *sherris*, "wine from Xeres," referring to the town where the wine was first made.

SHIITAKE, also called CHINESE BLACK MUSHROOM, GOLDEN OAK MUSHROOM, or ORIENTAL BLACK MUSHROOM, is an East Asian mushroom with an edible, meaty, tan to dark brown cap. It has a parasol shape, curved stem, and white gills. The tough stipe is inedible. The word shiitake is from the Japanese *shii*, "chinquapin/oak," and *take*, "mushroom."

> **HINTS** Dried shiitakes can actually have more flavor than fresh ones, because the sun-drying process brings out the umami flavor. You can buy them in packages and soak them for about 30 minutes just before you want to cook with them, which can make using them more cost-effective than buying fresh ones. Dried shiitakes can be stored in a tightly sealed container in the refrigerator or freezer. They will stay fresh for six to twelve months.

> Fresh shiitakes should be firm and plump. They should have no slimy spots or wrinkles (that means they're getting old). Store fresh shiitakes in a loosely closed paper bag in the refrigerator; they will stay fresh for about one week.

SHIRAZ, also called SYRAH, is a black grape/wine variety associated with the Rhône Valley region of France, as well as Australia and South Africa. Shiraz is named for a port in Iran, the former capital. Syrah is the French version of the name.

SHIRRED EGGS are eggs baked in a small shallow dish or ramekin with butter or cream and salt and pepper. When eggs are shirred, they are first baked a bit to set the white. For the second stage of cooking, cream or butter is added to the eggs to enrich their flavor and give them smoothness.

SHISH KEBAB is a configuration of marinated cubes of meat cooked on a skewer, usually with vegetables. The individual pieces of meat are called KEBAB, KEBOB, or KABOB. Shish kebab dates to 1914 and comes from the Armenian *shish kabab*, from the Turkish *siskebap*, "skewered roast meat." The best meat for shish kebab is leg of lamb or sirloin steaks.

SHOCK (SHOCKING), also called REFRESH, is to quickly stop the cooking process of blanched items, especially vegetables, by plunging them in ice water.

SHOESTRING POTATOES are potatoes cut in long, narrow slices, then deep-fried until crisp.

SHOOFLY PIE is a rich pie of Pennsylvania Dutch origin made of molasses or brown sugar mixed with flour, sugar, and butter. It is so named because people enjoying this molasses confection need to shoo flies away; the name dates to around 1935.

SHORE DINNER is a term for a meal of seafood.

SHORTBREAD is a rich, crumbly cake or cookie made with flour, sugar, and lots of shortening or butter. Shortbread, shortcake, and short pastry are made with shortening, "short" meaning that the added fat makes the dough easily crumbled. However, the term, which dates to 1801, originally meant an article of food in the form of a flat (usually round) cake made of flour, butter, and sugar, mixed in such proportions as to make the cake "short" when baked. Shortbread is generally associated with and originated in Scotland. The classic way of making shortbread is to press the dough into a shallow earthenware mold that is decoratively carved. After baking, the large round cookie is turned out of the mold and cut into wedges.

> **HINTS** Bake shortbread in the top third of the oven. This way you won't get too much bottom heat, which would cause the bottom of the shortbread to overcook before the top is done.
>
> ▌ Be sure to let the shortbread cool in the pan for 10 minutes before you flip the pan over to unmold it. This gives the delicate cookie a chance to firm up a bit. After cooling for 10 minutes, hold the pan parallel to and one inch above a wooden or plastic cutting board, face down, and unceremoniously drop it. This jars the shortbread and it drops right out of the pan.
>
> ▌ Slice the shortbread into serving pieces using a thin, sharp knife, while it is still hot. If you wait until it cools, it will become flaky and too fragile to cut cleanly.

SHORTCAKE is a dessert of a sponge cake or unsweetened biscuit base topped with fruit and whipped cream. It is also the name of a sponge cake round or biscuit that serves as a base for a shortcake dessert. Dating to 1594, the word first meant "a cake made short or crisp with butter or lard." The classic American shortcake is a large, sweet biscuit that is split in half, then filled and topped with sliced or chopped fruit and whipped cream. Shortbread is not to be confused with shortcake, which is similar to shortbread but can be made using vegetable fat instead of butter and always includes a chemical leavening agent such as baking powder, which gives it a different texture.

SHORTENING refers to fats used in making breads, cakes, and pastry because they make mixtures "short" or tender; in other words, it is an edible fat used to shorten (make tender and flaky) baked goods. The term mainly refers to a solid fat made from vegetable oils, such as soybean and cottonseed oil, chemically transformed into a solid state through hydrogenation. Vegetable shortening has a neutral flavor and may be substituted for other fats, such as butter, margarine, or lard, in baking pastry, cookies, and cakes. The "short" in shortcakes refers to the crumble-in-the mouth texture achieved by working the fat into the flour until small granules are formed. Solid vegetable shortening is 100% fat and adds tenderness, while its lack of liquids gives it more shortening power than butter. It is good for pie crust. Vegetable shortening is also good for creaming because it is able to trap more air than butter, which is only 80%–85% milk fat.

Pack solid shortening in a dry measuring cup.

SHORT LOIN is a portion of the hindquarter of beef immediately behind the ribs that is usually cut into steaks. This tender cut yields strip steak and T-bone steak. It lies in the middle of the back between the sirloin and the rib; the two main muscles in the short loin are the tenderloin and the top loin.

SHORT PASTRY or **SHORTCRUST PASTRY** is a type of soft pastry that breaks/flakes easily. Short pastry is lighter and crisper than regular pastry crust; it has some sort of fat added to make it soft and flaky.

SHORT RIBS, also called BEEF SHORT RIBS, is a cut of beef consisting of rib ends between the rib roast and the plate, from the chuck. Short ribs are around two inches wide and three inches long. They have very tough layers of fat and meat, and need long, slow, moist-heat cooking as in a slow cooker.

SHOTTSURU: see FISH SAUCE.

SHRED is to cut or tear into long, narrow strips.

> **CONFUSABLE** SHRED/GRATE. Shredding is reducing food to thin, narrow strips. Grating is reducing food to tiny particles. Shredded food is usually decorative, while grated food is created to blend, cook, dissolve, or melt easily.

SHRIMP is any of a number of small, slender-bodied marine decapod crustaceans with a long tail and a single pair of pincers. Certain species of shrimp are used for food. Etymologically, shrimp is from a Germanic root meaning "shrunken creature."

SHRIMP ESSENTIALS

> **CONFUSABLE** SHRIMP/PRAWN. Both shrimp and prawns are from the same family and the terms are used loosely. In the United States common usage is to use prawns for the larger animals and shrimp for the smaller. There is only one native American prawn variety; it is found in the southeastern part of the country (although it is now culti-vated in Hawaii), but not many are on the market. Anything from extra-large up might easily be called prawns in the market.

- To grill shrimp, thread them onto two skewers to prevent them from twisting.

- Select sweet-smelling, firm shrimp, still in the shell if possible. Most shrimp sold have previously been frozen and thawed, and should not be refrozen.

(continued)

Use raw shrimp within twenty-four hours, and store them in a plastic bag on a bed of ice in the refrigerator. Cooked shrimp may be refrigerated for up to three days. Frozen shrimp may be kept up to three months.

To refresh frozen shrimp, soak them in salted water for 10–15 minutes, then rinse.

It is not necessary to devein a shrimp for health's sake, but they do look better deveined. Remember that the intestinal vein is not the black nerve cord that runs down the inside curve but rather the one that runs down the exterior curve. The dark vein, while unsightly, can also have gritty material in it.

A shrimp cleaner tool removes the shell and vein in one motion and is recommended. To devein a shrimp without a shrimp cleaner, hold the shrimp under a slow stream of cold water. Run the tip of an ice pick down the back of the shrimp. This will leave the shrimp clean and whole.

The flavor of shrimp is located in the shell, and this is then absorbed by the flesh during cooking, so the shell should be left on during cooking to enhance the flavor. After the shrimp are cooked, the shell can then be removed, or left on for the diner to do the job. There is a difference in appearance and ease of eating when the shell is left on.

SHRIMP SIZES

MINIATURE (Bay) or extra-small (more than 70 per pound)	MEDIUM-LARGE (36–42 per pound)	JUMBO (21–25 per pound)
SMALL (51–60 per pound)	LARGE (31–35 per pound)	EXTRA-JUMBO (16–20 per pound)
MEDIUM (43–50 per pound)	EXTRA-LARGE (26–30 per pound)	COLOSSAL OR GIANT (10–15 per pound)

SHRUB is the name of a mixed drink made with citrus fruit juice, sugar, spices, and rum, brandy, or other alcohol. The name is a variant of the Arabic word *shrab*, "spirits/drink."

SHUCK is to remove a husk or pod, especially for corn. The word is also a noun meaning HUSK or pod. One can also shuck an oyster or clam from its shell.

> **HINT** You can shuck hard-shell clams with a knife or can opener; for oysters, use an oyster knife. Oysters can be shucked more easily if they are refrigerated for a few hours before the attempt. Let clams cool in the freezer for 5–10 minutes before you start, and it will be easier to shuck them.

SICHUAN CUISINE: see SZECHUAN CUISINE.

SICHUAN PEPPER: see SZECHUAN PEPPER.

SIDEBOARD: see BUFFET.

SIDE ORDER, SIDE DISH, or **SIDE** is any food served as an accompaniment to the main course, often on a separate dish. Side order is the same as side dish, but it is ordered in a restaurant or other eating establishment. This term was first recorded in 1725.

SIEVA BEAN: see LIMA BEAN.

SIEVE or **SIFTER**, also called STRAINER, is a kitchen utensil, usually wire, mesh, or perforated metal in a frame, for straining or sifting food in order to separate solids from a liquid or coarse particles from finer particles.

> **HINT** Remove liquid from a pot by putting a sieve in the middle, pushing solids down and to the sides. Use a ladle to scoop out liquid within the sieve's center.

SIFT is to put a foodstuff through a sieve, sifter, or strainer to separate coarse particles from finer particles. A sifter is mainly used to remove lumps from flour.

> **HINT** Sifting aerates the flour and removes large particles. If the recipe says "1 cup sifted flour," then sift before measuring. If the recipe says "1 cup flour, sifted," then measure before sifting. Sift flour with other dry ingredients to combine and aerate them so they distribute evenly in the batter.

SILVER BEET: see CHARD and SWISS CHARD.

SILVER DOLLAR PANCAKES are very small pancakes, usually three inches or less in diameter.

SILVER SALMON: see COHO SALMON.

SIMMER is to cook slowly and gently below 180°F or just at the boiling point (212°F); simmer as a noun is the state of simmering. A simmering liquid has bubbles floating slowly and gently from the bottom to the surface.

> **CONFUSABLE** SIMMER/POACH. Poaching is cooking food at 160°F–180°F. Simmering is cooking food at or below 180°F. Simmering requires careful temperature regulation so that the surface of the liquid shimmers, with a bubble coming up every few seconds. The temperature of simmering liquid is generally below the boiling point: around 180°F–190°F.

> **HINTS** Tiny bubbles barely breaking the surface is a gentle/low simmer. Larger bubbles moving rapidly is a brisk/full/rapid simmer.

> ▌ Recipes for stock generally call for simmering, so the fat and proteins released by meat or bones will not be emulsified into the liquid (as they might be if the stock were allowed to come to a full boil).

SIMPLE SYRUP is sugar and water cooked over low-to-medium heat while stirring until the sugar is dissolved and the mixture is clear. Simple syrup is usually a ratio of 1 cup of water to 2 cups of sugar. The longer the mixture boils, the thicker it will become. It is used as a mixer or sweetener for alcoholic drinks.

> **HINT** Making your own simple syrup is more economical than buying it at the store. You can make as small or as large a batch as you wish and store it in the refrigerator in a well-sealed bottle for around six months.

SINKER: see DOUGHNUT.

SIPPET is a small piece of toasted bread used for dipping in a liquid like soup or gravy. Sippet is also a synonym for CROUTON. The word dates to around 1530 and is a diminutive of sop.

SIRLOIN is the cut of the loin, especially beef, just in front of the round/rump. The word comes from the French *surlonge*, "above loin," as it is the cut of meat above the loin. It is an expensive prime cut of beef used for roasts or steaks. The sirloin is divided into the top sirloin, the most prized, and the less tender but larger bottom sirloin (typically what is offered when one just buys sirloin steaks); the bottom sirloin connects to the sirloin tip roast.

SIRLOIN TIP: see TOP SIRLOIN.

SKEWER is a long pin or stick, made of metal, wood, or bamboo, for holding meat, vegetables, or fruits in position while being roasted or grilled/broiled.

> **HINT** Bamboo or wood skewers should be soaked in water while you prepare food to put on them.

SKILLET, also called FRYING PAN, is a shallow, long-handled pan used for frying foods. Originally, skillet's meaning was the same as saucepan or stew pot. The word's origin is unknown, though there may be some relation to the Latin *scutella*, "dish/platter."

> **HINT** The best skillets for cooking fish fillets are made of stainless steel, heavy-gauge aluminum, or enameled cast iron. Grease the cooking surface before putting the fillet on it.

SKIM as a verb means to remove from the surface, especially a fat such as cream from the top of milk, or oil from the top of sauce. Skim or skimmed as an adjective means milk from which the cream has been removed.

SKIMMER or **SKIMMING SPOON** is a kitchen utensil used to skim fat from the surface of liquids, or to remove scum, food particles, or herbs from the surface of broths or stocks. A skimmer is generally long handled and spoonlike, with a large, round, flat bowl. There is also an Asian or wok version and one for tempura.

SKIM MILK is milk that has had the cream removed; the original term was skimmed milk. As a general rule, products labeled "skim milk" have less than 0.5% fat. Low-fat or semi-skimmed milk has a fat percentage ranging from 1% to 2%. Fat-free skim milk has only the casein micelles to scatter light, and they tend to scatter shorter-wavelength blue light more than they do red light, giving skim milk a bluish tint.

SKIN is a relatively thin but protective layer closely surrounding the flesh of a fruit or vegetable; the external protective membrane or covering of an animal's body; or a thin pliant surface that forms on the top of some liquids, e.g., on hot milk left to cool. It is also a verb that is synonymous with PARE.

SKIRT STEAK is one of two boneless cuts of beef from the lower part of the brisket: one is a boneless strip of beef cut from the plate/diaphragm muscle, and the other is boneless strip cut from the flank. Both are flavorful and tough compared to other cuts. The word skirt refers to the diaphragm or midriff of an animal. Skirt steak is the cut of choice for making fajitas, Cornish pasties, and Chinese stir-fry. It is best to either cook skirt steak very quickly or very slowly, because it is tough.

SLAW: see COLESLAW.

SLICE is a relatively thin piece cut from an object having some bulk or volume. To slice is to cut into relatively thin pieces, and also to cut with or as if with a knife.

SLICER or **SLICING KNIFE**, also called CARVER, is a knife or machine especially designed for slicing. A slicer has a long, slender, flexible blade and is good for carving poultry and whole fish. A slicer is distinguished from a chef's knife and bread knife by its narrower, thinner, and more flexible blade. Short models can be used for slicing raw fruits and vegetables, while longer ones are for meat (hams, roasts) and large poultry. The slicer is also handy for deboning large fish. The thinner the knife, the easier it is to use. The balance point of this knife should be at the bolster.

SLIDER is a miniature hamburger, first made popular by the White Castle fast-food restaurant (where it was originally spelled Slyder). The name comes from its size, as it can "slide" down the throat in one or two bites.

SLOPPY JOE is ground beef cooked in a thick, spicy tomato-based sauce and usually served on a bun. Ingredients can include onions, celery, green peppers, sweet pickle relish, sugar, Worcestershire sauce, and chili sauce. Early twentieth-century American cookbooks offer plenty of sloppy joe–type recipes, though they go by different titles. The origins of this dish are unknown, but recipes for the dish date back to at least the 1940s, and the *Encyclopedia of American Food and Drink* says the term first appeared in print in 1935. Its messy appearance and tendency to drip make "sloppy" an adequate description, and "Joe" is an average American name. In some places, it was first called a loosemeat sandwich.

SLOTTED SPOON, also called COOK'S SPOON, DRAINING SPOON, PERFORATED SPOON, PIERCED SPOON, SKIMMING SPOON, or STRAINER SPOON, is a large long-handled spoon whose bowl has perforations or holes so liquid will not be included in the spooned portion. It is made in various materials and with a handle from nine to fifteen inches long, sometimes with an end hook or hole for hanging on a tool rack.

SLOW COOKER, also called CROCKPOT or CROCK POT, is a lidded, electric casserole dish that cooks at low temperatures (300°F–325°F) over a long period of time. To slow-cook is to cook a food for several hours at relatively low temperatures, usually in this type of cooker.

> **HINTS** Brown meats in a skillet before adding to the slow cooker. Use the low heat setting for tough cuts.
>
> ▌Root vegetables should be cut in pieces no larger than 1 inch for the slow cooker.

SLOW FOOD is any dish or meal cooked with care and attention to detail, often according to traditional recipes and using few or no modern appliances like microwaves. It is basically food prepared in a conventional/traditional manner, as opposed to fast food. The term dates to 1974. Slow Food is also a nonprofit, member-supported, eco-gastronomic organization that was founded in 1989 to counteract fast food and fast life.

SLOW OVEN is an oven that is heated to a comparatively cool temperature, typically between 150°F and 300°F.

SLUMP, also called COBBLER or GRUNT, is a New England dessert made with cooked fruit, especially apples or berries, topped with a thick layer of biscuit dough or crumb (sugar, flour, butter) mixture. The dessert is referred to as a slump mainly in Vermont, Maine, and Rhode Island.

SLURRY is a thin, watery mixture of a starch (arrowroot, cornstarch, flour) and cold water in a ratio of one part starch to two parts cold water or other liquid, used as a thickener for sauces, and also for defatting sauces and broths.

SMEARCASE: see COTTAGE CHEESE.

SMELT is any of various small, silvery, bony food fishes (order *Salmoniformes*, family *Osmeridae*) that closely resemble trout and ascend rivers to spawn or are landlocked like its cousin the capelan. Smelt have delicate, oily flesh with a distinctive odor and taste. The word goes back least to at least AD 725 in Old English and has related forms in Danish, Dutch, Flemish, German, and Norwegian (the latter is for a small species of cod or whiting). Small smelt can be used in fritters or sautéed in butter. They can also be stuffed or dipped in batter and fried or baked. In the Charlevoix region of Canada, on the north shore of the St. Lawrence River, the locals fish for smelt from the docks to make a typical regional recipe: smelt pie.

SMITHFIELD HAM, which originated in 1908 in Smithfield, Virginia, is a lean, country-cured Virginia ham that goes through elaborate salt-curing, seasoning, hickory-smoking, and aging for six to twelve months. It is a long-cut ham (it includes all of the hog's hip and a long section of the shank part of the hog's leg above the knee) with a distinctive pungent flavor and salt content; it should be sliced paper-thin.

SMOKE or **SMOKE-CURE** is to flavor or cure meat, fish, or other foods by exposure to smoke. It is an ancient technique that preserves food, gives it deep color, and enhances its flavor. The process involves the absorption of smoke from smoldering fires and may or may not involve heat. Cold smoking (at a temperature from 60°F to 100°F) does not involve cooking the food. Hot smoking partially or completely cooks the food involved and uses a temperature ranging from 100°F to 200°F. Meat, poultry, and fish can be smoked, as well as cheese, vegetables, and sauces.

> **HINTS** Smokiness can be induced from the wood by soaking the wood for a half hour or more so that the wood will smoke rather than burn. Hardwoods such as oak, cherry, or hickory are the best kinds to use for smoking meats. Avoid using softwoods such as cedar or pine.

> ▌The most effective ways to flavor meats for smoking are to use dry rubs, pastes, or marinades.

SMOKED SALMON is salmon cured by heat-smoking over aromatic woods to give it a distinctive smoky flavor and a delicate texture. Smoking salmon is an ancient process involving hot or cold smoking. Different kinds of wood can be used, such as beech or evergreen branches, each imparting a particular flavor. Spices are added and sometimes a few drops of alcohol.

> **CONFUSABLE** SMOKED SALMON/LOX. Smoked salmon is cured in salt and sugar and then smoked. Lox is cured in salt, soaked to get rid of the salt, then lightly smoked.

SMOOTHIE is a thick drink made of fruit (like banana or berries) puréed in a blender with yogurt, juice, or ice cream. The term first appeared in print in 1977.

> **HINTS** Rather than using a conventional blender and pouring your finished smoothie into a glass, use an immersion blender. Add your ingredients directly into a tall glass and blend right there.
>
> ▌ You can add extra yogurt or ice cubes to thicken up a weak smoothie or you can try using frozen fruit.
>
> ▌ If your smoothie calls for fruit, plan ahead and use frozen fruit. Frozen fruit will blend better and make a thicker, colder smoothie. You can buy frozen fruit or freeze your own. Spread it out on a plate while it's freezing or the pieces will freeze together.
>
> ▌ You can freeze whole smoothies. Let them thaw in the refrigerator and you're ready to go.

S'MORE is a snack or dessert of toasted marshmallows and chocolate sandwiched between graham crackers. It is typically made over a campfire or outdoor grill but can also be made inside using a stove or microwave. The term may be a contraction of "some more" and it is an Americanism dating to 1934.

SMORGASBORD originally (around 1893) referred to a table on which open sandwiches are served; the word is a combination of the Swedish *smorgas*, "bread and butter/open sandwich," and *bord*, "table." Today, the meaning is a table on which an assortment of foods are served, synonymous with BUFFET, and a smorgasbord can include hors d'oeuvres, hot and cold meats, smoked and pickled fish, cheeses, salads, and relishes.

SMORREBROD or **SMØRREBRØD** is a Danish open sandwich consisting of a buttered slice of dense, dark brown rye bread (*rugbrød*) with a topping (*pålæg*) of cold cuts, pieces of meat or fish, cheese, or spreads. *Smørrebrød* is Danish for "buttered bread."

SMOTHER means to cook/steam in a heavy, tightly covered pan or pot with little liquid over low heat. Smother also means to cover closely or thickly, as with a sauce.

SMOTHERED STEAK, also called SWISS STEAK, is a thick, tenderized steak covered with vegetables and seasonings before slow-cooking.

SNACK is a light informal meal. Snack first meant "bite/snap (of a dog)," from the Dutch *snac*, "to bite."

SNAP BEAN: see GREEN BEAN.

SNAIL is a freshwater, marine, or terrestrial gastropod mollusk, usually having an external enclosing spiral shell, and the culinary term refers to the edible terrestrial snail usually served in the shell with a sauce. The word in Old English was *snæg(e)l*, ultimately of Germanic origin. The science and occupation of raising or growing snails for food are called heliculture.

> **HINT** Choose farm-raised snails, which have already been cleaned. There are also canned and frozen snails. Fresh snails should be eaten on the day they are purchased.

SNICKERDOODLE is a type of sugar cookie made with cream of tartar and rolled in cinnamon sugar. It is characterized by a cracked surface and can be crisp or soft depending on preference. Some people mistakenly refer to snickerdoodles as sugar cookies. The difference between the two comes from the use of cinnamon in snickerdoodles, which is balanced with cream of tartar to give these cookies their sweet, spicy flavor. The name dates to around 1889.

SNOW CONE, SNOWCONE, or **SNO-CONE** is a dessert of crushed ice molded into a ball, flavored with a syrup, and usually served in a paper cone. The term first appeared around 1969; there are similar confections all over the world, known by various other names. There are stories that during the Roman Empire (27 BC–AD 395), the Romans hauled snow from the tops of mountains into the city. They would add different syrups to make the first snow cones.

SNOW CRAB is an edible, long-legged spider crab (*Chionocetes opilio* and *bairdi*) of the cold North Pacific, used for food; it is especially important as a frozen seafood product.

SNOW EGGS: see FLOATING ISLAND.

SNOW PEAS are a variety of pea plant (*Pisum sativum macrocarpon*) that produces peas with thin, flat edible pods.

> **CONFUSABLE** SNOW PEA/SUGAR SNAP PEA. Snow peas have flat, edible pea pods that contain tiny peas; sugar snap peas or sugar peas have rounded pods and are a cross between snow peas and garden peas. Both are eaten in the pods and do not require shelling.

> **HINTS** Look for snow peas up to three inches long that are light green in color with smooth, firm skin. Stay away from snow peas that are overgrown, cracked, or wilted, or have small spots of rot. As with any tender garden vegetable, they are best consumed within two days. For longer storage, they can be

washed, drained, and refrigerated in a perforated bag away from strong odors for up to one week.

▌ No matter how you cook them—boiling, steaming, stir-frying, or blanching— snow peas cook in just 1–3 minutes. Quick-cooking will retain their vibrant color and vitamins.

SOAVE (pronounced SWAH-vey) is a dry white table wine of the Soave region of Italy, from Gargena and Trebbiano grapes. The Italian word means "delightful" and first appeared in English in 1935.

SOBA are buckwheat noodles, roughly the size of spaghetti, used in Japanese cuisine; it is the Japanese word for "buckwheat." Soba is mainly served either chilled with a dipping sauce or in hot broth as a noodle soup. Soba is traditionally eaten on New Year's Eve in most areas of Japan; the holiday noodles are called *toshikoshi soba*, which roughly means "end the old year and enter the new year soba noodles."

SODA or **SODA POP**, also called POP or SOFT DRINK, is a sweet drink containing carbonated water and flavoring. Soda also refers to ICE-CREAM SODA, a beverage made with flavored carbonated water and ice cream, usually served in a tall glass. It is also another term for sodium bicarbonate, BAKING SODA.

SODA BREAD is a term for any bread leavened with baking soda instead of yeast. This method is common in Irish bread making, and soda bread dates to approximately 1840, when bicarbonate of soda was introduced to Ireland. A cross is generally cut into the top of soda bread, and there are several theories as to its significance. Some believe that the cross was placed in the bread to ward off evil or to let the fairies out of the bread. However, it is more likely that the cross was intended to help with the cooking of the bread by allowing air circulation so that the bread would rise better.

HINT The buttermilk in soda bread dough contains lactic acid, which reacts with the baking soda to form tiny bubbles of carbon dioxide. Soda bread can dry out quickly and is typically good for two to three days.

SODA WATER: see CLUB SODA and SELTZER.

SODIUM is common table salt, a soft silver-white metallic element that reacts readily with other substances and is essential to the body's fluid balance.

SODIUM LABELS

SODIUM-FREE: 5 milligrams or less per serving.	REDUCED-SODIUM: 25% less sodium than the original version of the product.
VERY LOW SODIUM: 35 milligrams or less per serving.	NO ADDED SALT OR UNSALTED: No salt added during the processing (this does not mean it is sodium-free).
LOW-SODIUM: 140 milligrams or less per serving.	

SOFRITO or **SOFFRITO** is a sauce of sautéed onions, garlic, herbs, spices, and tomatoes. Sofrito (Spanish for "lightly fried") is the spelling in Spanish, Latin American, and Caribbean cookery, and soffrito is the spelling in Italian cookery, where the sauce is also called BATTUTO. The sauce is used to flavor stews and soups and can also include ingredients such as lime juice, coriander, oregano, parsley, celery, peppers, and carrots.

SOFT-BALL STAGE in candymaking is that point between 235°F and 240°F at which a spoonful of hot syrup dropped in ice water neither disintegrates nor flattens when picked up with the fingers. If the syrup has reached soft-ball stage, it easily forms a ball while in the cold water, but flattens once removed from the water.

SOFT-CRACK STAGE in candymaking is that point between 270°F and 290°F at which a spoonful of hot syrup dropped in ice water can be removed and pulled apart with the fingers. Soft-crack stage has been reached when the syrup forms firm but pliable threads.

SOFT DRINK, also called POP, SODA, or SODA POP, is a nonalcoholic beverage, usually carbonated. It is sold commercially in cans and bottles and often served cold. The term soda pop dates to 1863, and soft drink to 1880. The term soft drink was originated to distinguish the flavored drinks from hard liquor or spirits. Soft drinks were recommended as a substitute for alcoholic beverages in the effort to change the hard-drinking habits of early Americans.

SOFT DRINKS

BIRCH BEER	GINGER BEER	PHOSPHATE
BITTER LEMON	GINGER POP	QUININE WATER
CARBONATED WATER	ICED COFFEE	ROOT BEER
CLUB SODA	ICED TEA	SARSAPARILLA
COLA	LEMONADE	SELTZER
CREAM SODA	LIMEADE	SODA OR SODA POP
DANDELION AND BURDOCK	LOLLY WATER	SODA WATER
	MINERAL WATER	SPORTS DRINK
FIZZY WATER	ORANGEADE	SPRING WATER
GINGER ALE	ORANGE SODA	TONIC WATER

SOFT FOODS

A soft diet is useful when your body is ready for more than liquids during an illness but still unable to handle a regular solid diet. Soft food is easier to eat than regular food when the mouth, throat, esophagus, and/or stomach are sore. Some popular soft foods are listed here:

(continued)

SOFT FOODS

APPLESAUCE	GELATIN OR JELL-O	SMOOTH PEANUT BUTTER
BREAKFAST DRINK	ICE CREAM	SOFT BREAD
CANNED FRUIT	MACARONI AND CHEESE	SOFT CHEESE
COOKED CEREAL	MASHED POTATOES	SOFT FRUIT
COOKED FRUIT	MEAT LOAF	SOFT VEGETABLES
COOKED VEGETABLES	MILKSHAKE	SORBET
COTTAGE CHEESE	MUFFIN	SOUP
COUSCOUS	PASTA	YOGURT
CUSTARD	PASTRY	
EGGS	PUDDING	

SOFT-SHELL CLAM or **SOFTCLAM** is an edible clam with thin oval-shaped shell found in coastal regions of the United States and Europe, living buried in the mud on tidal mudflats. It is also called LONG CLAM, LONG-NECK CLAM, STEAMER, and STEAMER CLAM.

SOFT-SHELL CRAB is a crab that has recently molted and has a new shell that is soft and edible. In the United States the term dates to around 1844 and mainly refers to the blue crab (*Callinectes sapidus*). As crabs grow larger, their shells cannot expand, so they molt the exteriors and have a soft covering for a few days, when they are vulnerable and considered usable. Fishermen often put crabs beginning to molt aside, until the molting process is complete, in order to send them to market as soft-shell crabs. The Chesapeake Bay, shared by Maryland and Virginia, is famous for its soft-shell blue crabs. When eaten, soft-shell crabs are battered and deep-fried, sautéed, or grilled.

> **HINT** Crabs should be kept alive until immediately before cooking so they are fresh. Usually crabs must be eaten within four days of molting to be edible as soft-shell crabs.

SOLE is the right-eyed saltwater flatfish, and its lean, mild-flavored, flaky white flesh as food. Genuine sole are the true Dover sole, English sole, and turbot. Gray sole, lemon sole, rex sole, and the Dover sole of the Pacific are all flounders, which are inferior to genuine sole.

> **CONFUSABLE** FLOUNDER/SOLE. In the United States and Canada, the terms flounder and sole are used interchangeably. Petrale sole is a member of the flounder family.

SOMMELIER, also called WINE STEWARD, is a restaurant worker who orders and maintains the wine collection of a restaurant and usually has extensive knowledge about wine and food pairings. The French word means "officer in charge of provisions/steward" and is pronounced suhm-uhl-YEY.

SONKER: see COBBLER.

SOPAIPILLA (pronounced soh-payh-PEE-uh) is a Mexican/Spanish dessert of a piece of deep-fried puffed pastry, usually covered with or dipped in honey or syrup. The word dates to around 1934 and is an American Spanish diminutive of the Spanish *sopaipa*, "fried dough sweetened with honey," from *sopa*, "food soaked in liquid," but is ultimately from a Germanic source and Proto-Indo-European root. Sopaipillas are often served with ice cream, though there are savory recipes for sopaipilla, too.

SORBET (pronounced SAWR-bey) is a dessert or palate-cleansing, tart-flavored ice, usually of fruit juice. The word (which first appeared around 1585 as a synonym for SHERBET) is from the Italian *sorbetto*, from the Turkish *shorbet*, from earlier Persian and Arabic words.

> **CONFUSABLE** SORBET/SHERBET/GRANITA. Sherbet and sorbet are often used interchangeably, but a sherbet has milk products, and a sorbet does not. The purpose of sorbet when served between courses is to cleanse the palate. The difference between a sorbet and a granita is mainly one of texture. Granita is a fruit purée, made with simple syrup and perhaps a little lemon juice and a pinch of salt, that is frozen. It has less sugar, which means larger ice crystals. A sorbet is like a granita with the addition of beaten egg white and is usually finished in an ice-cream machine, which gives it a silky, creamy texture.

SORGHUM is any of a genus (*Sorghum*) of tropical grasses with solid stems bearing large panicles of paired spikelets with small, glossy grains. Sorghum is mainly used for grain and syrup.

SORREL is any of various coarse weedy plants with long taproots that are sometimes used as table greens or cooked as a vegetable. The name derives from the word sour because of the acid taste of the greens. Sorrel is also called common sorrel or spinach dock, and is actually considered more or an herb than a vegetable in some cultures. In appearance, sorrel greatly resembles spinach.

> **HINT** Sorrel will keep for only about three days in the refrigerator. The best place to look for sorrel is in specialty food stores, where it may be available fresh, puréed, or canned.

SOUFFLÉ is a light, fluffy dish of egg yolks and stiffly beaten egg whites mixed with savory ingredients like cheese and baked. It can also be a dessert made with fruit juices, chocolate, and vanilla. Soufflé is French for "puffed up" and comes from the Latin *subflare*, "to puff or blow up from below"; the word first appeared in English around 1813. The cooking temperature and the consistency of the soufflé base are the two critical factors. The soufflé base provides the flavor and contributes a reservoir of moisture for the soufflé's rise.

> **HINTS** A fallen soufflé will rise again if put back in the oven. The air bubbles are still there, along with the moisture, and both air and moisture will expand again as the temperature goes up.

> ▌ To cut a soufflé for serving, insert two forks back to back and gently pull it apart. Use a large serving spoon to transfer the portions to plates.

SOUFFLÉ

SOUP is a liquid foodstuff made of a vegetable or meat, poultry, or fish stock and often containing other ingredients, such as pieces of solid food, herbs, and spices. The word dates to around 1653 in English, and up until then this food had been called BROTH or POTTAGE. The origin of the word goes back to the Latin *suppare*, "soak," which came into French as *soupe*, "piece of bread soaked in liquid" or " broth poured on bread," before entering English.

SOUP ESSENTIALS

■ Homemade soup can be kept in a tightly covered container for two to three days in the refrigerator. Soup can be frozen for three to six months. Soup with potatoes cannot be frozen.

■ Season a soup only at the end of cooking. Cold soups require more seasoning than hot soups.

■ Alcohol can be used in making soup because the alcohol dissolves the fat and other compounds and results in great depth of flavor.

■ Curdling can be prevented when making soup with buttermilk by adding the buttermilk after the soup has been cooked.

■ Fat can be removed from soups by refrigerating overnight so that the fat congeals on top and can be lifted off easily. If the soup must be served just after preparation, then skim the fat off with a shallow ladle or skimmer, or drop a few ice cubes into the liquid and stir. The fat will cling to the cubes. Remove the cubes after a few seconds.

Alternatively, wrap ice cubes in a piece of cheesecloth or paper towels and skim over the top. The oil will adhere to the cloth or paper towels. Clear soups may be blotted with strips of unwaxed brown paper by floating the strips on the surface and then carefully lifting them off.

■ If a soup boils rapidly, the fat will emulsify with the stock and thus be difficult to remove, resulting in a greasy, cloudy soup.

■ Soup can be stretched by adding pasta, rice, barley, or beans, or by adding stock. Pasta should be separated when cooking for soup so it won't overcook and become mushy.

■ When making soup, you do not have to ensure that the vegetables used are fresh and crisp, because the soft ones that are no longer young, but not rotten, will result in rich flavor and consistency. Leftover potatoes should not be used for making soup, because the soup will then be cloudy.

Soup is a liquid savory food served at the beginning of a meal or as a light meal in itself. There are a few soups that make a heavy meal, like Italian minestrone or chunky seafood chowder. There are also cold fruit soups. Soup was originally the slice of bread on which was poured the contents of the cooking pot (then called potage). Soups can be broadly classified into clear or broth soups and thick or cream soups. Clear soups include bouillon and consommé. Thick soups include purée soups, bisques, cream soups, and velouté soups. Here is a sampling of the many varieties of soups:

ALPHABET SOUP	CONGEE	ONION SOUP
ASPARAGUS SOUP	CONSOMMÉ	OXTAIL SOUP
AVGOLEMONO	CORN SOUP	PEA SOUP
BEEF BROTH	CREAM SOUP	PISTOU
BEEF STEW	EGG DROP SOUP	POTAGE
BIRD'S NEST SOUP	FISH SOUP	POTATO AND LEEK SOUP
BISQUE	FRENCH ONION SOUP	POTATO SOUP
BORSCHT OR BORSCH	FRUIT SOUP	POT-AU-FEU
BOUILLABAISSE	GAZPACHO	RASAM
BOUILLON	GOULASH	SANCOCHE
BROCCOLI SOUP	GUMBO	SCOTCH BROTH
BROTH	HOT AND SOUR SOUP	SKILLY
BURGOO	LENTIL SOUP	SPLIT-PEA SOUP
CALLALOO	LOBSTER BISQUE	STOCK
CHEDDAR SOUP	MADRILENE	STRACCIATELLA
CHICKEN BROTH	MATZO BALL SOUP	TOMATO SOUP
CHICKEN NOODLE SOUP	MENUDO	TURTLE SOUP
CHICKEN SOUP	MINESTRONE	VEGETABLE SOUP
CHOWDER	MISO SOUP	VICHYSSOISE
CLAM CHOWDER	MOCK TURTLE SOUP	WONTON SOUP
COCK-A-LEEKIE	MULLIGATAWNY	
COLD SOUP	MUSHROOM SOUP	

SOUPSPOON or TABLESPOON is the larger of two spoons in a typical five-piece place setting, a spoon with a rounded bowl for eating soup. From the Middle Ages to the Renaissance, the tablespoon was the only spoon that appeared on the table and the only spoon used to eat foods such as soup, porridge, and pudding; hence the name tablespoon. Today, some people may call it a soupspoon when it is only used to eat soup, stew, or porridge. The soupspoon is placed on the right of the outside knife in a table setting. It should be laid on the underplate if there is one, and it can stay there securely when the dishes are cleared. It should be laid in the soup bowl if the underplate is too small to hold it securely. You are supposed to spoon the soup away from you when eating.

SOUR CREAM is cream that has been deliberately (commercially) fermented with bacteria (lactobacilli) in lactic acid. The term dates to 1855 in English.

HINTS Sour cream should always be kept refrigerated. Although sealed sour cream may be stored for up to two weeks beyond the sell-by date, it will lose flavor as it ages. Sour cream is not a candidate for freezing because it separates when thawed. Do not use the carton as a serving container. Remove what you need and return the carton to the refrigerator immediately. You may notice some liquid separation in sour cream after opening. You can either pour off the liquid or stir it back in. Any colored scum is an indicator of spoilage and the sour cream should be thrown away.

❙ Sour cream used as a thickener for hot sauces can easily curdle if the temperature is too high. Remove the food from the heat before stirring in the sour cream or add it during a very low simmer. Bring sour cream to room temperature before adding it to any hot liquid. To prevent curdling, you can also add 1 tablespoon of flour to ½ cup of sour cream used as a thickener.

SOURDOUGH is fermenting dough used as a leavening agent in making bread, and the bread made with this. Sourdough is named from the practice of prospectors who carried a lump of sour dough from each biscuit baking to start fermentation of the next batch. Today, fermenting dough is saved from one baking to be used for producing fermentation in a later one, thus avoiding the need for fresh yeast. The term in this sense is an Americanism from around 1868.

HINTS Three kinds of commercial sourdough starters are available in stores: dehydrated starters, freeze-dried starters, and specially packaged starter ingredients. All three require only water. When not in use, date and refrigerate the freshened or replenished starter in a sealed container. Fermentation is slowed during refrigeration, so the starter may not need to be used or freshened for a couple of weeks. Always bring it to room temperature and make sure it is bubbling before using (the process will take about 8–12 hours).

❙ To ensure a warm (80°F–85°F), draft-free place for the sourdough starter, place it on a sunny window, a high shelf, or a warm corner. Do not allow the starter to be subjected to direct heat sources or temperatures exceeding 95°F.

❙ Sourdough starter that has been sitting for a time will have a thin, alcoholic layer of clear/grayish liquid settle at the top of the batter. Old-timers referred to this alcohol as "hooch." Just mix it back into the starter. If this layer is green, blue, pink, or orange, discard the starter and start over. If the starter smells particularly sour or is too tart, add 1 cup of warm liquid and 1 cup of flour to 1 cup of starter and mix thoroughly. Pour off all but 1 cup of this batter. This is known as freshening or sweetening the starter.

SOUR-MILK CHEESE: see Cottage cheese.

SOUR ORANGE: see Seville orange.

SOUS-CHEF or **SOUS CHEF** is a head chef's assistant; it is a French word meaning "under chef." The sous-chef is second in command in a restaurant kitchen. Smaller operations may not have a sous-chef, while larger operations may have multiple sous-chefs. The usual duties include supervising the activities of specialist chefs, chefs, cooks, and other kitchen workers; demonstrating new cooking techniques and new equipment to cooking staff; possibly planning menus and requisitioning food and kitchen supplies; and possibly preparing and cooking meals or specialty foods.

SOUTHERN PEA: see Black-eyed pea.

SOUVLAKI is a Greek Kebab made with lamb pieces. The word dates to 1958 and is from the Greek *souvla*, "skewer." The plural is souvlakia.

SOYBEAN, SOYA BEAN, or **SOY** is a plant (*Glycine max*) of the pea family (Fabaceae) grown for its seeds, which contain much protein and oil. The seed contains 17% oil and 63% meal, 50% of which is protein. The most nutritious and most easily digested food of the bean family, the soybean is one of the richest and cheapest sources of protein.

SOY MILK is soaked, ground, and cooked soybeans that become a milky liquid suspension, and is then mixed with tofu. Soy milk has a distinctive taste, but it can be used the same as cow's milk in recipes. It is higher in protein than cow's milk and cholesterol free.

> **HINTS** Soy milk is available in whole, low-fat, enriched, and flavored versions. It may be kept in the refrigerator until one week after the sell-by date; it should be used within one week of opening.

> ❚ Soy milk tends to curdle when mixed with acidic ingredients like lemon juice or wine.

SOY SAUCE is a dark, salty liquid made by fermenting soybeans in brine; it is used in Asian cooking to flavor foods. It may contain wheat or barley. Soy sauce is a translation of two Chinese words that mean "salted bean oil." Light soy sauce is fairly thin in texture and light in flavor. Dark soy sauce often has added caramel and is darker in color, sweeter in flavor, and thicker in texture than light soy sauce.

> **CONFUSABLE** SOY SAUCE/TAMARI. Soy sauce is made of soybeans and wheat or barley, plus water and salt. Tamari is made from soybeans, water, and salt. Compared to soy sauce, tamari has a more intense, more complex flavor; has

a higher concentration of minerals; has a thicker consistency; and is darker. When wheat or barley is used to make soy sauce, it is more subtle though saltier. There is a difference between Japanese and Chinese soy sauce. Japanese soy sauce has more wheat in it and therefore is mellower, less salty, and more versatile. Chinese soy sauce is made with just a little wheat, is saltier, and often has a bit of molasses added for a slight sweetness.

HINT Soy sauce will keep indefinitely in a bottle in the refrigerator.

SPÄETZLE, SPAETZLE, or **SPÄTZLE** is egg noodles or dumplings made by pressing through a colander or coarse sieve and cooking the resulting irregular pieces in boiling water. The resulting noodles are drained and either mixed in butter, lightly pan-fried, or added to sauces or stews. This German word translates to "little sparrows." Written mention of späetzle has been found in documents dating from 1725, although medieval illustrations are believed to place this noodle at an even earlier date.

SPÄETZLE MAKER is a tool that is placed over the pot of boiling water—a flat, rectangular stainless stell and plastic shredder with a box that slides back and forth over the cutting surface. The box holds the batter, small pieces of which are shredded off through the bottom.

SPAGHETTI is pasta made into long strings. The word dates to 1849 in English and translates from Italian as "small cords/little strings"; it is a diminutive of *spago*, "cord/string." The singular is spaghetto and slang terms are spaggers and spag. Spaghettini is thin spaghetti. During the eighteenth and nineteenth centuries, people ate spaghetti with their hands. When the fork was invented, pasta became food fit for royalty as well, because it could then be eaten without a loss of dignity. The Italians say that a character of a man can be determined by the way he eats spaghetti. The perfect method for eating spaghetti or other long, stringy pasta is to twirl it around your fork. Use a spoon to help if needed. It is also acceptable to cut pasta with a knife and fork.

HINTS Spaghetti not made with semolina produces a softer noodle and will not hold up well when tossing. Most dried pasta doubles in volume when cooked, so 4 ounces uncooked spaghetti, angel hair, vermicelli, fettuccine, or linguine = 1-inch-diameter bunch of dried pasta = 2 cups cooked pasta.

For 16 ounces of spaghetti, you will want a pot that holds at least 5–6 quarts of water. Fill the pot three-quarters full with cold water, allowing at least 1 quart of water for every 4 ounces of dried spaghetti. Salting the water makes spaghetti taste better by bringing out its natural flavor. To keep spaghetti from sticking together, gently stir it in the water during the first 1–2 minutes of cooking. Do not rinse the spaghetti, as the starch that makes the spaghetti stick to itself also helps the sauce stick to the spaghetti.

SPAGHETTI SQUASH is a plant (*Cucurbita pepo*) bearing medium-sized, oval fruit with smooth yellow skin and flesh that is like strings of spaghetti once cooked. The term dates only to 1975.

SPAM is a canned, precooked meat product made by Hormel: it consists of chopped pork shoulder meat with ham meat added, salt, water, aspic, sugar, and sodium nitrite. The name Spam combines *sp* from spice and *am* from ham. The first can of Spam was produced in 1937 by Hormel Foods.

SPANAKOPITA or **SPANOKOPITA** is a traditional Greek pie of spinach, feta cheese, and seasonings baked in phyllo; *spanakopita* is Greek for "spinach pie."

SPANISH CHESTNUT: see MARRON.

SPANISH OLIVE is a young green olive that is soaked in lye, then fermented in brine for six to twelve months. Spanish olives are often pitted and stuffed with pimiento or garlic, and are often used in martinis.

SPANISH ONION (*Allium fistulosum*) is a large, mild and succulent yellow-skinned onion, often eaten raw.

SPARERIBS or **SPARE RIBS** is a cut of pork ribs with little flesh on them, baked or roasted with a spicy (barbecue) sauce. Spareribs got their name from spare, meaning absence of meat or fat, or perhaps from the German *ribbesper*, "pickled pork ribs roasted on a spit"; the term first appeared in English around 1596. Of the types of ribs, spareribs have the least amount of meat per bone but are among the most flavorful.

> **HINT** To speed up the cooking of spareribs without causing them to toughen or burn, you can presteam them in a pressure cooker, braise them in the oven, or precook them in the microwave.

SPÄTLESE is the grade of high-quality table wine above Kabinett in German wine classification; it is made from late-picked grapes and is typically medium-sweet. The name means "late harvest."

SPATULA is a kitchen utensil with a broad, flat, blunt rubbery/plastic blade, used especially for mixing or spreading. Spatula comes from the Latin *spathula*, a diminutive of *spatha*, "a broad blade to stir mixtures."

SPEARMINT is a garden herb (*Mentha spicata*) yielding an oil used as a flavoring.

> **HINT** Spearmint leaves lose their aroma after the plant flowers. Dry spearmint just before or right at peak as the flowers open; cut the stalk about one-half to three-quarters of the way down (leaving smaller shoots room to grow).

SPELT is a now-rare primitive species (*Triticum spelta*) of wheat with grains that do not thresh free from the chaff.

SPICE is any of various parts of plants with distinctive aromas and flavors used to season food. Spice seeds are the tiny aromatic fruits and oil-bearing seeds of herbaceous plants such as anise, caraway, cumin, fennel, poppy, and sesame. Spices are usually used dried, though some, such as chiles and ginger, are used in both their fresh and dried forms. Many of the world's highly prized spices are fragrant or pungent plant products cultivated in tropical and subtropical regions. The word spice is a shortening of the French *espice*, ultimately from Latin. The most expensive spices in descending order are saffron, vanilla, and cardamom. The three native spices to the Americas are allspice, chiles, and vanilla.

SPICE ESSENTIALS

CONFUSABLE SPICE/HERB. A spice (also called seasoning) is any substance used for seasoning foods; many herbs are used as spices, but not all. Herbs are usually the leaves or the whole of the plant, while spices are only part of the plant, commonly the seeds, or sometimes the roots or rhizomes.

■ A spice, garlic, or onion may be bruised to release the oils so the flavor better infuses the dish. Place it under the flat side of a chef's knife and strike the flat side of the knife carefully with the heel of your hand or your fist.

■ Buy spices in the smallest amounts you can.

■ Grind small quantities of a spice with a mortar and pestle or small food mill.

■ Heat, light, and air help disintegrate spices so place in tightly covered glass jars and place in a cool cabinet or in a drawer away from the heat. Properly stored, ground spices will keep for two to three years, leafy herbs for one to two years, and whole spices for three to four years. Chiles and paprika may be refrigerated. Spices should never be stored near a microwave or a range. The heat tends to cause a loss of flavor and color. Keep whole spices from sunlight, moisture, and heat.

■ Spices become bitter if cooked over high heat for more than a short time. It is not wise to add chili powder, black pepper, or similar seasoning agents at the beginning of the sautéing process.

■ To heighten the flavor of a spice, roast it in a single layer in a preheated 250°F oven for 10–15 minutes just before you plan to use it in cooking.

■ When you double a recipe, the spices should not be doubled as well. Taste first to make your judgment. Some recipe writers are not very exact; in addition, the intensity of flavors varies with the length and method of storage of the spice. Doubling could lead to an overspiced dish. Use caution and taste as you add. Small amounts specified in recipes are often approximate.

■ Whole or large pieces of spices can be easily removed from a liquid dish if they are added in a metal tea ball.

■ Toast whole spices just before grinding in a dry skillet over medium-high heat, then grind in a mortar and pestle.

■ Put a date on any bag or jar of spices when you buy it so you can keep track of its freshness.

SPICE VARIETIES

A spice is any of the many aromatic substances derived from plants that have a fragrant or sharp flavor and are used to season food. Most spices come from the East and the first spice introduced to Europe was pepper (from India), which long remained a rare and expensive commodity. The use of spices in cooking started with the Byzantines—probably to hide the fact that meat was spoiled or unflavorful. The spice route was important during the Crusades and also when British and Dutch trading companies worked hard to make money from spices. There are four basic kinds of spices: fresh spices, ground spices, spice pastes, and whole dried spices. Some well-known spices are listed here:

ALLSPICE	CLOVES	PARSLEY
ANISE	CORIANDER SEED	PEPPER
ANNATTO SEED	CUMIN	PEPPERMINT
BASIL	CURRY POWDER	PICKLING SPICE
BAY LEAF	DILL	POPPY SEED
BEAU MONDE	FENNEL SEED	RED PEPPER
BLACK PEPPER	FENUGREEK	ROSEMARY
BOUQUET GARNI	FINES HERBES	SAFFRON
CAJUN SPICE	GARLIC POWDER	SAGE
CARAWAY SEED	GARLIC SALT	SAVORY
CARDAMOM	GINGER	SESAME SEED
CAYENNE	JUNIPER BERRY	STAR ANISE
CELERY SEED	KOSHER SALT	SUGAR
CHERVIL	MACE	SUMMER SAVORY
CHILI POWDER	MARJORAM	TARRAGON
CHINESE FIVE-SPICE POWDER	MUSTARD	THYME
	NUTMEG	TURMERIC
CHIPOTLE POWDER	ONION POWDER	VANILLA
CHIVES	ONION SALT	WHITE PEPPER
CILANTRO	OREGANO	
CINNAMON	PAPRIKA	

SPICED TEA: see CHAI.

SPIDER is a cast-iron skillet or frying pan, especially the early versions with legs for using in a hearth fire.

SPINACH is a plant (*Spinacia oleracea*) of the goosefoot family, with large, dark green, juicy, edible leaves widely eaten as a vegetable. Spinach may come from the Persian *aspanakh/ispanak*, which is perhaps related to the Latin *spina*, "spine." Cooked spinach is more nutritious than raw spinach. The cellular walls of spinach are rather hard, and as a result many of the nutrients and vitamins of the spinach pass through the digestive tract imprisoned within these cells. Cooking breaks down the cellular walls and allows the nutrients to escape and thus be absorbed. Spinach has iron, vitamins A and C, folate, and beta carotene. During the Depression, Popeye the Sailor, the cartoon character who ate spinach for superhuman strength, had an impact on the taste buds of children. At that time, children ranked spinach as their third-favorite food behind turkey and ice cream.

> **HINT** Since most spinach is grown in sandy soils, residual sand has to be removed. To wash spinach, place it in a large pot of warm, not hot, water and shake gently. Keep repeating the process until no sand shows on the bottom of the pot.

SPINY LOBSTER is a large, edible marine crustacean having a spiny carapace but lacking the large pincers of a true lobster. A spiny lobster is also called CRAYFISH, LANGOUSTE, ROCK LOBSTER, SEA CRAYFISH.

SPIRIT or **SPIRITS** is a strong alcoholic liquor made by distillation, such as brandy, rum, or whiskey.

SPIT is a skewer for holding meat over a fire. To spit-roast is to cook by placing the spit over the fire, often turning it for even cooking.

SPLIT PEA is a dried variety of a yellow or green pea; it is a dried hulled pea (such as a field pea) in which the cotyledons usually split apart. It is mainly used for soup.

> **HINT** Split peas do not usually require presoaking before cooking.

SPONGE is a type of batter to which yeast is added, making it rather stiff; it is a soft mixture of yeast, liquid, and flour that is allowed to rise and then mixed with additional ingredients to create bread dough. Sponge is also the name of a whipped dessert containing egg whites, gelatin, and flavoring.

SPONGE CAKE is a light, porous cake made by beating egg yolks and sugar until fluffy, and then folding in beaten egg whites; the eggs are the only leavening agent in the cake. There is a large proportion of eggs, but no shortening in sponge cake.

HINT To cut a sponge cake, cut a circle in the center of the cake to the bottom, then slice into equal slices all the way around.

SPOON is a piece of cutlery with a shallow, bowl-shaped container and a handle. It is used as one of the three main eating utensils and also to stir and ladle liquid food. Spoons and forks together are known as FLATWARE. The word dates to 1340 and is from the Anglo-Saxon *spon,* "to chip." Spoons were the first eating utensils and are mentioned in the Bible. The first spoon was probably a depressed piece of stone or a gourd. By the Neolithic era, pottery was a known craft and scoop-shaped utensils were made of clay. The Egyptians crafted spoons in antiquity from cowrie shells mounted on stems of stone or wood, or spoons were carved from ivory or cast in metal. In the seventeenth century, the spoon bowl changed from pear-shaped to ovoid, taking on a shape similar to the elliptical form used today. Fourteen types of spoons have been identified by descending size: iced beverage spoon, oval soupspoon, dessert spoon, place spoon, cream soupspoon, teaspoon, five o'clock spoon, ice-cream spoon, citrus spoon, bouillon spoon, after-dinner coffee spoon, chocolate spoon, demitasse spoon, and salt spoon. The basic spoon of a place setting is the place spoon, an all-purpose spoon slightly larger than a teaspoon but smaller than a tablespoon. The length is 6½–7½ inches. When a portion of food is taken from a serving platter, a spoon is put under the food while the fork, with prongs down, holds and balances the portion on the spoon.

SPOON BREAD, also called BUTTER BREAD or EGG BREAD, is made of soft corn bread (and sometimes rice or hominy), milk, eggs, and shortening and served with a spoon. It is a southern U.S. dish and has the consistency of a pudding.

SPOTTED DICK or **SPOTTED DOG** is a steamed suet pudding containing dried fruit, such as raisins or currants. Spotted denotes the dessert's spotted appearance from the dried fruit, and dick may be a contraction of the word pudding (from the last syllable) or possibly a corruption of the word. According to the *Oxford English Dictionary,* the earliest documented reference is an 1850 recipe.

SPREAD is any tasty mixture intended to be spread, especially on bread and bread products; it also refers to any spreadable food.

SPREADS AND FILLINGS

Fillings consist of any edible layer placed inside a sandwich, cake, or other foodstuff. Spreads are soft, pastelike layers applied to breads or other foods. Sandwich spread is usually finely chopped vegetables or meat in mayonnaise. Spread is also a general term for butter, soft margarines, and low-fat spreads that cannot be called margarine. Some commonly used spreads and fillings are listed here:

(continued)

ANCHOVY PASTE	HAM SALAD	MAYONNAISE
APPLE BUTTER	HAM SPREAD	PEANUT BUTTER
BUTTER	HONEY	PRESERVES
CHEESE SPREAD	HUMMUS	SANDWICH SPREAD
CHICKEN SALAD	JAM	SOFT MARGARINE
CHICKEN SPREAD	JELLY	TOFU
CONSERVE	LOW-FAT SPREAD	TUNA SALAD
CREAM CHEESE	MARGARINE OR OLEOMARGARINE	TURKEY SPREAD
EGG SALAD		VEGETABLE SPREAD
FRUIT BUTTER	MARMALADE	
GOOSE LIVER/PÂTÉ	MARSHMALLOW CRÈME	

SPRINGERLE (pronounced SPRING-uhr-lee) are anise-flavored German cookies with an embossed design made by pressing the dough in a mold or using a stamped rolling pin before cooking. The name springerle means "little knights." Springerle are unusual in that they may use hartshorn (ammonium carbonate or baker's ammonia) as a leavening agent, though many recipes omit it in favor of modern leavening agents. The cookies are hard when first baked, and are packed away to ripen for two to three weeks; during this time, they become tender.

SPRINGFORM PAN is a circular, metal cake pan with a straight-sided rim containing a spring that can be unfastened to easily remove the cake when done, especially cheesecake. The springform pan comes in various materials; it may be flat or fluted, tubed or untubed, and is usually five to twelve inches in diameter. The side has a tongue and latch and the bottom is just an insert. The pan is used for baking all types of cakes, especially those that would be difficult to remove from a solid pan.

> **HINT** Check to make sure that the bottom and sides of a springform pan are securely attached before pouring batter inside.

SPRING GREENS is a British term for COLLARD GREENS.

SPRING ROLL is a type of small egg roll with minced vegetables and sometimes meat in a light, cylindrical wrapper of thin egg dough, that is not deep-fried. Spring rolls traditionally are smaller than egg rolls and have a lighter, more delicate pastry wrap. The term dates to 1943.

> **CONFUSABLE** SPRING ROLL/EGG ROLL. A spring roll has a thin, often transparent, flour wrapper, while egg rolls have thicker wrappings. Spring rolls tend to be vegetarian, while egg rolls sometimes contain meat. Spring rolls, so named because they're traditionally served on the first day of the Chinese New Year (in early spring), are smaller, more delicate versions of the egg roll.

SPRINKLES, also called JIMMIES, are tiny bits of candy or chocolate that can be used to decorate food like doughnuts, ice cream, and cupcakes.

SPRITZER is a mixed drink made of wine mixed with a sparkling water. A North American coinage dating to around 1961, it is from a German word meaning "a splash."

SPROUT is a young sprout of various plants such as alfalfa or mung beans that is eaten as a vegetable or in salads, especially in Asian cuisine. Sprout is also short for BRUSSELS SPROUT.

> **HINT** Buy sprouts as fresh as possible in bulk rather than packaged. You must be careful of salmonella and *E. coli* with sprouts, and they must be cooked. Keep sturdy ones in an airtight plastic container in the refrigerator for up to three days. Keep delicate ones in a perforated plastic bag in the refrigerator for up to two days.

SPUCKIE: see GRINDER.

SPUD: see POTATO.

SPUMANTE: see ASTI SPUMANTI.

SPUMONI is a molded, Italian-style ice-cream dessert, usually containing three layers of various colors and flavors and chopped fruit or nuts; two layers are ice cream and one layer is sweetened whipped cream. It is similar to Neapolitan ice cream and was introduced in the United States by 1929. The word is from the Italian *spuma*, "foam." Sometimes whipped cream or beaten egg whites are added to an ice-cream layer. Spumoni is cut into slices and sometimes served with a sweet sauce complementing the ice-cream flavors.

SPUN SUGAR: see COTTON CANDY.

SQUAB is the flesh of a fledgling (not yet flying) pigeon or dove, often braised, broiled, or roasted.

> **HINT** Squab should be kept in the coldest part of the refrigerator for up to two days. Freeze if keeping longer than that.

SQUASH is a broad category of any of numerous annual, tendril-bearing trailing plants of the genus *Cucurbita* grown for their fleshy edible fruits. Squash is a shortened form of the Narragansett *asquutasquash*, "eaten raw," from *asq*, "raw/uncooked." The old-fashioned terms summer squash and winter squash are not meaningful today.

Summer squash are on the market all winter, and winter squash are on the market in the late summer and fall, as well as winter. Most winter squash are vine-type plants whose fruits are harvested when fully mature. They take longer to mature than summer squash (three months or more) and are best harvested when cool weather arrives.

HINTS Squash should be firm and unblemished. Buy the hardest squash you can find, with fat full stems and unshiny skin.

▌ Summer squash can be kept in a perforated plastic bag in the vegetable crisper of the refrigerator for up to three days. Winter squash can be kept in the refrigerator for up to one week. Whole winter squash can be kept in a cool, dark place for months.

SQUASH VARIETIES

SUMMER	WINTER	
CHAYOTE	ACORN SQUASH	HUBBARD SQUASH
COUSA SQUASH	AMBER SQUASH	KABOCHA SQUASH
CROOKNECK SQUASH	ATLANTIC GIANT SQUASH	LAKOTA SQUASH
CUCUZZA, BOTTLE GOURD, OR CALABASH	BANANA SQUASH	LONG ISLAND CHEESE SQUASH
GLOBE SQUASH	BUTTERCUP SQUASH	PUMPKIN
PATTYPAN OR SCALLOP SQUASH	BUTTERNUT SQUASH	SPAGHETTI SQUASH
SCALLOPINI	CALABAZA	SUGAR LOAF SQUASH
TINDA	CUSHAW	SWEET DUMPLING SQUASH
YELLOW SQUASH	DELICATA SQUASH	TABLE QUEEN
ZUCCHINI	GEM SQUASH	TURBAN SQUASH
	GOLDEN NUGGET SQUASH	

SQUASH BLOSSOM is an edible flower found on squash plants. Squash blossoms are quite perishable. Both the male and female blossoms of winter and summer squash varieties can be used interchangeably. The male blossoms appear at the end of thin stems and the stamens should be removed first. The female blossoms form at the end of the buds that grow into squash and are often harvested with the tiny, nascent squash still attached.

HINT Squash blossoms can be put in one layer on paper towels on a baking sheet and refrigerated for up to twenty-four hours.

SQUID is a ten-armed, carnivorous cephalopod mollusk with a long, tapered body; some small squid are used as food. Henry David Thoreau first mentioned squid as food in 1865.

> **HINTS** Squid should be shiny and firm, with a fresh ocean smell. The membrane should be gray. Squid can be refrigerated on a bed of ice for up to two days.
>
> ❚ It is not necessary to remove the ink sac of a squid before cooking; removal is optional. However, the ink can impart a briny taste and most cooks do remove the ink sac. If they use the ink, they incorporate it into a sauce.

STANDING RIB ROAST: see PRIME RIB and RIB ROAST.

STAR ANISE is a small Asian tree (*Illicium verum*) bearing edible, anise-scented, star-shaped fruit. The small, hard seedpod looks like an eight-pointed star and is used whole or broken into individual points as a spice in food dishes.

STAR FRUIT or **STARFRUIT**, also called CARAMBOLA, is an acidic fleshy, orange fruit of a small shrub of the wood sorrel family; the fruit has five prominent ridges and in transverse section appears as a five-pointed star.

> **HINT** Star fruit should be firm and have shiny skin with a touch of green. Keep star fruit at room temperature until golden. Once ripe, they can be refrigerated for a couple of days.

STARTER, also called APPETIZER, is defined as food or drink to stimulate the appetite. Starter is also a culture containing yeast or bacteria that is used to start the process of fermentation or souring in making dough, butter, or cheese.

STEAK is a thick slice of meat (though the word can be applied to a slice from a large fish), especially beef, cut for broiling or frying. The term is also sometimes used for a patty of ground meat that is broiled or fried. The word steak seems to be related to the Old Norse *steikja*, "roast on a spit," and *stikna*, "be roasted," and was first used in English in the fifteenth century. A fresh cut of meat is red on its surface and brown inside, because when myoglobin is denied oxygen it first turns purple, then turns to a brown tinge. When the butcher makes a retail cut and wraps it in plastic, the newly exposed surface has access to oxygen and turns red. If you cut open a piece of meat it, too, will turn red. But with further aging, it will start to brown again. The most tender cut of beef available is the filet mignon.

■ A steak should be turned over on the grill when the upper surface begins to be very moist.

■ You should always brown the exterior surface of a steak for flavor because the light heat results in a reaction similar to caramelization of sugar. Searing a steak will not appreciably reduce the juice loss during cooking. The purpose of searing steak is to make the meat taste better. Before you sear steak, have the meat at room temperature, with both the broiler and the broiler pan preheated, and pat the meat dry. You can also use a heavy, unlined pan. The pan should be very hot to prevent the steak from sticking. You can also sprinkle the pan with salt before adding the steak to help prevent sticking and favorably affect the flavor.

■ There are conflicting views as to when to add salt to steak—before or after cooking has begun—and how much to use. The best compromise is to cook the steak on one side, then turn it over and salt one side. Finish cooking and salt the other side.

■ You can determine whether a steak is rare, medium, or well done by touching it instead of cutting into it: rare steak feels soft with very little resistance, medium steak gives a slight resistance but springs back into place, and well-done steak feels firm. To check the internal temperature of a steak, hold it with tongs and slide a meat thermometer through the side of the steak; 120°F–125°F is rare, 130°F–135°F is medium-rare, 140°F–145°F is medium, 150°F–155°F is medium-well, and 160°F and above is well done. You can use the same method for hamburgers.

■ Slash the edge of a steak at ¾-inch intervals to keep it from curling as it cooks.

■ Bring steaks to room temperature before cooking to speed the cooking time.

■ Keep the smaller part of a T-bone or porterhouse over the cooler part of the grill fire; the strip (the larger part, to the right of the bone) should be over the hottest part of the fire.

STEAK FRIES are large, thick, flat or wedge-shaped French fries.

STEAK KNIFE is a sharp, usually serrated, dinner knife used for cutting beefsteak.

STEAM is to cook something in the steam of boiling water, often in a steamer or on a rack over boiling water. Steamed milk is produced with a steam wand on a coffee/espresso machine, and tastes better and sweeter than milk heated by any other method.

> **HINTS** Food can be steamed in the microwave when it is tightly sealed in parchment paper. Food can be steamed in the oven when tightly sealed in foil.

> ▌ Boil the water, then add the food to be steamed. Cover and cook. Once the water is boiling, lower the heat to bubbling. If steaming for a longer time, periodically check to make sure the water has not boiled off. Put a coin in the base of the steamer, because if the water gets low, the coin will start to rattle. Make sure

the water does not touch the food or the container holding the food that you intend to steam.

STEAMER is a cooking utensil specifically for the purpose of steaming food, such as vegetables. It is usually a covered pan with a perforated base that fits on top of a saucepan of boiling water so that the food inside is cooked by steam. Steamer is also a soft-shell clam that is steamed in the shell.

> **HINT** Let a bamboo steamer air-dry for twenty-four hours to ensure that it is completely dry.

STEAM TABLE PAN: see HOTEL PAN.

STEEL, also called CHEF'S STEEL, HONING STEEL, or SHARPENING STEEL, is a type of nonelectric knife sharpener that is basically a ridged steel rod. The rod is rounded with longitudinal ridges. A sharpening steel is highly useful for honing knives and scissors, but it requires care and some expertise. Steel is also an alloy of iron with small amounts of carbon, used to make utensils and pans.

STEEP means to let an item such as a tea bag or tea leaves sit in a liquid to extract a flavor. This is also done with herbs and spices to extract or intensify the flavors.

STEEPER: see TEA BALL.

STEINPILZE: see PORCINI.

STEM CABBAGE: see KOHLRABI.

STEW is any dish that has been slowly simmered in liquid; stewing tenderizes meat, fish, and/or vegetables and blends the ingredients. Stew is from the Old French *estuver*, "to steam," and originally meant a stove, heated room, hot bath, or cauldron. Most stew meat comes from the forequarters or chuck (shoulder, ribs) or the upper hind leg or round. The round is best for tenderness and flavor. The best beef cuts for stew are short ribs, large end of brisket, top round, and chuck; the best veal cut is shoulder; the best lamb cuts are shank and shoulder; and the best pork cuts are butt and hock.

STEW ESSENTIALS

CONFUSABLE **STEWING/BRAISING**. Braising and stewing are similar procedures, but braising is done with a large piece of meat, such as a roast, while stewing is the same process with small pieces.

■ The liquid in a stew should almost cover or cover the food.

■ A stew recipe can be halved, but when halving, reduce the amount of liquid by

(continued)

one-third instead of one-half. A stew recipe can also be doubled, but when doubling multiply the liquid by 1½, not 2, to avoid a soupy dish.

■ If you use a wine for making beef stew, use a young, fruity, full-bodied, inexpensive red of decent quality, such as a California Cabernet Sauvignon, a red Zinfandel, a Chianti, a red from southern France, or a Shiraz from Australia. You should not use wines labeled "cooking wine" because they are usually not very good.

■ Stews should be thickened at the end of cooking because thickened mixtures easily stick and burn. You can thicken the sauce of a stew by concentrating (reducing) the volume of the sauce using cornstarch or arrowroot, or adding a small amount of instant mashed potato flakes or rolled oats. Flouring the meat before browning also thickens the cooking liquid, which means that when the meat is done the sauce is ready, too, but this is less desirable because the meat will not brown as well.

■ The fat content can be minimized in a stew by cooking it very gently at a bare simmer so that the fat will melt off the meat and flow into the liquid. Then chill the stew and skim off the hardened fat.

■ You can speed the cooking of a stew by cutting the meat into smaller pieces. You can also reduce the cooking time of a stew by adding ½ cup of strong tea.

TYPES OF STEW

Stewing is long, slow cooking in liquid with a low temperature. The ingredients are covered with liquid and a generous proportion of flavoring ingredients, such as onions and root vegetables. Stewing is a method for tenderizing tough cuts of meat. Some well-known stews are listed here:

BEEF BOURGUIGNON	FISH STEW	OYSTER STEW
BEEF STEW	FRICASSEE	PEPPER POT
BOUILLABAISSE	GOULASH	POT-AU-FEU
BRUNSWICK STEW	GRILLADE	POTPIE
BURGOO	HOT POT	POTTAGE
CARBONADE	IRISH STEW	RAGOUT
CASSEROLE	JAMBALAYA	RATATOUILLE
CASSOULET	LOBSCOUSE	SALMAGUNDI
CHICKEN PURLOO	LOBSTER STEW	SLUMGULLION
CHICKEN STEW	MULLIGAN STEW	TZIMMES
CHILI OR CHILI CON CARNE	OLIO	TURKEY STEW
CHOWDER	OLLA PODRIDA	
COQ AU VIN	OSSO BUCO	

STICK BLENDER: see Immersion blender.

STICKY BUN, also called Honeybun, is a sweet, spiral-shaped bun, usually with cinnamon, raisins, and nuts and coated with caramelized coating or icing. It dates to 1909 in English.

STICKY RICE, also called GLUTINOUS RICE, is a short-grain variety of rice that sticks together when cooked. The stickiness of sticky rice is related to the length; in other words, the shorter the kernel, the stickier the rice will be.

STILTON or **STILTON CHEESE** is a rich, waxy, blue-veined English cow's milk cheese; it has a wrinkled rind and is white, firm, and crumbly. Stilton melts easily and is one of the few cheeses that freezes well. Stilton can be traced back to the early eighteenth century, and it has its own certification trademark and is a European Union–protected food name. Stilton takes its name from the village in Cambridgeshire where the original pressed, cooked cream cheese was first made and sold. It takes 136 pints of milk to make one 17-pound Stilton cheese. White Stilton is also a protected-name cheese and is made in a similar way to its blue cousin—except that no mold spores are added and the cheese is sold at about four weeks of age; it is a crumbly, creamy, open-textured cheese and is now extensively used as a base for blending with apricot, ginger, and citrus or vine fruits to create unique dessert cheeses.

STIR is to move a kitchen utensil, such as a spoon, spatula, or beater, through a food substance with a circular movement.

STIR-FRY is to fry small pieces of meat, vegetables, or other food rapidly in a small quantity of oil over high heat, stirring continuously, for a short amount of time; it is an important technique in Asian cooking. Stir-fry is also a noun for a dish cooked this way. Stir-frying can be done in a wok or a frying pan. The term dates to 1959 in English. Stir-frying is like sautéing, but the food is kept moving.

STIR-FRY ESSENTIALS

■ Oils with a high smoke point, such as peanut, canola, or safflower, are good oils for stir-frying. Olive oil is not a good oil to use for stir-frying because it can produce too strong a flavor and smokes at a low temperature. A pan is ready for the oil when water evaporates on contact with the heated pan.

■ Use a little cornstarch stirred into cold water and added at the end to thicken the sauce while stir-frying. Be careful not to overdo it.

■ When adding vegetables to a stir-fry, make sure you add any that require longer cooking first, like carrots and cabbage.

■ On a stovetop, use a flat-bottom wok or skillet, not a round-bottom wok or pan.

■ Freeze meat for 30 minutes before slicing for a stir-fry.

■ Cut items diagonally for stir-fries, as it gives you the largest surface area for crisping.

STOCK is liquid in which meat, poultry, fish, or vegetables are simmered along with herbs and spices; it is used as a basis for soup or sauce. Stock is also called

BROTH, though usually broth refers to a finished product, while stock is used as an ingredient.

HINTS A tall, narrow pot should be used for making stock, because such a pot has a reduced surface area, which will slow evaporation. You can also use a large pot with a pasta insert so that you can remove the solids after they have contributed flavor to the stock. When making a meat stock, cook at a low simmer and do not boil. Don't cover the pot, but leave the lid askew so steam escapes. Let stock cool uncovered.

▌ Measured amounts of stock can be frozen for cooking by premeasuring the stock before freezing, such as in 1- or 2-cup amounts, and labeling the containers. You can then thaw the stock as needed.

▌ The amount of carrots and peppers used in making chicken stock should be limited because these sweet vegetables can overwhelm the chicken flavor if too much is used.

▌ When you make stock, the bones should be cracked or sawed into pieces to facilitate the release of their flavoring and of their collagen (a thickening agent). The bones should be added to the stock while the water is still cold because a sudden plunge into boiling water would partially or completely seal the bones, and thus the tastes, aromas, color, nutrients, and thickening agents might not be released into the stock.

STOCKPOT is a large pot for cooking stock or soup.

STOLLEN is a sweet German yeast bread containing fruits, raisins, and nuts, traditionally made for Christmas. The word appeared in English around 1906.

STONE CRAB is a large, brownish edible crab (*Menippe mercenaria*) prized for the meat of its claws; it hides itself among rocks and its shell is rocklike. Fishermen usually twist off the claws and throw the crab back to grow new claws, which takes up to two years of the stone crab's ten-year lifespan. This does not inhibit the crab, as the claws are only for defensive purposes. Stone crabmeat has a firm texture and a sweet, succulent flavor. It is sold precooked, usually frozen, because the meat has a tendency to adhere to the shell if frozen raw.

STONE FRUIT is any fruit with flesh or pulp enclosing a stone.

STONE FRUITS

APRICOT	MANGO	PEACH
CHERRY	NECTARINE	PLUM
DATE	OLIVE	PLUOT

STONE-GROUND means ground between millstones (especially burstone) to make flour or meal that retains the whole of the grain and preserves nutritional content.

STOUT is a strong, very dark, heavy-bodied ale made from roasted malted barley, with a higher percentage of hops than porter. This word only dates back to 1677.

STRAIN is to remove something by use of a filter, screen, or sieve, usually by pouring a liquid through such a device to separate out any solid matter.

> **CONFUSABLE** STRAIN/DRAIN. Draining differs from straining in that you reserve the liquid when you strain and usually discard it when you drain.

STRAINER is a utensil specifically used to filter and retain larger pieces while smaller pieces and liquids pass through.

STRAINER SPOON: see SLOTTED SPOON.

STRAWBERRY is the red fruit of a low-growing plant (family *Rosaceae*, genus *Fragaria*). The strawberry fruit in the botanical sense is not a berry but an aggregate fruit; it is the greatly enlarged stem end in which are partially embedded the many true fruits, or achenes, popularly called seeds. Strawberries got their name because the plant "strews" its runners along the ground. The word originated in Europe in the eighteenth century.

> **HINTS** Avoid large strawberries in supermarkets. Look for smaller berries with rich red, glossy color and shiny green leaves. Also avoid those with white or green shoulders and brown or limp leaves.
>
> ❚ Slice less-than-perfect strawberries horizontally and add sugar.
>
> ❚ Use flat-end tweezers to remove strawberry hulls, or hull strawberries with a plastic drinking straw. Rinse strawberries first, then hull them.

STREUSEL is a crumbly topping for quick breads like coffee cake, made of sugar, flour, butter, and cinnamon. The word derives from the German *streuen*, "to sprinkle," and dates to around 1909.

STRING BEAN is any French or kidney bean with stringy fibers that must be removed but which are eaten in their pods. The string bean's individual beans are seeds. The fibrous string that once ran down the seam of a string bean has been bred out of the species.

STRING CHEESE is any cheese made in long strings twisted together; it is generally low-moisture mozzarella. Several different types of cheese are known as string cheese. It is peelable and when peeled, the pieces comes away in strings or strips from the larger cheese.

STRIPED BASS or **STRIPER**, also called ROCKFISH, is a marine food and game fish with dark longitudinal stripes that travels up rivers to breed.

STRIP STEAK, STRIP LOIN STEAK, or **STRIP SIRLOIN STEAK,** also called DELMONICO STEAK, SHELL STEAK, or NEW YORK STRIP STEAK, NEW YORK STRIP, is a small steak cut from the front/upper part of the short loin of beef. The strip steak consists of a muscle that does little work and so it is very tender, though not as tender as the nearby ribeye or tenderloin.

STROGANOFF or **STROGANOV,** also called BEEF STROGANOFF, is a dish of beef strips or ground beef sautéed with onion and cooked in a sauce of sour cream, seasonings, and mushrooms and served with noodles or rice. Stroganoff is named for Russian Count Pavel Stroganov (1774–1817), and an 1861 Russian cookbook gives the first known recipe. The name dates to 1932 in English. After the fall of imperial Russia, variants of the dish were brought to the United States and it became popular in the 1950s.

STROMBOLI is an American turnover of Italian bread dough filled with various cheeses, Italian meats (like pepperoni), and sometimes vegetables. It is somewhat similar to a calzone. There is a story that stromboli originated in 1950 just outside of Philadelphia at Romano's Italian Restaurant and Pizzeria. Its creator, Nazzareno Romano, supposedly named it for the movie *Stromboli,* starring Ingrid Bergman.

STRUDEL is a pastry made from a very thin sheet of (phyllo) dough rolled up with fruit filling and baked; the name literally means "whirlpool/eddy" in German because of its spiral cross-section. Strudel is of Austrian origin and gained popularity in the eighteenth-century Hapsburg Empire. The oldest strudel recipe is from 1696.

STUFF means to fill with a stuffing while cooking. Vegetables and eggs can also be stuffed.

STUFFING is a seasoned bread used to stuff meats and poultry.

> **HINTS** A stuffed bird needs to be roasted for at least 15–20 minutes longer than an unstuffed one of the same weight.
>
> ▌ If you refrigerate or freeze a cooked bird, remove the stuffing and freeze it separately, otherwise the stuffing cools down last and bacteria may have time to develop. Remove the stuffing as soon as possible after the meal.
>
> ▌ Since the stuffing expands as it cooks, you can safely stuff a bird by not over-filling it. About 80% of the capacity of the cavity is the maximum, or the stuffing

will begin to ooze out. You can make sure that all the stuffing of a bird comes out by lining the cavity with a piece of cheesecloth before stuffing, then pulling the cheesecloth out after cooking.

STURGEON is a large, bottom-feeding fish with a long snout and tough bony-plated skin, and its flesh and roe eaten as food. The word comes from Anglo-French and ultimately from Indo-European; the word had entered English by 1300.

SUBMARINE or **SUB**, also called GRINDER, is a large sandwich on a long split roll filled with meats and cheese, and usually also lettuce, tomato, onion, and condiments.

SUBPRIMAL CUTS are cuts larger than a steak, roast, or other single cut but smaller than a side of beef. The term also refers to the smaller cuts of meat obtained from the larger primal cuts of an animal, such as short loin, sirloin, and tenderloin from loin.

SUCCOTASH is a dish of cooked corn, lima beans, and butter or cream. The word is from the Narragansett *msiquatash*, "boiled whole corn kernels." Popular during the Great Depression, succotash is a traditional dish of many Thanksgiving celebrations in Pennsylvania and other states. In Indiana succotash is made with green beans and corn instead of lima beans.

SUET is the hard white fat around the kidneys and loins in beef, sheep, and other animals. In cooking, suet is an ingredient in some traditional puddings such as English Christmas pudding.

SUGAR is any of numerous sweet, colorless, water-soluble compounds present in the sap of seed plants and the milk of mammals and making up the simplest group of carbohydrates. The most common sugar is sucrose, a crystalline tabletop and industrial sweetener used in foods and beverages. Sucrose is found in almost all plants, most importantly in sugarcane (*Saccharum officinarum*) and sugar beets (*Beta vulgaris*). Minor sources include the sugar maple and date palm. The word sugar traces back to the Arabic *sukkar* or Sanskrit *sarkara*, through the Old French *sucre*. Sugar was an expensive luxury until 1747, when it was discovered that sugar could be extracted from the sugar beet. A teaspoon of sugar has 16 calories. Sugar does not act as a stimulant—just the opposite. In many instances it has a calming effect. A high sugar intake leads to the production of the brain chemical serotonin, which puts you in a peaceful frame of mind. Sugar in baking adds to the volume, especially when sugar traps air cells in the fat. It also aids in the functioning of yeast.

> **HINTS** To make sugar syrup, heat sugar and water together. For a thin syrup use three parts water to one part sugar, for medium syrup use two parts water to one part sugar, and for heavy syrup use equal parts sugar and water. Store for three weeks at room temperature or for six months in the refrigerator.

▌Sugar lowers the intensity of taste perception. Use a little sugar to make a bitter coffee less bitter, to make a salty dish less salty, and to counteract the acidity of tomatoes in soup or spaghetti sauce. Add a little vinegar to save an oversweetened dish.

▌To substitute dark brown sugar for light brown sugar, use ½ cup of dark brown sugar and ½ cup of granulated sugar for 1 cup of light brown sugar. To substitute confectioners' sugar for granulated sugar, use 1¾ cups of confectioners' sugar for 1 cup of granulated sugar.

ARTIFICIAL SUGARS AND SWEETENERS

There are two main groups of artificial sweeteners: bulk sweeteners and intense sweeteners. Bulk sweeteners, such as hydrogenated glucose syrup and sorbitol, are used as flavor enhancers in many processed foods. Intense sweeteners, such as aspartame and saccharin, have no calories and they produce their sweet taste by triggering specific receptors on the tongue. New chemically engineered products much sweeter than current products have been developed, such as sucralose, which is six hundred times sweeter than sugar, and alitame, which is two thousand times sweeter. These are the names of some artificial sugars and sweeteners:

ACESULFAME POTASSIUM	HYDROGENATED GLUCOSE SYRUP	STEVIA
ALITAME		SUCRALOSE
ASPARTAME	SACCHARIN	XYLITOL
CYCLAMATE	SORBITOL	

SUGAR COOKING STAGES

As a sugar syrup is cooked, water boils away, the sugar concentration increases, and the temperature rises. The highest temperature that the sugar syrup reaches tells you what the syrup will be like when it cools. In fact, that's how each of the temperature stages discussed below is named.

COATED: 212°F (to coat fruits in sugar).	HARD BALL: 250°F–265°F (hard candy).
SMALL THREAD: 217°F–221°F (almond paste).	SOFT CRACK: 270°F–290°F (butterscotch).
THREAD: 223°F–236°F (frostings, butter cream).	HARD CRACK: 300°F–310°F (nut brittle, toffee, cotton candy).
SOFT BALL: 235°F–240°F (fondant, marzipan).	LIGHT CARAMEL: 320°F–338°F (brittle, praline).
FIRM BALL: 224°F–250°F (caramel, toffee).	DARK CARAMEL: 350°F–360°F (coloring, sauces).

Sugar is any sweet-tasting carbohydrate formed naturally in the leaves of numerous plants, but concentrated mainly in their roots, stems, or fruits. Sugar can be extracted from trees like the maple—but the two main commercial sources of sugar are sugarcane, a giant bamboo-like grass of tropical regions, and sugar beet, a root vegetable of temperate regions. The word sugar in the singular usually denotes cane or beet sugar, the scientific name for which is sucrose. Different sugars vary in sweetness or sweetening power. These are some of the many varieties of sugar that are used today:

BARLEY MALT SYRUP	DEMERARA SUGAR	MUSCOVADO SUGAR
BEET SUGAR	FONDANT SUGAR	PALM SUGAR
BROWN SUGAR	FRUIT SUGAR	PEARL SUGAR
BURNT SUGAR	GOLDEN SYRUP	PLANTATION SUGAR
CANE SUGAR	GOLDEN YELLOW SUGAR	RAISIN SYRUP
CARAMELIZED SUGAR OR CARAMEL	GRANULATED SUGAR	RAW SUGAR
CASTOR SUGAR OR CASTER SUGAR	GRAPE SUGAR	REFINED SUGAR
	HONEY	REFINED SUGAR SYRUP
CINNAMON SUGAR	ICING SUGAR	SANDING SUGAR
COARSE SUGAR	JAGGERY	SIMPLE SUGAR
COMPOUND SUGAR	LIGHT BROWN SUGAR	SORGHUM
CONFECTIONERS' SUGAR OR POWDERED SUGAR	LIQUID SUGAR	SUPERFINE SUGAR
	LOAF SUGAR	SYRUP
CORN SUGAR	LUMP SUGAR	TABLE SUGAR
CRYSTALLIZED SUGAR	MAPLE SUGAR	TREACLE
CUBE SUGAR	MAPLE SYRUP	TURBINADO SUGAR
DARK BROWN SUGAR	MILK SUGAR	WHITE SUGAR
DECORATIVE SUGAR	MOLASSES	

SUGAR BEAN: see LIMA BEAN.

SUGAR BEET is the common beet (family Amaranthaceae) with a sweet white root that yields juice from which sugar is obtained. The sugar beet is second only to sugarcane as the major source of the world's sugar.

SUGAR COTTON WOOL: see COTTON CANDY.

SUGARPLUM, is also called BONBON, a piece of sugary candy.

SUGAR SNAP PEA, also called MANGETOUT, is a type of green pea with edible, crisp, rounded pods. Sugar snap peas are a cross between snow peas and garden peas and are eaten in their pods. Sugar snap peas differ from snow peas in that their pods are round as opposed to flat.

SUKIYAKI is a Japanese dish of thin beef strips (or chicken or pork) cooked briefly with onions, noodles, and other vegetables in soy sauce, sake, and sugar. Sukiyaki derives from the Japanese *suki*, "slice/spade," and *yaki*, "broil/grill."

SULTANA is a pale yellow, seedless grape used for raisins and wine, and also the name for the raisin of the sultana (also called GOLDEN RAISIN). Sultanas are slightly more tart than other raisins. Their name is simply an adaptation of the term sultana, meaning a sultan's wife, and was first recorded in the 1840s.

SUMMER PUDDING is a cold British dessert of soft fruits such as blackberries, raspberries, and strawberries, stewed and placed inside or layered between sponge cake or bread.

SUMMER SAUSAGE is a dried or smoked sausage that does not need refrigeration and gets its name from being made in the winter and kept until the summer.

SUMMER SAVORY is an annual plant yielding an herb popular in cooking. It is used more than WINTER SAVORY, which has a slightly more bitter flavor. Summer savory is a characteristic ingredient of Herbes de Provence.

SUMMER SQUASH is any of various fruits of the gourd family (*Cucurbita pepo melopepo*) that mature during the summer and are eaten while immature and before the seeds and rind harden. Summer squash are soft-shelled, with thin edible skin and seeds; examples are crookneck, pattypan, yellow squash, and zucchini.

> **HINTS** Thoroughly scrub summer squash under running water until the skin feels clean. Then cut off and discard the stem end and scrape off the other end. It is usually not necessary to peel summer squash; peel it only if the skin is unusually tough or the surface feels especially gritty after washing.
>
> ▌ Choose young summer squash with tender skin for freezing. Wash and cut in ½-inch slices. Blanch for 3 minutes, then cool, drain, and package in a zip-lock freezer bag leaving ½ inch of headspace before freezing.

SUNCHOKE: see JERUSALEM ARTICHOKE.

SUNDAE is a dessert of ice cream served with a sauce, often garnished with whipped cream, a maraschino cherry, chopped nuts, and fruit. The word sundae is probably an alteration of Sunday—either because leftover ice cream was sold on Sunday or because the dish was served only on that day.

SUN-DRIED TOMATO is a chewy, flavorful, dark red tomato that has been dried in the sun to remove most of the water content; it is often packed in oil. Twenty pounds of fresh, ripe tomatoes will dry down to just one pound of sun-dried tomatoes. Sun-dried tomatoes are used more in the United States as a gourmet ingredient than they are as a staple in Italy, where they were created.

> **HINT** Dry sun-dried tomatoes can be stored in a cool, dry place indefinitely in an airtight container.

SUNFLOWER SEED is the edible, long, tan seed of the sunflower used as food and as a source of oil. Sunflower seeds are sold encased in their black-and-white shells or already shelled—roasted, unsalted, or salted.

SUNNY-SIDE UP is an egg fried on one side only. The egg is not turned over in cooking and has a visible yellow yolk uppermost, hence the name. The *Oxford English Dictionary* dates the term to 1901.

SUPERFINE SUGAR, also called Bar sugar, Berry sugar, Castor sugar, or Caster sugar, is a sugar with finer grains than those of granulated sugar. It dissolves quickly and completely, leaving no grainy texture, which is ideal for certain recipes such as meringues, mousses, and soufflés.

> **HINT** If a recipe calls for superfine sugar for something that is going to be baked, you can substitute regular sugar. However, if it is clear that speedy dissolving is important, you're better off using superfine sugar. You can make your own superfine sugar by processing granulated sugar in a food processor or blender until powdery.

SUPPER is the evening meal, especially when dinner is taken at midday; it is also the name of the food served as a supper. Supper is also a light meal served late in the evening. Supper is usually a less formal meal than late dinner. Supper, a term used by 1275, started out meaning a meal of soup and bread and was originally spelled *souper*; the word is ultimately from the French *super*, "to sup." Late supper is the term for a light meal served to guests following an event.

SUPRÊME or **SUPREME** has several food meanings: (1) a rich velouté made with chicken stock, cream, and egg yolks (also called Sauce suprême); (2) a dish made or served with this sauce, such as boneless chicken breast (also called suprême de volaille); (3) a citrus fruit cut into segments, or a skinless, pithless citrus segment; (4) a bowl for serving cold foods that has an inner container for the food nestled in an outer container for crushed ice; and (5) a sherbet glass with a large bowl. For the latter two, the dessert or appetizer served in the dish may also be called suprême/supreme.

SURFACE-RIPENED describes cheese ripened on the surface when a harmless mold, yeast, or bacteria is applied to the surface. Examples are Brie, Camembert, and Limburger.

SURF AND TURF, **SURF-AND-TURF**, **SURF 'N' TURF**, or **SURF-N-TURF** is an entrée of a serving each of seafood and meat, especially steak and lobster. The term dates to around 1968. Surf and turf is a main course particularly common in British/Irish pubs and North American steak houses.

SURIBACHI: see MORTAR AND PESTLE.

SUSHI is a Japanese dish broadly defined as rice with raw fish wrapped in seaweed, but there are hundreds of variations. Small cakes of sticky rice are flavored with sweet rice vinegar, shaped by hand or wrapped in seaweed, and topped with pieces of raw or cooked fish, vegetables, or egg. It is usually served with wasabi (a green horseradish) and soy sauce. The proper way to eat sushi is in a single bite. In Japanese sushi means "it is sour" with *su* meaning "vinegar"—and the one ingredient common to all sushi is vinegared rice. Sushi is sometimes called a Japanese sandwich. Japanese sushi has a history of over a thousand years, but the term was not recorded in English until 1893. Nigiri is pieces of fish, shellfish, or fish roe over rice balls. Makizushi or maki is sushi rolled in seaweed. Temaki is hand rolls, sashimi is sliced/chilled raw fish without rice, and chirashi sushi is sliced/chilled raw fish served like sashimi but over a bed of rice.

> **HINTS** It is acceptable to eat sushi with your fingers or chopsticks; sashimi is to be eaten only with chopsticks. Eat sushi in one bite if possible, though two bites are acceptable. It is proper to mix a dollop of wasabi into the dish of soy sauce before eating sushi or sashimi. Sushi should be lightly swiped through soy sauce and never left to linger there.
>
> ▌ *Gari* (pickled ginger) is considered a palate cleanser and is eaten between bites or different types of sushi. It is not meant to be eaten in the same bite as a piece of sushi.
>
> ▌ Technically, one doesn't drink sake with sushi (or rice in general), only with sashimi or before or after the meal.
>
> ▌ When eating at a sushi bar, place the chopsticks in front of you, parallel to the edge of the bar, with the narrow ends on the *has-hi oki* (chopstick rest). While it is not as polite to place your chopsticks on the plate, if you do, place them across your plate, not leaning on your plate.

SUSHI INGREDIENTS AND TYPES

Sushi is composed of rice mixed with a dressing that makes it shapable in a mold or by rolling. Additional ingredients of this Japanese specialty include fresh or cooked raw fish or seafood and vegetables. Layers of sushi rice and prepared ingredients are pressed in a mold to make rice "cakes" or are wrapped in a sheet of nori seaweed and served in slices. Dipping sauce, mustard, and pickled ginger are typical accompaniments. The following list includes ingredients of sushi, types of sushi, and condiments served with sushi.

AKAGAI (red clam)

AMAEBI (sweet shrimp)

ANAGO (conger eel)

AOYAGI (yellow round clam)

BARA SUSHI (sushi rice and ingredients mixed together)

BOSTON ROLL (poached shrimp)

CALIFORNIA ROLL (crab)

CHIRASHI-SUSHI OR GOMOKU SUSHI ISO-DON (sushi rice bed with ingredients on top)

DATEMAKI (rolled omelet)

EBI (shrimp)

FUGU (blowfish)

FUTOMAKI OR FUTO-MAKI (thick, large, fat rolls)

GARI (pickled ginger)

GUNKAN (battleship roll)

HAMACHI (young yellowtail)

HIRAME (halibut)

HOSOMAKI OR HOSO-MAKI (small cylindrical pieces)

HOTATE (scallops)

IKA (squid)

IKURA (salmon roe)

INARI SUSHI (deep-fried tofu/aburage stuffed with sushi rice)

KAIBASHIRA (scallop or shellfish)

KANI (crabmeat)

KAPPA (cucumber)

KOBASHIRA (scallops)

MAGURO (tuna)

MAKI SUSHI (cylindrical pieces made with a bamboo mat)

MASAGO (caviar)

MASU (trout)

MIRUGAI (longneck clam)

NEW YORK ROLL (salmon or tuna)

NIGIRI SUSHI (fish over molded pieces of rice)

NORI (dried seaweed)

OKONOMI SUSHI (home-style nigiri sushi)

ONIGRI (rice ball)

OSHIZUSHI (pressed rice squares with fish on top)

PHILADELPHIA ROLL (salmon)

SABA (mackerel)

SASHIMI (raw fish)

SHIMESABA (marinated mackerel)

SHRIMP ROLL

SMOKED SALMON ROLL

SPIDER ROLL (crab)

SUMMER MELON ROLL

TAI (sea bream, porgy, or snapper)

TAKO (octopus)

TAMAGO (omelet)

TEKKA MAKI (tuna)

TEMAKI (large cone-shaped pieces)

TORO (fatty tuna)

UNAGI (eel)

UNI (sea urchin)

URAMAKI (medium-sized cylindrical pieces)

WASABI (hot green horseradish)

SUZETTE PANCAKE: see Crêpe Suzette.

SWEAT means to cook vegetables in fat over gentle heat so they become soft but not brown and their juices are concentrated in the cooking fat. Often, it is to cook slowly over low heat in butter, usually covered, without browning.

SWEDE or **SWEDISH TURNIP**: see Rutabaga.

SWEDISH MEATBALLS are meatballs simmered in stock and made with ground beef (or sometimes veal or pork), butter, beef broth, half-and-half, bread crumbs, and nutmeg. The Swedish word for meatball (*köttbullar*) first appeared in print in a 1754 cookbook. At that time, beef was considered a luxury, which meant this was not a common dish. The dish became popular in the mid-nineteenth century thanks to wood stoves and meat grinders. Swedish meatballs, smaller in size than those of Italy or Germany, are traditionally served with a cream gravy, buttered noodles or boiled potatoes, lingonberry preserves, and sometimes fresh pickled cucumber.

SWEET is one of the four basic taste sensations, the taste of sugar or honey. A sweet is any food rich in sugar.

SWEET-AND-SOUR describes any sauce or dish that combines sugar and vinegar (or lemon juice) in the flavoring. The term dates to 1723. The Cantonese probably originated the idea of merging the two different flavors. Sweet-and-sour pork is a popular treat on Chinese New Year's Eve.

> **HINT** There's nothing wrong with varying the quantities of sugar and/or vinegar in a recipe to either increase or reduce the sweetness of a sauce. In fact, differences in the flavor of sweet-and-sour dishes are found throughout China, with Cantonese dishes tending to be sweeter than those found in other regions.

SWEETBREAD is any edible glands of an animal—it is not sweet and does not involve bread. Sweetbread is often the pancreas or thymus of a calf, lamb, or other young animal that is soaked and fried, grilled, or sautéed. Sweetbreads are very tender and have a delicate, mild flavor. The best sweetbreads come from milk-fed animals, especially from lamb.

SWEET BUTTER: see Unsalted butter.

SWEETENED CONDENSED MILK: see Condensed milk.

SWEETENER is any substance added to food or drink to make it taste sweeter, especially a substance other than sugar.

SWEET ITALIAN PEPPER: see Pepperoncini.

SWEETMEAT is an old term for any food rich in sugar, such as candied or crystallized fruit, candy, and confections. The word meat originally meant food, so this term, dating to at least 1480, meant sweet food.

SWEET PEPINO: see Pepino.

SWEET PEPPER, also called Bell pepper, is the large, mild, sweet, thick-walled, bell-shaped pepper of a plant (*Capsicum annuum*); it is usually green or red, but is now available in other colors such as orange or yellow. This capsicum is often eaten raw.

SWEET POTATO is the fleshy, orange, tuberlike root of a climbing plant (*Ipomoea batatas*). A sweet potato is neither a potato nor a yam.

> **CONFUSABLE** SWEET POTATO/YAM. The sweet potatoes and yams in the stores are the same vegetable. True yams are not sold anywhere except a handful of specialty grocers—sweet potatoes are inside every mislabeled yam can. African slaves brought to North America saw the resemblance of the sweet potato to their native plant, the true yam or *nyami* (a tuber with a sweetish taste); hence our misnamed sweet potato.

> **HINTS** Sweet potatoes peak in fall and winter. Select firm, unbroken, unblemished potatoes. Sweet potatoes with darker-colored skins are usually more moist and flavorful than those with lighter-colored skins. Sweet potatoes keep for up to one week in a cool, dry place.

> ❚ Boiled sweet potatoes can be easily peeled if you don't peel them before cooking. When they are tender, remove them from the boiling water and immerse immediately in very cold water to stop further cooking, and the peels will come off easily.

SWEET RICE: see GLUTINOUS RICE.

SWISS CHARD, also called CHARD, CHARD BEET, and SILVER BEET, is a variety of beet (*Beta vulgaris cicla*) with a swollen root, grown as a vegetable for its edible leaves and stalks. It takes its name from the French *chardon*, "thistle." Swiss chard isn't native to Switzerland, but the Swiss botanist Karl Koch came up with the scientific name of this plant in the nineteenth century. The actual homeland of chard is the Mediterranean region, and Aristotle wrote about chard in the fourth century BC. Chard got its common name from another Mediterranean vegetable, cardoon, a celerylike plant with thick stalks that resemble those of chard. The French got the two confused and called them both *carde*.

> **HINTS** Choose chard that is held in a chilled display as it will be crunchier and have a sweeter taste. Look for leaves that are vivid green with no browning or yellowing. The leaves should not be wilted or have tiny holes. The stalks should look crisp and unblemished.

> ❚ To store, place unwashed chard in the refrigerator in a plastic bag. It will keep fresh for up to three days. If you have large batches of chard, you can blanch the leaves and then freeze them.

> ❚ Both the leaves and the central leaf ribs can be consumed. The stalks can be cut into two- to three-inch lengths and simmered in boiling, salted water until tender. They are generally served with butter and salt or a little wine and vinegar. The leaves should be chopped coarsely and cooked quickly in just the water that clings to them.

SWISS CHEESE is a hard, deep ivory to pale yellow cheese that originated in Switzerland and is known for its elastic texture, mild nutty flavor, and large holes (or eyes) that form during ripening. EMMENTAL and GRUYÈRE are more specific types of Swiss cheese. The term, first applied around 1822 to any cheese from Switzerland, became used more specifically around 1924 for the varieties with a pitted or honeycombed texture. The holes in Swiss cheese are due to carbon dioxide gas bubbles produced by bacteria during fermentation (aging). The longer the fermentation, the larger the holes. In general, the larger the eyes in a Swiss cheese, the more pronounced its flavor. This is because the same conditions that lead to large eyes—longer aging or higher temperatures—also allow the bacteria and enzymes to produce a stronger flavor. However, cheese with large eyes does not slice well, so some U.S. manufacturers make a product less aged and flavorful than imported cheeses of the same style.

HOW DO THE HOLES GET INTO SWISS CHEESE?

The cow's milk used for the original Swiss cheese came from cows in the Emme River Valley in Switzerland. Here's how Swiss cheese is made:

1. The curd, formed from rennet, is shaped into large wheels about three feet in diameter and about six inches thick.

2. The wheels are salted in strong brine and wrapped to prevent drying.

3. Complete ripening (three to six months) is done in humidity- and temperature-controlled rooms where the microbial enzymes slowly change the cheese's composition, texture, and flavor.

4. The enzymes *Streptococcus thermophilus, Lactobacillus bulgaricus,* and *Propionibacterium shermanii* are added in the ripening process to give Swiss cheese its characteristic flavors. The latter bacterium lives on lactic acid excreted by the first two bacteria, giving off large amounts of propionic acid and carbon dioxide gas.

5. The gas collects in large pockets to form the holes in the cheese.

SWISS STEAK, also called SMOTHERED STEAK, is a thick slice of round steak (a relatively tough cut of meat) dredged in flour and pounded or rolled, browned, and braised with tomatoes, onions, and other vegetables; sometimes cube steak is used. Though Swiss steak may have originated in Switzerland (where it is called *Schmor Braten*), the term actually refers to swissing—the pounding or rolling of a material in order to soften and tenderize it. Swiss steak should be tender enough to eat without a knife.

SWORDFISH is a large, edible, oily marine fish (*Xiphias gladius*) with a streamlined body and a long, flattened, swordlike snout. The flesh of swordfish is usually served as a steak.

> **HINT** When choosing swordfish, look for the little strip of dark meat to be red, not brown. If it is brown, the meat is old. Swordfish from the U.S. Atlantic coast tends to be a little rosier than Pacific swordfish; this is caused by its diet, which is mainly other fish plus a little squid. Swordfish is excellent for grilling and is always sold as steaks.

SYLLABUB is a type of drink made of cream and beaten egg whites whipped with brandy, rum, wine, or cider. Syllabub may be thickened with gelatin to be a topping or dessert. Syllabub is found in English by 1537, though the origin of the word is obscure. One story is that it traditionally started with a bowl of Sille sparkling wine made in Sillery in the Champagne region of France, which was placed under a cow that was milked into the bowl. Bub was Elizabethan slang for a bubbling drink, which this was.

SYRAH: see SHIRAZ.

SYRUP denotes any thick, sweet, sticky liquid, especially a solution of sugar and water boiled together or the concentrated juice of a fruit or plant, such as corn syrup or maple syrup. Syrup is also the sweet, thick liquid obtained in the process of manufacturing cane sugar or glucose. Imitation pancake syrups are made by adding maple flavoring to corn syrup.

SZECHUAN CUISINE, also spelled SICHUAN CUISINE, is a hot, oily, spicy style of Chinese cooking with pungency and spiciness coming from the use of garlic and chiles, as well as the unique flavor of the Szechuan peppercorn (also called Sichuan peppercorn). Peanuts are also a prominent ingredient in Szechuan cooking, and the spicy foods are often preserved through pickling, salting, drying, and smoking. Beef is somewhat more common in Szechuan cuisine than in other Chinese cuisines, perhaps due to the oxen in Szechuan Province in southwestern China. The terms are variously spelled *Szechwan, Sichwan, Sichuan*.

SZECHUAN PEPPER, also spelled SICHUAN PEPPER, is a tree or shrub (*Zanthoxylum simulans*) with spicy, two-valved, reddish, dry fruits that are used as a spice in Chinese cooking. The spice has a hot aniselike flavor and is one of the ingredients of Chinese five-spice powder. Szechuan peppercorns cannot legally be imported into the United States unless they are labeled "heat-treated."

TABASCO is the brand name for a very hot sauce made from a tropical American hot red pepper (*Capsicum frutescens longum*); it was originally made from peppers picked near the Tabasco River in Mexico. The pepper sauce that Edmund McIlhenny created started with seeds from those peppers, which he first planted on Avery Island, Louisiana, in 1868. After the peppers are picked, they are mashed and then mixed with a small amount of Avery Island salt. The pepper mash is placed in white oak barrels, and the wooden tops of the barrels are then covered with more Avery Island salt, which acts as a natural barrier to protect the barrels' contents. The mash is allowed to ferment and then age for up to three years; once aged, it is inspected by a member of the McIlhenny family and when approved, it is blended with high-quality distilled vinegar. Numerous stirrings and about four weeks later, the pepper skins, pulp, and seeds are strained out using three different-sized screens. The following year's pepper crop is insured by the McIlhennys, who personally select the best plants in the field during harvest. The pepper seeds from the selected plants are treated, dried, and then stored both on the Island and in a local bank vault as a hedge against any disaster.

TABBOULEH, TABOULI, or **TABOOLI** is a Middle Eastern salad of soaked bulgur wheat and finely chopped parsley, tomatoes, scallions, and mint leaves, with an olive oil and lemon juice dressing. The word is from an Arabic word meaning "spice/seasoning." Tabbouleh is traditionally served with romaine lettuce leaves to scoop it, or eaten with the fingers.

TABLE CREAM: see LIGHT CREAM.

TABLE D'HÔTE or **TABLE D'HOTE** means a restaurant meal or menu offering a series of courses at a fixed price. It is French for "host's table."

TABLE MUSHROOM: see BUTTON MUSHROOM.

TABLE SALT is a white crystalline form of sodium chloride used to season and preserve food.

TABLE SETTING refers to the way to set a table with tableware, such as eating utensils and dishware, for serving and eating. The arrangement for a single diner is called a PLACE SETTING. A silence cloth is a thick liner used under a tablecloth to protect the table and reduce noise and breakage of dishes and glasses.

> **HINTS** Serve and remove beverages from the right of each diner.

> ▌ The water glass is set directly above the point of the knife. A cup and saucer are placed to the right of spoons, with handles to the right.

> ▌ Place silverware one inch from the table edge. The knife is on the right, with the sharp edge toward the plate. Spoons are to the right of knives. Forks are on

the left, with the dinner fork closest to the plate and the salad fork to its left. Dinner plates are in the center of each place setting, one inch from the table edge. Bread plates are placed directly above forks, salad plates to the left of forks.

TABLESPOON is the spoon in a place setting that is larger than a teaspoon; it is used for eating soup and also for serving. The tablespoon is also a measuring utensil, technically ½ fluid ounce, 3 teaspoons, or 15 milliliters. The tablespoon started out in the mid-seventeenth century as the utensil for eating soup made with particles of food. In the second half of the seventeenth century, the shape of the spoon bowl changed from pear-shaped to ovoid, becoming more similar to the elliptical form used today. Tablespoon is abbreviated Tbsp/tbsp or tbp or T.

TABLE WINE is any wine of moderate quality suitable for drinking with a meal. The term dates to 1673 in print. Table wine refers especially to ordinary grape wine as opposed to stronger, fortified wine; sparkling wine; or wine made from other fruits or with added flavoring.

TACO is a soft baked or hard fried tortilla stuffed with fillings such as meat, cheese, chopped tomato, and shredded lettuce. Taco is Mexican Spanish for "roll/wad" or "stopper," alluding to its use as a light lunch to "stop" hunger; it dates to 1949 in English. The breakfast taco, found in Tex-Mex cuisine, is filled with meat, eggs, and/or cheese, along with other ingredients.

TAFFY, also called TOFFEE, is chewy candy made of brown sugar, molasses, or syrup that is boiled until very thick and pulled until it is glossy and holds its shape. The word taffy dates to 1817 and preceded toffee, which dates to 1825. SALTWATER TAFFY was first cooked in copper kettles over open coal fires, cooled on marble slabs, and pulled on a large hook on the wall. The taffy pull was a household enjoyment on Saturday nights, as well as an Atlantic City enterprise. Pulling taffy is designed to add air to the corn syrup and sugar confection. By draping ten to twenty-five pounds of cooled taffy over a hook and then pulling away from the hook, the puller stretches the taffy. When the taffy reaches a five- to six-foot length, where it might become too heavy for itself and fall off the hook, the puller loops the taffy back over the hook, folding it onto itself and trapping air between the two lengths of glistening candy. This process of aeration helps to keep the taffy soft and prevents stickiness. Pulled taffy was traditionally shaped by hand-rolling it on marble or wooden tables into a ¼-inch-diameter snake. It was then cut into two-inch lengths with scissors and, finally, wrapped in a precut piece of wax paper with a twist at both ends. All of this was done by hand and usually within the sight of the Boardwalk strollers who were eager to watch. Despite the name, saltwater taffy contains no saltwater.

TAFFY APPLE: see CANDY APPLE.

TAGINE or **TAJINE** is a slow-cooked Moroccan (North African) stew of meat or poultry and vegetables with spices. The stew is flavored with olives, preserved lemons or other fruit, garlic, and spices like cumin, ginger, pepper, saffron, and turmeric, and usually served with couscous. Veal, lamb, and pigeon are used in some recipes. Tagine is also the name of an earthenware cooking dish with a tall conical lid, used for slow-cooking this stew. The term dates to around 1898 in English and is Arabic for "frying pan."

TAGLIATELLE (literally "small cut-up things") is pasta cut into long, flat noodles, usually thin; it is sometimes called FETTUCCINE, though tagliatelle can be up to one inch wide. The word is from the Italian, *tagliare*, "to cut." Tagliatelle can be golden or green; the green version contains spinach. Taglierini are narrower and tagliolini are shorter variations of tagliatelle.

TAHINI is a thick, smooth paste of ground sesame seeds. The word is from the Arabic *tahana*, "crush/grind."

> **HINT** Place a jar of tahini upside down for a few days to redistribute the oil in the paste.

TAILED CUBEBS or **TAILED PEPPER**: see CUBEB.

TALAI: see KEFIR.

TAMALE is a Mexican dish of corn and cornmeal dough stuffed with a mix of ground meat, red peppers, and seasonings, then wrapped in corn husks or plantain leaves and steamed or baked. The word dates to around 1856 and is from the Nahuatl *tamalli*. Tamale is actually the plural form; the singular is tamal. Tamale is an ancient dish and was traditionally made with lard. The corn mixture may be coarse or fine, and soft or stiff. The dough and husks are tied and cooked in a steamer, though there are many variations.

TAMARIND is a long seed pod from a tropical evergreen with very acidic brown pulp that is eaten fresh, cooked with rice and fish, or preserved for use in curries and chutneys.

> **HINT** Fresh tamarind pods should bend easily. Pods will keep indefinitely in a cool, dry place.

TANDOOR or **TANDOUR** is a cylindrical clay oven used in Indian/Pakistani cookery. Tandoors are capable of high temperatures for fast cooking of roasts or baking bread. Fish and galettes can also be cooked in the tandoor. In India the tandoor is also known by the name of BHATTI because the oven was used by the Bhatti tribe of the Thar Desert of northwestern India and eastern Pakistan. It is also used to describe a shop that sells food cooked in this oven. The word, dating to around 1840, is based on the Arabic *tannur*, "oven."

TANDOORI means baked or cooked in a tandoor, usually after being marinated in a mixture of yogurt and spices. Tandoori cooking was popularized during the Muslim reign in South Asia, and it is thought to have traveled to Central Asia and the Middle East along with the Roma people, who originated among the Thar Desert tribes.

TANGELO, also called HONEYBELL, is a large, sweet, juicy fruit (*Citrus tangelo*) with pebbly skin, the hybrid of either a tangerine and grapefruit, tangerine and mandarin orange, or grapefruit and pomelo. The plural is tangelos. The tangelo's rind and flesh are both bright orange in color; it may or may not contain seeds. The rind adheres firmly to the pulp and is not easily peeled by hand. The skin of the tangelo is more resistant than that of the tangerine, but easier to peel than an orange. The tangelo is also called Honeybell because of its bell-like shape.

> **HINT** Choose a tangelo that is heavy for its size, with firm skin that is free of spots and bruises. Store tangelos in a cool place or in the vegetable crisper of the refrigerator. To avoid condensation, punch small holes in the plastic bag or leave it slightly open. If your tangelos are stored in the refrigerator, take them out and leave them at room temperature to increase their flavor before eating.

TANGERINE is any of various mandarin oranges with deep orange-red skin and easily separated segments. Tangerines got their name from Tangiers, Morocco, from which they were first imported.

> **HINT** Good tangerines are firm to slightly soft, heavy for their size, pebbly-skinned with no deep grooves, and orange in color. They are easy to peel.

TAPAS are small cold or warm snacks or appetizers, usually served with alcoholic drinks, originally in Spain. *Raciones*, Spanish for "rations," are larger helpings of tapas, which is Spanish for "cover/lid." According to *The Joy of Cooking*, the original tapas were the slices of bread or meat that sherry drinkers in Andalusian taverns used to cover their glasses between sips. This was to prevent fruit flies from hovering over the sweet sherry. The meat used to cover the sherry was normally ham or chorizo. Tapas keep the Spanish people fueled before their midday meal and in the evening before dinner, which generally does not occur until after 9:00 P.M.

TAPENADE is a Provençal spread consisting of capers, black olives, and anchovies made into a purée with olive oil and seasonings. The word comes from *tapéno*, "capers."

TAPIOCA is a starchy granular preparation of cassava root used to thicken puddings, soups, and other dishes. Tapioca comes from the Tupi-Guarani *tipi*, "residue," and *ok/og*, "squeeze out." This starchy plant, native to the West Indies and South America, is now cultivated worldwide and has many names, including AIPIM, BITTER-CASSAVA, BOBA, CASSAVA, KAPPA, MACAXEIRA, MANDIOCA, MANIOCA, MANIOC, SABUDANA, SAGUDANA, and YUCCA. In processing cassava, heat ruptures the starch grains, converting them to small, irregular masses that are further baked into flake tapioca. A pellet form, known as pearl tapioca, is made by forcing the moist starch through sieves; this is used in pearl or bubble tea. Granulated tapioca, marketed in various-sized grains and sometimes called manioca, is produced by grinding flake tapioca. When cooked, tapioca swells into a pale, translucent jelly.

TARO is an herb grown for its edible starchy tuberous root; its edible corms are cooked, pounded to a paste, and fermented for poi, a Hawaiian dish. Taro leaves and tubers are poisonous if eaten raw; the acrid calcium oxalate they contain must first be destroyed by heating. Taro is a Hawaiian word. Probably native to southeastern Asia, taro spread to the Pacific islands and became a staple crop. It is also consumed as a cooked vegetable and made into puddings and breads.

TARRAGON is an herb (*Artemisia dracunculus*) with sweet, bright green, aromatic leaves used as a flavoring. Its flavor is licoricelike and its origin was Siberia. The word may come from the Greek *drakon*, "dragon." Tarragon is a common ingredient in seasoning blends, such as fines herbes.

> **HINT** Tarragon plants need to be handled gently as they bruise easily. Fresh leaves have the best flavor. The leaves can also be dried; the dried leaves can be ground or kept frozen in plastic bags.

TART or **TARTLET** is a small open pastry shell with a fruit, jam, jelly, or custard filling; a tartlet is smaller and is usually served as a canapé. Tart is also the adjective for food or drink having a sharp and sour, but usually pleasant, flavor. Tarts are similar to pies and the names are often used interchangeably. Tarts are made with short rather than flaky pastry and are frequently baked "blind," or empty, and filled after baking. A flan is a tart made in an open-bottom pan that is placed on a baking sheet. Tarts and flans, which are usually straight sided, are often removed from their pans before serving, while pies are served from the pan.

TARTARE (literally "in Tartar style") describes a food (usually meat or fish) that is ground up or diced, seasoned with raw egg, capers, chopped onion, and parsley, and served raw.

> **HINT** Steak tartare is a potential source of bacteria, and therefore potentially dangerous, because of both the raw meat and the raw eggs. But in a good

restaurant, where the meat is chopped fresh and hamburger is ground ahead of time in a properly cleaned grinder, the danger is diminished. Raw eggs, however, have a danger ratio in the neighborhood of one in ten thousand.

TARTAR SAUCE is a mayonnaise-based sauce with chopped pickles and sometimes capers, onions, and parsley that is served especially with fried fish. Tartar sauce is a translation from the French *sauce tartare*, with *tartare* originally being a dish covered with bread crumbs and grilled and served with a seasoned sauce.

TARTE TATIN is a warm French upside-down pastry with the dough on top and caramelized fruit, usually apples, underneath. Two French sisters, Carolina and Stephine Tatin, created the tart at their hotel in the late nineteenth century.

TARTUFO is Italian ice cream or layers of ice cream in a hard chocolate shell, usually round. Tartufo is the Italian word for "truffle." The original tartufi (the plural form) were created just after the French Revolution and were shaped like mushrooms. Sometime during the Victorian era, the frozen truffle came about when the idea of molding ice creams into shapes such as flowers, fruit, and other foods became popular. Tartufo is usually composed of two flavors of ice cream, which are sculpted by hand. If there is a fruit in the middle, ice cream may be scooped out from the middle and the fruit placed inside, or fruit syrup may be used to paste the two scoops together. The shell is often chocolate but may be cinnamon.

TASTING is a small portion taken to try a food or drink. It is also a gathering for the purpose of tasting and comparing various kinds of drink, usually wine.

T-BONE STEAK or **T-BONE** is a thick Choice porterhouse steak taken from the small end of the loin. The name dates to 1916 and comes from the T-shaped bone that runs through the steak. Steaks with a large tenderloin are often called a T-bone in restaurants and steak houses. The USDA says that the tenderloin must be at least ½ inch (13 millimeters) thick for the steak to be classified as a T-bone. Due to their large size and the fact that they contain meat from two of the most prized cuts of beef (the short loin and the tenderloin), T-bone steaks are generally considered one of the highest-quality steaks.

TEA is an evergreen plant (*Camellia sinensis*) of Asia, and its dried and prepared leaves are used to make beverages. It is also the name of the beverage itself, hot or iced. The Amoy Chinese *t'e* became tea, coming through the Malay *te/the* into Dutch and then into English. Tea is also a light meal, especially in the late afternoon, at which tea is the usual beverage, as well as the name for a more substantial, early evening meal (also called HIGH TEA) that is often the main meal of the day. The three main types of tea leaves are black, green, and oolong—with white tea being a rare fourth type. Oolong tea is lighter than black tea and darker than green tea. There are many stories behind the origin of the the names of black teas. Pekoe literally means "medium leaves," and orange pekoe means "small leaves." Tea bags were invented around 1900 by New York tea wholesaler Tom Sullivan.

CONFUSABLE PEKOE/ORANGE PEKOE. The difference between pekoe and orange pekoe is the size and cut of the leaves used; pekoe are medium-sized, coarser leaves.

HINTS To make tea, heat the teapot with boiling water, then pour out. Add the tea in an infuser, then add hot water and cover the pot. Let steep for 1–3 minutes for green tea, 3–6 minutes for black tea, or 6–8 minutes for oolong tea. Swirl, then remove the infuser and serve. Remove tea stains with a paste of baking soda and water.

❙ Sun tea can be made in 2–3 hours. Tea bags or loose tea are placed in a container with water and put in the sun.

❙ Store tea in its packaging in an airtight container in a cool, dry place for up to one year.

TEA VARIETIES

Tea, the most universally consumed beverage, is made by infusing the dried leaves of an Asiatic evergreen shrub. There are two main varieties of tea plant, one from China and one from India, with numerous local varieties and hybrids. It is thought that tea cultivation originated in China around 3000 BC and spread to Japan around AD 780. Tea was not grown in India until the 1840s, and the first tea estate was planted in 1867 in Ceylon (now Sri Lanka). The beverage was brought to Europe in the seventeenth century by the Dutch and reached England in 1644 and America in the early eighteenth century. Some popular varieties of tea are listed here:

ASSAM TEA	DARJEELING TEA	OOLONG TEA
BLACK CURRANT TEA	EARL GREY TEA	ORANGE PEKOE TEA
BLACK PEARL TEA	ENGLISH BREAKFAST TEA	PEKOE TEA
BLACK TEA	FRUIT TEA	PEPPERMINT TEA
BOHEA	GREEN TEA	POUCHONG
BUSH TEA	HERBAL TEA	ROSE HIP TEA
CAMBRIC TEA	HYSON	SASSAFRAS TEA
CEYLON TEA	ICED TEA	SOUCHONG
CHAMOMILE TEA	JASMINE TEA	SUN TEA
CHINA TEA	LABRADOR TEA	TILLEUL
CINNAMON TEA	LAPSANG SOUCHONG	TISANE
CONGOU	LEMON TEA	WHITE TEA
CREAM TEA	MINT TEA	

TEA BALL or **TEA INFUSER**, also called STEEPER, is a small, perforated metal ball of two halves that snap together for holding tea leaves to be steeped in hot water.

HINT A tea ball can also be used for bouquets garnis.

TEAHOUSE: see CAFÉ.

TEAKETTLE and **TEAPOT** are both used for making tea. A teakettle is a kettle used for boiling water for tea. A teapot is a pot used for brewing tea. Technically, a teapot is for brewing and serving tea, not for boiling water—which is what a teakettle is for. A teakettle is not for brewing.

TEASPOON is the smaller of two spoons in a place setting; it is used for eating food and stirring beverages, and measures ⅙ fluid ounce or ⅓ tablespoon (5 milliliters). The word dates to 1686 in English. Tea was introduced to the European continent in the seventeenth century. To provide the right balance and weight for the small cups, the first teaspoons were about 4¼ inches long, a size similar to today's demitasse spoon. By the eighteenth century, tea was less expensive, so teacups were larger and so were teaspoons. Today, teaspoons are 5½–6¼ inches long and they are used only in informal dining.

TEMPEH is an Asian/Indonesian food of soybeans fermented with a fungus. Tempeh has a cheeselike texture, tastes somewhat like mushrooms, is high in protein, and is used as a meat substitute in salads and other foods. It can be sautéed, stir-fried, or steamed. The word was first recorded in English in 1966.

TEMPER is to slowly bring up the temperature of an ingredient by adding small amounts of a hot or boiling liquid, which prevents the food from setting or actually cooking. The tempered ingredient is then added into hot liquid for further cooking. It also means to moisten a substance so as to form a paste or mixture. Temper also means to bring chocolate to a condition where it has shine but no streaks. Chocolate is chopped, part of it is melted until it reaches a temperature of 110°F–115°F, the balance is added to that, the chocolate is cooled, and then it is reheated briefly to 88°F–91°F.

TEMPRANILLO (tem-prah-NEE-yoh) is a black wine grape used in fine red wines of Spain; it is used to make Rioja. There are over thirty synonyms for Tempranillo.

TEMPURA is vegetables or seafood dipped in egg batter and deep-fried; it is basically a fritter that is served with soy or other dipping sauces in Asian cooking. Tempura is not a Japanese name, but a name that evolved from the Portuguese *tempero*, "seasoning." The batter-frying technique used in making tempura was introduced into Japan by the Portuguese and Spanish in the late sixteenth century.

TENDERIZE is to make meat tender by beating it, soaking it in marinade, or sprinkling it with a special substance with enzymes (a tenderizer) that softens its fibers/tissues.

TENDERIZE

HINT If you cut the meat against the grain, this shortens any connective tissues, making the meat more tender. Tough meat should also be cooked longer and to a higher internal temperature to melt some of the tough connective tissue.

HOW TENDERIZERS WORK ON MEAT

Meats are composed of protein molecules, and cooking meat breaks down its large protein molecules. The connective tissue polymers combine with water and form smaller molecules that are easier to digest.

Meat tenderizers are composed of enzymes that chemically break down meat proteins. Meat tenderizers are usually made of papain, an enzyme in papaya.

TENDERIZING METHODS

Less tender cuts of meat can be tenderized before cooking by these methods:

MARINATING: Pouring a marinade mixture over meat and refrigerating according to directions.

MEAT TENDERIZING: Using a commercial tenderizing product that helps break down the connective tissue.

MOIST-HEAT COOKING: Cooking meat in a liquid for a long time at a simmer.

POUNDING: Using a meat mallet to pound from the center to the edges.

SCORING: Using a sharp knife to make shallow diagonal cuts across the surface.

TENDERLOIN is the most tender cut of meat—in beef, it is the cut from below the short ribs and made up of the psoas muscle; in pork or beef, it is the tender meat of the muscle running through the sirloin and terminating before the ribs. When left whole, the tenderloin is known as a fillet/filet. Filets mignons are steaks cut from the small end of the tenderloin.

HINT Pork tenderloin is one of the leanest meats available, and according to the National Pork Producers' comparison chart, it's nearly as low in saturated fat as chicken breasts. The main thing to remember when cooking pork tenderloins is not to overcook when roasting, since overcooking will cause the meat to dry out. It's a good idea to use a meat thermometer to test for doneness; cutting into the meat to test for color will cause too many good juices to run out.

TEQUILA is Mexican liquor made from fermented juices of the blue agave plant, a variety of MESCAL. Tequila's name comes from Tequila, Mexico, a center for its production. The only place tequila is made is in Mexico. Upon maturity, the pineapple-like base of the agave plant fills with sweet sap, or *agua miel* (honey water). The bases are steamed to aid in extracting the sap; this juice is fermented and then distilled twice to achieve the desired purity. Some brands are aged in oak vats, which allows the distillate to mellow and take on a pale straw color.

TERIYAKI sauce is a Japanese sauce made from soy sauce, mirin or sake, sugar or honey, ginger, and seasonings, and used as a marinade for meats that are then grilled, broiled, or fried. Teriyaki translates to "gloss/luster" and "roast." Teriyaki is also the word describing beef, chicken, or seafood marinated in or basted with this sauce and grilled or broiled. It's the teriyaki sauce that brings the shiny look (*teri*) to the ingredients. The key ingredient in teriyaki sauce is mirin.

TERRAPIN is any of a family (Emydidae) of terrestrial turtles and their edible flesh.

TERRINE is a meat, fish, or vegetable spread baked in a type of casserole dish, cooled, and then sliced. The bakeware is also called terrine. A terrine can be made of various materials and be rectangular, oval, or triangular in shape. Capacities range from one pint to two quarts. Terrine is French for "large earthenware pot."

> **CONFUSABLE** TERRINE/PÂTÉ. A terrine differs from a pâté in that the terrine is often sliced out of the container, while a pâté has been removed from its mold.

> **HINT** To unmold a terrine, dip a knife in cold water and run it around the edge. Wet the serving plate slightly so you can move the loaf to the center.

TETRAZZINI means served over pasta with a sherry cream sauce with mushrooms, sprinkled with cheese, and browned in the oven. The name dates to around 1920; the dish was named for an Italian opera singer, Luisa Tetrazzini (1871–1940).

TEXAS TOAST is double-thick bread that is buttered and fried in a pan or broiled. Popular in Texas and the states surrounding it, Texas toast is generally served as a side dish with Southern-style dishes such as chicken-fried steak, fried catfish, or barbecue.

TEXMATI RICE is an aromatic white or brown rice that is a cross between long-grain and basmati rice. Cooked Texmati rice has the appetizing aroma of popcorn and a subtle nutty taste.

TEX-MEX is used to describe cuisine that includes a blend of southern Texan and northern Mexican dishes. Ingredients unknown in Mexico are often added. Tex-Mex cuisine is characterized by the use of melted cheese, meat (particularly beef), beans, and spices, in addition to Mexican-style tortillas. Texas-style chili con carne, chili con queso, chili gravy, and fajitas are all Tex-Mex inventions. Tex-Mex first entered the English language as a nickname for the Texas-Mexican Railway, chartered in southern Texas in 1875; the first-known use in print of Tex-Mex in reference to food dates to 1963.

TEXTURE is a general term for the "fabric" or "feel" of food when cut, tasted, or touched.

TEXTURED VEGETABLE PROTEIN or **TVP** is a high-protein product made from processed soybeans that are formed into chunks or ground, and flavored to taste like meat.

THERMIDOR is a descriptor for lobster cooked in a cream sauce, returned to its shell, topped with cheese, and grilled/broiled, or covered with Mornay sauce and glazed in the oven. It was created in 1894 at Maire's, a Paris restaurant, on the evening of the premiere of *Thermidor*, a play. The name thermidor is also given to a dish of sole poached in white wine and fish fumet with shallots and parsley, and covered with a butter and mustard reduction.

THERMOMETER is an instrument for determining temperature. According to the USDA, temperature is the only way to gauge whether food is sufficiently cooked.

> **HINTS** Use an oven thermometer to check the oven's accuracy and hang it from the rack in the middle of the oven. If it is off by 25°F–50°F after 20 minutes of preheating, adjust the temperature. You can also have the oven calibrated by an expert.

> ▌ For checking the temperature of roasting meat, a small instant instant-read thermometer is better than a traditional one that is kept in the roast during the entire time in the oven. This is because the instant-read thermometer is more accurate and makes a smaller hole in the meat, allowing less juice to escape; it also allows you to check the meat's temperature in various places.

> ▌ A dial instant-read meat thermometer is for larger meat cuts. Insert it at least two inches into the center of the largest muscle or thickest portion of the uncooked meat. The thermometer should not touch any fat or bone or the pan. For thinner foods like burgers and chops, insert through the side of the meat to get an accurate reading. When the meat reaches the desired temperature, push the thermometer in a little farther. If the temperature drops, continue cooking. If it stays the same, remove the meat from the oven or grill. Cover the meat with foil and let it stand for about 15 minutes before carving.

THERMOMETER TYPES

CANDY/DEEP-FRYING THERMOMETER	INSTANT-READ THERMOMETER (DIAL OR DIGITAL)
DIAL OVEN-GOING MEAT THERMOMETER	MEAT THERMOMETER
DISPOSABLE TEMPERATURE INDICATOR	OVEN THERMOMETER
ELECTRIC OVEN-CORD THERMOMETER	POP-UP THERMOMETER
FORK THERMOMETER	REFRIGERATOR/FREEZER THERMOMETER

THICKEN is to make or become thicker with the addition of a thickener, such as cornstarch or flour.

THICKENERS

AGAR	EGG YOLK	ROUX
ARROWROOT	FLOUR	SAGO STARCH
BEURRE MANIÉ	GELATIN	STARCH
BUTTER	POTATO	TAPIOCA
CORNSTARCH	REDUCTION	TOMATO PASTE
CREAM	RICE FLOUR	VEGETABLE PURÉE

THICK MILK: see CLABBER.

THOMPSON SEEDLESS GRAPE is a variety of grape cultivated in the United States for eating and drying as raisins. It is also used to produce a very neutral white wine for stretching blends in order to make so-called jug wines. The grape is named for W. B. Thompson (1869–1930), an American horticulturist.

THOUSAND ISLAND DRESSING is a mayonnaise-based salad dressing with chili sauce or ketchup, chopped pickles, pimientos, hard-cooked egg, and spices. Culinary lore has it that Thousand Island dressing was named for the group of almost two thousand small islands of the St. Lawrence River. Thousand Island dressing is a variant of Russian dressing and is frequently used in Reuben sandwiches. The Big Mac sauce of McDonald's restaurants is a variation of Thousand Island dressing.

THYME (pronounced TIME) is a shrubby plant (genus *Thymus*) with aromatic leaves used as an herb/flavoring. It is a little minty and a little lemony. The herb is found mainly in the Mediterranean region, and the word comes from a Greek word meaning "to burn as a sacrifice."

> **HINT** The stems of thyme cannot be used.

TIFFIN is a British term for a light midday meal; it is a synonym for lunch.

TIKKA is an Indian dish of small pieces of meat or vegetables marinated in a spice and yogurt mixture and cooked on a skewer in a tandoor. It is a Punjabi/Hindi word and was first recorded in English in 1955.

TILAPIA is a freshwater fish of the cichlid family, originally African and now cultivated worldwide. The word may come from a Greek fish name used by Aristotle. Scottish zoologist Andrew Smith named the species in 1849. Tilapia is one of the most commonly farmed fish in the world. Tilapia have very low levels of mercury, as they are fast-growing, large, and short-lived fish that mostly eat a vegetarian diet and therefore do not accumulate mercury found in prey. There is research suggesting that farm-raised tilapia contain an eleven to one ratio of omega-6 to omega-3 fatty acids, a potentially dangerous ratio for people with certain preexisting medical conditions. Other fish, such as salmon, contain closer to a one to one ratio.

TILEFISH is a brilliantly colored marine food fish (*Lopholatilus chamaeleonticeps*) with yellow spots; the name comes from its resemblance to ornamental tiles.

TIMBALE (pronounced TIM-bull) is a mixture of poultry, seafood, vegetables, and noodles in a cream sauce that is baked in drum-shaped mold; it is also the name of the mold itself. Timbale (also called timbale case) is also the name for a type of fried or baked pastry shell shaped like a drum and filled with such a mixture. Timbale is French for "kettledrum."

TIN FOIL: see FOIL.

TIRAMISU, also called TUSCAN TRIFLE, is an Italian dessert of sponge cake or ladyfingers (*savolardi*) soaked with coffee and brandy or rum, layered with mascarpone cheese and zabaglione (Italian custard), and topped with cocoa powder. Tiramisu is from the Italian phrase *tira mi su*, meaning "pick me up," probably from the coffee and liqueur included in it. There is no documented mention of this dessert in English before 1982.

TIROPITA, also spelled TYROPITA, is a Greek pastry with layers of buttered phyllo and a cheese-egg mixture. The word is from the Greek *turopita*, "cheese pie," and was first recorded in English in the late twentieth century.

TISANE is a tealike beverage created by infusion of dried or fresh herbs, flowers, or leaves. It dates to around 1398 as a medicinal drink and originally was made with barley. The word's ancestors are the Anglo-Norman *tysanne* and the Middle French *ptisane, ptisanne, thysanne, tisaine, tisane, tisanne, tizanne,* and *tysaine*.

TOAD-IN-THE-HOLE is a British dish of sausages baked in a batter like that used for Yorkshire pudding, usually served with vegetables and onion gravy. The best English sausages to use for this dish are Lincoln or Cumberland sausages.

TOAST is to make the surface brown and crisp by heating in a toaster, oven, or fire. Toast is also a slice of bread that has been toasted. Toast points are triangular pieces of toast, often without the crust, used as the base of hors d'oeuvres and canapés.

TOASTER and **TOASTER OVEN** are small, electric kitchen appliances that toast bread and pastries. A toaster oven can function as both an oven and a toaster. Because a toaster oven takes little time to preheat, it is ideal for toasting several slices of bread at once and baking small amounts of food.

> **HINTS** Use wooden tongs or chopsticks to help remove food from a toaster.
>
> ▌ Blow out crumbs in the toaster with a can of compressed air.

TOASTING BREAD

Here's how a pop-up toaster works:

1. The user inserts bread into the pop-up toaster and pushes down a lever that lowers the spring-loaded rack on which the bread sits.

2. Pushing down the lever activates a timer that will keep the toast inside for the amount of time connected to the chosen toast setting.

3. Power starts flowing to the heating elements, which creates infrared radiation that toasts the bread.

4. A bimetallic strip warms up due to the heat around it or electricity passing through it—and one metal strip of the two expands and lengthens faster with heat than the other.

5. The expanding metal strip arches into a curve and eventually touches a contact to activate an electromagnet.

6. The electromagnet attracts a catch that releases the spring-loaded rack, which pops up the toast and switches off the heating elements.

TODDY, also called HOT TODDY, is a mixed drink made of liquor, hot water, sugar, and spices and served hot. Toddies are often distinguished by prefixing the name of the chief ingredient, as brandy toddy, gin toddy, rum toddy, and whiskey toddy.

TOFFEE, also called TAFFY, is caramelized sugar made into a candy that can be soft and chewy or hard and brittle. Brown sugar or molasses is boiled with butter to make this and sometimes flavorings or chopped nuts are added. It may have been invented in the sixteenth century by Marguerite Bourgeoys, who opened the first school in French Canada.

TOFU, also called BEAN CURD, is a food made of curdled soybean milk pressed into cake form; it has a cheeselike texture and no distinctive flavor. Tofu is offered in various styles, such as extra-firm, firm, hard, or soft; it is sold unflavored or flavored. Tofu is Japanese for "bean curd," ultimately deriving from the Chinese *doufu*, "rotten beans," from *dou* "beans," and *fu*, "rot/sour."

TOLL HOUSE COOKIE is a type of chocolate chip cookie, sometimes containing chopped nuts, named after the Toll House Inn in Whitman, Massachusetts, the source of the recipe, which was created around 1930.

TOMATILLO, also called Husk tomato, Jamberry, or Mexican green tomato, is the edible purplish fruit of the Ground cherry (*Physalis ixocarpa*), resembling a small tomato. It is native to Mexico and the southern United States.

> **HINT** Select firm, unblemished tomatillos with tight husks. Store tomatillos in a perforated plastic bag in the vegetable crisper of the refrigerator for up to two weeks.

TOMATO is a red or yellowish fruit with a juicy pulp from a plant (*Lycopersicon esculentum*) of the nightshade family; it is botanically a berry but is used as a vegetable. Tomatoes were first called *tomates* in French/Spanish, and when tomatoes first came to England, they were called love apples because they looked like apples and were considered aphrodisiacs. Those who say TOE-mah-toe for tomato are historically correct, as the word came from the Mayan *xtomatl*, with three syllables, though the ultimate source is probably the Nahuatl *tomatl*. Up until the early nineteenth century, some people still considered the tomato to be poisonous.

TOMATO ESSENTIALS

■ Try to buy local tomatoes in season (usually June through September). Out of season, choose plum and cherry tomatoes over hothouse tomatoes.

■ Keep ripe tomatoes at room temperature for up to three days. Do not keep tomatoes in the refrigerator unless they are cut. They should not be refrigerated because they are more flavorful when kept at 50°F or higher and less tasty when stored chilled.

■ Most mass-marketed tomatoes are inferior in flavor and texture to home-grown ones. Mass-marketed tomatoes are still immature and green when picked. This is done because the green, unripe tomatoes are less fragile and less perishable, and thus better for shipping. They are red when they reach the store because they have been gassed with ethylene. If they had been left on the vine to ripen naturally, they would have generated their own ethylene gas. Many stores carry vine-ripened tomatoes, which are better-tasting but much more expensive.

■ To ripen partially ripe or green tomatoes, let them finish their ripening process in a paper bag. This prevents the ethylene gas from the tomatoes from dissipating, and instead concentrates it. Be sure to pierce the bag with about six well-distributed holes, because in order to stay healthy, tomatoes need to take in oxygen and give off carbon dioxide. Alternatively, place green tomatoes stem end down between sheets of newspaper in a box and put the box in a cool place.

■ To prepare tomatoes for sauces, drop them into rapidly boiling water, immediately remove with a slotted spoon, and put into ice water. Then pull away the skin, cut in half, squeeze out the seeds, and coarsely chop. When you combine tomatoes in the cooking process with meat, the tomatoes' acid tenderizes the meat and gives it more flavor.

■ Chop canned tomatoes in the can with kitchen shears, or in a bowl using a pastry blender.

■ When substituting canned tomatoes for fresh, choose peeled whole tomatoes.

BEEFSTEAK TOMATO	GREEN TOMATO	PEAR TOMATO
CHERRY TOMATO	HEIRLOOM TOMATO	PLUM TOMATO
DETERMINATE TOMATO	HYBRID TOMATO	SAN MARZANO TOMATO
DWARF TOMATO	INDETERMINATE TOMATO	SUN-DRIED TOMATO
GRAPE TOMATO	PASTE TOMATO	TOMATILLO

TOMATO KNIFE is a small serrated kitchen knife for slicing tomatoes, sometimes with a forked tip for picking up or moving tomatoes. The blade is 4½–6 inches long. This knife goes through the tomato skin better than other knives. The forked tip can be used to core the tomato.

> **HINT** For cutting tomatoes, use only a knife with a stainless-steel blade, as tomato acid will stain carbon steel.

TOMATO PASTE is concentrate of puréed tomatoes sold in cans or at double strength in tubes. Tomato paste is tomatoes cooked for several hours, then strained and cooked longer to reduce them to a thick concentrate. The differences between tomato paste, tomato purée, and tomato sauce are texture and depth of flavor (the thicker the consistency, the deeper the flavor).

> **HINTS** Buy double-concentrated tomato paste in a tube so that you can keep it in the refrigerator and use it when you need it in a dish.
>
> ▌ Cut both ends off a tomato paste can and push out what you need with plastic-covered fingers. Store the rest in a zip-lock freezer bag in the refrigerator.

TOMATO PURÉE is cooked and strained tomatoes made into a thick liquid; it is used to add flavor and body to sauces.

TOMATO SAUCE is a sauce made with a purée of tomatoes (or strained tomatoes), sometimes flavored with minced onions, garlic, spices, or herbs. It is used in recipes and with pasta dishes. *Concassé* (French for "coarsely chopped") is a term used for uncooked tomato sauce in which the tomatoes are peeled, seeded, and chopped to small dice, medium dice, or large dice.

> **HINTS** A raw tomato sauce should not be refrigerated before using. Set it aside at room temperature, for it will lose its flavor if chilled.
>
> ▌ Good tomato sauce can be made with canned tomatoes, especially plum tomatoes. If you use canned tomatoes in making sauce, purée or press the tomatoes through a strainer to eliminate any chunky pieces.
>
> ▌ It is a misconception that the longer tomato sauce simmers, the better it is. The sauce will lose its best characteristics with overcooking, so the best flavor

comes from brief cooking. Cook the tomato sauce in an uncovered pan to prevent steaming and produce a rich, concentrated flavor.

TONGS are a kitchen utensil for taking hold of objects; they usually have two hinged legs with handles above and graspers on the ends. Tongs can be V-shaped or scissorlike and can be made of various materials. Types of tongs include ice tongs, jar lifter, micro-wave tongs, bread tongs, salad tongs, snail tongs, spaghetti tongs, steamer tongs, toaster tongs, and utility tongs.

> **HINT** Using tongs instead of a fork or your hands prevents you from piercing foods such as juicy meats.

TOP is to provide with a topping, a flavorful addition on top of a dish.

TOP LOIN STEAK: see NEW YORK STEAK.

TOP ROUND is a thick, lean cut of meat taken from an inner section of a round of beef; the cut is taken from inside the round, which is below the rump and above the upper leg. The top round steak's cuts are LONDON BROIL and the butterball steak.

TOP SIRLOIN, also called LOIN TIP or SIRLOIN TIP, is a lean boneless cut from the tender top loin of beef. Top sirloin steaks differ from sirloin steaks in that the bone and the tenderloin and bottom round muscles have been removed. American butchers call a thick top sirloin steak a chateaubriand.

TORPEDO: see GRINDER.

TORTE is a rich cake made with many eggs and frosted with grated nuts or dry bread crumbs as decoration. The word is from the Latin *torta*, "round loaf/cake." The most well-known tortes include the SACHER TORTE, LINZERTORTE, and French GÂTEAU. Tortes are commonly baked in a springform pan, and the element common to most tortes is sweet icing.

TORTELLINI are pasta in tiny ring-shaped pieces, filled with minced meat, vegetables, or cheese and served with a sauce or in a broth. Tortellini is Italian for "little cakes," from *torta*, "tart." They are made in different shapes and sizes and are called tortelli, tortelletti, tortelloni, and tortiglioni. The pasta may be made with eggs or colored with tomato or spinach. The legend is that a young apprentice pastry chef made them in the shape of a navel out of love for his mistress.

TORTILLA is a thin, flat unleavened Mexican bread made from cornmeal or wheat flour; the word is the Spanish diminutive of *torta*, "cake." Tortillas are cooked or baked, and usually eaten folded with a filling or made into tortilla chips. Corn tortillas have little or no fat; flour tortillas are softer, higher in fat, and more pliable. Tortillas are traditionally used to make burritos, chimichangas, fajitas, flautas, and quesadillas.

> **HINTS** To use up stale tortillas, cut them into triangles and make chips, or chop or shred them for garnishes.

> █ Corn tortillas should not be frozen because freezing dries them out. Flour tortillas will keep well in the freezer.

> █ Warm tortillas in a dry skillet, turning once, or wrap in a damp kitchen towel or dampened paper towels and microwave for 15 seconds for one or 45 seconds for a package. If you just want to unstick the tortillas in a package, 10–15 seconds is enough.

TORTILLA DISHES

A tortilla is a thin pancake made of cornmeal or flour and was named by the Spanish conquistadors in Latin America, where it is an important part of the everyday diet. The original method of preparation consisted of kneading the dough (*masa*) on a stone (*metate*), then shaping it into circles. Tortillas are always eaten hot, either on their own as bread, or filled with various ingredients, often with a piquant sauce. Some well-known tortillas dishes are listed here:

BURRITO	PAPATZUL	TORTILLA DE HARINA
CHALUPA	QUESADILLA	TORTILLA DE MAIS
CHILAQUILE	SOPA SECA	TORTILLA DE PATATAS
CHIMICHANGA	SOPES	TORTILLA WRAP OR TORTILLA ROLLUP
ENCHILADA	TACO	TOSTADA
FAJITA	TORTILLA CHIPS OR TOTOPOS	
NACHO		

TORTONI is a rich Italian ice cream often flavored with sherry or rum, chopped maraschino cherries, and almonds; it has been described as a frozen mousse speckled with crushed macaroons. The dessert is usually attributed to Giuseppe Tortoni, an Italian who owned the popular Café Tortoni in Paris in the early nineteenth century. The café, which was depicted by Eduoard Manet and mentioned by Honoré de Balzac and Guy de Maupassant, was known for its ice creams and ices. It's assumed that tortoni was one of the ice creams sold at the café. In the recipe that appeared in the *New York Times* in 1898, air is whipped into egg whites and yolks, and bolstered by the addition of hot sugar syrup. More air is whipped into cream, and the two mousses are folded together, then poured into a mold lined with crushed macaroons.

TOSTADA or **TOSTADO** is a tortilla fried until crisp, usually topped with a variety of ingredients like refried beans, vegetables, and cheese. Ultimately the word is from the Latin *tostare*, "to toast." In Mexico tostada refers to a flat or bowl-shaped tortilla that is toasted or deep-fried. It also refers to the finished dish using a tostada. The tostada was created when tortillas went stale but were still fresh enough to eat. Not wanting to waste tortillas, which were one of their staple foods, Mexicans spread beans, rice, meat, cheese, and vegetables onto old tortillas like an open-faced taco.

TOURNEDOS is a small, circular, boneless, round or oval steak cut from the tip of beef tenderloin. It often has a strip of bacon or suet fastened around it before cooking. Tournedos means "to turn the back" in French, because the dish originally was not placed upon the table but passed behind the backs of guests.

TOURNÉE KNIFE: see BIRD'S BEAK KNIFE.

TRAIL MIX is usually a mixture of dried fruits, oats or chocolate, nuts, and/or seeds; it is a food mix thought to boost energy. One type is GORP, "good old raisins and peanuts," a mix of granola, oatmeal, raisins, and peanuts. Trail mix is named for its use by hikers and walkers. Trail mix is mentioned in Jack Kerouac's 1958 novel *The Dharma Bums* when the two main characters describe their planned meals in their preparation for a hiking trip.

TRANS FAT, **TRANS-FAT**, or **TRANS-FATTY ACID** is an unsaturated fatty acid that has been produced by hydrogenation of vegetable oils. It is found in processed foods such as margarine, fried foods, puddings, commercially baked goods, and partially hydrogenated vegetable oils. Trans fats, also called partially hydrogenated oil, were created by chemists to replace butter and other saturated fats when saturated fat was first linked to heart disease. Today, we know they have proven to be worse than saturated fats, increasing the risk of developing heart disease, stroke, and type 2 diabetes.

TREACLE is another word for GOLDEN SYRUP, but is also molasses drained from vats used in sugar refining.

TRIFLE is a dessert of jam-spread sponge cake soaked in wine and served with custard sauce and/or whipped cream. Trifle gets its name from being a "light," or trifling, confection and is a dessert eaten on festive occasions. Recipes go back to the sixteenth century.

TRIMMINGS are any accompaniments or garnishes to a main dish. To trim is to decorate food, as with parsley or other garnishes.

TRIPE is the lining of the stomach of a ruminant, especially a cow (or ox or sheep), used as food. It derives from an Old French word meaning "entrails of an animal."

TRIPLE CREAM is a fresh, soft French cheese with at least 72% butterfat, made from cow's milk enriched with cream. Some triple creams are fresh, like mascarpone. Others are soft-ripened, like Brillat-Savarin, Boursault, Blue Castello, Explorateur, and St. André.

TRIPLE SEC is a type of curaçao liqueur made from orange peel, but colorless and less sweet.

TRIVET is a stand or holder upon which a hot pot or dish may be placed at the table during a meal.

TROPICAL FRUIT is any fruit grown in a region or climate that is frost free, with temperatures high enough to support year-round plant growth given sufficient moisture.

TROPICAL FRUITS

ACKEE	GUAVA	PASSION FRUIT
ASIAN PEAR	HORNED MELON	PEPINO
AVOCADO	INDIAN FIG	PINEAPPLE
BANANA	JABOTICABA	PLANTAIN
BREADFRUIT	JACKFRUIT	POMEGRANATE
CAMUCAMU	JAPANESE PERSIMMON	PRICKLY PEAR
CARAMBOLA	JUJUBE	RAMBUTAN
CHERIMOYA	KIWI	ROSE APPLE
COCONUT	LONGAN	SALAK
CUSTARD APPLE	LYCHEE	SAPODILLA
DURIAN	MAMONCILLO	SOURSOP
FEIJOA	MANGO	TAMARILLO
FIG	MANGOSTEEN	TAMARIND
GUARANA	PAPAYA	

TROUT is any of various freshwater salmonid game and food fishes, such as brook trout, brown trout, lake trout, and rainbow trout. Its edible flesh is mild flavored, lean, flaky, and white to pink/orange. It is a carnivorous fish and its name comes from the Greek *troktes*, "voracious."

TRUFFLE is both an edible fungus growing underground and a type of rich, creamy chocolate candy. The chocolate truffle is so named because the finished candy somewhat resembles the black and white truffles used for cooking. The fungus is fleshy, edible, and potato shaped; it grows underground and is regarded as a delicacy. The word is from the Latin *tufer/trufe*, "tuber."

TRUSS is to tie and/or skewer the wings and legs of a bird/fowl before cooking it. Trussing is also the term for tying meat, such as roasts, with string to hold a shape.

TSEE GOO or **TSU GOO**: see ARROWROOT.

TUBE PAN is a round cooking pan with a hollow cylinder or cone in the middle, used for baking or molding ring-shaped foods such as angel food cake. The tube actually serves a very important function, ensuring that the center of the food being baked will cook through thoroughly and that the center will be finished at the same time as the rest of the dish. With delicate cakes and other baked recipes, the tube pan prevents the unfortunate baking disaster of a cake with burnt sides and a raw middle. The air circulation through the tube also helps the contents cool quickly and evenly after baking.

TUK TREY: see FISH SAUCE.

TUNA is a type of very large marine food and game fish (genus *Thunnus*), including albacore and bluefin tuna. Tuna or tuna fish is the flesh of a tuna when canned for use as food, made into tuna salad, or cut into steaks. The word is from the Latin *tunnina*, "false tunny/tuna." "Dolphin safe" printed on the label of a can of tuna means that the nets used for catching tuna have a shield that prevents the dolphins from getting caught. The procedure is not 100% effective.

> **HINTS** Put patted-dry fresh tuna in a zip-lock freezer bag in the refrigerator over a bowl of ice for no more than twenty-four hours. Tuna can be frozen in this kind of bag for up to one month.

> ▌The color of tuna changes with the time of year it is. In fall, tuna caught in North Atlantic waters are high in fat after migrating from the south and so are lighter in color. Choose bright pink tuna steaks (too red means little fat and flavor; chocolate red means it is too old).

> ▌Water-packed canned tuna may have no less fat than tuna packed in oil; in fact, it may have more. For instance, white albacore tuna of one batch may contain five times more fat than that of another batch, depending upon the temperature and depth of the water in which the fish is caught. So check the label. One may have 1 gram of fat, while another may have 5 grams. Oil-packed may have 1 gram from the fish plus 2 grams from the oil for a total of 3 grams. Also, higher-fat tuna is usually not used for oil-packing. The sodium content does not vary between water- and oil-packed tuna. It is the same.

TURBINADO SUGAR is raw, light brown, coarse sugar that has been steam-cleaned; it is made from the first crystallization of cane juice and retains some molasses. Turbinado sugar is produced by crushing freshly cut sugar cane; the juice obtained is evaporated by heat, then crystallized. The crystals are spun in a centrifuge, or turbine (thus the name), to remove excess moisture, resulting in the characteristic large, light brown crystals. Turbinado sugar is similar in appearance to brown sugar but paler, with larger crystals, and in general the two can be exchanged freely in recipes. Turbinado sugar differs from refined white sugar in that it is obtained or crystallized from the initial pressing of sugar cane. In the United Kingdom, this sugar is sold as DEMERARA SUGAR.

TURBOT (pronounced TUR-buht) is a large, brownish European flatfish (*Psetta maxima*) and its edible white flesh. Both eyes are on the left side. The word is from the Swedish *törnbut*, "thorn flatfish," from the bony tubercles on its back.

TUREEN is a type of large, deep serving dish with a cover for serving soups and stews; the word is derived from the French *terrine*.

TURKEY is a large, gallinaceous bird (*Meleagris gallopavo*) with a fan-shaped tail domesticated for food. Turkey was originally the name for African guinea fowl and eventually for the Western Hemisphere fowl with which the earlier fowl was confused.

TURKEY ESSENTIALS

■ Store turkey in its wrapper in the coldest part of the refrigerator for up to two days. Fresh turkey can be frozen for up to six months.

■ Remove the giblets and neck (usually stored wrapped together in the body cavity) from the turkey. Rinse and pat dry with paper towels. Refrigerate at or below 40°F. Don't keep for longer than three days; less is preferable.

■ A turkey breast should not be covered with foil while roasting, as this will trap the steam and prevent the skin from crisping, but if foil is used, crinkle it so that it is not lying flat on the skin. A better alternative to foil would be a double layer of cheesecloth that has been soaked in melted butter, which would eliminate the need for frequent basting. You can also roast a turkey breast upside down (breast down) for the first hour, to keep it moist.

■ Refrigerate and double-wrap leftover turkey in plastic wrap to prevent it from drying out.

■ When buying a turkey, figure about 1½–2 pounds of whole turkey per person. Thus, for ten people a bird of 15–20 pounds is adequate, but should be larger if leftovers are desired. The amount to buy also depends on how many side dishes will accompany the turkey. The larger the turkey, the lower percentage of the weight is bone. Turkey with the best taste is over 10 pounds. Free-range or organic fresh turkey is best.

1. Let the turkey rest for twenty minutes after removing it from the oven.

2. Wash your hands and place the turkey on a cutting board. Make sure the roasting pan is right next to it.

3. Insert a long serving fork into the chest of the turkey, and with the sharpest available knife, cut whatever was used to truss the legs.

4. Remove the legs by pulling the drumsticks away from the body, find the thigh joints, and cut through the ligaments to separate the joints.

5. Then cut the breast by making a cut deep into it, parallel to the wing.

6. Slice down at an angle and cut off the entire breast.

7. Each of these pieces—the drumsticks, the thighs, the breasts—are then carved on the cutting board before serving.

TURKISH COFFEE, also called GREEK COFFEE, is a strong, usually sweetened, coffee made by boiling pulverized coffee beans. Coffee has affected Turkish culture so much that the Turkish word for breakfast, *kahvalti*, literally means "before coffee." Turkish coffee is normally prepared using a narrow-topped small boiling pot (basically a tiny ewer) called an *kanaka, cezve, dzezva, xhezve*, or *bríki*; a teaspoon; and a heating apparatus. The ingredients are finely ground coffee, sometimes cardamom, cold water, and (if desired) sugar. The coffee is served in a demitasse. Some modern cups do have handles; traditional cups did not, and coffee was drunk either by handling the cup with the fingertips or, more often, by placing the cup in a *zarf*, a metal container with a handle. Traditionally, the pot is made of copper; the size of the pot is chosen to be close to the total volume of the cups to be prepared, since using too large a pot causes much of the foam to stick to the inside of it. A moderately low heat is used so that the coffee does not come to a boil too quickly— the beans need to be in hot water long enough to extract the flavor.

TURMERIC (pronounced TER-muh-rikh) is the root of a tropical plant of the ginger family with a large, aromatic, deep yellow-orange rhizome, which is made into a spice. Turmeric is used extensively in the East and Middle East as a condiment. The word's origin may be the French *terre mérite*, "deserving earth," referring to its golden color. Used in cooking since 600 BC, turmeric was often used in biblical times to make perfume. Turmeric is almost always used in curry preparations and in mustard, which is what gives American-style prepared mustard its bright yellow color.

> **HINT** Turmeric should be stored in a cool, dark place for no more than six months.

TURNER, also called FLIPPER, is a kitchen utensil with a flat flexible part and a long handle, used for turning or serving food. The blade is wide and flat, and the handle is offset to the blade. It is incorrectly called a spatula and vice versa. Specialty turners are the cookie turner, crêpe turner, hamburger turner, lasagna turner, pancake turner, slicing turner, slotted turner, and triple or spreading turner.

HINT Avoid using a turner with too narrow or short a blade for a soft food that might fall apart when lifted.

TURNIP is a plant (*Brassica rapa rapifera*) of the mustard family with edible leaves and a roundish, light-colored fleshy root used as a vegetable. Etymologically, a turnip may be a "turned neep," neep being a word used for turnips or swedes, a similar vegetable.

HINTS Select firm, sweet-smelling, unblemished turnips. Baby turnips can be kept in a perforated plastic bag in the vegetable crisper of the refrigerator for one to two weeks. Larger/older turnips will keep for a few weeks in a cool, dark place.

Never salt the cooking water of turnips because it removes the sweetness of the turnips.

TURNIP-ROOTED CELERY: see CELERIAC.

TURNOVER is a sweet or savory foodstuff made by folding a piece of pastry over a filling. It is common for sweet turnovers to have a fruit filling and be made with a short (pie crust–like) or puff pastry dough; savory turnovers generally contain meat and/or vegetables and can be made with any sort of dough, often a kneaded yeast dough. They are usually baked but may be deep-fried.

TURTLE is an order (*Testudines*) of terrestrial or aquatic reptiles, some with the flesh used as food. There are also turtle candies, named for their shape, which are made from a combination of toasted pecans, smooth chocolate, and soft caramel.

TUSCAN PEPPER: see PEPPERONCINI.

TUSCAN TRIFLE: see TIRAMISU.

TUTTI-FRUTTI is ice cream containing a mixture of dried or fresh chopped fruits, which are usually candied. The term may also be used for a preserve made with various diced fruits mixed with sugar and brandy, or for a flavoring made of this. The word dates to 1834 in English and is Italian for "all fruits."

TWICE-BAKED refers mainly to potatoes that are prepared as follows: the potatoes are baked and cut open; the flesh is removed and combined with spices and other ingredients like butter and cheese; the potatoes are restuffed, then reheated/baked for a short time before serving.

TWIST is a small curled piece of citrus peel used to garnish or flavor a drink, especially an alcoholic one. Surprisingly, the term did not come into use until around 1958.

TYROPITA: see Tiropita.

TZIMMES or **TSIMMES** (pronounced TSIHM-his) is meat and vegetables, or just vegetables, sweetened with dried fruits and stewed or baked in a casserole with honey and cinnamon. The word is from Yiddish, from a German word meaning "light meal."

UDON (pronounced oo-DOHN) is a thick, white, round, or square Japanese noodle (similar to spaghetti) made from wheat or corn flour and often served in soup or broth. The term dates to around 1920 in English.

UGLI FRUIT or **UGLI** is a hybrid of a grapefruit and mandarin orange or tangerine, and is basically a large, sweet variety of tangelo with rough, wrinkled, yellowish skin and yellow-orange pulp. The taste is often described as more sour than an orange and less bitter than a tangerine. Ugli fruit ranges in size between a navel orange and a giant grapefruit. Ugli in ugli fruit is simply a spelling variant of ugly. Ugli fruit was discovered growing wild in Jamaica.

> **HINT** The light green surface blemishes of ugli fruit turn orange when the fruit is at its peak ripeness. Choose fruit that is heavy for its size and that gives slightly to palm pressure. Store at room temperature and use within five days or refrigerate for up to three weeks.

UMAMI is a taste that is characteristic of monosodium glutamate and is associated with meats and other high-protein foods like soy products and some Asian foods. It is sometimes considered to be a fifth basic taste along with sweet, sour, salty, and bitter—this fifth taste is also called savoriness. Umami is the Japanese word for "deliciousness" and it first appeared in English around 1979. The umami taste is due to the taste receptors' detection of the carboxylate anion of glutamic acid, a naturally occurring amino acid common in meat, cheese, broth, stock, and other protein-heavy foods; this amino acid is believed to activate a separate set of taste receptors.

UNBLEACHED FLOUR is flour that has not been artificially colored or bleached. Flour that is bleached naturally as it ages is labeled "unbleached." Unbleached flour is matured and bleached naturally by oxygen present in the air. While this process is very simple, there are some disadvantages. This method is somewhat unreliable and rather time-consuming, taking months to complete. The flour also occupies space in the producer's warehouse while maturing. This storage expense is costly for the producer and makes unbleached flour more expensive than bleached flour. Don't be misled into thinking that unbleached flour is chemical free. Many brands also use potassium bromate as a maturing agent. Many flour producers in the United States are phasing out the use of potassium bromate in favor of ascorbic acid, which is not a carcinogen. The nutritional value of bleached and unbleached flours are practically identical, and the two types of flour are generally interchangeable in recipes; however, they have a noticeable difference in consistency. Unbleached flour has a higher level of gluten than bleached, and therefore it is preferred when making yeast breads and sturdier baked goods. Bleached flour has a lower level of gluten and a finer grain; it generally produces a slightly lighter and softer product than products made with unbleached flour, so it is more commonly used when making delicate pastries. Many cooks also use bleached flour in products for which a white color is desired, as unbleached flour retains a more golden hue.

UNDERPLATE: see CHARGER.

UNLEAVENED means made without leavener (baking powder, baking soda, yeast); the term is usually applied to bread. Examples of unleavened bread include bannock, chapatti, lavosh, and matzo.

UNPOLISHED RICE: see BROWN RICE.

UNSALTED BUTTER, also called SWEET BUTTER, is butter prepared without salt. All butter is salted unless the label specifically says "unsalted," in which case it has absolutely no salt. Unsalted butter is preferred in cooking, especially baking, so the cook has control over the salt content, but is more perishable (salt is a preservative). There is a distinct taste difference between salted and unsalted butter.

> **HINTS** If you assume your salted butter has ¾–1 teaspoon of salt per stick (½ cup), you'll be erring on the side of caution in decreasing the quantity of salt you add to your recipe.
>
> ❚ Store unsalted butter in an airtight container in the refrigerator for up to two weeks.

UNSATURATED FAT is fatty acid that is in a liquid form at room temperature and is primarily taken from plants; this type of fat is generally referred to as an oil and is made up of two different types: monounsaturated and polyunsaturated. An unsaturated fat molecule contains somewhat less energy (that is, fewer calories) than a comparable-sized saturated fat. Examples of unsaturated fats are palmitoleic acid, oleic acid, myristoleic acid, linoleic acid, and arachidonic acid. Foods containing unsaturated fats include avocados, nuts, and vegetable oils such as canola and olive.

UPSIDE-DOWN CAKE is a batter baked on top of a layer of sweetened fruit, then turned upside down so the fruit layer is on top. Pineapple is a favorite for this and the term dates to around 1920.

UTILITY KNIFE: see PARING KNIFE.

VACHERIN or **VACHERIN CHEESE** is a soft cow's milk cheese with a nutty flavor and 45% fat content. Vacherin is also the name of a dessert of baked meringue or almond paste rings placed on a meringue or pastry base or on ice cream and served with whipped cream. The dessert owes its name to its shape and color, which resemble the cheese.

> **HINT** Vacherin should be stored in a cool, dark place and once opened it should be eaten quickly, as it rapidly loses flavor and fragrance.

VALENCIA ORANGE or **VALENCIA** is a variety of thin-skinned sweet orange with few seeds. Primarily grown for processing and juice production, Valencia oranges usually have two crops per tree, the old and the new. Valencia oranges are prized as the only variety of orange in season during summer. This orange was created by the Californian agronomist William Wolfskill on his farm in Santa Ana, and its name comes from the Spanish city of Valencia, known for its excellent orange trees. The success of this crop in Southern California likely led to the naming of Orange County. The Irvine Company's Valencia operation later split from the company and became Sunkist.

VALPOLICELLA (pronounced val-poh-li-CHEL-uh) is a light dry Italian red wine named for the valley where it was first made.

VANDYKE is to cut a jagged V-shaped or serrated decorative edge into a citrus fruit half, such as grapefruit or orange. The term is derived from the Vandyke collar with its deeply indented edging.

VANILLA is a tropical climbing orchid with highly fragrant flowers whose seedpods, called vanilla beans, are used to extract a flavoring agent. This long, thin pod is the fruit of a celadon-colored orchid, which, of over twenty thousand orchid varieties, is the only one that bears anything edible. Vanilla had been used to flavor *xocoatl*, the chocolate beverage of the Aztecs, long before the Spanish conquistador Hernán Cortés drank it at Montezuma's court. It is used in a variety of sweet foods and beverages, particularly chocolate, confections, ice cream, and bakery goods. Vanilla was thought to be an aphrodisiac because its pod resembled the vagina, and the word vanilla comes from the Spanish for "little vagina." Vanilla is the world's most popular flavor, but it is the second most expensive spice after saffron because of the extremely labor-intensive, time-consuming process by which it's obtained. There are currently three major cultivars of vanilla grown globally, all derived from a species originally found in Mesoamerica, including parts of modern-day Mexico. Until the mid-nineteenth century, Mexico was the chief producer of vanilla. In 1819, however, French entrepreneurs shipped vanilla beans to the islands of Réunion and Mauritius in hopes of producing vanilla there. Now Madagascar accounts for half of the global production of vanilla. "Vanilla flavored" on a label means that there is a mixture of pure and synthetic vanilla. "Pure vanilla" is the bean plus ethyl alcohol. "Imitation vanilla" can be almost any combination of chemicals, usually in an alcohol base, and may contain no vanilla. Ice-cream manufacturing is the largest culinary use of vanilla.

> **HINTS** To meet FDA standards, pure vanilla extract must contain 13.35 ounces of vanilla beans per gallon during extraction and 35% alcohol. Extracts can be stored indefinitely in an airtight bottle in a cool, dark place. Vanilla beans should be wrapped tightly in plastic wrap, placed in an airtight jar, and refrigerated for up to six months.

> ▌ To make homemade vanilla extract, place a split bean in a jar containing ¾ cup of vodka, seal the jar, and let it stand for six months.

> ▌ Heat diminishes the intensity of vanilla, so for prolonged cooking add it close to the end.

VANILLA VARIETIES

The term French vanilla is not a type of vanilla, but is often used to designate preparations that have a strong vanilla aroma and contain vanilla grains. These are some varieties of vanilla:

JAVA VANILLA: Least expensive and flavorful.

MADAGASCAR VANILLA (Also called Bourbon vanilla, from the time when Réunion was ruled by Bourbon kings): robust aroma and sweet flavor.

MEXICAN VANILLA: All-purpose sweet vanilla, but should not contain coumarin, which is toxic.

TAHITIAN VANILLA: Most fragrant and expensive vanilla.

WEST INDIAN VANILLA: Made from a different plant strain and grown in the Caribbean and Central and South America.

VARIETAL WINE or **VARIETAL** is a wine made principally from one grape and carrying the name of that grape.

VARIETY MEATS are the edible viscera, entrails, and internal organs of an animal; tongue and liver are among these.

VEAL is the flesh of a young calf, especially one to three months old, used as food due to its delicate flavor and fine texture. The USDA grades veal in six different categories; from highest to lowest they are Prime, Choice, Good, Standard, Utility, and Cull. The leg is the most desirable cut because it has solid, lean, firm-textured meat.

> **HINTS** Choose milk-fed veal with a creamy pink color. Free-range veal is redder and good for hearty dishes. Keep in the refrigerator for up to two days for ground, three days for chops or steaks, or four days for a roast. Veal that

is ground can be frozen for up to three months; other cuts can be frozen for up to nine months.

❚ Veal is more perishable than beef, so buy it only for immediate use. You can tell the difference between veal (traditionally from a calf under three months old, but today from a calf that can be up to twenty-six weeks old) and baby beef (three to twelve months old) by the appearance. If the meat is creamy pink, it is veal. If the meat is creamy red, then it is baby beef. The deepening of color comes from the calf's increased consumption of iron in its diet. Also look at the surrounding fat. The whiter and less yellow the fat, the younger the animal.

❚ When pounding veal, use a steady, moderate stroke, starting at the center and moving outward.

VEAL CUTS

BREAST	RIB	SHOULDER
FLANK	ROUND	SIRLOIN
LOIN	SHANK	TIP

VEGAN (pronounced VEHJ-uhn, but also VEE-gun or VAY-gun) is a person who eats no animal products in any form, in other words, a strict vegetarian; it is also an adjective describing this type of eating. Vegans are purists who refuse to eat all animal-derivative foods, including butter, cheese, eggs, and milk, and also will not use or wear fur or leather. The term was coined in 1944. It is difficult to maintain a good balance of essential nutrients on a vegan diet and great care must be taken to avoid dietary deficiencies in protein, calcium, iron, and vitamin B_{12}.

VEGETABLE may be described as any plant or plant part, other than a sweet fruit, suitable for eating. The word vegetable in its current sense dates to around 1582 and has very little meaning in describing plants botanically, other than to suggest their horticultural nature or culinary use. Its original use as an adjective meaning "having the life of a plant" dates to around 1400; the word comes from the Latin *vegetabilis*, "animating/ life-giving." Canned vegetables actually have more vitamins than fresh vegetables because they are processed more quickly after picking, while fresh produce loses vitamins and other nutrients as it ages. Even the heat of canning doesn't destroy many nutrients. But frozen vegetables are more nutritious than canned because the heat of the canning process destroys vitamins. Frozen vegetables are just as nutritious as fresh vegetables. Fresh vegetables often sit around for days before being sold and/or eaten and thus decrease in nutritive value. Most vegetables reach their first stage of maturity before they have completed their growth. If they are harvested at this point, they are more tender. Later the cell walls begin to thicken and the woody cellular substance, lignin, which cannot be softened by cooking, becomes more abundant. Fully mature vegetables also have more seeds. The following commonly known vegetables are actually fruits according to the scientific definition: cucumbers, eggplants, okra, peppers, pumpkins, squash, and tomatoes. The botanical definition of a fruit is the ovary of a plant, that is, the section of the plant that houses the seeds. However, the USDA makes the distinction that if you usually eat a food as part of the meal's main course, it's a vegetable. And it says that the food is a fruit if you normally enjoy it as a dessert or as a between-meal snack. Therefore, according to the government (at least to one department), cucumbers, eggplants, pumpkins, and tomatoes are vegetables. This latter definition was upheld by the Supreme Court, which made a decision because of questions about import duties. On a traditionally set dinner plate, the vegetable should be positioned at two o'clock. The starch should be positioned at ten o'clock.

VEGETABLE ESSENTIALS

- Some green vegetables, including asparagus, broccoli, and green beans, will be discolored or darken if they stand in acidic dressings or sauces. You also have to be careful about cooking acidic ingredients like corn or tomatoes with green vegetables, which will dull the green color.

- Adding a little sugar to the vegetable cooking water will bring out the flavor. Many vegetables have a better flavor when cooked in chicken stock.

- Plunging vegetables in boiling water for a moment and then putting them in cold water stops further cooking and thus keeps the color bright and the taste essentially raw. Baking soda also helps to maintain the vivid green because it is an alkali and neutralizes the discoloring acid. Some people discourage adding baking soda, however, because it also destroys vitamins (particularly C and thiamin) and softens the hemicellulose of the vegetable's cells, resulting in a mushy texture.

- Potatoes, tomatoes, and dry onions should not be stored in the refrigerator.

- Asparagus, head lettuce, and broccoli do not have to ripen completely on the vine.

- Never soak vegetables in water, as they will become soft and mushy. Rinse them in cold running water and then blot dry with paper towels. Alternatively, wipe them with a damp paper towel dipped in lemon water (for example, to maintain the whiteness of a mushroom).

- Water used for boiling vegetables should be boiled for at least 2 minutes before putting the vegetables in it, because this will cause the water to lose a large percentage of its oxygen. It is the oxygen that causes the vitamin C content to be reduced. Vegetables, like other foods, continue to cook as they cool down.

- Wax can be removed from the surface of vegetables by washing them with a mild dishwashing soap and then thoroughly rinsing. This will remove most of the wax.

(continued)

■ To preserve vegetables' nutrition, don't cut them up until ready to use, for exposure to oxygen saps the nutrients. Avoid boiling, because it leaches the nutrients into the cooking liquid; instead, steam or microwave vegetables. You can also use quick-cooking methods, such as stir-frying, as extended exposure to heat destroys the nutrients.

■ A roll or oblique cut can be done on round, narrow vegetables like carrots or zucchini: slice one end diagonally, then roll the vegetable over and slice again at the same angle. Repeat down the length of the vegetable, rolling and cutting at an angle.

■ To prepare vegetables for the microwave, put them on a plate or in a shallow bowl, sprinkle with a few drops of water, then cover loosely with a vented microwave lid or paper towel.

■ For tender vegetables, boil briefly, shock in a bath of ice water, then reheat before serving.

TYPES OF VEGETABLES

Vegetables are herbaceous plants cultivated for food. Depending on the species, different parts are eaten—the fruit, the seeds, the bulbs, the tubers, the germ, the roots, the stems, the leaves, or the flowers. Many of the most important vegetables were cultivated by ancient civilizations of either the Old or the New World. Some, such as cucumber, onion, potato, and sweet corn (maize), have changed so much through cultivation that it is hard to determine what their wild ancestors were like. These are some of the names used for vegetables cultivated today:

ACORN SQUASH	BROCCOLI	CHIVE
ADZUKI BEAN	BRUSSELS SPROUT	COLLARD GREENS
ALFALFA SPROUT	BUTTER BEAN	CORN
ARTICHOKE	BUTTERNUT SQUASH	COS LETTUCE
ARUGULA	CABBAGE	COURGETTE
ASPARAGUS	CANNELLINI BEAN	CRESS
AUBERGINE	CARDOON	CUCUMBER
AVOCADO	CARROT	CURLY KALE
BAMBOO SHOOT	CASSAVA	DANDELION
BEAN	CAULIFLOWER	EARTHNUT
BEAN SPROUT	CELERIAC	EGGPLANT
BEET	CELERY	ENDIVE
BEETROOT	CELERY CABBAGE	ENGLISH PEA
BELL PEPPER	CHARD	ESCAROLE
BLACK BEAN	CHAYOTE	FENNEL
BLACK-EYED PEA	CHERVIL	FLAGEOLET
BOSTON LETTUCE	CHICKPEA	FRENCH BEAN
BREADFRUIT	CHICORY	GARBANZO BEAN
BROAD BEAN	CHINESE CABBAGE	GARDEN PEA

GARLIC	PARSNIP	SOYBEAN
GLASSWORT	PATTYPAN SQUASH	SPINACH
GLOBE ARTICHOKE	PEA	SPRING ONION
GOURD	PEARL ONION	SQUASH
GREEN BEAN	PEPPER	STRING BEAN
GREEN CORN	PETSAI	SUCCORY
GREEN ONION	PIMIENTO	SUCCOTASH
GREEN PEPPER	PINTO BEAN	SUGAR PEA
HARICOT BEAN	PLANTAIN	SUGAR SNAP PEA
ICEBERG LETTUCE	POKEWEED	SUMMER SQUASH
JALAPEÑO PEPPER	POTATO	SUNCHOKE
JERUSALEM ARTICHOKE	PUMPKIN	SWEET CASSAVA
JICAMA	RADICCHIO	SWEET CORN
KALE	RADISH	SWEET POTATO
KIDNEY BEAN	RAMPION	SWISS CHARD
KOHLRABI	RED BEAN	TARO
LEEK	RED CABBAGE	TOMATO
LENTIL	RED PEPPER	TRUFFLE
LETTUCE	RHUBARB	TURNIP
LIMA BEAN	RICE	TURNIP GREENS
MANGETOUT	ROMAINE LETTUCE	WASABI
MANIOC	RUNNER BEAN	WATER CHESTNUT
MARROW SQUASH	RUTABAGA	WATERCRESS
MUNG BEAN	SALSIFY	WAX BEAN
MUSHROOM	SAUERKRAUT	WHITE BEAN
MUSKMELON	SAVOY CABBAGE	WHITE POTATO
MUSTARD GREENS	SCALLION	WILD SPINACH
NAVY BEAN	SEA KALE	YAM
NEW ZEALAND SPINACH	SEAWEED	YELLOW PEPPER
OKRA	SHALLOT	YELLOW SQUASH
OLIVE	SNAP BEAN	ZUCCHINI
ONION	SNOW PEA	
PARSLEY	SORREL	

BULB AND STALK VEGETABLES

Vegetables are usually classified on the basis of the part of the plant that is used for food. A bulb consists of a relatively large, usually globe-shaped, underground bud with membraneous or fleshy overlapping leaves arising from a short stem. A vegetable stalk is the main stem of an herbaceous plant. These are some well-known bulb and stalk vegetables:

ASPARAGUS	CARDOON	CHIVE
BROCCOLI	CELERY	FENNEL
BRUSSELS SPROUT	CHICORY	FINOCCHIO

(continued)

GARLIC	ONION	SCALLION
GLOBE ARTICHOKE	RADISH	SEA KALE
HEART OF PALM	RHUBARB	SHALLOT
LEEK	RUTABAGA	SWISS CHARD

LEAF VEGETABLES

BRUSSELS SPROUT	DANDELION	ROMAINE LETTUCE
CABBAGE	ENDIVE	SORREL
CELERY	GRAPE LEAF	SPINACH
CHARD	GREEN CABBAGE	SPINACH BEET
CHICORY	KALE	SWISS CHARD
CHINESE CABBAGE	LETTUCE	WATERCRESS
CORN SALAD	MUSTARD GREENS	WHITE CABBAGE
CRESS	RHUBARB	

ROOT AND TUBER VEGETABLES

BEET	JERUSALEM ARTICHOKE	SKIRRET
BURDOCK	JICAMA	SWEET POTATO
CARROT	KOHLRABI	TARO
CELERIAC	LO BOK	TURMERIC
CHERVIL	PARSLEY	TURNIP
CHINESE ARTICHOKE	PARSNIP	WASABI
GINGER	POTATO	WATER CHESTNUT
GINSENG	RADISH	YAM
GOBO	RUTABAGA	YUCCA
HORSERADISH	SALSIFY	

SEED VEGETABLES

BABY CORN	GREEN PEA	RUNNER BEAN
BEAN	KIDNEY BEAN	SNOW PEA
BEAN SPROUTS	LEGUME	SOYBEAN
BLACK BEAN	LENTIL	SPLIT GREEN PEA
BROAD BEAN	LIMA BEAN	SPLIT YELLOW PEA
CHICKPEA	MUNG BEAN	SUGAR SNAP PEA
CORN	NAVY BEAN	SWEET CORN
ENGLISH PEA	PEA	SWEET PEA
FAVA BEAN	PEANUT	WAX BEAN
FLAGEOLET	PINK BEAN	YELLOW SNAP BEAN
FRENCH BEAN	PINTO BEAN	
GREEN BEAN	RED BEAN	

VEGETABLE FAMILIES

CARROT FAMILY: Carrot, celery, parsley.

GOURD FAMILY: Cantaloupe, cucumber, pumpkin, squash, watermelon.

LEGUME FAMILY: Garbanzo, lentil, peanut.

LILY FAMILY: Asparagus, onion.

MORNING GLORY FAMILY: Sweet potato (not yam).

MUSTARD FAMILY: Cabbage, cauliflower, radish, rutabaga, turnip.

NIGHTSHADE FAMILY: Potato, tomato.

PEA FAMILY: Bean, pea.

ROSE FAMILY: Apple, apricot, blackberry, cherry, peach, pear, plum, raspberry, strawberry.

THISTLE FAMILY: Artichoke, endive, lettuce.

VEGETABLES WITH THE HIGHEST SUGAR CONTENT

Surprisingly, most vegetables contain sugar. Some vegetables are also high in protein, such as roots and legumes. Most fresh vegetables have a water content in excess of 70%, with only about 3.5% protein and less than 1% fat. The following vegetables are high in sugar:

ACORN SQUASH	CARROT	RUTABAGA
ARTICHOKE	CORN	SWEET CORN
BAKED BEANS	LEEK	TARO
BEETS	PARSNIP	WHITE RICE
BRUSSELS SPROUT	PEAS	YAM
BUTTERNUT SQUASH	POTATO	

VEGETABLE OIL is any of a number of liquid edible fats that can be extracted from a plant or the seeds of a plant, such as corn, cottonseed, peanut, rapeseed, safflower, soybean, and sunflower. Pale in color and neutral in flavor, vegetable oils can be heated to high temperatures.

HINT Spray vegetable oil on dried fruit before trying to chop it for muffins, cakes, or breads.

VEGETABLE OILS

Vegetable oils are extremely important in cooking. They are extracted either from seeds (soy, sunflowers) or from fruits (olives, nuts). Sesame and olive oils have the oldest origins and records show they were both used by the ancient Egyptians. The ancient Greeks also used olive oil.

Most vegetable oils are low in cholesterol, being made up of monounsaturated or polyunsaturated fatty acids. Others, like coconut and palm oil, contain almost as much saturated fatty acid as animal fats. These are some of the many vegetable oils available:

(continued)

ALMOND OIL	FLAXSEED OIL	PEANUT OIL
ANISEED OIL	GRAIN OIL	PECAN OIL
AVOCADO OIL	GRAPESEED OIL	PEPPERMINT OIL
BRAZIL NUT OIL	GROUNDNUT OIL	PINE OIL
CALENDULA OIL	GUM SPIRIT	POPPY SEED OIL
CANOLA OIL	HAZELNUT OIL	PUMPKIN SEED OIL
CASTOR OIL	HEMPSEED OIL	RAPESEED OIL
CITRONELLA	LAUREL OIL	RICE BRAN OIL
CLOVE OIL	LEMON OIL	SAFFLOWER OIL
COCOA BUTTER	LINSEED OIL	SESAME OIL
COCOA OIL OR CACAO OIL	MACADAMIA NUT OIL	SOYBEAN OIL
COCONUT OIL	MAIZE OIL	SPEARMINT OIL
COFFEE SEED OIL	MUSTARD SEED OIL	SUNFLOWER OIL
COPAIBA	NUT OIL	SWEET OIL
COPRA OIL	OAT OIL	TUNG OIL
CORIANDER OIL	OLEORESIN	TURPENTINE
CORN OIL	OLIVE OIL	WALNUT OIL
COTTONSEED OIL	PALM KERNEL OIL	WINTERGREEN OIL
EUCALYPTUS OIL	PALM OIL	WOOD OIL

VEGETABLE PEAR: see CHAYOTE.

VEGETARIAN is a person who does not eat or does not believe in eating meat, fish, fowl, or, in some cases, any food derived from animals, such as eggs or cheese, but subsists instead on vegetables, fruits, nuts, and grains. The term dates to around 1839 and was popularized by the formation of the Vegetarian Society in England in 1847.

VEGETARIAN TYPES

Vegetarians eat a diet that includes a wide variety of vegetables, fruits, grains, nuts, pulses, and their products. All forms of flesh (meat, fowl, and fish) are excluded from all vegetarian diets, but some vegetarians use milk and milk products. These are some terms describing different types of vegetarians:

FRUITARIAN: Eats only fruit.

LACTO-OVO VEGETARIAN OR OVO-LACTO VEGETARIAN: Eats dairy products and eggs.

LACTO-VEGETARIAN: Consumes milk but no eggs.

MACROBIOTIC EATER: Eats a vegan diet of seeds, grains, and organically grown fruit and vegetables.

OVO-VEGETARIAN: Consumes eggs but no milk.

PESCETARIAN OR PESCO-VEGETARIAN: Eats fish.

RAW FOODIST OR LIVING FOODIST: Eats an uncooked, unprocessed, organic diet.

SEMI-VEGETARIAN, DEMI-VEGETARIAN, OR PART-VEGETARIAN: Eats mainly vegetables and some meat.

VEGAN: Eats nothing made from animals or fish, including eggs, milk, and cheese.

VEGETARIAN: Chooses not to eat meat or fish.

VELOUTÉ or **VELOUTÉ SAUCE** is a smooth white sauce made with meat, poultry, or fish stock and a white or golden roux of flour and butter. The word is French for "velvety." Sauces derived from velouté are allemande, caper, mushroom, and poulette sauces (from veal velouté); aurore, ivoire, and suprême sauces (from chicken velouté); and bretonne, cardinal, and Nantua sauces (from fish velouté).

VELVET: see MILKSHAKE.

VENISON is the meat of a deer used as food; the word derives from the Latin *venari*, "to hunt." Venison has less fat and less cholesterol than beef.

> **HINT** The gaminess of venison can be eliminated by soaking it in a cola beverage overnight.

VERMICELLI is pasta like spaghetti but much thinner. It is the Italian plural of *vermicello*, literally meaning "little worm." Angel hair is a very fine variety of vermicelli. The term Chinese vermicelli is used to describe a type of Asian noodle that is sold dried and comes in varying widths.

VERMOUTH is any of various white table wines flavored with herbs and fortified with brandy. The word is from the German *Wermuth*, "wormwood," the name of the aromatic herb formerly used in the flavoring of the wine. It is useful in the kitchen because of its herby ingredients and can be stored almost indefinitely.

VICHYSSOISE is shortened from *crème vichyssoise*, "iced cream soup of Vichy" (a town in France), and it is a smooth, thick soup made with potatoes, leeks, onions, chicken stock, and cream, and usually served cold.

VIDALIA ONION is a large, white, sweet, delicately flavored onion with a thin yellowish outer skin; Vidalia onions are grown mostly in Georgia.

> **HINT** To preserve Vidalia onions for a longer period of time, wrap them separately in paper towels and refrigerate. Vidalia onions can also be successfully stored in the legs of clean, sheer pantyhose with a knot tied between each onion. Hang in a cool, dry, well-ventilated place. Keep Vidalia onions cool and dry at all times.

VIDURE: see CABERNET.

VIENNA ROLL: see KAISER ROLL.

VIENNA SAUSAGE is a small, spicy frankfurter, often served as an hors d'oeuvre or snack. In North America the term Vienna sausage has most often come to mean only smaller and much shorter smoked and canned wieners, rather than hot dogs. Vienna sausages are made by grinding meat such as chicken, beef, turkey, or pork (or blends) to a paste consistency; mixing the meat with salt and spices, especially mustard; and stuffing the meat into a long casing. The meat is then sometimes smoked, and always thoroughly cooked, after which the casings are removed as with hot dogs. The sausages are then cut into short segments for canning and further cooked. The term dates only to 1958.

VINAIGRETTE is a salad dressing made with oil and vinegar, plus salt, pepper, and other seasonings, including an emulsifier like mustard. The word is from the French *vinaigre,* "vinegar."

> **HINTS** To make vinaigrette, mix the seasonings together, then beat in the vinegar or lemon juice and finally the oil. When making the vinaigrette in a food processor, mix the oil and vinegar and then add the seasonings. To reduce the tartness of a vinaigrette dressing, add a little bit of sugar. Add a tablespoon of mustard to a vinaigrette and it will be smoother and creamier, and it will last longer. A vinaigrette should not be added to a salad until just before serving because the lettuce will wilt.

> ▌Make vinaigrette in a screw-top jar using three parts oil to one part vinegar, or four to five parts oil to one part lemon juice.

VINDALOO is a very hot Indian curry sauce with vinegar or wine, garlic, coriander, red chile, ginger, and other spices; or a dish of meat or shellfish cooked in this sauce. The word is from the Portuguese *vinho de alho,* "wine and garlic sauce."

VINEGAR is a sour-tasting pungent liquid containing acetic acid and is usually made by oxidation of the alcohol in wine, cider, or malt; it is used as a condiment or food preservative.

> **HINTS** Since vinegar is very acidic, bacteria grow very poorly in it, or not at all. However, vinegar will still deteriorate if exposed to air and/or heat. Keep it capped and store it in a cool, dark, dry place.

> ▌Vinegars can be flavored by adding slightly bruised herbs or fruit, heating the vinegar almost to body temperature, and sealing the bottle.

VIRGIN means obtained from the first pressing without the use of heat, and refers to an oil, especially olive oil. EXTRA-VIRGIN means made from the first pressing of highest-quality olives. Extra-virgin olive oil comes from virgin oil production only, contains no more than 1% acidity (oleic acid), and is judged to have a superior taste. Virgin olive oil comes from virgin oil production only, has an acidity of less than 2%, and is judged to have a good taste.

VODKA is a light, colorless, neutral-tasting alcoholic liquor with little aroma, distilled from a mash of rye or wheat, but originally made in Russia from potatoes. Vodka is literally Russian for "little water."

VOL-AU-VENT is a puff pastry shell that looks like a pot with a lid and is filled with a savory meat and sauce mixture, and sometimes with vegetables. It is French for "flight in the wind," due to the pastry's lightness.

WAFER is either a thin disk of unleavened bread, especially as used in religious observances, or any small, thin, crisp cookie, usually sweetened and in a rectangular, fan, or cone shape. The word derives from the French *waufre*, "honeycomb/wafer."

WAFFLE is a batter cake baked in a waffle iron that gives it a gridlike surface; the batter is like that of a pancake but the result is crisper. The word come from the German *wafel*, from the early Germanic word *wabo*, "honeycomb." Belgian waffles, which are often accompanied by fresh strawberries and whipped cream, are made on special waffle makers with very large, deep grids. Sometimes vegetables like French fries are cut in a waffle pattern, which is like a grid or lattice design.

> **HINTS** Keep waffles warm by putting them in a single layer in a 250°F oven.
>
> ▌ Chopsticks or wooden skewers can be used to carefully lift waffles from the waffle iron.

WAFFLE IRON is a kitchen appliance, electric or for stovetop cooking, that is hinged with two honeycomb-patterned griddles. The batter is poured in and the second side closed over it until the waffle is cooked. Stovetop waffle irons must be turned over once during cooking to finish the second side. The oldest waffle irons date from the fifteenth century and many were elaborate masterpieces.

> **HINT** An electric waffle iron may have interchangeable plates for making toasted sandwiches or pancakes, or for grilling/broiling. The cooking surfaces should be coated with nonstick cooking spray before use.

WAITER'S FRIEND see CORKSCREW.

WALDORF SALAD is a mixture of diced raw apples, celery, walnuts, raisins, lemon juice, and sometimes miniature marshmallows, with a mayonnaise-based dressing. It was named after the Waldorf-Astoria Hotel in New York City in the early twentieth century, and a maître d' there was said to have created it.

WALLEYE or **WALLEYED PIKE** is a freshwater food fish (*Stizostedion vitreum*) that is related to perch.

WALNUT is the edible, two-lobed seeds/nuts of a walnut tree (genus *Juglans*), including the English (or Persian) walnut and black walnut. The Old English *walhh-nutu*, meaning "foreign nut" or "nut of the Roman/Persian lands," became walnut.

> **HINT** To easily crack walnuts, place them in a saucepan, cover with water, and bring to a boil. Remove from the heat, cover, and let stand for 15 minutes. You will then be able to easily crack the shells.

WAND BLENDER: see IMMERSION BLENDER.

WASABI, also called JAPANESE HORSERADISH, is a strong-tasting green condiment prepared from the ground thick pungent root of an Asian herb (*Wasabia japonica, Cochlearia wasabi*, or *Eutrema wasabi*) of the mustard family and is similar in flavor and use to horseradish; it is also the name of the herb that yields wasabi. Wasabi is generally sold either in root form, which must be very finely grated before use, or as a ready-to-use paste (either real wasabi or a mixture of horseradish, mustard, and food coloring), usually in tubes. Fresh leaves of wasabi can also be eaten and have some of the hot flavor of wasabi roots. The burning sensations it can induce are short-lived compared to the effects of chiles, especially when water is used to remove the spicy flavor.

> **HINT** Once wasabi paste is prepared, it should remain covered until served to protect the flavor from evaporation. For this reason, sushi chefs usually put the wasabi between the fish and the rice in sushi.

WASSAIL is a hot mulled drink made with wine, beer, or cider, along with spices, sugar, and usually baked apples. It is served in a large bowl and used for drinking and wishing health to others on festive occasions, especially on Christmas Eve and Twelfth Night. The word comes from the Middle English *waes haeil*, "be in good health" or "be fortunate."

WATER is a colorless, transparent liquid, chemically a compound of hydrogen and oxygen. The FDA classifies bottled water as a food and thus regulates it.

> **HINTS** Alcohol will lower the boiling temperature of water, for it has a boiling point of 175°F. So if you substitute a fair amount of wine for the water in a recipe, extend the cooking time by 5%–10% to compensate for the lower temperature.

> There is no difference in temperature between lightly and vigorously boiling water. At the boiling point, the temperature remains constant within 1°F. However, with vigorous boiling, more heat is transferred, which shortens the cooking time. The disadvantage of cooking food in vigorously boiling water is that there will be a loss of fuel, nutrients, and flavor because boiling water violently knocks the food pieces against each other, but this is not negative for some foods, such as pasta.

WATER BISCUIT is a thin, crisp, unsweetened biscuit made from flour and water. Water biscuits are bland, as they do not contain fat.

WATER CHESTNUT, also called CHINESE WATER CHESTNUT, is the edible, crunchy stem of a Chinese water plant (*Eleocharis dulcis*), often used in Asian cooking. The water chestnut's brownish black skin resembles that of a real chestnut, but its flesh is white, crunchy, and juicy.

HINT Select water chestnuts that are very hard and have a little sheen. Refrigerate in a plastic bag for up to one week.

WATERCRESS is a cress plant (*Nasturtium officinale*) with slightly peppery, dark green leaves; it is used in salads or as a potherb.

> **HINT** Avoid watercress that is drooping or tinged with yellow. Keep it in a perforated plastic bag in the refrigerator for up to two days.

WATERMELON is large oblong or round fruit (*Citrullus lanatus*) of the gourd family with a hard, green rind and sweet, juicy, pink-red (or sometimes yellowish) pulp containing many seeds. The seeds may be speckled or solid and are variously colored. Watermelon is 92% water. A watermelon is really a berry and it was first written in 1615 as two words. The history of watermelons is long: there is a Sanskrit word for watermelon, and fruits were depicted by early Egyptian artists more than four thousand years ago. The rind is sometimes preserved as a pickle. Seedless watermelons are not really seedless—they just contain far fewer seeds than regular watermelon and the seeds are soft and pale. The first seedless watermelon was created in 1939 by crossing a diploid watermelon with a tetraploid one, creating a plant with triploid seeds, which means many fewer seeds.

> **HINTS** A large pale yellow patch is a sign that a watermelon was left on the vine longer and may be ripe and sweeter. A resonant thud when you knock on the watermelon says it is full of juice. Keep whole or cut watermelon in the refrigerator. Watermelon does not mature after it is picked, so it is important to choose carefully.
>
> ▌ Store whole watermelon in the refrigerator for up to one week, or in a cool, dark place for four days.
>
> ▌ Store chopped watermelon in a salad spinner to avoid sogginess. The juice from the watermelon drains from the spinner basket into the bowl and can be easily dumped out.

WAX BEAN is a variety of string bean grown for its edible, waxy, golden pod. It is also called BUTTER BEAN.

> **HINT** To store wax beans, wrap in plastic and refrigerate in the vegetable crisper. Use within one week for optimum quality and taste. Cook fresh beans as little as possible to maintain their texture.

WAX PAPER or **WAXED PAPER** is water- and grease-resistant paper that has been treated with wax of paraffin; it is used in cooking, preparing, or wrapping food. The term dates to 1844.

HINT Rub a jar rim with wax paper to transfer wax to the jar and prevent food from dripping or clinging to it.

WAXY RICE: see GLUTINOUS RICE.

WEDGE: see GRINDER.

WELL-DONE or **WELL DONE** means thoroughly cooked and pertains to meat. No redness remains when meat is well done. Well done cuts, in addition to being brown, are drier and contain little or no juice; the loss of juice is simply due to evaporation, and can be prevented by cooking in water (braising), which yields juicy, well-done meat.

WELSH RAREBIT or **WELSH RABBIT** is buttered, toasted bread or crackers with melted Cheddar cheese, milk (and sometimes beer or ale), mustard, Worcestershire sauce, egg yolk, and seasonings. There are variations, but the key ingredients are toast and cheese. The dish may have been so called because it was resorted to when (rabbit) meat was not available.

WHEAT is any of several cereal grasses (genus *Triticum*) with erect spikes containing grains that can be threshed free of the chaff, especially bread wheat (*Triticum aestivum*), a cultigen with large, nutritious grains. From this grain, flour is made into cereals, breads, pastries, cakes, and other products. Durum wheat (*Triticum durum*) is used in making semolina, macaroni, and noodles, and club wheat (*Triticum compactum*) is a soft wheat used for cake, crackers, cookies, and pastries. Wheat comes from the Proto-Germanic root *khwaitijaz*, meaning "that which is white." Wheat flour contains glutenin, the protein in bread that expands into elastic strands known as gluten to capture the gases released by the yeast during kneading, rising, and baking. Wheat is the main source of flour because wheat is the only grain whose proteins form a gluten strong enough to produce raised breads. Hard wheat is low in starch and high in protein and is used to make bread and strong flours. Soft wheat is lower in protein and higher in starch and is used to make makes cake, pastry, and weak flours.

WHEAT VARIETIES

Wheat is a a cereal grass used to produce flour and semolina that can also be eaten cooked or crushed. Wheat was cultivated in Neolithic times; the Egyptians, Greeks, and Romans used it to make bread. It is the premier cereal grass of southern and western Europe. Some varieties of wheat are listed here:

BUCKWHEAT	EMMER WHEAT	STARCH WHEAT
BULGUR WHEAT	GERMINATED WHEAT	SUMMER WHEAT
CLUB WHEAT	HARD WHEAT	WHOLE WHEAT
COMMON WHEAT	MACARONI WHEAT	WILD WHEAT
CRACKED WHEAT	SOFT WHEAT	WINTER WHEAT
DURUM WHEAT	SPELT	
EINKORN WHEAT	SPRING WHEAT	

WHEY is the watery part of milk produced when raw milk sours and coagulates, separating from the thicker part (curds), as in cheese making. Sweet whey is manufactured during the making of rennet types of hard cheese like Cheddar or Swiss. Acid whey (or sour whey) is obtained during the making of acid types of cheese such as cottage cheese. Whey is used to produce ricotta, brown cheeses, Messmör/ Prim, and many other food products. It is also an additive in many processed foods, including breads, crackers, and commercial pastry. The word whey comes from an Indo-European root meaning "slime/muck."

WHINBERRY: see BILBERRY.

WHIP means to beat (egg whites, cream) with a fork, whisk, beater, or mixer so as to incorporate air and make frothy. Whip is also the name of a dessert made of whipped cream and sugar, stiffly beaten egg whites, and gelatin or fruit.

> **HINT** Hand-whipping helps the fat surround the flour and retain suspended air bubbles, creating maximum volume in the baking mixture.

WHIPPED CREAM is cream that has been beaten until light and fluffy.

WHIPPED POTATO: see MASHED POTATO.

WHIPPING CREAM is cream that has enough butterfat (30%–40%) to be whipped The high proportion of butterfat causes it to stiffen when whipped. Whipping cream is sometimes called HEAVY CREAM.

> **HINTS** When making whipped cream, begin with thoroughly chilled cream. Chill the mixing bowl and beaters. Whip the cream on medium speed. Add sugar and any flavorings when the cream is mostly whipped, and the cream will whip to a higher volume. Cream is whipped when soft peaks form. Use cream that has either a 36%–40% butterfat content (heavy cream) or 30%–36% (light whipping cream). Evaporated milk whips to three times its volume.
>
> ▌ If you add a pinch of salt to cream, it will whip better.

WHISK is a kitchen utensil consisting of curved or coiled wire loops fixed in a handle, for whipping foods such as egg whites or cream. Whisk, the verb, means to whip a soft or liquid substance with a fork, whisk, or other utensil. The word is from an Indo-European root meaning "twig/broom," as the first whisks were made of twigs or straw.

> **HINTS** Mix and aerate dry ingredients separately with eight to ten strokes of a large wire whisk.
>
> ▮ Use a straight whisk for smooth sauces; a balloon whisk for egg whites, cream, and light batters; and a flat whisk for stirring a roux or deglazing a pan.

WHISKEY or **WHISKY** is an alcoholic liquor distilled from the fermented mash of grains, usually barley, corn, or rye. Whiskeys are distinguished by grain, yeast, water, blending, method of distillation, the proof at which the mash is distilled, and age. Whiskey obtains its characteristic brown color from four sources: coloring matter from the barrel, oxidation, charred barrels, and the addition of caramel for color adjustment. The Scottish and Irish Gaelic *uisge beatha*, "water of life," was respelled *whiskybae*, then shortened to whiskey.

> **CONFUSABLE** WHISKEY/WHISKY: Whiskey and whisky are synonymous. The Scots and Canadians spell whisky without the *e*; the Irish and Americans spell whiskey with the *e*.

WHITE is a mass of albuminous material surrounding the yolk of an egg; it is the transparent part of an egg that turns white when the egg is cooked. White also describes wheat flour that has had the bran and germ removed, something made from white flour, coffee served with milk or cream, or wine made from white grapes.

WHITE CHOCOLATE is a blend of cocoa butter, milk solids, sugar, and vanilla. It is used in candy bars and baking and coatings, but is not technically a chocolate because it contains no chocolate liqueur or cocoa powder. The new definition of white chocolate, effective as of 1988, is that there must be a minimum of 20% cocoa butter. Prior to 2002, the FDA, by definition, did not consider white chocolate to be a chocolate. In 2002, the FDA amended its standards of identity to include white chocolate as a chocolate if certain requirements are followed.

WHITEFISH or **WHITE FISH** is any of various white or silvery, edible freshwater food fishes similar to trout but with a smaller mouth (genera *Prosopium* and *Coregonus*, as well as *Caulolatilus princeps* and silvery fishes of the minnow and carp family). The beluga or white whale is also sometimes called whitefish. White fish includes any fish with pale or whitish edible flesh. Examples of white round fish include cod, coley, haddock, hake, pollack, sea bass, and whiting. Members of the white flatfish group are halibut, flounder, John Dory, plaice, sole, and turbot. Other white fish include bream, torsk (also known as cusk), and pouting.

WHITE KIDNEY BEAN: see CANNELLINI.

WHITE MEAT is any meat that is light-colored after cooking, especially that of chicken, turkey, or pork. The term dates to 1752.

WHITE MUSHROOM: see BUTTON MUSHROOM.

WHITE RICE is rice from which the outer husk/hull and bran have been removed by milling. Long-grain white rice has slender grains that steam to a light, fluffy consistency. Short-grain and medium-grain varieties have a stickier consistency when cooked.

> **HINTS** For tender, fluffy rice with separate grains, choose long-grain white rice. Use a little less water than the recipes call for if you want fluffy rice. The ratio of rice to water should be a little less than one to two. To make fluffy rice, leave the cover on the pan after the rice is cooked (tender to the bite), remove the pan from the heat, and let it stand for 5–10 minutes. Then fluff the rice with a fork and serve. Another method for fluffy rice is to bring lots of water to a boil, add the rice, cook until just barely tender, then drain the rice in a colander. Return to the hot pot and cover; let stand for a few minutes to steam.

> ▌ Try using chicken broth, vegetable broth, or beef stock if you'd like more flavor. It all depends on what you're serving with the rice.

WHITE SAUCE is a pale-colored, milk-based sauce, thickened with butter and flour or cornstarch, and variously seasoned or flavored. The term dates to 1723. There are five mother sauces in French cuisine, including béchamel, a smooth white sauce made from milk and thickened with a roux of flour and butter. White or cream sauces are basically variations of this mother sauce.

> **HINT** Light stock, cream, or a combination may be used in place of the milk in white sauce.

WHITE TEA is the uncured and unoxidized tea leaf made from the young, silky, white-haired buds growing on the same tea shrub that produces green and black tea; white tea needs little processing and therefore is very high in polyphenols and antioxidants.

WHITE WALNUT: see BUTTERNUT.

WHITE WINE is wine with a yellowish to amber color derived from light-colored grapes. It may also be made from dark grapes whose skins, pulp, and seeds have been removed before fermentation. White wines are made from the grape juice and grape skin of green, gold, or yellowish grapes or from just the juice (not the skin) of select red grapes. White wines mature faster and fade faster than reds. White wines are often consumed with lighter meals like lunch, smaller dinners, and appetizers, or as an aperitif by themselves. They are more refreshing and lighter in both style and taste than the majority of their red wine counterparts. The "big eight" when it comes to white wine varietals are Chardonnay, Sauvignon Blanc (also called Fumé Blanc), Riesling, Gewürztraminer, Pinot Gris/Pinot Grigio, Semillon, Viognier, and Chenin Blanc.

> **HINT** White wines are best presented in narrower glasses, as the sharper taper at the top of the glass allows for better aroma concentration of more delicate white wines. Optimum white wine serving temperatures are between 45°F and 50°F.

WHOLE GRAIN is any grain that has been hulled to remove the outer husk, cleaned, and possibly roasted. Whole-grain (the adjective) means natural or unprocessed grain containing the germ and bran. Whole-grain products can be identified by the ingredient list. Typically, if the ingredient list has "whole wheat," "whole meal," or "whole corn" as the first ingredient, the product is a whole-grain food item. On the other hand, terms such as "enriched" and "bromated," among others, could indicate that the food lacks whole grain. The following names indicate whole-grain products, in accordance with federal government regulations: whole wheat bread, macaroni, spaghetti, cracked wheat (as an ingredient, not as part of a name as in cracked wheat bread), crushed wheat, whole wheat flour, graham flour (as an ingredient, not as part of a name as in graham crackers), entire wheat flour, whole durum flour, and bulgur (cracked wheat). Whole grains contain the entire grain kernel—the bran, germ, and endosperm. Examples include whole wheat flour, bulgur (cracked wheat), oatmeal, whole cornmeal, and brown rice.

WHOLE WHEAT uses all parts of the wheat berry in the flour, including the bran, germ, and the endosperm.

WHOOPEE PIE or **WHOOPIE PIE** is a baked good made of two round, mound-shaped pieces of chocolate cake with a sweet, creamy frosting in between. While considered a New England phenomenon and a Pennsylvania Amish tradition dating to at least the 1930s, they are increasingly sold throughout the United States. The filling is generally of one of two types: a thick, sweet frosting made from Crisco shortening combined with confectioners' sugar, or, more conveniently, a dollop of marshmallow crème.

WHORTLEBERRY: see Bilberry.

WIENER: see Hot dog.

WIENER SCHNITZEL, also called SCHNITZEL, is a breaded veal cutlet that is fried and often garnished with lemon, capers, and anchovies in the Viennese style. Wiener schnitzel is German, from *Wien*, "Vienna," and *Schnitzel*, "cutlet," literally meaning "Vienna cutlet"; the English term dates to 1854.

WIENER WINKS: see PIGS IN BLANKETS.

WILD LEEK: see RAMP.

WILD MARJORAM: see OREGANO.

WILD ONION: see CIPOLLINI.

WILD RICE is the seed of a tall, aquatic grass of North America; it is not a true rice. The unpolished dark brown kernels have a rich nutlike flavor and texture. It has been called water oats, water rice, and Indian rice. Wild rice is sold as a whole grain; it is never refined. During preparation it is fermented to develop its nutty flavor. It has more protein than white rice.

WILD WILLIES: see PIGS IN BLANKETS.

WINE is the fermented juice of grapes, used as an alcoholic beverage and in cooking. Wines have various colors (red, white, rosé) and sugar content (sweet, dry). Wines may be effervescent (sparkling) or noneffervescent (still), and are sometimes strengthened with additional alcohol (fortified). Wine was first mentioned in *Beowulf* and is from the Latin *vinum*, "wine." Though known by the ancients, wine was not drunk in its matured form until the development of the bottle and cork in the late seventheenth century. A wine cork puller is also called an ah-so.

> **HINTS** An expensive (high-grade) wine is not necessary for cooking, just one that is good enough to drink by itself. The wine need not be the same that is served with the meal, for the cooking process will change the taste, but should usually go well with the wine being served alongside the meal. Wine should be added about a half hour before a braised or stewed dish is finished to give the flavor time to integrate. To speed up the process, the wine can be gently warmed before adding. Add sherry or Marsala to soups in very small quantities just before serving, or what will be tasted is the wine and not the flavors of the soup. The amount of wine used in cooking should be limited, or it will dominate the taste of the dish and dilute the desired effect.

> ▎The enemy of wine is oxygen from the air, which, once the bottle has been opened, is in contact with the wine. To keep leftover wine from spoiling, the less space between the wine and the cork or the stopper, the better. You can pour the

remaining wine into a smaller bottle so there is little or no air space. You can also use a special pump to exhaust the air. In addition, refrigerate the wine or at the very least keep it cool.

❚ Put a room-temperature bottle of red wine in the refrigerator for 20 minutes before serving. Remove white wine from the refrigerator for 20 minutes before serving. Wine should stand upright for 1 hour before decanting so that any disturbed sediment can settle to the bottom of the bottle. The wine should be swirled before tasting to release its aroma.

WINE MAKING

1. Wine grapes are harvested.

2. The grapes are crushed and pressed.

3. The grape juice (must) is mixed with wine yeast found in the grapes themselves and begins to ferment. The wine yeast changes the sugar in the must to alcohol.

4. The must is exposed to air since the wine yeast thrives on oxygen.

5. The temperature of the fermenting grape juice is controlled.

6. When fermentation stops (depending on the grape), the juice is transferred to large wooden vessels called casks.

7. The wine is matured through common clarifying/stabilization steps: racking (transferring wine to a clean tank to remove it from lees, wine sediment); centrifugation (using gravity to pull particles from the wine); filtering to clarify and sterilize; cold stabilization through chilling to prevent tartrate crystals from forming; and/or putting in additives to clarify and balance the wine.

8. The wine is blended for balance or to augment its complexity or correct faults. This can be done by interplanting different grape varieties and harvesting and crushing them together, or by separately crushing, pressing, fermenting, and aging several different grape varieties and adding them together before bottling.

9. The wine is bottled. Sterilization is present at every stage in the bottling line.

10. The bottles are then aged, anywhere from a few days to several months to decades. Storage conditions at this point are the same as for any cellared wine: dark and vibration free, with constant cool temperatures ranging from 50°F to 68°F.

SIX S'S OF WINE TASTING

1. See (sight) the wine.

2. Smell the wine.

3. Swirl the wine.

4. Sip or slurp the wine.

5. Swish and savor the wine.

6. Swallow the wine.

WINE VARIETIES

The grape is the fruit of the vine, growing in bunches on a stalk. It has green, yellow, purple, white, and black varieties; white and black are used to make wine. Wine is a drink made from the juice of the grape; the sugar in the fruit is converted into alcohol by the action of yeasts in the process of fermentation. Wine's history is as old as civilizaton, and wine had been created in Mesopotamia and Egypt by 4000 BC. After the voyages of Christopher Columbus, grape culture and winemaking were transported to the New World. Almost all wines are labeled by the region of production, maturity of the fruit, variety of grape or type of wine, and year of production, and they can be further distinguished by color, sweetness, and aroma. Here are some of the names used for the many varieties of wine available today:

ALSACE	CHRISTI	MADEIRA
ALTAR WINE	CLARET	MALAGA
AMERICAN WINE	COLD DUCK	MARSALA
AMONTILLADO	CONDRIEU	MATEUS ROSÉ
AMOROSO	CÔTE DE NUITS	MÉDOC
APPETIZER WINE	CÔTE RÔTIE	MERLOT
APPLE WINE	CÔTES DU RHÔNE	MOSEL
ASTI SPUMANTI	DANDELION WINE	MOSELLE
AUSTRALIAN WINE	DÃO	MULLED WINE
AVELEDA	DESSERT WINE	MUSCADET
BARBERA	DOLCETTO	MUSCAT
BARDOLINO	DOURO	MUSCATEL
BAROLO	DRY WINE	NAPA VALLEY WINE
BEAUJOLAIS	EMPIRE WINE	NATURAL WINE
BERGERAC	ENTRE-DEUX-MERS	NAVARRA
BLANC DE NOIR	FORTIFIED WINE	NIERSTEIN
BLUSH WINE	FRASCATI	NOBLE WINE
BORDEAUX	FRUIT WINE	OLD WINE
BORDEAUX BLANC	FUMÉ BLANC	OPORTO
BURGUNDY	GERMAN WINE	ORANGE WINE
CABERNET SAUVIGNON	GEWÜRZTRAMINER	ORVIETO
CABINET WINE	GRAVES	PAUILLAC
CALIFORNIA WINE	GRENACHE	PINK WINE
CANARY WINE	HERMITAGE	PINOT BLANC
CAPE WINE	HOCK	PINOT GRIGIO
CARBONATED WINE	JOHANNISBERG RIESLING	PINOT GRIS
CHABLIS	JUG WINE	PINOT NOIR
CHAMPAGNE	LACRIMA	PLUM WINE
CHARDONNAY	LAMBRUSCO	POMEROL
CHATEAUNEUF-DU-PAPE	LIEBFRAUMILCH	POMMARD
CHENIN BLANC	LIGHT WINE	PORT
CHIANTI	MACON	POUILLY-FUISSÉ

(continued)

POUILLY-FUMÉ	SAUTERNES	TABLE WINE
RED BORDEAUX	SAUVIGNON BLANC	TAPESTRY RED
RED WINE	SEKT	TAWNY PORT
RETSINA	SHERRY	TOKAY PINOT GRIS
RHINE WINE	SHIRAZ	VALDEPEÑAS
RHÔNE WINE	SOAVE	VALPOLICELLA
RIESLING	SPARKLING WINE	VERMOUTH
RIOJA	ST. ESTÈPHE	VINHO VERDE
ROSÉ WINE	ST. JULIEN	VINTAGE WINE
RUBY PORT	STRAWBERRY WINE	VOUVRAY
SACRAMENTAL WINE	STRAW WINE	WHITE CABERNET
SAKE	SWEET WINE	WHITE WINE
SANCERRE	SYLVANER	WHITE ZINFANDEL
SANGIOVESE	SYRAH	ZINFANDEL

SHERRY AND DESSERT WINES

Sherry and dessert wine are fortified wines. Sherry is of Spanish origin and has a distinctive nutty flavor. A dessert wine is a sweet wine served with dessert or sometimes after a meal. Dessert wines have an alcohol content that ranges from 14% to 24%. Grapes for dessert wines are grown and processed in such a way that the sugars are concentrated in the grape, allowing the wines to have a higher level of alcohol and a sweet flavor. Typical dessert wines include cream sherry, sherry, Madeira, Marsala, port, and vermouth. Some sherry and dessert wines are listed here:

AMONTILLADO SHERRY	MADEIRA	SAUTERNES
AMOROSO	MALAGA	SERCIAL
AUSLESE	MALMSEY	SHERRY
BUAL	MANZANILLA	STRAW WINE
CANARY WINE	MARSALA	SWEET SHERRY
COMMANDARIA	MEDIUM SHERRY	SYLLABUB
CREAM SHERRY	MONBAZILLAC	TOKAY
DRY SHERRY	MOSCATO	VERDELHO
FINO SHERRY	MUSCAT	VERMOUTH
FORTIFIED WINE	MUSCATEL	VIN DE PAILLE
GRENACHE	OLOROSO	VINO DE PASTO
ICE WINE	PALO CORTADO	VIN SANTO
JEREPIGO	PORT	
LATE HARVEST RIESLING	SANGAREE	

WINE STEWARD: see SOMMELIER.

WINE VINEGAR is vinegar made from wine. The word is derived from the French *vin aigre*, "sour wine." Vinegar is made by bacterial activity that converts fermented liquids such as wine into a weak solution of acetic acid. Wine vinegar generally has a complex, mellow flavor that is less acidic than those of other vinegars. Vinegars can have an acetic acid content of 5%–18%, and wine vinegar is generally in the 5%–10% range.

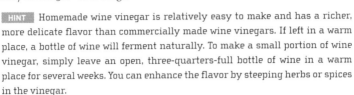
> **HINT** Homemade wine vinegar is relatively easy to make and has a richer, more delicate flavor than commercially made wine vinegars. If left in a warm place, a bottle of wine will ferment naturally. To make a small portion of wine vinegar, simply leave an open, three-quarters-full bottle of wine in a warm place for several weeks. You can enhance the flavor by steeping herbs or spices in the vinegar.

WINTERGREEN is a creeping shrub of the heath family with spicy, red, berrylike fruit and shiny aromatic leaves that yield wintergreen oil. It is so named for the fact that its leaves remain green in winter.

WINTER MELON is any of a variety of muskmelon vines (*Cucumis melo indorus*) bearing fruit with a smooth white rind and sweet flesh that is white, pale green, or orange. Mainly this term refers to the CASABA or HONEYDEW.

WINTER SAVORY is a mint plant yielding leaves used as an herb in cooking. It is used less than SUMMER SAVORY, because winter savory has a slightly more bitter flavor.

WINTER SQUASH are any of various fruits of the gourd family with hard, thick rinds and dense, firm, edible, yellow to orange flesh that mature in the fall and can be stored for several months. Winter squash include acorn squash, banana squash, buttercup squash, butternut squash, calabaza, golden nugget squash, Hubbard squash, pumpkin, spaghetti squash, and turban squash.

> **HINT** Winter squash arrive late in the growing season and they have a long shelf life, so they've long been a staple in winter and spring, when other vegetables are harder to come by. Unlike summer squash, winter squash must be cooked. They're usually baked or steamed, and then sometimes puréed. Select squash that are heavy for their size.

WISHBONE is the V-shaped furcula bone found between the breasts of a chicken or other bird. The tradition of two people pulling the bone from a cooked bird while making a wish (the person left with the larger part is granted his or her wish) started in the mid-nineteenth century.

WITLOOF: see BELGIAN ENDIVE.

WOK is a large, bowl-shaped metal pan with a curved base, used for stir-frying, steaming, and braising food in Asian cooking. The name first appeared in English in 1952.

A long-handled spatula shaped like a small shovel is the best kind of stirring tool for a wok, but any kind of long-handled spoon will work.

▌ Stir-frying in a wok on an electric stove is practically impossible, because only a limited amount of heat is produced and it hits only the very bottom of the wok. An electric wok works better than a stovetop wok, but only to a limited degree.

▌ When choosing a wok, look for a large one (twelve to fourteen inches) with deep sides and a rounded bottom, made of heavy carbon steel that will take high heat and not scorch food.

WONTON or **WON TON** is a small pocket of dough or dumpling with a savory filling such as minced meat or fish and spices, either deep-fried or boiled as a side dish or in a broth soup called wonton soup or won ton soup.

HINT As wontons are being prepared, keep those that are finished under a slightly damp towel so that they don't dry out.

WORCESTERSHIRE SAUCE is a thin, pungent sauce of soy sauce, vinegar, tamarind, and spices, originally made in Worcester, England. Worcester grocers John Lea and William Perrins coined the term for their Worcestershire (or Worcester) sauce. Lea and Perrins made up the first batch of the Worcestershire sauce and were not impressed by the taste. The sauce was placed in jars and sent to the cellar for storage. A few years later, after stumbling across the jars, they decided to try the sauce again. To their surprise, after aging, the sauce was delicious.

WORSTJES IN DEEG: see PIGS IN BLANKETS.

WURST is German for "sausage." German wurst, or sausage, comes in two basic categories: fresh sausages and slicing/spreading sausages. Fresh sausages are either uncooked or cooked once, and need recooking or reheating. Most sausages are made of pork, veal or beef, bacon or ham, egg, pickling salt, and spices, and are then cooked in water and sometimes lightly smoked. Some are made of cooked ingredients that are then cooked a second time after being stuffed into links, and may also be smoked. Slicing and spreading sausages are ready-to-eat, cold cut–style sausages, fully cured. Some are firm and are best sliced, but there are also soft sausages made for spreading.

YAKITORI is a Japanese dish of grilled, skewered, marinated chunks of meat (often chicken) and vegetables. The Japanese word derives from *yaki*, "grilled," and *tori*, "fowl." There are restaurants in Japan that specialize in yakitori and offer a range of these kebabs.

YAM is the edible, starchy tuberous root of various plants (family Dioscoreaceae, genus *Dioscorea*), used as a staple food in tropical areas. Despite the physical similarities between a yam and a sweet potato, the vegetables are botanically distinct; nonetheless, moist-fleshed varieties of sweet potato are often called yams in the United States. The word yam can be traced to Portuguese, but its origin is uncertain beyond that.

> **HINT** The true yam is not widely available in the United States, but may be found in African, Japanese, or Latin grocery stores. Yams should be very hard and have no cracks. A fingernail scratch should reveal juice. Yams can be stored at room temperature for up to one week.

YAM BEAN: see JICAMA.

YAM CHA: see DIM SUM.

YANKEE BEAN: see NAVY BEAN.

YEAST refers to a leavening agent containing yeast cells that is used to raise dough in making bread and to ferment beer and wine. Yeast is a single-celled organism that reproduces asexually by budding or division; as it grows, it converts its food through fermentation into alcohol and carbon dioxide, and when it feeds on starch or sugar, it gives off carbon dioxide gas as it converts its food to energy. The gas is trapped in a gluten mesh and causes dough to rise.

> **HINTS** Store active dry yeast in jars or envelopes in the freezer. Compressed fresh yeast in foil-wrapped packages is more perishable and will keep in the refrigerator for only ten days. It can be frozen for up to two months. Defrost yeast at room temperature and then use immediately.
>
> ▐ After the first rise, punch down yeast dough by pressing down with both hands. If you are removing the dough to shape it before the second rise, or if the recipe does not require a second rise, there is no need to punch it down. Punching down redistributes the yeast and expels carbon dioxide bubbles. It also keeps the gluten from becoming overstretched or broken.

There are three types of baker's yeast:

ACTIVE DRY YEAST: in jars or packages in regular or quick-rise/rapid-rise formulas.

COMPRESSED FRESH YEAST: One cake is equivalent to one package of active dry yeast.

INSTANT DRY YEAST (also called EUROPEAN YEAST): Three times more powerful than regular dry yeast.

YELLOW BERRY: see CLOUDBERRY.

YELLOWFIN TUNA, also called AHI, is a very large food fish (*Thunnus albacares*) with pale pink flesh; it is larger than albacore and has a flavor slightly stronger than that of albacore.

YOGURT, YOGHURT, or **YOGHOURT** is a thick, semisolid food made from milk fermented by a bacterium (*Lactobacillus bulgaricus*), offered in various flavors including fruits and in various consistencies and sweetnesses. It originated in Turkey and the word entered English around 1625. Frozen yogurt is made from low-fat or nonfat yogurt plus skim milk or milk and cream; this dessert's stabilizers take the place of the fat.

YOLK is the yellow of a bird's or reptile's egg, containing protein and fats that provide nourishment for the developing young. As a food, yolks are a major source of vitamins and minerals. They contain all of the egg's fat and cholesterol, and almost half of the protein. The yolk is sometimes separated from the egg white and used in cooking for dishes and sauces such as mayonnaise, custard, hollandaise sauce, crème brûlée, and avgolemono.

YORKSHIRE PUDDING is a popover of northern British origin made with unsweetened egg-and-flour batter and baked until it is puffy, crisp, and golden; it is baked in roast beef drippings. Yorkshire pudding is traditionally served with roast beef or prime rib, gravy, roasted potatoes, a green vegetable, mustard, and horseradish sauce.

YUCCA or **YUCA**, also called CASSAVA or MANIOC, is a plant of the agave family.

HINTS To use fresh yucca, peel away the skin with a sharp knife to expose its white flesh. This flesh can then be cut into pieces for boiling, frying, or baking. When cooked, yucca contains a tough, stringlike fiber throughout its middle section. This string is too hard to be eaten and can be easily removed from the cooked yucca by stripping it away from the softer flesh. Yucca is often made into fries and chips.

▌ Skinless, precut yucca is available in grocery or ethnic stores in frozen prepackaged bags. To use this type of yucca, follow the package instructions for cooking. Frozen yucca typically takes about 10 minutes to cook; overcooking the yucca tends to make it mushy.

YUKON GOLD potatoes are large potatoes with golden, buttery-tasting, waxy flesh; they are best served boiled, baked, or mashed. Yellow-fleshed potatoes are common in Europe and South America. In fact, yellow-fleshed potatoes are actually considered the norm in most countries outside North America. The University of Guelph in Canada spent years crossbreeding a North American white potato with a wild South American yellow-fleshed variety to create the Yukon Gold, the first Canadian-bred potato to be marketed and promoted by name. The university received a Canadian license for the potato in 1980 and it was then exported to the United States. There are other gold-fleshed potatoes on the market, including Yellow Finn, Michigold, Donna, Delta Gold, Banana, and Saginaw Gold, but none of these have achieved the name recognition of the Yukon Gold. Yukon Golds are slightly flat and oval in shape with light gold, thin skin and light yellow flesh. They can be identified by the rosy pink coloration of the shallow eyes. Anthoxanthins are the compound that gives the gold potato its beautiful yellow color.

YUM CHA: see DIM SUM.

ZABAGLIONE, also called SABAYON, is a light whipped Italian dessert of egg yolks, sugar, and Marsala wine beaten over hot water until a foamy custard forms, and usually served over cake, ice cream, or pastry. The name is Italian for "egg punch," possibly from an earlier drink. Zabaglione has its own special tall copper pan or pot with a rounded bottom to allow for continuous whisking while cooking.

ZEPPELIN or **ZEP**: see GRINDER.

ZEST is a thin piece of the colored portion of citrus peel used as flavoring; the aromatic oils in citrus zest are what add so much flavor to food.

HINTS Organic lemons gives the best zest because they don't have a wax coating. When choosing a fruit for zesting, look for firm, dry, and fresh fruit, without any wax covering. Citrus fruit should be prepared for zesting by washing it with warm water and scrubbing it with a brush to make sure any wax is eliminated.

▌To grate a lemon without losing too much zest in the holes of the grater, place a piece of parchment paper over the grater to act as a barrier. Alternatively, use a zester if a fine grate is not necessary.

ZESTER, also called Citrus ZESTER, is a kitchen utensil with a stainless-steel head with five tiny cutting holes that removes only the colored outer portion of the peel, leaving the pale, bitter pith.

ZINFANDEL is a dry red table wine from California and the small black grapes from which it is made. The term dates to around 1880.

ZITI is a type of smooth or ridged tubular medium-sized pasta. It is the plural of *zito/zita*, "piece of tubular pasta," probably short for *maccheroni di zita*, literally meaning "bride's macaroni." Baked ZITI is a popular baked Italian American casserole dish made with ziti and sauce. Zitoni is a wider version of ziti.

ZUCCHINI, also called Courgette, is a variety of summer squash with dark green skin; it is shaped like a cucumber and is used in various ways as a vegetable. The word is the Italian diminutive of *zucca*, "gourd."

HINT Choose a blemish-free zucchini about eight inches long, as it will be young and tender compared to bigger ones. Store zucchini for up to three days in a perforated plastic bag in the vegetable crisper of the refrigerator.

ZUPPA INGLESE is a dessert of sponge cake flavored with rum, topped with custard or pudding, covered with cream, and garnished with fruit. Zuppa inglese is, literally, Italian for "English soup"—but this dessert is an Italian version of an English trifle.

ZWIEBACK is a type of sweetened bread baked first as a loaf and later cut into slices and toasted; hence the word is German for "twice-baked."

PERFECT FLAVOR PAIRINGS

ALMOND: anise, apple, apricot, asparagus, banana, blackberry, black currant, blueberry, butternut squash, cardamom, cauliflower, cherry, chicken, chili/chile, chocolate, cinnamon, coconut, coffee, fig, garlic, ginger, grape, hard cheese, hazelnut, lamb, lemon, melon, oily fish, olive, orange, peach, pear, raspberry, rhubarb, rosemary, saffron, shellfish, strawberry, white chocolate

ANCHOVY: beef, beetroot, broccoli, caper, cauliflower, chili/chile, coconut, egg, garlic, hard cheese, lamb, lemon, lime, olive, onion, pineapple, potato, rosemary, sage, soft cheese, tomato, watercress, white fish

ANISE: almond, apple, asparagus, bacon, banana, basil, beef, black currant, carrot, chicken, chili/chile, chocolate, cinnamon, coconut, cucumber, egg, fig, goat's cheese, grape, hard cheese, lamb, lemon, melon, mint, mushroom, oily fish, olive, orange, oyster, parsnip, pea, pear, pineapple, pork, rhubarb, saffron, shellfish, strawberry, tomato, vanilla, walnut, washed-rind cheese, white fish

APPLE: almond, anise, bacon, beetroot, blackberry, blueberry, butternut squash, cabbage, carrot, celery, cinnamon, clove, coriander, hard cheese, hazelnut, horseradish, liver, mango, nutmeg, orange, peanut, pear, pineapple, sage, shellfish, soft cheese, vanilla, walnut, washed-rind cheese

APRICOT: almond, cardamom, chocolate, cinnamon, cumin, ginger, goat's cheese, hard cheese, lamb, mango, mushroom, orange, peach, pork, raspberry, rosemary, vanilla

ARTICHOKE: bacon, hard cheese, lamb, lemon, mint, oyster, pea, pork, potato, prosciutto, shellfish, truffle

ASPARAGUS: almond, anise, egg, hard cheese, lemon, mint, mushroom, oily fish, orange, pea, peanut, potato, prosciutto, shellfish, truffle, white fish

AVOCADO: bacon, blue cheese, chicken, chili/chile, chocolate, cilantro, coffee, cucumber, dill, grape, grapefruit, hazelnut, lime, mango, mint, nutmeg, oily fish, pineapple, shellfish, soft cheese, strawberry, tomato

BACON: anise, apple, artichoke, avocado, banana, beef, bell pepper, blue cheese, broccoli, butternut squash, cabbage, cardamom, chicken, chili/chile, chocolate, clove, egg, hard cheese, horseradish, liver, mushroom, onion, orange, oyster, parsley, parsnip, pea, pineapple, pork, potato, sage, shellfish, thyme, tomato, truffle, washed-rind cheese, white fish

BANANA: almond, anise, bacon, cardamom, caviar, cherry, chicken, chocolate, cinnamon, coconut, coffee, egg, hard cheese, hazelnut, parsnip, peanut, pear, pineapple, vanilla, walnut

BASIL: anise, chicken, clove, coconut, egg, garlic, goat's cheese, hard cheese, lemon, lime, mint, raspberry, shellfish, soft cheese, tomato, walnut

BEEF: anchovy, anise, bacon, beetroot, bell pepper, blackberry, blue cheese, broccoli, cabbage, caper, carrot, celery, chili/chile, cinnamon, clove, coconut, coffee, dill, egg, garlic, ginger, hard cheese, horseradish, lemon, lime, liver, mint, mushroom, oily fish, olive, onion, orange, oyster, parsley, parsnip, pea, peanut, pear, pork, potato, shellfish, thyme, tomato, truffle, walnut, watercress

BEETROOT: anchovy, apple, beef, caper, chocolate, coconut, cumin, dill, egg, goat's cheese, horseradish, liver, oily fish, onion, orange, pork, potato, walnut, watercress

BELL PEPPER: bacon, beef, chicken, chili/chile, egg, eggplant, olive, onion, shellfish, soft cheese, tomato

BLACKBERRY: almond, apple, beef, goat's cheese, peach, raspberry, vanilla, white chocolate

---

BLACK CURRANT: almond, anise, chocolate, coffee, mint, peanut, soft cheese

---

BLUEBERRY: almond, apple, blue cheese, cinnamon, coriander, lemon, mushroom, peach, vanilla

---

BLUE CHEESE: avocado, bacon, beef, blueberry, broccoli, butternut squash, cabbage, celery, chicken, fig, grape, grapefruit, mushroom, peach, pear, pineapple, sage, truffle, walnut, watercress

---

BROCCOLI: anchovy, bacon, beef, blue cheese, cauliflower, chili/chile, garlic, hard cheese, lemon, peanut, pork, walnut

---

BUTTERNUT SQUASH: almond, apple, bacon, blue cheese, chestnut, chili/chile, cinnamon, ginger, goat's cheese, lime, mushroom, nutmeg, pork, rosemary, sage, shellfish

---

CABBAGE: apple, bacon, beef, blue cheese, carrot, chestnut, chicken, chili/chile, egg, garlic, ginger, lamb, nutmeg, onion, potato, shellfish, smoked fish

---

CAPER: anchovy, beef, beetroot, cauliflower, cucumber, goat's cheese, lamb, lemon, oily fish, olive, parsley, potato, shellfish, smoked fish, soft cheese, tomato, white fish

---

CARDAMOM: almond, apricot, bacon, banana, carrot, chocolate, cinnamon, coconut, coffee, coriander, ginger, lamb, mango, pear, saffron, vanilla, white chocolate

---

CARROT: anise, apple, beef, cabbage, cardamom, celery, cinnamon, coconut, cucumber, cumin, hazelnut, olive, onion, orange, parsley, peanut, walnut

---

CAULIFLOWER: almond, anchovy, broccoli, caper, caviar, chili/chile, chocolate, cumin, garlic, hard cheese, nutmeg, potato, saffron, shellfish, truffle, walnut

---

CAVIAR: banana, cauliflower, chicken, egg, hazelnut, lemon, oyster, potato, smoked fish, soft cheese, white chocolate

---

CELERY: apple, beef, blue cheese, carrot, chestnut, chicken, egg, horseradish, lamb, nutmeg, onion, oyster, peanut, pork, potato, prosciutto, shellfish, soft cheese, truffle, walnut, white fish

---

CHERRY: almond, banana, chocolate, cinnamon, coconut, coffee, goat's cheese, hazelnut, lamb, peach, smoked fish, vanilla, walnut

---

CHESTNUT: butternut squash, cabbage, celery, chicken, chocolate, lamb, mushroom, pear, pork, prosciutto, rosemary, vanilla

---

CHICKEN: almond, anise, avocado, bacon, banana, basil, bell pepper, blue cheese, cabbage, caviar, celery, chestnut, chili/chile, cilantro, coconut, egg, garlic, grape, hard cheese, hazelnut, lemon, lime, mushroom, onion, oyster, parsnip, pea, peanut, pear, potato, saffron, sage, shellfish, thyme, tomato, truffle, walnut, watercress

---

CHILI/CHILE: almond, anchovy, anise, avocado, bacon, beef, bell pepper, broccoli, butternut squash, cabbage, cauliflower, chicken, chocolate, cilantro, coconut, egg, eggplant, garlic, ginger, goat's cheese, hard cheese, lemon, lime, liver, mango, mint, oily fish, olive, orange, oyster, peanut, pineapple, pork, potato, shellfish, tomato, walnut, watermelon

---

CHOCOLATE: almond, anise, apricot, avocado, bacon, banana, beetroot, black currant, cardamom, cauliflower, cherry, chestnut, chili/chile, cinnamon, coconut, coffee, fig, ginger, goat's cheese, hazelnut, lemon, lime, mint, nutmeg, orange, peanut, pear, pineapple, raspberry, rose, rosemary, strawberry, thyme, tomato, vanilla, walnut, watermelon, white chocolate

---

CINNAMON: almond, anise, apple, apricot, banana, beef, blueberry, butternut squash, cardamom, carrot, cherry, chocolate, clove, coconut, coffee, fig, ginger, grapefruit, lamb, lime, mint, orange, peanut, pear, pineapple, pork, soft cheese, strawberry, thyme, tomato, walnut, watermelon

CLOVE: apple, bacon, basil, beef, cinnamon, coffee, ginger, hard cheese, onion, orange, peach, pork, tomato, vanilla

COCONUT: almond, anchovy, banana, basil, beef, beetroot, cardamom, carrot, cherry, chicken, chili/chile, chocolate, cilantro, cinnamon, dill, egg, lemon, lime, mango, peanut, pineapple, pork, raspberry, shellfish, smoked fish, strawberry, vanilla, white chocolate, white fish

COFFEE: almond, avocado, banana, beef, black currant, cardamom, cherry, chocolate, cinnamon, clove, coriander, ginger, goat's cheese, hazelnut, orange, rose, vanilla, walnut, white chocolate

CILANTRO: avocado, chicken, chili/chile, coconut, coriander, cumin, garlic, goat's cheese, lamb, lemon, lime, mango, mint, orange, parsley, peanut, pineapple, pork, potato, shellfish, tomato, watermelon, white fish

CORIANDER: apple, blueberry, cardamom, cilantro, coffee, cumin, garlic, goat's cheese, lemon, olive, orange, pork

CUCUMBER: anise, avocado, caper, carrot, cumin, dill, garlic, goat's cheese, melon, mint, oily fish, onion, peanut, pork, rhubarb, shellfish, strawberry, tomato, watermelon, white fish

CUMIN: apricot, beetroot, carrot, cauliflower, cilantro, coriander, cucumber, egg, lamb, lemon, lime, mango, mint, oily fish, pork, potato, shellfish, washed-rind cheese

DILL: avocado, beef, beetroot, coconut, cucumber, egg, lamb, lemon, mint, mushroom, oily fish, pea, pork, potato, shellfish, smoked fish, white fish

EGG: anchovy, anise, asparagus, bacon, banana, basil, beef, beetroot, bell pepper, cabbage, caviar, celery, chicken, chili/chile, coconut, cumin, dill, ginger, lemon, mushroom, nutmeg, oily fish, onion, oyster, parsley, pea, pork, potato, prosciutto, sage, shellfish, smoked fish, tomato, truffle, vanilla, watercress

EGGPLANT: bell pepper, chili/chile, garlic, ginger, lamb, nutmeg, prosciutto, soft cheese, tomato, walnut

FIG: almond, anise, blue cheese, chocolate, cinnamon, goat's cheese, hard cheese, hazelnut, liver, mint, orange, prosciutto, raspberry, soft cheese, vanilla, walnut

GARLIC: almond, anchovy, aubergine, basil, beef, broccoli, cabbage, cauliflower, chicken, chili/chile, cilantro, coriander, cucumber, ginger, goat's cheese, hazelnut, lamb, liver, mint, mushroom, oily fish, olive, onion, parsley, pork, potato, rosemary, shellfish, soft cheese, thyme, tomato, truffle, walnut, washed-rind cheese, white fish

GINGER: almond, apricot, beef, butternut squash, cabbage, cardamom, chili/chile, chocolate, cinnamon, clove, coffee, egg, eggplant, garlic, lemon, lime, mango, melon, mint, oily fish, onion, orange, pork, rhubarb, tomato, vanilla, white fish

GOAT'S CHEESE: anise, apricot, basil, beetroot, blackberry, butternut squash, caper, cherry, chili/chile, chocolate, cilantro, coffee, coriander, cucumber, fig, garlic, lamb, lemon, mint, mushroom, olive, pear, raspberry, rosemary, thyme, walnut, watercress, watermelon

GRAPE: almond, anise, avocado, blue cheese, chicken, hard cheese, melon, peach, peanut, pineapple, pork, rosemary, soft cheese, strawberry, walnut, white fish

GRAPEFRUIT: avocado, blue cheese, cinnamon, orange, pineapple, pork, shellfish, watercress

---

HARD CHEESE: almond, anchovy, anise, apple, apricot, artichoke, asparagus, bacon, banana, basil, beef, broccoli, cauliflower, chicken, chili/chile, clove, fig, grape, mushroom, nutmeg, onion, orange, parsnip, pea, pear, pineapple, potato, sage, shellfish, tomato, walnut, white fish

---

HAZELNUT: almond, apple, avocado, banana, carrot, caviar, cherry, chicken, chocolate, coffee, fig, garlic, pear, raspberry, rosemary, strawberry, vanilla, white fish

---

HORSERADISH: apple, bacon, beef, beetroot, celery, oily fish, oyster, pea, potato, smoked fish, tomato, white fish

---

LAMB: almond, anchovy, anise, apricot, artichoke, cabbage, caper, cardamom, celery, cherry, chestnut, cilantro, cinnamon, cumin, dill, eggplant, garlic, goat's cheese, lemon, mint, nutmeg, onion, pea, peanut, potato, rhubarb, rosemary, saffron, shellfish, thyme, tomato

---

LEMON: almond, anchovy, anise, artichoke, asparagus, basil, beef, blueberry, broccoli, caper, caviar, chicken, chili/chile, chocolate, cilantro, coconut, coriander, cumin, dill, egg, ginger, goat's cheese, lamb, lime, mint, oily fish, olive, orange, oyster, parsley, potato, rosemary, saffron, shellfish, smoked fish, thyme, tomato, white chocolate, white fish

---

LIME: anchovy, avocado, basil, beef, butternut squash, chicken, chili/chile, chocolate, cilantro, cinnamon, coconut, cumin, ginger, lemon, mango, mint, oily fish, orange, peanut, shellfish, tomato, watermelon, white fish

---

LIVER: apple, bacon, beef, beetroot, chili/chile, fig, garlic, oily fish, onion, sage, truffle

---

MANGO: apple, apricot, avocado, cardamom, chili/chile, cilantro, coconut, cumin, ginger, lime, mint, orange, peach, pineapple, rhubarb, shellfish, white fish

MELON: almond, anise, cucumber, ginger, grape, mint, orange, prosciutto, strawberry, watermelon

MINT: anise, artichoke, asparagus, avocado, basil, beef, black currant, chili/chile, chocolate, cilantro, cinnamon, cucumber, cumin, dill, fig, garlic, ginger, goat's cheese, lamb, lemon, lime, mango, melon, mushroom, oily fish, onion, orange, parsley, pea, peanut, potato, raspberry, strawberry, watermelon

MUSHROOM: anise, apricot, asparagus, bacon, beef, blueberry, blue cheese, butternut squash, chestnut, chicken, dill, egg, garlic, goat's cheese, hard cheese, mint, oily fish, onion, oyster, parsley, pork, potato, rosemary, shellfish, soft cheese, thyme, tomato, truffle, walnut, white fish

NUTMEG: apple, avocado, butternut squash, cabbage, cauliflower, celery, chocolate, egg, eggplant, hard cheese, lamb, onion, oyster, parsnip, potato, saffron, shellfish, tomato, vanilla, walnut

OILY FISH: almond, anise, asparagus, avocado, beef, beetroot, caper, chili/chile, cucumber, cumin, dill, egg, garlic, ginger, horseradish, lemon, lime, liver, mint, mushroom, onion, parsley, pea, pork, potato, rhubarb, rosemary, shellfish, thyme, watercress

OLIVE: almond, anchovy, anise, beef, bell pepper, caper, carrot, chili/chile, coriander, garlic, goat's cheese, lemon, orange, potato, prosciutto, rosemary, shellfish, tomato, thyme, white chocolate, white fish

ONION: anchovy, bacon, beef, beetroot, bell pepper, cabbage, carrot, celery, chicken, clove, cucumber, egg, garlic, ginger, hard cheese, lamb, liver, mint, mushroom, nutmeg, oily fish, orange, oyster, pea, pork, potato, rosemary, sage, smoked fish, thyme, tomato

ORANGE: almond, anise, apple, apricot, asparagus, bacon, beef, beetroot, carrot, chili/chile, chocolate, cilantro, cinnamon, clove, coffee, coriander, fig, ginger, grapefruit, hard cheese, lemon, lime, mango, melon, mint, olive, onion, peach, pineapple, rhubarb, rosemary, saffron, strawberry, thyme, vanilla, walnut, watercress, white fish

---

OYSTER: anise, artichoke, bacon, beef, caviar, celery, chicken, chili/chile, egg, horseradish, lemon, mushroom, nutmeg, onion, parsley, pork, watermelon

---

PARSLEY: bacon, beef, caper, carrot, cilantro, egg, garlic, lemon, mint, mushroom, oily fish, oyster, potato, shellfish, smoked fish, walnut, white fish

---

PARSNIP: anise, bacon, banana, beef, chicken, hard cheese, nutmeg, pea, pork, potato, shellfish, walnut, watercress, white fish

---

PEA: anise, artichoke, asparagus, bacon, beef, chicken, dill, egg, hard cheese, horseradish, lamb, mint, oily fish, onion, parsnip, pork, potato, prosciutto, rosemary, shellfish, smoked fish, white fish

---

PEACH: almond, apricot, blackberry, blueberry, blue cheese, cherry, clove, grape, mango, orange, prosciutto, raspberry, strawberry, vanilla

---

PEANUT: apple, asparagus, banana, beef, black currant, broccoli, carrot, celery, chicken, chili/chile, chocolate, cilantro, cinnamon, coconut, cucumber, grape, lamb, lime, mint, pork, potato, shellfish, tomato, vanilla

---

PEAR: almond, anise, apple, banana, beef, blue cheese, cardamom, chestnut, chicken, chocolate, cinnamon, goat's cheese, hard cheese, hazelnut, pork, prosciutto, walnut, washed-rind cheese

---

PINEAPPLE: anchovy, anise, apple, avocado, bacon, banana, blue cheese, chili/chile, chocolate, cilantro, cinnamon, coconut, grape, grapefruit, hard cheese, mango, orange, pork, prosciutto, raspberry, sage, shellfish, strawberry, vanilla, white chocolate

---

PORK: anise, apple, apricot, artichoke, bacon, beef, beetroot, broccoli, butternut squash, cabbage, celery, chestnut, chili/chile, cilantro, cinnamon, clove, coconut, coriander, cucumber, cumin, dill, egg, garlic, ginger, grape, grapefruit, mushroom, oily fish, onion, oyster, parsnip, pea, peanut, pear, pineapple, potato, rhubarb, rosemary, sage, shellfish, thyme, tomato, truffle, watercress, watermelon

---

POTATO: anchovy, artichoke, asparagus, bacon, beef, beetroot, cabbage, caper, cauliflower, caviar, celery, chicken, chili/chile, cilantro, cumin, dill, egg, garlic, hard cheese, horseradish, lamb, lemon, mint, mushroom, nutmeg, oily fish, olive, onion, parsley, parsnip, pea, peanut, pork, rosemary, saffron, shellfish, smoked fish, tomato, truffle, washed-rind cheese, watercress, white fish

---

PROSCIUTTO: artichoke, asparagus, celery, chestnut, egg, eggplant, fig, melon, olive, pea, peach, pear, pineapple, sage, tomato, white fish

---

RASPBERRY: almond, apricot, basil, blackberry, chocolate, coconut, fig, goat's cheese, hazelnut, mint, peach, pineapple, strawberry, vanilla, white chocolate

---

RHUBARB: almond, anise, cucumber, ginger, lamb, mango, oily fish, orange, pork, rosemary, saffron, strawberry, vanilla

---

ROSEMARY: almond, anchovy, apricot, butternut squash, chestnut, chocolate, garlic, goat's cheese, grape, hazelnut, lamb, lemon, mushroom, oily fish, olive, onion, orange, pea, pork, potato, rhubarb, watermelon

---

SAFFRON: almond, anise, cardamom, cauliflower, chicken, lamb, lemon, nutmeg, orange, potato, rhubarb, shellfish, white chocolate, white fish

SAGE: anchovy, apple, bacon, blue cheese, butternut squash, chicken, egg, hard cheese, liver, onion, pineapple, pork, prosciutto, tomato

SHELLFISH: almond, anise, apple, artichoke, asparagus, avocado, bacon, basil, beef, bell pepper, butternut squash, cabbage, caper, cauliflower, celery, chicken, chili/chile, cilantro, coconut, cucumber, cumin, dill, egg, garlic, grapefruit, hard cheese, lamb, lemon, lime, mango, mushroom, nutmeg, oily fish, olive, parsley, parsnip, pea, peanut, pineapple, pork, potato, saffron, smoked fish, thyme, tomato, truffle, vanilla, walnut, watercress, white fish

SMOKED FISH: cabbage, caper, caviar, cherry, coconut, dill, egg, horseradish, lemon, onion, parsley, pea, potato, shellfish, soft cheese, watercress

SOFT CHEESE: anchovy, apple, avocado, basil, bell pepper, black currant, caper, caviar, celery, cinnamon, eggplant, fig, garlic, grape, mushroom, smoked fish, strawberry, tomato, truffle, walnut

STRAWBERRY: almond, anise, avocado, chocolate, cinnamon, coconut, cucumber, grape, hazelnut, melon, mint, orange, peach, pineapple, raspberry, rhubarb, soft cheese, tomato, vanilla, white chocolate

THYME: bacon, beef, chicken, chocolate, cinnamon, garlic, goat's cheese, lamb, lemon, mushroom, oily fish, olive, onion, orange, pork, shellfish, tomato, white fish

TOMATO: anchovy, anise, avocado, bacon, basil, bell pepper, caper, chicken, chili/chile, chocolate, cilantro, cinnamon, clove, cucumber, egg, eggplant, garlic, ginger, hard cheese, horseradish, lamb, lemon, lime, mushroom, nutmeg, olive,

onion, peanut, pork, potato, prosciutto, sage, shellfish, soft
cheese, strawberry, thyme, vanilla, watermelon, white fish

TRUFFLE: artichoke, asparagus, bacon, beef, blue cheese, cabbage, cauliflower, celery, chicken, egg, garlic, liver, mushroom, pork, potato, shellfish, soft cheese

VANILLA: anise, apple, apricot, banana, blackberry, blueberry, cardamom, cherry, chestnut, chocolate, clove, coconut, coffee, egg, fig, ginger, hazelnut, nutmeg, orange, peach, peanut, pineapple, raspberry, rhubarb, shellfish, strawberry, tomato, walnut

WALNUT: anise, apple, banana, basil, beef, beetroot, blue cheese, broccoli, carrot, cauliflower, celery, cherry, chicken, chili/ chile, chocolate, cinnamon, coffee, eggplant, fig, garlic, goat's cheese, grape, hard cheese, mushroom, nutmeg, orange, parsley, parsnip, pear, shellfish, soft cheese, vanilla, washed-rind cheese, watercress

WASHED-RIND CHEESE: anise, apple, bacon, cumin, garlic, pear, potato, walnut

WATERCRESS: anchovy, beef, beetroot, blue cheese, chicken, egg, goat's cheese, grapefruit, oily fish, orange, parsnip, pork, potato, shellfish, smoked fish, walnut

WATERMELON: chili/chile, chocolate, cilantro, cinnamon, cucumber, goat's cheese, lime, melon, mint, oyster, pork, rosemary, tomato

WHITE CHOCOLATE: almond, blackberry, cardamom, caviar, chocolate, coconut, coffee, lemon, olive, pineapple, raspberry, saffron, strawberry

WHITE FISH: anchovy, anise, asparagus, bacon, caper, celery, cilantro, coconut, cucumber, dill, garlic, ginger, grape, hard cheese, hazelnut, horseradish, lemon, lime, mango, mushroom, olive, orange, parsley, parsnip, pea, potato, prosciutto, saffron, shellfish, thyme, tomato

Index

Note: Main entry terms appear alphabetically in the book and are not included in this index.